The World of Count Basie

Also by Stanley Dance

THE WORLD OF DUKE ELLINGTON
THE WORLD OF SWING
THE WORLD OF EARL HINES
THE NIGHT PEOPLE (with Dicky Wells)
DUKE ELLINGTON IN PERSON
(with Mercer Ellington)

THE WORLD OF
COUNT BASIE

Stanley Dance

DA CAPO PRESS

Library of Congress Cataloging in Publication Data

Dance, Stanley.
  The world of Count Basie.

  (A Da Capo paperback)
  Reprint. Originally published: New York: C. Scribner's
Sons,c1980.
  "Selected discography": p.
  Bibliography: p.
  Includes index.
  1. Jazz musicians — United States — Biography.
2. Basie, Count, 1904–   . 3. Jazz music — United
States — History and criticism. 4. Big bands — United
States. I. Title.
ML385.D26 1985   785′.42′0924 [B]   85-12901
ISBN 0-306-80245-7 (pbk.)

This Da Capo Press paperback edition of *The World of Count Basie*
is an unabridged republication of the edition published in New York in
1980, here supplemented with a note to the Da Capo Edition.by the
author. It is reprinted by arrangement with Charles Scribner's Sons.

Published by Da Capo Press
A Member of the Perseus Books Group
http://www.dacapopress.com

14 13 12 11 10 9 8 7 6 5 4

To the Holy Main

Acknowledgments

Interviews with Harry Edison, Gus Johnson, and Gene Ramey were supported by the National Endowment for the Arts Jazz Oral History Project, and excerpts from these interviews appear by permission of the artists.

Part I of the Count Basie section originally appeared as *The Kid from Red Bank* in *This Is Jazz*, published by George Newnes Ltd., and is reproduced by permission of Syndication International Ltd.

The Dicky Wells chapter, originally entitled *Basie Days*, is from *The Night People* by Dicky Wells as told to Stanley Dance (Crescendo, 1971). Copyright 1971 by Stanley F. Dance. Reprinted by permission of Taplinger Publishing Co., Inc.

The interviews with Marshall Royal and Snooky Young first appeared in *Jazz Journal* in March and April 1962, respectively, and are reprinted with that magazine's permission.

Part II of the Lester Young section is reproduced by permission of *Melody Maker*, London.

Part II of the Lockjaw Davis section, originally entitled *Two-Career*

Man, the Frank Wess chapter, originally entitled *Wess Points,* and Part II of the Basie section, originally entitled *American Institution,* are reprinted by permission of *Down Beat* magazine.

The interviews with Sir Charles Thompson, Al Grey, and Lockjaw Davis (Part I) are reprinted by special permission of Robert Asen, publisher of *Metronome.*

The Buck Clayton and Eric Dixon interviews first appeared in *Jazz* and are reprinted by permission.

Permission to quote from *Living in a Land of Extremes: Melting Pot or Mosaic?* by Joe B. Frantz was granted by the Southwestern Library Association, Southwestern Mosaic Project, for whom it was written under a grant from the National Endowment for the Humanities.

CONTENTS

List of Illustrations

Introduction

Like *The World of Duke Ellington, The World of Swing,* and *The World of Earl Hines,* this book consists largely of interviews with musicians. It is not meant to stand as a biography of Count Basie, and I am presuming that the reader brings some knowledge of Basie and his world to the book. The oral historical method affords the reader many different views of Basie's career and lets aspects of his life emerge that might remain hidden in a straight, chronological account. While the musicians generally confirm each other in matters of fact (venues, recording session personnel, etc.), they sometimes contradict each other in matters of opinion (why, for instance, Basie is reluctant to take solos). Also, of course, the time at which a musician gave an interview affects his narration of the events. For example, when I interviewed Frank Foster in 1961, he was a virtual newcomer to Basie's world—and this fact no doubt colors his interpretation of that world. Now, almost twenty years later, this experienced, adventurous musician would probably recall that world differently. But Foster's early statements reveal a spontaneity that might be lost in an updated retrospective.

In the introduction to *The World of Earl Hines,* I wrote that interpretation was left to the reader. What I wanted then, as now, was to
have the musicians speak as directly as possible to the reader. A
running commentary from the interviewer, particularly if it conflicted
with the musicians' statements, would serve no useful purpose. There
are many interpretative histories of jazz and most of them suggest that
their authors' experience of the music is radically different from that
of the men and women who made the music. Generally, the musicians'
evaluations have an authority that their interpreters seem to lack. The
musician may sometimes be more impressed by technical virtuosity
than critics are, and he may, too, show a reluctance to fault or
condemn a colleague, but the *degree* or tone of his praise is usually a
reliable guide to quality.

The World of Count Basie is made up of two parts. Count Basie, to
my way of thinking, represented the First Wave from Kansas City and
Jay McShann the Second. Each brought with him an innovator
destined to exert an enormous influence on the whole course of jazz.
With Basie, it was Lester Young; with McShann, Charlie Parker. But
above and beyond this, the relationship of one to the other, and to a
common tradition, tells us much about both. In the course of *The Last
of the Blue Devils,* a documentary filmed in Kansas City, Basie says:
"I'm glad I got out of here as fast as I did, because he was breathing
down our backs so hard. We had to get out and move over and let this
cat in—Jay McShann."

This was a rather generous exaggeration, but a very few months
after Basie left for Chicago and New York, in 1936, McShann began
his important engagement at Martin's-on-the-Plaza.

The interview with Gene Ramey portrays the Kansas City scene at
that time with much clarity. The great popularity of Andy Kirk's band
is noted, but its style, with more emphasis on ensemble playing, was
closely related to that of bands in the East and contrasted sharply with
those of Basie and McShann, which were much more loose-knit, as was
Bennie Moten's in its last year.

The Basie and McShann "books," or repertoires, consisted mainly of
"head" arrangements, a large proportion of which were blues. Soloists,
backed by ensemble or section riffs, were extensively featured, and
particular attention was paid to the role of the rhythm section. So close
was the stylistic relationship of the two bands that three of McShann's
key musicians (Gene Ramey, Gus Johnson, and Paul Quinichette)
subsequently worked effectively and comfortably with Basie. The
shared roots and, for some years, the parallel courses of the two bands
explain the inclusion of the McShann section. Interviews with Eddie

Barefield, Sir Charles Thompson, Snub Mosely, and Melvin Moore further illustrate the music scene in the Southwest.

Jazz in that part of the country is a far larger subject than was originally recognized, and some knowledge of its history and landscape is essential to an understanding of the Basie band. Early jazz writers tended to focus their attention almost exclusively on New Orleans, Chicago, and New York, but first Dave Dexter and then Frank Driggs began to reveal the musical potential of the Southwest. While it is true that no really impressive records emanated from there prior to 1932, the work of talented individuals could certainly be heard on the relatively few records that were made. Bennie Moten's band, which recorded quite prolifically from 1923 onward, offers little of artistic significance on its Okeh and Victor records until its rhythm section is enhanced by the presence of Basie and bassist Walter Page. Even before their arrival, though, the band's personnel included musicians who made valuable contributions to Basie's band and to jazz in general, such as Eddie Durham, Ed Lewis, Joe Keyes, Lips Page, Jack Washington, Ben Webster, Eddie Barefield, and Harlan Leonard, not to mention singer Jimmy Rushing. Moten himself appears to have been an undistinguished pianist, but he was a capable leader and organizer. Basie referred to him in *The Last of the Blue Devils* with affection: "He was a very warm, very lovable man. . . . Bennie taught me an awful lot, by just watching him. I mean, I had no idea that I was watching him for any *reason* at all, but just that I was crazy about him. I had no thoughts of fronting any band while I was with Bennie."

Nevertheless, after Moten's tragic death, Basie soon found himself leading a group with a nucleus of musicians from that leader's band.

The joint interview with Basie and guitarist Freddie Green in *The World of Swing* revealed some of their beliefs regarding swing and tempos. Green joined Basie in 1937 and, apart from a brief interval in 1950, has been with him ever since—the longest tenure of any sideman in the band. His role in the rhythm section is of great significance. In Basie's view, "it holds things together." A reserved, dignified man, Green was born in Charleston, South Carolina, where his close friend, Lonnie Simmons (tenor saxophone and organ), got him his first professional job with the Nighthawks. Another friend, trumpet player Samuel Walker, whose father taught at Jenkin's Orphanage, helped Green to learn to read when he began to play banjo. Although he was not a member of the famous Jenkin's Orphanage Band, this friendship led to his first experience of "the road" when he toured with the band —along with Cat Anderson—as far as Maine. Green went to New York in 1930 and stayed with an aunt, in whose house he became familiar with rent parties and stride piano. He worked as an upholsterer by day, and at night in an after-hours club, the Yeah Man, where the manager advised him to switch to guitar. "Lonnie Johnson came in one night and upset me," he recalled. More invaluable experience came when he worked at the Exclusive Club with Willie Gant, a stride pianist. Gant had a huge repertoire and Green had to learn to accompany singers in all kinds of keys. Because there were no drums, maintaining a good beat was essential and, since there was room in the club for dancing, tempos were important too. When John Hammond heard him at the Black Cat in Greenwich Village in 1936, he was working with Kenny Clarke (drums), Lonnie Simmons (tenor saxophone), Fat Atkins (piano), and Frank Spearman (bass), Clarke's stepbrother. He auditioned for Basie at Roseland and got the job, thus determining the pattern of his life. Acoustic, rhythm guitar is seldom heard in the few remaining big bands, but Freddie Green's continues to be a vital part of the Basie band's pulse.

In their joint interview, Basie and Green were almost equally guarded in naming their favorites, but there are two bands that Basie consistently refers to with the greatest respect and admiration—Duke Ellington's and Jimmie Lunceford's. His liking for the latter is incomprehensible to many, for Lunceford's was a "show" band that emphasized arrangements and the ensemble. Lunceford's performances could be considered almost the antithesis of the loose, open kind that were Basie's original specialty, and its liking for "two-beat" rhythm, as opposed to the even four-four of Kansas City, was another major point of difference. Yet as Basie well knew, having encountered it in more than one ballroom, Lunceford's was a band with a flair for danceable tempos and a rare ability to swing, not so much, be it noted, on the flagwavers that excited white audiences, but on medium and slow tempos.

It is customary to divide Basie's career as a bandleader rather arbitrarily into two periods: one before he broke up his big band in 1950, the other after the brief period when he led a small group. The band's character changed considerably during the forties as a result of the departure of Lester Young, Jo Jones, and Walter Page, but the new band of 1951 closely resembled that of the late forties. The three individuals most responsible for a change of concept and direction later in the 1950s were Marshall Royal, Neal Hefti, and Joe Williams.

According to Hefti in a *Billboard* article (July 18, 1964), Basie wanted to get out of the "riff-raff rough" and develop a stage band that could appear on the Ed Sullivan Show! Although it never became a show band in the sense that Lunceford's was, it did become much more of an ensemble band, partly because soloists of marked individuality were less common than a quarter-century before. Hefti's neat, well-crafted arrangements, and the polished performances that Royal, as deputy music director, exacted from the band, all resulted in a new identity that has been maintained for more than twenty years, often in rather pale imitations of such Hefti originals as *Li'l Darlin'*.

Apart from Hefti's, successful arrangements were contributed from outside the band by Benny Carter and Quincy Jones, but, as in the early days, much of the best and most appropriate writing came from men in the band, such as Ernie Wilkins, Frank Wess, Frank Foster, Thad Jones, Eric Dixon, and Bobby Plater. Wilkins's and Foster's settings were of great significance in launching Joe Williams and his blues repertoire.

For many readers, especially those overseas, the Southwest may need defining geographically, culturally, and ethnically. The importance of its six states as background to the music and musicians discussed in this book will soon become evident, but the Southwest is not the entity casual references in jazz writings often suggest. It is well described in *Living in a Land of Extremes: Melting Pot or Mosaic?*—an essay written by Joe B. Frantz, Director of the Texas State Historical Association:

> Citizens in the eastern portion of the region descend from the Old South rather than the West, and the mixed culture is black-white rather than red-brown-white. Texas itself is split—an outreach of the Old South in the eastern one-third of the state, a combination desert-mountain area in the western two-thirds. Or you can split Texas laterally (as well as horizontally). North Texas is WASP country, heavily white Anglo-Saxon Protestant. The farther south you go in Texas, the more it becomes Catholic and Mexican and brown. Like Texas, Arkansas is bifurcated—Old South in the east and hillbilly and western in the west. Oklahoma, the most Indian of the southwestern states, has a southeastern area it calls "Little Dixie," while its northwestern panhandle knows no cultural difference from the plains of the Texas Panhandle. New Mexico varies from the forested mountains with their isolated towns, still redolent of colonial Spanish days; to the Indian pueblos, mainly in the north; to the pervasive desert that offers little to the person who can't afford to irrigate or mine it. Arizona has natural wonders that suggest emptiness punctuated by spectacle, most notably in the north; relieved by the grasslands and forests of the White Mountains and Oak Creek Canyon across the center; and the more genteel Patagonia rolling region in the south. Phoenix and Tucson sit in the middle of the state like twin hubs of a giant wheel, with the desert on all sides—

meccas for sunshine seekers. Here are two of the fastest-growing cities in the nation, with all of the pleasures and problems of people who represent extremes—wealth and poverty, youth and age—ethnic differences, and the political range.

In short, every subsection of the Southwest has its own cultural pattern, its own personality.

Basically, the region is tri-cultural though the components of that three-way culture vary. Arizona and New Mexico are Indian-Mexican-Anglo. Texas is Anglo-Black-Mexican, and Louisiana is French-Anglo-Black. Arkansas and Oklahoma tend to have only two principal cultural groups, but again the pattern varies. Arkansas is black-white, while Oklahoma is red-white, though each has elements of other cultural/ethnic groups.

This diversity means not only that the Southwest is enormously interesting culturally, but that stereotypes must be discarded to move from area to area within its six-state confines. Thus the notions of the Southerner's religion, black or white, as stemming from one of the more evangelical denominations loses its credibility in Louisiana and eastern Texas where both blacks and whites may be Roman Catholic. And the generalizations about the soft Southern speech lose authority in a region where French, Spanish, German, and many Indian dialects are commonly spoken.

Four of the six states have a cattle and cowboy heritage—Texas, Oklahoma, New Mexico and Arizona. But looking farther back, the American cowboy, that star of screen and penny dreadfuls, learned to ride from the Mexican, who learned from the Spanish, who learned from the Moors. The heritage is Moorish-Spanish, as are the original cattle and horses that stocked the grasslands of those future states. Even the terms are Spanish-derived—lariat for *la riata*, calaboose from the Spanish *calabozo* and the French *calabouse, cafecito* from the Mexican-Spanish diminutive for coffee, chaps from the Mexican *chaparreras*, canyon from the Spanish *cañon, cayuse* from the Cayuse Indians, and so on and on. That most typical Texan, the cowboy then, is a derivative of other cultures and so are his cattle and horses. He descends from the Spaniard and the Indian who handled cattle over vast stretches of land that had inadequate roads and few railroads.

Irrelevant as much of this may seem to jazz, it was through this huge, dusty region of plains, deserts, and mountains that the old cars and raggedy buses full of jazz musicians moved. The musicians who endured the hardships of those rough roads and their inadequate accommodations were a resilient breed and singularly free from self-pity. Weathering the Depression with hardy independence, they simultaneously shaped new, innovative forms of musical expression on the traditional framework of the blues. Their counterparts of today, whose experiences are considerably less harrowing, call this "paying their dues."

In conclusion, I wish to acknowledge the contribution made to this, and to my previous books, by my wife. Her constant help and, in particular, her familiarity with the Basie band's early days were especially valuable in the present case. She was also responsible for the interviews with Gus Johnson and Jimmy Witherspoon. I am, of course, greatly indebted to all the musicians whose voices are heard here, and I much appreciate the cooperation of my friends Chris Albertson, Frank Driggs, and J. R. Taylor. And as before, Mrs. W. J. Boone's customary skill and meticulous care in transcribing interviews have been very important in the realization of this book.

—STANLEY DANCE
Vista, California

NOTE TO THE DA CAPO EDITION
When this book was first published in 1980, Count Basie had given me the impression that his own book was imminent. Because I knew he had been working on it for a long time with Albert Murray, I did not press him for further material. He had already generously written a foreword to *The Night People*, which Dicky Wells and I put together, and a conversation with him and Freddie Green introduced *The World of Swing*. In any case, I visualized my book as complementing his, as saying things he could or would not say himself.

Despite my clear disavowal of any such intent in the introduction, I was astonished when some reviewers expressed disappointment that it was not a biography. My conception of the book was that it portrayed the world in which Basie lived his professional life, the people who worked with him in it, and the kind of people they were.

—STANLEY DANCE
Vista, California
April, 1985

The World of Count Basie

PART 1

Count Basie

(BANDLEADER AND PIANO)

I

In 1936 the world of jazz was dominated by the "big band"—a term employed to describe a group usually consisting of five or six brass, three or four reeds, and four rhythm. Its success largely depended upon acceptance by the dancing public, and this for several years had been regularly forthcoming from black audiences. Now, leaders like Benny Goodman, Tommy Dorsey, and Bob Crosby were taking their versions of the same idiom to white audiences. The Swing Era was under way.

The best bands at that time were led by Duke Ellington, Jimmy Lunceford, Chick Webb, Fletcher Henderson, Earl Hines, Don Redman, and Claude Hopkins. These bands, their soloists, and their arrangements were the real pacesetters. There was plenty of variety in their work, yet out of the heat of competition, out of the "battles of swing," standards had been set and a general conception of the big-band sound and program developed. Although these were still unashamedly "dance" bands, they were often to be found playing from theater stages and accompanying increasingly ostentatious floorshows in nightclubs. As a result of this, and because of the growing importance of radio as a means of publicity, there was a definite tendency in jazz toward elaboration and decoration.

Upon this world, and upon New York in particular, the band Count Basie brought from Kansas City at the end of 1936 made a startling impression.

It was, however, by no means an entirely favorable impression. The band's business, as Basie saw it, was to provide swinging dance music. Opening night at the Roseland dancehall—formerly the scene of Fletcher Henderson's triumphs—found Basie facing the band across the piano with his back to the audience! This was no studied slight of the kind fashionable among the boppers a decade later. Rather, it denoted a single-minded concentration upon the work in hand, and perhaps more than a little nervousness, for the magic-carpet transfer from Kansas City to Broadway, engineered by critic John Hammond, had a quality of dream about it. Would Basie wake up and find himself and the band on their way back to Kansas City? What would the cats from the bigtime bands have to say when they dropped by to dig the music?

Many years later, Basie recalled one of the band's first New York reviews. It went like this: "If you think the reed section is out of tune, listen to the brass, and if you think the brass section is out of tune, listen to the band."

Yet even before the problems of intonation and ragged section work were overcome, the band had become the rage among the better informed. Its success resulted not so much from what it did as the way in which it did it. Its formula was not a new one. It took the big-band mixture as before and shook it in a newly effective way. The riffs (figures that the reed and brass sections played behind soloists and in climactic ensembles) were no new discovery. They had been long known and practiced by the Eastern bands, as Basie, a native of Red Bank, New Jersey, well knew. What he brought to them was above all a new emphasis. His band's performances were rhythmically intoxicating—and lean. Fat, in the form of commercial concessions or exotic coloring, was conspicuously absent. The essence of the big-band idiom was presented unadulterated, without equivocation. And, miraculously, it was accepted.

It would have seemed incredible in 1936 that twenty-odd years later there should be only two big jazz bands in regular existence. Had that possibility been entertained, it would have seemed reasonable enough that one should be Duke Ellington's. But that the other should be Count Basie's—that, too, would have seemed incredible!

"My favorite band is Count Basie's all the way. He is direct. He keeps it simple and sincere, and swings at all times."

These views were expressed in 1958 by trombonist Eli Robinson, himself a member of Basie's band from 1941 to 1947. They sum up very aptly the qualities that account for Basie's enduring popularity.

The main source of inspiration in the band has always been the rhythm section. Much credit must be given to such other members as that great-hearted bassist, the late Walter Page, the inimitable guitarist, Freddie Green, and the peerless drummer, Jo Jones. "You may think you're the boss," Basie once said, "but the drummer is really the head man; when he isn't feeling right, nothing's going to sound good."

However that may be, it is an inescapable fact that Basie's piano is always the heart of his rhythm sections; he makes the drummer feel right, and does much more than set tempos and feed soloists. Even in the first demonstration of the potency of the new Kansas City brew, Basie's piano played an extremely significant part. This demonstration, overlooked in several otherwise painstaking studies of Basie, took place on December 13, 1932, when Bennie Moten's Kansas City Orchestra recorded ten titles for Victor, among them *Moten's Swing*, *Toby*, *Lafayette*, *Prince of Wales*, and a salacious *Two Times*. These performances gave record buyers a foretaste of what New York was to experience in 1936. They showed the kind of revitalization the Moten band had undergone, and they showed the Count striding and swinging with an abandon that was wonderfully contagious.

The continual stress on the rhythm section's role and the importance of swinging are fundamentals to which Basie remains steadfast, but this does not mean that he is unaware of superficial changes in jazz. His reactions to the bop onslaught were illustrative of this: "You got to bop for the kids," he said. "They're the ones who support you. I want to play a lot of things that start off with a little bop figure, build into a real shout and then come back into the bop theme. Of course, there'll be solos. I'm for bop solos so long as they show sense. But if a guy is gonna play good bop he has to have a sort of a bop soul."

Basie, of course, never had a bop soul.

Two years later, after referring to the need to provide "a little taste of bop," he was saying, "We still keep a beat in the back line, relaxed and solid, behind the horns. So it doesn't matter what they do up front; the audience gets the beat."

Six years later, he was recounting some of his greatest musical thrills: "My biggest thrill as a listener came one night back in, I think it was, 1951.

"The so-called progressive jazz was going big then, and here comes Duke Ellington on opening night at Birdland. He had just revamped his band, and no one knew just what he'd have. We all dropped in to catch him—and what we heard! What a thrill that was!

"The Duke was swinging. All this 'progressive' talk, and the Duke played the old swing. He scared a lot of people that night. It was just wonderful. Of course, the Duke has always had the greatest band at all times. There's never been another band for me, year in and year out."

Other thrills that he recalled at the same time, as provided by Art Tatum, Louis Armstrong, Fletcher Henderson, and Jimmie Lunceford, were consistent with the same viewpoint and clearly indicated in which direction his sympathies lay. To him, Duke was "The Master," Art Tatum "The Boss," and Louis Armstrong, affectionately, "Pops"—"I can listen to Louis play or sing or talk or anything. . . ."

Nevertheless, his attitude to past and present is essentially realistic. "You don't sit still anymore. You got to go. Are you gonna fight to stand still?" he asked in 1948. "Maybe you don't convert entirely. You have to retain your identity, but you get points for effort."

When Basie played in concert halls, for instance, he sometimes felt the need to include in the program show-stopping material of a kind unsuitable at dances. Playing in concert halls has similarly required a far greater degree of instrumental polish and precision, and this has often resulted in a reduction of that remarkable feeling of spontaneity the early bands conjured up when riffing as an ensemble or behind soloists.

In the beginning there was a tendency for the band's success to be credited to its two tenor stars, Lester Young and Herschel Evans. Since then, Basie has always featured a couple of tenor soloists, such as Buddy Tate, Don Byas, Lucky Thompson, Illinois Jacquet, Paul Gonsalves, Paul Quinichette, Lockjaw Davis, Frank Wess, Frank Foster, Jimmy Forrest, and Eric Dixon. "I've always been queer for tenor men," he says.

His ability to come up with "unknown" star talent time after time is a reflection of his alert listening habits. Listening to music, with him, is a major pleasure, not a duty. He remembers those who favorably impress him, and when the time comes he sends for them. The extremely popular singer Joe Williams, whose reputation has been made with Basie, is a case in point.

Yet it is perhaps in the way his music has retained its essential identity, despite occasional diplomatic and partial conversions, that his character is best revealed.

Underlying as unpretentiously relaxed and frankly hedonistic an exterior as any in jazz is Basie's rare and wholly admirable resolve, a holding fast to purposes. His own personal success is the consequence of this resolve, but far more important has been his influence upon the whole course of jazz. By keeping it "simple and sincere," and swinging "at all times," his music has provided a guiding light in the chaos of the past two decades.

It might even be argued that his influence was greater than Duke Ellington's during the postwar period. Ellington was a source of inspiration rather than an influence, evolving creatively out of himself, little affected by the change and decay around him. Basie reflects change more because, unlike Ellington's, his repertoire has consisted of the compositions and arrangements of many different writers, among them Buck Clayton, Eddie Durham, Jimmy Mundy, Buster Smith, Tab Smith, Don Redman, Sy Oliver, Andy Gibson, Buster Harding, Nat Pierce, Neal Hefti, Ernie Wilkins, Johnny Mandel, Manny Albam, and Frank Foster. But like Ellington's, his music acquired its truth and identity in performance.

Buddy Tate, who went on to lead one of the best small jazz combinations, was featured by Basie as tenor soloist for longer than any other musician. He was once asked how he liked his position. "I like playing in this band," he replied. "It's been a real pleasure ever since I joined Count."

Dicky Wells, who was with Basie for ten years, is one of the greatest trombone stylists and a veteran with experience in several of the finest big bands. Looking back over his career up to 1958, he said without any hesitation, "Count was my favorite big-band leader. I can't say one bad thing about him."

Arranger Ernie Wilkins, while a member of the band, said, "You know, sometimes we can't wait to get on the stand, and we hate to quit when the night is over."

Endorsements of this kind justify Basie's care in building his bands. "I think it's important to have a likeable guy, a happy sort of guy as well as one who is a nice musician. Those things," Basie said in 1952, "put together, make a happy band."

The enthusiasm of his men also stems very much from the fact that Basie, again like Duke Ellington, plays jazz for kicks, for his own pleasure. And, like Duke, he doesn't stand in front of the band waving a baton. He is in there, a part of it, contributing, prompting, suggesting, a playing member.

Offstage, too, there is no false dignity, no attitudinizing. Dressing-room exchanges are conducted on the men's own terms, whether angry, serious, or humorous. An argument may grow heated and involve such original and picaresque language that even Basie grows excited. Eventually, he will discharge a verbal barrage and then relapse, with almost disconcerting suddenness, into tranquillity. In a serious discussion, he will be considerate, sensitive to another's point of view, shrewd in judgment, and, above all, disarmingly modest.

The wit that finds expression in his stimulating piano interjections is a natural part of his conversation. It may be drily deflationary, a comment upon a pretentious or mistaken idea, or it may be provocatively intent on extracting the maximum pleasure from an amusing situation.

Before leaving London after his second successful British tour of 1957, he had some last-minute shopping to do. Having made a number of discerning purchases for his wife, he sought a particular kind of fur gloves for his daughter. Nowhere could they be found. Mitts were recommended as best for kids.

"Yeah?" Basie queried. "How're they going to count in the wintertime?"

In East Anglia one cold night, the band had hungrily descended upon a small and humble café. Lockjaw Davis regarded a dish of ill-shaped pastries on the counter. Several squadrons of flies were using them as emergency airstrips, landing and taking off with rapidity and agility.

"What are those?" Lockjaw asked the waitress, pointing at the dish.

"Flycakes, man," said Basie, long before the official reply was forthcoming.

Typical of his quietly effective comebacks to criticism was that made when he quitted Alan Freed's rock 'n' roll radio show. Basie and band were undoubtedly miscast in this series; the friction began, it is rumored, with his refusal to play Freed's conception of suitable arrangements. When the parting of the ways came, Freed announced magnanimously, "He has the greatest band in the country, but it isn't a dance band."

A statement of this kind could have had a damaging effect on the band's bookings for dances, and Basie mildly demurred.

"I think people were dancing before rock 'n' roll," he said.

Nevertheless, he was not blind to the worthwhile aspects of rock 'n' roll, and on another occasion he made this comment: "It's been good for the bands. It got the kids dancing again. Right after the war I thought everyone had forgotten how."

The shy, unassuming person that this world-famous band leader essentially is can also sometimes be seen in the novel role of host at the elegant bar that bears his name on 132nd Street in New York. Early in 1958, after extensive remodeling and redecoration, the bar opened with a trio led by his friend and former tenor soloist, Lockjaw Davis. A great attraction in this group was Shirley Scott, a brilliant young organist. Somewhere, unobtrusive in the background, was the benign figure of Basie. There was no piano in the house, so he was inevitably asked to play the organ.

"Not after her," he said, grinning, and pointing at Shirley.

The earliest part of Count Basie's professional career is not, unluckily, documented by records, but the evidence of it is clearly heard in his subsequent music. In New York in the mid-twenties, he had been influenced by the "stride" piano school, of which such men as James P. Johnson, Fats Waller, and Willie (The Lion) Smith were natural leaders. As recently as 1957, he made a record called *The Kid from Red Bank*, in which the exciting characteristics of the stride style were still rewardingly prominent. This style was a full, two-handed one, and Basie employed it at the 1932 session with Bennie Moten, mentioned earlier.

Between 1927 and 1936, Kansas City obviously exerted its special influence on Basie. He recalls it as "a good town for music with joints up and down 12th Street—all the way out to the Paseo—where folks could go and listen and dance. Bennie always played a foot-pattin' beat. Never anything you couldn't dance to."

Emerging as leader of his own band, he increasingly developed the personal style by which he is identified today. This style originated during choruses devoted to the band's rhythm section when Basie contributed isolated notes and chords, or short phrases, with electrifying effect. The success of these choruses was such that Basie came to build nearly all his solos in this idiom, playing very brief phrases in the right hand with occasional punctuations from the left, while bass and guitar provided the regular sustaining rhythm that was normally the left hand's function. It sounded casual and relaxed, but his timing was so wonderful that the rhythmic result was unusually stimulating. The apparent simplicity, and an ironic quality of understatement, made the style ideally suitable for the interpretation of the blues.

The blues have always been Basie's forte, slow and moody, rocking at an easy, dancing pace, or jumping at passionate up-tempos. Nearly all his greatest successes have been blues, from *One O'Clock Jump* to *Every Day*. It is through the blues that jazz communicates most warmly and surely, as he well knows.

Nowadays he does not take as many solos as his admirers wish. It is a matter of modesty again, not laziness. He has excuses, reasons, and suggests that his style is too familiar. Then he will come up with an intimate, moving performance like *After Supper*, full of the old mastery and magic. He is even more reluctant to feature himself on organ, although this one-time protégé of Fats Waller probably plays the organ to better effect than any other musician in jazz. He was egged into playing the instrument at a concert in Paris in 1954. Four years later he was admitting he had not played it publicly since. Recordings like his version of Buster Harding's *Paradise Squat* should, however, be sufficient to convince anyone that the organ has its place in jazz.

But so long as Basie is at the piano, leading a band, we may be sure that we shall hear a lot of blues, at good tempos, and swinging. For that, in an era when basic jazz values are often forsaken, we should be profoundly grateful.

(1960)

II

As his musicians took their places on the stand at the beginning of the evening, Count Basie ran his hands over the keyboard. The treble sounded reasonably true, the bass like a deranged guitar.

"You never heard a piano like that before in your life, did you?"

"No."

"Vietnam!"

He tossed the word over his right shoulder as he and the rhythm section began to set the tempo for the opener. The brass came in with a great, powerful exclamation that took the crowd's breath away and left it bright-eyed with excitement.

Another night had begun. Another night in more than thirty years of nights, back and forth across the land—across the world.

What does a life of that kind demand beyond talent and stamina? A certain kind of temperament? Melancholic, sanguine, phlegmatic, choleric? None of these is common to the enduring triumvirate of Basie, Ellington, and Herman, but each leader is slow to anger, patient, and able to put on a good face when things go wrong. More important, each has an unfailing sense of humor.

Basie's humor is dry, unhurried, and terse, and it is delivered off-hand, deadpan. If it goes unheard or is lost on the listener, he doesn't seem to care. The satisfaction in a witticism, for the true wit, lies more in the thought than in its expression, and certainly more than in any laughter it may arouse.

Another night. The band was grouped compactly in the corner of a large, almost empty club. The weather was bad and the house prices were outrageous. The band was swinging softly and beautifully before coming up into the climax.

"You gotta play *April in Paris!*" bawled a drunk at the bar.

"I know it," Basie answered, without turning around, without accent, the voice modulated, apparently genial, but full of irony to anyone who knew him. They played *April in Paris* next, and one-more-timed themselves into intermission.

Another night, backstage at Carnegie Hall, a story Basie's friend and confidant, Teddy Reig, tells with relish. It illustrates the kind of folksy repartee Basie enjoys, and it came at the end of some straight-faced ribbing.

"You're making my knife nervous!" Basie told Big Mama Thornton.

"And you've got my pistol shakin'!" the blues singer replied.

Yet another night, in 1968. "A man of very few words," in the phrase with which he comically introduced singer Richard Boone, Basie had gallantly accepted an invitation to address the New York chapter of the Duke Ellington Society. ("You know you're not going to get a speech.") Later he sat, like a Daniel among hungry lions, and answered questions.

"What is the attitude of younger guys coming into a band with players who are much older?"

"They're very eager and interested—and they get old, too."

"Was Charlie Christian known as a comer in those days? Most of us hadn't heard of him until he got to New York."

"Don't say 'most of us.' Say 'most of you.' "

"Will you tell us a little bit about your childhood?"

"No, I will not."

"How did you get your nickname?"

"Which you mean? Count or Bill?"

"Did you get a chance to hear Ethel Waters at the Cotton Club?"

"The Cotton Club! I couldn't get in!"

"Are you going to make any more albums like *Battle Royal?*"

"I'd certainly like the invitation. It was one of the greatest experiences of my life, apart from being scared to death. At first, you know, they had planned it quite differently. We were to make a side, and then Duke was to make a side. Now I've been knowing this guy for about seventy years, and I know what he can lay on you when he gets ready, so I thought it would be a lot better to augment the two bands. But he's a nice guy! Just because he can drop trouble all over you, he doesn't necessarily do it."

"How many Ellington compositions have you in the book?"

"Anytime we think we can get away with it, we play one. We play *All Heart* and a lot of others he doesn't play now, and I'm very happy about that!"

"When did you first hear Ellington?"

"Well, I remember my father taking me to hear my cousin Edward . . ."

(Tit for tat. "I remember when I was a little boy, I stood on the other side of Fifth Avenue," Ellington would claim, "and heard him playing in Edmond's.")

Behind the modest, almost shy manner, and the relaxed humorous twists of speech, there is, of course, a serious, sensitive person. No one can have said more fitting words at Art Tatum's passing than Basie.

"It's bad enough when a man and a friend dies," he said. "When a man dies with all that talent, it's a disgrace."

He listens to pianists, of course, with particular interest, as these comments on Newport, 1967, show: "Earl Hines had us all spellbound backstage. He hasn't lost anything and he hasn't got dated, because he's a real originator. Don Ewell was terrific with Willie The Lion, too. I was glad to hear him play *Handful of Keys*, because Nat Pierce has done an arrangement of it for us. Don didn't miss a note."

At record dates, he may delegate authority to the arranger and Marshall Royal, the straw boss, but when he intervenes he is decisive. After several takes at one session, dissatisfied with a passage for brass, he got up from the piano and addressed his trumpets forcefully: "Lean on that as hard as you can—and harder than that!"

As is well known, racing is among his preferred forms of recreation. One summer, he pretended a good deal of irritation with Willard Alexander for booking him into Atlantic City before racing began there. It meant a long drive to Monmouth Park in New Jersey each day. When he and Harlan Floyd got back to the club one night, Freddie Green was standing outside enjoying the evening air.

"How did it go?"

"Real well. A horse in the last race called *Fiddler's Green* paid seventeen to one."

Freddie smiled his biggest smile, remembering his predecessor in the band, Claude Williams. Claude, who played violin as well as guitar, had been nicknamed "Fiddler."

Although Basie always speaks warmly of Fats Waller, and the encouragement and organ tuition he had from him at the Lincoln Theater, the Harlem scene obviously didn't have the impact that Kansas City's did.

"For twenty-five blocks, there used to be joints, sometimes three or four doors apart, sometimes every other block," he recalled. "There were burlesque shows, too, and all this was established before I had a band, before I even started to work there. There was an awful lot of good music, and it was like everything happened there. It was the first place I really heard the blues played and sung as they should be, and I heard all the great old blues singers of the twenties. This was all in Kansas City, Missouri. There was a big difference across the bridge, because Kansas City, Kansas, was dry."

Jimmy Rushing, who was subsequently his singer for fifteen years, played an important part in his early career.

"I didn't audition Jimmy," Basie continued. "Jimmy auditioned me. I was in Tulsa, Oklahoma, with a little show—Gonzel White and The Big Jamboree. We used to ballyhoo out on the sidewalk before each show, move the piano out, play a few tunes, and say, 'Right inside, folks!' The Blue Devils were in town at that time and Jimmy happened to pass by. He invited me up to the hall that night, when I met Walter Page. They let me sit in, and that was how we got acquainted."

After his period with the Blue Devils and Bennie Moten came the Reno Club. "Basie told me he thought he'd try getting a band together," Jimmy Rushing remembered. "At first, he had a little combo, just rhythm and two or three horns. Then they started jam sessions and began to broadcast. Blue Monday got to be a big night—Sunday night, Monday morning—at the Reno, and they wanted to put a rope between white and colored, but Basie said, 'Oh, no, we don't go for that!' And there never was any trouble. Blue Monday started as a thing for entertainers. We'd send out invitations to the other clubs around, and everybody would come in and blow, or sing, or dance. The other clubs started the same thing on different nights. Basie was very successful at the Reno, and the band increased in size. He was always very conscientious about his music, and Walter Page was like a daddy teaching some of the boys to read."

"I had had a little organ thing going each afternoon," Basie supplemented, "and then I was lucky and got a sustaining date with the band. That's when I got a professional nickname. Dick Smith, one of the announcers then, said, 'Listen, we've got the Earl of Hines, the Duke of Ellington, the Baron of Lee, and Paul Whiteman is the King of Jazz. So you be the Count with His Barons of Rhythm.' The first part stuck."

On his way from California to New York, Buck Clayton stopped off in Kansas City to see his mother. Lips Page had just quit Basie. Clayton joined the band at the Reno Club and was with it for two months there, until it left Kansas City on Halloween Night, October 31, 1936, right after playing in a battle of bands with Duke Ellington at the Paseo Ballroom.

"Our reputation before we came east," Buck Clayton has explained, "was built on nine pieces, and I don't think we ever had a bad night in

Kansas City; but when we added five or six men it made a lot of difference. The band had to be enlarged to go on the road, but it slowed everything down and made it sluggish. . . ."

The aid of John Hammond, Willard Alexander, and Fletcher Henderson helped the band through difficult days, and when men like Benny Morton, Dicky Wells, Harry Edison, and Earle Warren came in, it began, Clayton added, "to sound like a good big band."

A great period in jazz history ensued. The 1936 Roseland engagement in New York did not insure the band's acceptance, but after it played the Famous Door there was no doubt anywhere.

As Basie tells it, talent was acquired almost casually, but it is his good ear and careful listening that brought that talent together.

"Someone had recommended Prez," he recalled. "He was working up in Minneapolis, and we had sent for him to join us. It was the strangest thing I ever heard, and the greatest. We got Herschel [Evans] from California while we were at the Reno, too. In those years, he represented 'soul.' That's where *he* was—a beautiful saxophonist.

"Somebody from St. Louis mentioned a drummer with the Jeter-Pilars band by the name of Jo Jones. We sent him a telegram, and he came to us and played two nights. The third night, there was no Jo Jones. 'What happened?' I asked. 'The boys came for him,' they said, 'and took him back to St. Louis.' But he got away and was with us until he went in the army.

"Freddie Green joined when we were working at Roseland. John Hammond came by one Sunday afternoon and said he had a guitarist he wanted me to hear. It seemed strange to audition a guitarist, but we went down to the dressing room. He was on the bus the next day when we went to Pittsburgh, and he's been with us ever since. Freddie Green is Mr. Hold-togetherer!

"When we were at the Brass Rail on Randolph Street in Chicago, with Clark Terry and the small group, Joe Williams used to come around and sing one song in the last set. Then we came back with a big band to the Trianon Ballroom, and Jonesy [Reunald Jones] came in very excited one night. 'You ought to hear this cat singing down there,' he said. 'Okay, tell him to come up here!' So Joe came, and you know what happened. He broke it up. To me, he's the tops. He's not limited. He can sing anything. We weren't doing any good, but then that thing came out—*Every Day*—and put us back on our feet.

"Sonny Payne was recommended to us, and he was pinchhitting for Gus Johnson, but he knocked a home run. Now we have Harold Jones, a young guy out of Chicago. He swings, and that's very necessary. The drummer is the boss of the band, not the bandleader. If the drummer's not right, nothing's happening."

The episode with Clark Terry and the small group in 1950 separates the story of the Basie band into two different chapters, and more definitely than might be expected of such a brief hiatus. Before 1950, despite many personnel changes, the band retained much of the character of the original. It was looser, and the contributions of the individual soloists, as compared with that of the ensemble, were stressed more. From 1952, as the new personnel stabilized, there was more emphasis on ensemble precision, and a very high standard has consistently been maintained in this area ever since. A perceptible difference in the two groups' approach to tempos was perhaps accounted for by the different nature of the audience. "A big difference between now and the thirties and forties is ballrooms," Basie said. "Everybody has converted over to jazz concerts, and there's a different atmosphere altogether."

Significantly, Basie never seemed to have difficulty in finding talented musicians, not men already established as stars, but men who would gain international fame in his band. Thad Jones, Joe Newman, Benny Powell, Ernie Wilkins, Frank Wess, Frank Foster, and, later, Al Grey were among those who grew greatly in stature during the fifties.

The band of 1968 was a well-balanced unit, and hardly less endowed than the band of the fifties. Each horn section had a first-class leader—Marshall Royal, Gene Goe, and Grover Mitchell. Each section boasted attractive soloists—Al Aarons, Sonny Cohn, and Oliver Brashear on trumpet; Harlan Floyd, Richard Boone, and Bill Hughes on trombone; Marshall Royal and Bobby Plater on alto; and Lockjaw Davis and Eric Dixon on tenor. And on baritone, the vastly underrated Charlie Fowlkes was the anchor man. Despite drum changes, the ticking heart of the band—the rhythm section—with the worthy Norman Keenan on bass, still provided the healthiest pulse in jazz.

Keeping a band of this quality together is evidence enough of leadership. It was never easy, and the itineraries, even with occasional aerial assistance, are still tough. One month in 1968, for example, the Basie band went from Florida to North Carolina, to Kansas, to Oklahoma, to Texas, to California, to Arizona, back to Kansas, to Iowa, to Illinois, to New York, and to Connecticut. Jumps and journeys may not be good for morale, but the leader makes them, too.

Transportation is a part of the enormous financial problem facing all big bands. They have to move to work. Other aspects of the same problem explain albums on which the band accompanies singers or records material unworthy of it. The reality of the conditions within the record industry must be taken into account. But at night, when the audience is right, everything is changed, and a big book of jazz instrumentals is opened up. For example, in the sympathetic atmosphere of one of Gene Hull's Bridgeport presentations, a program included

Cherry Point; Cottontail; Lonely Street; Bye, Bye, Blackbird; Li'l Darlin'; Shiny Stockings; When Your Lover Has Gone; Moten Swing; Every Day; Boone's Blues; King Porter Stomp; Satin Doll; Jumpin' at the Woodside; All Heart; Blues in Hoss' Flat; Whirlybird; Squeeze Me; Nasty Magnus; The Midnight Sun Never Sets; The Sidewinder; and Why Not?

Such a program, with its arrangements by Neal Hefti, Frank Foster, Eric Dixon, Sam Nestico, Nat Pierce, Bobby Plater and Quincy Jones, suggested that, like any other institution, the Basie band is too often taken for granted. And it *is* an institution, an American institution, a jazz institution. Its policy has changed only superficially in more than three decades. It still stands for forthright, swinging music, and the responsibility for it belongs to the man who, in Duke Ellington's words, "is still the most imitated piano player around."

(1968)

Jimmy Rushing

(VOCALIST)

"Both my parents were musical. My mother played and sang in the church choir. So did I. My father played trumpet in a brass band. But I also had an uncle, Wesley Manning, who used to play and sing in the sporting houses—forbidden territory to me—and he'd come home at night with a hatful of money. *Tricks Ain't Walkin' No More*, which I recorded in 1956, was a song he used to sing in the houses. He was the one who taught me to play the blues.

"I used to go by the red-light district on my way to school, and I'd see the girls in the windows, looking very pretty. I was eager to get in there, and one day I knocked on a door and a girl let me in.

"'What can I do for you?'

"'Well, . . .' I began, looking around, but not knowing what I was looking for.

"'Aren't you too young to be in here?'

"'I guess I am, but when I'm passing I often hear the blues.'

"'Can you play?'

"'Yes.'

17

" 'Then sit down and play.'

"So I sat down at the piano and played, and everybody gathered around, and I guess I was satisfied; but if my daddy had passed by there, that would have been *it!*

"He had bought me a violin and he had forbidden me to touch the piano. When he left the house, he'd lock the piano and give my mother the key. We'd watch him away, and then she'd give me the key. When he came back at night, he'd say, 'Get the violin out!' But I wouldn't know anything. It got to the stage where I just couldn't play it, and he told me, 'If I ever catch you on that piano again, or dancing, I'm gonna run you away from home!' I had really tried, but I was gone from there in about two weeks! He lived long enough to see my success with Basie, and he agreed to it, although he never said so. But he'd have a smile on his face and say, 'Well, I guess you're doing OK.'

"He didn't approve of blues like Bessie Smith's. That was honky-tonk music to him. I was official pianist at our high school 'drags,' as we called dances in Oklahoma City, where I was born on August 26, 1903. Then I went to Wilberforce University, where I met quite a few great pianists, but my biggest thrill was when I met Jelly Roll Morton.

"The first time I left home, I went to Chicago and heard a lot of bands and musicians. I liked roaming around by myself, and I went through states like Ohio and Texas, wherever I heard of bands and singers that were making an impression. Then in 1921 I left home again and went to California, where I sang professionally for the first time. That was in a little club with the Sunnyland Jazz Orchestra. Buster Wilson was the pianist. Papa Mutt Carey, Buddy Petit, Ed Garland, and a whole lot of New Orleans fellows were out there in the early twenties. When I went to the club where Jelly Roll Morton was playing, I thought he was the greatest thing I ever heard; so I made myself acquainted and we got to be real chummy. One night I was hired as intermission pianist and *he* played drums, although I could still only play in three keys. In those days, when a party came in a club, got himself seated and ordered a drink, the entertainers would ask if there was anything particular he wanted to hear. So on this occasion one of the girls wanted me to change keys—I guess she had a cold. I was swinging away in E-flat and she said, 'Change to B-flat,' but I just kept on playing in E-flat. She came back and called me everything under the sun. Jelly Roll spoke up then. 'Don't worry about it,' he said. 'I'll play for her.' He was a great fellow.

"There's a difference between the blues of the New Orleans guys and anyone else, and the difference is in a chord, but I can't figure the name of it. It's a different chord, and they *all* make it. I know people stamp

New Orleans as the home of the blues, but I don't because I found the blues everywhere in my travels. In the old days, a lot of people used not to like the blues. If you played blues, you were a nothing to the public—but they were always a kick to me. They always had a good feeling. Guys would walk around with guitars and mandolins, playing and singing the blues on the streets and on the corners. The blues tells a story in itself. It can make you happy or give you a feeling to swing. Here, lately, it's gotten to the place where they've given it a new name—'soul music.' It's always been a *soul* music.

"I heard a good blues singer we knew as Cut as long ago as 1918, in Tulsa, Oklahoma. He had a little band and they played blues in the sense we know it today. Their theme song was *When You Come to the End of a Perfect Day.* They played it at medium tempo, and people flocked to hear them. Cut had drums, sousaphone, trumpet, alto and tenor saxophones. They'd play dances during the week at Nails Park, and the place was always packed. There were after-hours spots they would go to, too. Mostly they played blues, twelve-bar blues, with a few pop songs of the day thrown in. They were not from New Orleans. Most of them were born right around Tulsa. Ernie Fields was around, too, and he had two bands at that time.

"Although I could only play in three keys, I made a living playing piano, but after a time everything began to sound alike to me, and it was then they told me to sing. I was working with Carrie Williams, a very good blues singer out of Chicago. During intermissions, she had to sing suggestive songs like *My Daddy Rocks Me.* She called on me one night and I nearly died. The first number I had to sing was *You Gotta See Mama Every Night or You Can't See Mama at All.*

"When I got homesick and came back from California, in 1926, I worked in my dad's hamburger stand and got to be a pretty good cook. It was a good business, but I used to listen to records and go see the touring shows, and music kept calling me. By 1927, the Blue Devils were getting very big in the state, and when they heard me sing one night I was gone again! We toured all over the Southwest and were recognized as one of the top bands.

"There were no microphones in those days, and unless you could overshadow the horns they wouldn't let you sing. You had to have a good pair of lungs—strong!—to reach out over the band and the people in those big dance halls. Later on, they brought in megaphones for singers like Rudy Vallee, but the crooners and sweet singers couldn't make it before that. As I remember, microphones came into use around 1933, and then you got a different type of singer like Orlando Robeson with Claude Hopkins, and Dan Grissom with Jimmie Lunceford. There was a very good Texas blues singer with Troy Floyd's band called Kellogg Jefferson. He was a kind of male Bessie Smith, but he could also sing high and almost in an opera style.

"Scat singing was just beginning to catch on with the public because of Louis Armstrong. George 'Fathead' Thomas, with McKinney's Cotton Pickers, was a good ballad singer *and* a scat man. A lot of singers tried to copy Louis, but not very successfully. George Thomas was one of the notable exceptions. He was the first I heard sing *I Want a Little Girl*. He did a marvelous job on *Baby, Won't You Please Come Home* and *If I Could Be with You*, too. When he was killed in an accident, I had a chance to take his place, but I couldn't because I had just joined Bennie Moten. I was well known in that part of the country by then, and Bennie's records were coming out on Victor.

"The first record I ever made was *Blue Devil Blues* by the Blue Devils when Walter Page was the leader. A guy had come to Kansas City from Chicago to make records for Vocalion. The number on the back, *Squabblin'*, was Basie's tune.

"Basie had come to the West with a show. He couldn't play the blues then. He was an 'actor' when I first saw him. They would bally-hoo in front of the show, take a band and play a number, and have fellows singing. They would be out on the street, and Basie would explain the show as a crowd gathered around. We'd stand through all the ballyhoo until Basie would play. 'That guy's crazy,' we'd say, because he played so good.

"The first time he heard the Blue Devils, we were ballyhooing on a big truck in Kansas City. There was a lot of that in those days. Wherever you were working, you had to go out and ballyhoo for the place. Coming back from downtown, we struck up with a good blues. Basie heard this and thought it was a record, but somebody told him, 'No, that's the Blue Devils!' He ran down and met all the fellows. Not long after, he quit the show and joined our band.

"The best band in Kansas City in those days was reckoned to be Bennie Moten's. We battled all the bands around, but he avoided us until we caught him one night and tore him up. Then he began to take guys from the Blue Devils when Walter Page had trouble with book-ings. Basie went first, then Lips Page and I. Later, Walter Page broke up his group and joined Bennie, too. We also got Ben Webster, and Moten's band was soon more exciting than it had ever been before. But those were difficult times, in the thirties, and business was just beginning to get better for us when Moten died during an operation for tonsils. After Basie got a little band together at the Reno Club, we still had to scuffle for a while till things clicked for us.

"Bennie Moten had been very well established in Kansas City, although he had started out with just three pieces. I guess the kids would die today if they heard just a piano and drums in a place that would hold six or seven hundred people. The pianist would sing and the drummer would sing, and then they'd sing duets together. They'd play blues and foxtrots. There were fellows then that never did get to the limelight, you know. Did you ever hear of the human-voice whistle? They'd have those and it would sound like someone singing. George and Julia Lee were one of the best teams you could ever hear. Around '23 or '24, Alphonso Trent and Troy Floyd had bands of six or seven pieces in Dallas, more or less what they'd call Dixieland bands today. Different bands and different entertainers were popular in different parts of the country in those days. Work was plentiful in the Middle West. Grant Moore worked out of Omaha and played in Chicago, around Minneapolis, down in Iowa, in Idaho, and all like that. He had great musicians and would play picnics, dances, boat trips, and excursions, for colored and white. Besides all the bands already established there, Bennie Moten and the Blue Devils would play in Kansas, Oklahoma, Tennessee, and Texas. But because most of the recording was done in the East, they never got quite the same attention.

"I used to listen to Alphonso Trent's band whenever I could. Though they played for both races, the dances were always segregated. They were one of the top attractions and played at the Adolphus Hotel in Dallas for years, but they had to use the back door and go up on the freight elevator to the roof garden where they worked. They had a real routine, and for most of the years they could work at the best hotels in Texas. People knew them from their broadcasts. The rest of the time they would tour through states like Oklahoma and Colorado, or take a vacation. They were much better off than most of the guys who were gigging around. They powdered up and had beautiful clothes and automobiles. There weren't many personnel changes in that band.

"There was more harmony in the bands then. I was offered all kinds of money to go with Trent, but I stuck with the Blue Devils and Bennie Moten. We had a lot of good musicians who were offered good jobs in the bands that were making the big money, but they stayed because we had a better time together. Sometimes, when the Blue Devils finished playing a dance, after the cost of the hall, placards, and traveling expenses had been deducted, and the take was split 60–40, we had done so badly that the man gave us his part because he wanted us back. Maybe rain had stopped the crowd turning out, but he knew we had top musicians. Whether we each had a dollar and thirty-six cents coming, or seven dollars and ten cents, we knew we all had the same, and we were happy. It was averaged out and divided up in front of us. Maybe when we played a Fourth of July breakfast dance it would be as much as forty dollars apiece. They'd keep a bank to pay for gasoline and the notes on the cars. In a cooperative like that, if a guy was late we'd bawl him out just as quick as any manager would.

"Lunceford had something like that at one time, but you won't find it anymore, because now a man thinks he has to have more money once he's a soloist. It used to be thumbs down on that. A man took a solo because he *could.* If a guy started drinking or coming late, he'd get three warnings, and then he was replaced. There were no ifs or buts. But sometimes, when we had maybe run through our reserves, whoever was in charge of them would say, 'We haven't much in the kitty, fellows, and it doesn't look as though we are going to make anything tonight, so you had better grab your girls.' Then we'd beg those girls, and in those days, if they liked you, they'd feed you and give you a small piece of money.

"When it came to parties, we used to be like one big family. If one couldn't go, none of us would! People liked to entertain the band. That really began when Basie first started with us; but later, what with being around New York, mixing with other musicians, and with the guys who were taking the solos feeling they ought to have more money —well, it wasn't the kind of band I had originally come out of. New York is something else. Guys wouldn't think of rehearsing without putting in a charge. In Kansas City, when a man wasn't working and was asked to rehearse, it was always, 'Sure!' But here it's 'Forget it, man!' The music game used to carry a certain amount of brotherly love, but it isn't that way now.

"As I said, Basie couldn't play the blues when he first came to Kansas City (and he wasn't 'Count' then), but he soon caught on when he heard Pete Johnson and some of the other great blues players around. In fact, he soon became, with Pete, the best of the blues pianists. Of course, Jay McShann is one of the very best still around today. I tried to get Columbia to send for him when I was recording, but I haven't been able to persuade *anyone* to do that yet. I don't know what it is, but there are some players who come out of the West, the Midwest, who play just exactly what you want. Others, you can't tell them what you want. If I say, 'No, change that chord,' they don't feel it that way and it's something different. There's also the question of touch, and time!

"Now, Earl Hines is a good one. He may say he can't play the blues, but he will for me. He used to play for Chippie Hill at the Golden Lily and the Sunset in Chicago. Guys like that are not always comfortable playing their natural style. They feel they've been playing it so long they need to dress it up to make it sound different today. And that's not good. It's a serious thing that they are made to feel they have to be different. Regardless of everything, Earl Hines is Earl Hines, a great pianist.

"Nat Cole is another one for playing the blues. He was a great admirer of Earl Hines, and you have to remember that. I used to sit down at night and listen to Earl for hours in after-hours spots. He was a pacesetter in Chicago for years, and everybody tried to play like him.

"This business of switching styles can't be done honestly by one man. As soon as he can play his instrument well, he can express himself, and all his life he has only one self.

"Basie used to please people with his piano, but he got away from it when bop came along. He got shy. I used to say, 'Come on, Basie, play one!' He'd say, 'Oh, man, I can't play no more.' But Basie can play a whole lot of piano still. When people asked me about it, I would say, 'Well, Basie's gotten lazy, and he hides behind his band.' That was only partly true. We used to go to house parties where he wouldn't be criticized, and Basie would play. How he played! Oh, God! You hear him on Bennie Moten's *Lafayette* and *Prince of Wales*. That's true Basie. But he wouldn't play like that now any more than the man in the moon. What if it's old, if it's good? He could still do it, but I think he got a little self-conscious about his playing. I know when I was with the band he would lay out and let the band take it on down. The record companies used to fight with him. 'The people want to hear the piano,' they'd say. 'That's what they want.' And that's why those Kansas City Seven records sold like they did: because there was some Basie on them.

"You could take Basie, Duke, Earl, Nat Cole, and Erroll Garner, and out of all of them Garner would be the only one not self-conscious about his playing. The others couldn't even play in the way they were raised in, although if they did you would hear some of the finest of music. For instance, people kind of frown on stride piano, even though it's hard and they can't play it.

"I worked with Ralph Sutton in California. I hadn't worked that way in years, with just piano and drums, and I was so well pleased. Ralph carried such a heavy left hand, it sounded like a bass. We broke the show up for two weeks and I didn't feel tired once. I've seen the time when I've had five or six pieces in there, but they wouldn't carry the time the way he did playing stride piano.

"I've been trying to get Ralph and me together as a combo for the past year. He can play all the stuff like Willie The Lion. I wanted to have him with a small combo in Toronto, but the guy there couldn't see it. In a way, Ralph doesn't even need drums, but he can be more relaxed when he can hear that beat all the time and he doesn't have to play so hard. It's the same with me. I'm more relaxed when I can hear the beat clearly all the time I'm singing.

"To go back to the old days, to the twenties . . . I remember when we had a small combo of seven or eight pieces. The sousaphone was just beginning to go out, and they were bringing in the bass fiddle. We had a drummer who used to beat the side of a leather case and get a sound like a rimshot. Believe me, that kind of beat does something to you. When a guy took a solo—a 'Boston' in those days—everybody in the band used to hit that beat; and on a swing tune you were home free. You had no worries. Then they brought the after-beat in on the high-hat, and now drummers like Sam Woodyard are bringing it back with rimshots. I like it, especially on a going-out chorus. Sometimes, when the drummer is playing fast—not clear and definite—the average guy in the horns can't hear the beat and gets lost. Many times I've heard musicians like Earle Warren and Dicky Wells say, 'What's the matter with the drummer? Why doesn't he stay in there?' When you've got a big ensemble going, you've got to be able to *feel* those drums, not just hear them. I've noticed on a lot of records you hear all top but no bottom to the drums. You must feel that bottom, and they should put a microphone on the bass drum.

"Not that they used the bass drum the way they ought. I walked behind a drummer on stage one time, and he had his right foot wrapped around his stool.

" 'What's wrong, man?' I asked him.

" 'What?' he said.

" 'What do you use that foot for?'

" 'I don't use that no more.'

" 'I'm not going to tell you how to drum, man, but give me that four,' I said.

" 'Oh, yes, yes . . .'

"Even before I heard Chick Webb, the drummer with the Blue Devils, and all those in the other bands in the Midwest, used to play that four on the bass drum. They all played but one way. Where they got this thing about neglecting the bass drum and carrying all the time on top, I don't know. A lot of young people don't know what's missing. They've been brought up without it and they don't know how it should be.

"Alvin Burroughs, who was with the Blue Devils, and later with Earl Hines, was one of the great drummers. He came to us from Little Rock, Arkansas. Another drummer who was the Jo Jones and Gene Krupa of the day before yesterday was A. G. Godley. He was with

Alphonso Trent's band for a long time until he quit playing and went to work. They used to use those little sock cymbals with their hands. (You can hear them on *Squabblin'* by the Blue Devils.) They used to shove the spotlight on A. G. Godley and he would drum for half an hour, years before Buddy Rich. There was another fine drummer out of Chicago, in Grant Moore's band. We used to call him 'Jeans.'

"In the old days, too, you could name almost as many good women pianists as men. Besides Mary Lou Williams, there were Countess Johnson and Julia Lee in Kansas City, another girl in Oklahoma, and a girl out of Minneapolis. But apart from pianists, there were never too many girls who could play in bands.

"So today [January 23, 1963] I was surprised to find that Patti Bown could sit in with a big band. I knew she had worked with Quincy Jones, but she was so relaxed on my date. And you can't be relaxed unless you know what you're doing. I think this album* was sort of on the new side for me, compared to what I had been doing. We have a little touch of the 'progressive' in it. It's all right for pop tunes, and I think people will like it, but I wouldn't get away from the things that made me popular in days gone by.

"When we went out with Basie once in the forties, he had changed his style to a certain extent. He had a bunch of new arrangements, and some fellow yelled out, 'Come on, Count! What the heck! You trying to sound like Stan Kenton?'

"I always say that Basie had a style he never should have changed. He came back to some extent, and he keeps it pretty simple, but the public grows with you and likes to hear you the way you came up. Once you've established yourself, they don't want you to get too far away from there. When I talk to people in the audience, they so often tell me, 'I have all your old records, and I won't let anybody borrow them.' Or, 'When I want a big kick I play the old arrangements—you and Basie.' It's dangerous to get too far from what they identify you with.

"I understand how fly-by-night things like bossa nova are introduced and promoted, but when they've gone you've got to get back to the main source—the blues. I can sing anything I want, maybe two or three songs before the blues, but the minute I begin *Goin' to Chicago*, or something like that, I hear that scream start. So if I told a guy who requested *Goin' to Chicago* that I didn't sing it now, or said I couldn't remember it—that would be very funny.

"I play the Playboy clubs and a lot of other clubs across the country, but I never thought the time would come when I would go up on the

* *Five Feet of Soul* (Colpix 446).

bandstand, call this or that familiar number, and have some of the cats on the stand say, 'Don't know it!' And they don't. They're younger musicians and most of them don't know anything farther back than Charlie Parker.

"I've been asked several times, 'What's going to happen to American jazz?' It's a big question. 'Well, Jim,' people ask, 'what will happen when you and Duke and Basie have gone?' We are not the patterns anymore. Years ago, when you heard a pianist, you'd say, 'He sounds like Earl Hines.' Or it might be Fats Waller, or Pete Johnson, the boogie-woogie man. You don't get that anymore. Musicians are afraid to pattern themselves on the great artists for fear someone will tell them, 'You sound like so-and-so.' Everybody's trying to create I don't know what. Maybe I should say a style of their own; but they try so hard to be different that they lose the soul.

"I met a fellow out in Detroit some years ago, a pianist who could play his ass off. He was very good. He came to New York, went to Juilliard, finished there, and went out on his own. Now when he plays for you, he mixes in the progressive style and augments the blues chords. That causes trouble, because you can't add to the blues. But it's *different*, even if he does lose the blues! The blues are just the old church chords, two- or three-part harmony, and that's all. When he makes the big chord, it's something else, and he loses the feeling.

"When I get to singing, with someone like that behind me, I may be feeling pretty good, but he'll strike one chord and take everything away from me. Such a lot of beautiful songs and solos have been built around the blues chords that the big chord seems like a big mistake to me.

"There are not as many good blues pianists as there used to be, but Jimmy Smith—though he plays organ—is a real blues man. He builds his whole repertoire around the blues. Ray Bryant is a very good blues pianist today, and so is Sir Charles Thompson, if you can make him play it. The 'progressive' kick has changed many people. A lot of musicians feel they're obsolete if they play the way they really should, the way they were taught years ago. They think that makes them 'webby,' as though they'd got spider webs on them! Not Basie, though. It's amusing. Sometimes, when he takes a solo, and then the band comes in, it's like two entirely different things. *He* is true to his first love in music.

"When I go in front of an audience, I'll admit I sometimes have a certain amount of fear in me, because maybe the people are not going to accept what I'm doing today. That's bad for any artist, especially if what you're doing is not in line with what's happening today. If you don't get the right amount of applause, you feel you're not doing the right thing, and you get nervous. Automatically, you begin to wonder if you're too old or passé, and that will work on you if you're not careful. It's not a matter of ability or, if you like, artistry. I remember singing *I Want a Little Girl* one night—and that's normally one of my big ones, after *Goin' to Chicago*—and the crowd just looked at me, as much to say, 'What is *that?*' That drug me. Other times, people know it and request it. But the performer always has his problems before he goes on. He tries to figure what will hit the crowd, like going for the jackpot. If I sing *When You're Smiling*, and they scream, I do another like that; and meantime someone will probably yell for *Goin' to Chicago*. When I get a good reaction on that, I go right into *St. Louis Blues*. It's surprising, though, how difficult it is to pick right.

"When I come out with a new album, guys will say, 'It's a typical Jimmy Rushing record.' Well, who else would it be? If I'm going to do blues, it's going to be a typical Jimmy Rushing record because I don't think any other way. It's impossible for me to be like anybody else. If it doesn't sell, if a guy doesn't like it, that's something else.

"I'm funny about recording something someone else has done and made a hit out of. When I did *I'm Walking Through Heaven with You*, I took the tempo a little up as compared with Lunceford's. I'm not being egotistical, but after I made *Goin' to Chicago*, a lot of people said, 'Nobody can sing that but Jimmy.' In the same way, I don't think anybody could make *I'm Walking Through Heaven* other than Lunceford's Dan Grissom; so if I'm going to record the same number I want a different tempo or something. Like this number of Billie Holiday's they wanted me to do. 'Oh, no,' I said, 'I have always cherished Billie and I don't feel anyone else could do the things she did.' The artist who establishes a number, in other words, has the edge. Like some of those Louis Armstrong made. Nevertheless, I love that song of his, *Someday You'll Be Sorry*, and I'm going to try to do that in my next album."

(1963)

Jimmy Rushing died June 8, 1972.

Lester "Prez" Young

(TENOR SAXOPHONE AND CLARINET)

Lester "Prez" Young haunts the pages of this book in the memories of those who knew and admired him. François Postif's famous interview with him, shortly before his death in 1959, was finally printed unexpurgated twenty years later in the French magazine *Jazz Hot* (nos. 362 and 363). The 1958 interview with Chris Albertson, which follows, is very different in tone, but not less revealing of the gentle, considerate person Young basically was.

The second, somewhat impressionistic section was written for the British magazine *Melody Maker* in 1956. It is included here primarily because Young liked it, and had his manager, Charlie Carpenter, write to tell me so.

I

Chris Albertson. First, I want to, if you can, talk about the old days. . . . You played with King Oliver for a year, didn't you?
Lester Young. Yes, about a year.

A. That was after Louis Armstrong moved away from the band, wasn't it?

Y. Many moons after, you know, because that was an older tribe than me. I came like in the middle of that.

A. Then you played with . . . Let's see, from there where did you go?

Y. From King Oliver? Then I played with a band called the Bostonians. They were out of Salina, Kansas. It was a nice little group, about eight or ten pieces.

A. Anybody we might know in the band?

Y. Oh, I'm sure you wouldn't. The boss-man's name was Art Bronson, so I know you never heard of him. He played piano.

A. Did you make your first records with Basie?

Y. Yes. My first records—I made 'em in Chicago.

A. With the old Basie band?

Y. Right. We were playing at the Grand Terrace.

A. Did you always play the way you did? Coleman Hawkins was *the* tenor sax man in those days.

Y. Yeah. . . . Well, I had a lot of trouble along in those days, because the people couldn't understand the way I sounded and they wanted me to play like Coleman Hawkins. Well, to each his own. So . . . I played in a band and there were about three boys from the West. They fired the trombone player . . . a great big envelope. Then they fired the trumpet player. When he was gone, well, I'm the third party. I know they're going to fire me, too. You dig? We were all from Kansas City, you know, and we came to New York and we weren't in the New York clique. So that made a difference. So I went to him and asked could I get a recommendation so I could split and go back home. So he did, and I went back, and then I started playing with Andy Kirk.

A. But you replaced Hawkins, didn't you, in the Fletcher Henderson band?

Y. Yes, I did.

A. Wasn't it pretty tough for you to replace him, when everybody was so used to the Hawkins style?

Y. Oh, yeah. I got all kinds of trouble, because most of the people would come out to hear him, and see me up there and listen to the way I sounded. . . . They were looking for him. I think he was in Switzerland, or Sweden, or something like that.

A. When did you first meet Billie Holiday?

Y. When I came to New York, in 1934. I used to live at her house, with her mother, 'cause I didn't know my way around. She taught me a lot of things, and got me little record dates, playing behind her, and little solos, and things like that.

A. You're her favorite soloist.

Y. She is mine, too. So that's a draw.

A. I understand she gave you the name Prez, didn't she?

Y. Yes, she did, and I gave her the name of Lady Day. So that was even.

A. I think she has said that her style of singing is formed after your style on tenor sax.

Y. Well, I think you can hear that on some of the old records. Sometimes I sit down and listen to them myself and it sounds like two of the same breed if you don't be careful, or the same line, or something like that.

A. Tell me, did you ever make records with Hawkins?

Y. With Hawkins? No, I never did.

A. You probably will some day. Now, is there anything you can tell us about Billie Holiday? Or any funny incidents when you were on the road with the Basie band?

Y. Oh, no, I couldn't think of anything like that. I just know we were all happy, always waiting to go to work, and things like that.

A. I was talking to Basie the other day, on this same show, and he was telling me that he preferred recording in the old days, when you had just one microphone. Now, he said, he has the rhythm section around the corner . . . and it's so confusing. Do you feel that way?

Y. One microphone?

A. Yes, in the old days, when they had just one microphone. Now it's become so technical. There are microphones all over the studio, and you're so split up. You're not together, the big band . . .

Y. I don't think I'd go for that. If you've got one mike, you've got to run over to the mike and play and then come and sit down, with only one mike. Now they make it convenient, with a mike here and a mike there, and a mike everywhere.

A. Did you use one mike when you recorded with Basie?

Y. Yes, that's true.

A. Well, several musicians whom I have interviewed have said the same thing, that they felt the spirit was more there in the old days, when you were recording. There were clinkers, but there was more feeling in the music because it wasn't so technical. Nowadays everything is technical, with high fidelity and everything, and they feel they just can't get into the right feeling.

Y. I still don't buy that. To each his own. No, I don't think like that.

A. What other bands have you played with?

Y. Well, with Teddy Wilson, records and things like that. I never played with him regular.

A. Do you have any favorite records of your own?

Y. No, I really couldn't say. When I get by myself, I just play them and enjoy them all.

A. Did you ever hear Bessie Smith? I'm sure you did.

Y. Yeah. I thought *she* was a wild lady with her blues.

A. Do you think there's anybody nowadays who can sing like her?

Y. Yeah.

A. Of the vocalists today, whom do you like?

Y. Oh, you left Bessie Smith, huh? Well, sometimes you think upon Kay Starr and listen to her voice and play one of Bessie Smith's records, and see if you hear anything.

A. You feel there is a similarity there?

Y. Yes, very much.

A. We have played Kay Starr records on this show, and she definitely does have a good voice for jazz. How about some of these new singers that are coming out nowadays?

Y. No. I can tell you really my favorite singer is Kay Starr. No . . . that's the wrong name. Her husband has a band. . . .

A. Jo Stafford?

Y. There you are! I'll go there. Yeah. And Lady Day. And I'm through.

A. Jo Stafford doesn't sing jazz, does she?

Y. No, but I hear her voice and the sound and the way she puts her songs on.

A. That's amazing. How do you feel now when you hear your old records?

Y. I think it was nice during those days. I have a lot of trouble on the bandstand, people coming to ask me, "How come you don't play like you played when you played with Count Basie?" Well, that's not progressive. If I'm going to stay there and play that same stuff year after year . . . I'll be an old man! I don't think like that, so I have to try to think of little new tricks and little new sounds and things like that—that's the way I do.

A. Are there any tenor sax men nowadays, newcomers, that you like especially?

Y. Well, I imagine I'll say I like them all. They all sound the same to me, because almost all of them went to Juilliard and whoever that teacher was, he taught them all the same thing. This one will start playing it, this one will pick it up and start playing it, the same thing. In my mind, the individual is going to come out and play for himself. Like, if you have thirteen people and the teacher teach all thirteen of them, you mean to tell me out of the thirteen he can't get *one* individual? That's the way *I* think.

A. So you don't have any favorites?

Y. Oh, no; I like them all. I like modern . . .

A. But you think there should be more individual styles?

Y. Yes, that's all.

A. How do you feel about Coleman Hawkins' style?

Y. Well, the way I look at him . . . he's the first person who played the tenor saxophone who woke you up and let you know there *was* a tenor saxophone. So when I see all the kiddies who are copying his style . . . That's about all I could say on that.

A. You don't think very highly of his style? It's not your type of music?

Y. Well . . . that's incomplete . . . !

A. You've traveled a lot with Jazz at the Philharmonic. How do the Europeans react to you? Do you feel any difference in your audience in Europe?

Y. They're very nice over there. I've been over twice.

A. Dizzy Gillespie feels that they appreciate the music more than the American audiences. How do you feel about that?

Y. I don't think I'll buy that. If a person likes you, they like you, and if they don't, they don't like you, that's all.

A. Do you ever play the clarinet anymore?

Y. Yeah. I just made some records for Norman Granz, about four or five or six months ago, on my clarinet.

A. I heard some records that you made with . . . was it Walter Page and His Blue Devils?

Y. Yes, many moons ago.

A. . . . *Way Down Yonder in New Orleans?*

Y. Right.

A. Are the records you made with Norman Granz the latest ones you've made?

Y. Well, the way we make records, Norman and I, he'd make so many records and then he'd put them in a vault, and he'd stash them away. Then when he wants to go and get them, he'll bring them out. And you can never tell when you'll hear one, 'cause that's his business, you know. So that's the way it is.

A. How do you feel about the reissue of the old Basie records? Do you ever go back and listen to the old records?

Y. Um-hum. I have some in my room, and I listen to them and try to dig little mistakes, little things that you could have done a little better.

A. We did a show on Coleman Hawkins the other day, two weeks ago, and we explained the difference between your styles and played one of your records, *Lester Leaps In,* with Count Basie's Kansas City Seven. That was a long time ago. Do you still play that number?

Y. I must have made about three or four different records of that.
That's just like a crib. I used to play it all night long.

A. Like Hawkins. They're always asking him to play *Body and Soul.*
So what are you doing now, just touring the States and playing various
spots?

Y. No, I've been off. I was a little sick and had to go to the hospital
and all that. I haven't worked since the fifth of August—I mean July.
This is my first week that I have. It takes a little time to build your
chops up.

A. Before we close, I want to ask what you think of Mahalia Jackson?

Y. I think she's great.

A. She has been compared with Bessie Smith. Do you think she could
sing like Bessie Smith if she sang the blues?

Y. That's a little deep for me. She's religious, right?

A. Yes. She won't sing anything but religious songs, but she has the
tremendous voice, very powerful voice.

Y. Yeah. I heard her . . . *Hold My Hand*, or something like that?

A. She has so many, I'm not sure . . . *He's Got the Whole World in
His Hand.* . . .

Y. Yes, something like that.

A. Thank you very much.

Y. It's a pleasure meeting you, Chris.

A. A pleasure meeting you.

(1958)

II

To some, Lester Young was the Trojan Horse of jazz, dragged into hot
and happy Troy by Count Basie and his carefree men. To others, he
was a voice crying in the wilderness, a herald of glad, cool times to
come. To others again, he was the lonely signpost at the meeting of
the ways, indicative of both, but committed to neither.

Whatever view you hold, the fact remains that in the jazz story
Young is one of those key figures whose style, nurtured in one era,
profoundly influenced the course of the next. We can look back now
and see how the brilliance that was Armstrong's leapt out of King
Oliver's orchestra like a Roman candle's fireball to presage the next
decade's solo idiom. And we can see now how Young's revolutionary
approach to sound, tone, and phrasing was full of implications of the
shape of things to come.

Young had the background. Born in New Orleans in 1909, his experience went all the way back to King Oliver, with whom he worked a year. After a phase in Kansas City, he took Coleman Hawkins's place with Fletcher Henderson in 1934, to the inevitable dismay of Hawkins's admirers. Returning to Kansas City, he joined Basie for the second time in 1936, and an epic four-year partnership began.

By that time Kansas City had made up its mind which way it wanted to go. It was swinging with uninhibited violence, with a direct, uncomplicated beat. When the Basie band came east, it had a rhythmically elemental quality which made even the best New York bands sound a little prissy. The heart of the band was the famous rhythm section, the heart of the rhythm section was Basie, and what stimulated Basie was Lester Young. No matter how much the band played, there was always that *duo* feeling between these two.

The driving, extrovert, rhythmic kick was not entirely Young's way. He needed the inimitable Basie rhythm behind him to insure the initial lift and subsequent freedom to fly (and never afterward was he afforded such security). Once away, however, soaring, his improvisations were to a considerable degree independent of the necessity to emphasize the beat audibly, although his musical heritage insured that it was always implied.

Hawkins had gone to Europe in 1934, but he had left behind the memory and influence of the style he had perfected during his decade with Fletcher Henderson. His was the big sound, with the rich, sensual tone, warm vibrato, incomparable rhythmic power, and unlimited imagination that assure him a place among the First Five of Jazz Giantry with any unbiased assessor. His seemed the ideal way of playing tenor, and with the exception of Bud Freeman, the Chicagoan whose tone approximated Lester's, all the leading tenor players drew inspiration from him. One of his disciples was Herschel Evans, who also played in Basie's band.

The rivalry between Evans and Young probably pushed both of them further in their respective directions than they might otherwise have gone. Evans has been overshadowed by Young, and as a result of his early death it is not always realized how great an artist he was; but the invention, the virtual creation of Young, was more readily apparent when contrasted with the approved and recognizable style that Evans played.

Compared with the big sound of the Hawkins tradition, Young's sound was diminished and light. He used far less vibrato. Where Hawkins was all power and confidence, Young was cool and detached. Irrespective of tempo, his melodic invention was always strange and haunting. On a jump number, he would impose a weird mood; a ballad was transformed into a nostalgic song, searching and mysterious. His phrasing was astonishingly varied rhythmically, rarely pushing, often lagging in a fashion new to the times and unique to himself. All of these qualities in the music were reflections of Young's unusual personality.

Those who knew him well would tell you that Young was no grabber or boaster, but essentially a gentle soul, a lover of beauty, of beauty as he saw it in beings, values, and things. Quick-witted, hip to everything of moment around him, experience had shown him the wisdom of detachment. He lived in a world of his own, accepting the fact that his highest, most idealistic values were out of reach. His fellow musicians were quick to sense the maturity of this acceptance and of its expression in his music. The young strive—with heat, anxiety, and impatience—for the impossible, whereas Young, like a wistful lover, was content to sing about it. Consistency of outlook and single-mindedness of approach sprang from this acceptance and his desire to come to terms with life. We may be sure that he would not have accepted many aspects of life had he had the choice, but that intuitive insight into cause and effect allowed him to practice tolerance while observing critically.

A sensitive person like Lester Young undoubtedly suffered much initially from those who compared his sound unfavorably with Hawkins's. It is a tribute to his artistic integrity that by 1940 he had compromised not at all. In fact, in an era when the tenor saxophone became the paramount solo instrument, his style was more influential than Hawkins's, earning him the nickname of "President" and its affectionate abbreviation, "Prez," and even influencing a singer like Billie Holiday, who tried to improvise in the same way. Charlie Parker admitted admiration but denied being influenced. That may be. Yet when the artificial attitudes of bop, physical and musical, were introduced, many of those attitudes had already been given expression with casual innocence by Young. He had made it quite clear where he stood. "I play a *swing* tenor." So he did, and so did his disciples, like Allen Eager, Paul Quinichette, Gene Ammons, and the late Wardell Gray, whenever the rhythm sections permitted. That Young liked more than a "listening beat" from his accompanists is evident from the superiority of his work with rhythm sections containing such swinging musicians as Count Basie, King Cole, Johnny Guarneri, and Teddy Wilson.

His cat-footed walk, his eccentric but unstudied stance, his hat, his exciting contributions out of a personal dream on a roaring J.A.T.P. stage, and his water pistol duels at Birdland all go to form the legend of the giant and genius that was Lester Young the President. On an inspired liner, David Stone Martin once depicted Lester and that famous Tower of Pisa. Lester was leaning the opposite way to the tower.

No copy-cat he!

(1956)

Lester Young died March 15, 1959.

Buck Clayton

"I first began to get interested in jazz when I was twelve. I was learning to play piano then in my hometown, Parsons, Kansas. It was a small railroad town of about eleven thousand people. The Missouri, Kansas & Texas Railway—the M.K.T.—had their headquarters in Parsons, and because it was a railway junction all the trains from Texas to Kansas City used to stop there.

"My father was a minister and a musician, and he taught me to play piano. He played tuba. Every Sunday, the church orchestra would rehearse at our house and the guys would leave their instruments there until the following week. So there were always plenty of horns to pick up and blow, and we had two pianos as well. A girl called Noreen Tate, who has been in New York, was in my father's band, too. She made some fine piano records with Sonny Greer playing brushes.

"Wild Bill Davis's father and mine were very good friends. They used to sing in the same quartet. He had a beautiful baritone voice and my father sang bass. Sir Charles Thompson's father was a church pastor, and they lived in Parsons, too.

"I suppose because I'd had the piano tuition, I was the one who organized a little six-piece band of kids aged from about twelve to sixteen. We had a drummer and the rest of us mostly played combs. We used to try to play tunes like *Hard to Get Gertie*, and we would maybe make a dollar apiece most weeks playing rent parties. We had a lot of records and the Bennie Moten and George E. Lee bands would play Parsons on their way through from Oklahoma to Kansas City. We also used to hear Coon Sanders on the radio, which we called the 'wireless' in those days.

"At one time, I liked George E. Lee's band best. He had a novelty band and they used to stand up and swing their trumpets around. Later, as a professional musician, I realized Moten had the better band. I'd take a girl to a dance at that time and not dance at all, but stand in front of the band and listen to the music all night long. She'd get mad at me, and the next day I didn't have a girl!

"I really got on the trumpet after one of George E. Lee's visits to Parsons. I met a fellow named Bob Russell who was with him. Although I had been very interested in trumpet, I had never really tried to play it. Bob had a very sharp personality, and he dressed well, and he had a mellophone and a slide trumpet—about five different horns. He talked to me and encouraged me very much, and at that time I had never heard Louis Armstrong, so Bob was really the very first trumpet in my life. I thought he was good then, but I haven't heard him since. I think he's out in Washington, around Seattle.

"Jazz was looked down upon in those days, but my father wouldn't be at the house parties! My mother told me she didn't want me to play jazz. There would be someone playing cornet down at a little dive, the Bucket of Blood, and somebody was always getting killed there. There was another place in Kansas City, the Yellow Front, and every Saturday night somebody would get killed in there, too. They tried to check the knives at the door as you went in, but people would be killed anyway. So my mother didn't want me to play in places like that, and I don't think she changed her mind about jazz until 1938 when I played at Carnegie Hall with Benny Goodman. There's no drinking at Carnegie Hall!

"I left home when I was nineteen, but I didn't leave strictly for music. A friend of mine had emigrated to California, and he wrote me so many pretty letters about how beautiful it was that I decided to go. So I ran away, and hoboed out there, and I stayed for four months, doing different jobs in a garage, a pool hall, a barber's shop, and washing dishes. I even took a chance on being a prizefighter. I had been a pretty good wrestler before I left home, but in those days wrestling wasn't like it is now. Then it was more in the style of the ancient

Greeks and a matter of different holds. I went to the gymnasium about twice, but I didn't like it. I preferred racking balls in a pool hall to prizefighting!

"When school time came around again, I went home, finished high school, got my diploma, returned to California, and really started my musical career there. I'll never forget the last job I had before I began playing professionally. I was working in a barber's shop in Los Angeles, and I was about nineteen. I had my trumpet and I knew how to run a few scales on it, but not well enough to play. When I got to California, there was a little band led by a guy called Duke Ellighew. (At that time everyone was trying to be like Duke Ellington.) He was a young cat, a trumpet player, about my age, and somebody told him about me. He asked me to come to a rehearsal at nine one Wednesday night. I was supposed to mop and sweep in the barber's shop after eight o'clock. I decided to sweep it real good and hope they wouldn't notice it hadn't been mopped. The fellow who owned the shop had a cousin who wanted my job. I swept real good, split out, and went to the band rehearsal. The next day I go to the job and I'm fired. 'You didn't mop,' the guy says, and he gives the job to his cousin.

"So I go back to the band. They're only playing parties, one or two nights a week, but I was single and I could make it. I was living in a basement, paying two dollars a week, and I remember once I was thirty-two dollars behind in rent! I stayed with that band about six months until I got my first *real* professional job at a taxi dance—the Red Mill dance hall. After that I never went back to anything else. The band was led by Lavern Floyd, a piano player, and he'd heard about this little young trumpet player from Kansas City. I think I had been making around sixteen dollars a week with Ellighew and he could offer thirty-five. That was like a thousand to me. These were my first real professional jobs apart from once in Kansas when a five-piece band came through and the trumpet got sick. They came and got me. I couldn't play anything but *Dinah,* and I played that all night for five dollars.

"There had been quite a shift of New Orleans players to California, musicians like Papa Mutt Carey and Kid Ory. There were about eight taxi dances in Los Angeles at that time and Papa Mutt was playing in one of them. I liked the way he played with a mute very much, but he never taught me. He was very nice to me, but my father had taught me how to play scales and I think that was the only thing anyone ever taught me on the trumpet. From then on I had to go on my own, and I never had a lesson on trumpet. Another player I liked very much and used to listen to was Claude Kennedy from Texas. He was a whiz, but he died and you never hear of him now.

"I left the taxi dance hall for a fourteen-piece band led by Charlie Echols that played all the great big ballrooms. That was my first big band. Then Earl Dancer, a big-time Broadway guy, came to California from New York. He had put Ethel Waters way up on top and he came with offers to make movies, so we all left Echols and went with him. We had to eliminate Earl when we found out later that he was gambling with our money. Because I had been arranging for the band, they elected me leader. I already knew the keyboard, because of that piano tuition, and a fellow named Parker Berry showed me, 'This is the trumpet, this is the trombone,' and so on, and I had picked up on arranging.

"One of the things I remember from about this time was the earthquake in 1933. I went to the union that day and from there I went to the barber's shop, and the guy was cutting my hair when there was this rumbling like thunder. They had the radio on with Bing Crosby singing, and the announcer says, 'The next number you're going to hear is *You May Never Come This Way Again*,' or something like that. There was some more rumbling and the ceiling started cracking, and a mirror fell off the wall. The guy says, 'Earthquake!'—and I'd never had one before—but I was out of that chair and in the street very soon. The street-car tracks were buckling and bricks were falling off the hotels, but nothing hit me. There was a place that sold chickens nearby and I remember women going home with chickens tucked up under their skirts. That night, they had big bonfires going in the streets and everybody stayed around them, praying.

"I was twenty-one and a bandleader when I took the band to China. Teddy Weatherford came back with orders to take an American band to Shanghai—no particular one, just a good one. At that time there were really only two in California—Les Hite's and mine. Teddy liked mine and I don't think he could have gotten Les Hite's, because Les was at the Cotton Club. We considered it quite an honor to accompany Teddy Weatherford to China, and we found it very nice, very European —not wild. We hadn't anything to lose, but we did think it rather a daring step. The sidemen were going to make a lot of money, and in 1934, right after the Crash, a hundred dollars a week was a lot. So we went to Shanghai and stayed two years. Bumps Myers, Eddie Beal, Teddy Buckner, Baby Lewis, and Caughey Roberts were in the band.

"Teddy lived in a big house in Shanghai and my wife and I always went by his to eat. The White Russians were numerous in Shanghai then and they seemed to like to pile everything up with thick, white cream in their restaurants, which was another reason for preferring the food at Teddy's. I didn't learn Chinese and I had no desire to, because there are so many different dialects. It's like learning English in New York and going to Newark, New Jersey, and finding they don't understand what you're talking about.

"We played at the Canidrome Ballroom in the International Settlement. It was run by English people and everything was fine until we ran into some racial prejudice from Atlanta, Georgia. A fellow came in one night and called me quite a few obnoxious names. The place was so beautiful I couldn't believe what I heard. Anyway, I gave the downbeat for the next number, the band began to play and a bunch of girls from Hollywood—the Hollywood Blondes—ran out all over the floor. I went over to the table where this fellow was sitting, and it turned out he was a boxer and an ex-marine. Before I even got to his table, he popped me one between the eyes, and while I'm still shaking my head I'm aware the band is all jumping off the stand to get to him. So there's a big free-for-all and when it's over this guy is all beat up. He sued the place and we all had to go to court. One of our main witnesses was Madame Chiang Kai-shek. She always wanted to learn tap dancing and she was taking lessons from one of my trombone players. We testified and this guy lost the case and had to pay court charges and everything, but after that there was such pressure and prejudice that we left the place to avoid bringing more trouble to it. We had played many dances for the marines and had a lot of friends among them. Six months after the trial was over, they caught this guy—they called him a rat—and beat him, and left him draped over the steering wheel of his car. That's how he was found the next day.

"It was a big thing, and I have article after article about it in my scrapbook, but it cost us our job, and for three weeks afterwards I had to have a bodyguard if I wanted to go to a nightclub. The other place we went to—the Casanova—could only take half the band, so the rest of the guys went home.

"At the Canidrome, we had played for dancing every night, and every Sunday we had an afternoon matinee when we used to play quite a bit of classical music and things like Ravel's *Bolero*, and *Rhapsody in Blue* with Teddy Weatherford playing the Gershwin piano parts. We wore tails—we had gray, white, and black—and altogether it was a wonderful foundation for me. I remember I had to learn every note of that *Rhapsody in Blue* so that I could conduct it. Jack Bratton, who's now a druggist, and I used to write the arrangements.

"Eventually, we returned to Los Angeles, opened at Frank Sebastian's Cotton Club, and played there and at the Club Araby for quite a few seasons. I had seen China, California, and part of Mexico and

Canada, and then I got the urge to go to New York. I was hearing about the Cotton Club there and what was going on, and I tried to get my band to come east, but western boys like their home state and barbecue pits the way New York boys like their apartments and after-hour spots, so in the end I gave Eddie Beal all my arrangements and split.

"On my way east to join Willie Bryant, I stopped to visit and talk with my mother for a couple of days. Lips Page had just quit Basie and when I went back into Kansas City he had told Basie I was available. So Basie called me, said he knew I was going to New York right away, but if I waited two or three months I could go with him. I was with him two months at the Reno Club. We left Kansas City October 31, 1936, Halloween Night, the same night we had played in a battle of bands with Duke Ellington at the Paseo Ballroom. In our minds, we thought we had won the battle, but when we got on the bus to leave there wasn't one single friend of ours on hand to assure us we had. So probably we didn't, and knowing Duke as I know him now, I'm almost sure we didn't.

"Our reputation, before we came east, was built on nine pieces, and I don't think we ever had a bad night in Kansas City, but when we added five or six men it made a lot of difference. The band had to be enlarged to go on the road, but it slowed everything down and made it sluggish, because those extra men were not exactly the best musicians. Then Benny Morton, Dicky Wells, Harry Edison, and Earle Warren came in and it began to sound like a good big band. At first it was a disappointment, especially as compared with the band in Kansas City. Anyone who heard it there heard the swingingest band in the world. It was really a pleasure to play in it. Of course, we weren't making any money to speak of, but things were cheap then and I think my rent was only about three dollars a week. We always had fun some kind of way.

"From there we went to Pittsburgh and Chicago, and we opened in New York at Roseland just in time for New Year's, which I'll never forget. It was a sight that first New Year's on Broadway, in 1937. There were so many people.

"The band first started clicking in the Famous Door. We had made good changes and the band sounded well together. The place was small and we sat close together, and the low ceilings made the band sound beautiful, and it was a rocking place, and that's where business started picking up. Café Society was another valuable stepping stone.

"The first song I ever wrote for Basie was called *Baby Girl*. We never recorded it, but we—the nine pieces—used to play it and swing it. I wrote it for my sister's little girl. Others I did for Basie were *Red*

Bank Boogie, Taps Mills, What's Your Number?, Avenue C, and *Love Jumped Out.* I have arranged for Benny Goodman and Tommy Dorsey, and I did a couple of things for Duke. I wrote *Hollywood Hangover* when I was in the army, when I had plenty of time to write, which I didn't have with Basie.

"He was a leader all right, but not a harsh one. When someone got too unruly, he would eventually get stirred up and let him know he was the boss. He was very nice to work for, but he always knew what he wanted from the band and the arrangers. At the beginning, it used to take us so long to get through the arrangements. We'd have to help guys who didn't do so much reading, but who were great as soloists and were accustomed to the 'heads.'

"Lester and Herschel never said an unkind word to one another. There was some kind of feeling between them, but a lot of respect and no real animosity. I remember one time Herschel stopped speaking to me for about a month. I finally found out that he thought in writing my arrangements I was giving Lester all the tenor solos. All I was doing was giving the solos as Basie told me, and Herschel blamed me for it. I think Basie felt Lester showed the band off best when it was flagging and waving and carrying on, but for the mellow things—slow blues and sentimental numbers—he preferred Herschel.

"The only reason I played all those things with a mute with Basie was because he asked me to, and as he was the leader his wishes were like commands. When I came out of the army I was my own judge and I played like I wanted to. The funny thing about Basie was that he'd ask me to record with a mute, but when we got out on one-nighters he'd have me play the same thing open. I don't mind playing with a mute, but not all the time. I got so I hated the cup mute then. There's even a record called *Cup Mute Clayton* that I made with Ike Quebec. But there are some songs, like *Goin' to Chicago* and *If I Could Be with You* which I like to play with a cup mute. I played plunger when we recorded Jimmy Mundy's *Fiesta in Blue* in 1941. I remember I was the last trumpet to play it, the fourth one to try it. It wasn't written for anyone in particular, but Mundy seemed to like the way I was playing it. I don't often use a plunger, but there are times when I like it. I can play with mute *and* plunger, but a mute will make you tired. A bucket is the easiest, because it lets the air out, and it's the only one you can play practically like an open horn. Nowadays, you don't see many people use a derby like Snooky Young did with Basie, and I saw him use a cup mute like a plunger down at Birdland one night. He had his fingers sticking in there and he played in and out—something you seldom see. Ed Lewis used to do that. The buzz mute is uncommon now, too. I think that was invented when fellows couldn't get to growl like Cootie and Duke's men. A lot of trumpet players, corny ones, couldn't growl, so the only thing that would give them a somewhat similar sound was the buzz mute. Roy gave me one and I used to like it. It's made on the principle of tissue paper and the comb, but with wire. It makes a mechanical buzz, but nothing on the order of Cootie's sound.

"I was with Basie seven years before I went into the army. I was luckier than Lester. He didn't make the band and when his time came they shipped him down to Alabama. It nearly happened to me, too. I went up to the reception center where everyone goes to be screened. After that they send you anywhere in the country for your basic training, and then they ship you. Dave Martin, the pianist, was stationed at that reception center and he had a five-piece band without a trumpet, so they were glad to see me. I started playing with them for officers' dances and everything, and they canceled every call that came up for me to be shipped to Georgia or somewhere for basic training. 'Not in camp—on leave,' they'd say, and they did that so many times. When finally a requisition came to go to Camp Shanks where Sy Oliver was, they said, 'Okay.' Otherwise I would have gone many times before as a soldier, not as a musician.

"The main job of the band I was with was to be at the port when the soldiers got on the boat, and to play them away and make them feel good. We had to meet them when they came back, too. Some days, when we played a boat away, it was so cold the valves of the horn would freeze. Then they'd send us in to the stoves to thaw them out. We'd come out and blow for fifteen minutes until they froze, and then go back in again. We might be playing from five o'clock in the morning until ten o'clock and then be through for the day, or they might call us out again the same evening. We used to play *Lay That Pistol Down, Flying Home*, and numbers like that.

"We started out with about thirty-five pieces and it got down to where I was the last trumpet player in the band. That was because I was the last to go in. Sy Oliver was in charge and a top sergeant. Others in the band were Mercer Ellington and Joe Turner. Sy had to arrange military music for ten trumpets, and so on. Another of his main jobs was to do the arrangements for an army broadcast we did every week. He used to play trumpet in the band, too. We were at Camp Shanks, only forty-five minutes from New York, and I stayed at the Hotel Theresa nearly the whole time I was in the army. I'd come home most nights and we'd call up the camp in the morning and ask, 'Anything for us to do?' They'd often say, 'No,' and sometimes we'd stay in town two or three days at a time. Then we'd go and play one boat and come right back!

"At first, I liked it, because it was a rest, and it was good for me after the years with Basie, but I didn't like wearing the uniform all the time. I was always wanting to change clothes. There were the M.P.'s, of course, and at one time there was a law which said soldiers had to get out of nightclubs and bars at midnight. We'd have to get up and leave our friends there, even if we had nothing to do next day.

"We had a certain amount of military training, but the main thing we had to do was to rehearse. And I don't regard it as a period of musical stagnation, because we tried hard to make ours a very good band. In fact, we could have washed away a lot of civilian bands that came out to entertain the soldiers.

"When I got out of the army in 1946, I joined Jazz at the Philharmonic. I'd known Norman Granz a long time. He had taken a group up the West Coast, but the very first real cross-country contingent he had was three horns, three rhythm, and Helen Humes. The horns were Lester, Coleman Hawkins, and myself; the rhythm, Kenny Kersey, Billy Hadnott, and Jackie Mills. Trummy Young, Rex Stewart, and Illinois Jacquet came later. We didn't have sax battles between Prez and Hawk. I'd solo between them and keep them apart.

"From 1948 on, I free-lanced around New York and toured abroad. I played in the Savoy Ballroom with Jimmy Rushing's band, which was practically the same as the one I took to Europe. It included Emmett Berry, Dicky Wells, Buddy Tate, and Buddy Johnson. After that I went to the Embers with Joe Bushkin. When we went into Lou Terrassi's on 57th, between Broadway and 8th, Tony Parenti taught me Dixieland. I didn't know anything about Dixieland until the fifties! Tony took me to his house and taught me solos and routines. He had a little band, with Sandy Williams on trombone, and he needed a trumpet. I didn't know the songs, but some afternoons he and his wife would cook a big dinner, and I'd go by his house and we'd take off our coats, and he'd teach me four or five songs that day. We did that quite a few times until I had learned about twenty songs.

"Now how long would you say it takes a trumpet player to mature from the time he first starts playing? When I joined Basie, I had been playing just four years and I felt I shouldn't take Lips Page's chair. I like some of those early records, though. The one I made with Teddy Wilson and Benny Goodman of *Why Was I Born?* was all right as an example of melody, but when it came to real hot, authentic jazz, I didn't think I was good enough to follow Lips. He'd been playing a long time. Louis Armstrong had been playing a long time when he made the *Hot Five* records, too. I think if Basie had known I'd only been playing four years he wouldn't have hired me. I believe it takes a trumpet player at least twelve years to mature, and after that he should try to improve himself. I don't believe you should stop improving. Some fellows believe they've got as far as they can go.

"I think the trumpet player I used to sound most like, fifteen years ago, was Bill Coleman. We played together when I was last in Europe and we're very far apart now. Of course, I haven't said much about Europe here, because it's really a story on its own. I've made seven trips and I like it over there. There are some rough trumpet players in Europe, too, but the best are in England. All of Ted Heath's are good, and then there are Kenny Baker and all the trumpet-playing leaders of little bands. It's not that way in France or Sweden. There are very good musicians in those countries, but England has more good trumpet players. I don't know how you account for things like that, but then it's also strange that there was so much variety in the trumpet players who came up through the big bands, while the youngsters who have come up in little bands sound so much alike."

(1962)

Jo Jones

Jo Jones has a quicksilver mind and the interviewer soon discovers that he is not there to ask questions but to be instructed. Questions, in fact, are sometimes brushed aside, but more often they merely deflect his stream of consciousness unprofitably. What follows was taped one afternoon in Jones's hotel room on 49th Street in New York City.

"The average person who works from nine to five could not possibly go through what the professional and his body go through in one year—not physically, mentally, morally, or spiritually. Nobody has ever explained what it takes to perform, the driving force that makes a person get up on that stage and perform night after night. I've been in this business fifty years and ever since I was a kid I've been hearing this cliché that they come up with—*the show must go on*. A nine-to-fiver gets a headache and doesn't come to work. Or it's snowing outside and he says, 'I can't get to the office today.' Or he has an important meeting in San Francisco but he comes down with a cold and says, 'Can you postpone it? I'll be there next Wednesday.' That's all right in a set business that doesn't fluctuate much, but when we're booked to go somewhere we are billed, and don't nothing stop us. We're worse than the mailman. We're going to be there.

"Show business has to be more flexible, but I've always been interested in the fact that if you take a thirty-five-year-old or a forty-year-old professional to the businessman's doctor, he's going to be in better shape than the nine-to-fiver. I remember we tried a thing once with two or three people who followed the Basie band. They tried to do the same things they *thought* we were doing. They tried to drink as much as they thought we were doing, and they tried to carouse around with the girls like they thought we were doing. It was that old wives' tale about a musician having a quart of whiskey on one arm and a chick on the other. I'd just like to see a man go to bed with thirty different women in a given month!

"You can take the average musician, any guy that plays music, and he's better off than anybody in any other walk of life, I don't care who—doctor, lawyer, teacher, minister, businessman, or what have you. He doesn't need what they need. He'll come out of the hospital after an appendix or tonsil operation and get right up on the bandstand and play. The other guy has got to *recuperate*. You can check it with any reputable doctor who has musicians and performers—that goes for dancers and singers—as patients, and he'll tell you that in comparison the nine-to-fiver is in bad shape. You're right, irregularity may be good. They're forever trying to find out about our bodies. They give new medicines to the army, because the foot soldier has to go through circumstances and conditions different from those of the ordinary layman. If it's tried and proved on him, then the patent is approved."

"When I was starting out I tried to do everything. I tried to sing, to dance, to do dramatics, to play the trumpet, to play the sax, to play the piano. When a distant cousin of mine took me to hear Mr. Louis Armstrong in Chicago, I said, 'Well, that's the end of my trumpet playing!' When I went to the sax, I got smarter than the music teacher, but here comes Coleman Hawkins, so that was the end of that! Right afterwards I met Lester Young. So now I'm going to the piano, and I know I'm very great, but then I met Mr. Art Tatum, and that ended my piano career!

"When we started out as youngsters, a lot of us—like Johnny Hodges—were fortunate enough to be around our elders and we weren't allowed the luxury of playing around like teenagers, because we were around older people with experience. They didn't lecture us, but they showed us the way. The boy who stayed home with Mama and Papa had a good routine, but the people I'm talking of were passing on the benefit of their professional experience to us. When we got so smart that we knew everything, they'd let us go and jump off a cliff. But they'd have a net there to break our fall, and then they'd let us know we weren't so all-fired smart.

"I was just always a gypsy, and I had an unusual urge to be in carnivals or circuses. I wouldn't have gained the knowledge I have by reading. It took a whole lot of experience and a whole lot of *helping* to make me what I am, because I realize that personally, myself, I'm fifty people. We were very fortunate, and ofttimes those of us with certain backgrounds could sit down and talk about them, but as of today I don't know nobody I can talk to but Roy Eldridge, because there's nobody playing in the music business that has had the kind of experience he and I had. I used to talk a lot with my very good friends Sidney Catlett and Chick Webb, but they hadn't met the people, hadn't had the experience, hadn't been in the states, the villages, and the hamlets that I had. In my formative years I didn't rightly know where I was, because I didn't major in geography. All I knew, I was just traveling. And I was fortunate enough to have a whole lot of mothers and fathers, sisters and brothers, and aunts and uncles, out there in the shows. In the carnivals and circuses you had mostly European performers, and they'd tell you about different things to come, and they'd give you addresses. They'd find out where you were going, from one town to another, and you'd look up retired and semi-retired people and ask questions—that is, if you were going to be in the business. It was a sort of protective thing, especially when your time was taken up with your music, your instrument, and getting the precision you had to have. Our hearts bleed now for the kids coming up who don't have the dance floors and the theaters we had. They took them away. A boy asked me the other night to explain to his wife, who was twenty-five, what a chorus girl was! She didn't know."

"A friend of mine, who knows more about me than anybody, is Wilson Driver. When I first saw him in Atlanta, he had a xylophone, a cornet, a set of drums. Another multi-musician I remember was Jimmy King. They both impressed me, but I wasn't thinking that I'd play drums as a livelihood because I had other things on my mind. I saw many drummers, many banjo players, many guitar players, many tuba players, many violin players, many piano players, and to make me what I am I collected many mannerisms and moral things from them. 'Come on, kid,' they'd say, 'sit down and watch this.'

"I'd hang around theaters and spend all my time running errands for different people. I ran errands for Butterbeans and Susie. I'd mown lawns and I'd washed windows, but I was always asking, 'Show me how to do this.' They could only show me through their eyes, because my imagination wasn't keen enough to grasp the experience. I ran errands for chorus girls and soubrettes, too. Most clubs had three or four women who sang different kinds of songs for different kinds of people. You'd call to 'em and this one would come up and sing risqué songs, this one would sing the blues, and another would sing pretty songs."

"When we first came to New York, I told 'em I didn't want to know anything about a drum or a woman until I was ninety! I have yet to see a man who knows anything about a drum. And I haven't read or seen anybody who knows anything about a woman. All you can do is leave her happy. You can't satisfy her! Years ago Mr. Ellington wrote *A Drum Is a Woman*. And it *is* like a woman. Because there is a type of woman you can talk to, there's one you have to shake, there's one you slap, and there's another you have to break a chair over her head. Yet she still loves you—as much as she can.

"You never know what that drum is going to do, and it has fascinated me all my life. I remember my aunt taking me to a circus when I was a kid, and I can still feel that bass drum. Later, she bought me a snare drum, but I didn't ever think I would really play drums. When I really switched over to them was when I found the drummer was the highest priced in the orchestra, because it was required of him to know as much music as the conductor, the first violinist, the first trumpet player . . . So I began.

"Samuel 'Baby' Brothers told me what to do. He was going to Australia with Sonny Clay. I was fortunate to be in Omaha then, because there were a lot of musicians around to help me. I went to Hospe's Music Store and got vibes, chimes, and tymps, and I went to a couple of teachers who showed me how to do things.

"The one I learned more *music* from than anyone was Henri Woode. I roomed with him when I was with Lloyd Hunter's band. He played piano and accordion, and sometimes I wanted to get my pistol on him because he would have music paper spread all over and he'd be using the bed as a piano, writing and singing. 'This guy's going crazy,' I thought. I didn't want to go out and sit in the park! When we were on one-nighters in Iowa, I used to watch him. He'd come back in with another idea and start writing—with no piano. I picked up so many things with that ten-piece band, and he really gave me an insight into ear training.

"He was the band's musical director. In most cases you are either an arranger or a performer. Few people can ever be both. Even as of today, if Henri Woode brings in an arrangement to an orchestra, and he sits down in front, and you're looking at the music, there will not be one mistake. And when he stomps it off you will play it from start to finish, and you'll feel relaxed. All his arrangements are relaxed.

"I was sheltered by two or three people who told me to study music, to go down to catch classical music, to do this, to do that. These guys were pool-hall characters. You must remember the social conditions in the country at the time. One of them owned a pool hall and he caught me using profanity. 'You use that kind of language in my pool hall again, I'm going to hit you in the mouth!' So then I pawned the pistol, broke off my knife in a tree, and he took me to his home and gave me a key. The guy could speak five languages, and he said, 'I'm going to lock you in here with these books, and you will *learn*. No sneaking out, because I'm going to ask you about what everything is!' Then I asked, 'Why do you talk like this in your home, Ralph, and a different way in the pool hall?' He explained that the people he was dealing with—laborers and guys from the packing house—would not understand. But here was a guy who could speak Greek and Latin, and in the pool hall he was talking about 'dis, dat, and da other.' So the people I've met have been very responsible for and to me.

"The guy that played the bass drum in Mr. Sousa's band was a Mr. Helmich. Later, he played with the Goldman band in Central Park, and I had the pleasure of taking several drummers out there with some popcorn to get some music. 'Now they're going to do this,' I said, 'and I want you to hear this bass drum.' I used to love to go back after the concerts to see him, and I always tried to get him a nice stein of beer. The last time I saw him he was about eighty-three years old but still very immaculate and dap. He could take that bass drum just by itself and get eight notes out of it. He was the only one of his kind.

"Experiences around the people I met make me create, and I must play *music*. I try to keep my drums in tune, although I have a very hard bass drum. The reason Mr. Chick Webb took an interest in me was that he found out I played with a tympany head. In old pictures, when I used two tom-toms, you can see where I have tympany rods on. It's very difficult to tell an individual how to tune up his drums. Most of the guys in my formative years would play with one band for ten to twelve years, but after World War II a guy's over here for three months, over there for two weeks, and he never gets to play with one group of people over a period of years. You see some young musicians get together and they've a good group for about six months, then something happens and they break up. Somebody has told one of the guys he should get a group of his own. They should have pooled their resources to make it one solid thing."

"You have to remember social conditions as they were in Chicago in the twenties and thirties. It's no secret that the people who controlled things would demand and tell you what you were going to do. If you were going to survive, that's what you did. If they wanted your services, you played where they told you to play. You did exactly what they told you to do or you were dead. That's what happened to me one time. I have crushed fingers, you see? You've met Mr. Earl Hines. So far as I know, the man had to play with a knife at his throat and a gun at his back the whole time he was in Chicago. You tell those people you were taking your horn to get it fixed, and they'd say, 'Leave it here. We'll get it fixed.' They knew you might have been thinking of going to Kansas City or someplace else.

"Chicago never was like Kansas City. Which was worse? Not worse—it was good, clean, wholesome fun. You did what they told you, and that was it. You had no worries, remember, when you were working for *them*. You see, there was a dearth in the United States from 1926 to 1936. We lost more music then than the world will ever know, because we hadn't got tape-recorders and all that modern boom-boom-boom. There was so much music and so many musicians, but if you didn't belong to certain cliques, didn't do this, didn't work for this guy or that guy—then you were just out of it. So guys said, 'Oh, what the heck!' Some got day jobs. Some began to drink and became winos. Some got jobs in department stores or running an elevator, or in the packing house, in order to survive. Some just gave up, because they weren't allowed to play the way they wanted to play."

"When it comes to wealth, musical wealth, I'm the richest drummer that's lived in fifty years, because nobody ever had what I have. Nobody ever had the pleasure of sitting up with a band night after night that had a Herschel Evans, a Lester Young, a Harry Edison, a Buck Clayton, a Dicky Wells, a Benny Morton, a Freddie Green, and a Walter Page. No band ever had that. Well there was one, but Mr. Ellington was always for presentation. I'm speaking in the pure sense of jazz—they never had all that ability. Everybody in that Basie band was capable of standing up and playing with just the rhythm section.

"Jack Washington was the brightest thing in the reed section, but everyone was talking about Herschel Evans and Lester Young. Jack just stayed in the background but ofttimes when guys acted up Basie would let Jack play two or three choruses. If he let him play four or five choruses, there wouldn't be any other saxophone players up there. That's right. Ask Mr. Benny Carter when you see him!

"Mr. Benny Carter lived across the hall at 580 St. Nicholas Avenue, where I was across the hall from Willie 'The Lion' Smith. Herschel Evans and Jack Washington roomed together in the next building. Mr. Benny Carter had just returned from Europe and sometimes he'd be there listening when they were working out. When Jack picked up the tenor, Benny would be listening to *him,* and Herschel would be shaking his head. And at other times, when the guys couldn't play an arrangement, he'd be sitting there, looking straight ahead, waiting till they got through, and then he'd play it. I remember once, too, when somebody was fooling around, Mr. Walter Page left his bass, went down quiet as a cat, got the baritone, played the sax parts, and went back to his place. So what else is new?

"You must remember there were about four drummers in Basie's band. Besides Basie, there was Freddie Green, and later on there was Joe Newman. I didn't need to worry about Gene Krupa or Buddy Rich. I was catching hell sitting up there, trying to play in Basie's band.

"There will never be an institution like the Basie band that came to New York in 1936. Until we came, musicians didn't fraternize with one another. It was a very cold, clique scene. Because they didn't know any better, and they still don't. I can remember everything that came through Kansas City. I used to run up and say, 'You guys gonna sit in?' And they'd say, 'No, it's against our contract.' I'd laugh, because they better *not* sit in and play with nobody there.

"At that time in Kansas City a local band had to play opposite visiting bands, and when some met up with Basie's raggedy band they got egg on their faces. They'd rather have paid us and had us not play. You ask Earl Hines about the night his band and ours played together. Or ask Duke Ellington what happened the night Basie's band left Kansas City. Fletcher Henderson? McKinney's Cotton Pickers? They never had a rhythm section. Chick Webb? Great, but never had a rhythm section. Everybody went north, east, south, and west.

"We worked at it, to build a rhythm section, every day, every night. We worked alone, not with the band all the time. I didn't care what happened—*one* of us would be up to par. If three were down, one would carry the three. Never four were out.

"What other rhythm section? None. None. The greatest band I've heard was Mr. Walter Page's Blue Devils. I heard all the bands in '26, '27, '28, '29, '30. . . . I used to go to Detroit. I saw Edward's Collegians, Fletcher Henderson, McKinney's Cotton Pickers. I'd see them in Battles of the Bands, when they had five-band tours. I saw Blanche Calloway, Belton's Syncopators out of Florida. But I never heard a band like Walter Page's.

"Naturally, you know about Hot Lips Page, but Mr. Louis Armstrong and I used always to talk about one guy, Harry Smith, who took Hot Lips Page's place with Walter Page. When I saw him, I quit dancing. And I used to love to dance. But I just took a look at this man and did a very foolish thing. I didn't know he wasn't supposed to drink, and I just bought him all the whiskey my little money would buy. Later on they left and went to Kansas City. He was in a hotel. He drank and died. Harry Smith—he never recorded.

"When I first joined Basie, I played with him one night and I quit. 'I'm going back to school,' I said. There I was, sitting up there with all those fantastic guys. I went back to get my drums, and they implored me to go to Little Rock with them, and I did. See, Basie had two bands that never came to New York, but he never had a band after that, not a band like that one. I can't explain that band, because there's no record of it.

"It is very wonderful that the young musicians today have a chance to make records, good, bad, or indifferent. At least they get a chance to hear themselves, and they can improve. There were so many people back then that you never heard about. The East Coast guys didn't travel around much, didn't go in all the different places in the Midwest. It takes all types of people to make a world, but there are so many that come to mind that nobody ever speaks about. As Dizzy Gillespie was saying, I'd like people to know about me being an innovator. It's not quite the same as wanting credit. Please let me know I was the innovator of this, or that I started that."

"At one time I had about seventy-five records of Duke Ellington and I used to carry my record-player around. I think Freddie Green and I must have put words to about twenty of Mr. Duke Ellington's tunes, before anybody else thought about putting words to them. We'd just get in a room and play the records and find words to go with the tunes. He wrote a four-part thing called *Reminiscing in Tempo,* and everything is in it that you could ever get—the whole embodiment. And I'm supposed to be a connoisseur of Mr. Ellington, you know.

" 'What do you think of Duke Ellington?' somebody asked me once. 'Well,' I said, 'you know how this slavery started, and who started it— the Africans, the Arabs, etc. But Mr. Ellington is the only slaver I know. When the so-called white people act up, he'll write a tune and spank them. And when the black people act up, he'll write a tune and spank them, too. He just keeps *everybody* in line. He's a slave-driver if ever there was one! Every time some little moral or civil upheaval comes along, he sits down and writes something, scratches it off, and bang!' They used to say at the theaters, 'Well, Duke is all right, but he can't write nothing popular.' I'd go by and tell them everything he wrote was 'popular.' I'd have some of the things Freddie Green and I had written down, and I'd say, 'Look, here's some words.' But they forget, how easy they forget!

"In 1930, I had Duke's record of *Three Little Words* and I took it 'round to the Ritz Café to play on the juke box.

" 'That can't be a colored man,' they said.

" 'He's very colored,' I told them.

" 'Here's a band you should book,' I told Jimmy Jewell. 'They're making a movie, *Check and Double Check,* with Amos and Andy.'

"So when Duke did come to Omaha, he had to play uptown and downtown. Not that it made any difference because at that time it was still a checkerboard. But he played in the small places, and then the people just had to have him in the big places. He came back and played the *other* theater, and I'm looking at them playing *Mood Indigo,* and for two or three years Barney Bigard made the clarinet famous. This is where it gets ridiculous. I *know* what I've got in my scrapbooks, because this was before Benny Goodman. Well, he was playing in the studios or with Ted Lewis, and nobody wrote the truth about Bigard. I used to follow what they were doing. I went from Cleveland to Boston—650 miles—to catch two shows of Duke Ellington, and then I got on a plane and went back to Basie's band."

"There will never be an institution like the Basie band was when it started out. All these other people, they started out *with* something. But we were really behind the Iron Curtain. There was no chance for us. So there was nothing for us to do but play for ourselves. You see, in Kansas City you had ten or eleven bands, and the only band that came in there and made any impact was McKinney's Cotton Pickers. They had a thing going and it was a different thing. Of course, the brass was electrifying. But Don Redman left them shortly after that.

"Now Bennie Moten's band played one and three, but Walter Page's played two and four. Walter joined Bennie in 1932, as Jimmy Rushing and Basie had already done, and then other guys from the Blue Devils got into the Moten band. East and West—it became a wedding. Instead of one and three and two and four, it became one, two, three, four, and then it was like a lilt. That's how you got rhythm.

"The first night I played with the Basie band was in Topeka. Tommy Douglas, at the Cherry Blossom, had said, 'How would you like to join a band?' 'That would be nice,' I answered, 'but I don't think I'm ready yet.' But I left, and I had two quarts of whiskey coming to me, which I didn't drink. I took it home and put it in my suitcase. Then I went to Topeka and played with Basie's band. I was doing all right until they played *After You've Gone*. When Lester Young jumped up and took the second chorus, I was ready to go home. I went downstairs and sat in a cab, looking for them to give me my money. They came and begged me. 'No, no,' I said, 'I'm going home.' Then Walter Page, Joe Keyes, and Ben Webster got me in the gents' room in the hotel. 'You can't leave us,' they said, because they knew Mack Washington was going back to Bennie Moten. Then I took out a great big quart of whiskey and said, 'Here, y'all! I'm going to Omaha, Nebraska, to go back to school.' But I went with them to Little Rock anyhow!

"What had upset me? Well, when they played my heart leaped in my mouth. I just jumped out of my seat. I didn't know what they were doing. 'My God,' I said, 'what am I doing here?' There, in the Metropolitan Hall, Topeka, that band just floated me and threw me off!

" 'Mr. Basie,' I'd said, 'you got a nice band. I wish you a lot of luck.'

"But then they conned me in that outhouse, until I said I'd go for two weeks, which became fourteen years! I really didn't think I had the experience to play with them, because there was no music. They'd just call a tune and play it.

"The man who taught me how to think was Joe Keyes, the greatest first trumpet player. He was a very remarkable man. He knew everything, all the arrangements. He was from Texas, I think, and there was never anybody able to outthink Mr. Joe Keyes. He taught me how to read shows and he taught me how to change tempos. He sat next to me and said, 'Watch it!' He'd come to work and not speak to anybody. He'd get off work, drink two quarts of whiskey, and come back to work next night. He sat over there on that bandstand and if anyone got hung up, he knew the whole arrangement. He went straight ahead. In his later years, when he was going down slow, there was a band room down in the Braddock. Little trumpet players would catch him and buy him a drink. Then he'd take 'em downstairs and show 'em things. Those he helped could tell you how wonderful he was.

"Mr. Cab Calloway came and got him, bought him a uniform and bought him a brand-new horn. He played one show, pulled the uniform off, gave him his horn, and went back to the Braddock bar. 'It's no use, Cab,' he said. 'Your music is not interesting.' "

"Dancing? It helps to give me my sense of timing. If you notice, anything I play I have to play dancing and singing to it. Because I was never allowed the luxury of playing a tune unless I could sing the lyrics. My sense of timing and dancing helped when I had bad luck with my legs and had to switch to drums. The actual experience, to be around the thing in person, is what counts. Like in Kansas City, you had your farm teams. You played down here and then you graduated. It was like going from grade school, to high school, to college. You didn't just jump into a particular thing until you were ready. Here in New York, there were guys with horns who had no business on the bandstand. 'I played with Lester Young last night,' they'd be saying, 'I played with Roy Eldridge . . . I played with Charlie Parker . . . I played with Dizzy Gillespie. . . .' It wasn't like that in Kansas City. You had to wait until they asked for you to sit in. They had enough respect to say, 'We don't belong here. We're not ready to play in this league.'

"The other bands didn't have the flexibility we had. Everything Basie had was flexible. In those days we were thinking about nothing but music, not about going in and making a hit record, nothing like that. We exchanged ideas and there was a continuity that only got broken after World War II, or during it. We used to go around and show kids how to formulate, how to play fours, how to get more leverage out of what they were doing, and it was very wonderful.

"I went to a drum clinic once with Charles Mingus, for three days. I'd ask each of the kids, 'Why do you play like that?' One would say he'd seen Max Roach, another Philly Joe, another Art Blakey.

" 'How long you been playing, son?'

" 'Oh, four years.'

" 'Wait a minute! Have you played with the people Max (or Philly Joe or Art) play with? It's *who* you play with should shape the way you play.'

"When they heard Lester Young play, they said, 'Oh, Prez, he don't sound like he used to.' So I said, 'Well, who's he playing with?' Then when they heard the album he made in 1956 with Roy Eldridge, Vic Dickenson, Teddy Wilson, Gene Ramey, and me, they said, 'Wow, that's a difference!' Now that kind of thing is hard to explain, but people can understand when they hear it. And that's the reason I always want to tell promoters that, when they put something together, be sure to put compatible things together, like bacon and eggs. You don't just throw different people together and expect to get a performance, unless you know something about the experience *they* have had. They may set up a program in which one guy's not speaking to this other guy anymore. It is not a matter of hate, but of self-respect. If they're playing off a sheet, then it doesn't make any difference. All they've got to do is say hello. But when you haven't got a part, and you've got to play from here [heart], you'd rather not play with this other guy because you'll get in his way of thought. Always remember that we are playing our experiences, have got to project our experiences, of what we've had in common. We set that to music, according to the tune. When you say you want me to record with Earl Hines, it's okay. You bring in Al Hall on bass, and he and I are together, but I can't really bring Paul Gonsalves in on this record of our experiences because when *we* start going somewhere we haven't got time to explain our references."

"Basically, people are not bad. Some people do good because they know better. Others do bad because they *don't* know any better. They're ignorant of the facts, and two college degrees are not the answer. Intelligence doesn't mean the individual is wise. Let me point out a mistake that was made with Dick Wilson, the tenor player who'd been with Andy Kirk. He was in the hospital and he was not supposed to have salt, so all he'd ask everybody to do was to bring him a box of salt. So one of his visitors brought him a box and he put it in the drawer. After everybody had gone, he was eating salt in his food. The person who brought it thought he was doing good, you follow?

"People think they're being nice when they press drinks and hospitality on you, but some musicians don't know how to say 'No.' Now I may be the most disliked musician that has ever been in New York, because I don't visit, I don't go to parties, and I've never been in but three after-hour spots in the whole city. I'm a loner, a street boy, fifty years without a home.

"Then you have to watch for the eager beavers, the guys that really want to do you in. They go for the Academy Award every night. They *mean* to put a stumbling block in front of you. There's one statement I'm going to have printed, and I'd like the guys to stick it right on their door, where they'll see it as they go out: *There's nothing wrong with the music business that we ourselves can't cure.*

"Everybody who goes to a bar don't get drunk. But that *bar* is a detrimental thing. Everybody knows that. Then people began to make money off other things—the narcotics agents, the police, the shakedown artists. They said nobody but musicians used pot, until a few years ago, when they found out that in order to get some pot you had to go back to school, to grade school, that is. Marijuana has never been habit-forming and it has never hurt anybody in the world. In fact, they should hurry up and give me the concession, so that people won't be going around with catarrh, sinusitis, and all that. See that bag there? I had it full of marijuana once and I set it right down by Lester Young.

"'What do you want?' I asked.

"'Coca-Cola,' he said."

(1971)

Eddie Durham

(TROMBONE, GUITAR, AND ARRANGER)

"My daddy was a musician, a fiddler, and he played numbers like *Turkey in the Straw* at square dances. They'd have just him, nobody else, just a fiddle. He died when he was quite young and it was Joe, my oldest brother, who taught me and my other brothers. He subscribed to lessons from what was called the U.S. School of Music, and we were all able to learn pretty good from them. The system they had of teaching was a start, to train you, but it didn't go very far. Nobody knew more than two- and three-part harmony. A sixth was unknown.

"Roosevelt, my youngest brother, and I were about ten months apart. I was born in San Marcos, Texas, in 1906. I had another brother, who died in childbirth, and a sister four years older than me. My oldest brother went in the army during World War I, and it was when he got back that he was teaching us youngsters. He was with us a long time and we formed a family band, the Durham Brothers Band. Earl, who played saxophone and clarinet, eventually went to Con-

necticut and stayed there. Roosevelt remained with the minstrel shows
for a time, playing piano, but I sent for him later and we were together quite a while. Our cousins, Allen and Clyde Durham, were also
in the band. Herschel Evans was another cousin, and he joined us
in Dallas. He was playing alto then, but he couldn't read and we tried
to teach him. We put him on tenor and he was better on that than
on alto, but he never did read very much. We used four saxophones
in four-part harmony, and just about the first time down he didn't hit
on anybody else's note. So if he didn't play the note *you* played, he'd
found his own!

"After my oldest brother married, he organized Blanche Calloway's
last band for her. She made him a trustee and he went to Kansas City
and brought Ben Webster back. Joe was a technician and as fast on
cello as Oscar Pettiford was on bass. He was with Nat Cole for a little
while, and he was playing *some* bass! He was way ahead. When Nat
got on top, he tried to get him to go in his trio, but he just hung
around his wife and wouldn't leave. Then he was working in a shipyard and playing gigs, and he never really made the most of what he
had.

"I played banjo first, then four-string guitar. Later on, I added
trombone and six-string guitar, and played both in the band. I think I
could have been a kind of genius on that six-string guitar, but after I
started getting up in the world I divided my time between arranging,
composing, trombone, and guitar, not sticking to any one. Mostly our
band worked traveling shows. At one time we were with Doug
Moyne's Dramatic Show, a white show. They had a terrific piano
player named Neil Heller to accompany the singers, and they used us
to back up other things.

"After our band split up, I went with the 101 Ranch Circus on
trombone. Edgar Battle was there, too, and that's where I really
taught myself to write, to express my own voicing, because we had
a lot of horns to play around with.° The circus band was a big brass
band, a parade band. We had four trombones, two or three French
horns, and peck horns, but we didn't use all of them when we played
for the minstrel show. They had very good men in those days, and

---

° Edgar Battle claimed that the 101 Ranch Rodeo Show was comparable to the
Ringling Brothers or Barnum and Bailey circuses. It originated at the second
largest ranch in the country, the King Ranch in Texas being bigger. The performers and animals moved from city to city on a train, Battle said, of about
thirty cars. Over a thousand people were involved—"cowboys, Indians, Negroes,
white folks and Russian cossack riders." The musicians would sometimes play
from a big red wagon pulled by ten black horses.

they could read rings around me. They had trumpet players who could triple-tongue and double-tongue when they were playing high-powered marches.

"They could play a little jazz, but they stayed very close to the melody. I was trying to solo a bit, and it wasn't hard for me to learn the value of notes, but a guy who could swing a break was something new to them. So when we played for dances at night, I asked them if I could swing in the jazz breaks. They were all trained musicians playing solid trombone—no faking—so jazz breaks on trombone were different.

"The show used to be out at nine and we didn't leave town right away, so that gave us the idea of putting on a dance. The leader of the band said, 'How can we have a dance when we ain't got no piano?' We said we'd fix up something, so they got me some manuscript paper. I was just beginning to write and I wrote harmony for some of the horns so it sounded like a piano. We had saxophones in the minstrel show, and I'd use them, too. It worked out all right. We'd find some little hole in town and charge a quarter at the door. Each of us would make two or three dollars a night, so we were on our way!

"The minstrel show was like a sideshow and not in the big tent where the circus was. It didn't start till the big show was over. In the parade, the big band from the circus would come first, and further down the band from the minstrel show, and that would be playing the jazz."

After leaving the 101 Ranch band in 1926, Durham worked with many bands in the Southwest, including Edgar Battle's Dixie Ramblers in the 711 Show with singer Mamie Smith, and the Blue Devils.

"When I went with Bennie Moten in 1929," Durham resumed, "he had only three saxophones and two trumpets. Although I didn't care for the instrument, I was playing valve trombone in order to help the trumpets. I worked very hard, playing awful high with the trumpets to give a three-trumpet effect, then switching back to make a two-trombone sound. There was a lot of pressure on the brass, but those guys wouldn't play a sixth or a ninth chord. They were playing the fifth, tonic, and third, and they couldn't hear the sixth. So then Moten brought Lips Page into the band. 'What's he gonna play?' the guys wanted to know. 'He's all right, but we don't need another horn.' Then I stepped the band up to ninth chords, and they could hear a ninth better than they could a sixth. Lips was pretty true on his horn [trumpet] and he could hear the sixth, so I gave him that and played the ninth myself. That's how we started getting five-part harmony in the brass, and they came to see why we had needed another horn.

There was nobody playing *their* note, where before they'd been saying 'You playin' my note? Get off my note!'

"I remember when the band started swinging, but I can't remember the year. Walter Page had played sousaphone, but he played good baritone saxophone, too, and he started doubling on baritone and bass with the Blue Devils. I went down and heard what he was doing. I stayed just long enough to steal him, and then he came with us. He was playing baritone, but then I got an idea about the rhythm. 'Who wants a bass fiddle in a band?' everybody wanted to know. They preferred sousaphone in a dancehall, because you could hear it better. Without amplification, a lot of guys weren't strong enough on bass fiddle. But Walter Page you could hear! He was like a house with a note. He didn't have the best ear, but he worked hard, and the string bass was in demand. How was his sound produced? I think it's in the coordination of the stroke in the head. The bass is one of the greatest things in the world for rhythm, but instead of writing a two-beat bass on the fifth and tonic, I kept it moving on chromatics to the chord. It sounded good, but when they saw it on paper, musicians said, 'This has gotta be out of tune!' Walter Page is the guy that created that walkin', walkin' . . . I wrote it long, but I couldn't control and master that swinging motion till I'd been in the band a long time. Of course, Willie McWashington, Moten's drummer, was a two-four man. He played that Charleston beat and cut wood all the time.

"I used to get through with Moten around two or three in the morning. When Jo Jones came to Kansas City, I used to take my guitar and trombone and jam with him from four in the morning till eight or nine. He was playing that modern stuff and it sounded good. He was was sharp on it and he was really creating a style. I don't know where he got it from. He hadn't been east—he hadn't been any place. But he was something else! It was *natural* with him, and maybe he doesn't get enough credit for it now. As a solo man, Chick Webb was the best up to that time, but he was too weak physically to play a whole lot of rhythm. He should have had a deputy. If I were Basie right now, I'd get me a good piano player and just come out to make an appearance with two or three numbers. But I think if he didn't sit at the piano, the band would lose something. I doubt if anyone else can do what he does. He's got a style. You've got to give him credit. Everybody was playing *all* the piano they could play to get famous, and here comes Basie saying, 'I play as *little* as I can.'

"While I was with Bennie Moten, I played a straight guitar with a resonator. It was about the size of a ten-inch record, made of tin, and it went right under the bridge. When you hit it, especially near the mike, you got an electric effect, and it carried like a banjo. Later,

I made a record of *Honey, Keep Your Mind on Me* with Jimmie Lunceford, and it sounds like electric, but it wasn't.

"When I met Charlie Christian in Oklahoma, I had a straight guitar and would just go to the mike with it. He was playing piano, but he had a cheap old piece of guitar. I was there three or four weeks and he told me how much he liked guitar, but he didn't know a lot about it. 'You've got an awful stroke and conception for guitar,' I told him, 'but I can give you a lot of pointers. One thing, when you press the guitar, use a downstroke. You can get that punch like a saxophone. When you come up, it may sound legato, but it's staccato.' So he started that downstroke stuff, and not much more than a year later he was with Benny Goodman.

"Same way with Floyd Smith in Nebraska. He wanted to play guitar, and he could play a little, but he hadn't an instrument of his own. 'If you go talk to my mother,' he said, 'she might get me one.' So I was around a few days and when I went to see her she gave me the money. I went down to the store with Floyd and bought a guitar. About three years later *he* was so good that he claimed he was teaching guitar.

"Of all the arrangements I did for Bennie Moten, *Moten Swing* was the biggest. We were at the Pearl Theatre in Philadelphia when the owner, Sam Steiffel, complained about us doing the same things over and over again. 'You've got to get something else,' he said, but we didn't have anything else! When Bennie said we'd got to have a new number, I asked him to let me lay off one show to get it together for him.

"I went downstairs and Basie came with me. He was often my co-writer. He'd put a little melody in there, so he'd have an answer when Bennie asked me, 'What did he write?' This time he gave me the channel. Horace Henderson was there and saw me write it, in pencil. We took it upstairs and the band went over it once, and then played it on the next show. It stopped the show every time. When we went to the Lafayette in New York the following week, we played it as the last number, and it took seven encores. The manager said, 'If you play it one more time, I'm going to throw the doors open.' And that's what he did, threw them open to the street, and people crowded around the doors to hear us.

"One reason it was a big hit was the tempo. That was one of the main things I concentrated on, and so did Basie, but Jo Jones was the key man for tempos. I'd say to him, 'Jo, this number I wrote here—don't let the leader, don't let the band, don't let anybody ever change this tempo!' That was the secret of Basie's band—not to let the tempo get too fast or too slow. But one number they spoiled was

One O'Clock Jump. It was not a real swing-out number. It was meant to be played at a good medium tempo. One of the things that went wrong with the band business was that the bands got too wild in their tempos.

"Another trouble with the later musicians is that they don't want to bend a note. They want to hit the note straight. But Basie's guys bend the notes around the corner. That's why the band sounds so good. He lost all the powerhouse men he had, but the guys he's got right now make the band sound so far ahead of others. He may not have the soloists, but he's got showmanship in the voicing and flexibility in the way the arrangements are played. He has still got some of the style there in the rhythm section, but modern amplification makes problems. The mikes pick up the sax and brass sections so well that you have to watch out and step up the volume of the rhythm. I like the kid Basie's got on drums now [Harold Jones]. He plays quite a bit of rhythm, and he can swing. The band swings *him* quite a little bit, too. I think Basie likes that, when you've got the band swinging the drummer. What could the drummer do but swing on an arrangement like *Moten Swing*? The band is based on hot licks, and the arrangements he played the other night at Roseland were all hot licks. The drummer can play all those licks along with the arrangement.

"To go back a bit, after I left Bennie Moten in 1933, I went to New York to join Willie Bryant's band. Teddy Wilson, Benny Carter, and Cozy Cole were in it, and I wrote arrangements like *Chimes in the Chapel*. Teddy Wilson was always late to rehearsals, and when he came in he'd find me at the piano, stretching those big chords. 'Stay right there!' he'd say. 'Don't get up!' He was always kidding me about that.

"After about a year, I got in the union and went with Jimmie Lunceford. Although I had never met him, he had been trying to get me for some time. There were two trumpet players in his band from Kansas City—Paul Webster and Eddie Tompkins—and we'd worked together and were buddies. Paul was always telling Lunceford, 'I gotta go get that guy,' and when we met I'd just tell him, 'Oh, I'll see you in New York.'

"I first caught the Lunceford band at the Apollo Theatre. There was nobody could play like that band! They would come out and play a dance routine. The Shim Sham Shimmy was popular then and six of the guys would come down and dance to it—like a tap dance, crossing their feet and sliding. Then Willie Smith would put his bonnet on and sing a sort of nursery rhyme. Eddie Tompkins hit the high notes and did a Louis Armstrong deal. Then they had a Guy

Lombardo bit and a Paul Whiteman bit. See, they imitated bands. The lights would go down next and they'd all lay down their horns and come out to sing as a glee club. They had solo singers like Henry Wells, too. The next number, they'd be throwing their horns and hats up to the ceiling. That was all novelty, and I liked it. So I joined them, as a trombone player and an arranger.

"I always liked the trombone sound in the circus band. And I liked the instrument because a guy could make it sound like he was crying. I just liked trombone players from the start—Big Green, Jimmy Harrison, J. C. Higginbotham, Joe Nanton with Duke, and later on, because he was sweeter, Lawrence Brown. Then I got crazy about Tommy Dorsey. He had a wonderful tone and it didn't sound gooey. I was crazy about Trummy Young, too, and I think he has been underrated. And then, yeah, there was Dicky Wells, who took my place in Basie's band. I liked all these guys, but I didn't copy any of them. The instrument itself moved me for inspiration. I didn't play many solos with Lunceford, because the section needed support in that band, so people didn't know too much about me. That was like Jack Washington with Basie. He was a good team man and he was fast on his baritone, but if you don't get up and take solos people don't know what you contribute.

"Sy Oliver and Eddie Wilcox were writing for Lunceford, but they'd had only three trumpets, two trombones, and four saxes before. They hadn't had much experience with wider arrangements, and few of the bands had more instruments than that. When Dan Grissom, the singer, played sax, he used to double, but now I fixed him a part of his own. I wrote a few things for them like that, stepping it up to five saxes. I showed Wilcox how to voice that way, and coached him with the sax section. I was also teaching Willie Smith how to voice for the instrumentation we had, and he was even willing to pay me. He wrote one or two things like *Running Wild*. Now we could have six brass, too, and I could handle that without any trouble. Where they had arrangements already set up, I wrote a part for myself, sometimes in the bass and sometimes above, but either way to get that extra note. I had a good range and could play it, but it was hard to set some of their earlier arrangements in six-part harmony. When Trummy Young eventually took my place in the band, they had to give him three weeks to go over the repertoire so he could get with my parts.

"I didn't get too much recognition for the numbers I wrote, and some weren't well recorded. I could write flagwavers like *Harlem Shout*, and they always opened and closed the show with a number of mine. When we were at the Larchmont Casino, there was a moving stand that used to excite people. The opener was always crescendo and loud. The band would be sitting on this stand, about a foot higher than the regular stage, and as they hit, the stand started moving forward, right up to the edge of the stage. It used to scare some people. They'd jump up and want to get out.

"I was with Lunceford about three years, and then Basie came to New York to play in Roseland at the end of 1936. They came to me and said he needed new numbers in my style. Although Lunceford was getting top money at the Larchmont, he was only paying about seventy dollars a week at that time. He wasn't a crook, but he always thought the leader should make all the money. A few weeks before he died, he told a reporter that that was where he made a mistake, that he had found out the men should make money, too.

"To cut a long story short, Willard Alexander offered me seventy-five dollars a week to play with Basie, and another seventy-five to write for the band, so it was a hundred-and-fifty a week. News got to the papers that I was on notice, so they booked a battle of music between Basie and Lunceford in Hartford, Connecticut, the night my notice expired. The radio stations were talking about this man who had been with Basie, then with Lunceford, and was now going back with Basie. 'He's going to let us know who's going to knock who down,' they said. I don't remember how the 'battle' came out. Basie could swing and he had Jo Jones, but though Lunceford's was a show band, it could swing, too. Nobody could wash Lunceford away at that time. Nobody! I had some swinging numbers in his book, and then they'd go back and put novelty on top of them.

"That night, when we packed up, the valet switched my stuff to Basie's band. We went to the Ritz-Carlton in Boston. That's where I started writing, and where we made *Blue and Sentimental* with Herschel Evans. Of course, Basie's was strictly a rhythm band, not an entertaining band like Lunceford's, and it wasn't as big, but they started adding guys.

"I had written things when I was in Kansas City with Bennie Moten that were in Basie's book. For instance, there was *One O'Clock Jump*, but we originally called it *Blue Ball*. Back then, it meant you've got the blues and ain't having a ball! Buster Smith in the reed section worked on that, and it was really a three-way deal. I was always looking to do something else with the trombones, always looking for a counter-melody. They used to call me 'Circus Guy' in those days. 'Here comes ol' Circus with all his slurring,' they'd say, but later they started liking it, and all the horns started doing it. Four weeks after I left to come east, Moten had a tonsil operation, and he died. There wasn't anything wrong between him and me. We were close, but I just wanted a little eastern air.

"During the year I was with Basie, I got a lot of ideas off him. He has a lot of hidden talent, but he'd only go about four measures, and that's all. Just enough to know the song. He was contributing enough to be acquainted with the arrangement when you wrote it. If I could have got him to go along—his ideas along with mine—he'd have twice the stuff he has now. He wanted the arrangements simple, to swing, not what they'd call 'far out' today. When I was with Lunceford, I could stretch out with my own ideas and put anything down, like on *Running a Temperature* and *Bird of Paradise*. You can be ahead of the public all the time, so they never catch up with you. Stan Kenton stayed ahead for a while.

"I had agreed to go with Basie for a year, and I guess I could have stayed longer, but I had really been with Lunceford too long. He was a college man, a different kind of leader. Nearly all the band were college men, and I never heard a word of profane language with them. But Basie's was a regular type of band like all the others, and it got to the point where I couldn't stand much of the radical stuff. The fellows were nice in Basie's band, but his attitude was different to Lunceford's. The only guy I knew to come near Lunceford was Glenn Miller. Tommy Dorsey was rough, rougher than Basie. I'd made tours opposite him with Lunceford. 'What's the matter back there?' Tommy would shout, and then he'd throw a trumpet player out of the bus and leave him on the highway. Things like that. Basie didn't bother after his men, but he wanted to have a good time all the time, and he wanted me to have it with him. 'You've been working so long,' he'd say. 'Now's your chance. Let's have some fun!'

"When I left Basie, I fooled around, arranging for Jan Savitt, Artie Shaw, and Ina Ray Hutton. I remember Ina asking me one day, 'Eddie, why do the two tenor saxophones have to be separated like that?' It was a good question, because all the bands used to put the two tenors and the two altos together, but all of a sudden they began putting one tenor on each end of the saxes. It began with Lester Young who couldn't sit beside Herschel, because he didn't like that vibrato in Herschel's tone. That's what started everybody doing it, even though they didn't know why they were doing it.

"I got a band of my own in 1940 and had guys like Joe Keyes, Buster Smith, Ben Smith, Eddie Williams, Doles Dickens, and Arthur Herbert in it. The president of Local 802 told me it was too smooth for a colored band, and that I'd be more successful if I went with Glenn Miller. I actually had two styles. I could swing or play sweet as any white band. I had a white boy playing first alto, and that was the trick. White boys have thin lips and get a very pretty sound on saxophone, and this boy could make the whole section sound like him. That band was so good that when we played Pleasure Beach all Connecticut state was trying to get in the park, and we were hurting the business of the big names they'd hired. But in the end I let them talk me out of it. I was having trouble, so I let the band go and carried my book to Glenn Miller.*

"Then I got the girls' band together. That was the only way I could stay out of the army. I met an old West Indian guy, a politician, who got me with the Treasury Department's bond drives. So long as I kept the girls' band, I'd be deferred from the army every six months for the duration. And so long as I gave some service to the USO, the Treasury Department cooperated with whatever agency I was with. I did one day a week for them and six days for myself. I played all the camps and did over four thousand miles in Canada for the Canadian government. For four years during the war I was the only leader who had a sleeper bus and used gas from the government. That's how I got involved with the International Sweethearts of Rhythm!

"After that, I got a six-piece band of my own together and went on the road for nine years with Wynonie Harris and Larry Darnell, a couple of blues singers. I had to treat them both like babies, but I could always handle people. Wynonie was wild, really radical, and he drank a lot, but I had a big old athlete on the show as bodyguard and bouncer. He'd run all the women out, drag Wynonie out of bed, throw him over his shoulder, and put him in the car. Wynonie liked that! He knew this guy would break the door down to get him. He'd do Larry, too, the same way.

"My resistance was very low when I came in from traveling with those guys; and I just retired from music for about ten years. I had a few dollars saved up and I played a few jobs out on Long Island, but I wouldn't go anywhere. I looked all right, and I wasn't too disgusted with the business, but I had had pneumonia and it took me a

---

* For a 1940 *Down Beat* story by Dave Dexter, Durham variously cited as his best or favorite arrangements the following: for Lunceford, *Harlem Shout, Honey, Keep Your Mind on Me,* and *Lunceford Special;* for Basie, *Topsy, John's Idea, Jumpin' at the Woodside, Out the Window, Sent for You Yesterday,* and *Swinging the Blues;* for Shaw, *My Blue Heaven, Sunny Side of the Street,* and *I've Got the World on a String;* for Savitt, *Tuxedo Junction, Wham, Dear Old Southland, Turkey in the Straw, Blues in the Groove,* and *It's Time to Jump and Shout;* and for Miller, *Sliphorn Jive, Wham, Glen Island Special, Tiger Rag, Baby Me,* and *I Want to Be Happy.*

long time to get over it. I gradually regained my strength and I've played a few concerts in the last four or five years. Right now, I think I'm going to start playing again. I've made two or three arrangements for the big band Edgar Battle has been organizing. The only fault with Edgar is that he has still got flexible musicians, who can play anything, on his mind. You've got to kind of forget that. I don't think you can pick up fellows of that kind today. You've got to condense your arrangements and simplify them a little, so these guys can play 'em. He's going to be a long time finding guys who can play like they used to play."

(1971)

Earle Warren

(ALTO SAXOPHONE)

Earle Warren was born in Springfield, Ohio, on July 1, 1914, the second son in a musical family. His father played mandolin and piano, his mother piano and guitar, an older brother drums, one sister piano, and another violin. When he was ten he began three years of piano tuition, but his father also bought him a banjo-ukulele, which he played on the family band's weekend engagements.

Warren, Sr., was a truck driver and an enterprising man. He had a small gym in which he trained fighters, and he taught both sons to box. Later, he presented and danced in minstrel-type shows at local affairs. One Christmas he bought Earle his first saxophone, a C-melody, on which he played in the school band before switching to tenor in an Elks band. Out of the latter, a nine-piece group was formed, which became known as Duke Warren and his Eight Counts of Syncopation. Earle played alto saxophone in this band. His father booked and promoted it energetically, and the band soon became well known in the territory around. Eventually it merged with another Springfield group and grew to fourteen pieces. Its size necessitated working farther

afield, and during the ensuing period Earle Warren worked with
Fats Waller and the Mills Brothers, encountered many musicians later
to become famous, such as Roy Eldridge, Chu Berry, and Joe Thomas,
and led his own group called the Varsity Seven.

After graduating from high school, he left home to work around
Columbus before joining a band led by Marion Sears (the older
brother of Al Sears) at the Furnace Club in Cleveland. It was an
after-hours spot run by gangsters, and the working hours were tough,
from 10 P.M. to 6 A.M. each night, but the money was good. So was
the experience, playing for a show with dancing girls, a comedian,
and other acts.

"Art Tatum was working at another club around the corner," Warren
recalled. "It was a place called Jimmy Jones's, down the street from
the old Majestic Hotel, right off of Central Avenue. I had heard of
him before, in 1931, when I went to Detroit to play at a food show
in an auditorium—one of those things where people showed what
they grew. Musicians told me about this young, blind man in Toledo
who played such remarkable piano. I made up my mind to search him
out, especially since Milton Senior, a fine saxophonist from my hometown, was in Toledo. Milton's dad played tuba and they both had
been in our Elks band. Milton had gone on to play with McKinney's
Cotton Pickers.

"The whole reed section from the Sears band—two altos and Andy
Anderson on tenor—used to go down to Jimmy Jones's after we got
through. Art Tatum was the featured attraction, and that's where the
jam sessions started, in the early wee hours of the morning. The Jeter-
Pillars band was also in Cleveland then, playing the Creole Club, and
Harry Edison was with them.

"After an election and a few shakedowns, Jimmy Jones's club began
to lose business. I didn't understand the politics involved with that,
but Art went to play in a little house off of Cedar Avenue, around 89th
Street. It was among some little shacks, and the man had a bar, a few
tables around, sawdust on the floor, and an upright piano with a little
dim light over it. That became the new after-hours spot. It was one of
those old-time upright pianos. It was kept in great condition and it
made a beautiful sound. Of course, Art would make *any* piano sound
good. We visited there all the time, and I used to sing *Body and Soul*,
Once in a While, and other songs of the day with him. We would split
any tips we made right down the middle, because he could use the
money the same as I could!

"All the big bands that came through—Glen Gray, Jimmie Lunceford, Jimmy Dorsey, and Paul Whiteman—had heard of Art Tatum,

and sometimes you couldn't get in the place, because it was really only a house. The people with money would sit at the tables, and the price for drinks was quite a bit for those days, like a dollar or a dollar-fifty. Art would have beer lined up on top of the piano, and he would play there six or eight months of the year. Those were lean days for black artists on radio programs, but I think it was Jimmy Dorsey who got him featured in a kind of jazz spectacular. Jack Teagarden used to come there and play, because he loved Art. So did Don Byas, and they played together in New York.

"Jam sessions there used to go on until seven or eight in the morning. Art was a good feeder and didn't get in the way. When it was his time to play, he'd really play, but then he'd come up to the service end of the bar and start arguing about football. Art loved to discuss the football and basketball players that to his mind were the greatest. He used to go to games, too, and when people hollered he'd know someone was running. One eye was better than the other then, and he could hold an envelope up to the light and tell what was written on it. And he could tell the difference between a one, a five, or a ten when he was given money. He hit a couple of guys that got cute. He was no baby. He was a man, and a fine one. If you hit a guy good, whether you can see or not, he doesn't want to come back for more.

"If a cat could play, Art loved to hear him. I never saw him show any particular partiality, although I know he loved to play with Don Byas. Of course, he didn't want to play with some lane,* because that would have been a waste of everybody's time, but otherwise he was wide open. He was just a lovely man to know and be around. Even as early as when he was at Jimmy Jones's, he used to get a lot of respect. He'd come in and hobble over to the piano with that funny walk of his, sit down and take himself a drink of beer, run a couple of quick arpeggios, and start off with something smooth, like *Deep Purple*. He had a God-given talent, like Erroll Garner, but Art always sounded schooled. I don't know how much of Fats Waller and Earl Hines there was in Art's style, but I used to see and play shows with Fats Waller when I was at a club in Dayton, Ohio. He came out of Cincinnati, where he was on WLW, a radio station. I didn't hear too much Fats in what Art did, except when he wanted to 'walk' on the piano.

"His knowledge of chord changes, and the way he'd go 'in and out,' as we say in jazz, were what impressed me. On a lot of his records you can hear how he carried progressions outside and then brought 'em back. 'Where's he going?' you'd say, and then he'd come back in so beautifully. One fellow that got very close to him was Lanny Scott.

---

* An inadequate performer, a square.

Whenever Art went to New York or somewhere else, Lanny would take his place. And often Lanny would sit beside the piano, and when Art got up Lanny would take his seat. He used to kill me, but he lost quite a bit of it when he came to New York. Communication is a wonderful thing. It keeps thoughts alive that haven't particularly originated in your own mind. When you're in communication with someone like Art Tatum, he stimulates many different thoughts. Away from real stimulation, you lose a lot of real things, real sounds. Art would come up with chords and changes an ordinary mind wouldn't think of.

"I think Don Byas was one of the few instrumentalists that really grasped what was happening. He learned those changes and his knowledge of his instrument was affected. After they had worked together on 52nd Street and Don left, it was hard for anybody else to work with Art. I think that background and Art's influence helped Don blossom out and become a stellar saxophone player. Only God can bring forth a forerunner, a man of a special type like Tatum. It was the same thing with Prez, Lester Young. No sound or approach to the tenor prepared us for him, because Hawk was *it* before he arrived."

"I first heard of Prez when I was in Cleveland, years before I ever dreamed I'd hear him. Leroy 'Snake' White had told me, 'Boy, if you ever get a chance to hear Lester Young . . . !' He'd known him as an alto player but knew he'd tried out for Fletcher Henderson on tenor. Fletcher, having had guys like Coleman Hawkins with a heavy sound, found Prez a little light. I was working in Sandusky, Ohio, when I first heard him over the air with Basie from the Reno Club. 'Boy, this guy is playing!' I said. And then there was Herschel Evans, too, with his big Hawkins sound.

"Leroy 'Snake' White always bragged on Lester Young. Leroy was a great trumpet player out of Des Moines via Minneapolis, with a background in bands like Zack Whyte's and Walter Page's Blue Devils. He knew what he was talking about. When I eventually joined Basie, I swear to God I had cold chills, because I never heard anything so fabulous in all my life. Prez had an approach to his horn that has been carried on down, but there are so many guys who would have given a right toe or something to embellish on their horn and come up with original ideas the way he did. He knew changes like nobody's business, and he was, of course, a great advocate of Art Tatum.

"About his tone, I should say I knew he had previously been an alto player, but I'd also heard Bud Freeman and Eddie Miller, who had tones just a little different but formed almost the same way. The inimitable sound coming from this man was a matter of the echo chamber and the lipping of the mouthpiece. By that I mean the nasal quality, up in your jaws, and the way you feed the reed. Buddy Tate had a different sound. Herschel Evans was *his* love and he tried to get a sound like his, but he wound up with a sound you can always tell is Buddy Tate's. But he got the job with Basie because he played more like Herschel than anybody we'd ever had. I studied singing and I know that the chamber within you is what determines an inimitable sound. It's from you personally, in the way you deliver it, in the way you feel, in your expression, and in the way you let the sound resolve and go through the chambers of your head.

"Lester was from the Deep South and he'd played in little jazz groups, including his father's family band. Probably his first horn was the cheapest or quickest thing he could get his hands on, and that way he may just have happened on the alto. I never heard him play it, but as an alto player myself I could always hear how fabulous he could have been on that, too. In fact, I'm sure that if he had gone back to alto he would have been world renowned in the same way. I don't know why he switched to tenor, but situations call for certain instruments. I've played tenor and baritone at different times, and with Basie I played alto and baritone—Jack Washington and I together. A guy wants to keep a job!

"The first time I heard Prez in person was in the early spring of '37. He came through Cincinnati with Basie and, to be honest, he didn't impress me at all. Herschel impressed me much more, because I was able to *hear* more. Prez turned his horn up in the air like he was smoking a pipe! Some idiotic idea he'd got, but it amused me greatly. It was a different story when I joined Basie. Jack Washington was sitting between me and Prez, and Herschel was next to me, and I could hear everything. 'Ee, shuckins!' I said. 'He's blowing, baby!' And Prez blew right on into world fame, you believe it!

"Herschel had been an alto player, too, but when he heard Coleman Hawkins he didn't want any more alto. He got him a tenor and worked on it. Hawk showed what the instrument *could* produce, but when I first heard him with Fletcher Henderson he used to play real high on that horn. In later years, he never played what you call those altissimo notes.

"I got the chance to meet Hawk when the Henderson band was in Cleveland in 1933. I remember Jeff [Hilton Jefferson], Procope, Dicky Wells, Pop Smith, Bobby Stark, and John Kirby were in it. Smaller sax sections could maybe move more, but when we went from three to four it opened up more of a basic harmony spread, which gave the reed section more substance. Then Duke came along with Harry Carney as *the* baritone player, but back in the twenties the baritone was thought of as a parade-band instrument and there just weren't real baritone players around. If you wanted a good subtle sound, you would get the alto players to double. That's what we did in Basie's band. A lot of people don't remember when I played baritone. Jack and I would be playing two baritones alongside two tenors to get a dark, deep sound on ballads. Then I'd go back to alto and he'd stay on baritone. The baritone is sort of harmonically based with the trombone, and at that time we had only three trumpets and two trombones so it gave a little more depth. One band that really used to make the baritone travel was Ozzie Nelson's. He had a sensational baritone years ago named Charlie Bubeck. Whoever wrote the arrangements put the alto and the baritone on the same melody. Duke did that quite a bit, and when he wrote that way Harry Carney could be the lead. It was an effect, but not everybody could get that sound because nobody else had a Harry Carney. For a while, some bands had baritone and bass saxophone, but that went out because the sound lacked finesse, was too guttural. A baritone is not an easy saxophone to play, in any case. Some people say, 'You play one saxophone, you play 'em all.' But that's not true.

"Alto saxophone players are usually either playing lead or third to a lead. There are good lead altos and good third altos, but a third alto very seldom makes a good lead alto. He's underneath, a follower; he lays right there with you, and his concept of his position is reverent. He accepts it and he does all he can to be right under the first man. Some guys get to be beautiful at that. But there are some third altos who want to be first altos, who play *over* because they're afraid they're not being heard. They say to themselves, 'Well, I don't like the way he [the lead] played that passage, so I'm going to see if I can't kind of influence him.'

"Years ago it used to be one-three-five harmony—first alto, third alto, and the fifth part for the tenor. Then arrangers began to find different ways of handling chords, whereby they could voice a reed section into four-part or five-part harmony at times, not that they didn't double on other horns in the band, but it gave body when it came to five saxophones. Saxophone choruses were very interesting in the thirties and forties. But all at once there was a change, more emphasis on trombones and not too much on the melodic sound of saxophones, except in solos. The battle of the tenors began to be the thing, and you could almost forget alto players. Some who had established themselves earlier, like Johnny Hodges, survived. What happened to me in the Basie band was that I got all the bridges, eight bars in the middle of everything. The only number I remember opening up on was *Out the Window,* and I got a lot of compliments for that."

"I was relieving Al Sears in his band at the Cotton Club in Cincinnati when Basie came. Al at that time played alto and clarinet, and well. He had to go to Detroit for the weekend and I had a seventeen-piece band down the street at the Sunset. I'd get my band started and go up and play the show at the Cotton Club. Basie and his band would play between the shows, and while they were on I'd go back to the Sunset. On the Sunday there was a matinée, and I played all the afternoon, and they heard me. I was reading the buttons off the music, and all our stuff was real bouncy but with a lot of sixteenth notes.

"After we closed, Herschel Evans came over to talk to me. Caughey Roberts had put in his notice, because he was getting lonesome and wanted to go back to California. I decided I would go with Basie and I joined him in Pittsburgh in April. Caughey played on a couple of days but then he was gone and I never saw him again until he came back for a hot minute as third alto. Buster Smith was also in the band for a month or so in 1938, the year his arrangement of *Blues I Like to Hear* was recorded. He was like Ben Webster. He would always go home to visit his mother. If he knew she was all right, he was all right, and then he'd come back to New York.

"I was twenty-three, younger than most of the guys in the band. I'd met Jack Washington, Ben Webster, and Eddie Barefield years before, when they were with Bennie Moten. They used to come to my home when they were stranded in Cincinnati during the hard times of 1932. One time they'd be there and they'd be real sharp. The next time they'd be kind of shopworn and their horns would be in pawn. Different things happen. Dates are canceled and hotel bills are due, but everybody's got to eat! Some took out on the lam, and others pawned clothes as well as horns.

"Cincinnati used to be called 'The Gateway of the South,' and all the bands used to stop off there. There was a Greystone Ballroom in Cincinnati just as there was in Detroit, and everybody wanted to play there. The big fabulous place was Castle Farms, but they didn't play many colored bands at that time. Colored bands used to play dances in the South, but you would be harassed, insulted, and not respected. You could play wonderfully, but they'd still make very derogatory remarks about you. It was a most grievous time.

"The Basie band was very insecure when I joined. Willard Alexander had something to do with the booking, but there was no money.

Three of the boys in my band had left to go with Walter Barnes when he offered them eighteen dollars a night, but they and Walter all got burned up in a fire in Natchez. I had gone to the secretary of the Cincinnati local and found that about sixty dollars was scale for a musician on the road, but when I first went with Basie I was making $6.25 a night. After Social Security came into effect, I made seven dollars a night—the nights we worked. I hadn't been making much with my big band, and after the Cincinnati flood the city was in terrible condition. Further, I had married in 1934, so I had my responsibilities!

"There weren't many black hotels around in those days, so we had to walk up and down the street in the black neighborhoods trying to find a room. If they knew you were a musician, a lot of people weren't going to give you a room even when they had one. But because of so many bands traveling through so many territories, there came to be more rooming houses and that's where we would have to stay, but they'd charge three-and-a-half or four dollars, and that was quite a bit of money then.

"When we finally got to New York, I moved into the Woodside Hotel, on 142nd Street, with Ed Lewis, the first trumpet player. He was a great big cat and I was real small then. We roomed together and I think we paid about six dollars a week. I'd go across the street where they'd have bologna or liverwurst. You could get that, an egg or two, some toast and a cup of coffee for a quarter then. Whenever I broke a dollar, I'd save three dimes in my little piggy bank in order to be able to eat later. Sometimes I didn't have a nickel to ride the subway, although I was with Count Basie's band!

"When they told me we were staying at the Woodside Hotel, I pictured a big, palatial place with a circular driveway in front. So when we pulled up in front of that hotel I almost died. A great big cat was sitting in the middle of the lobby. There were a lot of ballplayers and a guy who had worked with Basie for a long time, by the name of Jack Castor. He was like the bellhop, the impresario *and* the greeter. The band had stayed there before, when they played the Apollo, so all the guys knew what it was like. June Clark, the trumpet player, and the Mills Brothers' sister were there, along with a lot of show people. There were cooking facilities in some rooms, and a big kitchen where people could cook and take food up to their rooms. Jack Washington's wife, Jimmy Rushing's, and Ed Lewis's all lived there. It wasn't by any means luxurious, but it was like a music house, and we rehearsed in the basement. When we really started cooking in 1938, after the records of *Every Tub, One O'Clock Jump,* and *Jumpin' at the Woodside* came out, things improved and I brought my wife to New

York. We moved to where we could have our own little place, and everything became quite nice.

"I wasn't what the cats call a 'straw boss' at the beginning. I don't like that word, anyway. Up until the time he went into the army, Buck Clayton was the assistant conductor. He had had bands of his own, just as I had, and any time we did shows and stuff he conducted. The Holy Main [Basie] didn't want to be bothered with that anyhow. He wasn't much interested in conducting for an act because his name was becoming quite well known and he wanted to have his time for himself."

"Herschel was a most likeable guy, and he and Prez really weren't bitter enemies. Herschel was outspoken. He was a man. Little things that happened between him and Prez were of no great consequence. So far as sitting on the bandstand and not talking to one another— that's a lot of hogwash. Like guys would say to me, 'Man, that Prez. . . . I dug the way he walked. Is he kind of on the lady side?' So many times, I've had to tell them, 'No, definitely not.' There's no way in the world I can accept that. At one time, he, Walter Page, and I were all three living in one room, and I was so tired of looking at chicks running in and out of there I was sick. So I tell guys not to talk to me about Prez in that way. He nearly got arrested once on a train going out to Long Island, when a guy started hitting on him. Prez almost cut his suit off him, his army suit. He didn't bother anybody ordinarily. He wouldn't even say hello if he didn't know you.

"I remember when Lady Day was in the band, and how it would be some hard nights when Prez was blowing his brains out. We'd be soaking wet when we finished and got on the bus. If he had been able to cop a bottle, he would have his little gin. The first thing he'd do was come walking up the aisle with the dice in his hand, shaking them in everybody's ear. 'Sweet music,' he'd say, 'sweet music!' He had his special seat on the bus like everybody else, but now they'd be shooting dice, rolling 'em all up under the seats and everywhere. Usually he'd be the first one broke, and when that happened he'd go on back to his seat and sit down. He was just a beautiful cat.

"We had a softball team and Prez was the pitcher. He threw a backspinning ball which made the guy hit the ball on the ground. I played shortstop, Herschel was first base, Jack Washington was second, and I forget who was on third. We used to practice on the roadside in the spring when we were down south, and all through Texas.

"We were down in Columbia, South Carolina, one year, and we had a bus from America Orchestra Service over in Jersey. Little Jimmy

LeMarr was our driver, and if we didn't have him we weren't happy. We were crazy about him. He had a lot of gall and he was our mainstay. If something happened to the bus, we'd be out beside the highway with our gloves for batting practice while Jimmy fixed it. This time we were running up and down, and the ball went over two or three times into a field where a guy had some wheat planted. Meanwhile, Prez, Freddie Green, Lady Day, and Shad Collins had made a little trip, you know, in seclusion. All at once we see this guy coming up the road on a motorcycle, a big South Carolinian. When he got through getting himself off that cycle, he must have been six foot six and about 240 pounds. Maceo Birch was our manager then, and when he saw this cop coming he ran in the bus, pulled his hat down over his head, and made like he went to sleep. Jimmy was up under the bus when this guy asked, 'Who's in charge of you so-and-sos?' We pointed to Jimmy and he kicked him on the foot. 'What's the matter with you?' Jimmy said, coming out from under.

" 'I want you to get these so-and-sos out of here. This ain't no place to play! You better get that thing fixed right quick.'

"There was nothing to do but grab the bats, the ball, and the gloves and go on about our business. Prez and the others showed up just as we were getting back on the bus, and the cop told them to get moving, too. I don't like to embellish on things like that, but at the time it was quite scary because we knew what Columbia, South Carolina, meant in those days. We went over to a place called College Inn in Allen, hoping they'd have rooms where we might stay, and then we played the big Columbia auditorium, where the white people sat on one side and the Negroes on the other. Some people would want to dance, and others would throw money to 'em and act like a bunch of nuts. It was embarrassing. The band was beginning to gain fame and we needed scenes like that like a hole in the head.

"When we were in Memphis, playing a theater, Freddie Green left the window open. Somebody broke in and stole a brand-new coat he'd just bought, and the long black coat Prez always wore with his porkpie hat. Freddie had a little black spring coat and a trenchcoat as well, so whenever Hawk was really asking for them,* Prez would be trying to wear Freddie's trenchcoat and Freddie would be in his spring coat. We used to make fun of them and call them the Dootsie Twins.

"When Buddy Tate came to the band, he had an overcoat that came down around the ankles. He'd come out of Omaha from Nat Towles' band, and he'd just had a case of pneumonia. He was wearing long

---

* Whenever the weather turned really cold.

drawers, too. We'd see him outside crossing the street to the hotel, and the wind would be whipping that coat every which way. 'Whew,' he'd say when he got inside, 'that wind tore me up out there!' It seemed as though everybody had a joke to tell on somebody else in those days.

"Noble Sissle had been looking for a saxophone player before I joined Basie, but I didn't care for his style or the way he dominated his men. He was quite forceful in his language, and I guess it was just a lingo out of New York, but I was from Ohio, the Midwest, and if a person can't talk to me like I'm a man I don't have any respect for him. After I'd heard Basie, I figured that was *it*, anyhow, but even in that band I met the kind of talk that ran racial—bad words, and calling each other names. 'Well, wait a minute,' I said, 'I don't dig this. We never used that kind of language around where I lived.' So I cut that off. But I had the same problem Willie Smith had with Jimmie Lunceford, until people had seen him a few times and the word was brought out.

"People who didn't know me, even Negroes, assumed I was white. Years before, I'd played with an Italian guy who was darker than me and called himself Richard Sherman. There were his cousin, a couple of Jewish boys, a Pole, and an Irish kid in the band, but we were all real close and it didn't matter what race or denomination the other was. Only the leader and his cousin knew what *I* was. When we played the Pick Hotel in Owensboro, Kentucky, I did all the negotiating with the peckerwoods there. 'Mussolini's in town,' they said when we arrived in dark blue suits and yellow ties! Later I went back to Owensboro with Basie and I was scared to death. But musicians came by and said, 'Warren, we remember how you played here, and we know dog-gone well the best thing you ever did was get in a band with a bunch of niggers. You've got that kind of sound, and when we saw your picture in *Life* magazine we knew you were going to be the happiest man alive.' It made me laugh more than anything else, but when some of those hillbilly characters came to New York they wouldn't even speak to me anymore! Somebody must have told 'em, 'Man, are you kidding? He's colored, like everybody else in the band.'

"I got a lot of harassment from my own people. I objected when they started calling me 'white folks,' 'redneck,' 'albino,' 'peckerwood,' and other nicknames. I know Willie Smith would sometimes get quite venomous when they pulled that on him.

"In 1937 and '38, when I wasn't making any money and was trying to squeeze out a living, I stayed in the little old crummy places I had to stay in. Some of them were terrible. I got eaten up by bedbugs, and you had to keep one eye open all the time to keep from having your stuff stolen. I roomed with other guys in the band, and altogether I paid my dues, but when I got my raise I stayed in nice hotels.

"We came into Lincoln, Nebraska, one time, and it was so hot. There was a little white-run hotel near the station that accepted bands. Of course, it *had* to be down by the tracks! The band jumped out and went to this place, but we couldn't get rooms. I walked straight up the street with my clothes, bag, and horn to the Lincoln Hotel and checked in for $4.50—a nice room with ice water running out of the spigot, and big fans in the window. That night I told Basie, 'Come by and see me. I've got two beds, beautiful fans, and everything. Ain't no use sleeping some place where you're going to smother to death! Come by like you're talking business with me, and you can have four or five hours' sleep before we leave.' But he wouldn't do it."

"I first met Harry Edison in Columbus, on Long Street, and we struck up a friendship. He was just a young fellow out of high school, playing with some little band around there. Then he disappeared and I didn't know where he had gone, but when I got to Cleveland in the fall of '33 he was playing at the Creole Club in the Jeter-Pillars band. After an election, a new regime came in, the racketeers were washed away, and the club scene kind of dissolved. Next time I saw Harry, he was with Lucky Millinder's band in New York. Dicky Wells, Herschel, Harry, and I all lived in the same place, 2195 Seventh Avenue. It was strictly a show business building, run by Mrs. Cotton and her husband, two lovely people. Jimmy Jones, the bass player who used to be with Noble Sissle, Emmett Berry, and a lot of dancers lived there. My wife and I had kitchen privileges downstairs, and we used to eat with Mrs. Cotton, who was a very kind lady.

"Anyway, with us all in the same place, we managed to get Harry Edison over to the Basie band. He really added zest, fire, and punch to the trumpet section. I still maintain he's one of the world's greatest. He was a good reader and no novice. He already had a style of his own, and he was good fanning a derby to make hanh-hanh sounds. He and I were about the same age, and we used to wrestle and roll over the yard. He played short-center on the softball team. Sometimes we'd get mad at one another, but there were no fights. We were just like brothers. Just like Buck Clayton. I see Buck every Wednesday when I go to the union and I put the whistle on him. He'll cock an ear, because everybody from the old Basie band will recognize that whistle, even if they're in Istanbul. Where did it come from? From Prez. It says, 'I want you to get way back, babe!'

"It was Prez who named Harry 'Sweets.' I don't know why. You couldn't ask Prez why he did anything. He called me 'Smiles,' because when I play saxophone I smile, from the embouchure. 'Man,' he said, 'you're about the smilin'est son-of-a-gun I ever saw. I'm gonna call you Smiles.' Then he changed it to 'Smiley,' and later to 'Smile.'"

"I think Basie's more projective now. He's got more confidence in his position than in the olden days. Then he was more like one of the guys, an ordinary cat, but everybody loved Basie. Everybody knew he could play. Man, he was no dummy setting at that piano! And when he spoke up, expressed an opinion, everybody listened. You must understand that nobody in that band was a novice, and nobody was just a guy who came in gangbusting. That never worked anyhow. Basie started the band, although I heard years before that it was actually supposed to be a thing between him and Walter Page. That's beside the point, because it takes a leader. I don't think Basie got himself into a position to be a leader until about two or three years after the band was really going. He never was a forceful arbitrator, nor a disciplinarian. He'd wait till something just blew up, and then he'd tell the manager, 'Here, give him his notice! Tell him to take a walk.' He's always been a gentleman, but he can blow up like anybody else.

"I'm the godfather to his daughter, Diane Catherine, and my wife, Clara, was the godmother. Adam Clayton Powell was the pastor that baptized Diane. That was back in 1944. We stayed close together until I felt it was time for me to get out and try to help myself. It was like a sorry day, and I got a lot of venomous and nasty remarks from people I never expected them from.

"I had some money saved up and a whole, good band waiting for me in Cincinnati. My trombone player, Bob Kennerley, put it together. A guy named Murray Deutsch, who used to manage Woody Herman, became my manager, and Paul Ash of the Roxy Theater was taking out a $100,000 insurance policy on me and putting $50,000 behind the band. He liked my playing and singing, and he thought I had potential as a new bandleader.

"Mr. Ash and I went to Moe Gale's office when Ralph Cooper was there. Moe came on with the real funny Italian talk. So I said, 'Now, wait a minute. I don't need your money. I've had bands since I was sixteen years old. I want to know if you will take me as a prospective money-maker for your organization.' He had the Savoy in New York and the El Grotto in Chicago. But he turned me down, although Jimmy McCarthy, the publicist, had already got my picture in the papers all across the country. It seems that Moe and Paul Ash had had some words over Connie Stevens sometimes. Paul went to other agencies, and Willard Alexander naturally closed the door on me.

"I went to Cincinnati, but before I got there Moe Gale had sent somebody to take most of the men for Billy Eckstine's band. I got together twelve pieces and worked for the mother of Ezzard Charles, the prizefighter. She had what they called a coliseum on Ninth Street. Erskine Hawkins came through a couple of months later and said, 'Boy, where'd you get this band?' But we weren't making any money and I ended up with six pieces in New York, at the Concord—Charlie Lewis on trumpet, Bob Kennerley on trombone, a new piano player, Kenny Johnson on bass, and Khalil Mhadi on drums. From there we went to the Paradise in New Jersey, then to Kelly's Stables in New York for six weeks, after which we went up to the Savoy in Boston. We rehearsed all the time and emphasized jazz. I had a trio singing and wrote little original things myself. Charlie Lewis and I would sit down and arrange the format for certain tunes. I kept that group for two-and-a-half years, and did very well with it, but then in 1946 my wife became *very* ill with cancer. It just washed her away, and she passed in '51.

"I hadn't been in the service during the war, because I had terrible ulcers, starting in 1939. It may have been a nervous situation, but I can't recall being worried. In 1947, I got a telephone call and went back to Basie. Preston Love, who admired everything I played and tried to play just like me, was there. He fitted very well, but I took his place in Omaha. C. Q. Price was third alto and he wrote good. He never was promoted on alto, and I don't think he was justly paid for what he did do in the band, but he was so withdrawn—a rather timid, yet nice man. Another saxophone player nobody knew or recognized was a boy named Marvin Johnson, who was in the Basie band at the same time as Don Byas. He and his brother had a little combo in Los Angeles, and he was a marvelous player. He was in the post office, and he was only with us a few months, but he was on that record date when I sang *Time on My Hands*.

"Tab Smith and I got along beautifully. He would play first on the arrangements he wrote, and play all the alto solos on them. Nothing wrong with that. He and Buddy Tate were real close friends. He was a formidable musician, a nice guy to know, with an even personality and no animosity toward anyone. You never heard him talk about anything he disliked. He just took life as it came, and he was happy with Basie, but that was his last big band. He left to go out with a small group. His mother and sister were in St. Louis, where he had property.

"Playing in those days wasn't particularly healthy, especially in those old tobacco barns down south where there was so much dust and everything. I got sick in 1948 and the doctor told me not to blow anymore. 'If you lost a finger, you'd still be a doctor, wouldn't you?' I asked him. 'Well, that's the way I am. I'd rather die blowing than sit around moping away.' So I came back, and I've been blowing ever since.

"Of course, the war years brought so many changes. Jo Jones, Jack Washington, and Buck Clayton went in the army. We had a whole lot of different tenor players, including 'Sam' Byas (that's what we always called Don), Paul Gonsalves, Dexter Gordon for a little while, and Weasel Parker. Weasel is from Akron, and we got him from George Hudson's band. But everything was getting too difficult, so in 1950 Basie dissolved the band. Since then I've done all kinds of things, mostly with small groups."

(1969)

Dicky Wells

"Basie sent for me in 1938 and told me to come by his house, because Herschel [Evans], Lester [Young] and some of the fellows in the band liked my blowing with Teddy Hill.

" 'Okay,' I said, 'but how about you?'

" 'Well,' Basie said, 'so long as they like you, you must be okay.'

"We went to play in a country club in Plainfield, New Jersey. It was a small room.

" 'Come on,' Basie said, 'take your axe out, and sit down and blow with the cats. See if you like it.'

" 'Where's my music?' I asked.

" 'Sit in and see what happens,' he said.

"I took Ed Durham's place and they had only the two trombone parts for Dan Minor and Benny Morton.

" 'Grab a derby and start fannin'!' Basie called.

"I was so busy getting my kicks, because Billie Holiday was there, and Jimmy Rushing, and Herschel Evans, as well as Prez. Herschel and Prez had their battle going, and it was the swingingest band I had been

86

in since Fletcher's. Basie would start out and vamp a little, set a tempo, and call out, 'That's it!' He'd set a rhythm for the saxes first, and Earle Warren would pick that up and lead the saxes. Then he'd set one for the bones and we'd pick that up. Now it's our rhythm against theirs. The third rhythm would be for the trumpets, and they'd start fanning with their derbies. (Derbies were very effective with brass sections then, and it's too bad they're so little used now. Derby men like Lips Page, Sidney De Paris, and Harry Edison could always make your insides dance.) The solos would fall in between the ensembles, but that's how the piece would begin, and that's how Basie put his tunes together. He had a big band, but he handled it as though it were six pieces.

"When we got through, Basie asked me how I liked the band. I told him I was crazy about it.

" 'Am I hired?' I asked him.

" 'I didn't fire you, did I?' was his answer.

"It took me quite a while to pick up on some of the psychology he used. He was the first leader I ran into who used jokes as hints, along with nicety, to whip you back into line—maybe damned near too late! I found out afterwards that his motto was: 'I'm not going to fire you— you're going to fire yourself.' Just about the only way I had seen cats whipped back in line in Louisville was when others whipped out their shooting irons or blades. The leader I first worked with, the one who was pocketing the other half of my weekly pay, carried the longest rod in the world. It should have had wheels on it. He said he had it for pink-toes, but he must have been color blind because I've seen him pull it on some pretty dark pink-toes. Anyway, give me Basie's style as a leader and I can make it.

"It was a happy band. Even when Herschel and Lester weren't speaking, they were the best of friends! There was so much humor in that band. It was like being part of a family. And all kinds of people liked Basie. Sometimes there were so many millionaires on the bus there wasn't room for the guys to sit down. Walter Page was very popular, too. Carloads of people used to come long distances just to hang out with him. I'll tell you another thing. We were a clean band. When we played hotels, we didn't leave the stand littered up with cigarette butts and chewing gum. They used to be so surprised they'd say, 'Hey, didn't you guys work here last night?'

"Soon after I joined, we went into the Famous Door. It seemed that everything they had then turned out to be a hit, like *Jumpin' at the Woodside*, and *One O'Clock Jump*, and *Doggin' Around*. And Jimmy Rushing had his hit songs, too, like *Good Morning Blues, Sent for You Yesterday*, and *Don't You Miss Your Baby?* Billie didn't stay long,

but she had her songs going as well. This was about the time she began
to make a name for herself on records.

"We were supposed to be in the Famous Door six weeks, but we
stayed three months. Basie and I had a little spat there one night, and
he told me to go home until he sent for me. I thought he would
never send for me, but he did. So I went back after a couple of days
and was there until the job ended, when I was supposed to quit. He
asked me if I wanted to stay a bit longer and go on the road. The
band was swinging, so I said, 'Yes.'

"The bus left from outside the Woodside Hotel. Herschel was
sitting in the front and he started cursing me out right away:

" 'You knew you weren't going to leave in the first place, and here
you come dragging back! Get the hell in the back of the bus and set
your red ass down.'

"He made me kind of angry, but the other guys said not to pay him
any mind, and soon we were all smiles. He turned out to be one of
my best friends, and they used to call him, Buck [Clayton], and myself
brothers, because we were about the same height and color. I soon
seemed to settle in in that band, although the only guy I'd known
before was Benny Morton. I remember him coming to Louisville with
Fletcher, and everybody marveling about how well he played.

"So we went out, and that was the beginning of my eleven years
with Basie—what was supposed to have been six weeks. We went
touring, mostly in the South, because Basie didn't cover the wide area
he does now. In fact, he almost never goes south now.

"The band gradually took on a lot of arrangements as well as the
heads. Don Kirkpatrick, the pianist, used to bring in arrangements
while we were at the Famous Door. He was a wonderful writer. Now,
Herschel was a slow kind of reader and didn't care about reading at
all. So after we had spent about three hours rehearsing, Basie would
call out that night:

" 'Get out that number Kirkpatrick made!'

" 'I can't find my part,' Herschel would say.

"We'd all be down, looking under the stands, and Basie would be
looking through the piano music. Herschel would be real busy helping
Basie look for it, but after the gig he'd tell me:

" 'Man, I tore that damn thing up and sent it down the drain—all
them sharps and things. I didn't feel like fooling with that.'

"That happened three or four times, until Basie got wise. He said,
" 'I believe that rascal's tearing up our music.'

"But I don't think he ever actually *knew*. Herschel would wait until
after rehearsal and tear it up, six or seven sheets for saxophone. Well,
he read slow, but that was one of the reasons why he swung so much.

I asked Fletcher Henderson once why he wrote so much in those keys like B-natural and C-sharp, and he said he'd been doing it so long because it meant less notes and the band would swing more. Sandy Williams verified that later on. He said when he left Fletcher he couldn't read fast in flat or natural keys.

"Basie really began to get a book together when Ed Durham was in the band. Basie and Ed would lock up in a room with a little jug, and Basie would play the ideas and Ed would voice them. Durham could write real well then, as he did later for the Glenn Miller band. After Durham left, Basie began to buy different arrangements from outside. Even so, Basie always played a big part, because he would cut out what he didn't like, what wasn't Western style, just as he does today, until he got it swinging. He always said you could swing a piece no matter how fast or slow it was. He always believed in making people's feet pat, which is one reason he still has a swinging band. And he had that feeling for tempo. He'd start the band off, maybe fool around with the rhythm section for thirty-two bars, until he got it right, and then it would stay that way right through.

"I don't think the Basie band had anything *new* except the idea of the two tenors. After all, Fletcher had swung just about everything that could be swung. Maybe Fletcher's things were a bit more polished, but Basie had those tempos like Bennie Moten had. Bennie's brother used to play accordion and I believe it helped to groove the band. If you were standing in a corner, you'd hear it coming through with the rhythm. Ed Durham contributed a lot, too. He didn't write too complicated and he voiced so open, like Jimmy Mundy, and I think it caught the dancers better. Now Don Redman and Benny Carter wrote tough parts for trumpets, but their style couldn't be better for trombones. Benny's writing for saxes was something else, and there was no limit to what Don would write if he could pick his men.

"Basie's two battling tenors were two of the best, and the crowd went for them. I heard them going like that at the Cherry Blossom when I was in Kansas City with Fletcher Henderson. Plenty of bands had two trumpet soloists or two trombones, but not two tenors. I noticed their effect for the first time when we played the Paradise Theater in Detroit, a place like the Apollo. As soon as Herschel stood up, before ever he went down front, the people would start yelling. The same when Lester stood up. I think that started the tenor sax duet within a band. Before that it had been drums and trumpets. The flute's popular now, but I think it's more of a novelty. It has more of a symphonic sound, but that's the way it's gone lately, as though everyone wants to see how technical he can get. So they've tried to squeeze the older sounds under the rug. The older people you used to see, you may see now in a ballroom, dancing to a band like Buddy Tate's. That they can understand. The more Buddy swings, the sooner he fills the floor. And the blues still fills it up. I always remember Buchanan at the Savoy saying, 'The best band is the one that keeps the floor filled.'

"Herschel had a kind of first tenor sound that made a real contrast with Lester's, and Herschel was playing that way before he ever heard Hawk in person. When Buddy Tate, Lucky Thompson, Don Byas, and Paul Gonsalves were in the band, though they were tops, there was never the same contrast. It's pretty hard to duplicate the original, especially when the original is perfect—and that it was. Wow, what a team! I think, though, that if any of the fine fellows with real tenor tone, like Don, Paul, Lucky, Jacquet, or Buddy, had been on the scene *at first*, it would have been pretty much the same. Don, Lucky, and Paul were supreme technicians. Illinois Jacquet was an all-round man with something of Herschel's style. Buddy was tops for gut-bucket, and he had a lot of Herschel in his playing, too. Those three, Herschel, Buddy, and Illinois, all came from Texas, and they have that big Texas sound.

"Buddy came in when Herschel left, and Basie liked him because he had a quality like Herschel's. So had Illinois, but there was never again quite the same effect, although Basie always had a contrast going. He wouldn't put Don Byas and Lucky Thompson together, or Don and Paul Gonsalves. He aimed for two different sounds and styles. He had fine tenor players, but it was as though he was really lucky the first time. He could never get that flavor after Lester left, but at least the first two gave him a pattern. He came closest to it when he had Paul Quinichette.

"Basie is always listening, and he's the one who gives the band its character. Like if I had a band, and he and I bought the same arrangement, and rehearsed it with different bands, when we came to play it most people wouldn't know it was the same arrangement. He'd have whittled it down, maybe only kept the introduction, though he'd have paid good money for it. So it was Basie music! As great as Don Redman was, he'd rearrange his arrangements, too. Basie told me once about one of mine:

" 'That's good, but you've got enough there for fifty arrangements.'

"When he'd finished tearing it up, I didn't know it, but it was swinging.

"Andy Gibson wrote things for the band like *Tickle Toe* and *Beau Brummel*. He knew about Basie's way with arrangements, so one night he brought one in written on a bit of paper about the size of a postcard.

" 'Turn it over when you get to Letter B,' he said.

"Basie had gone to the phone. When he came back he heard us playing this number, said it was swinging, and wanted to know what it was. When he saw the size of it, he said, 'This one must be on the house, man!'

"So I think the real difference between the Basie band and most others was in the way they broke down arrangements the way they wanted them. Sometimes, Benny Carter's bands sounded almost too perfect. That's the funny thing about jazz. You may rehearse until you're hitting everything on the head, and here comes a band like the Savoy Sultans, raggedy, fuzzy-sounding, and they upset everything. 'What am I doing here?' you wonder. But that's the way it is. That's jazz. If you get too clean, too precise, you don't swing sometimes, and the fun goes out of the music. Like Fletcher's arrangements—they'd make you feel bright inside. You were having fun just riding along. You could almost compare it to a lot of kids playing in the mud, having a big time. When the mother calls one to wash his hands, he gets clean, but he has to stand and just look while the others are having a ball. *He's too clean and he can't go back.* Same way when you clean up on that horn and the arrangements are too clean: you get on another level. You're looking down on those guys, but they're all having a good, free-going time.

"Basie's book was probably more varied in the old days than it is today. Buck Clayton used to know just what to write for the guys, and Basie would often suggest the number he wanted. Besides Andy Gibson's things, Don Redman wrote some good ones like *Old Manuscript* and *Down, Down, Down.* I wrote *Stay Cool* and *After Theater Jump.* He used to play my *Kansas City Stride* every night, too, the one we recorded on V-Disc. One of the last the band recorded was *Just a Minute. Dickie's Dream* was Lester's tune. He made it up in the studio. We hadn't got a title for it, so John Hammond said, 'Let's call it *Dickie's Dream.*' I sometimes get a request for it, but until recently I had forgotten how it went.

"When the band first came to New York, it was pretty rough, but the time at the Famous Door ironed out quite a bit of that. Each section used to iron out its own problems. And then we used to have different guys for different chairs, sometimes maybe two first men. Like in Smack's band: Joe Smith wouldn't play first, nor would Louis. Today, everybody wants to be so great on their horns technically that they can say, 'I play first.' I once heard Sy Oliver say, 'If a man can't play first, I don't want him.' That's all right, but if everybody can play first you end up with a similarity of sound in solos. When you had definite first, second, and third chairs, I believe you got more of an individual flavor in the different solos. I go along with each playing *some* first, but there should be a key man. If everyone plays first, what about cats like Louis Armstrong, Buck Clayton, Emmett Berry, Bill Coleman, Bobby Stark, Bix Beiderbecke, Red Allen, Jonah Jones, Bobby Hackett, Miles Davis, Dizzy Gillespie, and Harry Edison, all of whom I consider great? There are many more, not to mention saxes and bones, who have a beautiful color (musically), who are also great and don't play first or care to do so.

"Now, Arthur Pryor, who had a band like Sousa's and started lip vibrato for trombone, was one of the greatest trombone soloists, but he always kept one or two of the best first bone men in his band. He used to demonstrate trombones for Conn, and he gave me lessons about 1936, when I was with Teddy Hill. Keg Johnson and Claude Jones went to him, too. He was one of the best artists, but when he was teaching you just had to watch and listen. He was so very fast, you had to tell him to slow down. There was nothing stiff about his playing; he was very flexible.

"Basie was one of the best to work for. He takes quite a bit, and then he may get mad and explode. Could be that you're on the way out and don't know why. Well, it's a poor guy who doesn't know he has done wrong and keeps doing it. Basie's pretty easygoing, but he still lets you know who's boss. He doesn't want you to drink too much on the job. That is, he wants you to be careful. I think Prez was about the only man he let have a taste on the stand, and he always hid it and wouldn't make it obvious.

"I don't think Basie plays enough piano solos today. One guy in the band used to kid him and say, 'Man, I hear you reaching way back!'

"He acted as though he were kidding, but he meant it, and that was no good, because Basie is kind of shy, and sincere about his work.

"Whether it's old-fashioned or not—and I don't think it is—the real question is, is it good? A lot of new-fashioned things are no good. That's what I like about European audiences. They don't just want the newest, they want the best. The Basie rhythm section could still be featured by itself like it used to be, because it's still a good rhythm section.

"When we were at the Lincoln Hotel in New York, the owner, Mrs. Kramer, was fond of swing, and she'd pull up a table near the stand. She especially liked the rhythm section, and sometimes they'd play alone for maybe an hour, and Basie would tell us we could leave for a while, and we'd be in the bars around, drinking.

"One of the things that keeps tension down in a band is a drummer who plays for the band, and for the soloists, rather than for himself. Basie's rhythm section used to be so light, and so strong, that it was a real inspiration. My idea of a rhythm section is one you feel or sense, one that doesn't disturb you. In the forties, some of the drummers got so technical they spoiled everything. Before he died, Shadow Wilson told me that before he went with Basie he had one way of playing in mind—the latest thing, that was it! Then he got hungry and found out, and began playing with a beat to satisfy the band. He was very versatile and a good drummer, and he played for the musicians on the order of Big Sid. At its best, the Basie rhythm section was nothing less than a Cadillac with the force of a Mack truck. They more or less gave you a *push*, or a *ride*, and they played no favorites, whether you were an E-flat or B-flat soloist.

"It was at the Lincoln that Prez got his little bell. If somebody missed a note, or you were a new guy and goofed, you'd hear this bell going—*'ding-dong!'* If Prez was blowing and goofed, somebody would reach over and ring his bell on him.

"'Why, you . . .' he'd say when he'd finished.

"Jo Jones had another way of saying the same thing. *Bing-bing-bing* he'd go on his cymbal rod. When you first joined, you would take it kind of rough, but later you'd be in stitches with the rest, and take it as a joke. They'd ring a bell on Basie, too. And if Prez saw someone getting angry, he'd blow the first bar of *Runnin' Wild*.

"Harry Edison named himself 'Sweets' because he was so rough, always kidding, hiding your hat, and things like that. Sweets, because it was the opposite of what he knew he was. He and Prez just about named everybody, and when Prez named anybody the name stuck.

"Basie was 'The Holy Main.' That meant 'tops' in the way you'd apply it to someone you greatly admired. Buck Clayton was 'Cat Eye' and Snooky Young was 'Rabbit.' Ed Lewis was 'Big D.' George Matthews was 'Truce,' and Benny Morton was 'Mr. Bones.' After Benny left, I became 'Mr. Bones,' but before that I had been 'Gas Belly' on account of my troublesome stomach. Freddie Green was 'Pep.' Walter Page was 'Big 'Un,' or 'Horse.' Jo Jones was 'Sampson.' Buddy Tate was 'Moon,' and Herschel was 'Tex.' Rush was 'Honey Bunny Boo' or 'Little Jim.' Earle Warren was 'Smiley,' and Jack Washington was 'Weasel.' Emmett Berry was 'Rev.,' and Eli Robinson was 'Mr. Eli.' Jimmy Powell was 'Neat,' and Helen Humes 'Homey.' It was Prez who named Snodgrass, the manager, 'Lady Snar.' Everybody had one of those names.

"Herschel worked up to the day before he died. I think it was dropsy. He swelled up so he couldn't get his hat on. It could have been cured if he had gone to the doctor earlier. Everybody loved him.

"Helen Humes did well as Billie's successor, and her blues style fitted the band. Even her pop songs had a blues flavor. She and

Jimmy Rushing used to get along well, telling tall tales and keeping the bus in an uproar all the time.

"Jimmy used to come aboard the bus with a bag of food, chicken or something. We'd be leaving around two o'clock and he would wait until everybody was asleep, snoring, and then open his chicken bag. I was sitting behind him one time, hungry, and saw his jaws working, so I touched him on the shoulder.

"'Ah, man, I thought you were asleep! Here, fool, eat this and go to sleep.'

"He passed me a very small bit of chicken. I'd wait a couple of nights and then touch him up again.

"Rush is a big man, but he's real light on his feet and can move fast. The only time that I saw Rush depressed was when his wife or mother was sick. He's something like Earl Hines. Earl may have troubles, but he doesn't let you know it. Earl told one of his guys once, 'You may have holes in your shoes, but don't let the people out front know it. Shine the tops.' And Rush never forgets anything. He can tell you exactly what happened twenty, thirty years ago.

"Basie kept going all through the difficult period when most other big bands broke up. Somehow, he always managed to get good transport and accommodation during the war. But then conditions caught up with him, too. It began to get rough some time before he cut down to six pieces. The band wasn't drawing, things were rough all over, and guys were coming in and out of the band fast. He asked me if I wanted to stay, and I appreciated it, but by that time I had had enough of the road, so I told him I thought I ought to stay home for a while.

"Before that I had been out of the band for some time. I had my tonsils removed, because they kept swelling, and I also had stomach disorders. That was because I was drinking quite a bit, trying to stay together. I guess anyone but Basie would have fired me long before. He didn't want to have you on the bandstand if you felt bad, and I'd lay off a week or two, and he'd tell Lady Snodgrass to bring me my money! After I'd had my tonsils out, Lester's burst on him. That was in Chicago. They got the house doctor in the hotel, and Prez said afterwards, 'Where the hell did you get that cat from? He must have been a horse doctor, cutting away at all the wrong places in my throat!'

"He got better, but he took it pretty hard when he had to go in the army."

(1970)

Harry "Sweets" Edison

(TRUMPET)

"My mother and father separated when I was six months old. My father was a Hopi Indian, a very handsome man, and I only saw him once or twice when I was about seven, but I still have a vivid picture in my mind of how he looked. My mother worked very, very hard, at two jobs, so my grandmother was my babysitter until I was five, when she died.

"I was born in Columbus, Ohio, on October 10, 1915, but after my grandmother died my mother sent me to my uncle, Robert Woodard, in a little place called Beaver, in Kentucky, ninety miles from Louisville. Do you remember a tune I wrote for Basie called *Beaver Junction*?

"My uncle was married to my mother's sister, and her folks were called Schultz, a German name that doesn't seem befitting to blacks, but they were all mixed up and there were so many Schultzes in one little Kentucky city that it was called Schultztown. My uncle was a coal miner and a farmer. Everything we ate and accumulated, so far as the house was concerned, we grew. There was so much work to do! I had to hoe the garden, I had to plow, and I had to feed the chickens.

We grew sweet potatoes, tomatoes, corn, sugar cane—just about everything. I had a paper route, on a horse. My uncle had to get to the mine early, so I had to get up first and light the fire to warm the room. When I got home from school, around four in the afternoon, I'd have to work in the garden, and study. I could always tell when my uncle was on his way home, because I could hear his horse hitting the bridge to the farm. Then I would have to get water and feed the horse. My life was no different from that of any child whose parents were farmers. If I had to do it over again, I wouldn't want to change a thing. It taught me something. But my uncle was lord and master of his house. Whatever he said, he meant.

"He had a pump organ and he would have me play something for him every day. He'd sent away for books from a mail-order store, and he'd just picked up some knowledge of music. He taught me the scales, and he was always trying to form a band among the youngsters in Beaver. When he succeeded, we went to little country towns like Bowling Green, Owensboro, and Hartford. We even went across the Kentucky border to Indianapolis, which is not far. There were usually ten or twelve in the band. I had gotten to where I finally played organ good enough to play in Sunday school! But my uncle had an old York cornet lying around, an old beat-up thing, and it intrigued me. After he got the valves working, he sent away to Louisville to get a mouthpiece. He taught me the scales on it, but after a while I laid it down and started playing trombone. Then I went back to trumpet. I still hadn't learned to read well, but the scales were a foundation, and you never get away from basics.

"Our little band would get on a wagon and play for church fairs, what they called chautauquas, an Indian word for a gathering. Every woman would make something—a pie, a cake, potato salad—and bring it to a kind of church bazaar. We'd play marches, like *Washington Post March*, but no jazz. I was about eight or nine. There was some Dixieland music around there. I used to stand outside a place we called a dancehall—a shack, really—and listen. They had a couple of banjos, a washboard, and a tub with a post and string on it like a bass. They had something going, and they had everybody dancing. It was jazz, and it sounded good to me.

"Then I used to listen to all the records of the old blues singers like Bessie Smith and Blind Lemon Jefferson. And I happened to hear Louis Armstrong backing up Bessie Smith. That was for me! That was where it all started, the direction I wanted to go. Louis Armstrong has been my idol ever since.

"When I was about eleven, I got typhoid fever. There was no swimming pool there, but on the way home from school we'd pull off our clothes and jump in those old ponds, so the water probably had something to do with it. I was deathly ill, burning up with fever, and the doctors gave up and said there was nothing they could do. My mother came from Columbus, and my great-grandmother, who lived to be 108 years old, said she'd use her last resort in medication. She got some fresh cow manure, made a tea out of it, and they gave me that tea all day long. I was delirious and didn't know what it was, but that night my fever came down. The doctor was absolutely amazed, but I had no strength left and almost had to learn to walk all over again. Old people like my great-grandmother had a lot of remedies. They'd dig up roots and make a tea that did more good than medicine. She was always giving me herbs, and there must have been something in the grass the cows ate that was good for my fever, just like the way they got penicillin from mold. They'd use tobacco as an antidote for wounds, and once when I was hit on my forehead by a baseball bat, my great-grandmother took soot out of the stove and filled the cut with that. I think the trumpet was a body-builder for me after that typhoid, too, because when you blow you exercise your lungs and your heart.

"My aunt played the organ in the church, and she could read. She played all the hymns and she helped me, but she was so busy most of the time. A woman's work was really never done in those days. She worked all day, every day. My uncle would be tired, too, when he got in, but Saturday and Sunday were his days to do what he wanted, mostly on the farm. But if the boys in that little country town wanted to know something about music, or wanted to rehearse, he would leave everything. He loved music.

"One of my most glorious moments came after I joined Count Basie in 1938. We played a dance in Owensboro, about thirty miles from where I was raised. My aunt and uncle came in a horse and buggy to see me. My uncle was so proud! He came up to the bandstand and told everybody, 'I taught him! What he's doing today, I taught him!'

"When I was twelve, my mother took me back to Columbus, Ohio. There was a fantastic trumpet player there, a friend of Sy Oliver's, named Pete France, and he and I became friends. But I still wasn't really enthused about trumpet, not even when my mother bought me a new horn, an Olds. I think it took her about five years to pay for it, at fifty cents a month. I loved *sports*, and got a letter in school for baseball, but after a couple of tackles in football I went back to trumpet. Pete France had joined the band at Central High School, and I began to play in it, too, because we could get in the football games free.

"At that time *all* the big bands came through Columbus. It was a big dance town and they had a fantastic dance hall called Valley Dale.

Blacks couldn't go in there, but we could stand outside the fence and hear the bands playing. I heard Louis Armstrong, and when Bennie Moten played there I met Ben Webster and Hot Lips Page for the first time. I was living next door to a beautiful girl, and when I was coming from school one afternoon I saw Lips sitting on the porch talking to her. Musicians were getting all the girls at that time, and here was one accomplishing overnight what I'd been trying to accomplish for years. Of course, the girl was much older than me, but that's when I decided to be a trumpet player! Then, too, I loved the way musicians dressed. They had style about them. They wouldn't come out on the street unless they looked the part. Ben Webster had big shoulders, but he had Little Caesar coats with padded shoulders, and when he put them on he looked like a football player. His shoes were always shined, too, and altogether musicians had an entrée to conversation with a lady the average layman would never get.

"When Pops [Louis Armstrong] came to town in his early days, he was so sharp! The compass of a trumpet was reckoned to be from low C to a high C, and to play over that was considered impossible, but here was a man doing the impossible, hitting three or four tones above the impossible. When he came the first time, my mother asked the manager of the Palace Theater if I could be allowed backstage to hear him. This was downtown and blacks were not allowed in the place. We had a theater of our own. Columbus was segregated, but the schools were mixed. We all played together, but after school the white kids went to the white part of town and the blacks to the black part. I had two or three white friends, and when I go back they are still my friends today. One of them used to stay at my house some weekends, and some weekends I'd stay at his. So I grew up not having that complex about being black or white, although I was very concerned about not being able to hear Louis Armstrong!

"Some of the symphony musicians thought he played a freak horn to get those high notes. Some trumpet players used to make the hole smaller with chewing gum to play higher, but then they couldn't play low. Pops was getting all *over* his horn, playing high *and* low. Anyway, the symphony musicians went to the first show at the Palace Theater, and he showed them his horn and mouthpiece, and even let them blow the horn. It was not the horn, but the man behind it.

"As I was standing in the wings, Louis announced that he was going to play *Tiger Rag*. Since some of the audience still thought he played a trick horn, he had a local trumpet player come up and play it first. Then the band started out, and I never heard a man blow like that in my life! He hit two hundred high Cs, and they counted them as he went around the stage, and he ended on a high F. It looked like the lights shattered when he hit that note. He had phenomenal chops and they never went down, not even when he traveled by himself, just barnstorming. 'Who can play?' he'd ask. 'We're playing a dance tonight.' They had some pretty good musicians around Columbus, and he'd get four or five of 'em. There was a trombone player called Archie White who'd been with Jim Europe years before. There was John Hooks, a fantastic trumpet player. Sy Oliver was around, and a good saxophone player named Paul Tyler. He played in Earl Hood's band, and Johnny Hodges knew him well. The neighboring cities were good dance towns, too, and bands used to station themselves in Columbus. Cincinnati was ninety miles. So were Akron and Dayton. Cleveland was a hundred-and-fifty and Steubenville only sixty. Columbus is the capital of Ohio—Ohio State University, the state penitentiary, and the capitol are all there. Besides Valley Dale, there was a Greystone Ballroom, another called Lane Askins, one on Long Street in the black neighborhood, and both the Pythian Temple and the Masonic Hall were used for dances. So every night there was a different band to hear, and there were always a lot of good musicians around in Ohio.

"Paul Tyler lived next door to my mother's home and he heard me playing all the time, so one day he asked me to a rehearsal of Earl Hood's band. Hood liked me and I joined his band, playing around Columbus and Chillicothe, mostly Saturday nights. He'd tell me, 'You're playing for experience,' and wouldn't pay me. I'd be so sleepy on Monday, I wouldn't have my homework done. My mother, who had bought me a trumpet and a tuxedo, thought Hood was mistreating me, and when she eventually went to see him he started paying me thirty-five cents a night! We were playing dance music and everybody was taking solos. One night I just started playing one myself on *Limehouse Blues*. Everybody turned around asking, 'Who is this kid?' That was my debut as a soloist.

"I continued going to school until a band called Morrison's Grenadiers was organized. Some rich family of that name loved music and backed it, and they got the best musicians, like Sy Oliver, Jimmy Crawford, and Joe Thomas. They were going to Cleveland for an engagement at the Cotton Club, and they asked my mother if I could go. She agreed, so long as I came back and went to school. We were eight pieces, and later we added Jimmy Miller on guitar. There were all kinds of clubs in Cleveland, and that was where I first met Art Tatum. He was playing at Val's in the Alley. There were other very good piano players there, too, like Lanny Scott and a man named Pickett who married Rose Murphy, the Chi-Chi Girl. I was nearly sixteen and music had gotten in my blood, but my mother came and made me go back to Columbus to school.

"The Alphonso Trent band from Texas had been doing one-nighters until Trent got sick in Bangor, Maine. He went back to Fort Smith, Arkansas, and the band broke up in Columbus. It was a very good band, and two of the saxophone players, James Jeter [alto] and Hayes Pillars [tenor] decided to get a band together again. My mother agreed for me to go back to Cleveland with them, and we started playing in the Creole Club. That's where I met Basie's wife, Catherine. She was a dancer in the club. We were all youngsters then, but we became friends and she would take me out to her mother's house, Mrs. Morgan's, and feed me quite a bit.

"Then we got another job at the Heat Wave Bar in the Majestic Hotel. Besides Jeter and Pillars, Snub Mosely was playing trombone, A. G. Godley was on drums, and Slim Waters was on tuba. Slim was from Jersey, and he could play tuba like other guys played trumpet. In fact, when we got off at four in the morning we would go places, and he would jam with the trumpet players. Wherever there's an underworld, there's plenty of money, and there were a lot of speakeasies there where you could buy whiskey. The town was flourishing, and that attracted musicians. Caesar Dameron, Tadd's brother, was a good saxophone player at that time, and Poison Gardner, a piano player and entertainer, was also at the Heat Wave. But there was no one like Art Tatum. He was a genius from the time I first knew him.

"The Ohio State School for the Blind was on Parsons and Main, right across the street from me in Columbus, and he graduated from there. They taught him to read braille first, and then to read music in braille. He certainly got some of his training there, but I think he was born with a gift and went to that school to improve it. In later years, he did have more finesse, but he always knew how to keep people involved. The more he played, the more you listened—and drank. There was no hour to quit in those days, but you had an hour to start, usually nine o'clock, and you left when everybody left the club. Art would play till ten, eleven, or twelve o'clock in the daytime. I know we were making only twelve dollars a week in Cleveland, but they had a kitty and we'd get five or six dollars a night in tips. Naturally, Art did better than that.

"I was getting pretty confident by this time, but we mostly played heads. The reading you had to do was not complicated, but more like what beginners play today, at least as compared with what you're expected to do now in the studios. I never forget when McKinney's Cotton Pickers came to Cleveland. They had Roy Eldridge, Billy Bowen, Teddy Wilson's brother Gus, Clyde Hart, and Cuba Austin. Roy came in after us one night and carried us from place to place. He almost made me want to quit. What chops he had, and how he could play! He and Pops were the only two people I ever heard who could play continuously like that. The longer they played, the stronger they got. Pops could play for hours and hours, never miss a note, and never crack or anything. He had good tooth formation and a perfect lip for playing. And he was just so far ahead of his time. It was absolutely amazing how a man could pave the way fifty years ago, and here we are, still playing his things. For any trumpet player to play a decent solo, he's got to play something Pops played. Dizzy still plays things Pops played. They can call it be-bop if they want to, but he was playing it in the thirties.

"The Jeter-Pillars band stayed in Cleveland about a year and then went to St. Louis for two or three years. We added George Hudson on trumpet there, and Carl Smith, a trombone player we called 'Trombone Smitty.' When he left, Gus Wilson took his place. He was a better musician than Teddy then. Besides trombone, he could play good piano and write beautifully. After A. G. Godley left, we got Sidney Catlett on drums, and when our bass player decided to stay in Cleveland we got Jimmy Blanton. Then Sidney Catlett got a call to join Fletcher Henderson in Chicago, so that was when Jo Jones and Walter Page joined us. Chester Lane, who now works with Teddy Buckner at Disneyland, was on piano, and Jimmy Miller was on guitar. Gene Porter, a tenor player who had been with Earl Hines, was also added.

"Some stories have put me in Alphonso Trent's band, although I never met him. I have also been connected with Eddie Johnson and His Crackerjacks, but I never did play with them. They used to come through Columbus and I got to know Hal Baker quite well. The first time I heard Tab Smith play was in that band, and later he recommended me to Lucky Millinder.

"Where we were playing in St. Louis was the Plantation, a big club with fantastic chorus girls. The girl I'd been going with left before I did, to dance in the New York Cotton Club. I guess I would have stayed if she hadn't left, but then Lucky Millinder sent a telegram and tickets to a friend of mine, Harold Arnold, who was playing tenor with the Crackerjacks. Lucky had wanted some other St. Louis trumpet player, but Harold suggested I go with him. So I got on the train and went to New York, where Tab Smith told Lucky I was a good trumpet player.

"I think I stayed with Lucky about six months before I joined Basie. Lucky had a good band. He had Charlie Shavers, Carl Warwick, Billy Kyle, Tab Smith, Don Byas, and Andy Gibson. O'Neil Spencer was on drums, but when he got sick Walter Johnson took his place. We played opposite Basie in Baltimore, and we played an arrangement I'd written called *Every Tub.* It upset the crowd before Basie could get on the bandstand. 'Where in the hell did these guys come from?' he asked.

"Lucky fired me for Dizzy Gillespie. Charlie Shavers and 'Bama Warwick had played with him and they were good buddies. I was from St. Louis, you know! But Dizzy and I got to playing *Body and Soul* in some place in Philadelphia one night, and I made a little noise, so Lucky hired me back and Dizzy went to Teddy Hill.

"Then Bobby Moore, who was with Basie, took sick. He was a good trumpet player, but he had trouble with his teeth, and they had a bit of a problem replacing him. I was staying at the same boarding house as Jo Jones and Herschel Evans, and they recommended me to Basie. So I joined his band at the end of 1937.

"Lucky had a guy named Chappie Willet who used to write such hard arrangements, but when I got with Basie everything seemed to be head arrangements. I bet they didn't have ten manuscripts. I still wanted to learn more about music, so I recommended Andy Gibson, who made *Louisiana, Tickle Toe, The World Is Mad,* and all those arrangements.*

"Basie's was not an ensemble band. Everybody in it was a soloist. I think Basie had become the leader because he was very popular in Kansas City. It was logical, too, in an era of piano-playing leaders like Duke Ellington, Earl Hines, Fletcher Henderson, and Claude Hopkins. They could direct from the piano, but if the bandleader played tenor or trumpet he had to hire another to play while he was directing.

"By this time I guess I had developed a style. I didn't have the chops to play like Louis Armstrong or Roy Eldridge. To play high as they did is partly a gift, but you also have to be dedicated to practicing to play high. Red Allen was one of my idols because he played in the register of the horn I love to play in. I think he thought the same way I did, too. Jeter and Pillars were both very good musicians, and they stressed quality in their band. You had to have tonal quality and you really had to express yourself on the lower part of your horn. They had more of a sweet band—not like Guy Lombardo—and after the show at the Plantation we'd play for dancing, mostly stocks of show tunes and numbers like *The Continental.* It was a white club, and blacks weren't allowed in there. They had a special door for us. It was the same old thing, the same old South, just like the song! But there wasn't much room for playing solos in that band, and it wasn't at all like Bennie Moten's or McKinney's Cotton Pickers. I didn't forget about Pops and Roy, but I was only a kid and this was a job where I tried to play with the tone and quality they wanted.

* For more details on Gibson's career, see *The World of Swing.*

"When I got with Basie, I was still playing that way, and in the lower register, which is why Prez started calling me 'Sweets.' At first I tried to play pretty all the time, and I took a lot of solos Buck Clayton got the credit for.* He already had a name, but people hadn't heard of me. It didn't matter then who got the credit, just so you got to play. If you didn't swing, Basie would take the solo away from you and give it to someone else. Prez had a bell he would ring, and that was the cue that the solo was not for you.

"What a thrill it was to play with that band! It was the greatest thrill of my life. We couldn't wait to get on the bandstand at night. It was just like a horse prancing to get out on the racetrack. We were nervous if we weren't on the bandstand. I don't think there is a better bandleader on earth than Basie. He's a very humorous guy; he's easy to get along with; and he knows how to handle men. He knew how important the soloists were at that time, and he didn't try to make an ensemble band out of it. He loved to hear Prez play, and he loved to hear Herschel play. He liked to hear Buck play, liked to hear me, and he liked to hear Jo Jones. He was and is the greatest for stomping off the tempo. He noodles around on the piano until he gets it just right. Just like you were mixing mash and yeast to make whiskey, and you keep tasting and tasting it. Or you're making a cake and tasting the mix to make sure you've got the ingredients and everything to the point where you know it's going to be all right. Freddie Green and Jo Jones would follow him until he hit the right tempo, and when he started it they *kept* it. They knew where he was going at all times, but if the tempo was too fast he would bring it down gradually, not abruptly, so nobody would ever know. And if it was too slow, he would bring it up until it was *just* right.

"Of course, Walter Page contributed a lot, too. He was a good musician and a teacher from the University of Kansas. Besides playing bass, he was also a fantastic baritone player. He started that 'strolling' or 'walking' bass, going way up and then coming right on down. He

---

* On Basie's early records, Harry Edison has solos on *Sent for You Yesterday; Every Tub; Now Will You Be Good?; Swinging the Blues* (second trumpet solo); *Texas Shuffle; Shorty George; Panassie Stomp; Jive at Five; Rock-a-bye Basie; Jump for Me; Twelfth Street Rag; Miss Thing; Pound Cake; Riff Interlude; Hollywood Jump; Let's Make Hay; Louisiana; Easy Does It* (second trumpet solo); *Blow Top; Super Chief; Moten Swing; What's Your Number?; Five O'Clock Whistle; Broadway; Stampede in G Minor; Rocking the Blues; Wiggle Woogie; Beau Brummel; Jump the Blues Away; Tuesday at Ten; 9:20 Special; H & J; Tom Thumb; Something New; Platterbrains; Feather Merchant; It's Sand, Man; Ain't It the Truth?; Taps Miller; Avenue C; Queer Street; High Tide; Lazy Lady Blues* (obbligato); *Bambo; Stay Cool; Open the Door, Richard* (vocal); *One O'Clock Boogie; Guest in the Nest; Money Is Honey;* and *Just a Minute.*

did it on four strings, but other bass players couldn't get that high so they started making a five-string bass. That rhythm section would send chills up me every night. The whole band would be shouting, and then all of a sudden everybody would drop out for the bridge and there would be just the rhythm with Page's bass going up and down. Oh, my goodness! That was the greatest band that's ever been on earth! I've never heard any other swing like it did.

"We were all very close in the band. You couldn't just say, 'This is my best buddy.' Buck was a very good friend. Freddie Green is about the closest friend I have. Basie is a good buddy to me, and I always looked upon him as a father. When I joined the band, he just took a liking to me. I used to listen to him, because I had no fatherly advice when I left home. He took me everyplace in New York and introduced me to Duke, Don Redman, Clark Monroe, Benny Carter, and Chick Webb—to the whole scene. It was a thrill to meet James P. Johnson and all the people I had read about and admired without thinking I'd ever be shaking hands with them. I met them through Basie, and he introduced me to the older dancers in New York at that time. I'm really grateful to him for my whole career. I was with him from '38 to '50, but I still go back to him. There's a chair in that band I consider mine. I'm sure anybody still active that has been in the band can always go back. He'll make room for you.

"Early on, I put in my notice. There was so little written music that I wasn't accomplishing what I wanted to accomplish. I wanted to read well and be a really good musician. I told him that nobody could play those head arrangements like Ed Lewis and the guys who had been in Bennie Moten's band. Every night I was trying to pick me a note to play.

" 'Well, you sound good,' Basie said.

" 'But I don't know what note to hit,' I said.

" 'Well, if you find a note tonight that sounds good, play the same damn note every night!'

"That was the beginning of a beautiful friendship.

"Basie gave Coleman Hawkins all the respect in the world, and he respected Chu Berry and Joe Thomas, too, but it was Lester Young's playing that he *loved*. Everything Prez did was a classic. Like the names he had for different people. He nicknamed Basie 'Holy,' the Holy Man, the Holy Main, the Main Man—Holy, because he was the bandleader and did the paying! He named Billie Holiday 'Lady Day,' Earle Warren 'Smiley,' and Herschel Evans, because he came from Texas, 'Tex.' He had a name for everybody, and a knack for doing comical things. He'd be the first to start a crap game on our old bus, and the first to go to sleep. We were so short of space, we'd take turns sitting on the outside seat so we could stretch our legs in the aisle. Sometimes, when we were all asleep, he'd wake up, take the dice, and shake 'em in everybody's ear all down the bus, saying, 'Sweet music, sweet music!' He'd get another crap game started, but he would be the first one broke. Originally, he didn't drink or smoke at all. When he first left Kansas City, he had an old cob pipe he used to hold in his mouth, but he never had any tobacco for it. New York is so fast you have to have a lot of willpower to stay within the bounds of your teaching. In later years, after he started drinking, he never ate anything. He might order a good meal, take a bit of this and try that, but then leave it. He never had what you'd call a good appetite, and alcohol will take your appetite away. His body was just saturated with alcohol, and Coleman Hawkins was the same way towards the end.

"We got an engagement at the Strand on Broadway, and it was our big chance. Basie wanted a production number and Jimmy Mundy did an arrangement on *I Struck a Match in the Dark*, which Earle Warren was to sing. When the lights went out and Earle started, we were all supposed to strike a match and light up the stage. Well, when Earle made his introduction, Prez struck a match, held his part up, and set fire to it! That was the end of that. He didn't like Earle Warren's singing, and he always imitated singers and made a comedy out of it. He liked Helen Humes and Jimmy Rushing, but after Billie Holiday left we didn't really want a singer anyway. The singer was just an ornament on the bandstand in those days, more of an accompaniment to the band. Sing a chorus and sit down! Now it's the singers' era and the band is an accompaniment. Most of those making the money, to me, are not good singers. If you put Ella Fitzgerald and Sarah Vaughan aside, I'd say Streisand is one newcomer who can sing. Frank Sinatra, Billy Eckstine, Carmen McRae, Peggy Lee—the ones that sang with the old bands—were better singers than today's crop and had something of quality in what they did. The record companies take all the equipment and put it behind somebody who doesn't have quality, but they won't take that equipment to make someone who already sounds good sound better. The electronics are the worst thing that ever happened. If you've got quality, you don't need them to make you sound good, but take them away from some of today's musicians and they'd be absolutely horrible to listen to. I once made an album of thirty-six tunes in three hours with Ella Fitzgerald. Art Tatum would make several albums in a day. But I read where they've given Stevie Wonder a year to make one album! They're really trying to wash out black music. They'll promote any kind of mush, but not jazz. Rock 'n' roll is strictly white music. Country music came way after the blues, because cowboys came way after slavery! Norman Granz is the only man I know who really promotes jazz.

"I just wish they would give the originator credit while he's living. To me, Coleman Hawkins is just as great as Thomas Edison. He originated something on tenor saxophone that had never been heard before. Louis Armstrong broke all the rules of trumpet, and Duke Ellington broke all the rules of those who said you cannot play dissonant chords because they're displeasing to the ear. There's only one Dizzy Gillespie, but the beginning of most of the white soloists' prominence was bebop. Dizzy started playing the trumpet like a virtuoso, with a lot of notes, and there were many white players who had been taught to get over their horns fast. What they couldn't do was hit one note, or two notes, and make it sound effective by putting a lot of feeling in it. That was the beginning of a lot of white musicians, who didn't have to have quality to play. Charlie Parker could swing, but his swing was getting over his horn—speed. But when it came to melody, nobody in the world could play like Johnny Hodges. He could play a melody note for note and make it absolutely expressive. And nobody could play a melody as *pretty* as Ben Webster. There was no quality in Charlie Parker's tone, not like there was in Johnny Hodges', Benny Carter's, or Hilton Jefferson's. Jeff was magnificent and a schooled musician, but he never got the recognition. I can't allow for an imitator. There's no substitute for originality.

"I think there's nobody more influential on tenor players today than Lester Young. More than Coleman Hawkins now. Prez would try anything on the bandstand, anything he thought of. He maintained that if he didn't try it there, where was he going to try it? If it didn't work in the first instance, you kept playing it until it did. It was like an experiment, and the bandstand was his proving ground.

"We used to do like three hundred one-nighters a year, because we had no place to sit down and play. Jimmie Lunceford had the Cotton Club, and when he came out of there he would go on forty weeks of theaters, where we had fifty weeks of one-nighters. But one time we were supposed to battle Lunceford in Hartford, Connecticut. He came out from New York in a big, air-conditioned Greyhound bus. We came from Pittsburgh, Pennsylvania, to Hartford—a long ride, and we were so tired. Basie said, 'Well, I'm tired like everybody else.' Willie Smith was one of the warmest guys you could ever meet, and Joe Thomas was very friendly, but most of the guys in Lunceford's band didn't even speak to us. We were only Count Basie's band, and we got out of a ragged bus, but when we got on that bandstand we started jumping and showering down. Prez played like he'd never played before. Before you knew it, Lunceford and all his guys were coming up to the bandstand. We put a hurting on them that night and washed Lunceford out of the dance hall.

"Our head arrangements sounded good, because we had them so well together, but as musicians were added to the band we had to have written music. We had to rehearse and learn it. Because you're looking at the music when you're playing, you don't have the freedom you had when everything was head. Therefore you lose a little of your feeling. Yet when you've got your own notes and *know* what you're playing, you are more at ease. As more instruments were added, the band became more musical and more of an ensemble. Today, the band is strictly an ensemble band, and one thing I think Basie misses, too, is soloists, because he was always used to having solos.

"After Prez went in the army, and didn't come back, Basie got musicians who could read and blend in with the sections better. In the late forties, Jimmy Mundy and Don Redman were writing for the band. Buck Clayton was doing a lot of writing, and Benny Goodman gave Basie some of Fletcher Henderson's arrangements. All that required more rehearsals than we were used to. Quite a few of the tunes we recorded were mine, like *Every Tub, Sent for You Yesterday,* and *Jive at Five.*

"While I was in the Jeter-Pillars band, Gus Wilson and I had become very good friends. He was a beautiful arranger and I used to ask him questions. How do you voice the altos? How do you put the trumpets here? The E-flat scale is different from the B-flat scale, and he'd tell me where to put the note to experiment. 'After you hear it one time,' he'd say, 'change it and put it in a different perspective, a different place.' So I started doing that, and sometimes it sounded pretty good, but after hearing what guys like Benny Carter wrote, I kind of got discouraged. I love to play, and the only man I know who writes as well as he plays is Benny Carter. He can make a living doing either one.

"After I went to New York, I went from place to place, listening to solos by Charlie Shavers, Roy Eldridge, and Erskine Hawkins. Erskine had a style and fantastic chops. He was promoted as the Twentieth Century Gabriel, and in those days playing high and reaching the stratosphere on your horn was popular, even if it wasn't tasteful. The musician I really liked in his band was Dud Bascomb, a remarkable trumpet player.

"All the big bands were collapsing. Only Duke's ASCAP rating kept his going, and he was paying good salaries even when other bands were in trouble. Johnny Hodges was making five or six hundred dollars a week when we were getting fifteen dollars a night.

"I left Basie when the band broke up. Little groups had begun to take over, dance halls diminished, and people didn't dance anymore. When we played we became more like a concert band, and in the clubs people would just sit and drink. It was nightclubs instead of dance halls. So in 1950, Basie formed a small group with Clark Terry and Serge Chaloff. Clark had been in the trumpet section a year or two, and it had been a very good section with Snooky Young, Emmett Berry, Clark, and myself. Snooky was a more flexible trumpet player than Ed Lewis, and the new arrangements we were getting required flexibility. Right now, I think Snooky's the best first trumpet there is. He's a good soloist, too, and good soloists make better first trumpet players than just strictly first trumpet players because, although they may be the most reliable guys in the world, when it comes to bending a note, and being flexible, and phrasing as only a soloist can, the first trumpet who is also a soloist has an edge. Snooky once had a band of his own in Dayton and *had* to be a soloist. Then he took it to the Three Sixes in Detroit, and he had to solo there, too. When Basie had only three trumpets—Ed Lewis, Buck, and me—Buck wouldn't play first, and I wouldn't because Buck wouldn't, so Ed had to play it all. But after I got a band of my own and came out to California, I had to play a lot of first parts.

"The first thing I had to do when I left Basie was join Local 802, because we'd been a traveling band all those years and the only members of 802 were guys like Dicky Wells and Benny Morton who lived in New York. A lot of people wondered why Basie didn't take Dicky Wells, myself, and older guys out of the band, because he had enough soloists to keep the thing going. Somebody must have sold him a bill of goods for him to take Serge Chaloff and Buddy De-Franco! We didn't even know he had a small band till Freddie Green, Ted Donnelly, and I met one afternoon. 'Man, how come you-all aren't going to Chicago?' somebody asked. 'Basie and them just caught a plane to open up some bar in Chicago.' I said, 'You got to be kidding!' and Freddie said, 'Aw, that can't be true.' But we found out it was.

"That's when I became almost hysterical. It's very easy to be a sideman. The bandleader has to get all the work. All you have to do as a sideman is lie around until you get up to play, or until you get a telephone call saying, 'We're leaving at four o'clock tomorrow and we'll be out for three months. Get your things packed.' All those years with Basie, I didn't have to worry about work. I'd been irresponsible and I'd depended on him just like I would on a father. I was twenty-one when I joined him just before Christmas in 1937, and now it was 1950 and I was a married man. I was afraid and really depressed. I didn't know where I was going to get any money from.

Nobody knew what Basie was thinking. He hadn't said, 'This is it. You go your way and I'll go mine, because it's come to the point where I just can't afford the big band any longer.' Yet it happened for the best, because it made me realize I'd got to look out for myself.

"I played around New York with all kinds of people and I recorded quite a bit. I went out with Jazz at the Philharmonic. With Coleman Hawkins, I went to Toronto and Cleveland. We were good friends and I played with him a lot of times. It was an experimental period in music, I think, because everything was happening. I couldn't understand what some of the guys were playing, but I never said anything. Who's to say who's right and who's wrong? But if it was not understandable to a musician, how could the average person understand it? The right hand was coming into prominence with the piano players in the small groups. The left hand was like the drummer's right foot. It went from bass drum to no bass drum, from left hand to no left hand, just that quick. It went from holding one note to making a whole lot of notes on your horn. It went from making a simple chord to putting in a flatted fifth, or a thirteenth, or a suspended note, or whatever.

"I always play the melody before I start improvising. One of the hardest things to do is to play straight melody without deviating from a note. You can originate a lot of little things around the melody without changing it till people don't know what you're doing. I'd rather be a mediocre originator than a perfect imitator any time."

Harry Edison's career from 1950 onward was one he could scarcely have anticipated. In 1952 he became Josephine Baker's musical director and toured with her for a long time, spending six months at El Patio in Mexico City. Deciding to settle in California, he became acquainted with Nelson Riddle. Although at first reluctant, he gradually became involved in studio work and persevered until he was completely accepted. He credited much of his success to Riddle's patience and the help of established studio trumpet players like Mannie Klein. He began recording with Frank Sinatra in 1952 and was in the band that accompanied him on the *Wee Hours* album, which Edison considers the singer's best. At Sinatra's request, he continued to record with him for six straight years, often with headphones at a mike separate from the trumpet section. He was thus free to make his own muted trumpet commentary on the singing. Soon in demand as an accompanist for other singers, he also recorded with Nat Cole, Margaret Whiting, Bing Crosby, Jerry Lewis, Billy Daniels, and Ella Fitzgerald, not to mention with jazz musicians like Shorty Rogers, Ben Webster, Arnold Ross, and Conrad Gozzo. He was featured in the film *Jammin' the Blues* and also played on the sound track of such movies as *Step Down to Terror, Houseboat, The Girl Most Likely,* and *Lady Sings the Blues.*

As a result of the popularity Sinatra's records brought him, he went to New York in 1958 and formed his own group consisting of Jimmy Forrest (tenor saxophone), Jimmy Jones (piano), Joe Benjamin (bass), and Charlie Persip (drums). After signing with Roulette Records, Edison opened at Birdland, where he often played opposite Count Basie's band. When Joe Williams left him, Basie thought it would be a good idea to put the Edison quintet and Williams together. It was a successful combination until the singer decided to operate on his own with just a trio in support.

The sixties were a busy time for Edison. He toured Europe several times, with Norman Granz's Jazz at the Philharmonic, George Wein's Newport package, and as a guest alumnus with the Basie band. Returning to Los Angeles, he again became involved in studio work. He did *The Hollywood Palace Show* with Mitchell Ayres for three years, playing all kinds of music in what was essentially a variety show. Other television shows followed, with Della Reese, Frank Sinatra, Rosemary Clooney, Bill Cosby, Don Rickles, Leslie Uggams, and Glen Campbell. He was also on many record dates during this period, and, having got his own group together again (with Jimmy Forrest), he played extensive engagements in Las Vegas and Los Angeles.

In 1977 he teamed up with Lockjaw Davis, an old associate and Basie alumnus. Usually picking up local rhythm sections in the cities they played, they began to tour the world with great success. This gave Edison opportunities to indulge his taste for history and art; much of his spare time abroad was spent in art galleries, museums, and historic buildings. (His discriminating taste is, incidentally, indicated by the excellent prints of Constable, Goya, Rembrandt, and Van Gogh paintings that adorn the walls of his apartment.) One of the most exciting experiences of his life was a tour of the Middle East made for the U.S. State Department in the Bicentennial year. As a member of a quintet led by Benny Carter, he appreciated the VIP treatment they received, but most of all he enjoyed seeing the Blue Mosque and St. Sophia's in Istanbul, the beauty of Isfahan, the Nile, the pyramid at Karnak, the Sphinx, the treasures of Tutankhamen, and a little town where Jesus walked. Perhaps this breadth of interest helps account for the fact that Harry Edison is today one of the most renowned and best preserved of all the Swing Era's famous trumpet players.

(1979)

Bennie Moten's Orchestra, 1931. Left to right: *(front) Vernon Page, Count *asie, Lips Page, Ed Lewis, Thamon Hayes, Eddie Durham, Woodie Walder,* *uster Berry, Harlan Leonard, Booker Washington, Willie McWashington, Jack* *`ashington; (rear) Bennie Moten, Buster Moten, Jimmy Rushing.* (Courtesy mmy Rushing)

The Blue Devils, Oklahoma City, August 10, 1928. Left to right: *Lips Page,* *uster Smith, unknown, Walter Page, unknown, Willie Lewis (piano), unknown,* *rnie Williams, unknown.* (Courtesy The Last of the Blue Devils Film Co.)

3. *Count Basie.* (Stanley Dance collection)

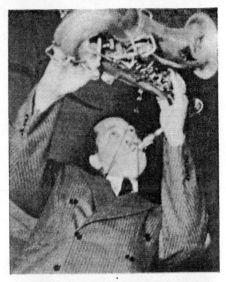

4. *Lester Young.*
(Courtesy Dicky Wells)

5. *Buck Clayton.*
(Courtesy Dicky Wells)

6. *Earle Warren.*
(Courtesy Earle Warren)

7. *Walter Page.* (Courtesy Dicky Wells)

8. *Dicky Wells in Harlem.* (Courtesy Dicky Wells)

9. *Edgar Battle, Valentine Billington, and Eddie Durham with the Seven Eleven and Mamie Smith Show, 1927.* (Courtesy Eddie Durham)

10. *Count Basie and Freddie Green.* (Courtesy Freddie Green)

11. Count Basie and Billie Holiday.
(Courtesy Dicky Wells)

12. Left to right: *Jo Jones, Walter Page, Buddy Tate, Count Basie, Freddie Green, Buck Clayton, Dicky Wells.* (Courtesy Freddie Green)

13. *Count Basie and His Orchestra, 1941.* Left to right: *(front) Ed Cuffee, Dicky Wells, Dan Minor, Helen Humes (vocal), Count Basie, Buddy Tate, Tab Smith, Earle Warren, Jack Washington, Don Byas; (rear) Harry Edison, Al Killian, Ed Lewis, Buck Clayton, Jo Jones, Freddie Green, Walter Page.* (Stanley Dance collection)

14. *"America's Number One Band,"* 1941. (Courtesy Dicky Wells)

15. Left to right: *(front) Count Basie, Buddy Tate, Earle Warren, Jack Washington, Lester Young; (rear) Walter Page, Freddie Green, Benny Morton.* (Courtesy Freddie Green)

16. *Count Basie and Duke Ellington.* (Courtesy Columbia Records)

Buddy Tate

(TENOR SAXOPHONE AND CLARINET)

"Pilot Grove in Texas is where my parents and grandparents came from. It's between Dallas and Sherman, which are about fifty miles apart. There's a place called McKinney and a little town called Van Alstyne. Pilot Grove is out from Van Alstyne, one of those in-between stops in north Texas near the Oklahoma line. My grandfather was a very good businessman and he taught all four boys the importance of owning property. There's a whole country of Tates down there. At one time my father owned three farms. He gave one to his brother and sold another to my mother's brother. My father was pretty well-adjusted and he left my mother straight with all the farm paid for. He was forty-six when he died, and I was three.

"I had two brothers, one ten years older than me, and the other eight years older. I also had a sister who was six years older. I was the baby, and I think I was kind of spoiled, although at the time I thought they were the meanest people in the world! We had plenty of cattle on the farm, near Sherman, when I was born in 1915. We had everything and hardly had to go to town to buy anything. My mother canned, and we had a big smokehouse with hams and sausages hanging in it. When we killed hogs, we'd still have hams from the previous year. We had good water from a spring that never failed. My daddy and granddaddy had fixed it with cement all around.

"My two brothers weren't really old enough to run the farm when my father died so my mother had to have help. When I was about twelve, she told me we were moving into town, three miles away. It broke my heart. We were leaving a brand-new house, and I loved that farm and the outdoor life. We had horses to ride and I could go hunting whenever I liked. I even liked walking through the woods on the way to school with fifty or sixty other kids. Mother had a hard time keeping me in the city at first, but she rented the farm to a friend, a school teacher who farmed and taught. We had five hundred acres and we grew cotton, wheat, corn, and grain. After my brothers died my sister sold some of it, but I think we still have nearly four hundred acres. Now the government has taken over and they only let you cultivate so much of your land. Farmers are always independent and they don't like that because they can't always cultivate enough to live comfortably.

"One of my brothers played piano, and the other played C-melody saxophone. I used to listen to them and I wanted to play, too, but not saxophone. I liked the sound of trombone better, and I got an old curtain rod with the rings on and I used to slide the rings up and down, imitating a trombone. I'd stand around and watch my brother change reeds on his saxophone, but he'd never let me touch it.

"When I started listening to the radio, I used to hear Guy Lombardo, and then Alphonso Trent over WFFA from Dallas. They used to broadcast every night from the Adolphus Hotel, a fine, exclusive place. That was a band, man! We had a Victrola, too, and I used to listen to all of Bessie Smith's records. Mother loved music and she liked those records, but she had so many that after a while when my sister and I got tired of some of them we'd take them and sail them through the air, throwing them at each other.

"We used to have what people called picnics, or chittlin' suppers. We could stay up all night and make as much noise as we wanted, when we were out in the country. My brothers would play and I wanted to join in so badly. Sometimes, when my brothers were away, I'd sneak in and try to put a reed in the saxophone and play it. I broke up so many reeds he'd box me upside the head. Finally, he went to school in Dallas and was working on the side. When he came back one time he had bought me a brass alto saxophone.

" 'Okay, now,' he said as he gave it to me. 'You want to play so bad, you've got to get a teacher and learn *how* to play it!'

"There weren't many teachers around in those days, but there was a boy called Emmett Malone, a brilliant musician who played trumpet. Where he got his knowledge from, I don't know, and he never really made it, but he knew chords and changes inside out. And all kinds of times. He used to try to tell me about times like twelve-eight, but it sounded like Japanese to me. He taught me how to read. He gave me books and wrote out scales for me to practice. I had a good ear and my mother would pay him, but we could never keep him at home long. Three months, six months, and then he'd be gone. When a minstrel show or a circus came around, he'd run off with them.

"Eventually we had a little family band. Malone was the only one in it not related to us, but he was engaged to my cousin. He always wanted his own band, and later we played with him a little while when he was in Sherman. But by then ours was better and more popular.

"We used to rehearse by listening to records. I remember how we listened to Pops [Louis Armstrong] playing *West End Blues*. Then we got records by the Coon-Sanders Kansas City Nighthawks. They could swing! In those days you could get stock arrangements with the solos all written out just like on the record. That was a help, but I can remember how we scuffled with Coon-Saunders' *Brainstorm* and Fletcher Henderson's *Deep Henderson*. What we couldn't read, we'd clap our ear to on the record. And we would slow the record down so that we could get it. We rehearsed every night and we were tight. We must have had a hundred numbers, and the band got to be pretty popular, playing dances.

"We got us a manager, a white fellow named Red Jackson, a college kid, and after about a year we added another saxophone. His name was James Johnson, and he played good violin as well as C-melody. My cousin, Roy McCloud, played trumpet; another cousin, Hazel Jones, played piano; Ralph Arterberry, a third cousin, was on drums; and Bernice Douglas, a boy despite the name, played banjo. Leroy Porter was the original banjoist, and he had had a lot to do with getting us together and getting us jobs because he worked uptown and people asked him about music. Leroy was another cousin, but when we started playing from stocks we got Bernice instead because he had a good piano foundation and played beautiful chords.

"I must have been thirteen or fourteen when we started playing dances for all the high schools. Bernice and the drummer were about my age, and nobody more than three years older. As soon as we began to make some money we started buying uniforms. At one time we each had seven of them. Then we bought tuxes, and we used to wear spats with them. I'll never forget that—tuxedos and spats! When we'd go to a town and fall out of the car, people would just stare at us. Man, we were so sharp! We spent all our money on ourselves, and we were making good money. Families were making it then on ten dollars a week, because you could get a loaf of bread for a nickel, but here were we making twelve dollars a night!

"Those were the days of territory bands, before the booking agencies monopolized everything. You could rent a hall for twenty-five dollars, and after all the expenses for placards and everything had been paid we'd split the swag down equally. Sometimes we'd give the leader five or ten dollars extra for the work he'd put in. That's the way it used to be.

"As our band became popular, they started asking for us farther afield. We went to Oklahoma City all the time, and all over Texas. We traveled in cars with wide running boards and on one side we'd have a rack with all the instruments lined up on it. You couldn't get out that side. We'd have something to cover the instruments so they wouldn't get splashed. We had a Model T Ford and no one but me and the manager could drive it. I remember lots of nights when the manager didn't go with us and I had to drive home, and all those cats in the car would fall asleep.

"There were two towns we could always expect to make fifteen dollars apiece—Ardmore, Oklahoma, and Paris, Texas. Bonham, between Paris and Sherman, was a good town, too. It was Charlie Christian and Nipsey Russell's hometown, and I guess the population was around 25,000. We'd just play dances in a hall. Put up our placards, go in and start playing, and people would start dancing. A lot of white people would come, but they just listened and didn't dance, although eventually we were playing more white dances than black.

"There were four or five colleges in Sherman, where I was raised, and they always paid a good, flat guarantee. Red Jackson was booking us into all of them, because he had connections.

"There were five or six white theaters there, too, and each had a band, but they were all white musicians, playing for the pictures. There was a saxophone player named Frank O'Banner who played one of those theaters, and he had a beautiful sound. He used to come to our dances.

" 'You play so pretty,' I told him one time.

" 'But I can't play jazz,' he said. 'Man, if you snatch this sheet of music away, I'll have to fold up.'

" 'Well, I can't handle that sheet . . .'

" 'That's nothing,' he answered. 'I'll see to that. Why don't you come to see me?'

"This was after Malone had left, so I used to go around midday and stay sometimes till he had to leave for the theater at 2:30. The first thing he taught me to do was transpose, playing from the piano sheet music, playing a tone-and-a-half down. Sometimes, if I'd goofed my money off, I'd miss a week and tell him I had had to go out of town, but he'd know when I was lying and he'd want the truth. When I told him I didn't have the money, he said, 'Don't you ever let that stop you from coming. Money isn't why I have you here. I want you to continue. Someday you may remember what I've done.' I don't know what help I was to him, but I'd have him taking solos and getting off. He's in another business and doesn't play anymore, but his father lived on in Sherman and I used to go by and see him when I was home.

"So Malone and O'Banner were my two teachers. They got me where I could go for myself after that. They really put me ahead, because so many of the guys weren't reading then.

"Sherman was swinging in the twenties. It was a good dance town. It seems as though one of the name bands would come up from Dallas every week. It was a rare treat to hear Alphonso Trent. I remember seeing Rudolph Valentino at the Adolphus Hotel one day when I happened to be in Dallas. He was touring the country in patent leather boots! I heard Paul Whiteman's band the same day at the same hotel, and my brother got me backstage to see Bix Beiderbecke and Frankie Trumbauer. Whiteman's band had come in for the automobile show, and I think he had thirty-six pieces. Frankie Trumbauer had a style, and a lot to offer. He and I became real friends in later years when I used to go to Kansas City with Basie. He was in aeronautics there and he would come backstage and stay all day. The first time I ever spoke to him—in 1927 or 1928—he said, 'Practice. You don't get this overnight.' He was a beautiful person. In 1942 he said, 'I remember you, the kid your brother brought backstage. I see you practiced!' I have a box of reeds he gave me in 1943. He bought them in 1924 and I keep them—in a sealed box—for sentimental reasons. I didn't use them because they were for C-melody, but they still *look* good!

"He used to tell me some of his experiences with Paul Whiteman. He had his own plane and used to fly to his gig. One night they were opening at some big hotel in San Francisco. On the way his plane developed engine trouble and it ended up falling on the hotel they were to play. He *swore* this was the truth, that the plane just sat right on top of the hotel. 'See this?' he said, pointing to a scar on his nose. 'This came from that.'

"I used to visit my aunty in Dallas and stay with her. She had a big house and some of Alphonso Trent's boys roomed with her, including

Gene Crook, the banjo player who lives across the street [in Harlem].
It was a terrific band and they had a terrific drummer in A. G. Godley.
He was the first real *solo* drummer I ever heard. That band was always
some mess! Later on, Trent had Snub Mosley, Peanuts Holland, Sy
Oliver, and Stuff Smith.

"Our little band, which we called McCloud's Night Owls, lasted
four or five years. It seemed longer to me then. After we hired the
saxophone player who doubled on violin, we decided we had to have
a trombone player. One of our friends who used to go to the Holiness
churches said, 'I have just the fellow for you guys! You ought to hear
him play. He's a good salesman, too. He can get on his belly and play!'
So we figured we should go and listen to him. We could hear this cat
a block away, he had such a big sound. He could swing, and he could
read. 'He really does sound good,' we said, but when we asked would
he want to join us he said, 'I can't play good enough for your band.'
But we talked him into it. I can't remember his right name, but we
called him 'Booley.'

"Next we added another alto player, Leo Wright's father, whose
name was Mel Nash Wright. By this time, I was playing tenor as well
as alto. When we found we couldn't keep Booley, we got Booker
Ervin, Sr., in his place. Augusta Arterberry, another cousin, came in
on sousaphone, and Rudolph Collins on trumpet. Rudolph was good,
but not an Emmett Malone. We couldn't keep Emmett, he was so
brilliant. So here we were, up to ten pieces, a big band and very popular. We were buying stocks, listening to Fletcher Henderson's records,
to Alphonso Trent's broadcasts, and making up heads of our own.

"My main influence on tenor then was Prince Robinson. I loved that
cat! He was doing some things that were complicated. I always remember him on McKinney's Cotton Pickers' records—*I Found a New
Baby, Zonky, There's a Rainbow 'Round My Shoulder*. He was a pioneer, but he didn't keep up. In those years, though, he was out there
with Hawk, and his modulation on *Zonky* used to knock me out.

"On alto, my two idols were Harris Erwing and Booker Pittman.
Booker was the grandson of Booker T. Washington and he played in
a band led by Fred Cooper. Booker was a daring, pretty boy, who
could outplay everyone. The chicks were crazy about him. Then he
was in The Blue Moon Chasers with Budd Johnson. They had eight
or ten pieces when we had only six. We heard them when they came
to Sherman, or when we went to Dallas. The Erwing brothers had a
family band in Kansas City, but their parents were from Sherman.
When I heard Harris in the twenties, he was just the best alto I had
heard in my life, but he never did learn to read. Buck Clayton played

with them, and they went out to Los Angeles. Marshall Royal heard Harris and dug him, too. He said I was right in my opinion of him.

"Marshall's daddy was a bandmaster who played everything. I always knew about Marshall because his mother was from Denison and he was born in Sapulpa, Oklahoma, but I didn't get to meet him till I went to Los Angeles with Basie in 1939. He had a band of local musicians playing *One O'Clock Jump* to greet us on arrival, although the Palomar had burned down the night before we were supposed to open. Charlie Barnet's band lost all its instruments.

"Back with our ten-piece band . . . I was still going to high school, but I was getting that fever. I wanted to play with people like Budd and Booker. Then T. Holder and His Clouds of Joy came to Denison and Sherman. When I heard them I said to myself, 'Man, I have to get with one of those bands!' You get to the stage where you figure you're not learning anymore. Holder was a fine trumpet player who had left Alphonso Trent and organized his own band. He had Theodore Ross and Fats Wall on altos, Slim Freeman on tenor, Big Jim Lawson on trumpet, and Andy Kirk on sousaphone. They were working in Tulsa just before Christmas, and T. took off with all the payroll to see his wife in Dallas. He came back after three or four days, and he hadn't spent any of the money, but the guys called a meeting and made Andy Kirk the new leader. So T. went back to Dallas and formed a second band with Budd Johnson, Booker Pittman, and a boy named Fred Murphy, who looked like Cab Calloway and played alto almost as well as Booker except that he wouldn't play lead. T. had Eddie Tompkins, Eddie Durham, and Jesse Stone, too, and it was a terrific band. Later on, when I was with Andy Kirk, Andy told me T. came through Oklahoma City and looked him up. Andy's band was scuffling and T. said, 'Well, I want to wish you a lot of luck. I've got two or three jobs you can have.' Andy said, 'After me taking his band, for the guy to come by and offer us work like that . . . well, you just can't say anything bad about him.' When T. got to Kansas City, Jesse Stone took the band over. That's that territory thing again. Jesse had had a band there and was better known.

"In the meantime, I left home and went to Wichita Falls with the Night Owls. There was an oil boom and a lot of sporting people there who were spending money like water. It was winter, and *cold*. We went to play a week, but Roy McCloud and I decided to stay and make some money. The other guys quit, because they wanted to go to school, and home. We were making over sixty dollars a week, and it cost only about four dollars a week for a room and three meals a day. I felt I couldn't turn that down! I had one year more to do at school, but I kept thinking that I had time to make that up, and I had my heart set on being a musician anyway. Ross and I joined a band called the St. Louis Merrymakers and one of the musicians in it was Herschel Evans. I had met him a couple of years before when we were playing a job in Van Alstyne. He was in a band coming from New Orleans called TNT, or Trent Number Two! Trent was so popular that they named themselves after him, hoping some of his luck would rub off on them. Where we were playing was a ballroom near the highway, with a swimming pool and everything. There were hundreds of people around, so they decided to stop and join in the fun. Then they asked if they could sit in, and we wanted to hear them, of course. They had so many instruments, those cats would scare you to death! Even if they couldn't play them all too well, they had saxophones standing around like a show. They had lights in the drums, too, and the bass drum head looked like a reflection of water in the ocean. It all made the bandstand look so pretty!

"Herschel had heard about me from my brother in Dallas. He was playing alto then and had about a thousand rubber bands around his instrument, but while all the other guys looked beat he was immaculate, sharp as a tack. He always looked good. He'd been riding all day, but his clothes were pressed and he was a picture of health. . . . He was a good alto player, and he sure did play that night! He was still playing alto in Wichita Falls, where I was playing tenor.

"Then Troy Floyd came out there. He was from Dallas and he'd been working the Gunter Hotel in San Anton', another big white hotel. He had got a job at Shadowland, a ballroom about eighteen miles out of San Anton'. That was when they had roadhouses where people could get drunk. You'd drive five miles up some country road off the highway to a place that turned out to be a beautiful nightclub. The police never came by.

"Troy heard Herschel play on Fletcher Henderson's *Stampede*, and Herschel killed that thing! Troy took him, although he didn't read too well. When they needed an alto later, Herschel told me to come to San Anton' and take the job. 'We'll alternate,' he said, and we both played tenor and alto with Troy.

"While we were out there, the Alphonso Trent band came to San Anton', to play a dance. Herschel asked Troy to lay him off that night.

" 'No,' Troy said. 'If you take off it will cost you five dollars.'

" 'Here's my five dollars right now,' Herschel said.

"Everybody in the band wanted to take off, but the manager of the club told Troy, 'If they do, I'll hire the band you're going to hear.' But all the local bands in San Anton' did take off that night. This was when A. G. Godley had gone to the Blue Devils and Alvin Burroughs had taken his place. Stuff Smith was in the band, and Sy Oliver was director.

"After four or five months, I went back to Dallas, and that was when T. Holder came back from Kansas City to put together his third band. I joined him, playing tenor. Sam Price was on piano, and we had a wonderful drummer named John R. Davis. Red Calhoun, who was Money Johnson's cousin, played brilliant alto. He taught himself everything and he could write anything he heard, so that it sounded just like Duke. He played the blues better than anybody I ever heard in my life. He never left Dallas, wouldn't go any place else, but he could really have made a name for himself had he come to New York. He died of cancer a few years ago, about the same time as Willie Smith. Besides T. playing trumpet, we had Norris Wilson on trombone. When we went to Bonham, Texas, to play the fair, we ran into a college band out of Austin. It was led by Wesley Smith, a fiddle player. Lloyd Glenn was on piano, and there were three Corley brothers—one played tenor, another trumpet, and the third trombone and sousaphone. Wesley had about twelve pieces, but he knew T. had this big, beautiful reputation, so he asked him if he would take over the whole band. When T. became leader, I went along with him, for five years. In 1930, I hired Earl Bostic for him! He had sat in and cut everybody one night. He could do anything on alto, and he could write like crazy.

"When T. Holder's band broke up in 1933, Wesley Smith organized a band for Victoria Spivey. She and Nina Mae McKinney had just made the picture *Hallelujah*, about the first black movie ever produced. Victoria opened a show in Dallas called *Tan Town Revue*, and then we played the circuit of vaudeville houses all through Oklahoma, Texas, Arkansas, and Missouri. Half the band came out of T. Holder's, the other half from Troy Floyd's. We had Joe McLewis on trombone, Nat Towles on bass, a pianist named Jeffrey Perry, and John Humphrey on drums. John was a great drummer, not a soloist but a rhythm man who never varied an inch. Al Johnson was on trumpet and Slow Wilson, C. Q. Price's uncle, played alto. Wesley played fiddle, of course, and he was also a very nice arranger.

"After that, Nat Towles, Al Johnson, and I went to Little Rock to work with Ethel May's band. In those days they used to put an attractive girl in front of a band to sing and direct, and that was what Ethel did. About the time her band broke up, Basie brought a band to Little Rock and I joined it. As I understand it, Bennie Moten hadn't any bookings and agreed for Basie to take most of his band for an engagement in Little Rock. When Moten picked up some bookings, the fellows began slipping off one by one. Lips Page went first. Then

I met Jimmy Rushing one morning about three o'clock. He said he was going downtown to the drugstore, but I knew there was none open at that hour in Little Rock. He was sneaking off to the bus station, you know, to catch a bus! That's the way guys would leave a band in those days. I stayed because I knew I could go home any time I got ready. I called Nat Towles in Dallas and told him the band was breaking up. 'Doesn't anybody need any money?' he asked. 'This cat I'm working for over here has got so much, you can have anything you want.' When Buster Smith and Joe Keyes found they could get as much as a hundred dollars, we three went back to Dallas. Towles sounded like Santy Claus to them. The others all went back to Kansas City.

"Nat Towles was working for a gangster who was really pulling the strings. He owned twenty-six nightclubs in the city. One of them was called The Big House, and it had bars inside so it looked like a prison. We all wore striped prison uniforms, and it was there I met Bonnie and Clyde and Pretty Boy Floyd. That gangster loved me, said I had potential, but I didn't want to be obligated to him. T-Bone Walker was with Towles then, and he was the one who used to go out on the floor and make all of the money for us.

"Now, after Fletcher Henderson got rid of Lester Young, they sent to Kansas City for Ben Webster, who was with Andy Kirk. When Basie heard Andy needed a tenor player, he said, 'Man, we just left one down in Texas. Send and get him.' So Andy sent me a ticket, and I told Towles I was going to leave. No contracts in those days! Do you know, I walked around with the ticket in my pocket for about a month, trying to make up my mind! Dallas was jumping, and we were really swinging every night. The money was no better with Kirk, but in the end I went, just to see what was going on in Kansas City. The Kirk band had a good reputation by then [1934]. Mary Lou Williams, John Williams, and Pha Terrell were in it. We went east and through New York State with Mamie Smith, playing theaters, and we were booked into the Vendome, a very popular place in Buffalo. Then we played dances as McKinney's Cotton Pickers. McKinney had a lot of dates but he had nobody to play them because he had lost his band. He would just make a brief appearance on drums, but he was a good businessman, just like Troy Floyd. When Don Redman fronted the band, I don't think McKinney did anything!

"The Kirk band broke up in Cincinnati, and I decided to go back to school, to Wiley College. They'd give you a scholarship if you had an interview and agreed to play in their band—one of those deals! Joe 'Trombone Buddy' McLewis, who was later with Earl Hines for years, went with me. He was way ahead, a hell of a trombone player. He was Henry Coker's idol. Some of the others there were Tom Pratt, a bass player who could have been another Jimmy Blanton; Duke Groner, who was to be singer and director with Nat Towles; Walter Duncan, a fine trumpet player who's now a doctor; and Earl Bostic.

"Most of us were in there to be in the band, and just jiving. We toured a lot for the school, and for the football games. I see my mistake now. I could have got a lot of theory, and I'm sorry I didn't study to be a teacher. Bostic tried his best to get me to do that. He became a teacher there, and although he was only a year or so older, he later taught Joe Newman. Joe seemed so much smaller and younger then, but when you saw them together in later years they looked to be the same age.

"When we came out from Wiley, about everybody who'd been in the band went with Nat Towles—except Joe McLewis, who went with Clarence Love and Eddie Heywood. Nat was from Louisiana and had originally worked out of Monroe and New Orleans. Now he got some bookings in Omaha. I think Duke Groner had something to do with it. He was a house-stopper, a singer with a high voice like Orlando Robeson, only I liked him better. He used to sing *Trees* and *I'm in the Mood for Love*, and women would just fall out.

"We made Omaha our headquarters and were there three years. We just took that territory over. We played all through the Dakotas, all through Minnesota, and we'd go as far as Chicago. It was very good dance country and mostly one-nighters. We'd go sometimes to a place that looked like a barn in the middle of a field. They were cultivating all around, but inside it would be a fine ballroom.

"We had a sleeper bus, like a Pullman car. There was a cab up front and then seats you could let down like a bunk. There was plenty of room and next to the cab a huge closet with shelves where we put all our uniforms and instruments. There was a john on it, too, and altogether it cost Towles a lot of money. A fellow in Sioux City, Iowa, made it, and not long afterwards all the big bands started getting them.

"There were about four big black bands in Omaha besides ours— Lloyd Hunter's Serenaders, Red Perkins', Ted Adams', and Warren Webb's. When we came there, we just cut them down to nothing! Lawrence Welk was working for the same agency as us, and he was already very popular with his polkas.

"Sir Charles Thompson, Henry Coker, Fred Beckett, and Money Johnson weren't part of the Wiley Collegians, but they joined us there. In those days we all called Money Johnson 'Satch.' 'Money' is a New York nickname. (Later on I got him in Basie's band, in Chicago.) Bob Dorsey, from Lincoln, Nebraska, was formerly a piano player, but he, Lee Pope, and the boy who played with me, Lem Talley, were good saxophonists. Then there was a trombone player named Archie Brown.

He played just like Tricky Sam, but nobody ever got to know anything about him. Debo Mills was the drummer the band always needed.

"Towles had a big book and I learned to read a lot in that band. It was harder music than Basie's, because it was an entertaining band and we did everything, all with a lot of class. We did ballads, and we had good singing groups like Lunceford. Then, too, we had so many guys who could write well. Sir Charles was writing every day. C. Q. Price was terrific, and so was Weldon Sneed, the trumpet player. He was Erskine Hawkins's first cousin. They look alike, and he had real strong chops like Hawk. We used to have two or three arrangements on one tune. For example, *Dinah, Dinah No. 2,* or *Dinah No. 3;* or 35A, 35A–2, 35A–3. This was unusual, and if we played *Dinah* three times in one night the tempos and treatment would vary very much. It was a very interesting band and ready for the big time. We used to beg Nat to go into New York, but he wouldn't and then the boys kind of lost interest. Sir Charles left. Then Coker went to Honolulu. I had a choice to join Basie or go with him to Honolulu. Francis Whitby, a very good tenor player, went in my place, and they made barrels of money over there.

"After I had left Towles, Horace Henderson, Emmett Berry, and Israel Crosby went out to Omaha and took Nat's band, took everybody.

"Basie had sent for me. I didn't know that Herschel Evans had died, didn't even know he had been ill, but I *dreamed* he had died and that Basie was going to call me. That's the truth, so help me God. I had married in Omaha in 1936 and I told Vi, 'Honey, I dreamed Herschel died and that I was going to New York to join Basie.' It happened within a week or two. I still have the telegram Basie sent me.

"When I joined the band in Kansas City, Prez said, 'Come on, Lady Tate, let's go have dinner!' We went to a little place where we always ate in Kansas City, and you know what he ordered? 'I'd like a bowl of red beans and rice,' he said, 'and give him the same.' He didn't give me a chance to order!

" 'Have you been keeping up on your horn?' he asked.

" 'Well, I've been trying,' I answered.

" 'If you're playing anything like you did the last time I heard you, it'll be your gig.'

"This was 1939 and he hadn't heard me play in five or six years. He had kind of settled down and was faster than when I'd heard him before. That time I'd come into Tulsa with the *Tan Town Revue* and he was in the same hotel. He was with King Oliver and he'd checked in that morning and had just gotten to bed. Downstairs in the Small Hotel (the biggest colored hotel in the country), they had a room where you could jam, so I went and woke him up. 'I'm going to make this cat play some this morning,' I told our piano player, Jeffrey Perry. He came down, and I wish I could hear again what came out of that horn! I listened, and then he had me play. He dug what I did and he told me so, which is what he meant when he spoke of the last time he heard me.

"There were plenty of tenor players who wanted the gig with Basie. 'Lots of ladies have eyes,' Prez said, and mentioned the names of several guys who could have had it in terms of reputation. But Basie had remembered me, and had sent for me!

"We played a colored dance the first night, and I'll never forget how those cats sounded and how they swung. They had Skippy Williams traveling along with them, and he wanted the gig, too. We'd each play a while, and he'd say, 'I hope you make it.' He was a beautiful cat, and sincere, and I felt badly when they hired me because he had wanted the job so much.

"The next night we played Kansas City University—a white dance— and the kids kept asking for *Blue and Sentimental*, which had been Herschel's showcase. Basie looked down at the piano and asked, 'Hey, do you know that?'

" 'I can try,' I said.

" 'E-flat,' Basie said, and made the introduction.

"I walked out to the mike and it seemed like a mile. I knew *Blue and Sentimental*, because I'd listened to the record often enough, but I'd never played it. Everybody danced as I played and it broke the house up. All the guys in the band stood up and shook my hand when I finished. 'You're in,' they said. Everybody, that is, but Prez. He just looked up and winked.

"We had kind of a long tour, and then we came into New York and made records like *Rock-a-Bye Basie* and *Taxi War Dance*. I'd never been to New York, and the band had been out so long doing one-nighters that all the guys were glad to get in. I'd never seen a station as big as Pennsylvania Station before, and the guys were all going this way and that way, running and grabbing cabs. I was standing there with a pocket full of money, not knowing where to go, when I saw Prez standing in a corner. So then he looked out after me, carried me along in his cab, got me a kitchenette right next to him and Mary at the Woodside Hotel.

" 'I knew you didn't know where to go,' he said. 'The ladies are excited. They haven't seen their Madam Queens for a long time. You understand?'

"He was a beautiful cat and he had a lot of class. When he was on the road, he'd have a ball, but when he was in New York he'd stick with his old lady, just as though he were a one-woman man.

"What set him on the road to ruin? I've often tried to figure that out. We were in the band together from '39 to '41, when they let him go because he wouldn't make a record date on Friday the thirteenth. He had his superstitions. He came back in the band in '43, when they fired Don Byas. The reason for that? Well, Ben Webster came down one night when we were at the Hotel Lincoln, and he sat in Don's chair and played. I never heard anyone sound like that in my life, and all the cats flipped over Ben. Poor Don went across the street and got stoned!

"Prez worked until they got him in the army. The way he was drinking whiskey, I didn't think they'd ever take him, but he was healthy then and he passed *every*thing. He had a big, healthy chest and, although he smoked, he didn't inhale. But the army did him in. He was actually a jolly, happy cat, but he got sad after that. They put him in the brig and kept him there a long time. He had made that movie, *Jammin' the Blues*, for Norman Granz, before he went in, and Norman used to send him money all the time he was in there. If you ever did Prez a favor, he never forgot it in his heart.

"Prez had beaten induction for quite a while. Like a lot of guys would say, 'Well, I wasn't at that address when . . . I'm traveling with this band all the time.' When we opened in Los Angeles that year, there was a sharp young cat there who kept looking at Prez and Jo Jones. That wasn't unusual, because they were stars. He sat there drinking whiskey all night, but when we got through he came over and said, 'You, Lester Young, and you, Jo Jones, I have to serve you with these papers. Be down at the Induction Center tomorrow morning!'

"They thought Prez was crazy down there, because he was talking his special kind of talk, like, 'Well, boot, then.' . . . 'I see you got hangman's eyes.' Or: 'I'm with you, ladies.' They thought he might be putting on an act, so they passed him.

"When they went in the army, Buddy Rich took Jo's place and Artie Shaw played Prez's part until Lucky Thompson came in the band. Artie had just given up his navy band, but Buddy was working with Tommy Dorsey in Hollywood. Tommy started early in the evening and got through about ten, when Buddy would come over to the Plantation, a big ballroom in Watts, where we were playing. It was packed every night and Buddy was our drummer till we got Shadow Wilson. Artie Shaw was playing tenor parts on clarinet, but Basie wouldn't let *us* play clarinets. I think the only clarinet player he really liked was Benny Goodman, although he used to let Rudy Rutherford play, and Rudy was playing his ass off in those war days.

"When Lucky Thompson arrived, he continued the Byas approach. Lester had naturally been featured more than me, and Lucky was in his chair. Lucky quit when he decided he wanted to stay on the Coast, and then Illinois Jacquet came in. I'd heard him—and Arnett Cobb— when I went to Houston with Nat Towles. They were with Milt Larkins. Norman Granz offered Illinois all that money to play in Jazz at the Philharmonic, so he left and later Basie got Paul Gonsalves.

"We didn't have cliques in the Basie band. Everybody seemed to dig each other. If a cat really got out of line, he'd be over in left field by himself. Then he would come on back in. When we had a disagreement, everybody would help straighten it out on the bus right then and there. Basie was like one of the guys and he'd have a ball with us, but we always knew when he was serious, when he meant business.

"The band broke up in 1948, right after our engagement with Billie Holiday at the Strand on Broadway and 47th. The bop era was coming in and people were confused. Rhythm and blues and rock 'n' roll were getting big, too. Packagewise, bop hadn't really gotten big, but the booking agencies started sending out packages of five or six attractions, each one able to hold its own. It got harder and harder for a band operating by itself when people could see a bunch of acts for maybe just a quarter more.

"I'd been with Basie for ten years, but by the time Murray Bloom, the road manager, called and said the band was getting back together and they were going to rehearse I'd make up my mind I wanted to try something else and stay around New York. After I'd put my transfer in with the union, I soon had all kinds of gigs coming in. There were single dates and a lot of recording.

"I worked with Lucky Millinder at the Savoy for three months. I don't know where he got it from, but money didn't mean anything to him. If he wanted you, he'd pay what you asked. Tab Smith was making four or five hundred dollars with him when most people were asking no more than two hundred and fifty. Lucky hated it when I wouldn't go out on the road with him, but I quit and went to work with Lips Page. He had a good, eight-piece band and we were playing theaters. That's where I met Skip Hall, the piano player. Lips had Vinnie Bair-Bey, a good alto player, Flat Top Wilson on bass, and Herbie Lovelle on drums. When jobs ran out for Lips, Billy Shaw— God bless him—got me some dates, and I asked Lips if I could use some of his guys. He said he didn't mind, and I got Irvin Stokes on trumpet. While we were in Philly, Lips got some work and was peeved with me because he couldn't get his guys back.

"Next, I took Sam 'The Man' Taylor's place in a band led by Ted Fields at the Celebrity Club in Freeport, Long Island. Ted was a drummer who had been to Europe with Sam Wooding. I was living in New York then and I used to hate going way out there. It was too damn far!

"Then Jimmy Rushing got a good nine-piece group together and took it into the Savoy. He had guys like Buck Clayton and Jimmy Mundy writing for him, and the band was very popular for a while.

"After that I was in Lucille Dixon's band at the Savannah Club in the Village for about a year. The front line was pretty—Taft Jordan, Tyree Glenn, and me. Jimmie Evans played piano, Lucille bass, and Billy Smith drums. It was a big club with a floor show, and packed every night. There was a line of girls, about fourteen of the prettiest chicks you ever saw in your life, three acts, three shows a night.

"Irving Cohen, the owner of the Celebrity Club in Freeport, had another club with the same name on 125th Street in Harlem, and he called me one day. He'd noticed that I didn't drink, and he wanted me to take a band in there. He said 'booze was getting the best of all the guys' in the group he had. I couldn't leave Lucille Dixon right away, but after a couple of weeks I opened with Pat Jenkins [trumpet], Shorty Haughton [trombone], Ben Richardson [reeds], Skip Hall [piano], Flat Top Wilson [bass], and Fats Donaldson [drums]. That was in 1950 and I've been there nearly twenty years. That's been my main thing. Eli Robinson took Shorty's place in '53, and we've had several changes in the rhythm section—Sir Charles Thompson, Sadik Hakim, Johnny Acea, and Kenny Drew on piano. Everett Barksdale played fine bass guitar for a time, and he used to break it up with *One O'Clock Jump*. He is a well-schooled musician, and when we had to play a waltz he'd add things, build rich chords. The old piano was always out of tune, so I ended up with George Baker playing electric guitar instead.

"I have to play what the dancers want at the Celebrity. If they're mostly kids, I have to play more boogaloo or James Bond–type things. It's getting so I can play less jazz as time goes by, but I play as much as I can—to their beat. So long as the rhythm is there, they dance to that, and it doesn't matter what the horns play. Sometimes we get people who say we don't play loud enough. What they really want is three guitars amplified to the point where you can't hear yourself talk! But when European fans come over, the Celebrity is one of the first places they go to, and they want to hear jazz. On the other hand, I've never seen any of the well-known New York critics there. The band nevertheless got quite a reputation, so that we'd be hired for social dances at downtown hotels and ballrooms. Depending on the size of the room, I might have to augment to meet the minimum number of men the union required. They usually send a delegate around and if I were not employing the full number I'd be in violation. So that's when I'd have a gig for some of my old friends in the Basie band.

"The last time I saw Prez was at Newport. I'd gone up to play with Benny Goodman in a big band. That was the time the guys got high, played badly, and really let him down. The trumpet players threw their derbies down on the stand while he was trying to make an announcement! John Hammond asked me to stay over to play for Billie Holiday the next night, with Buck Clayton, Jack Teagarden, Georgie Auld, and Pee Wee Russell. We played for Joe Turner and Chuck Berry, too. And Prez came up from Birdland. A friend brought him in a big Cadillac. He was already so weak, he just dragged his case along. We were rehearsing when he came in, wearing that big hat. He'd had a lot of trouble finding the tent, and we were just about ready to quit.

" 'Voo,' he said, standing in the entrance.

"Everybody burst out laughing, he was so funny.

" 'I don't want to hear any of you bitches laughing,' he said. 'I had a helluva hard time finding this molly trolly. I'm tired, and you're all laughing.'

"I didn't know what he meant by 'molly trolly,' but that's what he called the rehearsal. When we finished, he sat at the back of the tent for several hours and drank a little.

" 'Lady Tate,' he said, 'I really don't dig you laughing at me! But I want you to be like my manager and get my money for me. Take out a hundred and send it to my wife. Don't say a fucking thing except, "Hundred dollars, Lester." They're going to dock me at Birdland tonight. They didn't want me to come, but I needed the money.'

"It was three hundred and fifty dollars.

"I went on first that night and later we played together. After it was all over, I went back to New York with him in the Cadillac. We got lost and it took us eight hours from Newport. He talked all the way. I remember parts of our conversation.

" 'You know,' he said, 'I never really made it on my horn.'

" 'Don't feel like that,' I said.

" 'I never really made it on my horn,' he repeated.

" 'What are you talking about? You and Coleman Hawkins have more imitators than any tenor players in the world. They play like you *or* him. So you know you made it.'

" 'But the *other* ladies, my imitators, are making the money!'

" 'You shouldn't say that. I'm not a booker, but I could sell you, because they know you everywhere in the world. The only thing is, you haven't taken care of business like you should have.'

"He was my friend, and I didn't pull any punches when I told him that.

" 'Yeah, I guess you're right,' he said.

"Just a few months later he was dead."

(1969)

Helen Humes

(VOCALIST)

"I was in Bessie Allen's Sunday School band in Louisville, along with Dicky Wells, Jonah Jones, and Bill Beason. I had had piano lessons from a German teacher, but I tried to play trumpet in the band. I didn't really care for it; so when we went out on trips to some of the small towns around I'd play piano in the little jazz group we called The Dandies.

"A lot of us kids in Louisville started singing as soon as we could talk. I used to sing all the time, but I guess I really began seriously at the Baptist church down the street. My father and mother both sang there, and they'd sing duets together right here in this house. My mother had been a schoolteacher, and she was half Cherokee. Her name was Emma Johnson. They used to call my father 'Judge,' because he was in and out of the courthouse all day. He was among the first black attorneys in the city, and he did well in real estate. Besides this house, he owned a farm and other property at one time. He was John Henry Humes, and he had a reputation for being kind to people. I

129

was an only child, and we were a *very* happy family. My parents were always so good to me.

"Our little band would sometimes play at the Palace Theater, and when they had amateur contests I'd slip off and go down there. I remember that the first song I ever sang in public was *When You're a Long, Long Way from Home*; and the first song I sang with a band—in 1926—was *I'm in Love with You, That's Why*.

"It was at the Palace Theater that a guitar player by the name of Sylvester Weaver heard me. He had made records for Okeh and knew Tommy Rockwell, who was producing for that company. He told him I sounded like Ethel Waters; but I was only fourteen, and nobody had influenced me at that time.° We had a piano at home, but no record player or records, and I didn't know anything about Ethel Waters. When I got to hear her later, I preferred her to others, and I've always liked pretty songs, torch songs. Bessie Smith and Ma Rainey were too bluesy for me, but people have always tried to make me a blues singer, right from my first record date.

"Mr. Rockwell had my mother and me go to St. Louis, where I recorded *Black Cat Blues, A Worried Woman's Blues*, and a couple of sides that were not issued. I don't know whether the record sold anywhere else, but I know people around home bought it. When Mr. Rockwell wrote us and wanted me to go on the road in some show, Mother told him no—I had to go to school. But she and I went to New York and I made a second lot of records. Then we came right on back.† Of course, I didn't know then what the words of the songs really meant.

"After I got through high school, I took a business course and worked in my father's office. Then I got a job at the first black bank in Louisville, typing and doing shorthand. I had no idea of making a career in music, but I *knew* I didn't want to keep typing! So then for a time I was a waitress in a place called the Canary Cottage, a lovely place right down in the heart of town.

" 'Have you ever worked before?' the man asked me when I went in first.

" 'Yes, but only in nightclubs,' I told him.

" 'Well, go into the kitchen and get me a demitasse cup,' he said.

"I didn't know nothing about a demitasse cup, but I asked somebody

---

° On the early records, Helen Humes sounded more like Mildred Bailey, whom she had never heard and who made no records until a couple of years later.

† The titles were *If Papa Has Outside Lovin'; Do What You Did Last Night; Everybody Does It Now; Cross-Eyed Blues; Garlic Blues; Alligator Blues; Nappy Headed Blues;* and *Race Horse Blues.* Discographies credit J. C. Johnson as the pianist, but John Hammond recalled a conversation with James P. Johnson, who remembered the session and spoke enthusiastically of the singer.

and they showed me. When I went back with the cup, he hired me right away.

"'You work with the captain today,' he said.

"So I worked with the captain, and the next day he gave me a station of my own. I was so *happy!* I loved that work, and I was there until I left home to go to Buffalo. I went there to visit Margaret Stewart and her husband, Luke, who was a terrific banjo player. He's retired now; but I heard from him last week, and I asked him why he didn't get his guitar out and do something. He goes to visit Jonah Jones all the time. They were in the same school, and they're real buddy-buddies.

"We went to a club in Buffalo called the Spider Web, where Al Sears had the band. 'Make her go up there and sing,' Luke said to Margaret. I was scared, because this was a large place and I hadn't been out in front of an audience like that before. But I got up and sang, and they liked me so well the man asked me would I come and work.

"'Well,' I said, still scared, 'I'll come back tomorrow and let you know.'

"I went back and stayed for I don't know how long. Then I left and went over to the Vendome Hotel, where Jonah Jones, Luke Stewart, Stuff Smith, Joe Thomas, and all of 'em worked. I was in Buffalo a couple of years, and then I came home. I never was a person to stay away from home too long. Later on, I would always make it my business to come home once or twice a year.

"The following year, I went back to Buffalo, just visiting, not working; and from there I went to Albany. Virginia Scott and her husband, George, were there, and I got to know them when they were in Buffalo. He was a saxophone player, and she was a singer and a dancer. She would do splits, high kicks, and all that kind of stuff. I worked in a club there, but I can't remember the name. While I was back in Louisville again, some man called from Cincinnati. He wanted me at the Cotton Club, and when I got there I found Al Sears had the band —a lovely band, eight or ten pieces. Basie came through in 1937 and heard me sing. He said Billie Holiday was going to leave, and he asked if I'd go with the band.

"'Well,' I said, 'what does it pay?'

"'Thirty-five dollars.'

"'Oh, shucks, I make that here and don't have to go no place!'

"A bit later Al Sears took the band to New York, and I went with 'em. Al got a job with Vernon Andrade's band at the Renaissance, and I would go up there and sing. I guess Basie had told John Hammond about me, because I think John heard me at the Renaissance for the first time. He asked Al and Vernon to see if they could get me to join Basie.

"In the meantime, they had had an amateur contest at the Apollo, and I had come in second. The girl who won sounded *just like* Ella Fitzgerald. She had listened to all Ella's records; and Ella was the biggest thing in show business then, along with Billie. I was happy to be second, but it was like an audition for Basie, because after they had tried that girl he came after *me*. I was glad he did, although the pay was still thirty-five dollars a week, which is what all the guys in the band were getting. Our salaries went up to ten dollars a day when we were on the road, and a little more when we worked theaters. We went into the Famous Door on 52nd Street, and that was where the band really took over. I was with Basie four years, and when I left I was getting more than thirty-five dollars!

"One thing I always remember about Basie was what happened when we were traveling in the South. They have a lot of wooden bridges down there, and when we came to one he would have the bus stop. Then he'd get out and walk across.

" 'What about the boys and me?' I asked him one time.

" 'You can get off if you want,' he said.

"Jimmy Rushing sang all the blues and originals with the band, and I got mostly ballads and pop songs, some good, some not so good. I did *If I Could Be with You; Someday, Sweetheart; Don't Worry 'Bout Me; All or Nothing at All; Between the Devil and the Deep Blue Sea; Sub-Deb Blues;* and a number by Leonard Feather called *My Wandering Man.* My very first record with the band was *Dark Rapture*, but before that I had recorded with Harry James. He used about half of Basie's band on those sessions—Buck Clayton, Herschel Evans, Earle Warren, Eddie Durham, Jack Washington, Walter Page, and Jo Jones. I sang on *I Can Dream, Can't I?; Jubilee; Song of the Wanderer;* and *It's the Dreamer in Me.* That was before Harry had a band of his own.

"Jimmy Rushing and I were close friends in the band, and we always kept in contact. I had a Christmas card from him a while back, and then it seemed right after that they sent an announcement that said he had passed. 'Well, for pity's sake,' I said. I thought of all the laughs and good times we'd had. We made some records together for Columbia out in California, but I don't think they ever were issued. Irving Townsend was in charge of the session, and I remember we did *Outskirts of Town.*

"I used to pretend I was asleep on the Basie bus, so the boys wouldn't think I was hearing their rough talk. I'd sew buttons on, and cook for them, too. I used to carry pots and a little hot plate around, and I'd fix up some food backstage or in places where it was difficult to get anything to eat when we were down South. Playing cards was the best way of passing time on those long trips, but sometimes when I won money from them I found I had to lend it back! I wasn't interested in drinking and keeping late hours, so that part didn't hurt me. But my kidneys couldn't stand the punishment of those long rides. I was too timid to ask the driver to stop when I should have. Then, too, I got tired of singing the same songs year after year.

"So I went home to Louisville, but I hadn't been there long when John Hammond called me to go into Café Society in New York. I had Mr. Teddy Wilson to accompany me, and you know that wasn't bad at all! Then I had Art Tatum for a while. My goodness, that was such a ball! Sometimes he'd play too much, but then I'd tell him: 'Wait a minute now! Give me a chance. Just play something pretty.' He understood, and we were really good friends. It was nice working down there, and I was at Café Society several times. But I remember one time they had a picture of me in the paper right next to some movie star, and in the picture I looked so *fair*.

" 'Miss Humes,' the headwaiter said when I went in that night, 'there's a gentleman waiting to see you.'

" 'Okay,' I said. 'I'll be out in a few minutes when I've got my things on.'

"When I came out, the headwaiter took me over to the man.

" 'Oh, you're colored!' he said, and he looked so shocked.

" 'I certainly am,' I said, and just walked away from him.

"He continued to sit at the bar, but we didn't speak again. I don't know who he thought I was, from looking at the paper, but I'm telling you, you meet some weirdos in this business.

"I was driving through Arkansas one time with my cousin, his wife, and their little girl. The baby wanted to go to the rest room, so I drove up to this gas station and asked, 'Do you have a toilet we could go to?' The man said, 'Yes, back there.' So I said, 'Well, fill the car up with gas.' When I found there was no bathroom, I came back and asked where it was.

" 'Didn't you see it?' he said.

" 'No, I didn't.'

" 'Well, they must have it locked.'

"Then my cousin remembered he knew a doctor three blocks down; and when we came back there was this old gas attendant and the police.

" 'That's the woman, that's the woman!' the attendant shouted. 'She was talking back to me.'

" 'Don't talk to me like you're talking to some of these kids around here,' I said, 'because I came to you like a lady, and you're gonna come to me like a gentleman.'

" 'Well, you know, you're down South now,' the police said.

" 'I was born in the South and I know exactly where I am.'

" 'Well, let's go on and try to forget it,' the police said.

"There are diehards down there, of course, but then you meet others who are just so wonderful.

"Besides Café Society, I also worked on 52nd Street and at the Village Vanguard. It was while I was at the Vanguard one year that I got to thinking that I wanted to be back in Louisville for the Derby. I didn't want to leave Max Gordon without anybody, so I ran around trying to find a singer for him. Somebody suggested Pearl Bailey, and I went all over Harlem looking for her and finally found her. She went from the Vanguard to the Blue Angel, and I don't think she has ever looked back since. She's a wonderful entertainer, and I was so happy for her.

"After I left New York, I went on another tour through the South to New Orleans in a package show. Then I went out to California in 1944 with Connie Smith, the piano player. She was from Atlanta, Georgia, and she had a left hand like a man. The way she hit those keys—oh, she could play! We worked as a team at the Streets of Paris and just upset everything. The people loved us. Lately, she's been playing cocktail piano in hotels.

"I also worked with Nina Russell out there. She played piano and organ.

"I stayed out in Los Angeles and did four or five seasons with Jazz at the Philharmonic. I made a few records and had hits with *E-Baba-Le-Ba* and *Million Dollar Secret*. I never got a nickel of royalty out of *Million Dollar Secret*, but I did get between three and four thousand dollars out of *E-Baba-Le-Ba*. When I asked the Modern people about *Million Dollar Secret*, they said they didn't know it was selling, that somebody must have been selling it 'under the table.' Knowing those fellows, I knew better, but what could you do?

"While I was on the Coast, I played a part in Langston Hughes's *Simply Heavenly*. It didn't last long, but I always remember a review that said, '*Simply Heavenly* is simply Helen Humes.' My voice was used in three movies, *Panic in the Street*, *My Blue Heaven*, and *The Steel Trap*—as well as in the television version of *Come Home, Bill Bailey*.

"In 1952, I was working at a club in San Francisco when I got a phone call from Dorothy Johnson, a very dear friend of mine. We sometimes say we're sisters.

" 'Well, now,' she said, 'you might as well get yourself together, because you're going to Australia!'

" 'No, I ain't going to Australia,' I said.

" 'Yes, you are, because I told the man you were going.'

" 'You better call him and tell him something different.'

" 'You're going with Red Norvo. I know you'll enjoy it.'

"I had met Red casually when he and Mildred Bailey were together. (And I just loved the way *she* sang.) So I met Red again up at the office and we got everything all signed up. 'Oh, Helen,' he said, 'there's nothing to it. You'll like it.'

"But I was scared to death about going that far. I thought the little plane we were in would never make it. At that time you didn't have great big planes like today. 'If I ever get there,' I kept saying to myself, I think I'm going to stay, 'cause I don't want to come back like this.' They have good musicians in Australia, and after Red had put a quartet together we went over big and had a wonderful time. The promoter wanted me to stay and work by myself, but I told him no, that I had to go back home—because I didn't want to make the trip alone! And Red Norvo had some more work lined up for us here. By the time I went back, in 1962, they had jets and everything, and I didn't mind going by myself. I had a very good Australian group to accompany me, and we played clubs and major hotels for thirteen weeks. The third time I went, in 1964, I stayed ten months, and they tried hard to get me to become a citizen.

"In 1962, I toured Europe with the first blues festival package. T-Bone Walker and Memphis Slim were big names over there, and we did very well. Then I was out in L.A. again, working in Redd Foxx's club, when Mama took sick in '67. I went back to Louisville, and she died soon afterwards. My father was sick, too, and I knew I had to stay. I knew it was what I was supposed to do. I haven't sung since. I got a job in an ammunition plant and, you know, I enjoyed it, enjoyed being with the people there. When we got laid off, I still had my father to care for, and in the afternoons I'd drive with some other women to bingo games. I don't know what Louisville people, particularly the older people, would do without bingo.

"I caught Eubie Blake on the tube the other night, and, gee, he was good—just full of life! This is a funny business. People get out of the picture, and then first thing you know they're big again. I don't know what Newport will do for me. I hope you're right; but it's been so long since I've even tried to sing. I might get a piano back here and rehearse by myself. That would be a way of trying to remember some of those songs."

(1973)

The preceding interview took place in Louisville in 1973, when the writer succeeded, on George Wein's behalf, in persuading Helen Humes to participate in a tribute to Count Basie at the Newport

Jazz Festival. Her appearance was a great success, and it was followed by records, lengthy engagements at The Cookery in New York City, at prestigious clubs and hotels all around the country, and frequent European tours. Her cherished father, who had encouraged her to resume singing, died in 1975, at the age of ninety-six.

In preparation for a European tour, Helen sent a list of her preferred songs for arranger Buck Clayton's consideration, as follows:

> *Between the Devil and the Deep Blue Sea*
> *'Deed I Do*
> *You're Driving Me Crazy*
> *Don't Worry 'Bout Me*
> *Honeysuckle Rose*
> *Mean to Me* (use verse)
> *Someone to Watch Over Me*
> *I Wish You Love* (use verse)
> *Today I Sing the Blues*
> *I've Grown Accustomed to His Face*
> *A Hundred Years from Today*
> *If I Could Be with You One Hour Tonight* (use verse)
> *Million Dollar Secret*
> *Woe Is Me* (a cute calypso)
> *Kansas City*

A charmingly modest note added: "I love the old songs, but the keys I had them in may be too high now. Anyhow, tell Buck my low note is G under middle C, and C above. That will leave me room to play around, because after I sing a while I get clear and higher. Please see if Buck can pick me up a copy of *You've Changed, I Could Have Told You So*, and *You've Got Your Troubles, I've Got Mine*. I like those songs, and one of these days I'm going to sing *I'm Satisfied*, Duke's song that Ivie Anderson used to sing so good. I loved it from the time I first heard it, but nobody ever does it now."

Like the late Louis Armstrong, Helen Humes takes pleasure in what is now almost a lost art: she writes lively and informative letters.

Snooky Young

Count Basie was relaxing in his dressing room before a concert at Carnegie Hall. The conversation touched on tempos, his own preferences and those of different audiences; on the sight-reading ability of today's bands as compared with those of yesterday; and, inevitably, on personalities within his present group.

"Snooky Young? He's very likeable, and wonderful, and dependable," he said warmly.

"Snooky's a gentleman and very pleasant to work with," Buck Clayton had said a few days earlier. "He has a good lip and he's very consistent. In fact, I'd say he's one of the most dependable trumpet players in the business."

"Snooky'll just stand up in the section to take his solo," Emmett Berry remarked on another occasion, "and not come down front. He doesn't have to. He's the kind of trumpet player who can wash everybody away."

Public recognition of the talents engaged in jazz is a haphazard matter, but the musicians themselves judge more surely and have

longer memories. Records, fortunately, can often prove the validity of
their opinions.

For instance, the two choruses on Basie versions of *Who, Me?* may
be compared with the two on Lunceford's *Uptown Blues*, which
marked Young's recording debut. Not a few years lie between, but the
polished young musician with Lunceford and the seasoned professional
with Basie are clearly the same man. There is the same artistic integrity
in the solos, the same poise, the same disciplined imagination, the
same precise articulation, and the same brilliancy and beauty of tone.

Young was born and raised in Dayton, Ohio. The first instrument he
remembers playing was an unlikely one, a zither, but he came of a
truly musical family, one that actually operated a "family band."
Young's father played saxophone and taught the children music. His
mother played banjo, and later, as it became more popular, guitar. His
sister, Mary Louise, played piano, and he and his brother, Granville,
trumpet.

"Granville and I had a teacher named Ed Sanders, who played in
the old Don Redman band and used to come to Dayton," Young recalled. "He took a liking to us and really taught us how to play trumpet.
Granville is older than me and there's always been a lot of controversy
among our friends. Some of them claim right today that he was a better
trumpet player than me. He played with Floyd Ray's band in later
years, but he gradually gave up music. He shouldn't have done it,
because I think he had a wonderful future ahead of him.

"When I first went out from home professionally, in the family
band, it was with a road show called *The Black and White Revue*.
They added a drummer, another saxophone, and one or two pieces to
our band, and we accompanied the show, but we were an act in ourselves. A drummer called John Godley played with us around home
but didn't go on the road. He always said he was a cousin, but he
really wasn't any relation at all.

"We went south and got stranded. My father had to take all the
blame for that! But I met a couple of people there who were a help to
me in terms of experience. I played with Eddie Heywood's father
(Eddie Heywood, Sr.). He was a fine pianist and arranger and at that
time he was writing for shows and everything. I also played with
Graham Jackson, who had a band in Atlanta, Georgia, and because I
was so young he featured me out front.

"It took us six months, but we came back from there to Dayton
together, the whole family, and we weren't in any hurry to leave again.
While we were on the road, we'd had a tutor, but now I went back to
school again. I did a lot of playing at night, in clubs and so on, while

I was still in school. I was generally considered fairly advanced for my age and I played with the Wilberforce Collegians before I graduated from high school.

"Louis Armstrong used to come to the Palace Ballroom in my home-town, but I wasn't old enough to be allowed inside. I used to stand in the street—and even the street would be crowded!—and Louis would be playing the most beautiful trumpet I ever heard. This was before air conditioning became so general, and in the summer all the windows would be wide open, and you could hear all right. So when I first began to play, Louis was my influence. I liked the way he played melodic things as well as the 'hot' solos. I thought a lot of Roy Eldridge, too, and though I liked what Dizzy played I never tried to play like him. There are guys like Charlie Shavers and Clark Terry whose work I'm crazy about, and you can't beat those men, but my main influence was Louis.

"After the Collegians, the next band of any size I worked with was Chick Carter's. If it could have stayed together, I think it would have become famous. Most of the musicians in it—like Gerald Wilson, Booty Wood, Ray Perry (who played alto and fiddle), and Eddie Byrd, the drummer—went on to make their names in other bands.

"My next move was to get married, and in that same year [1939] I joined Jimmie Lunceford. Gerald Wilson had gone into that band about six months before and had told Lunceford about me. My wife's cousin had gone to school with Lunceford, and I think his friendship helped me. Gerald always admired my playing, thought I should go places, and used to tell Jimmie, 'If you ever need a trumpet player, I have a young kid around here who can play.'

"It was a great break for me, because Lunceford's was one of the top bands then. I was only twenty and, although I hadn't had so much training, I had had a lot of experience. I replaced Eddie Tompkins, the first trumpet, and I had to play lead. I really wanted to be a soloist, a 'hot' man, and I did get plenty of solos, but since that time I've played lead in most of the bands I've been in. I think I must have been cut out to play first, and now I really like it.

"But it was different in those days. They usually had a lead, a growl, and a get-off man, but today the lead is thrown about more. In fact, I don't think one man could play lead on *every* number in today's books. So much of what we play is upstairs that it would wear one man down. They used to have a high-note man (Lunceford had Tommy Stevenson and then Paul Webster), but now the lead is expected to take care of the high notes. They'll write an F or a G or an A right on the lead sheet, but before, when they wrote an A or a high B-flat, they'd write it for third or fourth chair, the high-note man.

"There was a time when it was a thrill to hear a high note, but now you hear high notes all night long. I think sometimes the arrangers make a mistake in taking such advantage of the musicians' ability to play more. You don't get so much contrast from the brass if you don't have them playing soft and pretty as well. And if the listener gets tired of high notes, you can bet the trumpet player does, too! It's a kick to play them, but if you have to keep pounding them all night, it gets kind of rough."

Young was with Lunceford for nearly three years, and besides the famous *Uptown Blues* he was heard as a soloist on records like *Dinah*, *Twenty-Four Robbers*, *Wham*, *Blues in the Groove*, *Red Wagon*, *It Had to Be You*, *Swingin' on C*, and *Monotony in Four Flats*. "It was a good band," he said, "one of the greatest I was ever in, but what with the war, and the older guys leaving, there was a lot of confusion. When I left and went back home, I asked for the navy, because all my friends were stationed up at Great Lakes, and I was accepted and passed physically fit, but they never called me.

"Count Basie came through Dayton at a time when Buck Clayton was sick with tonsils, and he asked if I would play in the band for about a month until Buck was well. I think that was how I made my way with Basie, because he liked my playing, but the next time I joined him it was to take Al Killian's chair, not Buck's, and at a time when the lead was split between Al and Ed Lewis.

"I went back to Dayton and gigged around for a while. Then I was on the road with Lionel Hampton for about a year. Next, I went out to the Coast to join Lee and Lester Young. They had a trumpet player by the name of Paul Campbell. I stayed at the house with Paul and got to like him, so I wouldn't take the job, because he liked it. I gave Lee back the money he had sent for me to come out and joined Les Hite. Gerald Wilson was with Hite, and I consider Gerald my closest friend, so we were back together again. Eventually, when things began to slow down, we moved the whole trumpet section over and joined Benny Carter—Gerald, Walter Williams, Jack Trainer, and myself.

"While I was out on the Coast, I played in most of the musical sequences in the pictures Lena Horne was making, and I was the off-screen trumpet in *Blues in the Night*. I like the Coast, but things haven't broken yet. I really don't think they've improved *that* much.

"I stayed with Benny until Basie came out and Al Killian was leaving. So I took Al's place, and that was when I was first really one of Basie's men. Later, Gerald Wilson came up with an idea for forming a big band, so I went out to the Coast again and joined him. We came east and played New York, but things got rough for the band in Chicago and St. Louis, and Basie took me back again.

"In 1947, I quit the road, went home, and organized a seven-piece band. I had four rhythm and three horns—trombone, tenor, and my trumpet. Slam Stewart was on bass and Eddie Byrd, who was with Louis Jordan a long time, was on drums. My sister played piano and later on my younger brother, Don Leroy, came in on drums. Booty Wood played trombone for a while, until he formed his own group with three trombones, and he had a good thing there. I gave Frank Foster his first job after he came out of Wilberforce University. Charlie White did the arrangements, and we always tried to keep a big-band feeling in the writing. We traveled all around the territory, in Michigan, Ohio, Indiana, and Kentucky, played all the best places, and I think it was the best band in that area. We opened the Flame Show Bar in Detroit, where we also accompanied Billie Holiday, and we played the Club Valley there. In Dayton, we worked the Classic, a club which ran shows and big names.

"Every time Basie came through Dayton he would ask me to come on back, and I always told him I wasn't coming back anymore. Finally, he called me one day in the fall of '57 when, I guess, I was pretty low in mind, because I said 'yes,' although all the other times I'd been saying 'no.' When I quit the road in 1947, it was to be home and to bring up my three children. They grew up during that ten years. It was a gap in my career, but I thought it was the right thing to do, and I wasn't forgotten completely—not by Basie, anyway.

"I've written a few tunes but I've never done any arranging. One Basie recorded, a little swing thing, called *Let's Have a Taste.* Another I did with Freddie Green a few years ago was called *Free Eats.*

"I feel very happy about being back on the scene. I got attached to the big-band sound and I like playing in a big band better than in a small group. There was a period when I wanted to blow all the time, but now I like to listen to the other guys and I don't care about solos the way I once did. What I really like is to hold the section together, to get that section feeling."

"It's probably only because he's so valuable in the section," Benny Carter said at the end of a Basie record session, "that Snooky hasn't received his due recognition as a soloist. He's equipped to solo well in so many ways. He can play with wonderful expression, as he did on *Pensive Miss,* or he can play real, swinging jazz—just whatever's required. He's an outstanding musician and a powerhouse in any trumpet section."

(1962)

Joe Newman

"My daddy was a musician in New Orleans, where I originally came from. He played in the first Negro band to have a sustaining radio show in New Orleans, on WWL. The band was known as the Creole Serenaders and was approximately six pieces. The three Bocage brothers played in it—Peter, Charlie, and Henry. Peter played trumpet and doubled on violin. Henry played tuba. Charlie used to sing. I didn't like his voice, and there were many other people who didn't, but they still went along. My dad played piano, Louis Warnick played alto and clarinet, and a guy we called Mr. Martin was on drums. During the Depression, they played at the famous old Absinthe House. Before that, I remember, they'd played in a jitney dance hall, where they had girls and the band segued from one number right into another. Men would come in and buy tickets to dance with these girls. They also played in Gretna, just across the river, and my sister and I would go over when they played dances.

"There were six of us children, four girls and two boys. My father and mother both married twice, and they each had two children in their first marriages. My sister Georgia and I were the children of their second marriage. We all lived together and I never could find the slightest bit of difference between us except in terms of complexion. My mother was a Creole, very fair, and with very straight hair. My father was much darker, more Negro. The children of his first marriage were dark, my mother's very fair. My sister and I have the same complexion.

"We had two pianos in the house, one a big, regular upright that would play rolls, the other a big concert grand. The grand was kept locked, but we found how to open it with a pair of scissors. My father discovered we were doing this because the little brass ring that fitted in the keyhole got loose and would fall out. So he forbade us to touch it after that.

"I began by studying drums for about two weeks, but I never cared too much for them. This was around home. I originally wanted to play tenor saxophone. The guy who impressed me most on tenor was Dick Wilson, with Andy Kirk. With the exception of Herschel Evans, I don't think anybody captured that particular style. It really got to me, but I think the style is lost now.

"I always wanted to play music. I can remember times I used to sit up, or *try* to sit up, to hear Louis Armstrong. He used to come to a club called the Club Forest, out near the Jefferson Racetrack. On a few occasions, too, I heard Earl Hines broadcasting from the Grand Terrace. These bands were my beginning, and later the Benny Goodman and Count Basie bands. They all fed my desire to play tenor saxophone. One day I found some zinc pipes that had elbows on them. They curved like the neck of the tenor saxophone, and the bottom curved up like a bell. In the center there was an extension that came out, another pipe, and I used to put my fingers over this, I used to blow it as you would blow a trumpet, and I'd get tones out of it, all with my lip.

"Soon we formed a little band that played birthday parties in the neighborhood, getting maybe five dollars for the whole band. My brother imitated a trumpet with a kazoo, which he had inserted in a can and fitted with a regular funnel, like a trumpet bell. We had one real instrument, a banjo, which belonged to Ernest Penn, whose father was a minister. Ernest could really get over his instrument, and his solos at that time, to me, were amazing. Then my father bought my brother a Conn cornet, one of those horns with a key on it so you could change to A-flat and back to B-flat. He also bought a clarinet for my sister.

"They began giving free music lessons in the high school, but my brother got so he didn't really want to play the instrument. He fooled with it for some time, but then he would take it away from home, hide it under the bridge, and pick it up on his way back from school. Then it got so he didn't take it at all, and it just laid around the house until I picked it up and learned to play tunes on it.

"Sometimes the Creole Serenaders would rehearse at our house, because my father was more or less the leader. One night I went in the back yard, sat on the steps, and started playing along with them. The musicians heard me and came out to see what I was doing. They suggested to my father that I ought to have lessons. The teacher who started me off was David Jones. He had played saxophone and mellophone on the riverboats with Fate Marable, and he gave me very good backgrounds. He had a band of students, most of them older than me, some very much older. We used to rehearse on Sundays. It was a dance band, but it never worked much. Guys in it used to come and get me for gigs. They were like fathers to me and never let me do anything wrong.

"After the Jones band, I remember working in an uptown section of New Orleans with a drummer called Big Warren, who was always smoking cigars. The piano player was Percy Washington, and we used to rehearse at his house most of the time. We played for dances, picnics, or whatever the occasion was. Many weekends, too, I used to play in small groups at beer taverns—like trumpet, saxophone, banjo, bass, and drums. All this was experience.

"I guess I was seven when I began playing cornet. I've been playing all my life, really! There's a special day in New Orleans called McDonald's Day, in memory of a guy who had donated a lot of money to the public schools. All the schools would go to his monument and lay flowers, and all the school bands would play. Earl Bostic had become bandmaster at my school and had started the first band there. I was a tiny little guy, about eight, and he stood me on a chair to solo on a tune called *Washington and Lee Swing*. It was a march, and I always remember that because it was the first solo I took in public. We gave concerts in several different sections of the city. I guess I was pretty versatile at that age, because I also used to do tap dancing and a little singing at concerts and school affairs. We had a quartet for dancing, and other schools like Hoffman Junior High would send for me and my buddies. We'd walk there, nearly ten miles from our school, but our instructors would let us out maybe an hour early. I've really walked all over New Orleans.

"Our closest neighborhood theater was the Tivoli, in Zion City, but my parents would never let me go by myself. The father of one of my friends owned a truck, and on Friday nights he'd pick all of us children up and take us to the show. There was a Buffalo Bill serial then, and I'd have a fit if I missed a week and didn't know what had happened. The point of this is that the theater started having amateur contests. It was part of a chain in New Orleans, and each week there would be a contest in one of the theaters. So I started at the Tivoli, did nothing but play my trumpet, and won second prize. After that I went to a lot more contests, won five or six first places, several seconds, and some thirds. The older brother of one of my friends used to go with me as guardian and manager. It was a nice little hustle for me, because I was able to give this guy a small fee. By this time I was thirteen or fourteen and going to high school.

"I left New Orleans for the first time when I was fifteen. I had met Allegretto Alexander, a marvelous piano player who had worked with Fate Marable on the *St. Louis* riverboat. He was in charge of the music department at St. Francis Xavier University. I was christened Catholic, and that's where all my background comes from. I think it's a very good background and both my kids are Catholic. I'd like for them to come up in Catholic schools. Although I was still in high school, Allegretto had heard of me and the amateur contests. He also happened to be a very good trumpet player, and he took me out on a tour through Mississippi, Alabama, and Texas with the Xavier University Swing Band. My mother came to see me off that particular morning. We traveled in cars, and if we hadn't had to play a return engagement in Mississippi I would have seen her alive again. She died of heart attack the morning we got back. My sister saw me from across the street and burst out crying. I was very close to my mother, and when my sister told me what had happened I came as close to passing out as I ever did. I remember I went down on my knees, and then I came back up.

"Now after my first year in high school, I had a problem with the Sisters, the school instructors. They didn't think a high school student should play with a college organization. I was also playing jobs at weekends, and sometimes during the week at the Rhythm Club with Henry Horton's band. Then I got a wire from Alabama State Teachers College in Montgomery. A young man from New Orleans who was attending school there had told them about me. It was a state-supported school and they used to give scholarships to musicians and athletes. I finally convinced my father to let me go. He didn't want me to go at first, but I was pretty disgusted after my mother died.

"I was at Alabama State a little more than three years. I was in the band the first summer when it toured all through Ohio and then made the big jump to Chicago, where we played in the Beacon Ballroom. The following year I decided to go home for vacation and stay a while. I went by bus, and while I telephoned my father to pick me up I left my bag outside the booth. Somebody stole it and I was really upset, because he took my horn as well. They finally caught the guy, but it soured me and I went back to school after a week, to play with the band, although they didn't tour that year.

"The band got to be so good before I left that we could go to a town like Dayton, Ohio, when Lunceford and all those bands were there, and *still* have a packed house! We used to copy arrangements from Lunceford's and Basie's records, and we'd have others that some of the guys wrote. I remember one in particular on *Avalon* that Dick Hailie wrote. He later became music instructor at Florida A & M. There was another guy named Handy, a funny looking guy whose parents were at Tuskegee Institute. He came down to Alabama State because it was known to have the best band. As a matter of fact, in Erskine Hawkins's time, before I went there, they had three bands, the Collegians, the Revelers, and the Cavaliers. Just before I left, we had two very good bands, and everybody thought a great deal of my playing ability.

"We used to hitchhike to different towns to hear touring bands, and some of the guys went to Birmingham—about a hundred miles away—to hear Lionel Hampton's band. I had a bad cold and couldn't go, but Leroy Williams (we called him 'Monty Googoo,' and he was Cootie Williams's brother) and Isaac Livingston, who played trombone with the Revelers—they found out Hamp needed a trumpet player and they spoke highly of me to him. Hamp asked me to come up to Atlanta, Georgia, the next night. I didn't have any money, nor did my two friends, but they pawned some of their clothes to get me the fare and some money to go up and let Lionel Hampton hear me. So I took the train up, and Hamp said I was to join the band, but he would let me know when. For months I didn't hear from him. I got my father to get me a card from the New Orleans local, because he was on the board of directors. So I was ready.

"The purpose of college bands like ours was to create funds to help keep the school running properly, because state support didn't represent enough money. The music was just a means to our tuition. I had a place to stay, I had my meals, I had doctor care, and I had my books—I didn't pay anything. My parents gave me spending money and some to buy clothes. But by this time it was in my blood to leave.

"Some of us decided we would form a band from the better musicians in both bands. The music belonged to the guys anyway, because the school only gave us the paper to put it on. We took the arrangements and left. The fact that Erskine Hawkins had done it earlier gave us a little inspiration. We made a contract with Dillworth Attractions, an agency in Atlanta, and they sent a bus for us. I hadn't quite made up my mind to leave then, but the guys packed my bags and carried me bodily on the bus. They also said that if I went I could be leader of the band. So I went, although it was supposed to be Joe Morris' band. Joe was a trumpet player, too, but I fronted the band and was really the leader.

"We got to Miami and played our first date in a club owned by Bill Rivers, a pretty wealthy Negro. When this guy Dillworth messed up some kind of way, Rivers decided to furnish our keep. We worked in his place weekends and he took over the band, buying stands and uniforms for us and putting us in hotels and private homes. He was a wonderful guy. We were there two or three months, and then Lionel Hampton got in touch with me again. So now I didn't know whether I wanted to leave or not. I spoke to Bill Rivers about it, and he said it was my decision to make but he offered to buy me a wardrobe, a diamond ring, and any kind of horn I wanted if I stayed. In the end I decided to go, and I joined Lionel Hampton in Chicago early in 1941. I was eighteen then.

"Lionel had formed his band on the West Coast the previous year, and we had heard it on the air. He had a lot of good men like Ernie Royal on trumpet, Dexter Gordon on tenor, Jack McVea on baritone, Marshall Royal on alto, Ray Perry on violin and alto, Vernon Alley on bass, Sir Charles Thompson on piano, Irving Ashby on guitar, and Shadow Wilson on drums. They had something different, and they were really swinging. But what chiefly influenced me in going with them was Illinois Jacquet. Most of the guys who were from Texas in our band knew him, and they all spoke very well of him and his ability.

"I stayed with Hamp till December 1943, when I went with Basie at the Lincoln Hotel. What encouraged me to go with him specifically was Lester Young and Jo Jones. Hamp's band was at the Famous Door, over the House of Chan, back of Birdland and on Seventh Avenue. The night we closed, Jo Jones came by and said Buck Clayton had to go in the army, and would I come and sit in with the band? Basie decided to keep me, and I worked with his band a year or so until I decided to stay in New York and get my union card. I was with Cootie Williams about a month, and we did theaters in a package deal with Ella Fitzgerald and the Ink Spots.

"During the time I was getting my 802 card, Basie was in California. By this time he had Illinois Jacquet and Shadow Wilson, so when he called me I went out, rejoined the band, and came back with them to New York. I stayed with Basie until Jacquet decided to leave and form his own group, and I went with him. At first there were just the two of us. We'd go to different towns and hire a rhythm section. One night we played a dance for Norman Granz in Washington, D.C., and that was where Leo Parker joined us. He was one of the best modern baritone saxophonists. He used to make it pretty hot for Jacquet, without knowing it. He loved Harry Carney, and Harry would tell him things. Leo really *manhandled* that baritone, but he got messed up, which was a shame. Later he contracted TB and one of his lungs collapsed. He had a tune called *Mad Lad*, and I made several record dates with him.

"After a time, Jacquet wasn't getting enough work, so I went with J. C. Heard's band at downtown Café Society for almost a year. I took George Treadwell's place. It was the last job he worked as a musician before he went with Sarah Vaughan and took over her affairs. J.C. had a very good band: Big Nick Nicholas on tenor, Dicky Harris on trombone, Jimmy Jones on piano, Al McKibbon on bass. We started off well, but a little incident came up when we took off and played a benefit at the Apollo. Barney Josephson, at Café Society, was pretty torn up about it when we got back to the club. J.C. had a six-month contract and when it was up Barney wouldn't renew it. I went back to Jacquet for about a year, and then rejoined Basie in January of '52. I'm still with him, and I've had many happy, lovely days with the band.

"I haven't said much about my own musical influences. The first and biggest, of course, was Louis Armstrong. I went to hear him when I was still in grade school. He was playing at the fairgrounds, and I got on my old man so there wasn't anything for him to do but give me the money to go. Somebody must have told Pops about me, because he gave me a mouthpiece. I also became interested in Fats Waller. They used to play his records on the radio, and my sisters were crazy about him. He was so jolly in his way of putting tunes over. But Louis Armstrong was my first idol, and the biggest influence of my whole career. I liked everything about him—his singing, his playing, and what he played, all seemed very colorful to me.

"After Louis, I guess it was Roy Eldridge, because I had a picture of him on the door at home where I could look at him. I used to hear him on the radio, and they were hopping, one of the hottest groups you could ever hear. When bop, Dizzy Gillespie, and Charlie Parker came along, I realized that what I was hearing was something very advanced, but I didn't quite get with it at first. A lot of it I didn't understand, and some of it I didn't like. But now I think the world of Dizzy and admire him. He's one of the greatest, personally as well as a musician. I like the way he treats me and other people around him. If there's anybody to follow Louis in the public's mind and eye, it will be Dizzy Gillespie, in spite of his clowning.

"I don't like some of the things Louis says and does, but to be his age and still able to do what he's doing today—well, I don't think there's a person living as great as he is. Most of the trumpet players who've come behind him have failed to realize that Louis made it all possible. I'm not trying to get on a soapbox about it, but this is the way I feel. There are guys younger than me who don't feel this way about him, because they don't know what he accomplished and can't see what I've seen through *experience*. There are so few musicians today who could really play in bands like Basie's. They don't have the background, and they haven't had the opportunity to hear the old stuff. There are guys in the band right now who never heard Lunceford's band, and that, to me, seems fairly recent compared to a lot of other things. We have a younger influence in the Basie band now, but the old flavor's still there. The changes mostly reflect the work of the arrangers.

"People throughout Europe are more serious-minded about jazz and not, in general, as prejudiced about it as the American public. A lot of our critics, and the younger fans, frown on older guys like Louis Armstrong. The only reason I see why Basie's band is as well received as it is is because there aren't many other big bands. We've had the opportunity to reawaken the older people's interest, and by surviving we have attracted a lot of youngsters too. We've been criticized in many ways. Some writers have said the band plays good ensemble but doesn't have any soloists. That's usually because they're prejudiced in favor of a more modern type of soloist. But as I was saying about Louis, it took the other styles to make the new styles possible. They couldn't have been if the guys hadn't listened to what went before. From Louis came Roy, and from Roy came Dizzy. Dizzy was imitating Roy at one time. It takes a while for a musician to realize what he really wants to play, what he wants to do on his instrument, and where he wants to go.

"Dizzy is more mature now and knows where he's going. A lot of guys *don't* know where they're going. They're not sure. . . . Some of them don't know the first thing about music to begin with, and then there's the matter of jumping on the bandwagon. A lot of people like Basie because the majority likes Basie. Apart from Duke Ellington's, there are so few other bands really surviving.

"We always play music that can be *felt*. At many places we've played, the people could not dance, but they *wished* they could. It's the beat that really gets under people. Of course, a lot of people want to be critics, but there aren't many critics who have the nerve to say, 'Well, I don't think much of Basie now.' There was one who compared us very unfavorably to the old band and said that we were *nothing*, but he lied, because he'd come in, sit down at ringside, and pat his foot all night! His feeling, when he wrote his article, was just a sentimental feeling.

"Musically, anything that isn't melodic doesn't really impress me. No matter how much you vary music, you've got to have a melodic line somewhere. You don't get over to the ordinary listener if he can't remember some part of what you've played. By the same token, how many of the people who claim an abstract painting is the greatest can tell you what it is?

"There's a type of person who wants to be right all the time, wants to be *with* whatever's happening. So many different types of people follow music. Some do, not because they love it, but because it provides an outlet for them. Like when we play Birdland, a lot of guys and girls come down there of the sportin'-life type. They come because at different times the band has had a following of a lot of chicks that came around not because they like the guys but because they like what we play. I think women are more true in their convictions about music than men are. They're more apt to say what they really feel than men. Then, too, a lot of men who come to Birdland don't give a damn about us, but come to make contacts with those girls.

"People also follow music because they think it's glamorous. I did, too, at one time in my life. But recognizing it for what it is, I love music for what I feel in my heart, not because somebody else likes it. There are some musicians I don't care for, just as there are probably some who don't care for me, but if I can't say anything good, I won't say anything."

(1960)

Preston Love

(ALTO SAXOPHONE)

"I joined Count Basie's band as Earle Warren's temporary replacement on September 6, 1943. Except for the fact that Rodney Richardson had recently taken Walter Page's place, and that Lester Young was absent, most of my early heroes of the band were still there. All of the early Basie aura and atmosphere were intact, and the band was still at an absolute peak. Everything about playing with a 'name' band was new to me, and the six weeks I spent in it were utopian.

"The band was still playing nearly all the great hits from the early years when Basie 'exploded' on the music scene. I owned all his records and had listened to them ecstatically thousands of times. I had also heard them on network broadcasts and in person. It was like being in heaven to play the first alto part on *Swingin' the Blues, Goin' to Chicago, Harvard Blues, It's Sand Man, More Than You Know, One O'Clock Jump,* etc. The first time I played *Moten Swing* with the band, I could hardly restrain my emotion and excitement when Dicky Wells began to blow those incredible and uniquely colorful obbligatos behind me. The other trombone men became a bit annoyed at my youthful enthusiasm as I fidgeted around and exhorted 'Mr. Bones' to 'pour it on!'

"*Moten Swing* had a special meaning for me, because when I was with Lloyd Hunter's band in 1941, Lloyd and some of the older members of the band sharply criticized Basie's recording of the number. They said Buddy Tate's tenor part stood out as loud as the lead alto's in the organ harmony behind Sweets Edison's trumpet solo. They also found it unforgivable for the lead trumpet and lead alto sax to play the same melody notes, doubling together as they did in the last chorus. With all my youthful zeal, I would remind Lloyd and the older guys that it was stupid to become analytical where great art and jazz were concerned. The final product is all that counts, regardless of how the artist arrives at it. And they had to concede that in spite of breaking rules, Basie's *Moten Swing* was beautiful, soulful and that it 'sure did swing.'

"I was barely twenty-two in 1943 and it was understood that I was only 'spelling' Earle Warren. My ability to imitate him closely, my youth, and enthusiasm for the band made me quite a novelty, so that I became a kind of pet with the older Basie band members. I enjoyed that immensely! The more experienced men by this time took for granted such things as the high-class mode of travel, the fancy ballrooms, nightclubs, and theaters, but they were all novel to me. I felt my life and musical experience were absolutely complete when we played a one-nighter at Castle Farms in Cincinnati and I made my first coast-to-coast broadcast. I could hardly believe that Omaha's 'Love Boy' was in Earle Warren's chair, broadcasting over WLW with Count Basie.

"During this 1943 period we played a one-week stand at four theaters and two weeks of one-nighters. My last week was at the Apollo Theatre in Harlem, where Earle Warren played some of the shows and I did the others. At that time it was the ambition of all black musicians to play the Apollo, so naturally I was very excited to be there. An even bigger thrill was in store for me, because Lester Young rejoined the band, taking Don Byas's place. This was my first and only opportunity to work in the same reed section with my favorite tenor sax player, one of the geniuses of jazz history. I could hardly play my part, because I kept glancing to my left to observe Lester and his unique playing pose. We opened with an up-tempo version of *Swingin' the Blues,* and at the first notes of his famous recorded solo the whole house went wild!

"Playing for stage acts as at the Apollo was another first in my musical experience. Backing comedians, dancers, acrobats, magicians, and other kinds of performers was so new and different from playing in ballrooms or for listening audiences. I loved the variety of music and changes of tempos theater acts required. Basie's band put the same feeling and personality into the show music as they did into their own repertoire. To me, in 1943, playing shows seemed to represent the real big time of the band business.

"My six weeks ended all too quickly and abruptly for me. I had just begun to feel comfortable with the repertoire and to relax a bit. In that era, the Basie mystique was probably matched only by that of Duke Ellington's. There was a personal style about everything these two bands did, including their dress, their slang, their humor, and the relationships within the personnel. Earle Warren, or 'Smiley' as he was called, was part of all this, so I couldn't help feeling like an observer. I never really felt like an insider, but my enormous admiration for Earle and the band did give me a special status in the Basie 'family.'

"As an alto man, I also admired other lead men. I rated very highly Willie Smith with Lunceford, Otto Hardwick with Ellington, Hilton Jefferson, Milt Yaner, and a young man I heard with Fletcher Henderson called George Fauntleroy. So long as Willie Smith played in the context of the Lunceford style, I admired him as much as Earle Warren, but when I heard him later with Charlie Spivak, Duke Ellington, and Harry James, he sounded less impressive. In fact, I think Willie played far below his own personal standard in every setting I heard him in outside that of the Lunceford band.

"Apart from who was the best or greatest alto sax man, Earle Warren's sound and conception were for my taste always ideal, but I question whether his style would have fitted the Lunceford band, where the reeds used straight tone without vibrato and put more emphasis on the 'moaning' quality.

"After Earle returned to Basie in late October 1943, I went back to Omaha and worked with Lloyd Hunter a couple of months. Trevor Bacon, Lucky Millinder's singer, had heard me at the Regal Theatre in Chicago with Basie, and he urged Lucky to send for me. On January 4, 1944, I received a train ticket from Millinder, and I joined his band two days later at the Fay's theater in North Philadelphia.

"Millinder's band was not the equal of Basie's, but it was a fine one, and now I had the opportunity to work with Tab Smith, whom I had seen playing third alto next to Earle Warren when Basie played Omaha in 1940 and 1941. I worked with Millinder intermittently until April 1945, and I made my first recording in May 1944 with his band. We made five sides for Decca, including Wynonie 'Mr. Blues' Harris's first records, *Hurry, Hurry* and *Who Threw the Whiskey in the Well?* The other titles, on which Judy Carol sang, were *Darlin'*, *Lover Man*, and *I Just Can't See for Lookin'*. Judy was born Winelda Carter and, like Wynonie, she was from Omaha, so that made three of us.

"When the Millinder band was in New York, I would hang out with Basie's musicians if they were in town, too. I would go down to the Lincoln Hotel or backstage at the theater, wherever they were playing, and I was more awed by the band and Earle Warren than ever. My dream of playing in Earle's chair seemed remote, until one day in the spring of 1945 he told me he was going to leave and form his own band, and that his chair would then automatically be mine. I quit Lucky Millinder in a state of jubilation and went home to Omaha. Basie called me on May 25 and I set out for New York again the next afternoon. My ecstatic family and incredulous friends were at the railroad station to see me go, and it would have been a really triumphant moment if my brothers had been there, but I was the only male member of the Love family in Omaha during these wartime years.

"When I arrived in New York, I took a cab to the Braddock Hotel at 126th Street and 8th Avenue, where I had stayed before. Then I took the subway downtown to the Roxy Theatre, where Basie was playing. The band was on stage and I eased into a place between the curtains only a few feet from the reed section. (The wings of a theater are by far the best vantage point from which to hear an orchestra.) Buddy Tate was nearest me, and when he caught sight of me he nudged the other sax players—Earle, Jimmy Powell, Lucky Thompson, and Rudy Rutherford (on baritone sax). Jimmy had been alto in the 1943 band, and I had worked with Lucky briefly in the Millinder band in 1944.

"There were several new faces in key positions in this wartime Basie band, but it was still fantastic, and still *Basie*. Shadow Wilson had replaced Jo Jones when Jo went in the army, but Basie, Freddie Green, and Rodney Richardson were there as in 1943. Karl George on trumpet and J. J. Johnson and Ted Donnelly on trombones were the only members of the brass new to me. Jimmy Rushing acted as my 'guardian' at this point, and Earle Warren encouraged me about my future in the band, counseling me on negotiations with Basie management. When the Roxy engagement ended, we left for a one-nighter in Johnstown, Pennsylvania. Earle came down to see us off in the charter bus in front of the Theresa Hotel on 125th Street. I detected a little melancholy in his manner, but he couldn't know how happy he had made my life.

"This 1945 band was a formidable group of musicians, but without Jo Jones, Jack Washington, Walter Page, Buck Clayton, and Earle Warren there had to be a difference. I constantly measured my performance against Earle's, and came up very short in my own estimation. I actually resented it when fans and columnists compared me favorably with that great man. One reviewer caught us at a Cleveland theater and wrote: 'At least Basie's reed section has gotten together, thanks to the presence of a fine young lead sax man who replaced the erratic Earle Warren.' I called him the next day and told him that he knew nothing about lead sax, that Earle was the greatest lead man in history, and that to compare me with him, especially in Basie's band, was stupid. After many years and much more experience, I am even more amazed at lead men like Earle and Willie Smith. They are as incredible in their way (of leading a section) as were geniuses like Art Tatum, Lester Young, Charlie Parker, and Clifford Brown in their solos.

"On October 15, 1945, I had the great personal thrill of making my first records with the band at CBS in Hollywood—*Queer Street, Jivin' Joe Jackson, High Tide,* and *Blue Skies.* That night, our road manager handed out a new itinerary for our trip back east. My heart almost stopped when at the top of the list I saw 'Orpheum Theatre, Omaha, October 22–28'! Ever since I was ten years old I had been going to the Orpheum to see all the famous bands and their stage shows—Duke Ellington, Cab Calloway, Erskine Hawkins, Jan Garber, Lucky Millinder, Charlie Spivak, and for the first time, Count Basie. To go from the poverty of the Love Mansion and Omaha's ghetto to the Orpheum stage seemed too far-fetched to a black kid of my generation. Nearly every kid I knew, musician or not, had dreams of performing on that glittering stage some day. The Orpheum simply represented the 'big time' of Omaha.

"I began counting the seconds when the Union Pacific *Challenger* pulled out of Los Angeles and headed east for Omaha. Union Station seemed to be crowded with members of the Love family and friends. They were there to greet me and Buddy Tate, whom they thought of as an ex-Omahan. If Jo Jones hadn't been in the army, there would have been a contingent of his friends there, too. After directing some of the band members to the best rooming houses in the ghetto, I was whisked off to one of the nightclubs on the main street of the black community.

"North 24th Street was buzzing like a bee that night, with Count Basie's band in town and with a night off before the Orpheum opening. I almost got tired of taking bows at the clubs on the 'Avenue,' the term we used for the area of 24th and Lake streets, the main intersection in our part of town.

"My wife and I still maintained our Omaha apartment. She and our three-year-old son had been with me in California for three months, but they had left a few days ahead of the band's departure. I awoke earlier than usual, because I had invited Bill Doggett to breakfast. Being an early riser, he arrived promptly on time at ten A.M. He was traveling with the band as staff arranger, and occasionally Basie would let him sit in on piano. We had our bacon and eggs and set off in good time for the theater. I stopped on the way to pick up some accessories at the Hospe's Music Store, sauntered south on 15th Street, and turned into the alley leading to the Orpheum stage door.

"The movie was on and I could see that the band valet had been there earlier that morning to set up the bandstand before it began. The five chairs for the reed section were on the side nearest me. A lot of friends and well-wishers were standing around, but I finally found one of the better dressing rooms upstairs that Buddy Tate had staked out for himself and me. In a few minutes they called the 'half-hour' before the show so I changed clothes and warmed up my horn. It seemed like no time at all before someone yelled 'All on!' Down the steps and into my seat I went. Then I remember Basie's piano intro to *One O'Clock Jump* and his signaling 'Line Ten,' which meant for the reed section to begin its opening riff on the number.

"All the lights were bright on the stage and the curtain began to open as the moveable stage rolled forward. So here I was before a hometown audience at the Omaha Orpheum Theatre. Blacks were still 'requested' to sit in the balcony of downtown theaters then, but there in the front row were a gang of my life-long buddies, among them 'Brother' Joe Allen, Maxine 'The Red Fox' Parker, Basie Givens, Bernice Donaldson, and Bernard Butler. They cheered and pointed to me, and I could also hear a murmur of excitement from the balcony, where other ghetto friends were seated.

"After a short version of *One O'Clock Jump*, the band launched into an up-tempo number called *B-Flat*. For the next hour, Basie and his stage show had the audience wild with delight. He never gave any special recognition to band members when the band was playing their hometowns. That was the band policy, so I had only a short solo on each of the five daily shows—the eight-bar bridge Earle Warren had played on *Jumpin' at the Woodside* or the one on *Rock-a-Bye Basie*.

"Pop, the backstage doorman, soon learned I was a hometown boy by the visitors who came to see me. He had instructions from the management to curtail the number of people backstage, but he realized this was my moment of glory, so there would always be a crowd of my friends and relatives backstage, in the wings or in our dressing room.

"My mother had purchased a fine home in 1944 with money sent by my brothers, Norm and Dodda, from their army pay, and during the week my sisters gave several huge parties there for the entire Basie band and show cast. At each of these affairs, Jimmy Rushing and

Sweets Edison were the life of the party. What with playing piano and telling jokes, they kept everybody lively. I think of them as two of the cleverest individuals ever in show business.

"The night we closed at the Orpheum, we had to hurry to Union Station to catch a late train to Minneapolis, where we were to open at another Orpheum. I was very excited again at the thought of seeing my brother Dude there, when he would get to hear his kid brother play first sax with Count Basie for the first time. (When the band returned to Omaha the following year, it was an added pleasure for me because my two other brothers were home from the war in Europe.)

"Nineteen forty-six was really the most significant year of my stay with the band, because Jo Jones and Walter Page returned to reunite the famous Basie rhythm section. Jack Washington was back from the army on baritone saxophone, and in some ways this little giant was the greatest saxophonist ever to play in the band. If Buck Clayton and Earle Warren had only been there, it would have been one of Basie's best bands. In the summer of 1946, too, we 'discovered' a young tenor sax man named Paul Gonsalves, who replaced Illinois Jacquet, who had taken Lucky Thompson's place in October 1945. I never felt Paul's style fitted Basie's band ideally, but he was a true virtuoso and we became very good friends. Of course, he went on to distinguish himself in the great Duke Ellington band.

"Perhaps the most overlooked member of the original Basie band was Ed Lewis, the lead trumpet player. Ed played nearly all the lead on the 'classic' recordings when Basie had only three trumpets, Buck Clayton and Sweets Edison being the other two. In person, Buck or Sweets would occasionally relieve Ed by playing the lead on a riff or a prolonged number, but even after Basie added a fourth trumpet, Ed still played a predominant part of the lead.

"Much of the Basie sound was Ed Lewis. He 'grew up' with the original Basie style from Kansas City and captured the essence of the Basie feeling and the Kansas City charm. Ed had a sweet, delicate sound, but he played definitively. Basie's was the greatest swing band with the most relaxed feeling in jazz history, and Ed always swung like no other lead trumpet probably ever did. We always referred to his lead as 'funky,' far before the word came into common usage in connection with rhythm and blues.

'I rate Snooky Young as the greatest of all jazz lead trumpets. For power, finesse, and the ability to interpret a part, he is without equal. But in Basie's band, Ed's lead had a very special quality that fitted the Basie style. I heard Ed and Snooky together nightly for nearly three years, and although Ed was nearing the lower curve of his greatness as a lead man, he still gave a beautiful account of himself on the more characteristic Basie arrangements. He would still 'spit out' the lead on numbers like *It's Sand, Man,* just as he had years before. Then, towards the climax of the arrangement, the younger man, Snooky Young, would take over with high notes on 'shouting' out choruses.

"Ed Lewis gave his all to the Basie band during its rise to the top. He may even have burned his lip out by playing *all* the lead in the young powerhouse band of 1937, 1938, and early 1939. Unfortunately, his kind of dedication was never properly rewarded.

"Nineteen forty-six was really the last 'glory' year for the Basie band of the thirties and forties. Bookings were still good, crowds were still large, and the band still regularly played the most prestigious nightclubs, theaters, and ballrooms. However, storm clouds were brewing. Bebop was becoming the popular craze in jazz, and Basie hadn't had a hit record or anything dramatic happen in quite some time. When the war ended, the country's economy changed drastically. Early in 1947, as if at some prearranged signal, things declined sharply for the Basie band.

"After a tour of the West Coast, we played a one-nighter at a ballroom in Philadelphia on our way back to New York. It was late January of 1947 and the crowd and enthusiasm were much less than when we played there before. Before intermission I noticed a group of young fellows standing attentively in front of the reed section. Occasionally they would whisper to each other. From their manner I judged them to be young musicians from the same orchestra or local clique.

"At intermission, they beckoned me to join them in front of the bandstand. A spokesman for the group said, 'Man, we want to talk to you because you're a young cat. How can you stand playing those old-fashioned arrangements, man? Diz was here with his big band, and that's what's happening! Basie better get hip and get some new stuff. We know if you tell him what's happening, he will listen to a hip young cat!' Then one of them pointed to Buddy Tate. 'They don't play like that anymore,' he said. 'That other tenor man [Paul Gonsalves] can kinda get by, but that old cat has got to go!' The whole group laughed in agreement.

"I was twenty-five years old, the youngest member of Basie's band, but I felt nothing in common with these beboppers. But I did realize that the mania for change and newness in both show business and the music business had finally caught up with even my beloved Count Basie band.

"Looking back to that night in 1947, I wonder how those young musical 'revolutionaries' feel about youth, age, and changes in music now that they must all be in their early fifties. Buddy Tate has survived as a highly esteemed figure in jazz, but I wonder if any of that clique ever made a name for posterity to remember. Buddy always played tastefully in the purest jazz idiom, compensating for a lack of virtuosity with expression, a big sound, a driving beat, and by always telling a meaningful and unpretentious story in his solos.

"Bookings fell off sharply as 1947 progressed, as did the caliber of the places where we were forced to work and the size of the crowds. Some of the better bookings were retained, but there were more one-nighters, unpaid vacations, and 'short weeks' in which we worked less than five days for reduced salaries.

"In early June, Basie called a meeting and announced that summer bookings were few, but that his manager had the opportunity to book the entire summer season at the Club Paradise in Atlantic City if the payroll were reduced to meet the club's top offer. It meant a sharp reduction for all of us, but we agreed to it rather than go through the summer unemployed.

"Although the cost of living in Atlantic City was staggering, by careful budgeting all of us were able to have our families with us to enjoy the resort atmosphere. The hours at the Paradise were brutally long, but we had a fine show complete with Ziggy Johnson's revue and a line of attractive chorus girls. Like a well-conditioned athlete, any band shows the effect of a long location by becoming tighter, and on its better nights, the Count Basie band almost 'burned down' that little Club Paradise.

"Our competition in Atlantic City came from the other main black club, the Club Harlem, which presented the Coleridge Davis big band, Larry Steele's *Smart Affairs* revue, with twelve beautiful chorus girls, Moms Mabley, Billy Daniels, Top and Wilda, Derby Wilson, and others. The musicians and performers from both clubs soon had a wonderful rapport.

"Basie's band had a fine softball team organized by Paul Gonsalves, Jack Washington, Ted Donnelly, Sweets Edison, and me. We played several mornings each week after we got off at five A.M. We played teams from the Harry James, Charlie Spivak, and Louis Prima bands when they were working in Atlantic City. We also played teams made up of bartenders and waiters from the black clubs, as well as teams formed by the black policemen and firemen of the city. I played third base and Paul Gonsalves played shortstop. If you could have combined my ability to catch sizzling grounders with Paul's riflelike throwing arm, we would have had the finest shortstop–third-base combination in jazz. But Paul was prone to miss a few catches, and I always had the worst throwing arm in the world. We won only occasionally, but the games were great fun. The stands would be full of celebrities, because nearly every star of black show business visited Atlantic City during the season. Some of them would play with us for laughs, and after each game there would be a big party.

"Freddie Green, Ted Donnelly, my son, and I went crabbing once a week. We had bought ropes and crabbing baskets, and we would walk several miles to an inlet where we stood on a little bridge and caught hundreds of ocean crabs. Freddie was from Charleston, South Carolina, so he was right at home on the seacoast with crabbing basket in hand! He was also a master swimmer. Emmett Berry, singer Bob Bailey, and I once made the mistake of trying to swim with him in the ocean. The three of us had a frightening time when we found ourselves far out beyond our safe limits.

"Snooky Young, his wife, and three children, C. Q. Price (the third alto man) and his wife Mildred, together with my wife, son, and me, shared a three-bedroom apartment, which reduced our costs to a minimum. The three families worked out the cooking arrangements very harmoniously, considering that there were ten of us in a rather small space.

"The season at Atlantic City traditionally ends with Labor Day, but Basie's management got a booking at the Strand Theatre on Broadway in New York, so we closed at the Paradise on August 22. It had been a surprisingly enjoyable eight weeks.

"Hot Lips Page opened at the Paradise the day after we closed with a hastily put together band. We stayed one day to catch his opening with the same show we had played. Hot Lips had a much smaller group and most of his men were good jazz players, but not adept at reading show music. It was a disaster, though Sweets Edison got up on the stand with his trumpet to help them. Sweets even conducted some of the more difficult show numbers. When he played for dancing after the show ended, Hot Lips rewarded us with some of the richest, purest Kansas City blues I ever heard.

"We opened at the Strand August 25 with the picture *Deep Valley*, featuring Ida Lupino and Dave Clark. We had an excellent stage show with the Edwards Sisters [tap dancers], Lewis and White [Slappy White] comedians, and Pearl Bailey as the headline. This was Pearl's first Broadway appearance and she was sensational. But a weak movie on Broadway meant a short run, so the Strand gig lasted only two-and-a-half weeks. After a two-week 'vacation' without pay, we set out on a string of one-nighters. The Orpheum in Omaha passed this year, but we played a one-nighter at Dreamland Ballroom, where I first saw Basie in 1938 and where I auditioned to replace Earle Warren in 1943.

"This 1947 gig was enjoyable because all my family and hometown friends could stand right in front and chat with me between numbers. Jo Jones and Buddy Tate were still sensations in Omaha, so coming there was a pleasure for them, too. The visit was marred for me by the fact that I had the only argument with Count Basie that I ever had. He called all the members of the band to the office during intermission to discuss salaries for the rest of the tour, and somehow the road manager maneuvered the conversation to make it appear I was being mercenary. I told him and Basie that, if they couldn't pay my full salary, they could leave me in Omaha right then and there. I was contrite afterwards, because Basie seemed surprised and disappointed by my outburst.

"From Omaha we went to Denver for a one-nighter and then to the Rainbow Rendezvous Ballroom in Salt Lake City for a week. The ballroom afforded Basie valuable air time on a coast-to-coast network. I never quite got over the miracle of broadcasting on the networks, which enabled my family and friends to listen to us at the very moment of our performance thousands of miles away. By this time I had made hundreds of broadcasts with Basie, but it remained a novelty to me till the end.

"We went to Los Angeles from Salt Lake City in our private railroad pullman car. Our arrival at Union Station had previously always been triumphant, with crowds of friends, relatives, and fans to greet us. But this November morning in 1947 there was only a handful, although Les Hite, Basie's faithful friend and admirer, was on hand. Les was formerly leader of the top big band on the Coast in the thirties and early forties.

"I realized then that the Basie magic was waning, but there was worse to come. We opened for a week at the Million Dollar Theatre, which had once been an ornate and prestigious venue, but it was on lower Broadway and it had declined. The Orpheum, where we had previously played, was on upper Broadway and was considered a higher-class place. Furthermore, attendance at the Million Dollar was far below what we had enjoyed at the Orpheum.

"Next, we went off for some weeks of one-nighters in northern California, Oregon, Washington, and Vancouver. We played a week at the Golden Gate Theatre in San Francisco. In nearly all these places we had played to enormous crowds in 1945 and 1946. I had also played some of them in 1944 when I was with Lucky Millinder and we played from Seattle down to San Diego. Now we were playing to far smaller audiences than Lucky had drawn. I was alarmed and I felt personally affronted by any serious threat to the sacred Basie 'thing.'

"We returned to Los Angeles for a four-week stand at the Meadowbrook Club in Culver City, which had been the Casa Mañana when we triumphed there in 1945. (Previously, during Les Hite's great days, it had been Sebastian's Cotton Club.) After the first week, the owners told Milt Ebbins, Basie's personal manager, that they couldn't honor the remaining three weeks of the contract because of the miserably poor attendance. Ebbins reached a compromise whereby the band would work only three nights over the weekends. Everybody in the band had to accept a large reduction in salary, and, with Christmas approaching, spirits were very low. The lack of enthusiasm on the part of the fans was also damaging to morale, but this didn't touch me deeply, because I was still with Basie and felt sure something would turn up to improve the band's fortunes.

"On the first night of the last three-day arrangement, I arrived at the club with Jimmy Rushing in the jitney we shared each night. Milt Ebbins was in my dressing room and he motioned for me to closet with him.

" 'Prez,' Milt began, 'Earle is coming back to the band.'

" 'I had heard rumors about that,' I said. 'I even heard the tape Basie made telling Earle that he missed him.'

"Milt became all flustered and protested nervously, 'No, Prez, Basie loves your playing and wants you to stay on and play with Earle. Isn't that what you've always wanted, to play in the same section as your man?'

"I knew the gesture of offering me the third alto chair was half-hearted, because C. Q. Price had become an important member of Basie's arranging staff. I had personally gotten C.Q. into Lucky Millinder's band in 1944, and was instrumental with Buddy Tate in getting Basie to hire him, so I wouldn't have done anything to cause his dismissal, even if I had felt the third-chair gesture was sincere.

" 'Listen, Milt,' I told Ebbins, 'this band is Earle Warren's home. As long as Basie has a band it should include Earle as first alto if he needs a job. Furthermore, I wouldn't play third alto under anyone, including Earle, and I think you and Basie both know this.'

"We could hear Basie signaling the band from the piano, so I asked Milt to excuse me and started to put my alto and its stand together before heading for the stand. As I came around the back of the band shell, I could see Earle Warren hurrying across the dance floor with his sax case in hand, heading for *his* chair in the middle of Count

Basie's reed section. He had arrived in Los Angeles earlier that day without my knowledge. I rushed to greet him in front of the bandstand. We exchanged a few warm words, and within seconds I was listening to the greatest first alto sax man in the world, in the band that was now made complete again by his presence."

(1978)

Marshall Royal

(ALTO SAXOPHONE AND CLARINET)

"Without Marshall Royal," said Sir Charles Thompson in 1961, recalling his days with Lionel Hampton, "it wouldn't have been the band it was. I looked to him as to a father musically, although sometimes his criticism made me so mad I could have cried. Later on, I saw its value. Several of the younger musicians disliked him for it, but they had such poor tones it was pitiful. He told them there was more to it than just blowing their horns, and he taught them about breathing together. He is one of the greatest musicians in the world. He can read any kind of music, play any kind of music, and he is—something few people know today—a genius on clarinet."

Some weeks later, Count Basie and his orchestra were playing at Birdland, a spot recognized as their New York home. While there, they were in the habit of rehearsing once a week. At two o'clock in the afternoon, the club presented a very different picture to that at two in the morning.

Thad Jones was at the piano. One or two musicians were on the stand, the others scattered in little groups at the tables. Benny Powell and Henry Coker were getting their kicks playing music out of a book for tuba by Don Butterfield. Marshall Royal did not appreciate their efforts and called the band together.

"You sound as though you were auditioning for the Salvation Army," he told them.

The band began to run through a new number and soon had the measure of it. Marshall turned around in his chair and gave some instructions: "At the end there, you guys make sure you push that right in tempo, so they don't think you're pulling out on them."

Other members of the band became impatient to give the number a real performance and began to call the leader:

"Base!"

"Basie!"

"Count!"

In answer to the last, shouted through Frank Foster's cupped hands, Count Basie emerged from the washroom in vest and trousers, carrying his electric razor. He bowed courteously to the band and took his seat at the piano.

The rehearsal rolled. Afterwards, at his hotel, Marshall Royal had this to say about his life and times.

"My father was a bandleader and music teacher. He played all the reeds, all the strings, and some of the valve instruments. He was a good musician. My mother was a pianist, and there were instruments around me all my life. I slept behind the piano on the overcoats from the time I was a month old. We had a kind of family orchestra, and my uncle played in it. Outsiders were recruited for the larger engagements, but the nucleus was always the family band. Everybody around my house was a musician, so I had to be one, and I *wanted* to be one. I knew nothing but music. That was it from the go, and I've never regretted it, never a day. I don't know that I could live without music.

"My father started me on violin, and I was very fortunate in being able to get any kind of tutoring I wanted right at home. That is, except in the case of my advanced styling, and then I studied with a graduate of the Paris Conservatory. I loved to play baseball and football when I was a kid, but the utmost in my mind was to be a good musician, and it was part of the deal at home that I always practiced before athletics. I used to practice hard, even when I was only seven or eight years old, sometimes at night after my parents had gone to bed, from nine to one or even two in the morning. The violin isn't loud, anyway, and I would put a mute on it. I'd be there playing what I wanted to play, and I liked it. I guess if I picked the violin up now and practiced for a couple of years I could be a good violinist. It goes, you know, if you don't keep up. It's the hardest instrument of all.

"I gave up the violin when I got into high school and started playing clarinet, and then saxophone. (I played a little guitar on the way, too.) I made the change for strictly economic reasons. Violins weren't popular. I used to play pretty things, and waltzes, on the violin in the orchestras when I first started out. In those days, most saxophone players were violinists who had changed over. Hardly any Negro orchestras were using violins in any capacity. Of course, orchestras like Paul Whiteman's still did, but they were larger, and they were founded on concert principles and on a more legitimate type of playing. The violins could do very well with the type of music that was written at that time. There was no getting hot, loud, and blary. Bands like that would have a full section of four fiddles. People danced then, and there were more waltzes.

"Saxophones hadn't been delved into very far. They weren't very good. They weren't made well. They were using C-melody saxes, rather as a substitute than as an instrument on its own. The real good sound of the tenor saxophone didn't come until Coleman Hawkins produced it. He had a different approach to the sound of the horn. Before him, they'd used a whole lot of wavery vibrato, and slap-tonguing.

"There were a few guys who started playing well on the alto, like Frankie Trumbauer. I was very conscious of him, long before I heard of Benny Carter. There weren't too many Negro orchestras being recorded then. In the early twenties, you could just about count on your fingers all the Negro dance bands that had ever recorded. There was Fletcher Henderson, of course. I can remember getting records of his like *Fidgety Feet* and *Sensation* in 1927. That was a turnover period in jazz then—arranged jazz, rather than everyone taking off for themselves.

"I think Benny Carter has always tried to play correctly, as I have. That may be why you hear a similarity in our lines and formations. I had never even heard a record of Benny's until 1940 or 1941, and I didn't meet him until World War II, when he had a band out on the West Coast. I was brought up there, although I was born in Oklahoma.

"While I was in high school, the music teacher came up one day and said someone called up and wanted a small group to work at the opening of a school market. They told him what *they* wanted, a drum, a saxophone, a trombone, and so on, six or seven pieces.

" 'You play saxophone?' he asked.

" 'Yeah,' I said, although I'd never played one in my life till then. But I'd been playing legitimate clarinet and there were always saxophones at my house. My uncle had a couple of them, and my father had two or three lying around. So I went home and got my dad's alto, and asked him how to play the scale on it. He told me, showed me how to use the octave key, showed me that it was built in octaves, so that once I'd learned one scale, all I had to do was press the octave key and play an octave higher. I practiced for one evening and started playing the next day. They had a platform out front, and music and bright lights to attract people to the opening. We had no arrangements. We just played the popular tunes of the day. One I remember was *Varsity Drag* from *Good News.*

"After that, I went into taxi dance halls, and I worked at night all during the time I was in high school, with different small bands, six, seven, or eight pieces. We'd get off at one or two o'clock in the morning and I'd have to make that class at eight o'clock. Not enough sleep maybe, but you can get a pretty fine education from seeing and meeting people when you're an entertainer. And you can systemize anything. When I got home from school in the afternoon, I would go to bed. I wouldn't run around. If there was a track meet or a hard baseball game, I'd stay out for that, but I'd still try to get home to sleep a couple of hours. I did that all through high school, and I learnt how to get two hours here and three hours there, and I've always done that. That life didn't harm me physically at all. I was always athletically inclined and I tried to keep my body in pretty good condition.

"There are two things that I think are overdone in this world— eating and sleeping. You really don't need as much sleep or as much food as most people get. So far as food is concerned, this is the land of plenty. Quite poor people here often have some of the fullest tables you've ever seen.

"After the taxi dance halls, I started working nightclubs. I'd be sixteen or seventeen. I went pretty fast, because I had a good background, and when I started working with professional musicians, I was competent to do so. I worked with Curtis Mosby, and then I had eight or nine years with Les Hite. With Les Hite, I was a sort of straw boss for the first time. As a straw boss, I rehearse the band. I try to make it sound good, and that's what I enjoy doing. If I succeed, that's another feather in my cap, and I'm very happy.

"I had complete charge of the rehearsing and putting together of Lionel Hampton's big band. I joined him in October 1940 and stayed until September 1942, when I enlisted in the navy and became straw boss of a very, very good band. During the war years, there was a shortage of good men around, and if I hadn't gone into the navy, I wouldn't have remained with Hamp. I would have become rich by being a bandleader myself! By now, I might have retired with my laurels! There were more people getting by with little talent during World War II than at any time in the history of music. There were people who were garbage collectors or street sweepers who went back to music because most of the good musicians were of draft age and in the service. The bands that were on the road during the war weren't too good, and that goes for colored and white bands. The bandleaders on the road were struggling, but you could work day and night if you wanted to.

"When I came out of the navy, I went with Eddie Heywood. The big-band scene had become pretty bad. Why? Well, the band business here has always depended on new dance crazes, but there hasn't been a good dance invented in the last twenty-five years where you didn't need to be a gymnast to do it. On top of that, during the war they took up all the floors with tables to serve drinks, so there was no place for the people to dance. That created a listening audience, which is good in a lot of ways, but if you have no dance, dance bands can't exist. They turned some halls into cocktail lounges and bars, and most of the big ones just went under. Then there was the influx of Latin American bands with their dances.

"Today's young people haven't discovered the big band yet. How're you going to get them to discover it? I wish I knew. You take the kids who came out and heard us at Freedomland. The only thing they ever hear is those six- or seven-piece bands playing rock 'n' roll. So when they hear a big band, it's new to them, but they like it. I think there has to be more in-person and TV exposure of big bands. They should take them for some of those summer TV replacements. That's where Freedomland was very good for music. 'Gee, I like this!' young people were saying. 'Why haven't I heard about this before?'

"I left Eddie Heywood at the Three Deuces in New York and went back to California. I set down at home and only worked recording and studio jobs. I did that for about five years without ever leaving Los Angeles, and I made a very logical-type living. Now young fellows like to go around and jam, and that's fun during a certain period of your life, but after a number of years you look back, you get to be a family man, and you see this guy who went to school with you is now a doctor, and that one is now a lawyer. Each can provide well for his family, and his wife doesn't want for many things, so if you're going to be a real family man, around your mother and your wife, you'd better get down to business and make a real business of this thing. That was how I felt. Although it may become a matter of hard, cold business, you try to get your enjoyment along with your business. Uppermost in your mind is how to have a better type of existence for your family. I try to go about it with a real business attitude, but I'm still doing something I like. I'm doing exactly what I want to do and making my livelihood at the same time.

"I never did much writing. It didn't appeal to me, and then there was the eye strain in writing all those little old notes. I like to play, and to conduct, and to mold an orchestra. That's a different thing. I know enough about arranging and the fundamentals to correct a score, to read a score, and to know what's happening at all times, which is all I'm interested in knowing. So far as doing the writing—that's for the birds!

"I'd like to be sitting in one of those good studio bands in Hollywood, really making it well, because I like to play a whole lot of different things. I don't like just to swing hard all night. I like to play pretty things, too, and I like to play in big bands—thirty or forty pieces— where I have big sounds all around me and different things going on. That's my taste in music. I like contrast. I played in some of those studio bands and enjoyed it very much, but during the time I was trying to invade the field, there were no Negroes in those studio groups. I was one of the first, in the thirties and into the forties. It's a little better now, but it isn't that good.

"When I first came out with Basie, I did it more as a lark. I thought I would come out six months or so and then go back. I took Buddy De Franco's place, playing clarinet with Basie. It was a seven-piece group for about four months after I joined. Then the old Basie standards were revived. The big band was formed and it snowballed. I started to enjoy my work and stayed.

"I consider Basie is a friend of mine and I've always tried to keep my working conditions with him on a level of friendship and respect. In the early stages of the big band, it was just a matter of helping him. I will do anything with anyone I work with that will help to make the job better, easier, and more successful. Basie and I work together on a handshake proposition. I'm not contracted to him. I'm just the same as any other man in that band. Every band has to have a kind of deputy leader and my job may go a little further than that at times. I direct the shows in the theaters, rehearse the acts, put 'em together, and try to keep things going. I've done that kind of stuff all my life and know how it should be done. I just try to do a good job. So many people, who have resented at the time what I've told them to do, have come back in later years and thanked me, and that in itself is some- times enough reward. I remember working with kids like Illinois Jacquet and Dexter Gordon for the first time. I was eight years older than them, and that was a lot when they were only eighteen or nine- teen. I was only in my twenties, but I was a 'veteran'!

"When I joined Basie, I didn't have the least idea I'd be out here on the road, going into my eleventh year, not by any manner of means. In fact, I would have made a wager against that happening.

"My wife lives in L.A. and is very wonderful in her outlook on me. She wants me to be happy and she knows I'm happy when I'm playing my horn. Periodically she visits me, and periodically I go home, but she has been so great about the whole thing. A lot of guys I worked with in the early years, who were very good musicians, were told by their wives: 'I want you at home. If you're going to be a married man, you've got to be at home with me.' Well, the only reason the girl was attracted to the musician in the first place was probably because he was sitting up there on the bandstand playing music. After they get married, she forgets that and wants him home. She says she's lonesome, tells him she wants something secure, and takes him out of the band business 'You get yourself a job in the post office,' she says. 'You work twenty years and you can set down with a pension.' I look at a lot of those fellows and see the unhappiness deep inside them because they couldn't further their musical career. They were supposed to be musicians in the first place. Many of them have advanced well in terms of money, but money isn't everything. You've got to have peace of mind.

"I'm not minimizing the bad side of this. I'd like to be home right now for a couple of weeks, to be around things that are mine, to sleep in my own bed, and not wake up in some hotel room wondering, 'Where am I? What city am I in?' That happens quite often. Just to sit at home and look at my own TV, to ride in my own automobile, and to eat off my own table—that would mean a lot. The band may play on the Coast about once a year, for two weeks, a month. We used to play Vegas, but we haven't done so now for a couple of years.

"This band Basie has had the last eight or nine years has been an exceptionally happy one. They're wonderful guys, some of the nicest I've ever worked with, and there's been very little turnover, so that it's more like a family. We have our little ups and downs from time to time, but it all smooths out. And it's a very mature band. There are no teenagers in it. At this time, there's only one fellow even in his twenties —Al Aarons. He's a very nice boy and a good musician. This isn't a young band and that is one of the reasons for its success. There's enough age in it to give it stability, which is very important if you're going to keep a big band. Nowadays, the average young musician of the new era, who has been on the road three or four years, thinks it's time he became a bandleader himself. And if he's fortunate enough to get one album out, then he's really going out on his own. It's pretty hard to keep a youngster down if he gets a hit going, and I'm not censuring him, because if he can make a quick buck, then more power to him; but you need a bunch of settled people in a big band.

"In a big band, you play what's given you. I sat up in this one three or four years before I was given a solo to play. You don't worry about it. The main thing is to be able to play it when they give it to you. You're not trying to prove anything. It's mostly kids who are always trying to prove things, and that's because they feel insecure. Doesn't that apply in any phase of life?

"All four guys in a trumpet section should be able to play lead. That keeps the weight, the physical strain, off any one guy. The same thing should apply to trombones. There isn't the physical element with the reeds as with the brass, so the reed section may be led nearly all the time by one man. There's just a little more exertion to playing lead. You have to think a little harder and be more precise.

"There aren't many lead altos out now. Mostly the studios grab them. Willie Smith has always been considered an excellent lead alto. George Dorsey is wonderful. He was out on the road with Basie when Lucky Thompson was in the band. Benny Carter and Hilton Jefferson are two of the best. There are a lot of wonderful guys who can play lead alto, but they mostly have white-collar jobs and are not out on the road.

"In this day and age, the bands are at the discretion of the arrangers, and you get so much that is driving, driving. . . . The reason you like *Segue in C* is because some forethought went into it, both as regards the shape of the arrangement and the tempo. Even though the Basie band is expected to drive and shout, you can call one particular number on any dance floor anywhere, in any club or at any concert, and you will get instant applause at the start of the number. Overall, it's as popular as any Basie has in his book. We've been playing it for years —*Lil Darlin'*.

"You find out from requests what people want. A lot of people who come to Birdland would have us blast on every number. Sometimes, when we play a soft, easygoing number, we are almost forcing it on them. They seem to want a feeling of tension. And you could have a great big, roomy place, four times as big as Birdland, and people would stay away in droves. People like to feel all cluttered up. You don't believe it, you get a little restaurant and fine food, just a few stools and only five or six tables, and people will come and stand in line to get in there. When the manager renovates the place, enlarges it so they can have all the room they want, then they'll stay away—in droves. Same thing with music. You give them what they want in a place where they're all close together, and they feel they're a part of it, and they get mass hysteria. A person may come there not intending to enjoy it, but merely to say he's been there. Soon, he's patting like the rest. He's caught something from the people at the next table. But you'd be surprised the requests we get. If we played only requests, we'd play loud, blaring numbers all night long.

"It's strange, but when bands like Lunceford's were playing dances and one-nighters, there was more variety in the music than now, when we have a 'listening' audience. They had to play four or five tempos, and there was a dance for each of those tempos. You would think there would be more variety with a listening audience, but the people are sitting there waiting for something to happen, and it seems that to keep them going you've got to keep driving. Each set gets to be like a performance on its own. Some people only come into Birdland for the last set. They know exactly when to come in. (3:15 to 4:00 is the last set.) We get a lot of musicians at the bar then, but there are also a lot of music lovers who come in at 2:15 to catch the last two sets. Sometimes they're better than the first two, and sometimes they're not. Sometimes the guys are all fired up then, and sometimes they're tired.

"Music, like anything else, has its fads. One year, one instrument is top in the public's estimation; the next year, it's another one. For instance, there was the Louis Armstrong era, when everybody was mad about trumpet. Then you get along to the mid-thirties and it's clarinet —Benny Goodman, Artie Shaw, and a few others. The clarinet won public acceptance and people learned to know and appreciate the instrument's sound. It's almost the same with dogs. A year or so back the fad was for cocker spaniels. Now it's for poodles. Further back, it was for wirehaired fox terrriers, and airedales, and police dogs.

"If the clarinet seems a bit out of fashion now, you have to remember that it is a hard instrument to play. That is, to play freely. Most things originally set up for clarinet were stereotyped and supposed to be played from one certain angle, but when you go to play in jazz, you have to take off in all directions. Then the clarinetist who is not thoroughly prepared on his instrument is always afraid of the squeak. It's a fine type of precision instrument and that squeak is always waiting.

"The reason you hear more squeaks on tenor is because the players are involved in experimentation. They're trying to do something different. To get into something else, they may go beyond the realm of the tenor saxophone.

"I always play Boehm system on clarinet. The difference between the sound of the New Orleans musicians, who played the Albert system, and those who later played Boehm, didn't have much to do with the system. They sounded different because the style of playing and conception of sound were different, but that had nothing to do with the system itself. If they took enough time to learn the Boehm system, they would sound just the same way. The Boehm system is a reconstruction of the old Albert system and it has so many advantages.

"In this era, one instrument that has been really prostituted is the flute. There are guys playing flute parts on recordings who should never be on the instrument, because flute is a beautiful instrument which takes time and a lot of courage to play correctly. Just because a guy owns one and studies for a year doesn't mean he can go out and do a good, acceptable job on it. It doesn't make sense to me. It has become a gimmick in jazz, although there are only a handful of players in the world who can play jazz flute. We're fortunate to have a good one in our band—Frank Wess. There are so many so-called flautists!

"I've always tried to keep an open mind with my music. If you get to liking one soloist too much, you almost invariably tend to dislike someone else. I've tried to sort of space my feelings with regard to soloists by taking the good parts of each and ignoring what I didn't like. I don't necessarily look to reed soloists as my favorites just because I'm a reed player. I like to listen to excellent trombonists, and I like good bassists, and guitarists. I like to go all over the field. I've always tried not to be influenced much by others. There's always a certain amount of anyone that will rub off on you. For that reason, I've never had a record collection. I believe if you listen to one person long enough you'll unconsciously start playing like him. I listen to different people for short periods, so that I won't be taking their soul. That's a bit of a roundabout approach, but most people take it exactly the other way. I don't like copyists. I think each person is supposed to be his own individual self. I enjoyed listening to Charlie Parker very much, but I don't think I would have enjoyed playing what he did, because his line of thinking was different to mine. That's not saying anything he did was wrong. I just didn't want to play the way he did. Through the years, I've enjoyed Johnny Hodges and Benny Carter very much, and some of the things Jimmy Dorsey did. Besides Frankie Trumbauer, I used to enjoy Bix Beiderbecke and Eddie Lang. They had something going and they could play their instruments. I always appreciated Bix's *In a Mist*. He showed a little of his inner self. He had an inner beauty that was all right, and he played good piano.

"I worked with Lawrence Brown on the Coast and I thought he was one of the greatest trombonists that ever lived. He developed an entirely new outlook towards trombone. I never forget a thing he did with Paul Howard in 1929 called *Charlie's Idea*. I was still a teenager then, but I used to follow those bands. There's another trombonist out there I've always admired, a beautiful musician—Murray McEachern. Then I always admired the way Don Byas played tenor saxophone. We used to play and jam around together when he first came out from Oklahoma in the thirties. That's the kind of horn I like. Now Lester was a wonderful stylist, but if I played tenor I would like to play like Don. As for trumpets, there was no one to surpass Pops in his day. Then came Roy Eldridge, and he was wonderful. I like Dizzy and Miles. They all have something to offer.

"I'll eventually go home to California, the place I love the most. The studio position may improve, but a lot of young fellows will have come up. The only thing about those studios is that they want you to be a jack-of-all-trades—alto, tenor, alto flute, bass clarinet, baritone, and so on. I never thought that was quite correct. I thought a man should be hired for what he could do best, rather than for his ability to play a lot of instruments."

(1962)

Lockjaw Davis

(TENOR SAXOPHONE)

I

"You got him!" Count Basie exclaimed, as though relinquishing a not-unwelcome responsibility. "He was talking to me all the way from Idlewild to London."

Eddie "Lockjaw" Davis had just arrived in England for the first time. His tenor solos, sang-froid, and relaxed stage personality soon made him a great favorite with British audiences. During his free hours, he patiently interested himself in the ways of the natives. Maybe they had been doing things in this fashion for centuries, but why? "Theirs not to reason why" was no answer. Davis wanted factual explanations.

A diligent searcher after truth from way back, he admits to being the despair of some of his early teachers. "I didn't want to be told about Columbus discovering America, or America discovering Columbus. 'Where,' I'd ask them, 'did the Indian come from?' Same thing with the pyramids. They'd tell me who built them, when, and where, but they couldn't tell me *how* they were built."

175

An individualist with a naturally nonconforming mind, Davis is also a remarkable conversationalist with a formidable vocabulary. Had writing been his métier, he would have made a great essayist. All one has to do is to suggest a subject, or raise a question, put a suitable jug in a suitable position, and sit back to catch the news in a stimulating form. Some excerpts from a recent dissertation follow.

"Starting an evening, before all the gallant faces that expect a great performance," he explained, "you know you can sway them with a serious look. The public tends to go along with the characteristics you display. If we get on the stand and there's a lot of laughter and discussion amongst ourselves—'What did you do last night?'—the audience tends to feel we are a lackadaisical group, that we're just clowning. Later in the evening, we can get away with it, because everyone has had a few drinks and is feeling more gay. Working in all kinds of groups and with all kinds of fellows, I've found that that first set is the hardest. It's especially hard to get in the mood before a stony-looking audience, one that's considering the kind of tie you're wearing, or whether your shoes are shined. I've known it to unnerve quite a lot of musicians, but as the evening wears on, they become more at ease, more acclimated to the room. What I find very odd is that this may happen after they've been working there every night for weeks before. Sometimes a funny comment or a funny gesture is required to make the fellows relax, because, after all, this is just one out of five sets. What are you going to do for the other four?

"The next amusing thing after that first set is that the people become a little more talkative, and in the intermission they are surprised to discover that you are able to discuss subjects other than music. This astounds them, and brings me to a pet peeve.

"Apart from the fact that he plays an instrument, the audience really knows nothing about a musician. If you take an athlete, a footballer or a baseball player, the fan usually has some idea what the man does in his off-season. He may sell cars or insurance, or he may work for a tobacco firm or a brewery. The fan learns about his hobbies, too. He likes deep-sea fishing, he's interested in electronics, or he teaches in school. All this brings the fan or admirer closer to the performer, and that's what is missing in music.

"Among musicians, for instance, we have intellectual and sportsman-like types. We have some fine golfers like Freddie Green and Sir Charles Thompson. We have many jazz artists who could endorse golf balls, golf bags, and such products, if the manufacturers knew about them. In the same way, we have many musicians who are interested in the technical side of radio. I know one or two who are deeply interested in electronics, and others who have taken the IBM course. Facts like that are never brought out. You are always asked, 'How did you start in music? Did you sell newspapers to buy your first horn? Or did you sell apples, or shine shoes?' That's all people get to know about the musician, nothing about his personal life, nothing about the grown adult except when he violates the law, or something like that. JAZZ MUSICIAN COMMITS . . . the headline says, but when it's a baker, a butcher, or a plumber, the occupation isn't mentioned.

"If a musician saves a dog from the ASPCA, we don't read about that. If he saves a kid from being run over by a car, we won't read about that either. It's just the natural act of a citizen. When his services are required for a benefit, how often is the fact that they're given free mentioned? The distance he had to travel to make it, the sacrifice of a money-paying gig—these are taken for granted.

"The jazz musician in the eyes of the public is a villain!

"He's good copy in that role for the journalist, but if the public were told a bit more about the problems, a bit more about backstage, then I think there would be a higher appreciation of him. Various manufacturers would take a different view, too, and consider musicians for endorsing products.

"Now why doesn't the jazz musician endorse certain products?

"Tobacco, alcohol, and gasoline, for instance, are very much a part of his life, and he has had enough experience to know about differences in quality. Sure there's a difference in gasoline! If I'm using regular, I can get more out of W than out of X, more out of Y than out of Z. The same thing goes for automobiles. When I had that _____, the service was the worst. The musician who's traveling needs immediate service. He doesn't want to wait for parts to come from Detroit. When you deal with _____, they have parts in every section of the country, so this is advantageous to the traveling musician.

"I've certainly been in the business long enough to endorse liquors and beverages! The ones which won't give you hangovers. I have experience *nightly*, and right now I would like to endorse Cutty Sark! I have also had so much exposure to different brands of cigarettes that I really *know* which taste like a cigarette should. I remember how great they used to taste and I know what brings out the flavor. Like they say, 'Come up for a _____.' Don't stay down in this dungeon with the smoke! Who works more dungeons than the jazz musician? He's always in some trouble in smoke-filled rooms. Yes, he knows when to come up! (He knows when to throw up, too, with some of those funny-style beverages!) I mean, don't ask an athlete about cigarettes. He's in the locker room having a shower. How would he know? Ask the musician in the dungeon!

"For the musician who knows he's going to be drinking during intermissions, there are two rules. One, he must drink something he can control or handle. Two, he must select something that will be kind to his stomach, because there's always the next day to consider. I have a program where I drink beer in the early part of the evening. After drinking several bottles, I find I become irritated and agitated, and this agitation is projected through my instrument. I always have an excuse, you see, because if my music sounds offensive I can put it down to the beer, and there is one brand that does make my stomach feel particularly wretched. Later in the evening, I switch to Scotch and milk, but if I started off on this I'd become lazy, too relaxed. I have proof of this. I took my tape recorder and recorded a number of my performances when I varied my drinking program. Yes, really—a scientific project! But haven't you noticed that a group which began very sharp sometimes sounds all dragged out in its later sets? That's because they haven't programmed their drinking. Some, of course, do sound better as the evening progresses and the crowd grows larger, but others just seem to wane.

"One of our trials is the patron who asks, 'When are you going to play my request?' just after you get through playing it. He feels he's entitled to hear a version note for not as on the record, and this difficulty particularly applies to the artist who records with musicians other than those he works with. I think it's very important that a musician who works regularly with a group should at least make some recordings with that group, because then he's equipped to talk to the patron and explain that he does a variety of things, and that the number requested was made with a studio group. It's like people who record with strings. They may get a wonderful effect, but when they go out to work without them, there's a hell of a vacuum. It's amazing how many patrons can't tell a big-band sound from that of a little band. They listen to a soloist on a record and pay little attention to the support, but when they hear him in person, without that support, they decide the soloist himself is lacking something. You hear all these arguments about the critics and the musicians, but the patrons are most ill-informed. They are the ones who pay the bills, so you can't be too harsh with them, but they really know so little.

"You so often hear announcements like, 'Our next number, ladies and gentlemen, answers a request,' and you know it is self-manufactured. Nobody has asked for it. But take Paul Gonsalves playing *Diminuendo and Crescendo* every night, twenty choruses or so. The fact that you have something the people really want to hear—there's nothing awful about that! And it isn't that long. It runs about fifteen minutes, and that isn't so laborious, either. For Paul, it's an outlet, something everyone welcomes in a big band, something you can stretch out on, where the soloist is not restricted to one or two choruses. Even if it's monotonous to the listener, it isn't to the artist, because he doesn't know when he's going to get to solo again. This he welcomes, really.

"I deliberately handle the horn the way I do, to show I'm its master! I've always noticed how delicately so many tenor players handle it, as though it were fragile, as though it commanded *them*. I try to show that I have command of the horn at all times, whether I'm playing or just holding it. You take charge, it's yours, and I want the audience to feel I'm in complete command. Otherwise you can give the impression the horn is too big for you, whether you play it well or not. The visual impression is quite important. Similarly, the guy who acts as though the keys don't work properly, or as though he has a bad reed, gives the public a poor impression. The musician who comes in and must tune up before he plays is only too likely to give a sad performance. The seasoned musician plays and then tunes after his horn has warmed up. Then he gets a true sound. You can tune your horn with your lip, anyway. If I put my horn too far in, I may play sharp, but if I don't take too much of a bite, all will depend on the pitch of the piano. When they start asking for that 'A' before they've even played, you can bet they're relying on nothing but technicalities.

"Working in the quintet with Johnny Griffin, we had two styles. You might have a situation where a guy tried to capture the audience by having a substandard colleague along, but we tried to present two guys who were considered good musicians and could get over their horns. Then it was up to the public to decide which style they preferred, and it gave them a chance to realize the range and capabilities of the instrument, which is why we played all kinds of material. It has been said that the tenor is a sluggish instrument. In fact, Charlie Parker used to say as much when he played with Earl Hines. It was too sluggish for him, but Don Byas proved you can fly with the tenor and still possess full quality. Its potentialities are enormous, and I think the patron got pleasure from making comparisons between two tenors where he wouldn't be able to compare the musicianship of, say, a trumpet and a tenor."

Dutifully skipping the newspaper-apples-shoeshine bit, it can be revealed that Davis began playing for $1.50 a night a few months after he bought his first horn. He joined Cootie Williams in 1942, played with Lucky Millinder, Andy Kirk, and Louis Armstrong, led his own group at Minton's for several years, was with Basie in 1952–1953 and again in 1957.

Largely self-taught, he credited Ben Webster with being his chief influence. Indeed, at one time, when they were playing together, Webster liked to refer to him as "Little Ben." The influence is most apparent on ballads, but at up-tempo Davis is very much his own man, and what Humphrey Lyttelton has termed his "slurred, insolent phrases" give to his interpretations an intensely personal character.

He realized the possibilities of pairing the tenor with organ when he first heard Wild Bill Davis, then playing as a single. He approached him about making records, but he was under contract, so Davis then engaged pianist Bill Doggett to play organ with him on his first tenor-organ session for Teddy Reig's Roost label. The date turned out so well that Doggett, who was accompanist for Ella Fitzgerald at the time, went right out and bought himself an organ. Billy Taylor and Jackie Davis also played organ for Lockjaw, but it was during the three-year period Doc Bagby from Philadelphia was with him that tenor, organ, and drums became a nationally popular combination.

"Nearly all the people who play organ in jazz have been converted from piano," Davis said, "and many of them knew so little they really cheated and exploited the instrument. Basically, it's the same keyboard, and there are only two things you must learn: the stops, which give you variations of sound, and the foot pedal, which is a substitute for bass.

"I got to the stage where I'd had enough organ. It was always controversial, because a lot of people thought it belonged to r. and b., and there's a faction that still refuses to accept the organ as a definite contribution to jazz. I made up my mind to go back to the conventional rhythm section, but rather than use brass I decided to revive the two tenors, because there had never been too much of that on records. There were Gene Ammons and Sonny Stitt, Wardell Gray and Dexter Gordon, but I don't believe any two-tenor unit stayed together so long and traveled the country as much as Johnny Griffin and I did."

(1961)

II

"You must be kidding," Count Basie said as he tore up the new business card he had just been handed.

This was not untypical of the reaction Eddie "Lockjaw" Davis met when he went to work as a booking agent for Shaw Artists Corp. in June 1963. Some of his closest colleagues among the musicians would not take the move seriously and laid bets that the job would not last six months. It would prove too boring, too tiring, or too monotonous.

"Another kind of reaction," Davis recalled, "was that I had a God-given talent and that I showed little regard for it by just stopping playing so abruptly. I had never considered it from a religious aspect. Then some people wanted to know if I was suffering from anything. Did I have some kind of bronchial disorder? Record fans kept dropping me cards. They were so disappointed, they said, and some suggested I was a defeatist. Did the popularity of other tenor players have anything to do with it? Some of the older musicians thought I had made a good decision, but they felt I should not have discontinued playing. They held that I should have tried to arrange my affairs so that I could still play saxophone as well as conduct business. But generally the comedy bit prevailed and Ben Webster even composed a poem for me called *Jaws the Booker*, which went like this:

> *Jaws is booking now,*
> *Jaws is booking now,*
> *Don't offer him a gig*
> *Or he'll blow his wig,*
> *'Cause Jaws is booking now."*

Later, as people grew accustomed to the idea, the repercussions were fewer and quieter. Just occasionally would someone ask Davis, "Are you still there?" or "Have you touched the horn recently?" Still, to many minds Davis's career was mystifying. Why should such a popular musician have ceased playing?

"There were several reasons why I decided to withdraw," Davis said. "And I prefer the term 'withdraw' rather than 'quit' or 'retire.' When you say 'quit' you mean you give up entirely, and when you say 'retire' it usually means you have reached a comfortable financial plateau. Neither applied in my case.

"I withdrew because I found myself becoming stagnant so far as musical progress was concerned. I was repeating a lot. It had to do with the fact that I was playing the same circuit and the same rooms, and that *had* become monotonous. Then I found I had a double job. I had to try to mold the youthful musicians into the type I'd been accustomed to working with. Oversaturation of records with insufficient variety didn't help either.

"Anyway, I began to lack enthusiasm and one club owner openly said I had become lazy. So I decided I wasn't enhancing the industry by my performances and I started thinking about getting into a different area, the booking agencies or the a. and r. field—working with musicians, but not necessarily playing."

The period of transition proved difficult for one who for two decades had worked by night and rested by day. "Acclimating to the other tribe—the nine-to-fivers—was a big problem for some weeks," Davis admitted; but he had an initial advantage in his familiarity with most of the rooms he was booking into and in his knowledge of the general background to the business. The hardest part, for him, was learning office procedure, the way a firm functions, and understanding the minds of those with whom he was now associated.

"It's a different way of thinking," he declared. "When you're working as a musician, you're in contact with people who are big spenders, busy drinking, gay, and out for recreation. In the office, the budget mentality rules with its problems of lunch money and carfare. The people are more settled and determined, and not as gay. You have to adjust to this and it's quite difficult if you've been accustomed to bartenders giving away drinks and all that sort of thing. Here, it was something if anyone gave you a coffee, but they could tell you all about fringe benefits and paid holidays, things I'd never given any thought to before. So now I became a member of the Budgeters Club, and when I went out at night I'd become so inhibited about spending that I was afraid of being called cheap. Yes, I was taking my daytime mentality out at night!"

Shaw Artists Corp. in New York was one of the biggest agencies and it handled such jazz artists as Miles Davis, Horace Silver, Art Blakey, John Coltrane, Sonny Rollins, Sonny Stitt, Roland Kirk, Oscar Peterson, Wynton Kelly, Hank Crawford, Shirley Scott, Milt Buckner, Wild Bill Davis, Bill Doggett, and Jimmy McGriff. Though well acquainted with them and their music, Davis found he also had to familiarize himself with a big roster of rock 'n' roll performers. The Coasters, the Drifters, the Contours, the Vibrations, the Sensations, the Shirelles, and the Miracles were only names to him, but now he had to know what they did, not to mention all the singles like Chuck Jackson, Jerry Butler, Marvin Gaye, Percy Mayfield, Major Lance, B. B. King, Fats Domino, Mary Wells, Gladys Knight, Maxine Brown, Betty Harris, Baby Washington, and Doris Troy. He had to check the record charts to see what hits they had last year and what they had going currently. He had to find out how many were in each group, whether they had any musical accompaniment of their own, and whether they were male or female. He listened to them on records and in theaters.

"Rock 'n' roll people," he claimed, "are active more in theaters and on one-nighters than in clubs. Some attractions appeal primarily to a colored clientele, others to a white clientele. We had one or two clubs with a basically white audience. We could send an r. and r.

group that had a big colored following and they would lay an egg there. And vice versa. We had expensive colored attractions that didn't draw a colored audience. It's a matter of taste and desire, but you cannot afford to make mistakes in that area, because it's costly for the club owner and it places the account in jeopardy. If you send the client a lemon, he assumes it was done deliberately just to raise the commission. When I had my own group, I used to say, 'You can afford a mistake on the bandstand, but you cannot afford one on the highway.' Now I found you could make a mistake in the office, but not one with the client.

"It was difficult, too, to sell an artist without a record. It didn't have to be a hit as long as he had made something. It's never a question of how good you are with a club owner, but of can you draw? A recording artist has a distinct advantage in that respect, but unfortunately there are a lot of good groups that haven't had the opportunity to record, and that makes it difficult to sell them. People used to call me as though I were a miracle worker, because I was aware of talent. When I found an artist with potential, the best I could do was to advise him on one or two record companies to approach."

The agency itself was divided into two sections: the Location Department, which served clubs on a weekly basis, and the One-Night Department, which handled dances and all jobs of fewer than three days. Each section had four agents, among whom the work was divided geographically. Davis was in charge of the East, as far north as Buffalo and as far west as Ohio, in the Location Department. An agent's major objective is always to route attractions in such a way that layoffs and big jumps are avoided. To this end, a booking slip was passed out every night to each agent and posted the next day in the route book. The agents could then see at a glance where each act was playing and know where and when to pick it up. In addition to the route book, there was a master book that showed specifics—the venue and the terms. "My three basic instruments as an agent," Davis explained, "were the route book, the master book, and the telephone."

Because he has a bigger and more detailed picture before him than anyone else, the agent obviously knows best about the general health of the business.

"According to the older hands," Davis said, "they've never seen it this bad, jazz or rock 'n' roll. Jazzwize, there's a combination of reasons. A lot of the club owners have found very few winners. The conduct of many jazz artists hasn't helped—the same old problems like showing up late, but also more profound ones. Jazz at one time was a happy thing, but now it has become so serious, even depressing in some instances. And there are too many experiments going on now.

The experiments should be in the studio, because you cannot expect an audience of musicians every night. Club owners claim there's a lack of entertainment on and off the bandstand. The relationship with the patrons is so distant. The artists stay in the bandroom during intermission or leave the premises, and the patrons feel this. The effect of a small group in a nightclub was to bring the artist and the patron close in a way big bands on a big stage never could. The patrons enjoyed this and it was a success. Today, a lot of them say they're almost afraid to go and ask the name of the artist's latest record.

"This need for entertainment can mean that the music will go in one of two directions. Maybe the older musicians and their values will be accepted again, or maybe the younger musicians will be groomed to realize the need for entertainment. Either way, it doesn't mean you have to become a clown."

Before Davis returned to music and Count Basie, he had begun to grow restless. As an agent, he could not perform before a live audience, but he was able to record and he thought a great deal about this as the backlog of his previously recorded material diminished. Shortly before he took Frank Foster's chair with Basie in 1964, he sized up the situation like this:

"I realize I had just as much security as a musician. My wife went along with my change of occupation because she felt it was important for me to have knowledge of another trade, in case I met with some accident or got so I didn't want to travel, but she prefers me to play. She says my personal habits have changed tremendously, that I have become more serious, more meticulous, and more grumpy. She has had to go through a transition herself, because when I was an active musician a lot of my time was spent on the road. Now she has had to acclimate herself to my grouchy appearance on a daily basis, and after twenty years this has been quite a job. I have really upset the household and all this can be eliminated if I go back to playing! It will only take a few days to pick up on the horn, and there's nothing, really, to compare with the musician's life for fulfillment and activity."

(1964)

Frank Wess

"You can play jazz on any instrument," Frank Wess said, "but you've got to have the feeling and conception for it. Where jazz and the flute are concerned, there's a whole lot more to be done on the instrument. The greatest flute players I've heard don't play jazz, but if we ever arrive at a really good academic flutist with an outstanding jazz conception, then the flute will really be appreciated in jazz."

Since he left Count Basie for the pit of *Golden Boy*, a Broadway musical, Wess had been studying again, and he reluctantly confessed that he had "made some progress." He was equally reluctant to discuss his own role in establishing the flute in jazz, yet there can be no doubt that the instrument's acceptance and popularity were very much due to his presentation as a flute soloist in the Basie band.

"Basie didn't know I played flute when I joined," he said, "but I used to practice during intermission all the time, and he couldn't help hearing me. So he told me to go ahead if I wanted to play any of my tenor spots on flute. The first number I was featured on—and that we recorded—was *Perdido*. Of course, in a band like that you don't have time to warm up. You've just got to pick the instrument up and blow."

Born in Kansas City, Missouri, Frank Wess began playing alto saxophone in 1932. His parents were both schoolteachers, and his father headed a family band. "They were not professionals," Wess said in explanation of his musical beginnings, "but there were always a couple of cornets around." When the family moved to Washington, D.C., he continued playing alto in Bill Baldwin's dance band at the Colonnades. After that, he went into the house band at the Howard Theatre under Coleridge Davis's leadership.

"It knocked me out to see in that issue of *Down Beat* [March 11, 1965] that somebody had heard and remembered Biddy Fleet," he said. "I heard him in Washington and he was a helluva guitar player. He came to New York and played with Bird, and all around, but now everybody seems to have forgotten him. I guess if he'd had more recognition he would still be playing, but he was something else. I heard both Paul Gonsalves and Irving Ashby playing guitar in a New Bedford club a few years later. The guitar went out, but it's back now!"

It was in Washington, too, that pianist John Malachi heard Wess playing alto and suggested he should be playing tenor.

"When I started on tenor, I found I liked it better," he explained. "I went back to alto later only because Basie asked me. I liked Chu Berry and Ben Webster, and I'd known Don Byas from the time I was ten years old in Oklahoma. He went to Langston University, in Oklahoma, and I went out there during the summer, studying saxophone. He had a band there—Don Carlos's—and he always played the same way. But Lester Young impressed me more then. He was my inspiration.

"I jammed with him in Washington, and he showed me a lot of things about the horn, and how to make some of the sounds he got that other people were not making. For a long time I played more like him and sounded more like him than anybody, and I played nearly everything he recorded. Then one day a friend of mine, just a guy who liked music, came around where I was playing matinees in Baltimore.

" 'You know what?' he said. 'You sound just like Prez. You'll never get any credit for that. Everything you play just makes him bigger.'

"That made sense to me, and I gradually changed."

Blanche Calloway's was the first widely known band in which Wess worked. At that time, it included Ray Perry, the violinist and alto saxophonist, and George Jenkins, the drummer. In the army from 1940 to 1945, Wess was with Billy Eckstine during 1946–1947. Gillespie and Parker had left by then, but Gene Ammons, Fats Navarro, Doug Mettome, Shorts McConnell, and, for a while, Miles Davis were in it while he was. There followed a few months with Eddie Heywood, playing alto, tenor, and clarinet. ("I had played solo clarinet in the army, but I didn't care for the instrument.") Next, he played with Lucky Millinder, and then for a year with Bull Moose Jackson. In 1949, under the G.I. Bill of Rights, he began to study flute in Washington, D.C., with Wallace Mann, the flute soloist of the National Symphony, and eventually he got his degree on that instrument.

"I had heard Wayman Carver when those records by Chick Webb and His Little Chicks first came out," he said, "and I was always interested in flute, but then I didn't have a teacher. Carver did quite a bit of flute playing with Chick, but I don't think too much of it was recorded. Cats have really been playing flute forever, you know!"

Wess went on to speak with respect of Albert Socarras ("a beautiful flute player, a legitimate flute player"); of Esy Morales and his flutter-tongued *Jungle Fantasy* ("That was beautiful"); and of contemporary players he likes, such as Sam Most, Jerome Richardson, and James Moody. He was always at pains to make clear a distinction between what is acceptable as jazz flute and what is good flute playing from the academic viewpoint. He liked the alto flute, with which he recorded on the Impulse *Kansas City Seven* album: "It's a little different to play, and it has a nice, warm sound in the lower register, but it doesn't carry as well as the C flute."

When he joined Basie in 1953, Wess was already quite well known to musicians, but his was a new name to the public. "I think Basie first heard me when I was with Bull Moose at Ciro's in San Francisco," he recalled. "We had a pretty nice band then."

He and Frank Foster together perpetuated the image of two contrasting tenor soloists that was an established feature of Basie's presentation, but soon something new was added in the sound and shape of the flute. Basie used the flute increasingly and effectively, but the greatest impression on the public was probably made in *The Midgets* by Joe Newman, where it was complemented by Newman's fast, muted trumpet. Scores by Frank Wess also came to occupy an important part in the band's book.

"I started writing arrangements in the forties," he said. "I went to the Howard University Music School, where they had a fourteen-piece band called The Swingmasters. Some of the musicians in it were Benny Golson on tenor sax, Bill Hughes and Morris Ellis on trombone, Rick Henderson and Emery Pearce on alto sax, Pee Wee Thomas on baritone sax, John Watkins on trumpet, Carl Drinkard on piano,

Eddie Jones on bass, and Bertell Knox on drums. I enjoyed playing with them. Bill Hughes, Eddie Jones, and I went on to Basie, Rick Henderson to Duke Ellington, Benny Golson to Dizzy Gillespie, and Carl Drinkard to become Billie Holiday's musical director. Besides studying at Howard, I had private lessons on the side at the same time, so I knew what I was doing when I began arranging.

"*Perdido* was the first I did for Basie, and I think *Segue in C* was one of the more successful. I did another on *Dancing in the Dark* that I thought was pretty nice, and among the last before I left were a bossa nova and a couple of blues things that haven't been recorded. The more you do, the better you can do it. It makes a difference when you're in a band, because you have that orchestral sound in your mind, and you know what each guy can do. A band personality takes time, but if you grow in it, that helps, too. I'll get back to arranging eventually, but there are a few other things I want to get straightened out first—my instruments, my doubles, clarinet, and bass clarinet. I want to be proficient on them rather than a soloist."

When he left Basie, he knew he was going into the pit band of *Golden Boy*. It was, like, a new life to him, and he liked it. The band, which included Aaron Bell, Eddie Bert, Jimmy Crawford, and Benny Powell, was good. He could live at home, and he had three children, the youngest of whom was to go to high school the following year.

"The chief difference is not so much in the regularity," he observed, "but in the absence of all that traveling. I'd been on the road since 1939, most of the time, and if there were an opportunity for me to go into a studio band, I'd like that. It's mostly section work in the pit, although I have a few little fills on flute here and there. But no jazz. Clarinet is required as well as flute and tenor, and I hadn't played clarinet for almost twenty years. The only reason I can think of why that instrument has gone out of favor is that it is rather difficult to play. Many of the guys who are really proficient on it are not on the road. Marshall Royal can play it, but I don't know that he wants to. I heard that record of *Kansas City Wrinkles* recently, and his clarinet sure sounded good on it.

"Most of the recording I've done since leaving Basie has been transcriptions. I have ideas I want to record. I'd like to do an album of swinging things on flute with muted brass, and tenor with strings, but I've been thinking instrumentally rather than in terms of writing lately."

Conscientious, thorough, versatile, and well schooled, Frank Wess is one of those undemonstrative musicians who are the backbone of the profession and of any band they happen to be in. At one Basie recording session, when Marshall Royal was away, he played all the lead alto parts on a series of new arrangements by Benny Carter. He was quite unruffled, despite the fact that Carter was playing third alto beside him.

(1965)

Frank Foster

"I was very assertive when I came into Basie's band in 1953, until I found out I wasn't as effective as I would liked to have been. I was relatively inexperienced and the band as a unit was very mature, getting on for twenty years old, and I soon realized that I had to alter if I was to fit. I had to learn to bend notes a certain way in order to blend with the section, and the section leader in particular. I had to learn all sorts of inflections on the instrument to blend not only with the reed section but also with the band as a whole.

"In the bands I'd played in before, everybody was on the same age level. When I had my own band, everybody was between the ages of fifteen and seventeen. Everybody was together, phrasewise and stylewise, and whatever other way you can think of. When I came into this band—it was a big break for me—the ages ranged from twenty-four to fifty-four.

"My original influences were Johnny Hodges and Benny Carter. I admired them a great deal and was conditioned to them. I was still in the lesson-taking stage when I was listening to them, but by the time

I really started playing, along came Charlie Parker on a record called *Swingmatism,* by Jay McShann. That was in 1941 and I was thirteen. It came like a natural thing to me, not revolutionary. Then, in 1945, I heard *Now's the Time* and *Billie's Bounce,* and that was the beginning, really, of a new era.

"A lot of fellows who switched from alto to tenor said the only way they could get away from Charlie Parker and go on their own was to switch instruments. I know that so long as I played alto I didn't try to sound like anything but Charlie Parker. But with me the change came out of necessity.

"When I was in college [Wilberforce University], they had two alto players in the band and needed a tenor. So I switched, and I liked it very much because it was different to what I'd been accustomed to for more than four years. It seemed to have more guts to it than the alto. It seemed like switching from a Chevrolet to a Cadillac, and I never got a chance to go back to alto.

"I should say that I started out on clarinet in a school band, a marching band, the football band. Then when I had my own band in my last year at high school, I still played clarinet. It's the best reed instrument to start out on, because it's harder than saxophone. After two years of clarinet lessons, I picked up an alto and played it in a few minutes. That's no unusual accomplishment, although it may sound like it.

"I will never completely escape the influence of Charlie Parker, because he played a little tenor himself and had a very pleasing style on it. I didn't hear him play much tenor, but some of the elements of his style that I absorbed are still evidenced in my tenor playing today. I loved Don Byas, and still do, but Sonny Stitt was the greatest influence. Strangely enough, I wasn't too much influenced by Prez. I didn't come to appreciate him until around 1954 or 1955. I got to know him during that period. He was already over the hill by then. His best playing was from the mid-thirties till the late forties. I was drawn to him through personal contact and on the basis of his early records with Basie. His tone, and the way of phrasing and execution had a lot to do with it, and even if he had lost a lot of what he had, he was always Prez up till the very end.

"But from 1949 to 1951, all I could hear on tenor saxophone was Sonny Stitt. I admired Wardell Gray's playing very much, but he could not penetrate too much because Sonny had me in his grips then.

"The next two years in the army were not a void, although there was not much association with the world of music as we know it. It was good experience and I don't regret it. I got to play quite a bit the last year and a half, in a combo and a large dance band. We played numbers Miles Davis, Charlie Parker, and Dizzy Gillespie had written, and we had a ball doing it.

"I joined Basie in 1953, a few months after Frank Wess. I didn't know how long I'd be there. All I knew was that I *wanted* to be there. Frank's style and tone resembled, say, Don Byas's, and perhaps Lucky Thompson's, whereas I brought to the band what was then referred to as the 'hard bop' style. It had been in the band before, because Wardell Gray played that style. Of course Basie had had Paul Gonsalves for a time, and then Eddie Davis, who gave him a contrast with Paul Quinichette.

"Whereas Wardell and others had fit the band very well, I didn't seem to fit too well with my style. I didn't think so, anyway. Frank Wess was smooth, and I had a little more drive, but there were certain tempos I couldn't fit into at all. I could only fit on the tempo of *Jumpin' at the Woodside*. The older men wouldn't let me do any ballads because I didn't seem to have the tone for them, and even on medium-tempo things I didn't seem to do too well. Much confusion resulted from this through '54, '55, '56, '57, and even maybe through '58. I was torn between styles and didn't consider myself as having one of my own at all. Sometimes I wanted to play like Ben Webster, and sometimes like Sonny Stitt.

"A grown man in his middle twenties is supposed to be going for himself so far as style is concerned. I had outgrown the Sonny Stitt influence and was trying to find something for myself, but what caused the confusion was my feeling that I didn't fit. I groped in the dark, practiced at home, and finally stumbled on a little technique. The end result was that I seemed—to myself—to emerge as a cross between several tenor players, namely, Ben Webster, Wardell Gray, Sonny Stitt, and some of myself. Sometimes I'd play like Ben Webster as a sort of burlesque on the bandstand, and Basie would like it and want me to keep on playing that way. But I couldn't keep it up because I'd always want to go for myself. Lockjaw can do it because that was his natural style. The natural style of Ben Webster and Lockjaw really appeals to Basie, and I guess I was too much from the new school. He called me 'Junior' all the time. I wanted to sound old, in one way of speaking, but I couldn't manage to sound old enough! I really did want to sound *something* like Ben Webster, but I still wanted to be myself! I liked the way he played, I liked that sound, I liked his way of getting over the instrument, and his tone was just beautiful. I've been striving for a beautiful tone for years and years, and it seems as though I'm only now on the threshold of acquiring a tone. I still don't consider myself adequate. I don't think a musician approaches his peak until he's around thirty years of age. He's arriving at maturity, acquiring better, smoother technique, better tone, and everything that goes with that. In his early twenties he's usually more conscious of technique than of anything else.

"The experience of playing with this band has been wonderful and very valuable. It's led me to sit down and try to figure out just what to do with myself. Had I played in small combos I would perhaps have emerged with a more definite style by now, but the mainstream-type influence of the Basie band helped me toward maturity. To a degree, style has to conform to the character of the band, unless you're such a great star that you can build it around yourself. I came to the band a very young man, relatively unknown, and I had to find my own way.

"What I think had a large bearing on the issue was the fact that much of my time was concentrated on arranging. Quite a few arrangers have had much trouble being good arrangers and instrumentalists at the same time. You'll find that most arrangers who play are not exceptional players. There are a few exceptions to that rule, too, but usually something somewhere is sacrificed by those who try to write *and* play. When you concentrate on the writing alone for a month or so, sometimes your playing will fall down, and vice versa.

"I met Tadd Dameron in the early fifties, but by the late forties I was influenced by his writing for ten-piece groups. He recorded a lot of things with a group that included Fats Navarro. What I admired about Tadd was not his unconventionality but the fact he wrote so pretty. His voicings were very beautiful. He wrote for Dizzy Gillespie's big band, and in recent years I've heard he had written things that were very adventurous.

"I wrote a couple of arrangements in the first two weeks I was with Basie. They didn't go too well. The first I wrote that did make it was *Blues Backstage*, and then another called *Down for the Count*. Both were written in the winter of 1953, and both were recorded for Verve.

"I maybe got too ambitious in my early arranging. I didn't want to change the style of the band but merely bring it some very original ideas of my own. Not all of 'em got across. I had had no tuition and was self-taught. My experience, in the beginning, was from playing in big bands around Cincinnati, Ohio, playing stocks and special arrangements by fellows in that area. I listened and analyzed what I was hearing. I had a pretty fair ear for chords and changes. I could pick up bits of knowledge here and there.

"My first arrangement was of *Stardust*, and it turned out pretty good. I wrote it for a big band in Cincinnati in '43 or '44. I didn't know what I was really doing, but they played it anyway. It was just hit or miss from then on, and I gradually developed. By the time I had my own band, I could sit down and write out parts in block harmony and make it sound pretty good.

"During my entire eight years with Basie, I've found that whereas one arrangement is accepted, the next one may not be. Basie himself decides. I've had rejected and accepted arrangements over the whole period! The unforgiveable sin so far as Basie arrangements are concerned is overloading. He will not accept an overloaded arrangement. What he always says is, 'Give me the simple life, baby.'

"There is a new emphasis on fast tempos for showing off technique and creating excitement. A fellow named A. K. Solomon wrote *Blee Blop Blues* and it was exciting to play. It was short—not long or too drawn out, and as a flag-waver it generated tremendous audience response because of all the screaming. It would swing if we played it a little slower, but we just keep it upstairs.

"But I have to say that Mr. Basie has not forgotten the groovy tempos. He still likes them, and flag-wavers remain a minority so far as the repertoire is concerned. The few flag-wavers we play *are* played often, and maybe the book has been replenished with enough groovy material.

"Of my own contributions, one of those I prefer is *In a Mellotone*, although *not* all of the fellows dig it too much. If it's late and they're tired, the trumpet players sort of drop in the closing chorus. But we won't go into that! One of my favorites is *Discommotion*. It's named on the new album, but that track actually is a flag-waver by Ernie Wilkins called *Basie*. A very sad mistake, so far as I'm concerned! I hope it's corrected soon. I don't like someone else to get credit for mine! I want any royalties I receive to be my own, too.

"Others of mine in the book that I like are *Blues in Hoss' Flat*, and then there's *Easin' It*. Basie likes both of those—the groove, the simplicity. There wasn't too much sweat writing *Easin' It* down, so as an achievement it's not much.* It's in that easy *groove* and the performance actually means everything. Sometimes you get a poor performance of a good arrangement because the fellows don't interpret it the way you wanted, or because you can't get across to them *how* you wanted it interpreted.

"In general, our rehearsals are very tiresome because we rehearse too many tunes at one rehearsal. By the time we get to the eighteenth

---

* The album entitled *Easin' It* (Roulette R 52106) makes an excellent introduction to Frank Foster, all seven compositions and arrangements on it being his work. He was also responsible for six of the arrangements on *Count Basie Swings, Joe Williams Sings* (Verve V-8488). Among other valuable works not mentioned above were *Who, Me?* and his most famous composition, *Shiny Stockings*.

arrangement that's been brought in, the fellows don't want to hear anything about how to interpret it! All they want to do is get out of there!

"We have a big turnover, but everything that gets in the book doesn't get played and some things in it get played too much. The turnover of arrangements comes from the fact that we have other arrangers in the band, like Thad Jones and Frank Wess, and Ernie Wilkins is still working for us. Then I like the whole album Benny Carter did for us (*Kansas City Suite,* Roulette 52056). Most of those are wonderful arrangements. He's a brass man as well as a saxophonist, but I think he used to use the trumpets more or less to punctuate the saxes.

"I feel I've neglected the trombone section quite a bit and I plan to do something about that in the future and make better use of the trombones. But three is a hard number to work with. There is so much more that could be done with four.* Ninety percent of the time I've used trombones as part of the brass section, and it doesn't give them enough exercise really. With one more trombone they could be an independent section, although you can get over that by using one or two saxophones with the trombones. No one section is a weak link in this band. Each section is excellent, and they should be featured more, as sections. I'm carrying on a personal campaign now to bring back the reed section, because I'd say in the past ten years reed sections have largely been neglected and brass has been heavily leaned on. I don't intend neglecting anybody in future, but I'm going to show off the reed section more in my arrangements. I don't think we could have a better section leader than we've got now in Marshall Royal.

"I know he plays great clarinet, but for one reason or another the instrument is neglected nowadays and is waning in popularity. In the heyday of the clarinet, of Goodman and Shaw, the flute was hardly ever heard except when Wayman Carver played it with Chick Webb. I guess that was long since forgotten, but in the fifties we had the return of the flute, which I think is a wonderful instrument. I have one. I don't play it well yet, but I shall one day. It seemed new on the scene, and I think the novelty of it appealed to the people.

"I would like to revive interest in the clarinet. There are several good clarinetists around, and it may still be more popular than I know it to be, because I don't keep up with trends unless they are very obvious and all over. I'm going to use clarinet more in the reed section. Whenever I can, I've been snatching a little practice on it, and I'm getting to the point where I can get over the instrument a little

---

* The section was expanded in 1963 and it has contained four trombones ever since.

bit now. I'm going to write a few little simple ditties—no real show-off music—on which the clarinet will be heard. You take *Blue and Sentimental,* on which Prez played clarinet. That is about the extent of what I play at this stage. You don't have to have all technique in the world to get a little color, and I think I can play enough clarinet to vary the shading.

"Neal Hefti, I think, gets more variety in the brass section than he does in the reed section. One nice effect was when he used flute and one trumpet in the harmony and one trumpet in the straight music. Other than that, he hasn't used the clarinet and he hasn't used any different voicings for the reed section other than the straight block harmony. Basie likes the simplicity, but I think you can still achieve a lot of effective color and have the simplicity he likes—and still have arrangements that will please the listeners. Simplicity has nothing to do with lack of color. You don't have to sacrifice one for the other. Color has just been omitted, and that's what we'll have to try to find.

"Perhaps for some listeners there are not enough holes left in the arrangements. If you listen well, you'll find quite a few arrangements we play in which there are some holes left. Basie himself would be mad if there weren't. It's a matter of taste, really. If I think the holes in an arrangement of mine are too filled up, I'll speak to the drummer about it and say, 'Leave it vacant here so the piano can tinkle, or something can happen, or the rhythm can just walk.' If it's too empty somewhere, I say, 'Fill this in.' I haven't really been displeased in this area, although sometimes I feel it could be done with more attention to shading, and a little softer at times. If it were done that way you wouldn't notice it as much as you do. In Birdland, I know, every mistake can be heard. In dance halls some of our mistakes go unnoticed, but in Birdland every mistake is right there, and noticed. Basie is not so fussy about it. We play the same everywhere, whether it's Birdland, the armory in Flint, Michigan, Carnegie Hall, or the Hollywood Bowl, which is for the most part, I guess I'll have to say, loud. But we do know how to shade, and we don't play loud *all* the time.

"Because of the intimate atmosphere in Birdland, if the fellow next to you laughs at you, the people at ringside will know what he's laughing at. I made a terrible mistake last night. I beeped when I should have bopped. I played a note that shouldn't have been there. I was all by myself, and I should have been arrested. Well, that happens. As long as there aren't too many of those to cause the boss to roll his eyes!

"A true jazz fan in Europe is one of the best that you can have sitting out there in front of you, but everybody who comes to listen isn't a true jazz fan. I've seen people bring their whole families, say three or four generations. Probably Grandma and Granddad came out of curiosity, as well as the little five-year-old child. They come and they sit and they clap—what you might call perfunctory applause. They don't always know what it is they're hearing, but they've heard about it and so they come to see what it's all about. Some are always converted.

"The *true* jazz fan in the United States is also an excellent listener, and in the past few years our listening audience has increased—and improved. That is, when we play a dance, there's a larger crowd gathered around the bandstand than before and a smaller crowd off at a distance dancing. Some stand there all night long. That picture has definitely changed from '55, '56, and '57. Jazz listening must have become more universal, because the outdoor jazz concert was something unheard of—by me, anyway—when I first joined the band. A lot of people come to the festival-type thing to listen, and a lot come to do other things."

(1961)

Joe Williams

(VOCALIST)

"My Number One son!"

That is how Count Basie introduced Joe Williams at Basie's seventy-fifth birthday party in Disneyland in 1979. The tall, commanding singer sprang up on stage to a roar of spontaneous applause, and he proceeded to excite an experienced audience of Basie's well-wishers from within the profession.

Although Basie has featured many singers with his band, and has accompanied even more, most of his followers think in terms of two only—Jimmy Rushing and Joe Williams. Since Rushing was a year older than Basie, he could scarcely qualify as a "son," but he was a major factor in the band's success during its early years, just as Williams was in the period that followed the recording of *Every Day* in 1955. The impact of this record was enormous, and Williams was immediately established in the public's mind as a blues singer.

But he had never thought of himself as strictly a blues singer. Although he had gained experience with bands led by Jimmie Noone, Lionel Hampton, Coleman Hawkins, and Andy Kirk before he joined

Basie, his repertoire was the normal mixture of popular songs, ballads, and standards. Rushing's chief successes were the blues he sang, but he, too, featured such songs as *Pennies from Heaven, Exactly Like You, London Bridge Is Falling Down, You Can Depend on Me, I Can't Believe That You're in Love with Me, I Want a Little Girl*, and *Blue Skies*. In Basie's case, the proportion of vocal blues was certainly higher than in those of the other major bands. While most of them played a considerable number of blues, it is curious how few were sung as compared with those performed instrumentally. The biggest hits of some of the more important bands were often blues in one form or another, such as Duke Ellington's *Things Ain't What They Used to Be* and *Diminuendo and Crescendo in Blue*, Fletcher Henderson's *Sugar Foot Stomp*, Erskine Hawkin's *After Hours*, Jimmie Lunceford's *Uptown Blues*, and Earl Hines's *Boogie Woogie on St. Louis Blues*, And there was certainly a profitable lesson to be learned from *Jelly, Jelly*, the Hines hit on which Billy Eckstine sang the blues.

It is important to recognize that social mobility upward had led many urban blacks to regard the blues as low class, as speaking of times and conditions best forgotten. Instrumentally, the blues still meant good music for good times, but the lyrics too often reflected rural origins. References to mules, cotton, and cornbread were not very relevant to city dwellers, except in Chicago, where newly arrived immigrants from the South abounded. And it was in the South, of course, that blues-playing groups like Buddy Johnson's, Louis Jordan's, and Roy Milton's could still tour successfully after most of the established big bands had broken up.

The blues boom of the fifties was largely supported by young whites. They did not, of course, approve of the conditions and hardships that lent authenticity to the accents and delivery of singers from the South, but the grim and often sordid background to the music that they enjoyed undoubtedly gave it savor. In effect, the North preferred the blues of the South and measured authenticity by its Southern and rural characteristics.

Trombonist Quentin Jackson once described the Basie band of the fifties as "a sophisticated blues band." With Joe Williams, the leader added a sophisticated blues singer to it, and then launched him with a song by Memphis Slim, a veteran but not unsophisticated blues artist himself. So evident a success was *Every Day* that Basie's supporters promptly divided into two camps.

"I went ape," said Nat Pierce, recalling the first time he heard Williams at Birdland. "As I was leaving, I met John Hammond coming down the stairs.

" 'Basie got himself a singer,' I said.

" 'Ah, I like Jimmy Rushing,' John answered.

" 'Wait till you hear this cat!'

" 'Nobody like Jimmy. . . .' "

Hammond's preference was not merely a matter of loyalty to Rushing. There was a generation gap, a difference of approach, a different conception of what was or was not authentic, and Joe Williams was well aware of it.

"There were a lot of people like that," he said, "and a lot of critics in England and Europe who were hostile. After the posters went up and signs were stuck on them saying, 'All Seats Sold,' the reviewers would write, 'Most of the applause was reserved for a singer, and he is no Jimmy Rushing,' and so on, blah, blah, blah. It took 'em a long time. It took them years before they finally decided: 'So it isn't Jimmy Rushing. But wait a minute—he's got something to say, and not only that, he says it well.' Some people just have preconceived ideas about things like that. They don't want to hear the band without Prez and Buck Clayton. That's *their* band. It's like when Duke had Ben Webster. 'How can it possibly be as good now?' they'd be asking years later when he had Paul Gonsalves. That's an example, I think, of a closed mind. When Ben himself went in that band, he brought a new sound to it, and I went out and bought those records like *Cottontail* and *Koko* before I'd even got a record player!"

The union recording ban of 1943, a crucial year in jazz history, prevented the preservation of many important musical developments. It may also have delayed the arrival of Joe Williams at center stage by a dozen years.

"Lionel Hampton had a singer called Rubel Blakely, who left Hamp's band in 1943," Williams remembered. "The manager of the Regal Theatre called me and said, 'Hey, I want you to join Lionel Hampton. He's going to pay you eleven dollars a night.' So I went and joined him in Boston. Man, what a band! Oh, my God! He had Joe Morris, Joe Newman, and Lammar Wright, and Joe Wilder was playing lead trumpet. Milt Buckner was playing piano and arranging. He had Arnett Cobb on tenor, Eric Miller on guitar, and George Jenkins on drums. Man, that band was cooking! I was with Hamp two or three months, but didn't get a chance to record because of the ban. Then I went back to Chicago, and I didn't mind, because Chicago was still Chicago in those days. Good Lord, *every*body was making some money!"

It was in Chicago, in 1950, that Williams first sang with Basie, during the period he was fronting a small group.

"I worked with him at the Brass Rail," he continued, "when he had Clark Terry, Wardell Gray, Buddy De Franco, and in the rhythm section, Freddie Green, Jimmy Lewis, and Gus Johnson. Talk about swinging! They'd get into some things that would swing you into bad health! Clark would play *any*thing, and so could Wardell and Buddy. Basie, Freddie, Jimmy, and Gus would just lay it on 'em. That was a lot of fun, and that was where I found out about responding to musical cues. I'd be someplace out in the room, and he'd give me that *ding-ding-ding-ding*. That meant the number might run another five minutes, so go to the bathroom and do whatever you have to do, but be ready to hit the stage as soon as it is over.

"Later on, in the fifties with the big band, when we got those long introductions to tunes, we no longer needed signals like that. *Every Day* had a four-bar introduction plus two choruses—twenty-four bars—and another four-bar interval in front, so I had plenty of time to get on stage for it. That was how Ernie Wilkins conceived and wrote the arrangement, and that's the way it's been ever since. Nobody said, 'Let's have it this way, in case Joe is in the back of the room!' The same thing with *The Comeback*. Basie plays two choruses and then the trombones come in—ba-*ba*-ba-*ba*-ba-*ba*—with that old-time blues figure in the bass, and then it's *I know my baby. . . .*

"Working with musicians like Frank Wess, Joe Newman, Thad Jones, Marshall Royal, and Benny Powell, there was never a lull, and I don't think there ever was a time when we felt we were being put upon or anything like that. You take care of your *own* business, of course. I never had any big problems, because I never felt I needed much, and I used to arrange for money to go home. There wasn't one cat in that band who was a drag. There was real esprit de corps, pride in what we were doing, in getting it right.

"We made some long trips, but they were fun, too. I remember some of the Birdland tours, and one in particular in 1957 when we jumped from Los Angeles to Texas. That was a *looooong* trip! There were no facilities on the bus to relieve yourself, so the bus would make what we called a Pittsburgh stop. We have pictures of all the guys lined up beside the bus, and turned towards it to take a piss. We have pictures of Sarah Vaughan getting out of the bus and running across a field to some bushes for the same purpose. Sometimes, when we were on a tight schedule, the bus driver would just open the door a crack, and we'd stand there and wail and let it go. Because of the companionship, it was a lot of fun, and there were a lot of jokes."

As his association with Basie lengthened, Williams felt a need for new material.

"When I had something new I wanted to do," he said, "I'd go to Basie and tell him, and he'd be so cool all the time.

" 'You don't need more music,' he'd say. 'You've got our arrangements, and you're breaking it up every damn night everywhere we go. What do you need more for?'

" 'I just want some new music,' I'd say.

" 'Well, okay, talk to my guys then,' he'd answer.

"So I'd get with Frank Foster or Ernie Wilkins, have an arrangement made, and do it that very night. Basie would sit there at the piano, look at me, and give me that nod. What I got from that was the knowledge that you have to do what you believe in. Man, you sometimes have to fight the person that's closest to you. You have to fight your *mother* sometimes! And your father! I consider Basie a father, but I had to fight him every inch of the way to get what I wanted."

Nevertheless, there was a time when Basie provoked an addition to the singer's repertoire.

"We were in Boston," Williams resumed, "and we went to a theater where Buddy Johnson and his band were playing. Buddy's sister, Ella, was singing *Alright, Okay, You Win,* and I was just kidding with Basie, talking about the way she was singing it. Later that night we were in an after-hours joint. I always remember that, because it was the first time Sarah Vaughan and I did a duet together. We did *Teach Me Tonight,* just for kicks. We were still sitting there when they played Buddy Johnson's record of *Alright, Okay, You Win.* Sonny Payne and I were kidding about this chick singing her head off. 'She sure sounds funky, doesn't she?' he said. 'Yeah,' Basie said, turning to me, 'and you ought to sing that song.'

"I thought he was kidding me, but he knew how to get my goat and make me angry. 'You ought to sing it,' he added, 'but you probably can't sing it as well as that bitch can.' He has a way of doing things like that, and it works with most guys.

"So I got with Frank Foster and he made an arrangement. I wasn't going to do it the way Ella Johnson did it. It suited her with her little cutesy ways, but it wasn't ballsy, and so far as I was concerned it didn't suit a male vocalist. So I changed it. After I recorded it, the people who wrote the tune recalled the sheet music, rewrote it the way I did it, and now everybody does it that way."

By 1960 the urge to go out on his own and do something different had become compelling. Williams gave Basie six months' notice, and when he left the band early in 1961 he had six months of engagements already set.

"We closed at the Apollo on a Thursday, and Joe Newman and I left the same night," he recalled. "I was to open at the Storyville in Boston the following Monday. Basie was great. He took the time off, blocked the date.out, and we rode up in the club car on the train together. We ate and drank all the way, and when we got out of our cab in front of the Bradford Hotel there was a sign which said *Count Basie Presents* in very small letters and *Joe Williams* in very big letters. Basie introduced me at both shows that night, and then went back to New York.

" 'I knew you'd be all right,' he said before he left. It was really beautiful. He's always been like my Number One fan."

Since then Joe Williams has become an international star in his own right, but the bond with Basie remains strong and there have been many happy reunions.

(1979)

Al Grey

(TROMBONE)

"I see a future in you, Al Grey, but you'll have to listen to me!"

Count Basie and Al Grey sauntered up the street from the club they were playing in Philadelphia.

"Well, okay, Chief," Grey replied.

"I can tell you, but you'll have to listen."

Grey listened, and continued to listen.

"Basie's been in the business so long," Grey said, "He *knows*, he really does know. He gives me ideas on how to play that plunger style. He mentions trombone players from so way back that I never heard of them, but he'll hum, and I'll listen, and when it strikes he'll say, 'That's it!' Like when we recorded *The Rare Butterfly*. He listened to the first playback and said, 'Yes, but I want a little more humor.' Other times he'll say, 'I want you to be more boisterous here,' or maybe 'a little more delicate.'

"I didn't have the feeling at first, but with him as an advisor to me, I do have it now. Trombone players ask me how to do it. It's a matter of how you move your fingers, moving them in and out on the plunger, letting the air leak to form different sounds. What I'm working on now is how to make words out of notes—more talking than 'yes,' 'what,' and 'no.' I think that can be developed quite a lot. The style can be very melodic, too. I listen to singers and often prefer to play more or less like a singer would sing."

Born in Aldie, Virginia, Al Grey came from a musical family. His father started him off on baritone horn when he was only four years old. In his high school band, he subsequently played and became very proficient on the E-flat tuba, but when he joined the navy and was sent to Great Lakes he realized there was no future on that instrument. Knowing bass clef, he decided trombone was the logical horn for him, so he took it up on his own, without regular instruction. "I used to have to get up early in the morning and practice," he said, "because I just couldn't make it." But two trombone players influenced him at that time. One he remembered only as Trombone Smitty from Detroit—"He could play!" The other was Rocks McConnell, who had been with Lucky Millinder. Osie Johnson, who was writing for the band then, also helped him greatly.

When he left the navy, he joined Benny Carter. Like everyone else who worked for him, Grey had the greatest respect for Carter: "He's an accomplished, finished musician, and the biggest thing about him from my point of view was that he taught me how to *phrase*. Then he played all of those instruments, and played all of them well. One day he decided to pick up the trombone. Though I was only a newcomer, I thought I sounded pretty good. So he played, and I was soon saying to myself, 'Well, well, you'd better take note here!'"

Jimmie Lunceford heard and hired Grey about the time Carter broke up his band and went to Hollywood. "I had to take Trummy's solos," Grey recalled, "and I even used to sing his numbers like *Margie* and *'T'ain't What You Do*. Trummy was one of my idols then. He was the first one I thought could really play trombone. I used to play his solos note for note and at that time he played so high I had to find another mouthpiece. I was the youngest in the band and they really had to hold me down. Bebop was popular at that time and they weren't going to have any bebop players in that band! But it wasn't bebop to me. It was just a difference in playing chord changes that had more notes in them, and being more familiar with them."

After Lunceford's death and a period with Lucky Millinder, Grey joined Lionel Hampton's band. Here he found quite a different atmosphere. "The fellows would sit up and clap their hands and pop their fingers, and Lionel would say, 'Gate, eh-eh-eh . . . pop your fingers, gate!' I couldn't see it at first, but it developed a different feeling, a stronger rhythmic feeling. It taught me the more human side of life, to be more jolly in music, something I didn't get with Benny and Lunceford. Theirs was more like the modern approach, more serious, where you concentrate on playing the music and nothing else, but somehow this gave me more feeling, more of what they call 'soul' today. The band had been together long enough to shake down, and there were great artists in it like Clifford Brown, Fats Navarro, Jerome Richardson, Jimmy Cleveland, Benny Powell, and Ellis Bartee. But I think everyone should have that experience, to be around someone who has as much rhythm as Hamp. Lucky Millinder had rhythm, too. He could clap his hands and get a beat that would make you stop and listen."

When he left, Grey went into studio work with Sy Oliver, an experience that reminded him somewhat of his period with Benny Carter. "Sy's was a brain made for music," he said, "and he made everyone stay up on their toes—no relaxing. That kind of work is more of a business matter, of taking care of music, and it can be kind of cold and impersonal, but it was good for me to be working alongside those studio musicians. They have finesse, but, you know, some of them believe Negroes can't play trombone. They say Negroes can play all the instruments *but* trombone. Of course, it's very different from a finger instrument, and I appreciate the difficulties violin players sometimes have, but . . ."

Next, Grey tried it with his own eight-piece group in the South. He accompanied singers like Bobby Blue Bland, Junior Parker, Willa Mae Thornton, Marie Adams, and Gatemouth Brown on Don Robey's record sessions and went out on tour with some of them. The band made good money but had little opportunity to play good music, and after three-and-a-half years he felt he was in a rut. He returned home to Philadelphia, where he at first found himself back in the same r. and b. groove. Then he worked with Arnett Cobb—"We had a nice little band, but we played good music, so we didn't get too much work."

After Cobb's automobile accident, the band dissolved and Grey joined Dizzy Gillespie's big band, in which he was very happy. "Dizzy," he said, "let everybody play, regardless of how well you could play—or how badly. He would give you a chance and let you blow. He brought me back to life really, because I had been hidden away down South so long. It was a family band—really together—and everybody just hated to see it break up." The spirit of gaiety and

humor that emanated from Dizzy was something Grey carried with
him when he joined Count Basie in 1957.

Grey has one of the biggest trombone sounds in jazz. He gratefully
remembers his high school teacher, Harvey Leroy Wilson, who taught
him the nonpressure system. ("It takes the pressure off your lips, but
it is a process," he explained with a grin, "of building the stomach,
which is why the stomach gets bigger all the time!") He feels the
plunger style retains the true character of the trombone, which has
tended to be lost. The production of the low notes at the bottom of the
horn is a function of the instrument, whereas those musicians who
think the idea is to play only high often sound like trumpet players
and lose a lot of color. The plunger up against the bell makes more
pressure and develops strength, which is why, Grey imagined, Cootie
Williams has one of the biggest trumpet sounds.

Plunger trombone has, of course, a long tradition back of it, a fact
acknowledged in the title of Grey's Argo album, *The Last of the Big
Plungers.* How he feels about that tradition, and how he came to help
extend it, he explained like this:

"When I was with Lionel Hampton, he had Sonny Parker singing.
He could holler the blues and he used to make me want to express a
happy humorous feeling. So sometimes I would get to play fill-ins with
Sonny. After I got comfortable with Basie, Joe Williams was singing
the blues one night at the Blue Note, and I was feeling pretty good,
and he hollered something that reminded me of Sonny. So I just
picked up the plunger and made a figuration. 'That's it,' Basie said,
'keep it in!'

"From there on, I started to develop the plunger. Some people think
it's a freak thing, but it's not. It's a development, because you can find
the same notes with the plunger as with the open horn. I think we
need more humor in music today, too, and I try not to play the same
note-for-note solo night after night, because that can become very
boring for the fellows around you. Sometimes I crack 'em up with
something quite different, and sometimes I know Joe Williams wishes
I'd keep the same little things in there so as not to distract him. He'll
turn around and look, but he'll keep on singing!

"I'm trying to set my mind on playing more of the true form of jazz.
I know about the technical side of music, but if you take too much of
jazz away you'll get back to something like symphony. Already some
music they call jazz is so intricate it has no warmth, no personal feeling to the heart.

"Sometimes people say to me: 'You're hamming it up. You're enjoying life too much. It's out of place. That's something that belongs to the past.' Other times when I don't feel so jolly the music can be just as sad. Then they'll ask, 'What's the matter? You're so nasty tonight. Something bothering you?' Sometimes the difference comes from taking a little stimulant. A jazz musician is surrounded by drink all the time, and it can release the emotions and help him to convey a message. It's just not natural to feel and play in the same mood always."

(1960)

Sonny Cohn

(TRUMPET)

"I was born in Chicago March 14, 1925. My father could sit down at the piano and play things by ear, but while he was working at Sears Roebuck, before he went into the Post Office, Omer Simeon persuaded him to buy a trumpet. I heard him tooting on the horn, but although he tried and tried and tried, he never really did anything with it. So he decided to put the horn up and wait till I was old enough to try it.

"When I was about eleven years old I started taking lessons with Charles Anderson, a guy who worked with my father. He used to come out to the house once a week, and I think he played trumpet in some local band that didn't amount to much of anything. Because they worked together, he and my father had a deal going and the charge was only fifty cents a lesson. I would more or less mess around and wouldn't practice, but I had a good ear. 'How does this go?' I'd ask him. He'd play it, and I'd cop my ear on him and play it right behind him. Gradually I got more and more interested. When I graduated from elementary school and went on into high school, I started playing with the little bands. I found out that little girls liked musicians and bands and everything, so I just went on from there.

"I have a brother and a sister, and I'm in between the two. My brother studied clarinet and saxophone, but he never did anything with it. My sister had piano, and she was pretty good. In fact, she can still play, can sit down and read anything she likes. She and I and a couple of other guys in the building where we were living got together and formed a quartet that we called Frances and Her Rhythm Kings. We used to play around at little social affairs on Saturday nights and make two or three dollars.

"One of the guys, Johnny Thompson, became pretty well known in Chicago. He played tenor and would have been a very, very good saxophonist, but he met with an unfortunate accident three or four years ago. I think he was on his way to work and tried to catch a subway train when something happened, and he was killed.

"Guys are funny about girls in a band, so eventually Johnny and I organized an eight-piece group with a piano player called King Fleming. (He has several albums out.) That's when I *really* started getting interested. We used to play a social dance every Wednesday at Union Park. We were still in school and this was indoors, like a field house. Admission was fifteen cents, and kids from all over the neighborhood would come. It started out with the band taking half and the park taking half, but it grew till we were each making about three dollars. That was good for lunch money and other stuff at school. The band began to get very popular, and some of the guys wanted to join the union and some didn't. That was where we came to the parting of the ways. It was still King Fleming's band, and it kept on going.

"At the time Roy Eldridge was working at the Three Deuces in Chicago. I was too young to hear him, but I always looked forward to a time when I would have the chance to work with guys like that. Then a couple of years ago he came into Basie's band and he inspired me very much. Of course, Johnny Thompson and I used to buy *all* his records when we were with King Fleming. I liked to listen to Buck Clayton, Sweets Edison, and Ed Lewis on the Basie records, to Tommy Stevenson, then Paul Webster, and then Snooky Young on Lunceford's. It's been almost like a fairy tale for me. It shows what time will do for you, because I've *played* with a lot of those guys. I've sat with Snooky for years, and I've played with Sweets. I've never played with Buck, but I've listened to him a lot, believe me. Of course, we listened to Duke Ellington's band, and Ray Nance. It's a funny thing, but Ray and I are both from Chicago and didn't really meet until I was in Basie's band, and then it was like we were old friends who'd been knowing each other all the time.

"Right after I graduated from high school, I started working with Richard Fox's band in Calumet City. That's when I got my first taste of playing for shows, and I learned an awful lot from Richard. He's still one of my dear, dear friends, and each time the Basie band comes into town I look up and see Richard Fox sitting in the audience.

"We started buying little stock arrangements when I was in King Fleming's band. There was quite a bit of reading to do with Richard, what with the pieces you had to play for the acts. That's when it really started coming for me. Along with this I was still practicing, but I seemed to spend most of my time getting to and from the job.

"I was still living on the West Side of Chicago, and I'd have to catch a bus at about six in the evening to get out on the South Side in time to meet the car at seven o'clock. We'd get to Calumet City about 8:30, hit at nine o'clock, and play till two or three. By the time I got home it would be six o'clock in the morning! This was seven nights a week. It was my first steady job, so I stood it for about five months, but then it got so I couldn't take it anymore and I had to leave Richard.

"Captain Walter Dyett of Du Sable High School, who taught some of today's great musicians, had a band of professionals who had been to the school. Even though I hadn't been to Du Sable, I worked in that band for over a year before I went in the service for eighteen months. When I came back, I worked with him again. It was like a club-date band. We'd play at the Parkway Ballroom, the Pershing Ballroom, Warwick Hall, and different clubs for social events, three or four nights a week. With this band, and by gigging steady as I did, you could make a nice little taste to live on. Captain Dyett's band was usually ten or twelve pieces—three trumpets, two trombones, three saxes, and rhythm. He made some of the arrangements himself, and he'd buy stocks. It was just a good, commercial band that worked all the time. A dollar was a dollar then, in '43–'45. I learned a lot in that band, and I think the fellow who influenced my playing more than anyone I worked with was Melvin Moore. He was a wonderful trumpet player. He lives in California and he's still active.

"I went in the army at the end of '43 and got out early in '45. They sent me to Fort Custer, MacDill Field, in Tampa and from there to Fort Myers. I was in the engineers, but I never got a chance to do anything because as soon as they found out I was a trumpet player they'd always make me the bugler! But I finally got in the 770th AEF band in Greenville, South Carolina. It was a good band, we stayed in one place, and there was comradeship among musicians. When the band was inactivated, I returned to Captain Dyett for six months and then went with Red Saunders.

"Red had just left the Club DeLisa and it looked like a step up and steady work. He had six pieces, and we worked at the Capitol Lounge for six weeks. Then we moved to the Garrick Lounge and the Downbeat Room, where Red Allen, Stuff Smith, and everybody had worked. We were at the Garrick Lounge for fourteen months, and it was one of the best jobs I ever had.

"Red was an excellent drummer. He had the reputation of being one of the greatest show drummers in the country, but with our six pieces we were more or less an act in ourselves. I guess the people just liked us, because we were drawing good. He had Leon Washington, a *very* good tenor saxophone player; Antonio Cosie was on alto; Mickey Sims on bass; Porter Derico on piano; and Red played the drums. When Cosie left, we got Nat Jones in his place. Nat plays a lot like Johnny Hodges and is just wonderful. He's still in Chicago. Why isn't he better known? Well, a lot of musicians in the Chicago area let music become their second means of income, because they get good jobs and don't want to travel. They have quite a few things coming, like commercials and that kind of stuff, so they can make it comfortably. But they're still good musicians! I think Nat has a good daytime job, but he's still active in the music business and works with one of the gig bands at weekends.

"After Nat came, we went to New York and played at Kelly's Stables for about six weeks in 1946. This was my first time in New York. We made some records that were quite successful, but after two years Red reorganized, formed a twelve-piece band, and went back to the DeLisa. I was there until it closed in 1958, and altogether I was with Red from 1945 to 1960.

"We played mostly show music at the DeLisa. Bill Davis was arranging for the ensembles then. Producers and choreographers are forever making changes up to the last minute, and you have to sit down and write arrangements right then and there. Bill would do that and they *always* came out beautiful. He had come to Chicago from Texas with Milt Larkins's band, and so had Illinois Jacquet. Another wonderful arranger was Marl Young. He wrote the arrangement for Miss Cornshucks's hit, *So Long*, and if I'm not mistaken he did some for Dinah Washington, too. We played things for a whole lot of different singers, like Lurlean Hunter. She's good looking, still sings, and I don't understand why she didn't break through, because everyone—including all the singers—knew how good she was. You could hear her voice on quite a few commercials, like those for White Rain, Campbell's soups, and the Jolly Green Giant.

"At the DeLisa, for her spots she would have arrangements by Osie Johnson and Pee Wee Jackson. They used to collaborate and they turned out some beautiful arrangements. Pee Wee was another excellent trumpet player. He and Freddie Webster worked together in the Lunceford band and were great friends. Pee Wee died too soon, but you can hear him on some of the old Dinah Washington records. One in particular I never forget is *I Can't Get Started*. Pee Wee and his big sound. . . . He and Freddie Webster could *play*. Another very good trumpet around Chicago was Shorts McConnell, who had been with Earl Hines. I think he had the misfortune to lose his mouthpiece. Anyway, something happened to him, because you never hear of him now.

"Chicago had its share of good musicians! You'd be surprised at the number of musicians and entertainers who have been working there for years and years, and you never hear about them. Harold Jones is from Chicago. I had heard of him but didn't meet him till he joined us on drums. I knew about Oscar Brashear because he was a pupil of Charlie Allen, a good friend of mine. Charlie's a very good teacher and makes all my mouthpieces. He was lead trumpet in the Earl Hines band, and right today he can still pick up the horn and hit those high notes.

"George Dixon, who was also with Earl, is another good friend of mine. We all belong to the same lodge. Because of my friendship with people like him, I know far more about the past than most musicians my age. I know more than just the contemporary styles. When the Red Saunders band started up again at the Club DeLisa, we had three trumpets, but for the last six years there was only one—me. We had good trumpet players in that band, like Charlie Gray and Nick Cooper, and I'm not ashamed to admit that I've learned something from everyone I've played with.

"I was working at a place called Robert's with Red Saunders before I joined Basie. They have a five-day law in Chicago—five days' work and two days off. Basie was in town, playing the Regal Theater, when John Anderson got sick. He had taken Wendell Culley's place. Someone called and asked if I'd be interested, so I went down, worked the rest of the engagement, and made a light rehearsal with them after they finished. 'Well, I'll see you,' I said, leaving. This was in November, and a couple of days later I got another call asking if I'd like to join the band on a permanent basis. I said I would, after the holidays. Something like that. Duke used to play the Blue Note before the holidays, and Basie would come in right after. I didn't have a wife then, because I'd been divorced a few years, and I felt I'd been living at home long enough, so I joined Basie on January 19, 1960.

"In the trumpet section then were Snooky Young, Thad Jones, and Joe Newman. I always thought of Joe as a human dynamo. He's always in there driving—always, never no letup. We got to be real close. Thad and I were friends even before he joined Basie, because whenever he came to Chicago he'd always come to the DeLisa. Every Sunday night–Monday morning, everybody would come to the breakfast show, which actually started at 6:30 in the morning. It was a huge place. You could get a thousand people in there. It was the first club with one of those hydraulic floors. When the show was on, the floor would go up, and when it was over it would go down and people could come out and dance. Show people knew it was a place where they could come after they finished work, see their friends, and have a good time. The DeLisa was important. After two of the brothers who ran it died, the other brothers tried to keep it going, but they had their problems. The club is still there under a different name, and it functions, but it's not like it was.

"How was it coming from a seven-piece band to Basie's? It didn't take long to adjust, and it was just the greatest. Especially with that dream section. Every now and then I had to pinch myself and ask, 'Is this really happening to me?'

"Snooky Young and I were friends, too, and we had something in common. We didn't volunteer, but if we were asked we could do it. I think I'm pretty well equipped, and if I'm asked I can cover it. Snooky, that son of a gun, *can* play everything. I sat beside him and was thrilled for two whole years. To me, he's the greatest, and I'll always sing his praises. He's got it! He plays the trumpet the way it *should be played*. We'd sit up there and he would make it just like it was *nothing*, those notes just ringing out of that horn! He thrilled me for two years. Some things trumpet players do, it looks like they're hard. Snooky does them like falling off a log—he makes it *look* so easy. He does everything right. You get out what you put into it, and he must put everything into it.

"When I joined this band, I was called on to do what Wendell Culley did—to play all the pretty things and play the lead on ballads. I inherited the solo on *Li'l Darlin'*, and off and on I would take the one on *April in Paris*. I alternated on *The Deacon*, and when we made the album with Benny Carter, I was assigned the plunger solo on *Meeting Time*. I was real happy about my role. In fact, I still enjoy it, and I've been here for nine years. It just doesn't seem like its's been that long![*]

"Today, the trumpet section consists of Gene Coe, Al Aarons, Oscar Brashear, and myself, and it has been going well over a year. It's a good section and we all get along. There's a fine human relationship. Gene's a very good lead man. Oscar is new, but he's just like one of the guys

---

[*] Ten years later, Sonny Cohn is still there, still apparently happy, and clearly a much valued part of Count Basie's organization.

from the old school, and that's rare in up-and-coming trumpet players. As for Al, he really hasn't had the recognition he should have had. He had been in the band about eight years, and he's like me—another trumpet player who's not pushy. He does what he has to do, but that doesn't mean he can't do more. I don't think there's anything Al can't do on that horn. He's technically gifted and very versatile. In the last couple of years he picked up the flugelhorn, and it's just beautiful.

"All four of us in the section now have flugelhorns. I like the instrument. It's good for solos. You really need a special flugel mouthpiece. A flugelhorn with a trumpet mouthpiece doesn't get that sound. A flugelhorn mouthpiece is deeper and the throat a little bigger. Charlie Allen makes all our mouthpieces and makes the rims the same as our trumpets, so it's the same feel even though the flugel mouthpiece is deeper. That way, going from one to another doesn't present a problem.

"Home is still Chicago, and when we have a week off I can indulge in my hobby, photography. I have my own darkroom and quite an expensive collection of cameras. I like taking pictures of kids. I have a daughter of twenty-five and a granddaughter. There are nieces and nephews, too, who are still young, so I have plenty of subjects to practice on. You don't have to say 'Smile!' You just let them do what they want to do and catch them when they don't know they're being photographed."

(1969)

Eric Dixon

(TENOR SAXOPHONE, FLUTE, AND ARRANGER)

"When I was about eight, I got into a drum-and-bugle corps on Staten Island, where I was born. They had to lie about my age to get me in, because I was small then. I was always interested in the melodic side of music and I started in playing bugle rather than drums, and I stayed in that band until I was about sixteen. I used to get a big kick out of watching the street bands with all the different instruments, and when I was a kid I used to walk beside the saxophone players. The instrument had caught my eye right away and when I was twelve I insisted that my mother buy me a tenor saxophone. I found a teacher who taught me fingering and the rudiments, and I think I caught on pretty quick because I always had a good ear. After a few years, he felt he wasn't qualified to take me any further, so he recommended a teacher in New York and I went to him every week for another five years.

"Music was a kind of hobby for me then and I didn't give it a thought as a way of making money. So long as I was living at home and going to school, I was torn between music and sports. Sport was very strong with me until I went into the service in 1951, and then the fact that I was well up on my horn helped me get into the army band after my basic training. Of the twenty-four months I was in the army, I spent twenty-two in the band at Fort Dix. This was when I realized that if I had gone to a school with a band of more or less this kind, I would have grabbed on to music much quicker. In those two years I really got into it. Sport gradually drifted away and it became music, music, music. . . . So in a way the army made a big turning for me. We played military music, but we also played jazz in the service clubs. Andy McGhee, who was with Lionel Hampton, was in the band, and so was Lou Blackburn, the trombone player.

"It was jazz from the beginning with me. I was an 'old school' lover —the tenor saxophonists like Don Byas, Ben Webster, and Coleman Hawkins. It was their sound and technique I liked, but most of all their sound. Right away, when I hear good sound, I'm captured. I go to hear Duke Ellington for the band and particularly Paul Gonsalves. Sometimes, when he's playing, I just stand there with my mouth open. He has such a wonderful sound, and he maintains it all the time. You occasionally run into a good musician who substitutes technique when, for some reason, he can't get the sound together. I can listen to someone like that for the sake of his technique, but sound is just very important to me.

"When I was in the service, I didn't play with the type of sound I do now, but more like Stan Getz. There was a fellow in the band who had a Don Byas sound, and whenever we were jamming I would notice it. It would overshadow everybody, no matter how well they knew their instrument, and no matter how much they played. When he played and was done, a well-spoken story had been told. So I listened to him and realized he was really taking charge. He was Henry Durant, from Newark, but I haven't seen him for years. I think he would have gone a long way in music had he continued, but he got off the track.

"I thought about music seriously when I was in the service, but when I got out I didn't know of anything I could get into! I had had a job before in a factory, packing dresses up, and they had told me I could go back, but I had decided I'd take a little time off first. The day after I came out, a fellow called me on the telephone who didn't even know I'd been in the army two years. He wanted me for a job at Copa City, Long Island, and it lasted four or five months, six nights a week. Mal Waldron played piano in the group at first, and then Al Richardson (Wally's brother). That was in 1953, but the job kept on going and I worked another in 1954 with Mal, Peck Morrison, and Frankie Brown. Later that year, I started working with Cootie Williams at the Savoy Ballroom. He had six pieces and I was with him seven or eight months. Then in 1955 I went with Johnny Hodges for about his last trip out—about three months—before he decided to go back to Duke. The following year, I was with Benny Green's quintet for a while.

"All this time I had wanted to go to Juilliard on the G.I. Bill, but when I went to the school I found they only allowed about two weeks off. This was at the time I was with Johnny Hodges, and he did a lot of traveling. Although I had wanted to study composition, I figured it was better to be out there, working, and getting myself a little recognized—or hoping to—than being two years in school. Finally, time ran out. You have only so long after you get out of the service. Deep down in my heart I regret it, because though I love to blow, I also want to write music. Although I haven't written for Basie's band yet, I can do it, and I've written quite a few arrangements for big bands, and I have them home. For a short while I used to rehearse a band. Freddie Hubbard and Julian Priester used to come. There were a lot of young fellows and they put the idea of writing to me. I was satisfied with what I did, but although it wasn't hard, a lot of those fellows hadn't had any experience of playing in a big band and they weren't blending together. Then, too, the arrangements were written for fourteen or fifteen pieces, and sometimes only ten guys would come by. Other times, I could have had two orchestra rehearsals a week. There are a couple of my big-band arrangements on Reuben Phillips's U.A. album—*Two by Four, Eric's Flute.*

"Even without a Juilliard background, you can make progress, and I found the biggest help was just listening to other arrangements. Some of the most famous jazz arrangers didn't have much training, because there weren't schools equipped to teach them in their day. Now you have to risk embarrassment to get good. You may write something you think is good, but when you hear it, it's awful. That sharpens you up, makes you get on the ball. It might not be all wrong, but you have to experiment, get laughed at, too, and everything else. My problem is that when I write I need a piano, and I never did have one. You need it when you're experimenting, just to strike a chord and see what it sounds like to your ear. When you have a piano and play it all the time, and you're familiar with the keyboard, you really know those chords you want to play, the voicing and everything.

"With a lot of groups you hear today, the rhythm section starts playing and then a horn comes in, but there's no real togetherness. Anytime there are six pieces and you have three horns, there can and should be an awful lot going on. It's so much better, too, from the fact that if one man has to be replaced you still have music. Of course, I've always liked big bands, but today there aren't enough to give young players experience. I was discussing alto players with some other musicians recently and we came to the conclusion that we knew of no one in our own age bracket—thirty to thirty-two—who could sit down and lead a saxophone section. That doesn't mean there isn't anyone, but men like Marshall Royal, Russell Procope, and George Dorsey are older, and when they were coming up there were a whole lot of big bands. Jimmy Powell is another very experienced saxophone player. Once, when Marshall had to go home on emergency leave, Jimmy took his place for two weeks. He was with Basie in the forties, and he has worked with Machito, Bill Doggett, and Reuben Phillips.

"I like big bands because you can always have something going on. I've been on a lot of dates with arrangers like Oliver Nelson, and Oliver is one of the finest today. I was on those *Afro-American Sketches* sessions, and I thought he did a wonderful job. He keeps very busy now, but he always tries to keep up on his horn. He told me Johnny Hodges and Jimmy Forrest were two of his idols. Before he writes an arrangement, he always likes to hear the group, to see what style will suit it. He asks you what you want. How much do you want happening behind you? He's very capable, and he's always on time with his music, not like some arrangers. He's very sincere, too, and if he gets his foot in the door he'll call the musicians he really wants.

"I also like Billy Byers as an arranger. I was on that Mercury album he did—*Impressions of Duke Ellington*—and it was very good for a studio band, but there's nothing like a band that works regularly together. If I get a band of good musicians, and we work together for a time, and then you get a band of the best studio musicians, your band still won't sound as good as mine. When somebody brings a new arrangement to Basie's or Duke's band, they feel it so much better, because they're accustomed to playing together. When I first joined Basie, I found a lot of things in the music were not written, the different bends and stuff you hear the saxophone and brass sections playing. It was difficult for me at first, because I would go straight ahead when they were bending, but when a new arrangement is brought in now I know what they're going to do. It doesn't take you long, if you can think in that Basie vein.

"That's getting too far ahead of my story. After Benny Green, I free-lanced for years and years. I was in the Apollo band with Reuben Phillips four years, and I always managed to work. Quincy Jones asked me to join at a time when I was working pretty steadily, but before ever I went with him I had been to Europe with Curley Hamner, the Cooper brothers, and Lloyd Mayers. We were with the Josephine Baker show in 1959 and worked a whole year in Paris. When we came back, in the Topa Club on 125th Street, I played tenor, alto, and trumpet. I always played all the saxophone family, but I never studied trumpet. (My brother had one when we were younger—I'm the young-est of four brothers.) At the end of 1960, Quincy was going over to Europe when we were working at the Purple Manor, and that was the trip Jerome Richardson didn't make, so Budd Johnson and I played tenors. It was an enthusiastic band and the book was very interesting. Maybe Quincy tried to do it the hard way, without a singer. Yet the people didn't dance to that band. On the biggest dance floors, the crowd would be packed all around the stand. I enjoyed the group and I stayed with Quincy until it broke up in November, after we were at Basin Street East with Peggy Lee and Billy Eckstine. I joined Basie in December [1961] when Budd Johnson left.

"The difference between Basie's and Duke's band is the greater variety of music that Duke has, but I think Basie's is the more con-sistent band. I've heard people say they've heard Basie's band sound better, but they always add that it still sounds good. Everybody in that Ellington band has a mood, and they have such moods it amazes me how well they can play together. And nobody is going to sound as good as that band when they decide to play. Buster Cooper is in the trom-bone section now and I think it was the right move for him. He's a good trombone player and the experience will help him. He was in Lionel Hampton's band before he joined Curley Hamner, but that's different, altogether different, although just about everybody you ever heard of was in Hamp's band at some time or other.

"Basie's band is another I enjoy being in. Maybe we don't look so interested in what we're doing *every* night, because—you know, one night here, one night there—sometimes we're awfully tired. But it's always pleasing, even if you wouldn't believe it from the facial expres-sions. If it didn't sound good, we wouldn't enjoy it. And I think Basie has one of the finest reed sections. His and Duke's are opposites, but both are distinctive. Before I joined, I could always tell Basie's by Marshall Royal's lead and Duke's by Harry Carney's sound. Harry has a way of playing which dominates the section just enough to give it Duke's distinctive character. Frank Wess is a very valuable asset to Basie's band, too. Quite apart from the flute, he's a good alto and tenor player, and he does a lot for the blending in the section.

"The way I came to take up flute was when I was in Cleveland with Benny Green. James Moody was in town and he spoke to me about flute, told me he would be around the rest of the week, and that I could borrow his, because he wouldn't have time for it. He showed me the fingering and after a week I was sold on the idea. Back in New York, I bought a flute, just a flute, so that I had one, and I kept it for about a year before I really decided to play it. I would carry it around, practice all day, walk from room to room. I practiced so much my mother would say, 'Will you please put that down and go *out!*' Even now I do it, when I'm sitting in my car at four or five in the morning on the ferry that carries you over to Staten Island.

"One night—this would be about 1956—I brought the flute out in Connie's, a little bar across the street from Smalls' Paradise. I was there several months, and, although all the musicians used to flock there, I don't think anybody ever wrote about it. I don't think it seated more than forty and weekends there would be lines of people waiting outside. Anyway, when I played the flute, the people applauded, which they shouldn't have done! I never studied the instrument, but I've learned one thing about it. There's a legitimate way of playing it, but you can't play jazz with a legitimate sound. I can get that legitimate sound—it's not the best in the world!—but it takes away on jazz solos. To get the jazz effect, you've got to bend notes in a way that isn't correct. A lot of things I play on flute now, such as the fingering, are wrong, but they get results and they sound right as jazz. If I went to a teacher, he would turn me all around, because he's naturally supposed to show you the correct method.

"I played clarinet on the Impulse album Basie made with the Kansas City Seven. I never studied that either, but I feel I could play much more if there was more opportunity. I think it's one of the most beautiful instruments in the world, and that's one of the things about Duke's band sound—he's always got those clarinets working. Basie's been using flutes, clarinet, and bass clarinet, too, and it's good, because it gives the band a whole new color. I don't know what it is about the clarinet—a mental block maybe—but it frightens me every time I pick it up. I can play a good enough clarinet solo to get by on, but it's not free the way I want it to be. There's always a tightness that gets me. It's one of the hardest instruments to play, much harder than flute, but the Boehm system is the easier. The fingering in some cases allows you two ways to make it, where on the Albert there's only one. I once talked to Barney Bigard, who has an Albert clarinet, and he showed me how there was only one way to make C-sharp, I think it was. It's difficult to make it on Albert, but after you've been playing as long as he has it comes to you. The way they make clarinets now with auxiliary fingerings and added keys, they've really simplified it.

"Quite apart from solos, the clarinet is so valuable in playing parts. You hear them come in in Duke's band and the whole mood changes. Duke has had a head start on everybody for years with the way he has used clarinets, and plungers, and his different muted effects. I think European audiences appreciate things like color in arrangements. I suppose people here do take jazz more for granted, but I would see the same people quite often in Paris while I was there with Curley

Hamner, and they were *always* interested. I've been over four times and those audiences made an impression on me. When Basie played all those folk parks in Sweden, you might have thought they were country people out there who hadn't heard much, but the funny thing is that they were calling every number we played. They'd call for *Segue in C*, and *Splanky*, and *Corner Pocket*. That *Segue* is a good number for listening or dancing.

"The flute has just been one of those things with me, but I'd like to get with that clarinet. We used to do a sort of life story of Josephine Baker in Paris, so we'd play some Dixieland, calypso, and so forth, and then I got to play clarinet. When we came back to New York, we added a saxophone and I used to write arrangements for the three horns. Curley still has the book. I'd very much like to do an album with four horns, and that's the kind of band I'd like to have one day, but where would we work? I know when I got into Basie's band, after being with Quincy, that I thought to myself, 'You know, you're pretty lucky working all the time like this!'

"I've always believed in being dependable, because I've been on gigs which were, shall we say, too cool. If a leader calls me and I accept it, then I'll be there, and usually ahead of time. I hate that being-late feeling. If I come in late, I can't do anything right. I feel wrong, even at a rehearsal. When I was working at the Apollo, I was nearly always the first one there, although the other fellows lived in New York and I came from Staten Island. I might be sitting there a whole hour, just doing nothing, but I was relaxed, which I wouldn't have been if I'd come running in at the last minute.

"And, yes, I have a nickname—'Big Daddy.' It began with my girl friend, and then the Cooper brothers started calling me by it. I always thought somebody told Quincy, but it just came to him, too, and now everybody calls me that. If ever I get a chance to make my own album, that will have to be the name of it!"

(1963)

Bobby Plater

(ALTO SAXOPHONE AND ARRANGER)

"In Newark, where I was born [in 1914], I started going to the theater when I was about twelve. I'd go three or four times a week—sometimes I'd sneak in—and usually I'd sit in the front row. I liked the sound of the saxophone and I used to get as close to the lead alto man as I could. They had only three saxophones in the band then, but I'd sit there all day and just listen to him. This was before I'd taken up an instrument, but I was there so much that it got so he knew me. His name was Clarence Adams, and he used to turn around and wink at me.

"A friend of mine had a brother who played saxophone, and I used to go to his place and listen to him practice. I told my father about it. (He used to play drums for what they called 'block' dances, when they roped off a portion of the street and had three or four musicians.) He got me a saxophone for a Christmas present, and my mother paid for the lessons.

"I studied and practiced regularly for about three years. After I found I could play a little bit, like most musicians I didn't want to

223

practice any more. So I stopped taking lessons, but I discovered later I should have gone on. There are certain things I'd like to do that I'm not able to do. That is, in the technique department. Then I took up clarinet, but I didn't study it long. Just enough that I could play a little on it. After all, you had to double. You couldn't get into a big band unless you did.

"I started out professionally by playing what they called 'house rent parties' in those days. Sometimes they called them 'parlor socials.' If you were short of the rent, you'd have little cards printed up that announced you were having a house rent party Saturday night. You'd hand them around among all your friends and neighbors. Usually, they'd have about three pieces playing. I'd get about three dollars, and the money they made they used to pay the rent. This gave me experience, and I got into everything I could get into. I was around seventeen, but I didn't work any steady job, just gigs. Don Lambert, the piano player, used to play at those rent parties sometimes, all by himself. He was very good, in a class with James P. Johnson and Art Tatum. He'd go from one place to another and sit in. He stayed right in Newark. That's where he liked to be, where he liked to play.

"I first got into a professional band when I joined a nine-piece local group called the Savoy Dictators. It was a good band, ten years ahead of its time. We made some records for Herman Lubinsky's Savoy label right there in Newark [*Rhythm and Bugs*; *Tricks*; *Heyfuss, Geyfuss*; *Jam and Crackers*]. Count Hastings, who was later with Louis Jordan, was the tenor player. The trombone was Howard Scott, and he was very good. We had two trumpets, Harry Mitchell and Chippy Outcalt. Chippy plays trombone now. The piano player was Clem Moorman; Willie Johnson was on guitar; Al Henderson on bass; and Danny Gibson on drums. They were the best musicians in New Jersey at that time. Chippy Outcalt and Clem Moorman did most of the arrangements, but I learned to get my hand in there and once in a while I threw one in.

"I never had any schooling in writing but picked up things as I went along. I wish I had had some tuition. Another hindrance is the fact that I can't play piano. If I could play piano, I could write more. I can hit a few chords, of course, but when I write I don't know what it is going to sound like till I hear it. So I am limited, and there are only certain things I can do.

"The Savoy Dictators worked in Newark and the vicinity, and occasionally we played New York. When the Depression came along, some of the guys had to take other jobs to make it. For about a year we had a ballroom in Newark called the Savoy. We soon had a good following and were at least able to pay our expenses, but in the end the band folded because we just couldn't keep the guys together.

"I was more interested in playing lead than soloing, so the guys I listened to were Earle Warren and Willie Smith. When I first heard Benny Carter, he was playing trumpet in a band of his own. I had gone to audition with another band on Broadway, and it was not until later that I listened to Benny on alto. I heard a lot of Johnny Hodges, and I was influenced by him also, and in those days I was more active as a soloist.

"When our band broke up, Count Hastings, a couple of others, and I had an offer to join Tiny Bradshaw. He was a road man and he had a band of about thirteen pieces, his singing being the feature. It was a good band, but we sort of took over the style of it because he had our key men playing all the lead.

"We played mostly in the South, all the way out to Texas, and ended up in Chicago. I'd had offers before to go on the road, but I'd never had the nerve. I used to hear about fellows getting stranded, and things like that. I stayed with Tiny about three years, and then I went in the army from 1939 till 1942. I was attached to an infantry outfit for three months' basic training, and then they put me in a band. Usually in an army band you just play marches and things like that for parades, but with an infantry outfit you have other duties. They took the whole division out to Fort Huachuca in Arizona, where they put me in charge of what they called the B orchestra, and left me to do the best I could.

"We had fourteen pieces and I enjoyed it, because military life can become monotonous, especially if you've been accustomed to playing music. Every now and then we'd go out and play a dance, so this was a good outlet. We went overseas to Italy and the Mediterranean Theater.

"As soon as I got back, I received a wire from Lionel Hampton. I guess he'd heard of me from men in his band who had been with Tiny Bradshaw. Herbie Fields was leaving and he needed someone to take his place. I went in as lead alto. Arnett Cobb was straw boss then, but when he left, about two years later, I became straw boss. I stayed with Hamp eighteen years. He had a good band, and I was satisfied with him. I was never one to jump around and make changes so long as things were going right. I'm not hard to get along with.

"Apart from Billy Mackel, the guitar player from Baltimore, I guess I was the guy who stayed with Hamp longest. There's nothing but good you can say about Billy. I didn't play many solos in those days and I didn't worry about it. I was content to play the lead and try to make everything go right. I had taken up the flute in the army, and I was ahead of the fashion when I played it with Hamp. I didn't do too much with it, but I still played it with Basie. The only time I play clarinet now is when we're playing for singers. The band doesn't play the arrangements with clarinet parts anymore. I think one of the big reasons why clarinet went out is because it is such a difficult instrument, and saxophone players just didn't want to be bothered with it. Just to play it straight is difficult, so that discouraged them, because they all want to solo. Then, too, arrangers stopped writing for clarinet. The only band today that features them is Duke Ellington's.

"The arrangements I wrote while I was with Hamp were mostly vocal arrangements, like for Sonny Parker, who sang blues and ballads. Except for a couple Hamp wanted, I didn't get around to writing instrumentals.

"When I left, it was because we weren't working enough and I couldn't make ends meet. He still had a large band, but every weekend we went to work there would be different men. So then I had an offer from Basie and I've been with him ever since.

"Two of the arrangements I've written for him are *Happy House* and *Tidbit*, and both of them have been recorded. I solo on the first, Al Aarons and Basie on *Tidbit*, which was more of an experimental dance arrangement. I'd never written for the band, so I just thought I would like to see how it would sound. I had done *The Hour of Parting* for Charlie Fowlkes before I joined the band, and I gave it to him, but we haven't rehearsed it yet. There are so many we haven't rehearsed—a book full of arrangements that just lay there! I've got another one called *Laughing in the Sunshine*, a hillbilly tune that sounds so much like *Can't Stop Loving You* that I put it on a commercial kick. We ran over it once.

"The most writing I'd done in years was when Lockjaw [Davis] approached me and asked me to write for an album he was going to record for RCA [*The Fox and the Hounds*, LSP 3741]. It was a few weeks before he left Basie, and it's pretty hard for me to say no to people. The good part was that he told me at a time when I didn't have to rush. It's hard when you're on one-nighters, better when you're on location. But when I have something to do, I go ahead and do it. I don't fool around and wait till the last minute. So I started on his project right away and had it done in plenty of time. The tunes were mostly standards like *When Your Lover Has Gone*; *Out of Nowhere*; *Bye, Bye Blackbird*; and *People Will Say We're in Love*. He had seventeen pieces and I thought the dates came off pretty well.

"I always get a kick out of Benny Carter—anything he does, playing or writing. I like Quincy Jones and Billy Byers, too. Of Hamp's arrangements, I liked Milt Buckner's the most. He was a genius. Eric Dixon is doing most of the arrangements for Basie now, and he's very talented. So is Frank Foster, who did *In a Mellotone*. Anytime you want to write an arrangement, as often as you want to, it's all right with Basie, but I don't feel I'm really qualified. I don't have the knowledge and I never did really try to write anything original, but Basie finally got eight out of me! He asked for eight, but I said I couldn't do all that. 'Well, do two for me,' he said. I did those, and then he asked for two more. 'You better ask somebody else,' I said, but he got two at a time until he had eight altogether!

"For me, it's very difficult if you're writing a whole album. You start repeating yourself when you write consecutively. The same things keep coming back to you. The writer needs time to do something else in between. It's just like a guy who gets up to solo, takes four or five choruses, runs out of ideas, and starts repeating himself. You're in one bag and you can't get out of it.

"My future? Well, I don't ever expect to be a great writer. My style, of course, was formed before Charlie Parker, but I still like to play. I'd like to stay with Basie.* I like being with this band, and I've always liked his bands since way back in the thirties. I hope they can continue to do some great things and that I can be a part of them. Sweets [Edison] has been a big asset since he returned to the band. He fits. A man can be a great musician in his particular bag, but not everybody necessarily fits this band."

(1966)

---

* Still with the band in 1979, Bobby Plater had become one of its key men, an able deputy and musical director who would conduct the band as necessary when the leader was at the piano.

Richard Boone

(TROMBONE AND VOCAL)

Count Basie used to introduce Richard Boone as "a man of very few words." Before those familiar with Basie's own terse conversational style could laugh, he completed the introduction by saying, "He has a message he wants to lay on you!"

Boone's message, hip, sly, and very amusing, was delivered in English, in his personal Boone language. It was the wittiest form of scat singing heard in many a long day, and his versions of *I Got Rhythm* and *Boone's Blues* provoked a hilarious reaction. On the blues, to everyone's surprise, the mountain jacks of Booneland yodeled instead of hollering.

It seemed that in Boone Basie had discovered someone who could partly fill the void left by Joe Williams. The singer was also a very capable trombonist, both in solo and ensemble, but unfortunately he stayed with the band only three years. After he recorded an album in Hollywood for Nocturne in 1969, all too little was heard of this talented artist.

"I was born in Little Rock, Arkansas, on February 23 or 24, 1930. There were no hospital records, and for eighteen years I celebrated the 24th as my birthday, but when I went in the army I had to get a birth certificate and the certificate said the 23rd. My grandmother assures me they got it wrong, that it was a weekend and when the midwife reported the birth on Monday she got the dates mixed up.

"My mother and grandmother sang in church, the New Hope Baptist Church, and that's where I began singing spirituals and hymns when I was five or six. I don't know anything about being a prodigy or anything like that, but I was considered pretty good. Until I was ten or eleven, I would go from church to church to sing solos. Different churches used to visit each other in those days with their choirs and featured singers.

"When I got to be twelve, I went to a high school that covered from the seventh to the twelfth grades. I started in the seventh, and that's when I first got an instrument. If you wanted to take up music, there was a particular day to go to the band room. When I got there, everybody had been before me and all they had was a trumpet with keys that wouldn't work—and a trombone. The trombone had never come into my mind before. What I had really wanted to play was tenor saxophone. I was always the skinny type, and my arms were long enough, but trombone—that's a hard instrument!

"I had two teachers, the first a Mr. Bowie. He's still active in St. Louis at one of the high schools as a bandmaster. The second was a Mrs. Robinson, and she was good, too. But I think the best musical training came after I went into the army. I volunteered when I was eighteen, and I played in Special Service orchestras. I was there six years, from 1948. I went to Europe, not Korea, which was very lucky.

"But before that I had played in a band led by Grover Lofton. He was from Little Rock, and he'd been in Chicago with Red Saunders, but he came home and formed a big band. There were few trombone players around, so I got in to make up the section, although I was only fifteen. So I went out on the road with him in the summer of '45. The following year, when I was still in high school, Lucky Millinder came to town. He was sponsoring talent contests through the South, and I won for the city of Little Rock—as a singer. By then I knew all the old pop standards and I won as a sort of ballad singer.

"I was scatting, too, in my way. Around 1945 I started listening to Charlie Parker, Dizzy Gillespie, and bop musicians. I was a young cat then and I naturally went to left field, to the way that was supposed to be ahead of the times. Diz used to scat, and I'm sure I heard Ella, so they must have had some influence on me. I knew about Cab Calloway, but I didn't know it was done by anyone much in earlier times. Only last night I heard a record of *Sweet Sue* by Satchmo on which Budd Johnson was scatting in 'viper's language.'

"What I was doing as a teenager couldn't be considered professional. I guess nothing can be professional unless you're earning money at it, even if your *standard* is professional! What I was doing was really for kicks. But in that contest I won, guess who won second place? Ocie Smith, who sang with Basie a few years ago. I always kid him about that. His father was some kind of government man who worked a few years in one city and was then switched to another. Ocie went to school in Little Rock, but I know other guys who went to school with him in a different city at a different time.

"For the finals of the winners in Lucky Millinder's contests in the Southern states, I went to Atlanta and took second place there. The winner was a singer from Mississippi who had recorded and been around, but I can't remember his name now. My second prize was a month's tour with Lucky, and I was able to take it because it was summer. The song I had sung in the contest was *Embraceable You*, and I did it as a straight ballad. I sang that and other tunes during the month. Some people said I sounded like Nat Cole, but I think that was because I was into that soft-type thing and did some of the songs he'd made popular.

"That was the way it went up till the army. Two of my six years were overseas. Seldon Powell, the tenor player, was in that Special Services orchestra. Eddie Fisher was attached to the band, Vic Damone was in the company, and I first met Pearl Bailey there. Stars would come over to perform for the troops. They'd join us in Munich, fix up a schedule, and travel with the band. It was seventeen pieces, just like Basie, and we played no marches or anything like that. It was a crazy band. So far as the army was concerned, all the cats were like deadbeats. Good musicians, you know, but cats that wouldn't be soldiers!

"There was no real tuition, but you learned things continually out of experience. There were periods allotted for individual rehearsals, section rehearsals, and then band rehearsals. There was a lot I didn't know about changes, chords, and structure up until then, but I learned all about that from the piano player in the band, Art Simmons. He opened my eyes to a whole bunch of things. There were other fellows in the band who helped me, too. I had to learn to read music fast, because the stars were bringing their own special music over. I wouldn't have traded the experience for a semester in college, or whatever. I learned about the keys and the songs, and how to play them right on the spot. When I joined Basie, he kicked off *Jumpin' at the*

Woodside the first night. 'What number?' I asked, and the guys next to me said, 'There's no music, man. Just make up your part.' Now if I hadn't had that army experience I might not have been able to pick myself up a part!

"When I finished in the army, I went back home to Little Rock, to college. It was a small Methodist school that had come into prominence because Elijah Pitts, the football player, had gone there. They had a pretty good music staff and that is where I got formal tuition and training. They taught you how to teach, and that was the thing for many black musicians in the South. They had a good thing going there, but it was basically an education-type program, with courses in psychology and child study. I just took all the *music* courses I could take.

"I was sick of Little Rock and there was no outlet there. I didn't like New York, and I still don't, so I went to Los Angeles. This was 1958. I had no money to speak of, but I didn't meet too many problems. It took me about a year to get around to knowing 'most everybody. I worked at the post office for six months, and I had another job with Magnetic Recorders, who sell tape recorders and that kind of stuff. I finally got established with enough gigs coming in so that I didn't have to work in the daytime. There were recording dates, too. Besides recording in the big studios, there were others where anybody could go in and record. So, for instance, when I got a song together and wanted to record it for a demo, I'd have to pay musicians fifteen or twenty dollars for a forty-five side. There was a lot of that going on in L.A. Cats were always putting things together.

The first gig I had in L.A. was five nights a week and I was making ninety dollars, singing. It was a club where they had dancing and a small group that played old standards, not rhythm and blues or rock 'n' roll. I worked there six months before any of the guys knew I played trombone! But there were all kinds of gigs to keep me going, and in '62 I got a chance to work with Della Reese in Las Vegas. Although I went to Sydney, Australia, with her, I didn't normally travel with her, but I'd join her when she was on the West Coast to play in Vegas, Reno, San Francisco, and at the Grove in L.A. She carried her rhythm section with her everywhere and just picked up other guys in the area. She usually had three trombones and three trumpets, guys like Bud Brisbois and Buddy Childers. Buddy, who was first trumpet with Stan Kenton at one time, borrowed $5,000 from Stan to buy a plane and wrecked it next day. That was the kind of cat he was, always drinking.

"Streamline Ewing called me several times to take a job for him when he had so much work he couldn't make it. He'd got the studio thing in L.A. sewed up. There are a lot of guys there you don't hear much about, but they're working all the time in places like San Bernardino, Pasadena, Santa Monica, or Pomona. I don't think I would have left for anybody but Basie.

"He was in L.A. and they had a party for the band at Memory Lane. I went over and sat in with the group that was playing—I didn't sing. They got to hear me that way, and I met some of the guys. Jaws [Lockjaw Davis] was in charge of hiring and firing then, so I said to him, 'Well, look, man, if you're ever out on the West Coast and need a trombone player, give me a ring.' That was what happened when they were out there again about a year later. I think Jaws knew from Sweets that I sang, and some of the other guys had probably heard, because I often used to go around places and sing. But I was hired as a trombone player.

"We were still out in California a couple of months later when Basie started out one night with an elaborate concert-type intro and then went into the blues. Everybody wigged out, because it was the first time he had done it. Usually, when he plays his intro, all the guys know just about what the tune is to be, but they were sitting there wondering this time. It was a nightclub, the atmosphere was very nice, and he was playing the blues real slow.

" 'Hey, man, why don't you sing some blues?' Jaws suggested.

" 'I don't really know too many blues,' I said, 'but I know a whole bunch of standards.'

" 'Well, do like they did in the old days. Make up something.'

"That's how it began. I sang a few words and scatted a bit. And I got a laugh. We got going into it, and finally we took it out. The ending was also groovy. I had never worked on it at all, but I really started thinking about it when Basie called it again the next night. From then on he would call it almost every night, which finally got it around into some shape. I had sung tunes like *Bye, Bye Blackbird*, where I sang the words for a chorus and then scatted another, but never like this where the words and the scatting were all mixed in a format. I've got a thing going, I know, but I'm really getting tired of it now. I guess I've got as much ego as the next musician, but I very seldom push things too much, especially where I myself am concerned. I might tell you I can do such and such a thing, if you need me to do it sometime, but I probaby won't mention it to you anymore. If I didn't think I could do the thing good, or well enough to tell you, I wouldn't tell you. That's the way I am with my singing and playing. Like I can half play trombone, you know. But to go into a businesslike thing of selling it—well, that's something musicians don't seem to have, and they say they should have.

"Since I've been in the band, three or four vocalists have come and gone. I really feel that I can personally fill that spot, but at the same time I feel that Basie is the leader of the band and, if he doesn't hear it, I'm not going to bug him. After all, I was hired as a third trombone player. I didn't know they were getting rid of Bill Henderson till the night he was getting ready to leave. Sometimes the cat didn't get to sing but one set a night, depending on where we were playing. Maybe carrying a singer is like carrying one more guy than they need. That was what I thought.

"I've been singing that blues for eighteen months, as well as the up-tempo thing. I felt I had to get me something new, so I sat down and worked on *Some of These Days*, and wrote an arrangement. I've done quite a bit of arranging, but not much for a big band. Out on the Coast, when we were recording those demos, many of the guys were singers who got a tune in their heads but didn't know much about music and needed a musician to write it down. I'd ask them how many pieces they wanted, how much money they wanted to spend. Usually it would be a working sketch, the simplest form with some notes for the horns. I knew how to voice things and I feel if I were really serious, and took enough time, I could probably turn out a good arrangement. So, anyway, I intended making this one for *Some of These Days*, but there were a couple of hard spots in it, so it was kind of refused. I never got a chance to clean up those spots, because we didn't get around to rehearsing it again. The idea of it was okay, I was convinced of that. So I said to myself, 'The only way I can get this one in is to let Frank Foster or somebody else arrange it, and then when they try it again I at least have Frank's arrangement on my side!'

"Maybe things are different now from what they were in early jazz. I think there was more love going on between musicians than there is today. You have to be *known*, and it's difficult to be known unless you are recognized as a successful musician. That's how it is with arrangements, too, but I've heard arrangements by people who are accepted that I don't dig at all. They'll accept a cat who is a good musician but who is also a junky known to mess up on the bandstand. He might not show up at all, but still they'll accept him quicker than some guy they haven't heard who plays very well. And I think that's bad.

"Of course politics gets into everything today, and I think there's more politics than love. I don't think you can put seventeen musicians together now and have them come up with good head arrangements like they did in the old days. They don't have that much love for each other—everybody is competing. I really try to stay out of that bag!

"There were no trombone players that really influenced me. Every once in a while I get a compliment that substantiates this. Now I like all the good trombone players that everybody knows, but when I was coming up I used to listen to the tenor players. That's what I wanted to play. Sometimes a musician will tell me that when I solo my ideas aren't like trombone ideas, but have more of a tenor feel. I don't get to solo much here, but I figure that will come in the next couple of years, although I don't plan to stay with Basie as long as some of the guys have. You get to play more in a small combination.

"One of the guys I worked for in L.A. was Dexter Gordon. We were at the Zebra Lounge a couple of months and we made an album for Jazzland called *The Resurgence of Dexter Gordon*. I liked it, and not just because I was on it. I think Coltrane must have been influenced by Dexter. Coltrane was more modern, but Dexter was doing that screaming thing way back, when they were having the battles of tenors. He was one of the tenors I admired, and then there was Gene Ammons. For big-tone tenor on slow tunes and ballads, you can't beat him. He's been 'in' about five years now, and that should be enough to get a parole. I have a feeling Gene came up against the wrong person on the political scene in Chicago. A cat can not like you, and if he's big enough he can wipe you out, no matter what profession you're in. You can't make it anymore. And maybe for some little thing. Like you went out with his girlfriend, or something.

"Wardell Gray's case was much the same. Of course, it was supposed to be an overdose, but the talk before was that he'd burned the people in power, who supply the heroin. He'd done something wrong, not enough to kill somebody, but from their point of view they figured they'd snuff him out.

"Another tenor player I liked in the early days, when I was eighteen and up, was James Moody. I got really hung up on buying him. And I was really hung up on buying Bird, too, although he played alto. My age thing really starts with Bird.

"Now, I guess, my mind is more on singing than trombone, because of this scat thing, because it seems to be something profitable. Vocalists joining bands make more money than musicians. They jump up and do a couple of tunes, and they can dance all night. That was a nice thing Basie did for me on the Merv Griffin show. There was no mention of trombone. He just said, 'I got a singer I want you to hear.' I went over to thank Merv the next day, and he said it was a gas and hoped I'd be back. Like I said, I don't like to drag myself posing the business angle, running around trying to find out who got the money for my appearance. The night before the show, someone comes and says, 'Hey, you're on the show!' That's what makes me so mad with this business. The same thing happened when we went in the studio and recorded *St. Louis Blues* and *Frankie and Johnny*. Out of a clear blue sky they say, 'Hey, we're going to record your two songs.' Businesswise, you're supposed to discuss a contract price, but am I going to argue when I haven't been heard singing on a record? Am I going to hang up the whole bit while we go in the office? That album was produced by Teddy Reig, a kind of difficult guy to get along with, who likes to shout. So that's where it is.

"My position right now is something like it was eighteen months ago. I came as a trombone player, and if I wasn't discharging the job right I'd have been gone from there. I take solos on *Hitting Twelve* and *In a Mellotone*, but about the time I get up it's time to sit down. The whole thing is rough, making it as a singer *and* a trombone player.

"Like when I joined the band, I wasn't all that naive, but I had visions of the guys getting together when they weren't working. I really thought the kind of thing might go on like you see in the movie, where the guy is playing his guitar in the bus. But these guys never go out to jam. I can understand it to some degree, because they work so hard and never have too much time, but it's still difficult for me to grasp inasmuch as I still want to play. That's where jazz ideas are born, in jamming. They're not born in a pen. Not really with the writer or composer either."

(1967)

Nat Pierce

(BANDLEADER, PIANO, AND ARRANGER)

"I've been arranging for Count Basie, off and on, for twenty-nine years, ever since I first met him in Boston in 1950. He had given up the big band and was working with a small group made up of Clark Terry, Wardell Gray, Buddy De Franco, Freddie Green, Jimmy Lewis, and Gus Johnson. Each last set at the Hi Hat Club, Basie would ask me to sit in, and that was a great thrill for me! I was about twenty-five years old, and whether it was a small group or a big band made no difference. It was Count Basie's, and that was more than enough for me!

"Some producer had the brilliant idea of making an album called *Count Basie Plays the Melody,* so Neal Hefti sent up arrangements of 'Golden Oldies' like *Confessin'* and *Little White Lies.* I went to a rehearsal at the Hi Hat, and Basie was sitting there at the piano as they rehearsed and rehearsed and rehearsed. The parts had been made by a professional copyist, but they were obviously having trouble. After a while, Basie called a break and sat down at a table with me.

" 'I've just found out the bass player can't read,' he said, 'and he's been with me three years! I was playing the bass notes on the piano part, and he was playing different notes.'

"I couldn't believe it. Maybe he *felt* some different notes? Those guys were supposed to be professional musicians who could play whatever was put in front of them.

"Serge Chaloff became an added attraction with the group while they were in Boston, and I think he stayed with Basie about six months. So they had four horns and four rhythm. It was really a gorgeous band, and they had some beautiful arrangements. They did the tunes of the day, bebop tunes like Charlie Parker's *Donna Lee*. Basie would play *Indiana* in front, and then the horns would come in. They all had the so-called bebop thing down, but this group sounded different to all the other bebop bands in that the rhythm section was playing straight ahead. The drummer wasn't too outside, because Gus Johnson just swung, like Jo Jones and people of that kind.

"I had my big band in Boston at the time, so Wardell, Buddy, and Serge came over and helped me rehearse it. We were very into bebop then, and we knew all the hottest licks of the day. We had heard Dizzy Gillespie's big band and Billy Eckstine's, and it was a kick for all of us in the Boston area to hear their wonderful arrangements and marvelous soloists like Fats Navarro and Budd Johnson. But when Count Basie showed up with this small group, it was frightening. 'How come these guys are playing bebop with a swing-type rhythm section?' we asked one another.

"At that point, Clark Terry was one of the beboppinest trumpet players of all time, but he could also play *On the Sunny Side of the Street* and *Confessin'* like Louis Armstrong. Buddy De Franco could play like Benny Goodman and the way Jimmy Hamilton used to with Duke Ellington. Wardell Gray was simply one of our gods in those days. He kind of consumed the styles of Coleman Hawkins, Lester Young, and Charlie Parker, and came out with one of his own. His nickname was 'Waistline,' because he weighed about ninety-eight pounds. I wrote an original for him called *Mosquito Knees*. And then Serge Chaloff was one of the masters of the baritone, and he has not been credited with all he could do. He could play fully as well as Harry Carney in the section, and a more fluid, or more modern type of solo than Harry. He was the first breakaway on baritone, and he spawned people we have today like Gerry Mulligan, Art Pepper, and Nick Brignola. When you hear sensational musicians like these as a young man, they make an indelible impression on you.

"Basie told me he was going to start another big band in a little while, and he said he wanted me to write some arrangements. Charlie

Mariano, Sonny Truitt, and I wrote some, gave them to him, and never thought anything more about 'em. Soon after that I went with Woody Herman's orchestra, and towards the end of 1951 we heard that Basie had gotten his band together one more time, with Marshall Royal, Joe Newman, Paul Quinichette, Gus Johnson, and people like that. When I went to hear them, they were playing my arrangements, and I said, 'Oh, wow, that sounds great!' Then a record came out called *New Basie Blues*, which I recognized as my tune. I went to see Jack Bregman of Bregman, Vocco and Conn, the publishers, and after some discussion I got my first composer credit on a big-time record with a big-time orchestra.

"As the years went by, and we floated around the East Coast, I'd go and see Basie and he'd ask me to write this or that. But he had Neal Hefti, Ernie Wilkins, Frank Wess, and Frank Foster writing for him, so he didn't really need my things and they tended to get phased out. It was maybe ten years later, after I'd left Woody's band the second time, that Basie asked me to write arrangements for a whole album of tunes by pianists. I wrote them for some of Horace Silver's numbers, for Willie 'The Lion' Smith's *I Want to Ride the Rest of the Way,* for Jelly Roll Morton's *King Porter Stomp,* and for Fats Waller's *Squeeze Me* and *Handful of Keys.* When I showed up where they were playing, Basie said, 'Oh, Nat is here. We must play his arrangement of *Handful of Keys.*' And he played the shit out of it! Then he said, 'I got to tell you something about the modulation into the second strain,' and other things like that. He was thinking of *Handful of Keys* as he had learned it when he was a young man and a disciple of Fats Waller.

"Around this time, too, I wrote *Willow, Weep for Me* for Roy Eldridge, and a tune called *Mr. Softee,* but Roy never played them, because he had left Basie before I turned them in. When Harry Edison came back in the sixties, he played them. I also wrote a number called *Open All Night,* which opened that show, *The Sound of Jazz,* in 1957 when Basie had an all-star band. I had written all the music on that show—the arrangements, that is—and much later the band Frankie Capp and I lead recorded the arrangement of *Dickie's Dream* for Concord. During the fifties, I also made a lot of records with idols of mine like Freddie Green, Joe Newman, Milt Hinton, Shadow Wilson, and Jo Jones. We were trying to get the old Kansas City kind of rhythm section.

"When I'd go to see Basie's band, I often used to sit by the piano and watch him play. On one occasion I noticed that he suddenly laid out on a certain chord.

" 'Why did you do that?' I asked him.

" 'I'm going to murder that chord,' he answered.

"To be technical about it, let's say the chord was a C-minor seventh with a flatted fifth. He didn't know that chord. But if I had written an E-flat-minor sixth, which has the same notes in it, he would have played it. So I decided that was the way to go.

"I wrote a few more arrangements and went to his recording sessions. Once, when he was called to the telephone, Marshall Royal said, 'Nat, sit in here and play this tune.' So I played it, and from the booth they said, 'Okay, next tune.' But Count Basie wasn't even in the room. In the same way, I recorded *There Are Such Things*—an old tune from the Tommy Dorsey time—with Sarah Vaughan for Roulette Records, and a number that happened to be in six flats, *Tell Me Your Troubles*, with Joe Williams, but my name was not on the records. To me, it just remained a thrill to be involved with the band over the years.

"It seems that every time Basie blinks his eye, cocks his head, or something, I end up playing the piano. It's exciting, because to play piano in a piano player's band is something that doesn't normally happen.

"I had the opportunity to go out in 1972 with Stan Kenton's band. It was not exactly my cup of tea, but I was not trying to do my Woody Herman or Count Basie act there, and somehow it jelled. It was a marvelous experience to have. On a few occasions during my time, I even sat in with the Ellington orchestra. These are things that don't pay the rent, and the landlord couldn't care less, but they are very important in my life.

"I found out that even today, in 1979, Count Basie's orchestra will play only a certain type of material. In other words, if you write an original tune, you must frame it on a sequence of chords Basie already knows, because he is not going to sit down and learn a lot of strange things. He'd rather sit outside and listen to the band play through the arrangement, and then jump in if he feels comfortable. Way down deep he hears something that is very important. If it doesn't fit with his band, he'll stop the arrangement in the middle and call another. I've seen arrangements by Sam Nestico, Billy Byers, and Quincy Jones stopped right after the introduction, because they didn't suit the way he felt at the time. It's a strange thing, but after being with Woody Herman for many years, I know he feels the same way. And I presume Duke felt that way, too. There are a lot of rejects from the Basie and Herman orchestras out here, arrangements they *knew* were not going to happen. Maybe five or ten years later, with a different sound, the arrangement might happen. Maybe it was written too late and they had bypassed it, or maybe it was too soon. Everybody has his own conception of arranging, but although Basie and Woody were not arrangers, and never wrote anything down on paper, they knew how to edit. They were the greatest editors of all time!

"Many of Duke's arrangements, of course, were written in sections. If he didn't like one section, he threw it out and wrote another, and added that to what was already acceptable. So he edited in his own way, just as Basie and Woody do in theirs.

"I feel very privileged to be Basie's Number One substitute pianist. That's what *he* told me I was. We have a special thing between us. We don't talk about it or publicize it. But there's no way I could ever play the amount of piano he's played in all his years in the music business. There's no way I could play *Prince of Wales* and all the things he did with the original Bennie Moten band. It would be absolutely impossible. People think Basie just goes *ding . . . ding . . . ding*, but I've heard him really play that piano.

"Back in my Boston days, I had a little upright piano in my humble apartment near the Hi Hat Club. One night he came over and played *Handful of Keys* in a direct copy of Fats Waller's version. Fats was his man, and later he watered Fat's style down to where it became the Count Basie style, but on a lot of the earlier records he played with two hands. Today he is seventy-five, God bless him, with maybe a problem that he calls arthritis, and I'm twenty years younger, but sometimes when he really wants to play . . . then it's like a spark, or when you get your car tuned up. He may not be the most accurate piano player of all time, but for rhythm, time, and swing, he is one of the greatest in the history of jazz piano. There have been some great ones, too, like Mr. Earl Hines, Mr. Art Tatum, and my very favorite, Mr. Nat 'King' Cole. They may know or have known more tunes than Basie knows, and all kinds of other things he doesn't know, but don't let anyone try to outswing him! I think there's only man left in this day and age who could, and that's Jay McShann. He's a monster! Erroll Garner was one of the great swing giants, but I wouldn't want him in a contest with Fats Waller, Jay McShann, and Art Tatum. Pete Johnson was regarded as a boogie-woogie pianist, but I wouldn't want to put him in the same room with Jay McShann and Basie and tell the three of them to just go ahead and play piano, because there would be a terrible mess and no way of deciding who did the most swinging.

"Of course, jazz critics—not so much jazz historians as jazz critics— always say, 'I like this,' or 'I like that,' and that's anybody's prerogative. But I think that if you had to show up in the same room as those three piano players, and decide who blew away whom, it would be quite impossible. Nobody could really say who was best or better of three such individuals such as they. But today, who could tell the difference between Keith Jarrett, Chick Corea, and Herbie Hancock? That is what the alleged or so-called jazz music has come to. And to Cecil Taylor, who was thrown out of Boston for playing thirteen-bar blues. He should be in the country-and-western bag, down in Nashville. But there are still giants out there, like Barry Harris and Al Haig. Barry Harris is like a disciple of Hank Jones and Tommy Flanagan, and he puts it all together. He's some kind of piano player! I can never approach the kind of thing he does, nor can Count Basie.

"Nobody much ever gave Nat Cole any great credit. He was a disciple of Earl Hines, and Earl came out of nowhere in the twenties, and there was no one before him who did what he did. After him came Erroll Garner, another true genius. I know that word is used very loosely nowadays, but I was on a record date with him when he said something very important. The red light went on and he started to play. The red light went off and he kept on playing. Everybody waved to him from the booth, and when he eventually finished they said, 'Erroll, we turned off the light. You were supposed to stop.' He looked at them and said, 'I couldn't stop. I wanted to find out how *it* would come out.'

"Now whether you believe in God or not, 'it' implies that there is some higher power upstairs. That's heavy stuff, I know. But *how would it come out?* In other words, he had no control over what he was playing at the time. Maybe he hit a couple of strange notes here and there, but there was no doubt he would work his way out *through none of his own effort.* 'It' came from another place. 'It' worked itself out.

"I'm sure that was how it was with the great musicians like Louis Armstrong, Lester Young, Bix Beiderbecke, Charlie Parker, and George Gershwin. And Gershwin was a great *pianist*, a favorite of Fats Waller and Art Tatum. They sat down and improvised to the point of no return. I'm sure Duke Ellington had the same feeling on certain occasions. Billy Strayhorn was also a great pianist in my opinion, of the same kind that people considered Gershwin to be. He could play up and down that piano! So many to remember! And I've hardly mentioned that happy-go-lucky guy with the strongest left hand anybody ever had. Nobody could smooth out the rhythm like Fats Waller.

"I go back to William James Basie. He knew those other guys were playing pretty good, and he knew he couldn't challenge Fats Waller or Earl Hines. He didn't have the same kind of gift from above, but he did have a very nice rhythm section. So he decided on something original and said to himself, 'Once I start off and play a bit, I'll just let them roll, and then I'll throw in a note or two here and there.' All of a sudden the world changed! They already had Benny Goodman, the King of Swing. Now they had Count Basie, the Jump King of Swing. What did 'jump' mean? There were a lot of tunes written with 'jump' on the end of the title. The jump was Kansas City, although Count Basie was never a Kansas City pianist in the way that Pete Johnson, Jay McShann, Mary Lou Williams, or Julia Lee were. They lived and grew up in that area. Count Basie was from New Jersey, but he walked in there like a renegade and ended up with the whole thing, so that writers made him the epitome of Kansas City jazz. When he became famous, they made all the other bands try to play in his fashion, and it didn't work. The feeling was different. Even today, they make records of Jay McShann playing *Jumpin' at the Woodside* and whatever, but that's not the way Jay goes. He goes with the blues and Pete Johnson. He's the only one left who can play that certain type of blues piano. Ray Charles has tried to for the last fifteen or twenty years. He started out like a poor man's Nat Cole and then became a 'genius.' I've never believed he was a genius. If you went into a corner saloon and listened to him play the piano and sing, you'd walk out in five minutes, or earlier. It would be that horrible. But if Jay McShann were in there, playing and singing the blues, you might stay all night.

"When Basie showed up at the Grand Terrace in Chicago in 1936, he had some little-known head arrangements like *Moten Swing* and *One O'Clock Jump*, and a few blues. Fletcher Henderson had been in the Grand Terrace while Earl Hines was out on the road, and he gave some arrangements to the young Basie orchestra, because he knew that if they didn't make it on this gig it would all be over, and they'd have to go back to Kansas City and the Reno Club. So now Basie and his guys took the same arrangements Fletcher Henderson and Benny Goodman had played, but how different they made them sound! The notes were the same and maybe even the conception was the same, but the *individuals* in the band made that difference in the sound. Duke had found that out years before with Johnny Hodges, Harry Carney, Cootie Williams, and Lawrence Brown, but now Basie arrived with his impeccable rhythm section, with a type of rhythm never heard before. You might almost say that Swing was born then, because they swung in the *true* sense of the word.

"Changing, but bringing some of the roots with you, is what it's all about. But who is swinging now? We have all kinds of combos playing all kinds of atonal groups of notes, but what would they do if they had to go in a country club and play a dance? We've got great musicians today, but they don't play any music to get those feet going out there! It's impossible to explain, but something happens between an audience and a band, a kind of electricity. It's one to one, you and me, and that's the way it goes down. That's the reason the big-band era happened. Later on it died, because it got too strange and many of the groups refused to play dances. It had nothing to do with rock 'n' roll, rhythm and blues, punk rock, or the Beatles. When you get up on that stand, you've got to have the right tempo and the right music to tear up the world!"

(1979)

PART 2

Jay McShann

(BANDLEADER, PIANO, AND VOCAL)

"Look. I'll be frank with you," Earl Hines said. "I want to hire that guy Bird, Charlie Parker. You don't know what to do with him. Let me have him and I'll make a man of him."

Jay McShann was remembering the night Hines had come out to hear his band in Washington, D.C. "He wanted one or two of my trumpet players, too," he said. "Bird owed me so much by then that I told Earl he could take him if he paid me the money, made a man of him, and let me have him back. Bird didn't want to leave, but I told him to try it for a few weeks. 'If you like it, just stay on,' I told him, 'and if you want to come on back home, come on back home.' Eventually he left, because for one thing he was going to get more bread than I could afford to pay him. Later on, I saw Earl at a Sunday afternoon jam session on 52nd Street in New York. He threw up his hands when he saw me and said, 'That's the worst man I ever met in my life! He owes everybody money. Come get him!' Earl had bought Bird a saxophone worth four or five hundred dollars, and Bird really had him crying the blues! It was true, too, that he owed quite a bit. In those days

he would take another cat's horn, pawn it, and then take the ticket to
him and say, 'Man, you want your horn? Here's the ticket!' "

McShann is a pianist and bandleader whose reputation has been
overshadowed by the immense legend surrounding Parker, whom he
brought to New York in his band in 1942. With his ally Dizzy Gillespie, the saxophonist was chiefly responsible for the idiom known as
bebop that radically transformed the character jazz had assumed
during the Swing Era of the thirties. The importance subsequently
attached to their innovations by critics and musicians helped obscure
the fact that McShann was—and remains—one of the great players
in the swing tradition. That he is modest, retiring, even shy partly
accounts for the lack of recognition. But a long documentary film on
Kansas City jazz now in preparation, *The Last of the Blue Devils*,
should do much to rectify this. When he found himself billed by the
film's title during his last New York appearance, he was mystified,
because he had never played with the legendary Blue Devils band in
Oklahoma. The title, nevertheless, was not inappropriate. Ralph
Ellison has explained in *Grackle* that "blue devils" was the name given
to those who cut wire fences during range wars in the West, and it is
not hard to hear in McShann's music a love of the loose, loping freedom of yesterday.

When his band first arrived in New York, it was to play at the
famous Savoy Ballroom in Harlem opposite Lucky Millinder, an established leader with a band full of experienced musicians. They took
one look at the "ragged" band from Kansas City, listened to its
"ragged" ensemble work, and decided they had nothing to fear.

"During the first two or three sets we came up with some stocks and
sort of played around," McShann recalled. "So then Lucky said to his
guys, 'We're going to get ready to blow those Western dogs off the
stand!' My cats saw his musicians going into their books [of arrange-
ments] and asked me, 'What're *we* going to reach?' I told them we'd
hold off another set, but after Lucky's guys had really carried on, mine
began to get restless. Now we had a number called *Roll 'Em* that we
used to play for about twenty-five minutes, and if we got it going,
moving right, we would extend it to thirty minutes or more. This particular night my cats—mostly young and wild—were so eager that we
just turned them loose and played that number ten minutes into
Lucky's time. That broke the house up! Lucky came back on the
stand and fired seven of his guys right there. I guess it was just a
gesture, but he did it. He took me out afterwards to some night spots,
and we hung around for a while and had a little taste. 'Man,' he
kept saying, 'you cats came and blew me out tonight.' He wanted to
know where he could get the music of some of the tunes we played.

'We don't have any music to lots of 'em,' I told him. 'We just put them together out of our heads.' "

This encounter was not untypical of what were known as "battles of bands," and it was not the first time Western groups had humbled some of New York's best. Earl Hines and his Chicago-based band had done it on several occasions, and Count Basie's had set a precedent for McShann when he came from Kansas City in 1936. Basie's was not then notable for polish and precision, but it had a superior rhythm section and a great gift for swinging. Like McShann's, it's outstanding innovative personality was a saxophonist, Lester Young, whose reputation in retrospect has also tended in some quarters to diminish that of the band. Yet no matter how great his sidemen, Basie himself was always the rhythmic heart of the group, just as McShann was of his. And it is significant that so many of the period's best bands were led by pianists, such as Duke Ellington, Earl Hines, Claude Hopkins, Fletcher and Horace Henderson.

McShann's career as a bandleader, so full of promise in 1942, was cut short by World War II. He was drafted in 1944 right from the bandstand in Kansas City.

"We had a marvelous crowd that night," he said with a wry smile, "about six or seven thousand people. An FBI guy came up about 11:30 and served papers on me. There were two red letters on them—two 'I's—and when I asked what they stood for, he said, 'Immediate Induction, and that means we go right now to Leavenworth!' I asked my manager to take care of the band's book, but we lost the whole of it that night. Two guys came in and told the caretaker of the auditorium that they were to pick up the band's things, and I never did find out what happened to that trunk of music.

"I was in antiaircraft for thirteen months. When I got out of the service, I still had the big-band sound on my mind, and I tried it again, but it had become too expensive. Most of the dance halls were using combos of five or six pieces, so I had to cut down, and I went out to California. Since then it has been small groups for me nearly all the time."

Jay McShann was born in Muskogee, Oklahoma, in 1916. Although a small town, it is the birthplace of such notable jazz musicians as Don Byas, Barney Kessel, Walter "Foots" Thomas, and the Ellington bassist, Aaron Bell. McShann was nearly twelve years old when Bell's mother began teaching his older sister piano. The family could not afford lessons for both children, but after singing and whistling the melodies his sister played, McShann found out how to reproduce them on the piano. The same thing happened when she began to play organ at their church, but there he had to be careful to open the hymn book at the right place and pretend to read the music. He also began to listen to the piano players on blue records, and to bands on the radio like Earl Hines's from Chicago. ("I would tell the folks I was going to do some studying, so I could stay up and listen to Fatha Hines, but I wouldn't be studying at all. When Fatha went off the air, I went to bed.") He heard the famous Kansas City band of Bennie Moten at local dances, but it was one led by Clarence Love that really fired an ambition in him to play jazz. He still could not read a note when he finished high school and went off to Fisk University in Nashville.

"I was trying to play football there," he said, "but it didn't work out too well because I went out on that field and got my fingers hurt. Then some fraternity was having a party and couldn't find anybody to play for it. A friend of mine told them about me, and they came and asked me. I told them I knew only three or four tunes. 'That's okay,' they said. 'You just keep going from one to another.' That was how the gig went. After I'd played my four tunes, I'd go back to the first and on down to the second, third, and fourth—all night.

"Then things got a little rough. We had tried to get jobs to help us through school, but I got despondent and decided to hobo back home with a buddy. After a week in Muskogee again, everything seemed so dull that I told my dad I thought I would go to Tulsa. He said if things didn't work out to contact him, and he'd get me back.

"Soon after I got to Tulsa, I was passing a hall where I heard some guys rehearsing. It was Al Denny's band—about twelve pieces—and they had no piano player! I went in, sat and listened to them, and memorized the tunes they played. When they started talking about what they were going to do for a piano player, I went up to see one of them and said, 'Look, man, I think I can play those tunes.' He said, 'You can? Well, come on up then!' They put the music in front of me and they thought I was reading it. 'Man,' they said, 'we've got a cat here who can read, and fake, and everything!' I had a good ear, but they soon found out I couldn't read. Then they helped me, and I learned fast.

"That was really how I got into music. I was fifteen years old. I stayed in Tulsa with Al Denny until I got a chance to go to Arkansas City with a small group. I worked there a year or so and then decided to get a little more education at Arkansas City Junior College. I fooled around until my money ran out. I used to raid the landlady's icebox at night after everybody had gone to sleep. When she got smart and emptied it, I realized I was going to have to get out, and I went to Oklahoma City."

There he joined Eddie Hill and His Bostonians. They worked at a ballroom in Shawnee and then went to a resort in the mountains twenty miles outside of Albuquerque. The band broke up in 1934 and McShann returned to Arkansas City, working for the first time in a duo with a drummer. Eventually the club closed and he set out for Omaha, where he had an uncle. When his bus made an hour-long stop in Kansas City, he visited the Reno Club, and bassist Billy Hadnott persuaded him to stay. He got a job in a trio with Elmer Hopkins on drums and Ed Lewis, who later made his name with Count Basie, on trumpet. After that he was in Dee Stewart's band in a downtown club, and in another piano-and-drums duo at Wolfe's Buffet, where blues singer Joe Turner sometimes joined him. Turner and boogie-woogie pianist Pete Johnson were two of his greatest pleasures in Kansas City, which soon became McShann's second home. It was there that drummer Jesse Price gave him his nickname of "Hootie." Some connected this with his liking for hootch, or "ignorant oil," but his close friend, bassist Gene Ramey, also related it to his habit of staying up at night with the hoot owls.

"After I got through where I was playing," McShann recalled, "the joints were still going till five or six in the morning, and I'd go around and hear everybody. It was so exciting I'd not want to go to sleep, because I was afraid I'd miss something! I heard Mary Lou Williams with Andy Kirk at Fairyland Park; and when Basie came back to Kansas City I finally had the chance to hear his band."

He worked around the city from 1937 to 1940 and had a long engagement at Martin's-on-the-Plaza with a seven-piece group that included Earl Jackson, Willie Scott, and Bob Mabane on saxophones, Orville Minor on trumpet, Gene Ramey on bass, and Gus Johnson on drums. This was to be the nucleus of his big band, and it was enthusistically reported on by Dave Dexter, a young writer on the Kansas City *Journal-Post* who later became editor of the influential *Down Beat* and was much responsible for focusing attention on McShann.

"Charlie Parker worked with us for a time then, too," the pianist continued. "He had joined George Lee's band and gone down to the Ozarks for two or three months. There's nothing to do in the Ozarks, but he said he went there to 'woodshed.' I'd say he went through a quick transition there, because when I was walking along the street one day I heard this unfamiliar saxophone sound. 'Who could that be?' I asked myself. I figured I knew everybody's sound then, but I'd never heard one like this. So I went up and there was this cat, back in town, blowing altogether different. He was soon upsetting all the musicians around, and anyone who was in Kansas City in those days just loved to see Bird come in with his horn in that sack under his arm. They liked what he did, even if they didn't understand it. He

asked to join our group, and he was with us five or six months before
he decided to go to New York. That's when he went on his own, just
standing around, looking and seeing. He told me how thrilled he was
to stand across the street and see the Apollo Theatre. He looked New
York over, came back, and joined Harlan Leonard's band.

"This was in '39, and I was just beginning to organize a big band.
Dave Dexter begged me to keep the small group and let everything
stay as it was, but I always wanted a big band. When I got a job at
the Century Room, I had to get me some more musicians, so I went
to Omaha and got some of Nat Towles's men. It was Mr. Bales, an
insurance executive who had helped me before, who gave me the
money to do that. All the other monies, for uniforms and everything,
came out of the band. A lot of people think that Johnny Tumino, who
was booking us, did that, but the band carried itself, particularly
when we had hit records later. Unfortunately, I didn't improve as a
businessman. I lost the value of money with that big band. If a guy
told me he badly wanted a new horn, I'd tell him, 'Okay, go get it!'
We hadn't been together long when we had a battle with Harlan
Leonard. Charlie Parker made up his mind where he wanted to be
that night, put his notice in, and joined us two weeks later.

"He was an *interested* cat in those days, and I could depend on him
to take care of the reed section. He'd be mad at the guys if they were
late for rehearsal. Then one night we had played a couple of numbers
before he showed, and I knew he was 'messing around.' But he was
strong mentally and physically, and it was some years before he
started deteriorating, before his habit really began wearing on him.

"He got his nickname when we were driving through Texas. The
car we were in hit a chicken and he made us stop. He got out, picked
it up, and had it cooked that night at the hotel where we were staying.
And he insisted we eat what he called 'that yardbird' for dinner. From
then on he was known as 'Yardbird' or 'Bird.'

"Tadd Dameron heard us play an arrangement he'd written for Harlan Leonard, and he liked the way we played it better. The difference
was in the phrasing. We played it long and singing. That's where the
'first' man is so important. If he's singing, everybody sings along with
him. Our first man was either Charlie or John Jackson. So long as we
were playing from a written arrangement, I had John phrase it, but
when it was a 'head' tune, then Bird phrased it. He set most of the
riffs on the heads, too. Bird didn't have the tone John had, but he had
so much feeling. Some people used to think I was crazy when I told
them he was the greatest blues player in the world. Everything he
played, even when he played a sweet tune, it was the blues. As compared with Johnny Hodges, he'd play a dozen notes where Johnny

played one, but he'd make you like 'em, so that made up for the difference in tone.

"I always say his *peak* was when he was with my band. He played *more* then. If anything, he *lost* when he got involved with the 'stuff' and got so far out. No one who heard it ever forgets the time we were broadcasting from the Savoy Ballroom and playing *Cherokee*. The engineer on that broadcast must have been a musician, because he told me to keep right on, and we played right through the theme. Bird was straight then and he really had his chops. I knew how remarkable it was and I tried to get John Tumino to record him, but Bird was ahead of his time. When we went to New York we had a heck of an arrangement on *Body and Soul*, and Bird would blow that *Body and Soul* till there wasn't anything else to blow, but the people wouldn't even clap their hands. Then Jimmy Forrest would take over, and the house would break up when he got through. It used to make me so mad! I know that was an audience of dancers, but believe me our rhythm section was giving them a solid beat.

"We had a lot of music, but we had twice as many head arrangements that had been put together on the stand or in rehearsal. The guys were young and they could remember where we were going if we wanted to stretch a number out for twenty or thirty minutes. That was how our style was shaped. Sometimes the rhythm section would play three or four choruses by itself in front. That set the band up, and by the time the horns came in they were rarin' to go. We used to play *Willow, Weep for Me*, and the way we did it made people ask what it was. '*Sport 'Em Up*,' we'd tell them. We'd be playing the same chords, but with all different riffs. And when we came to the out chorus, the reeds would be doing one thing, the trumpets would be doing one thing, and the trombones another— but not clashing! Some of the written arrangements may have been more stiff and formal to begin with, but by the time our cats were through with them we were back to playing our way!

"Bird was with me four years, but he changed in that time. His heart wasn't like it was at the beginning of our big band. He had got into the habit of going to places like Monroe's in New York with his horn under his arm. There he might blow just a couple of tunes and then step off the stand for a taste. With me, too, his time had been going bad—showing up late, and so on. Gene Ramey would say to me, 'Let me handle it. I'll get him here on time.' They were very close, and Gene would go by and check him out. He tried, and I went with it for a time, until it began to have a bad effect on the other guys.

"I let him go at the Paradise Theater in Detroit. I'd been warning him, because those pushers would be hanging around, standing in the wings and wherever they could get to him. This time, I think he had an overdose. Now he used to have bad feet, and when it came time for him to solo he went out to the mike in his stocking feet. I was sitting at the piano, wondering what all the people were laughing at, and there he was with his big toe showing! He went back to New York with Andy Kirk, and then joined Earl Hines.

"He and Dizzy Gillespie were responsible for launching bebop, but there was a big difference between them. Both of them could run up and down the horn and play a lot of notes, but nobody could play a whole bunch of notes and swing like Bird. Swing is strange. I put it this way: some people have to walk the chalk line, while others walk the same distance but don't have to walk the chalk line. You either swing or you don't. Swing is free. Blues is free. Latin rhythm is a structured thing. That guitar player, George Benson, can play Latin rhythms—and swing. There are plenty of good musicians in jazz who can't swing, and it's often because they get too technical to swing.

"One night a band swings more than another night. My theory is that if the guys have a full dinner thirty minutes before they go on the stand, they're not going to do anything because they can't coordinate. One's fuller than another! Another's overstuffed. Catch them when they've just got off the bus and haven't had anything to eat if you want to hear what they can really do. They play better and coordinate better.

"At one point, we were short of bookings, so we took some dates with Don Redman, who would stand out front of the band with his baton. Some of the cats had been griping, saying if things didn't pick up they'd have to go home. What was funny was that they played so well one night that Don said to me, 'Man, listen, don't worry about nothing. The way those cats played tonight, ain't nobody going nowhere! Don't you believe what they're saying."

Records played a curious trick on the McShann band and its potential audience. When the band recorded for Decca in Dallas, the producer was less interested in its jazz repertoire than in blues. *Confessin' the Blues* and *Hootie Blues* were made by just the rhythm section with vocals by Walter Brown, who sang in a nasal, rather uneventful manner. It was a manner, however, with which people could clearly identify. Not everyone wanted dramatics. When the two titles were issued back to back on a seventy-eight, they proved a smash hit, reputedly selling half a million copies. This unexpected success dictated a pattern, and very few of the band's best arrangements, written or oral, were ever recorded. In later years, having also been responsible for the discovery of singers like Al Hibbler and Jimmy Witherspoon, McShann would answer requests for Walter Brown's blues by singing them himself, and singing them very much better.

After cutting down to a small group again, McShann enjoyed considerable success in California, and it was there that he met the renowned pianist, Art Tatum.

"Art could really play the blues," he insisted. "To me, he was the world's greatest blues player, and I think few people realized that. The way I found out was when we used to hang out together, around about '47. I'd do his driving when we went out, because he couldn't see well, and when he stayed out late I had to do the explaining to his wife, too. We'd go to Hollywood and listen to Duke Ellington when he was in town, and then we'd go to our hideout, an after-hours place where they had a piano and sold booze. He thought I could play the blues, and after he got to feeling pretty good he'd tell me, 'Go play the blues!' So I'd play, and he'd sit and listen. If I did something he liked, he'd start popping his fingers. I'd keep it going strong, because I'd want him to play. After a while he might get up and go in the kitchen, and then come back to where the piano was. I'd finish up right quick then, and sit down. He never did want anyone to ask him to play. It took something out of him. You had to prime him a little and wait until he got ready. As a rule, he'd play all that old technique stuff first, but when he settled down he played blues. He was a great piano player, a great technician, and he felt the blues and could play the blues."

McShann reflects the importance of this friendship in the way he plays the blues today. He will close his eyes, shake his head from side to side, rock on the piano stool, and deliver the blues with unrivaled authority. Although he plays with tremendous rhythmic vitality, it is not with the heavy, pounding touch associated with many blues pianists. His is much lighter, more akin to Tatum's, and he is by no means limited to blues and boogie-woogie as some suppose. He plays ballads and standards with refreshing originality, his knowledge of harmonics being much in evidence. This results in part from his decision to "go back to school" in 1952, to Kansas City Conservatory, where he studied under Dr. Francis Boubendork and Dr. Herb Six.

"I knew that sooner or later I would have to settle somewhere," he said. "I looked Chicago over, but I thought I could maybe do a better job of raising the three kids, and seeing they got their schooling, in Kansas City. I worked around there five years or more, sometimes with a six-piece group, sometimes with a quartet or trio. We went with the punches. As the kids grew up, I started moving out more. We often played three months of the year in Lincoln, Nebraska, and we also went into Iowa, Michigan, Minnesota, and the Dakotas—cold country!"

Since a first visit in 1968, he has toured Europe several times and is as much appreciated there as in his natural habitat, the Great Plains. New York doesn't see him often. The city is probably too abrasive for one of his genial, unassuming personality. But in 1977 he was finally presented with an appropriate group at Michael's Pub, where for three weeks the swinging was as intense, and the values as fresh and undated, as any experienced in Manhattan for many a long night. Then he was gone to Kansas City again, unconsciously fulfilling the kind of blues lyrics he delivers with such droll nonchalance: *Sorry, baybay, but I can't take you!*

(1970 and 1977)

31. *Joe Williams.*
(Courtesy Red Saunders)

32. *Sonny Cohn.*
(Courtesy Red Saunders)

29. *Catherine and Count Basie at Basie's seventieth birthday party, New York, August 21, 1974.* (Courtesy Jack Bradley)

30. *Nat Pierce and Count Basie at Disneyland, 1977.* (Photo by Mal Levin, courtesy Nat Pierce)

27. *Carnegie Hall reunion, January 15, 1966. At microphone: Ed Hall (clarinet) and Joe Turner (vocal). At side of piano: Harry Edison, Buck Clayton (trumpets), Buddy Tate (saxophone). First row, left to right: Eric Dixon, Bobby Plater, Marshall Royal, Billy Mitchell, Charlie Fowlkes. Second row: Norman Keenan (bass); Freddie Green, Harlan Floyd, Grover Mitchell, Richard Boone, Bill Hughes. Third row: Jo Jones (drums); Gene Goe, Sonny Cohn, Al Aarons. (Courtesy Columbia Records)*

28. *Count Basie and Lockjaw Davis. (Courtesy Jack Bradley)*

24. *Billie Holiday and Snooky Young.* (Courtesy Snooky Young)

25. *Eric Dixon* (left) *and Frank Wess* (right). (Courtesy Impulse Records)

26. *Harry Edison* (left) *and Earl Hines* (right). (Courtesy Georges Braunschweig)

22. *Count Basie's Orchestra, 1958. Eddie Jones (bass); Freddie Green (guitar); Sonny Payne (drums); (left to right) Thad Jones, Snooky Young, Wendell Culley, Joe Newman (trumpets); Henry Coker, Al Grey, Benny Powell (trombones); Billy Mitchell, Frank Wess, Marshall Royal, Frank Foster, Charlie Fowlkes (reeds); Count Basie (piano).* (Courtesy Willard Alexander, Inc.)

23. *Frank Foster.* (Courtesy Jack Bradley)

19. *Helen Humes at the Oceanic Hotel, Sydney, Australia, 1964.* (Courtesy Helen Humes)

20. *Dicky Wells and Benny Morton.* (Stanley Dance collection)

21. *Buddy Tate.* (Courtesy Jean-Pierre Tahmazian)

17. *Count Basie's Orchestra, featuring Jimmy Rushing. Preston Love is third saxophonist from the right.* (Stanley Dance collection)

18. *Jo Jones.*
(Stanley Dance collection)

Gene Ramey

(BASS)

"Where I was born in Austin, Texas, April 4, 1913, is now Breckenridge Hospital, so I call that a personal monument to myself. Austin was a very small city then. There had been an oil boom thirty miles away, and there were great ranches around. A lot of cotton was grown in those days, but now the government has limited how much they grow.

"On my birth certificate it says my father was a teamster. He was a horse trainer. He'd take colts and train them to pace, train them for saddling, for the wagon, and for working. When he died, he was a regular farmhand and did all the plowing and everything. He worked for General Hamby, one of the baddest men Texas ever had. He was one of those men who would ride his horse into the saloon and shoot out the clock and all the lights. Anyone who wanted to protest was shot, too. On Sunday afternoons, he and his wife would ride in the gig and my father would drive. General Hamby had two black and white .45 revolvers and he could shoot birds off the telephone wire as they were riding along. Pow! There goes another bird! In the fifties, he killed three men and was put in a home. He must have been in his nineties, but he wrecked that home. He couldn't get that wildness out of his blood.

"My mother was a housewife, but she also did laundry. She'd take her three boys and my baby sister when she went to wash in people's backyards. My sister would have some toys to play with, my mother was on the wash, my older brother was on the old black pot you boil clothes in, and my other brother and I were on the two rinses. I was on the pot nearest my mother, which always gave her a chance to pop me when I didn't do right. But I took advantage of the fact that I was the baby boy! I was more or less a midget and kind of sickly, so when she told me to bring an armload of wood I'd grab my stomach and say, 'My stomach feels bad.'

"There were eight sisters and three brothers on my mother's side, and five of the sisters were good piano players. Somebody loaned my mother one of those old foot organs, and today I know how difficult some of the songs she played were, like, *He Married Another . . . O Dee . . . Three Little Babes Lost in the Woods . . .* and *Ball and Cabbage.* That last one was more like a reel in the South, and the people would be doing their dance to it.

"My grandfather, John Glasco, was half Comanche Indian. My grandmother came from Madagascar at the age of four or five. All she remembered was being put on a sailing ship that howled like a monster. She owned a restaurant right in the heart of downtown Austin, and my father's half brother owned another a couple of blocks down the street. Everybody called my grandmother Mother Glasco, and she managed to give her kids a good education. She brought them up in the church, and they must have done lots of singing and playing. My only surviving aunt recently retired as organist for Ebenezer, the largest black Baptist church in Austin. She had the number one choir there for years.

"My Uncle John married a lady named Leila Johnson, who was a first cousin of Jack Johnson the prizefighter. Their daughter, Nannie Mae, played classical music, was a featured artist with the Chicago Symphony, and became president of some kind of music society. She travels all over the country. There was a younger daughter, whose name was Bunch—we called her 'Dootsie'—and she also made her way in music. She played piano and sang. After I left Texas, she joined a trio and they became pretty prominent. She was Ivy of Ivy, Verne, and Von, who sang with Floyd Ray's band. She was the one who sang the solos, and she visited me when they were passing through Kansas City. When the band broke up, the trio continued successfully with one playing guitar, another piano, and Ivy the bass. They played bits in a couple of movies, too.

"Another cousin of mine was Louise Jones. She and her husband were both great musicians. Her son, Parrish Jones, was the one Kenny Dorham learned from. He played trumpet, and he was one of the greatest in the country, but he wouldn't leave Texas. He took up teaching, but he played jazz and Diz [Gillespie] and them were afraid of him. He passed away, very young, last year.

"There was music on the Ramey side of the family as well. Grandfather Jack Ramey was a whiz on violin. They said I took after him, the way he'd have his foot patting the ground. I can't play unless I pat my feet. My father played banjo and sang in a quartet, but he was more of an athlete. He died before I was four, in his early forties. I remember how my sister and I would be waiting at the front gate when he came home, and he'd take us down to the store and buy us candy. And I remember somebody picking me up to see him in that old, brown, wooden casket, and I kept saying, 'Why doesn't he wake up and take me to get some candy?'

"The Glasco children would go out with us to pick cotton where my father had worked. When we finished picking, we'd sit outside the cabin singing and telling stories until maybe midnight. We'd harmonize and sing all those old, good church songs—and some funny songs, too. That was where I composed my first song:

> *I went down the street and saw some pretty women,*
> *Don't nobody care about me?*
> *I went down the street, and I had patches in my pants,*
> *Don't nobody care about me?*
> *I woke up one morning, and I had cornbread and beans,*
> *Don't nobody care about me?*
> *I woke up this morning, and I had wet in the bed,*
> *My mother beat my back so bad, it sure did hurt.*

"They used to ask me to sing that song, and I'd sing it all over. Then I'd get out there and preach. I could roar, and get down there and say, 'Oh, brother, don't you want to go to Heaven?' Everybody knew I was going to be a preacher, because I could preach when I was five years old. I could tell ghost stories, too, and scare them all, but I'd scare myself more.

"I got some of the preaching from going to church, and also from all the camp meetings around us. The St. John's Association had one every summer, and so did a Holiness church about a block from our house. My brothers used to help park the cars of the white people who came to watch and listen to the singing, shouting, and speaking in unknown tongues. It used to be in a great big pasture, and the church appreciated the white people because they'd get a good collection, but there was always that color line. The whites would stand *outside* the tent, and the blacks would stay out of the way so they could see.

"Now the funny thing about Texas is that it's such a *plains* country. When we stopped singing outside our cabin, we could often hear another family singing three miles away! Sometimes we'd all get together and sing. My brothers and cousins would form a ring and start clapping their hands. Then one at a time they would get out in the middle and do a buck dance. They called that 'getting off the puppy's tail.' They danced flat-footed and my brothers got very good at it. They also had little team things where they would all do some particular step together, and they formed vocal quartets. Ira Glasco went to sing in the Deluxe Melody Boys Band, which played around Austin and did some touring. They started about 1926 and went up to '30 or '31. They were all local musicians.

"When George Corley took the band over, it became George Corley and His Royal Aces. There were three Corley brothers. George played trombone, Reginald trumpet, and Wilfred some other instrument. I started working in that band at the end of '31, and I stayed till I went to college. I borrowed some things called timber blocks—not *temple* blocks. They were like a xylophone, like the African ones, and I started to try to play them, picking up things as I went along.

"At school, I'd played field drums in the Boy Scouts, and I'd sung in a quartet. We had a Sergeant Willis there who was really terrific on drums and the ukulele. He interested me in getting a trumpet, and I learned to play ukulele. My brothers and sister used to get every record that came on the market with jazz on it. I'd be sitting on the floor just like the dog on the record that was listening to his master's voice! Everyone in our family could sing, and we could hum and scat every note of Louis Armstrong's. My cousin Duke became like the Texas Cab Calloway. He had long hair like the white man has, and he'd throw it over his eyes and do all those contortions.

"I got most of my music fundamentals in Anderson High School from the lady who was the choir leader. She also taught the quartet I sang in. Trumpet was my first instrument, but I found I could never get the pressure to play more than an octave. When I was thirteen I began playing tuba. Austin was known as the Friendly City, and we were very blessed. We had a lot of help from the old people and ex-soldiers, and from whites who bought us uniforms. Every Friday night during the summer there was a band concert in the park by a black brass band of about twenty pieces. Mr. Timmons, a barber in town, played bass horn in that group, and he was my teacher.

"After the trumpet I went to baritone horn but found that was too much in between, so then I got a tuba, an E flat helicon. You don't have to squeeze your lips so tightly as with a trumpet, because you get more support from the mouthpiece. Now I belonged to a social club called the Moonlight Serenaders. Others I remember were the Wild Fire Sheiks and the Mystic Knights. They'd take it in turns giving dances for us teenage kids, and they'd have three or four pieces to play. Somebody got the idea we were paying too much for musicians, so they took money to buy instruments and we organized our own band. We became very popular because we had six pieces where the other groups could only afford three.

"I didn't really know how to apply what I'd learned in high school, but we'd practice all night. The neighbors would complain about us boys playing all out of tune. Eugene Love, who later played piano with Sammy Holmes's band, took an interest in our group and had the patience to make us go over the music till we got it right. We soon had enough showmanship to fool the people. Then Sammy Holmes and his La Palm Orchestra came in. Herschel Evans played in that band, and Buddy Tate says he did, too. Sammy used to hire me for jobs when I wasn't busy. I couldn't play much, but that was how I first met Herschel. He came from a little town not far away. At that time there were a lot of road shows and carnivals. They'd hire musicians, get them so far, and drop 'em. Maybe they'd get up in the middle of the night and leave them. Herschel may not have been stranded like that, but there were many cases of musicians who were.

"Now when I got with George Corley's Royal Aces, I took the place of a learned sousaphone player who was also the coach on the school football team. That's when they started calling me 'Warm-up Ramey.' That coach always gave me pants that were too big for me, and about two minutes before the game would end he'd holler, 'Ramey, warm up!' And I'd be running down the sideline, and never get in the game. But my cousin's husband was the basketball coach, and I got to be like a star on his team.

"When my schooldays were over, I got a kind of musical scholarship to Western University in a suburb of Kansas City. I left Austin August 18, 1932. I had to work my way through. I'd had experience in Texas picking cotton, picking turkeys, shining dirty cowboy boots on the street, and working as a dishwasher, but an uncle, who was a house painter by trade, had also taught me painting. So when I got to Western a friend of mine and I took over the furnace room and those

big boilers. We also painted all seven buildings on the outside. Everybody was afraid of those scaffolds, but we'd get up there, three stories
high, and do the whole thing, windows and everything.

"I started getting music jobs right away on the side. I remember
going to the music store and getting stocks of Jimmie Lunceford's
White Heat and something by Duke Ellington, after I had organized
a fifteen-piece band. Buddy Anderson [trumpet] was in it, and
Lawrence 'Frog' Anderson played trombone. We mostly rehearsed.
It was a kind of outlet for us, but when Alf Landon had his political
campaigns some of us got on a flat-bottomed truck and played for
him.

"On Labor Day that first year they had a Battle of Bands in
Kansas City. I think they had eight bands and they started about
seven o'clock and played till three in the morning. It was very exciting. Bennie Moten was usually the boss in those days. After Bennie
died, Andy Kirk ran away with it, but the Blue Devils were always
bad and the Southern Serenaders were a powerful group. Then there
was George E. Lee with that mighty voice, and later on they had
Thamon Hayes. Sometimes Alphonso Trent would come up from
Dallas, when he was available. Incidentally, an uncle of mine was
head bellboy at the Adolphus Hotel where Trent mostly worked.

"I went to Western University to study electrical engineering, but
after the first year the school lost its credit rating. So then I thought
I was going into a journalism course, and ended up getting a certificate
in printing. I didn't get a chance to write anything, but I learned how
to run a printing press! I took a course in arranging and public school
music with Marie Little—what you'd *teach* in the elementary grades.
But Little Jack Washington was a graduate of Western University
and I used to go over to his house. He showed me everything about
reading.

"I was still a tuba player when I got to Kansas City, but I made the
switch to string bass in 1933. I didn't have nerve enough to go out
in the open with it, but I played it with my band until late '34. They'd
had a real big band at Western at one time and there was a storeroom
full of instruments. Guy O'Taylor was director of the band and he just
told me to get what I wanted. I took a bass, and then I went back
and asked if I could have a saxophone as well. So I was learning both
instruments at the same time. O'Taylor was a good violin player who
worked with Basie at the Eblon Theater where Basie played organ
and accompanied the silent movies. We had an eighteen-piece marching band, and eight of us played for assembly every morning.

"I've had guys ask me why I didn't learn to play the bass properly, because they sometimes see me with two fingers on one note. That's because I was born double-jointed. I have no pressure in the balls of my fingers. When they talk of my 'long' notes, it's partly due to that, but I never gave up the big-band style until about three years ago. In fact, guys ask me do I still have my strings a half-inch off the finger board. You had to do that, had to keep it up high, because you didn't have a mike in those days. But I never appreciate the guys who wanted the bass fiddle to stand out all alone in the rhythm section. I like an *even* rhythm section, not the bass dominating. You listen to Basie's rhythm section—it was all balanced, the drums didn't sound any louder than the guitar, the piano, or the bass. Then all of a sudden, around '47 or '48, they started making the bass dominant and noisy with all those amplifications. It was wrong. The *drummer* is hired to carry the tempo. He can decorate, but it's up to him to hold the tempo. Back when bop came in, Curly Russell and I were the most hired guys on 52nd Street, because that was when drummers began to put their foot in their pockets. It didn't matter how fast the tempo was, or how ragged it got. So they had to have a strong bass player to carry that beat while the drummer was decorating and actually stealing the solo in places from the horns. It became an exciting thing and it was accepted.

"But the man I adore most, Walter Page, saw things differently when he created the Basie rhythm section. When they were first playing together after Jo Jones came, he would constantly tell them to remember that that drum is not supposed to sound any louder than the piano or the unamplified guitar. 'Now come on down,' he'd say. 'See if you can do all that stuff and come on down.'

"If you think back to the days of King Oliver, it was the drummer who swung the band. They had to have a bass horn, because the bass fiddle could not compete with that one-man rhythm section. All you could hear was the *pop-wop-wop-wop* of the bass drum, although the drummer was also playing the snare drum. I call that New Orleans style. Baby Lovett's a good example, and he's still a genius on those snares although he doesn't play with that heavy foot. Zutty Singleton played the snare and the rims, but later, in Chicago, he started playing the cymbals. In the Chicago style, the drummer not only used his foot, but played some on the cymbals. Of course the sousaphone could play as loud as the drummer, but he couldn't play those fast tempos. Happy Jackson, who lived outside Kansas City in Liberty, Missouri, was the baddest bass horn player in the world, and when it was played the way he did, the sousaphone could be felt as well as heard, even at those big battles of bands. But even before amplification, they started changing to bass fiddle because the bass horn would take up a whole truck bed. You couldn't unscrew that bell and fold it into a compact little thing. It was three times as big as a bass fiddle.

"Pops Foster and those guys in New Orleans had shown how the bass fiddle could be used if the drummer would come down a little bit. It could not be heard with that big foot. How splendid Sonny Greer and Wellman Braud sounded on Duke's early records. Sonny still has a heavier foot than Jo Jones, but the way they blended and swung showed that the rhythm section was *teaming*. Braud was strong. He might get close to the mike when they were recording, but there was no such thing as a mike in most little towns. And yet you could hear them. Lunceford's bass player, Moses Allen, mostly played two-beat, but he and ol' Crawford cut right through. They blended. I say no band was great unless it had a strong rhythm section. It had to have a motor.

"With the exception of Duke's, there weren't many that were great. Earl Hines had fine arrangements and sounded so beautiful on piano. He had a good rhythm section but it wasn't *even* till he got Alvin Burroughs. Neither Cab Calloway nor Fletcher Henderson had good rhythm sections at the time Walter Page was sitting down and telling the guys, 'Now listen, we gotta get the balance! You gotta stay out of the way, or we'll have to get rid of either the piano or the guitar.' This was right in Basie's lot, because when he came to Texas with Bennie Moten they would play places with only one piano. Moten would sit there and play the bass part, and Basie would play the treble. They learned how to stay out of each other's way, so there was no problem at all for Basie to stay out of the way of the guitar.

"Freddie Green, that famous guitarist in Basie's band, does not flirt with the chords. Chords can follow progressions. Or chords can just stay on rudiments, and that way people know where you are and don't have to clash with you. Why Freddie's so great is that he plays that fundamental chord and doesn't get in the way of the piano. When bop came in, they eliminated the guitar player because he was clashing with the piano. Then when amplified guitar arrived, not only did the piano player have trouble, but the bass player as well!

"I first met Walter Page at the battle of bands in 1932. He was there with his own Blue Devils, and a week or two later I saw him with Bennie Moten. I didn't learn any technical things about playing the bass from him, but I learned from him how to construct, how to support a soloist, and how to work with a rhythm section. What he showed me most of all was restraint. I'd stand next to him, next to the door leading out to the alleyway, and he'd tell me things. 'There's a whole lot I could do here,' he'd say, 'but what you must do is play a straight line, because that man out there's waiting for food from you. You could run changes on every chord that's going on. You've got time to do it. But if you do, you're interfering with that guy [the soloist]. So run a straight line.'

"He told me that, generally speaking, when you've got a slow tune and the melody goes up, the bass should ordinarily run his line down. If the melody is coming down, the bass should go up to put body in it. He taught me such things as building the second chorus and how to avoid a drummer that's gotten on the wrong beat—how to stay out there, and let him catch up, so that you find each other without showing him up.

"I valued what he told me very much, because I didn't have too much real music training. I bought a Frank Skinner book and pasted the chart from the middle of it on the bass fiddle. It showed the names of each note, and where your fingers should be, but I couldn't finger them like I should because of my fingers being double-jointed. It was a handicap, especially for speed and endurance, and when you're bowing you should really play on the ball of your fingers. With those fingers, I should have joined a carnival instead of a band!

"The bass player who preceded Jimmy Blanton with Duke for a short time was from Kansas City. His name was Adolphus Allbrooks, and I used to see him walking across the viaduct from Kansas City, Kansas, to Kansas City, Missouri, with his bass on his back. He was a great bass player, but he complained that Duke was using all the wrong chords. He was a great arranger, too, but he didn't want to consider that Duke was creating a new sound in music. He became a professor up at the University of Minnesota, but I guess he was too legitimate in his thinking because I believe he's the only guy who quit Duke. Everybody else wanted to get with him.

"Kansas was dry in the days I'm talking of, but Missouri was wide open. People who lived in Kansas went over to Missouri and raised hell. It was like some people say of New York—a place to go and have fun in, and then you get on out. But Kansas was a 'northern' state. Western University was right where John Brown brought the slaves across the Missouri River into Kansas. The schools were integrated in Kansas, too, but on the Missouri side you couldn't sit with the white people in a club unless the boss fell over backwards and said, 'Come over here and talk.' Like in the Reno Club, they would get Basie, Jo Jones, or somebody, and bring them over to the table.

"We'd go over from Western and have our little jam sessions. We heard Joe Turner at the Hawaiian Gardens, and then we'd go down to the Sunset Club. That was really something—about twelve feet wide and maybe sixty feet long. It was just like going down a hallway. They hired a piano player and a drummer to come on at midnight, but we'd get over there before that and sometimes there'd maybe be ten musicians up on the stand. That was where I first met Prez and Ben Webster. They took a liking to me, so they had me going over there every night. They'd fight it out till daylight, sometimes to ten o'clock in the morning. They were both three or four years older than me, but they noticed I wasn't a heckler. I'd just stand and listen to them, and not keep asking why or how they did this or that. Around nine o'clock in the morning, we'd go across to the Sawdust Trail, a dining room with sawdust on the floor, where all the musicians met. The Lone Star, where Pete Johnson was playing, was directly across from the Sunset. It was a nightclub, a little like Ryan's in New York, a little less crowded than the Sunset. The Sunset was not a bucket of blood, but you might see some fighting in it, and you'd have to break out of there. Anyway, after breakfast at the Sawdust Trail they'd get us back to college.

"Another place where we had after-hours jam sessions was the Subway, over on 18th Street. Piney Brown ran it and he was a big man in all that black neighborhood, although Felix Payne was actually the boss. Piney was a friend to the musicians and in with the politicians, because he could get you out of jail. Felix Payne had an open lottery right on the street, with a roulette wheel and everything. You could go right in there and gamble, and there was always peace, although that was the area where you found the hustlers and good restaurants. The only place that's still there is Matlow's Clothing Store. There isn't much musical life there now. It's scattered way out to the suburbs, but even in our time the clubs weren't all in one locality.

"Lester had a very spacey sound at the end of '33. In fact, I still try to play like that now. He would play a phrase and maybe lay out three beats before he'd come in with another phrase. You know, instead of more continuous staying on style, like Bird would play. Prez had kind of loosened up, but Ben Webster had not developed his style at all. I don't think he had really developed it even when he was with Teddy Wilson. I think Duke Ellington brought that out of Ben—he and Johnny Hodges. At that time, everybody thought Dick Wilson was next to Prez in Kansas City. I didn't know Dick Wilson that much, but one thing they held against him was that he liked to play the higher part of the saxophone. I liked the way Prez played tenor with an alto style, but everybody seemed to be a Coleman Hawkins fan then.

"I slipped away from school the night Hawk played at the Cherry

Blossom. Ben, Herschel, Dick Wilson, and three or four other local tenors were there, and Hawk was cutting everybody out. Until Prez got him. He tore Hawk apart. He tore Hawk up so bad he missed a date in St. Louis. Hawk was still trying to get him at twelve o'clock next day. Seemed like the longer Prez played, the longer that head-cutting session went on, the better Prez got. He played more creative things. The adage in Kansas City was—and still is—*say something on your horn*, not just show off your versatility and ability to execute. *Tell us a story, and don't let it be a lie.* Let it *mean* something, if it's only one note, like Louis Armstrong or Duke would do.

"Prez tore up Hawk, Herschel, and everybody else, and then got the job with Fletcher Henderson, but Fletcher fired him right away because of his tone. Everybody put him down, but he wasn't too proud to come on back to Basie. He was always nice and considerate. In fact, he was like my big brother. That tenor saxophone, that silver Conn he had in New York, was one I gave him, the same one they had given me at the university. He liked it best of all.

"He was going with the Countess, Margaret Johnson, at that time. She took Mary Lou Williams's place with Andy Kirk. She was very good, and everybody said she was better than Mary Lou. In 1935, I had been working with Oliver Todd's band at Frankie and Johnny's, where we played with our overcoats on because the man couldn't pay for the heat. Five of us then got a job in a club on 12th Street, and we persuaded her to play piano and act as leader. Countess Johnson and Her Band—the name made us a good draw. We had Orville 'Piggy' Minor on trumpet, Earl Jackson and William Scott on saxes, Bill Nolan as singer and drummer. In those days Earl Jackson was better than Bird or John Jackson. After we played a couple of places, we opened the State Line Tavern. I was still at Western University, but I'd graduated and taken a job as assistant engineer in charge of the generators and transformers that fed the laundry they had there. It paid only sixty dollars a month, but it was a kind of security. I was married and had a child, so that was why I had to have the other job with Countess Johnson.

"Those clubs on 12th Street ran from eight to four o'clock, sometimes to five, and I was getting very little sleep, not more than two or three hours. But being as talented and honorable as I am, I had found a very nice thing to do. I'd get down in the boiler room at Western University, stuff that thing full with coal, and go to sleep. Sometimes I could sleep five hours in the day, until somebody came running down saying, 'Listen, all the buildings are cold!'

"Countess Johnson didn't show any effort when she played. Her style was different, between Earl Hines's and Basie's but nearer to

Earl's. She was fast and powerful, and she said something. Of course, Earl was a strong influence not only in Kansas City but in Texas, too. All the gang at home used to make it to the radio when he came on from Chicago. We couldn't get New York too easily on those radios. We'd sit there all night listening to *Deep Forest, Rosetta,* and all that stuff. Earl was really a big influence all over the United States, bigger than anyone else since maybe Jelly Roll Morton. Some magazine had shown how he could stretch those tenths, and guys were saying he had had the webs cut between his fingers. He hadn't, but everybody was patterning after him and trying to stretch tenths!

"There was another band came on from noon to one from the Gunter Hotel in San Antonio, playing the nearest thing to nice, soft society swing. It was Herman Waldman's band* and at noon we would make it to a Chinese restaurant where they had the radio on. Sometimes, too, we'd hear Alphonso Trent's band from the Adolphus Hotel. Its success could be due to musical ability, but socializing ability was important, too.

"Basie's band built up their popularity on socializing. I mean the big following they had in and around Kansas City. But that whole band didn't believe in going out with steady black people. They'd head straight for the pimps and prostitutes and hang out with them. Those people were like a great advertisement for Basie. They didn't dig Andy Kirk. They said he was too uppity. But Basie was down there, lying in the gutter, getting drunk with them. He'd have patches in his pants and everything. All of his band was like that.

"The job with Countess Johnson lasted till she went with Andy Kirk's band. They went to New York, but she didn't live long after that. They brought her back home and she died shortly afterwards of what people thought was tuberculosis. She had made one record, with Billie Holiday. Prez was crazy about her, and I believe he got her on that date. Her brother, Roy Johnson, played bass with Lionel Hampton, but last I heard he was playing piano in Kansas City.

"Everett Johnson was another good piano player, and one of the cats who could stretch out Pete Johnson. They'd battle all night. He could really play barrelhouse and eight-to-the-bar blues, and at the time I'm talking of he was a little more popular than Pete. A whole lot has to do with who chooses whom. Andy Kirk was winning all the battles, but he didn't have the right people to give him a build-up. His was the most popular band in Kansas City, but Basie ended up with Benny Goodman and John Hammond behind him. You think Kirk's band didn't have the drive of Basie's, but I'd put it a different

---

* Not Herman Walder's, Gene Ramey insists.

way. Some bands—and I could name others in Kansas City—had too much orchestration. When you listen to the original Basie records, they sound so exciting. Sometimes it wasn't really the solo that made it exciting, but the riff backing t up that Buster Smith, Herschel, Jack Washington, or any of the fou. guys in the sax section set. That also left the soloist free. The horns weren't fighting to make that note on time, like in those real experienced bands of Duke, Lunceford, and Andy Kirk. One band that went to New York and didn't really make it, because it didn't do enough ad lib playing, was Harlan Leonard's. That was why Jay McShann's band outblew them every time. Jay would give us the first chorus and then turn us a-loose.

"After the job with Countess Johnson, I played in a band for a walkathon at the Pla-Mor Ballroom. No Negroes had been allowed there before that, and we just went in the back door, got up on the stand, and played while the people walked around so many hours a day, trying to outlast each other. It was more or less an offshoot of the carnivals and shows the bands used to do. When the medicine man came through town, they'd build a tent and have a band to go with the two-headed man and the billy goat with a dog's head. The Pla-Mor had brought in all the good white bands, but they canceled the other engagements of the company that had rented the hall and brought in the black band!

"Some people seem to think the Cherry Blossom was a ballroom, but it was the old Eblon Theater turned into a huge nightclub. It was on Vine Street, between 18th and 19th, directly across the street from the Booker T. Washington Hotel, which had become the most popular one for musicians. Next door to it, on the right, was the Kentucky Tavern, where jam sessions would usually start around two o'clock in the afternoon. 'Spook breakfasts,' we called them in Kansas City! Anybody who'd stay up all night we called spooks or ghosts. Jay McShann got the name of 'Hootie' because he'd stay up so late he was up with the hoot owls. They also used to say that he would hoot like an owl when he'd drunk some whiskey!

"I keep sidetracking, but after the walkathon I went with Bus Moten. His brother had died, and he was trying to get the Reno Club job after Basie had gone to New York. There was never all that much work in Kansas City. Bennie used to play places like Fairyland Park and then go out on the road. None of the bands stayed in Kansas City that long. They had a regular circuit, whether they were booking themselves or not. That's why we used to see them all in Texas. Not only Bennie Moten and George E. Lee—with those long, beautiful cars—but King Oliver, Louis Armstrong, and Cab Calloway, too. Earl Hines was so much in demand because of the broadcasts they'd have taken him on a Monday morning if they could have gotten him. Every time they came down, they'd steal musicians out of Texas and Oklahoma. That's how they got Lips Page and others.

"Bus Moten played piano *and* accordion, so he could take jobs where there was no piano. I wasn't too keen on his playing of either instrument. There are two kinds of piano players: one is a soloist, a single, and the other plays with the band. Buster would start a tune and then just go for himself. You had a better chance with the accordion when you were playing bass, because he was playing on the treble side. When he was playing both hands on the piano, it was kind of rough! I think Bennie may have been a better player, although I never heard him solo, but apart from his musicianship he was a good organizer and a good manager. He kept his bands together better than anyone else, even though he was robbed by eastern bands like Blanche Calloway's.

"I first met Jay McShann at one of the jam sessions in the Taproom on 12th and Paseo. It was an all-black club, one of those walk-in-off-the-street places. When they had spook breakfasts there'd be a houseful there, but normally they had three pieces. So far as a rhythm section was concerned, McShann's gang then was Billy Hadnott on bass and Jesse Price on drums, but I joined him on either the 18th or 28th of April, 1938, for a job at Martin's-on-the-Plaza. We had seven pieces—trumpet, alto, tenor, baritone, and rhythm. Pete McShann, Jay's cousin, played drums the first two weeks, because Gus Johnson, who had come back from Omaha, had to give two weeks' notice where he was working. Hadnott didn't want to join till Gus came in, but at the end of the two weeks McShann called him and said he liked what he got, meaning me. We became like bosom friends.

"We immediately began to get trouble from the white local in Kansas City. They started saying we were out of our territory according to a zoning law they made up quickly. The Plaza was a real ritzy part of the city, with beautiful homes, trees in the yards, gardens, and everything. There was a real estate man, a Mr. Bales, who was a good friend of Jay's, and he may have had some interest in Martin's. We played soft music from eight to ten o'clock. Then the waiters moved the chairs and tables in the restaurant and we played dance music—twenty minutes on and forty minutes off. We had a dressing room where we played cards, but none of us did much drinking because we wanted to protect the job. Jay started taking care of business there, too, but after we were through we'd get down on 18th Street and Vine, where the gang was, and he'd get tore up. And I'd have to take him home.

"They loved him at Martin's. They were promoting their chicken-in-the-basket then, and I made up a song about it to the melody of *Pennies from Heaven.* We'd sing it there and on the radio, and it turned out to be a great thing. Society people would come from all over to order this chicken that would 'knock you out.' Then McShann became so popular that we got on what they called *The Vine Street Varieties* at the Lincoln Theater, a show for black people that started about 12:30 at night and went on till around four in the morning. Besides our group, they'd have a comedian, a couple of singers, and maybe a shake dancer. People down at the radio show were trying to get McShann, and some afternoons we'd have to go down to the big music store where Thamon Hayes was by this time working as a salesman. Then Dave Dexter, a newspaperman, met him and fell in love with him. From then on, McShann was on his way.

"It was partly Jay's personality, but he was really playing the piano and he was appreciated by all sorts of people. When we were at Martin's, we played numbers like *Hawaiian Paradise, Over the Rainbow,* and *Sierra Sue.* We only played what you might call 'hot' tunes at certain times. So those who thought of McShann and Bird as only playing bluesy and jazz were wrong, but he didn't get a chance to record ballads until years later [for Master Jazz]. I can see improvement and a lot more variety in his playing, but it's a different kind of piano when you play with a rhythm section and when you play as a single. But back in those days he was really cooking, and I'd say he was as much of an influence on Bird as the other guys who supposedly taught him.

"By his own personality McShann created a happy band. The guys were like a family. Often I'd pick up *all* the guys, and after work we'd go back home or to some restaurant in town. You knew he was the boss, but you could sit down and talk with him or cuss him out. It was a real good feeling like that.

"McShann would hit some phrase at the piano and the others would pick up on it. Long before we came to New York he created a tune he never finished, called *The Master's in His Solitude Today.* He'd get half tore up and say, 'I'm the master, you know.' Then he'd play this thing, and that's where the flatted fifth started coming in. He didn't let it show, but it kind of hurt him when his own ability wasn't recognized. He mentioned it to me a couple of times. 'Everybody's introducing me as the man who discovered Charlie Parker,' he said. I tried to console him by telling him, 'It's coming. Twelve years ago they would hardly let you back in New York.' But he thinks it's the jokers in his life. When he went on that tour behind the Iron Curtain with the Charlie Parker package, he said those guys played him down so low that it was just getting to him. One guy was talking nightly as the authority on Bird, on how he learned to play, and McShann was treated as just another man in the band.

"When we went to Europe recently, we had the same kind of thing going, and I threatened to come home. Fiddler [Claude Williams] brought both his violin and his guitar, and he played them at the highest pitch he could get them. I spoke to McShann first, and then to Fiddler, and I said, 'You don't really have to play that loud. I think we are supposed to be a team, and one guy is not supposed to walk off as the individual god of this thing!' McShann was in charge of the show and he'd run it, but this guy was telling him how to play it and what he wanted played.

"McShann is a very easygoing person until he fills up, and then he blows up. I used to tell him, 'You can nip it in the bud, stop it before it goes too far. Do it easy, rather than wait till you get really mad and don't know what you're saying.'

"To go back to Martin's-on-the-Plaza. . . . We stayed there maybe three months and then switched over to the Continental. It was there in 1938 that McShann had an offer from Charlie Barnet, who wanted to hire me. I didn't know about it, but instead of telling me, 'Go ahead, be happy,' McShann hid me, stuck me off in the corner somewhere. I wouldn't have gone, anyway, because McShann had established a beachhead in Wichita and, thanks to Dave Dexter, we'd been voted promising new players in a *Down Beat* poll. Jay and I were brought to Chicago along with George Barnes, Anita O'Day, and a drummer who had won in his category. We were supposed to go for two weeks, but we stayed six.

"While we were away, we left the band under the control of Willie Scott, a tenor player who had that real business manner about him. Bird and Earl Jackson had been in and out of the band before, but when we got back we found Bird had hoboed to New York. It was then that McShann began organizing a big band with John Tumino, our booking agent. Tumino leased a club called the Century Room, and bought us fine uniforms—black coats with striped pants, like evening dress. We did pretty good there, and then Don Robey in Houston booked us on a tour down there in the latter part of 1939 or beginning of 1940. McShann just tore it up all over the country. Most of what we did were heads. Willie Scott was doing some arranging, but we used the same things we'd done with seven pieces, voiced them out for the other horns, and fixed little riffs. The only thing I remember Bird writing was *What Price Love?*—which we recorded as *Yardbird Suite*. We recorded it in Dallas for Decca, but we never heard anymore of it. 'This is a little far from the picture we have of

Jay McShann,' they said. 'We want some blues.' Each time we played it, they told us to go back to the blues, and a lot of things we did were made up as we went along. Walter Brown had the words for them.

"I never knew too much about Brown, except that he'd been in a federal CCC camp up around Topeka. The lyrics were different, but he sang more or less the same melody to everything he did. He even had a bad talking voice—completely nasal. He didn't have good diction, and people could misunderstand when he sang, 'Baby, here I stand before you with my heart in my hand.' Jay can sing in a nasal way, too, but you can hear the different tunes. Before Brown, we'd mostly had ballad singers. There were quite a few blues singers around Kansas City, but to us they all seemed like poor imitations of Jimmy Rushing and Joe Turner. After the record of *Confessin' the Blues* was such a big hit, it began to go over good wherever we played. The whole band played it, although on the record there was only a trio back of Brown. There was never one note written on it. In fact, Bird and I were supposed to have written *The Jumpin' Blues*. We sat down and started humming riffs that would fit. I got the first eight bars and he got the last four. Then Brown came in and sang, and as we rehearsed we fitted other riffs. Not a note was written on that, either, but it became McShann's theme song. Before that he used that mournful blues theme as on the Wichita recording.* That kind of thing may have typed us as a blues band. We used to reminisce about old tunes as we rode home in the bus. One somebody sang was *My Mama's Dead and My Papa's Across the Sea.* Sometimes in their solos guys would go back to something sad like that that had got to them.

"I have to say that when I first met Bird in 1934 he was a terrible saxophone player, but I could always get him to jam with me. Even when he was with McShann, and he was getting ready to get himself some drugs, I could always ask him to give me fifteen minutes to get our fingers together. Then he'd start playing and forget all about the other things.

"In the McShann years, Bird was generally in control of his habit. He wasn't scratching his face, which was always an obvious sign. It was very rarely you would see him nodding and that sort of thing, but you could tell. The other guys who were trying to be like him by using it were the ones who showed it worse. He was wise enough in his way, and while we were playing at Tutty's Mayfair in Kansas City he got all the guys who were following him to take a teaspoon

* *Early Bird,* Spotlite 120.

of nutmeg and a drink of water. You don't get high that same day, but for two or three days afterwards you'll be walking like a sick duck. The grocery store where Tutty bought his supplies told him, 'You sure must be baking a lot of cakes and pies!' But when Bird got to New York and was hanging out with Tadd Dameron, they were experimenting with everything. He was even soaking the reed in his mouthpiece in Benzedrine water. That was a waker-upper. The drug was a go-to-sleeper.

"I think Jay first heard him when he came back from working with George E. Lee. Basie's 'Jones-Smith' record had come out and Bird startled everybody by playing Lester Young's solo on *Lady Be Good* note for note. 'Here comes this guy,' the cats used to say. 'He's a drag!' They couldn't believe it, because six months before he had been like a crying saxophone player. Although one famous writer says Bird was not influenced by Lester Young, if you listen to him you can tell he was *completely* influenced by Prez.

"Buster Smith's influence was not so direct. At spook breakfasts, Buster would set the riffs. There might be one trumpet and ten saxophone players. Usually, when one horn sets a riff, the other guys play in unison with him, but with Buster the other horns had to harmonize. Then it would sound like a written chorus, and that's what you hear on records when Basie's band was jumping so good. Buster was noted for that, and for eliminating those who didn't get the harmonic notes right in the riffs. You may have played your solo well, but you had to get out and not play for a while. Buster would always do that at jam sessions where there were too many horns. The guys would take their horns to a table and listen to the heavy riffs he set. It made them think, yes, but it also showed the young guys that they had to learn to team as well as play a solo. The sections, too, had to learn to breathe at the same time. All this was inspiring to Bird, who learned many tricky riffs that way.

"Buster was also a great improviser. He didn't have the strong sound of Johnny Hodges, Bird, or Benny Carter. He had a soft alto sound, more like Charlie Holmes's when he was with Luis Russell, or Johnny Hodges's in the early days with Duke. But though it was soft, he was very good playing lead. And when Benny Goodman or any other clarinet players came into a spook breakfast, Buster would get his clarinet out and clean everybody up, including Benny.

"He was a nice, easygoing man, and still is. The last time I heard from him he was playing piano in Dallas. He told me once he was sorry in a way that he didn't go with Basie, yet I think it was Buster who really made the Basie band what it was, a riff band with very little music. They were so well organized that Benny Goodman and

John Hammond couldn't believe a small band like that could sound so big.

"In the McShann band most of the sax riffs were set by the two alto players, Bird and John Jackson. Buddy Anderson or Piggy Minor set the riffs for the brass. So we were really picking up on what Buster Smith had done. Then, of course, the simple blues is *it*. When I was talking about the different phases of jazz, I meant to say that we looked upon Kansas City jazz as like a camp meeting, completely imitated from one of those revival meetings, where the preacher is singing and the people are replying. It's something you're bound to feel.

"I have to admit that all bands had things they riffed by the time Moten came out with *Toby* and *Lafayette*. If we were rehearsing a stock at a McShann rehearsal, someone in the reed section might find a phrase that didn't swing. 'We're going to play it this way,' they'd say, 'to make it swing more.' Then, too, McShann built his band and his solos playing behind the beat. He would try to arrange it so that the melodic line was played just a fraction behind the beat, but so that we would catch up just before we got to the end of the phrase. If you listen to *Hootie Blues*, you'll notice how far behind the real tempo the horns come in. That gave it a lazy image and a bluesy sound.

"They riffed in the East, but the rhythm sections there until very recently had a metronomic beat. It didn't accent like the western beat with the sock cymbal. The eastern drummer would drive you crazy—*tick, tick, tick, tick,* like a metronome. The western beat gave you a chance to relax—and that came from those camp meetings again. That's why I said the rhythm section makes the band. Remember how the rhythm sections in Basie's band and Duke's band were beating the heck out of a song. Those horns *had* to play! Lunceford's rhythm section was very good, too, and with their two-beat rhythm they were the first movement towards the churchy feeling. The horns were playing in a unique style from the arrangements, and it was so relaxed you'd still be patting your feet in your sleep. Lunceford played a ballroom on Woodland in 1934. It was an old building, the Masonic auditorium. He had the whole house jumping. The people were dancing and swinging so hard the floor went down about six inches, and they had to cancel the dance! I used to hear Claude Hopkins's band from Roseland, too, and they *moved*. I remember when Don Redman came out to Kansas City with McKinney's Cotton Pickers. He had Cuba Austin on drums and they tore it *up*. I only heard Fletcher Henderson once, right after they introduced Israel Crosby, that great little bass player, and made *Chistopher Columbus*. Probably because I was so prejudiced in favor of Kansas City bands, I just wasn't impressed. There wasn't the same sort of looseness. The remnants of the Kansas City thing were slowly taken away from Basie's band as all those changes were made. Most of the guys were saying the looseness was going, but the powerful rhythm section held it together.

"To go back, it was the same way with Duke when he had Wellman Braud, Sonny Greer, and Freddy Guy. I remember when *Ring Dem Bells* came out. That was a totally different kind of rhythm section. For the first time you could hear the bass player coming through, and Sonny Greer knew how to team with that bass fiddle, because it wasn't as strong and couldn't cut through like the bass horn had been doing.

"Now when McShann, Gus Johnson, and I got together, we were slightly influenced by Basie, and I was definitely influenced by Walter Page. We used to talk and I would explain to them what Page had told me, about how we should team, how the drummers' foot should not be too heavy, and how the bass player should get a straight line where he could *push*. McShann was naturally talented in how to play with a band, and we began to find each other. During that first year, the horns would lay out lots of times and the rhythm section would just walk for five or ten minutes. We got a guitar player in 1940, but I think it was a fill-up because back in those days certain halls had to have a certain number of musicians.

"Before we went to New York to play at the Savoy Ballroom, we got a postcard from Lucky Millinder which said, 'We're going to send you hicks back to the sticks.' McShann had one of those big old long Buicks, and I was driving, with about five or six guys in it. I took what I thought was the shortest route to New York, up and over the mountains, instead of taking the Pennsylvania Turnpike. We struggled and struggled, but we finally got to New York, raggedy and tired. When we got up on the bandstand where the Savoy Sultans used to play, the people were looking at us like we were nothing. Lucky Millinder was on the main bandstand.

"Everything we had was shabby-looking, including our cardboard stands, and we only had one uniform—a blue coat and brown pants. But from the time we hit that first note until the time we got off the bandstand, we didn't let up. We heated it so hot for Lucky Millinder that during his set he got up on top of the piano and directed his band from there. Then he jumped off and almost broke his leg. Well, that opening was on Friday, the thirteenth of February, 1942. That Sunday we had to do a matinee at four o'clock. In fifteen minutes we played only two tunes, *Moten's Swing*, I think, and *Cherokee*. Bird started blowing on *Cherokee* at that extremely fast tempo. It was way up there. The program was going out on the radio and somebody in the studio called the man with the earset and said, 'Let them go ahead.

Don't stop them!' We played about forty-five minutes more, just the rhythm section and Bird, with the horns setting riffs from time to time. That night you couldn't get near the bandstand for musicians who had heard the broadcast. 'Who was that saxophone player?' they all wanted to know.

"From the Savoy we went to the Apollo, and then back to the Savoy, where we had an incident on a Sunday afternoon. Bird had gone over to Walter Brown's wife and gotten Brown's last five dollars! Brown came over while Bird was on the bandstand and they got into a fight. Each of them was so high, they never made contact. It was like a slow motion picture of a fight. They'd swing at each other and fall down. As a result, a guy came from Joe Glaser's office, gave us a lecture, and demanded that Charlie Parker be fired immediately. McShann had to let him go, but after a couple of weeks we were getting so many complaints that we got him back. I persuaded McShann to let me hire Bird, act as his agent, and look after him. He'd been working at Monroe's Uptown House, an after-hours joint, but not making any money.

"Then we went on a tour down South and had a lot of trouble. In Augusta the operator left with the money at half-time and the cops said we had to pay the rent of the hall, as well as the bouncers and people on the door, or go to jail. In Martinsville, Virginia, the same thing happened, and this time they were not only going to take us to jail but they were going to take our instruments and the bus as well. In Natchez, Mississippi, they put Walter Brown and Bird in jail for smoking cigarettes in a screened porch of the rooming house where they were staying. If they'd been smoking pot, they'd have been there forever, but Johnny Tumino had to go and pay twenty-five dollars each to get them out. When they joined us in Little Rock, they had knots on their heads big enough to hang a hat on. They had really taken a beating. Not that Bird had sassed the cops. He got us out of trouble many a time. I remember once we'd just got through Baton Rouge when the cops caught us. 'You Yankee niggers, huh?' they asked. Bird got up, turned out nice in well-fitting clothes, and started to tell them how his father had worked in Louisiana, all the while giving them a 'Yes, sir' or 'No, sir.' His father had never been there, but they ended up escorting us to the next town. He was talented at that sort of thing. With them, it was all a matter of making an example to keep blacks frightened. Like in Texas, when we were kids, they'd get some guy, tar him, lynch him, and drag him through the black neighborhood.

"By the time we got back to Kansas City, McShann and the band were mad and disgusted. Bird, Buddy Anderson, Orville Minor, Freddie Culliver, and several of them quit. Gus Johnson and I were among the few that stuck with McShann, but that was when Bird officially left. When we went out again, we picked up Paul Quinichette in Denver, and about that time Bird rejoined us. When we got to San Antonio, Paul and Walter Brown were arrested. They were out in a field picking that stuff! Bird was lucky that time and slick enough to get away.

"We picked up Al Hibbler in San Antonio, and when we came on back to New York we had three singers—Bill Nolan, Walter Brown, and Hibbler. Nolan sang the blues before Walter Brown, but he didn't have a nasty voice and was really a great ballad singer. Eventually McShann had to tell him it was too expensive carrying three singers, so Bill went back to Kansas City. Bird left permanently in the fall of '42 to join Earl Hines. I went by the Apollo Theatre in February 1943, when Earl was there. I had just left McShann's band, and Bird bought me a secondhand bearskin coat. 'Now I got some money,' he said, 'the first thing I'm going to do is buy you a coat!'

"I'd had a fight with Bob Merrill in McShann's band when we were in Boston with Don Redman fronting. Bob was supposed to have torn up a difficult piece of music, and he came in the dressing room and said, 'What are you going to do about it, so-and-so?' He had a pitcher in his hand ready to hit me and I got my knife and cut him in front of his ear all the way down to the chin. From that day, I've never carried a knife. I was so ashamed and disgusted with myself, I went back to Kansas City and got a job, first in a packing house and then in a railroad station.

"McShann kept calling me to come back, and I joined him in Chicago. I was with him till he went in the service, but there were guys I had helped get in the band who hated my guts because Jay liked to show me off and have me take solos. When he went away in the army, we were supposed to be billed as *Jay McShann and His Orchestra, featuring Walter Brown, under the direction of Gene Ramey,* but somebody came from the agency and said they'd decided we were taking too much of a chance that way. Until Jay came back, it was to be Walter Brown and His Band, under the direction of Gene Ramey. So I told them I was not going with that. The guys got mad, too, because nobody wanted to work under Walter Brown, who was very hard to get along with and a far worse dope addict than Bird. I understand six men got to Cincinnati, but the music had been lost and that was the end of that band.

"I worked about six weeks with Oliver Todd at the new Reno Club, out on Independence, going towards [Harry] Truman's home. Then the Luis Russell band came through, with Lil Green, the singer. He had lost his bass player, Ted Sturgis, and they asked me to go with him. Razz Mitchell was on drums, so we had a swinging rhythm section. Most of the guys were amateurs, excepting Charlie Holmes on alto and Howard Callender on trumpet. It was really a band put together to accompany singers, in a package. We also had Gatemouth Moore, a great blues singer, who became a pastor down in Memphis. Later on we had the Ink Spots and Ella Fitzgerald. They were all working out of Moe Gale's office, and we played the Apollo three times. I left them in October 1944. Barney Richmond, from Galveston, Texas, took my place.

"I saw Lips Page and he wanted me to stay in New York. I applied for my union card, which meant that I couldn't play with guys who weren't 802 members for six months. When McShann got out of the army, I explained what I was doing, and he understood. Lips Page gave me plenty of work, and I played with Ike Quebec and Noble Sissle, too. Then I worked steady with Ben Webster, and for a time with Tiny Grimes. It got so I was one of the most wanted bass players in New York.

"While I was working with Ben at the Onyx, Prez was across the street at the Spotlight. He was living in the Chesterfield, and I'd walk around there and we'd have breakfast together. He kept asking me to go with him, and when a job at Minton's with Ben folded, I joined him. This was in 1948, and Moe Gale sent us out on tours with six or eight pieces. We had Jo Jones, and Junior Mance on piano. While Prez was out with Jazz at the Philharmonic, I joined Miles Davis and we opened in Birdland opposite Lips Page. Then Prez came back and we had a quartet with Jo Jones and John Lewis.

"We worked at Birdland a long time, and whenever John Hammond came in Prez would say, 'Lady Ramey and Lady Jones, Tommy Tucker's in the house!' John Hammond would sit there with a smile on his face, and on many occasions he really made efforts to regain Prez's friendship, but he never did. Prez used to tell me things, because we were close. I was best man at his wedding and like the father of his children for a long time. He said he left Basie because he wanted a hundred-and-twenty-five dollars a week, and he [Hammond] said he wasn't worth it, or something like that. When Prez and Billie Holiday got together, all they'd talk about was John, and how he tore that band asunder when it was on its way to make it.

"Prez would go out for Norman Granz, but whenever he came back I would go work with him unless I was already committed. We renewed our old, tight relationship, and if I was working for somebody else and got off early I'd wait for him and take him home to his hotel, the Mark, on 43rd Street. He always talked about his cat. He called her Philharmonic. He said something one day that the cat didn't like, insulted her, and the cat jumped out the window from the eighth floor. He said it hurt him so badly.

"Prez, Ben Webster, and Roy Eldridge were the only people who were really vocal about the new rhythm sections. The other guys would say, 'Well, man, there's something new. I ain't going to put it down. I might have to go with it.' But Prez, Roy, and Ben played their solo in phrases, and when a guy dropped a bomb in the middle it killed the phrase. Prez would turn around and say, 'Just give me some tinkdee-doo.' He got rid of one drummer who was back there *soloing* behind him.

"In Kansas City, the rhythm section stayed straight, but in New York, we ran across this new thing Max Roach and them developed. That's how I managed to stay in there as long as I did, with Monk and Dizzy and all of them. They needed a strong bass to carry the beat while the drummer was carrying on. Oscar Pettiford was on 52nd Street and he did lots of work with those guys. He wasn't strong in the rhythm section, but it didn't bother him what they were doing. He could walk right on through it, too.

"Ben and Prez were vocal specifically about the drums. They didn't like what was going on in the rhythm section, and they didn't like the flatted fifths and that stuff. The fact that the piano player sounded like he was one-handed wasn't too bad, so far as the bass player was concerned. They couldn't play like Basie, who could play with both hands and still stay out of the way of the bass.

"Another thing that happened at that time was that the guys who drank whiskey were condemned by the guys on the other side of the street who used dope. They'd see Ben or Prez or Hawk half-drunk and say, 'Man, you a drag. You a damned drunkard.' You couldn't turn around and tell a guy who was high and bent all out that he was a dope addict, because that would be squealing! Drinkers like Ben and Roy used to talk about this. 'Man, this guy's hitting me,' they'd say, 'and I can't fight back.'

"One night the cops came and arrested twenty-four guys on 52nd Street. Sid Catlett and I often used to talk about it. We were hanging in the White Rose at intermission when it happened. 'Man, isn't it amazing,' he said, 'how those federal guys knew exactly who to pick up?'

"When the heroin users started coming out on the Street, it ended the career of lots of trumpet players who could have kept on working. With heroin came the idea that guys had to play with a straight

sound, a symphonic sound. They put everybody down who was playing the other way. Ben Webster had always used a buzz, but he just
eased out of it.

"I stayed with Prez, off and on, until 1957. He was married to a
white girl named Mary and he had sent for her when he was in the
army, in some town in Alabama, I think. He told me they put him in
their disciplinary barracks, and every night the guards would get
drunk and have target practice on his head. He named that *D B Blues*
after his experience—*Disciplinary Barracks Blues.* His style of music
changed after he got out. I think he'd had lots of blows on his skull.
He lost coordination of his speed. He still had the feel and everything,
but you'd see him finding a way to shortcut and get out of holes in his
solos. I think he had a *bruised* membrane in his head. He made a
record called *Up 'n' Adam* and it was like someday he was going to
find those guys who did it to him and knock them down. Later, I made
Down 'n' Adam with him, and that was where he'd got them down.

"His favorite phrase was, 'Nice eyes, no evil spirits,' but I think the
effect of that experience was lasting, at least until he married another
Mary, a colored girl, who gave him two kids, a boy and a girl. That
helped him pull out of it for a while, but then he started getting back
on the bottle and drank so much he lost his taste for food.

"In 1952 I was at Birdland when I had a call from Denver to join
Basie. 'You make the price right, I'll come,' I told them. When I got
there, it was a pleasure working with Gus Johnson again, and we had
a good time. I stayed there several months until I found different ones
in the band had formed a clique to get Gus out. I don't know what
was back of it, except that Gus had had a couple of run-ins with
members of the band, but I made up my mind I wasn't going to be a
part of it. Basie brought a fifth of whiskey up to my room in a hotel
in Detroit, and we talked and talked practically all night. He begged
me, but I said, 'Man, I'm leaving. I know what you're going to do.
You're going to get pressures on you, and you're going to let Gus go.'
He kept Gus until Gus got sick, and when he came back he didn't
have a job. Sonny Payne had it.

"I always kid Gus about the time when we were both singing in the
Trinity A.M.E. [African Methodist Episcopal] Church choir. His voice
is as light as mine, but I was singing tenor and he was singing the bass
line. When we were with McShann, I was the only one with a car,
but I never had it in the daytime because Gus would be over first
thing in the morning. In fact, I had a key made for him. He was having a ball, but so long as he put gas in it and brought it back in time,
I just let him have it.

"A big duty of the big-band drummer is to make those dynamics with the brass, while the bass player has to play along with the reeds unless the arrangement is written so that he marks those dynamics with the brass, too. Gus and I worked on that.

"With the big-band drummers, we'd have to say Sonny Greer and Jo Jones were the original bosses. Gene Krupa wasn't bad, and Buddy Rich is good but more or less an individualist. Shadow Wilson was one of my favorite drummers, an expert. He came in to cut a show while I was with Basie. In fact, I think the best solo I ever took was with Shadow, on *Audubon*, on Sonny Rollins's first recording date. Osie Johnson was a great drummer in a small band. Walter Johnson was good, but I wouldn't say he was a take-command drummer. Sidney Catlett was *the* boss.

"Sidney and I finally started working together in 1946 on 52nd Street. We played many jobs together, especially on Sunday afternoons where they featured 'All Stars.' Usually, we'd have Marlowe Morris on piano, but sometimes Sir Charles Thompson. Sidney was a man who could play anything, in the big band and the small. So could Kenny Clarke—'Klook'—who lives over in Paris.

"But I go back to Sonny Greer, Jo Jones, and Jimmy Crawford, because those cats made the rhythm section pop. They heard everything the brass was doing and they knew how to bring the band up. A rhythm section is not going to play the second chorus like the first chorus. In the first chorus they play more or less easy, and give the soloist especially a chance to find himself and relax, but in the second they're supposed to blow them out of the building!

"After Prez, I went with Roy Eldridge, Sol Yaged, and Cozy Cole at the Metropole for two years. Then I went to Europe with Buck Clayton, came back, and played with Cootie Williams at the Roundtable. After working with, first, Teddy Wilson, and then, Earl Hines, I got a job with Chase Manhattan Bank. I'd no sooner got it than I had a call from Louis Armstrong! But I decided to stay with the bank, although I continued to play weekends, mostly with Buck Clayton and Buddy Tate.

"I'd gone to school again, to the American Institute of Banking, and they gave me a job as a kind of teacher. Altogether, I worked in about forty different Chase banks. I went back to Europe in 1963 and took off in 1969 to go over with Jay for about a month. I retired from the bank at the end of 1975. Although I had a good record and many commendations from them, those people at Chase Manhattan didn't allow me any chance for promotion. I think it was more due to the race than my age.

"As soon as I got my release from them, I shipped my furniture, got in my car, and tore out for Texas. I didn't even have a chance to tell the guys good-bye. I bought a little farm and a home, so you might say I'm a farmer now, but I still play concerts and go to Europe with Jay McShann from time to time."

(1976)

Gus Johnson, Jr.

(DRUMS)

Gus Johnson was born November 15, 1913, in Tyler, Texas, the only son of churchgoing parents. They separated after a few years of married life, and his father went into the army during the First World War.

"We lived right by the tracks," Johnson said, "and I remember when his train passed by the house. He was hanging out the window, waving, and crying. I was about four then."

When his mother married again, he went with her and his stepfather to Beaumont, in southern Texas, close to Louisiana. He had already been drawn to the music he heard on the street or in the circus, and particularly to that of the drums. A drummer, Joe Bonham, lived next door in Beaumont, and when he found how interested his young neighbor was, he persuaded his mother to let him take him to rehearsal every other night.

"I learned everything they played," Johnson recalled, "just by listening. I couldn't read music then. One night the guy who played the bass drum couldn't make it, so Joe showed me the notes the bass drum played and the notes he played on the snare drum. I sat down and played the bass drum that night. I knew how the songs went. Of course, I was very excited, and my mother didn't want to believe my story till Joe Bonham came over and told her. Later, they had a parade and I played the bass drum again, walking down the street. They had the drum mounted on a little bitty wagon, which someone else dragged along."

Meanwhile, Johnson, Sr., had also married again. His new wife was an entertainer, and when the show in which she was dancing went to Beaumont, she took her stepson to see a performance. He was most impressed by the drummer who traveled with the show: "He played a solo that really knocked me out. He had a big bass drum with little Japanese tom-toms on the side. I was right there in front, and it was a great experience for me."

From Beaumont the family moved to Houston. A Dr. McDavid lived nearby, and his two sons had a jazz band that rehearsed in his house. They allowed Johnson to be present, and here again, a good listener, he added to his fund of musical knowledge. He went downtown and bought himself a little drum at the five-and-ten-cent store, and he used to play on this at home, humming to himself. Sometimes, too, he would accompany an accomplished pianist who was living in the same rooming house. He was also lucky enough to make friends with Holden DeWalt, whose father was head of the NAACP in the city and owner of the Lincoln Theater on Prairie. The theater mostly showed movies, but occasionally it presented a show, and it always had a six-piece pit band. Because he could get in free, Johnson went every day and sat down front where he could watch the drummer, Abner Jones. They eventually struck up an acquaintanceship.

"I see you in here all the time," Jones said. "You just watch. Can you play drums?"

"A little bit," Johnson answered.

"You want to sit in and play?"

Johnson was now twelve years old and, although he had practiced assiduously on a snare drum his mother had recently bought him, he was understandably nervous. Nevertheless, when the band played a "medium-slow" number he sat in and "kept time."

"Joe Bonham had shown me how to hold the sticks and everything," he said, "and anytime I came in the theater Abner would get up and just go out and talk to somebody he knew, while I took his place. As long as I kept good time, the band didn't mind. All I wanted to do was to play right along with them, and that's what I did—nothing fancy. And one day when I was playing they flashed my name on the screen as 'Abner Jones's protégé.' That really got to me.

"The DeWalts knew how much I liked the drums, and their son

and I were such close friends that they would take me when they went on vacation. With them, too, I was listening to good music all the time, because they had lots of records. Holden was taking violin lessons with one of the best teachers, a German. I'd see this teacher hollering at him—'Do this, do that!'—and eventually he gave up. My mother wanted me to take violin, too, but I couldn't stand that screeching. I took lessons in music and learned to read with a teacher in the Fifth Ward, a Mr. McMillan. I had to ride a streetcar over there, with my drum under my arm. We were living in Fourth Ward, and they didn't allow Fourth Ward guys in Fifth Ward. They asked me where I was going, and I'd say 'to take my music lesson'; but they didn't ask where I lived, so I never had any trouble.

"The DeWalts were the richest black people in Houston, but Mr. DeWalt was doing too much for the blacks in the city. The operator of the theater shot and killed him. He was paid to do that. That happened in 1929 after I left Houston. Mrs. DeWalt tried to run the theater, but it didn't last long. They opened a barbecue place and did very well for a time. When I went back in 1930, Holden and I plotted to get even with the man who killed his father, but his mother got wind of it and stopped us. We would have got him, too. They had caught him and put him in jail, but he got out very fast. Everybody knew exactly what had happened. The man is dead now; but that messed up things for Holden, upset him altogether, and later on I lost touch with him.

"When we went to Dallas, I went to the Booker T. Washington High School in north Dallas, and I got into everything there, although I didn't meet many of the well-known musicians from there till years later. T-Bone Walker was in much faster company, a rougher kid, always with his guitar, and already mature. Booker Pittman, the saxophone player, was at a dance hall, but he left Dallas and went to South America, where I met him years later. Buddy Tate was from Sherman, Texas, and I never saw him in Dallas. Illinois Jacquet lived in Houston's Fifth Ward, and I didn't meet him till I was with Jay McShann. Budd Johnson's from Dallas, but he's older than I am and I didn't know him. Same thing with Tyree Glenn, from Corsicana. I met and worked with him later in New York.

"I was in the glee club at high school, and we had a very good teacher—Professor A. S. Jackson, Jr. With him, you had to know the music first. He would have you stand up at the blackboard with your back to him, and when he hit a note you had to tell him what it was. I got so I could tell every note he hit. I have almost perfect pitch, like Henry Coker, the trombone player, who was in the same music class. Long and lanky, he had the trombone that had been his daddy's.

"After I finished school, I went to Kansas City to live with my dad.

That was the first time I'd seen him since he and my mother separated. He found out I was in Dallas and asked if I would come and stay with him a while. I had my mind on more schooling, and I went to Southern Junior College in Kansas City, Kansas. My father's brother, Uncle Charles, used to go to all the dances, and he would take me. I heard all the big bands there—Bennie Moten, Andy Kirk, George E. Lee . . . Joe Turner wasn't singing when I got to Kansas City. He was the janitor, cleaning up the place at the Lone Star. Later on, he tended bar, and after he had learned all the blues they started letting him sit in and sing. Pete Johnson was playing piano there, and I was sitting in with him the night I met Jo Jones.

" 'That's Jo Jones just walked in,' Pete said. 'He just joined Basie's band.'

" 'Oh, yeah?' I said. 'See if you can get him to sit in and play.'

"Jo had met Pete before. 'Oh, I'll be over after a while,' he said. He sat down at a table and was talking to different ones, and listening. Finally he came over and said, 'You play a nice drum. I'll take over now.' I think we were playing *I Got Rhythm*, and the way he played was something else. I never saw anything like it, the way he was with those brushes. It was as smooth as you'd want to hear anybody play; and it was just right easy. He was smiling, doing little bitty things, and he wasn't *working*. The personality and everything just knocked me *out!* I was standing there with a grin from one ear to the other. All I was doing was chin-chin-chin-chin, just rhythm, but he came on with all this flash and I was just petrified. I had seen Sonny Greer with Duke Ellington's band, with his chimes and everything, and he had been one of my idols; but for me it was Jo Jones from now on. Nobody else. He was it!

" 'Have you ever been to Omaha?' he asked afterwards. 'I'm sending a band there. Would you like to go?'

"It was a good six-piece band—piano, bass, Floyd Smith on guitar, Jimmy Keith on tenor sax, Paul King on trumpet, and myself. It was the first time I really left home and was out on my own. Jo Jones had told us where we could stay. A fellow named Henderson, a barber, had a house and we all had rooms there. After three months I left that band and joined Lloyd Hunter's. I had bought myself a set of drums from Wurlitzer in Kansas City, what they called a pony set. I loved that little old set and hated to turn it in when I bought a new, sparkling gold set in Omaha.

"I was twenty or twenty-one, and I was all tied up in the music. You could get cigarettes for five or ten cents then, but I wasn't messing with anything like that. I always liked straight bourbon, but I would drink only just so much. Lloyd Hunter's guys would get so drunk, I said I didn't know what I was going to do. Then the bass player left and they couldn't get another. I told Lloyd if he'd buy a bass I'd try to play it. He got his old drummer back, Debo Mills, and he got me a German teacher. I took two lessons. What I wanted to know was how to slap the bass, but he wanted to teach me how to *play* the bass.

"Before this, while I was going to college in Kansas City, I had a vocal quartet called Four Rhythm Aces. Roy Johnson played guitar and could chord on piano. His sister was Countess Johnson, who took Mary Lou Williams's place with Andy Kirk. She was *very* good. Our big thing was imitating the Mills Brothers, and the group was *together*. When beer first came in after Prohibition, we'd sing at places where they had little stands, and guys would throw us money. Then we got a program on the radio station for The Store Without a Name, a fifteen-minute thing every morning at seven o'clock. We had to be at school at eight, so we had to get down there real fast, but we got twenty-five dollars per man each week, and that was good then. I'm mentioning this because in the Four Rhythm Aces I had played some simple bass.

"When I left Omaha with Lloyd Hunter's band, the first thing they threw at me was *White Heat*, a fast number with a bass solo! In no time I had blisters on my fingers, and soon they were bleeding. So I had to wrap my fingers in tape; and then I began to notice that I didn't feel any pain. Eventually, I left the tape off. I enjoyed playing bass, but I didn't really learn how to play it properly. I could hit the right notes, but I was moving the whole hand, sliding up and down, instead of using the fingers.

"I stayed with Lloyd Hunter all of 1936, and when he got another bass player, a fellow we called Bassy, I went back to playing drums. It was a twelve-piece band, with Jimmy Coe on trumpet, Little Jimmy Byron on trombone, a fellow named McKinley on guitar, and Jimmy Bikewood was the tenor player. Lloyd was a good trumpet player, and he wrote a lot of the arrangements. Nat Towles had a good band, good musicians and arrangements that sounded like Jimmie Lunceford's, but we cut him one night at the Greenland Ballroom in Omaha because his drummer was the weakest guy in the band, one who didn't cut the mustard, as they said. Buddy Tate and Henry Coker were with Towles, and it was a really sharp band. They even had a sleeper bus; but they didn't swing like Lloyd's band. The dancers knew what was happening.

"Lloyd Hunter had good musicians, but they were kind of raggedy-like. They could play—until they drank too much. I remember we were playing off in some field near Pipestone, Minnesota. Everybody came from different little towns around, and it was *hot!* A guy brought a bucket of water with ice and then poured a whole gallon of straight alcohol into it. Lloyd's guys began drinking this and soon the band began to sound bad. They were missing notes and couldn't play their horns. I got mad and started cussing out Lloyd and all the guys who were drunk. I told him and everybody else they were fired. I fired the leader of the band that night!

" 'Okay, I'll just take my horn and go,' Lloyd said. He packed his horn up and walked out the door; but then it struck him that it was *his* band, so he came back in.

" 'You can't fire me,' he said. 'I'm the leader of this band!'

"After we finished the gig, he started talking about it: 'I've never had nobody to fire me out of my band before.' It didn't help that I was the youngest man in it.

"They just got on my nerves. I couldn't take it, but I got even one night in Nebraska. 'They going to get drunk,' I said to myself, 'I'm going to get drunk with 'em!' So I got drunk before I got to work. When we started playing, the whiskey hit me and I just threw up all behind the stand. The white guy giving the dance came up and asked, 'What's wrong, Gus?'

" 'Oh, my stomach,' I said, 'it's about to kill me!'

" 'Where'd you eat?'

" 'That little place down the street.'

" 'Don't you know better than to go down there? That place will kill you. Go out there in the bus and get some sleep.'

"I went out and slept for about half an hour, and then went back and finished the gig. It was my first time for anything like that. I never got drunk on the job after that. If I got drunk, it would be after I finished my work.

"I was with Lloyd about a year and a half. One night in Nebraska with him I always remember. There was a blizzard and it was thirty-two below zero. We used to switch about with the driving, and I was driving when I saw a snowdrift right across the road. I stepped on the gas to go through it, but it was like hitting a brick wall and I got stuck. We couldn't move any further, and it was lucky we couldn't because there were about twelve cars ahead of us. I had one of those big camel's hair coats they were wearing then, so I got out and walked about two miles looking for a house where we could get help. The baritone player put a second coat over his own and went looking, too. When he saw a light way across the fields, he started walking towards where he thought he saw it, and he found a house. A white guy came out with a wagon on a sled—no wheels—and took us to his house, and kept us there and fed us for a whole week before we could get out. There were thirteen of us altogether, and we just cuddled up and slept on the floor. The man didn't charge us a penny, but when we got to Omaha we sent him some money. They were real great out west then!

" 'Oh, Lord, help me,' I said as I was getting into that wagon, because I could barely move my feet.

" 'Ain't nothin' *I* can do for you,' Lloyd Hunter said.

" 'Oh, Lloyd, shut up!'

" 'Aren't you talking to me?'

"Lloyd was a funny cat, but a very nice cat!

"Anna Mae Winburn was singing with the band then and she had less clothes on than we did, but she didn't get frostbitten or anything. I think women can stand cold better than men.

"After a year and a half with Lloyd, I got a letter from Ernest Redd, or 'Speck' Redd, as they called him. He was a cousin of Red Perkins and had played piano in his band, which was another 'territory' band out of Omaha, like Lloyd Hunter's. Ernest was a very good pianist who could imitate Earl Hines and play a lot in Art Tatum's style. He had gone to Ottumwa, Iowa, and formed a little band. He had a couple of his brothers in it, John on tenor and Little Johnny Redd. Little Johnny played piano, too, and he could imitate everybody, but he was very young and still going to school. For his age, he was a genius. Later, he went to California and changed his name to Yolando Coloponto, or something like that. Francis Bates was on bass, Leonard Chadwick on trumpet, and my buddy Raymond Fields played alto, tenor, and clarinet.

"Ottumwa was only a small town, but we had a lot of fun. Leonard Chadwick and I had day jobs at Hart's Furniture Store, and I also acted as busboy at the only hotel in town. John Redd worked at a filling station, and Bates worked at a garage. We had all the jobs sewed up! I had been paying a dollar a week for a room in Omaha, but in Ottumwa I had to pay $1.35, with one meal a day included. I shared an attic room with Raymond Fields. It was in a sporting house, and we—the madam and the girls—all ate around one big table.

"I was making so much money, I sent for my mother to come to Ottumwa. I had been sending her money all along, but when I met her at the train station I found she had married again and had her husband with her. She'd kept that a secret, and I was as mad as I could be; but I found them a place to stay and got her a job at the club where we were playing. I was salty with *him*, but he turned out to be an A-1 guy. He's always been in my corner; and they're still together.

"Eventually I went back to Kansas City to visit my father. He worked for the Santa Fe Railroad and was always on the go. While I was there I saw Bill Hadnott, the bass player, who told me about Jay McShann starting a band. He said he was going to join it, and I said I would, too. I had never met Jay before, but they sent for me and Bill introduced us. Jay impressed me as a fine, jolly guy, and we soon opened at Martin's-on-the-Plaza, a swank place, but with Gene Ramey on bass, not Bill Hadnott. We had Orville Minor on trumpet, William Scott and Bob Mabane on tenors, and Earl Jackson on alto. Little Joe Coleman was the singer, and William Scott did the arrangements. Oh, it was a swinging little band!

"We used to have jam sessions at the house where Jay and I stayed on Park Avenue—Park Avenue, Kansas City. We'd rehearse first and then jam. Earl Jackson would get pretty juiced at times, but not enough to mess up. Jay was the only one that really drank a lot. Because we were in the same house, I often made him go to sleep. Then I'd wake him and put him in the shower and get him so he could play his job. He never did throw his weight around as a leader. He's always been an easygoing guy. You couldn't find anyone better than he is, and I don't say that because I played with him. But sometimes after work he'd get drunk, go home, and start raising hell with his wife.

" 'I'm going in and cook her head this morning,' he'd say.

" 'You want me to throw your hat in for you?'

" 'Oh, stop that, W.W.,' he'd say. 'You know good and well she's not going to do anything.'

" 'W.W.' was the nickname he gave me, but I don't know how he dreamed that one up. He had different little names for different guys.

"I had a Model A Ford and we would drive up and down the streets, doing about ten miles an hour, and he would speak to everybody we passed. That was his thing!

" 'Howdedo! How're you? You're looking so *beautiful* today!'

"I'm sitting up there behind the wheel, and people would think we were the nicest fellows in town. Then one day I had just turned my head to look at something and hit the back of a car in front. The bumpers hit each other, that was all, but the guy jumped out and came around.

" 'What the hell's wrong with you? Cain't you drive that car? Don't you have any brakes?'

" 'Yeah,' I said, 'don't you see the marks where I slid after I used them?'

"There was nothing more for him to say, so he got in his car and left. Then Jay turned to me and said, 'W., you drunk?'

"Charlie Parker joined us when we started the big band in 1939 at the Century Room. Before he got to be good, they wouldn't let him play anyplace, wouldn't even let him get up on the stand. But he went in the woodshed and after he came out he blew everybody off the stand! He didn't care nothin' about nobody! When we had our jam sessions, we would play a number in five or six different keys—what we call chromatics. We'd start in B-flat and then take just a half step to C, to C-sharp . . . Even McShann himself had to figure out these keys. Charlie would just run all through 'em. All the guys in the band would do the same, trying to keep up with him. He liked fast tempos, but sweet numbers, too, and he could play those if he wanted. He played altogether different then than he did later. When he went to New York he changed his style, but I liked the way he played his alto better when he was with Jay. His tone was different, and he knew what he was doing. When he got to New York he got on this bop kick.

"Everybody was mad with us when we came into New York, because we were late. The cars had broken down. Johnny Tumino had retreads on one car and they all blew off, so we had to buy new tires. We were supposed to have been at the Savoy at five that evening, but it was almost nine when we got there. We didn't have time to change clothes, so we just got up and played in what we were wearing. Lucky Millinder was on the stand and he had stayed there, playing, because he didn't know whether we were going to show or not. Charlie Buchanan, the boss, was mad and rolling his eyes, but when we started playing the floor started jumping. The jitterbugs were there and they were swinging back. We stayed in one tempo nearly all night long and at intermission Buchanan just ate us *out!* Lucky Millinder and his guys called us the Western Dogs, but we swung 'em off the stage! Lucky was a good front man and he was playing all types of tunes, fast and slow, but when we finally played some fast ones—that was it! Everybody came over to us and was glad to meet us.

"I was with Jay till 1943, when I was inducted at Fort Sheridan. They sent me down to Camp Rucker, Alabama, where I got in the 250th Army Band. My first sergeant was Joe Comfort, the bass player who worked with Harry James, Ella Fitzgerald, and Charlie Barnet. After I got out of the army I was with McShann's big band again at the Famous Door in New York, but then he wasn't getting the right money. I don't think it was so much a matter of the times being bad for big bands. The managers would tell the bandleaders they could get the same money for a smaller band. I think that was what happened to Earl Hines.

"Being in New York was always good for me to hear other famous drummers. I had seen Chick Webb in Kansas City when I was at the College Inn with Prince Stewart. He was a thrill, not only for his bass drum but for everything he did—his accents, beats, and all that. He was strong, and he had his drums tuned the way he wanted them. Then I met Sid Catlett at the Onyx Club, with Stuff Smith. He was real cool with his brush work—very fine, and a very nice guy. I was *very* happy to meet him, and he acted the same way, like he was happy to meet me, a little old western dog from Kansas City. When I came back after the army, everybody was talking about Hal West, another good drummer.

"I was staying with my mother in Chicago when I found out they needed a drummer at the Club DeLisa. Red Saunders was going on vacation and Jesse Miller was taking a band in to replace him for two months. It was a very good show band, with a lot of guys who had played with Earl Hines. This would be in 1945. After that Eddie Vinson sent for me. I met him at the Savoy when Cootie Williams was playing opposite us. Now Eddie was putting his own big band together. Dinah Washington was the singer, but he had to replace her when she got pregnant. It was a good band. We played the Apollo and the Savoy, and then we went out on the road in a package with the Ink Spots. When we came back, we went out again, playing dance halls. I quit in St. Louis, because Eddie was drinking and gambling a lot then and messing up with the money.

"I was back in New York in 1947 when Earl Hines wired me, and I joined him in Chicago. I knew some of the guys in the band, like Budd Johnson and Scoops Carry. Soon after I joined, we made some records that never came out.° He had three violins on the date, but it was a good session. The band soon broke up, and then I worked with Cootie Williams's small band at the Savoy. It was a fine group. Cootie had Arnold Jarvis on piano and Leonard Swain on bass, and we got Willis Jackson from Florida. I gave him the name of 'Gatortail,' because they say all that the people down there eat is alligator tail and rice!

"I went with Basie at the very end of '47 for an engagement at the Strand Theater, but while we were there Shadow Wilson returned and the office wanted him back in the band. Basie insisted I stay till the Strand job was finished, but Shadow took his former place again when the band went into the Royal Roost across the street for about a month. Then they went out on the road, and Shadow put his notice in and joined Woody Herman. So now Basie was without a drummer and he told Jimmy Rushing to call me.

" 'No, I ain't going to call him,' Rushing said. 'You didn't treat him right when he was here.'

"They got Butch Ballard in the meantime, but later on Basie came to see me himself at the Savoy, where I was back with Cootie. He said he was going to start a small band and wanted me in it. I asked how

---

° Several titles appeared on Bravo K 134 many years later.

much, and he offered $125 a week. When I said, 'No thanks,' he raised it to $135. I told him I'd let him know, and when he called me up later I said, 'Okay, I'll make it with you.'

"When we did the first job at the Brass Rail in Chicago, Freddie Green wasn't with us. There were just Clark Terry, Buddy De Franco, Bob Graf on tenor, Jimmy Lewis on bass, Basie, and myself. We were there about a month and we sounded good, but I missed Freddie because we were pals. I saw him when we got back to New York.

" 'Man,' he said, 'tell Basie to hire me back in the band!'

" 'Yeah,' I said, 'I told him already.'

" 'You kidding? All I do is dream about that band,' Freddie told me.

"I'm quite sure he meant it, too, and when we went out again he was in. We had Wardell Gray on tenor in place of Graf. Clark Terry was with us, and he was so versatile. He even played like Louis Armstrong on four or five numbers and just knocked Basie out. He used to sing *Mumbles* on the bus just like he did on his hit record, many years later. This was in 1950, and during 1951 we traveled all over from Boston to Seattle. It was a good little band; but Basie missed the sound of the rest of the brass just as I did, so he decided on a big band and reorganized.° I was in that band until December 22, 1954. On the 23rd I was in the hospital with appendicitis. I was there ten days or so when Basie wrote me to say he had got Sonny Payne and that he was doing a good job. Basie liked a lot of flash, and some of the fellows in the band thought Sonny was better than me because he was more of a showman. Charlie Fowlkes told me that later on he [Charlie] fell and broke his kneecap and Basie didn't hire him back either. The same thing happened to Marshall Royal when he had to go into the hospital. Moral: don't get sick!

"But it was okay with me, because right after that I went to work with Lena Horne and stayed quite a little while, and the money was good. But she had a kind of snarl when she was singing, and I thought I wasn't doing my job and that she was snarling at me! It was really just her way of putting a song over, but it used to worry me. I began to get pains, and the doctor told me I had heart trouble and couldn't play tennis. When I went to another, he took my blood pressure and asked what I was so uptight about. It registered then, right in my

° The band that opened at the Savoy in October 1951, opposite Jimmy Rushing's group, consisted of Basie, Freddie Green, Jimmy Lewis, Gus Johnson, rhythm; Idres Sulieman, Johnny Letman, Gydner Campbell, Tommy Turrentine, trumpets; Matthew Gee, Benny Powell, Jimmy Wilkins, trombones; Marshall Royal, Floyd Johnson, Paul Quinichette, Ernie Wilkins, Charlie Fowlkes, reeds; Bixie Crawford, vocal. Most of the arrangements were by Neal Hefti, Nat Pierce, and Buster Harding.

head, that what I was uptight about was the thought that I wasn't doing my job well enough. Lena had never said anything to me, and Lennie Hayton, her husband, had told me I was playing her numbers fine, but I went right back then and put my notice in at the Coconut Grove in Los Angeles.

"After that, I went to work with Ella Fitzgerald. She had her little ways, too, you know. She's self-conscious, which she shouldn't be at all, because she's so great. But she knew she wasn't as pretty as Lena, although she sounded better. Nobody's going to sound like Ella! Still, she's very sensitive, and if she saw you talking she might think you were talking bad things about her. I used to tell her all the time, 'Go ahead and sing. Nobody's talking bad about you. They love you!' She wanted people to love her, and she's beautiful, to me, but she was always trying to improve herself in everything she did. When Tommy Flanagan came with the group, we were playing some club in Cleveland, and the first night he was doing the best he could when she turned around and like to scared him to death. I saw it happen and just told her, 'Turn around!' I believe that pretty well shocked her, so afterwards I walked right behind her, waiting to hear 'You're fired!' But she had evidently gotten over it. 'This is his first night,' I told her. 'He doesn't know the numbers, and he's nervous.' It worked pretty good, because Tommy stayed on with her for years.

"I joined Ella in 1956 and I was with her nine years, till 1965. I really loved working with her. Norman Granz, her manager, is a great cat, too. Everybody's got their ways, but I like him. He knows what he's listening to and he knows his business. I never had any trouble with him—no problems whatsoever. Norman used to have dinners for the guys, and when I was in Boston with Ella his show featured Oscar Peterson, Count Basie's band, and Louis Bellson. He took everybody on the concert down to a Chinese place for an eating contest! Guess who won the contest? Eddie Jones, the bass player, couldn't eat any more. Basie couldn't eat any more. Oscar Peterson—he couldn't eat any more. But there was Louis Bellson, still eating up! He's terrific on drums, too. He plays so clean, till it sounds to me like he is reading it out of a book. And he can swing. Buddy Rich can, too. The first time I heard Buddy Rich was when I was with Jay's seven-piece band. He was with Artie Shaw, and the manager at the club suggested we try to get him to sit in. Well, he came over, and right then and there he was terrific. This was the first time I heard him, and I knew he outplayed Gene Krupa. We became friends, and later on, when I was with Basie's small group in Chicago, he came by.

" 'How'd you like a new set of drums?' he asked.

" 'Fine,' I said.

" 'Okay, go to Ludwig and tell 'em I sent you over.'

"I went next day, and the guy said, 'Oh, yeah—you're Gus Johnson. We've been looking for you. Pick out what you want!' Just like that. And that was the first set of drums *given* to me that way.

"As for Tommy Flanagan, I 'hate' him like I do Buddy Tate. That's our little thing together. We love each other, actually. Same with George Duvivier. He's another of my worst 'enemies.' If he walked into a record studio and somebody told him Gus Johnson was playing drums, he'd holler, 'Give me my bass and let me get the hell out of here!' I'd do the same if I saw him first and say, 'I can't play with *him*. Get somebody else or I don't make the gig!' Another time, I remember, we were going to California. I was driving his car and we had to stop for a light in downtown Denver. He was arguing about my driving, so I told him to get the hell out of my car—*his* Cadillac. He got out, slammed the door, and I drove off around the block. When I came back by where he was standing, I called, 'Hey, what do you know? You want to ride?' People looking on were amazed when he said, 'I don't mind if I do,' and then got back in the car.

"It's a different thing with Buddy Tate. I call him the Texas Pimp and he's always saying I'm 'messing with his women.' He has a very pretty daughter, and one night she came out to listen to the band. They were sitting together when I went over and said, 'My goodness! Won't you introduce me to the young lady?'

" 'Never mind that,' Buddy said. 'This is my daughter and I don't want to catch you hanging around *her!*' Then he turned to her and added, 'Honey, see that guy? Don't say nothing to him. Don't trust him. Don't turn your back on him! He's a dirty guy!' Then Buddy looked up at me and laughed."

By the time his engagement with Ella Fitzgerald ended, Gus Johnson was well known and well liked wherever jazz was heard. He subsequently worked with Woody Herman, Ralph Sutton, Zoot Sims, Gerry Mulligan, Al Cohn, and Stan Getz.

"The only somebody I had any worries with was Bob Brookmeyer. He would keep calling me 'Gussie.' So while we were in Europe I had to straighten him out." After an engagement with Peanuts Hucko in Denver, Johnson took Morey Feld's place in The World's Greatest Jazz Band during the period when its fortunes were directed by Dick Gibson. He also appeared at many of Gibson's famous jazz parties, and when he brought his wife and children along from New York in 1973, they liked Colorado so much that they moved out to Denver and have since made it their home.

Looking back over his long career, he named Ben Webster, Coleman

Hawkins, Chu Berry, Lester Young, and Dick Wilson as his "top" tenor players; Roy Eldridge, Buck Clayton, Clark Terry, Hot Lips Page, and Sweets Edison as his top trumpet players. "Cootie Williams was something else; and then there was Freddie Webster, with Lunceford, who had Snooky Young sitting right beside him, and they both could blow."

"My top alto man was Johnny Hodges," Johnson stated. "Nobody had his sound; and you know who loved him? Charlie Parker. Johnny had me on a lot of record dates, and I loved playing with him. 'You're just the guy I want to see,' he said a while back when I went by where they were playing. 'I'm making a date three weeks from now.' But he died before ever the three weeks were up!

"I played with Duke Ellington, too. Every time Sam Woodyard didn't show up, they'd call me. I think the reason was because I had played in Mercer Ellington's band four or five times, and he'd told Duke about me.

"Back in those days there were a lot of good bands. Things change suddenly in this country and big bands just might make a comeback again. I know a lot of kids around here [Denver] who like that sound."

(1979)

Paul Quinichette

(TENOR SAXOPHONE)

"My father was French, a kind of lend-lease surgeon. They brought him over to Denver, Colorado, to consult about something. He saw my mother, and they fell in love and got married. Because she was a Negro, his parents didn't want him to marry her, but that only made him mad. His surname was Quinichet, and he continued to pronounce it that way, although he added 'te' to make it look different.

"My parents weren't musical, but by the time I was ten my dad had me in a beret and knickers, with a clarinet on my arm. All I could do was Beethoven and Bartók—classical music. I had regular tuition and I could read around the corner. I went to Denver University and then for two years to Tennessee State College. They wanted me to play in the band and they told my mother they'd give me my tuition and everything free. So Mom took me down to Nashville, and she didn't know anything about that southern thing! I studied hard and then went back to Denver U. and graduated from there, a music major. I was burning the midnight oil a lot of the time, and asking myself, 'Why in heck do I have to study history, when I'm trying to be a good *musician?*'

" 'Listen,' they used to tell me, 'if you're a musician you've got to know history, art, and everything. It's not all just notes. When you are out there talking to the public, you can't just look stupid. You've got to be accomplished, educated, in other things, too.'

"I went for it, but my parents were disappointed when I turned to jazz. My mother wanted me to be a surgeon like my father. So when I rebelled, she didn't speak to me for years. But I bought her her first mink coat, and after that it was okay!

"I learned jazz from the oldtimers. They taught me, and then I kept going. I could read, but improvisation is another story. Yehudi Menuhin once said he wished he could improvise. He's a genius, but he can only play from the music. I think you learn to improvise by listening and practicing. You make a lot of mistakes, but you proceed by trial and error. You acquire stock phrases and riffs. That's a beginning, then you have to have a knowledge of the basic harmonic changes in the songs you're going to play. I was so frustrated at first that sometimes I'd go home crying, because I couldn't improvise like I wanted to. I guess it's really a matter of innate ability, or a bent to do it, and if you have it sooner or later it comes out. With me, it was a matter of experience. Then it all seemed to come suddenly to me.

"When I was coming up through the ranks, Lester Willis Young was living in Denver, working with a fellow named Art Bronson. He liked me and helped me as best he could. We used to practice together and everything. 'What do you think about *this* passage?' he'd ask. Or he might say, 'I don't like the way you played *that* passage. *This* way, see?'

"One time when I was playing at the Village Vanguard in New York, Mary Lou Williams and Ben Webster came down and tried to insult me. They were going to carve me. So Lester heard about it, and he had actually taught Ben how to play. 'You leave my man alone,' he told him, 'or I'll get up there and tear you up!' See, Ben was all bark and no bite. He wanted to show off, but he'd give you the shirt off his back. He insulted Joe Louis once in Sugar Ray's bar uptown, so Joe punched him right in the stomach. Pow! He didn't do that anymore! He was such a belligerent character, but he played wonderful saxophone.

"You know that Lester's father had like a carnival band? Irma Young played fantastic alto saxophone and Lee Young played drums. Louis Jordan's father had a carnival called The Rabbit Foot Minstrels, but Lester's father's band was more sophisticated and beat 'em up all the time. It was no contest.

"I started professionally with territory bands during the summer semester. Then I'd go back to school again. I played with Nat Towles and Lloyd Hunter out of Omaha, and I did some things with Bojangles and Ernie Fields out of Tulsa, Oklahoma. The first time I met Charlie Christian was during one of these summer 'vacations.' He was working with a girl named Anna Mae Winburn, who ended up as leader of the International Sweethearts of Rhythm. Those girls were good! They made Phil Spitalny look like a fool, and they messed up Ina Ray Hutton when she had a band, too. They came from all over, those girls, and they were playing! Some were Chinese, some were Jewish, and some were colored. When they went down south, they'd put dark makeup on so as not to run into trouble, and they had a big old matron, like a warden, and she'd lock those girls up at night!

"Sir Charles Thompson was with Nat Towles, and Neal Hefti used to bring his arrangements around. Jimmy Mundy was writing heavy arrangements in those days, and Neal used to say, 'Well, listen. It's gotta be light!' So even then he was doing those light and nimble things like he did for Basie years later. That must have been around 1938.

"When I finished college, I started traveling with bands like Lucky Millinder's and Shorty Sherock's. I was the only non-Caucasian in Shorty's band, and he was an Irishman drinking Bushmill's whiskey. One time, we were on the North Side of Chicago and he was hanging out with Jack Teagarden and Jimmy Dorsey. They got so juiced, he didn't show up for a week, so I had to take over the group until he sobered up and dried out. It was only a quintet, but they were very prejudiced on the North Side.

"I dropped the clarinet entirely because I couldn't make any money playing it, and I was a clarinetist first, but it was tenor people wanted to hear. I always liked Artie Shaw better than Benny Goodman. Buster Bailey could outplay Benny, too. Benny had Gene Krupa, Harry James, and Toots Mondello to back him up, but Artie Shaw had only Georgie Auld, out of Bunny Berigan's old band, behind him. My aunt had a record of Benny Goodman trying to play alto saxophone, and it used to crack me up. Now Rudy Rutherford, who has been playing with Earl Hines, is an excellent clarinetist, but he can't play the saxophone. Old Omer Simeon sure could play clarinet, but it went out of favor. The flute came in and it's not a good jazz instrument—too sticky, too tight. I never liked the soprano either—too raucous and brash a sound. When you look at the pictures of the old bands, all the sax players had several instruments in front of them, but they could only play one good.

"The old-timers, like Buster Bailey, played the Albert system. So did Artie Shaw. The Albert system was simpler, more like a saxophone, but when the Boehm system came in the old-timers couldn't get conditioned with it. That's why they say, 'Put the blame on Boehm.' But the Boehm has more range, three octaves, and that's why I chose it. I figured the Albert system was going to be obsolete.

"Josephine Baker came over here once when I was with Basie, and I had to pick up the clarinet again to play her arrangements. It was the same backing Valaida Snow. When Lester Young and I were practicing, we didn't have a Selmer or Leblanc from France, but an old metal clarinet. We called it 'the gas pipe.' It sounds just as good as the other kind if you know what to do with your embouchure and how to 'imaginate.'

"I don't play a Selmer saxophone to this day. I call my horn Matilda and I've had eight of them. This one, the eighth, is a collector's item, a Conn. I can get up over the brass section with it, even when I'm with Basie.

"'How can you get up over those brass riffs behind you?' fans and young musicians ask me.

"'I've got Matilda here,' I tell them. 'That's how.'

"When Prez came back from Paris, another company had given him a couple of horns and he gave me one of them.

"'Prez,' I said, 'this ain't doing nothing!' He put his down, too.

"Kansas City was only five or six hundred miles from Denver, and I just *had* to go there during the summer, to learn about this music. Mother would be sending the police out to haul me back to Denver, and she would be screaming at me when I got back, but I wasn't that dumb and nobody hurt me. Even the underworld people would take up for us musicians. So I met all the people like Joe Turner, Sammy Price, Charlie Parker, Al Hibbler, and Jay McShann. I ended up in Jay's band and in 1942 we went to the Savoy Ballroom, playing opposite Al Cooper's Savoy Sultans. We were so goddamned raggedy, the uniforms would whistle when the wind blew! But we blew those Sultans right off the stand!

"Jay McShann plays good piano, more than Basie actually. He's got that Kansas City shit! And when he plays boogie-woogie, even Sammy Price can't beat him. In fact, Sam is scared of him.

"Jay was always an easygoing guy. Of course, during the war we had transportation problems. If we were traveling by train to the next gig, and officers came aboard, we might have to stand up all the way. One time, when we were down in Tulsa, Jay hired two station wagons. 'Paul,' he said, 'I want you to drive this one. I'll sit in the back.' So I drove all the way from Tulsa to San Francisco, because we had a deadline to meet. I was taking no-doze tablets to keep me awake. We were using retreads, because you couldn't get new tires then. They kept blowing and we'd pull into a gas station, have them jack the wagon up, and put another retread on. The guy driving the other car kept as close behind us as he could. A sixteen-piece band and all the horns in two station wagons! Can you imagine that?

"I stayed with McShann until he went in the army. I was straw boss for the band. I had a portable typewriter and I had to write his letters for him, because he stayed juiced. That's why they nicknamed him Hootie. (It's a western term—gimme a drink of that hoot, gimme a shot of that red-eye.) I got so mad with him in San Francisco—he wouldn't buy the right uniforms—that I quit and joined Johnny Otis.

"Johnny had a full sixteen-piece band and Little Esther, who was about eleven years old. Preston Love was playing first alto and we were getting some of Basie's arrangements and recording them before Basie did. I was with Johnny Otis about two years. World War II was over and the bottom seemed to drop out of everything. I remember working on Sunset Boulevard with Benny Carter and Big Sid Catlett, and I remember being in a hotel room next to Sammy Davis, Jr.'s. We were so broke we were eating mustard sandwiches.

" 'Hey, man,' he says, whenever he sees me, 'how about them mustard sandwiches?'

"About this time Louis Jordan came to get me. He really wanted Wardell Gray, but Wardell had told him, 'Fuck you, you Uncle Tom, I ain't going to work for you!' But by this time Louis had his Tympany Five and he was a big shot. He told me once about when he was playing first alto with Chick Webb. Chick would let him go out and sing a couple of tunes. Apparently he was in the wings with grease and a stocking cap on his head. When he went out on stage, all the people laughed and he looked like a fool. I guess that started something, but he was considerable of a blues singer and in the year I was with him we made a whole lot of records.

"Next I went to Lucky Millinder at the Savoy Ballroom, which was owned by the Metropolitan Life Insurance Company. A lot of people don't know that. Ed Wilcox, who took over the band when Jimmie Lunceford died, had hired me, but Lucky had a good band and was paying his musicians more than Basie. Andy Gibson was writing most of the arrangements and they were good, never too ponderous. I always told Lucky he missed his calling, that he should have been a producer, like Ziggy Joe Johnson or Larry Steele, but he liked fronting a band and he'd stand out there on big old dice at the Apollo. When we were there, Mr. Schiffman wouldn't show the movie, but he'd show previews of what was coming and cartoons. There were no elevators backstage, so we'd hardly have time to run upstairs and change uniforms between shows. Remind me not to go there no more!

"I did go back again with Joe Thomas when he had a sixteen-piece band. He had been the tenor star with Lunceford.

" 'Come on, Paul,' he said, 'work with me. There won't be any solos for you, because I'm the feature.'

" 'That's all right,' I said. 'Just give me the money.'

"Now he's a funeral director in Kansas City, burying people, and he's got Cadillacs and all the money.

"Around this time I worked with J. C. Heard at the Village Vanguard. Sometimes I did dates with Lips Page and Red Allen playing those old Dixieland tunes I can't stand, but which are part of the game. That's where the money was at that particular time, and they'd help me and tell me where to go if I got screwed up. But Hot Lips Page stranded us up in Canada. I couldn't get out, couldn't pay my hotel bill. He had been juicing and gambling at those after-hours joints, and he'd gambled our money away. His wife worked for the First National City Bank and she bailed us out, but when he got home she wouldn't let him in the door! The next thing my doorbell was ringing.

" 'It's me,' Lips was hollering. 'Move over, move over!'

" 'Well look, Lips,' I said, 'I can't do this no more. To hell with ya. I'm going to Basie.'

"Basie sent Wardell Gray to get me. He was mad with Lucky Thompson, and Lester had told him, 'Paul will play my chair, not Lucky Thompson.'

"Wardell was a good saxophone player, but a junkie. Wardell disliked me, because like Stan Getz, Zoot Sims, and Al Cohn, he didn't really know Lester. Lester paid them no attention, but he and I were together, and he showed *me* how to do this and that. I think the others resented this and may even have been jealous of my good luck, especially when people started calling me the 'Vice-Prez.'

"Basie was doing the Kate Smith show then and everything was fine. He had Freddie Green—'Green Bay' or 'Pepperhead', as we used to call him—and I think he'd be lost without him. If you put the tempo too fast, Freddie kept it down there, always controlled. He's got it right there, in his wrist. And Basie listens to Freddie Green, one reason why he's still successful to this day. He might not listen to me, but he's going to listen to Freddie, because he knows that's where it is. Basie would stomp off the tune two or three times, getting it right, what I call the right slot, the right tempo. When Walter Page died, the only one he had left was Freddie, the only one he could rely on to keep tempo. After Gus Johnson left, he got Sonny Payne, who did all that trickerating like Lionel Hampton used to do before he started playing vibes.

"The reason I left Basie was because of the records I was making for

Mercury in 1952. There were no big hits, but they were fairly successful, so Basie said, 'All right, get out of the band. I'm going to be your
manager.' But James C. Petrillo, the boss of the union, sent Basie and
me a telegram which said in effect, 'You cannot have a monopoly on
a sideman.' So then Basie thought he would put it in his wife's name,
but Petrillo sent her a telegram, too! Meanwhile, Basie had hired Lockjaw and others for the band. They had families, too, and he couldn't
turn them down just because this caper of ours hadn't worked.

"Soon after that I got a call from Ralph Watkins to go into Basin
Street East with Benny Goodman. We had a lot of trouble. 'Benny
only plays fifteen minutes,' Ralph said, 'because when you guys start
swinging the people don't buy booze.' At any other joint, Benny had to
play forty minutes. Previous to this, Gene Krupa had said to me, 'Listen,
if you're going to work for him, get your money, because he's like a
horse trader. He's going to get you at the lowest price he can.' That's
the way he is, too. Gene also told me how when he did the concert
with Louis Armstrong, Benny was so mad because Louis had top
billing that he took a whole bottle of scotch and threw it up against
the wall!

"After the Basin Street engagement, he called me for some concerts.
I went to Montreal with him and I got a big write-up all on the front
page. Coming back on the plane he started screaming at me.

" 'Everybody thought it was *your* band,' he said.

" 'Well, thank you, Fletcher Henderson,' I answered.

"That was bad. So I told the truth on him and he didn't want to
hear it. He didn't hire me again.

"After that I got out of music, because they seemed to be booking
only rock 'n' rollers. Moe Gale was trying to talk me into being a
rock 'n' roll saxophone player, but I felt it was so wrong I couldn't
do it. I got a little poor then, until an investigator for the welfare department got me a grant from Nelson Rockefeller in Albany which
enabled me to take a three-year course as an electronics technician at
RCA. He knew I had been a ham operator at one time. I had got so
discouraged, I had to do something. If I had had a pistol, I would have
shot Elvis Presley right in the face! That's how I felt about it. I
figured I'd go to school and know two trades instead of one, but I fully
intended picking up my horn again. After I graduated from RCA in
1971, I gradually started back.

"Catherine Basie sent me a telegram asking me to take a group into
Basie's lounge uptown. There was no organ in the room, but she wanted
one. In a Harlem garage, all covered with cobwebs, I found her one
and I fixed it up. All went well till Arlene Francis, who had a television
show, went up there. Some woman took her white mink coat and left

a rotten old fox coat in its place. So now Basie was mad. He had to replace the coat, and he was saying, 'You shut this damn place up! If it won't be her, it will be someone else again. I can't keep paying for a lot of mink coats!'

"Later, I started working at a place downtown called Churchill's with Brooks Kerr and Sam Woodyard. The manager wouldn't let us play any slow ballads. So it was *Jumpin' at the Woodside* all night. I had two heart attacks down there, on the stand, working too hard, seven nights a week. I was tired, but I went to the West End Café and got a little attention. Then I went into Michael's Pub with Jay McShann, and made a few records. Now Matilda and I are looking for something good to show up."

(1977)

Jimmy Witherspoon

(VOCALIST)

"I was born in Gordon, Arkansas, August 18, 1923. My dad was named Leonard Witherspoon, and my mother's name is Eva. She's still living, in Stockton, California. My brother Leonard lives in San Francisco, and my sister Jimmie lives here in Los Angeles. Everybody in the family was musical, really. My mother and sister both played piano. My mother played in the Baptist church, and my daddy sang there, too. That's where I started singing, in the choir. I was singing a solo in the church when I was five years old, a song called *I'm Goin' Through*. I did it nearly every Sunday, and my mother played piano for me.

"My father was a brakeman on the Missouri Pacific Railroad for twenty some years, and we could ride a pass anywhere in America and Canada. He died when I was about six years old. I went to school in Arkansas, but when I was sixteen I forged my mother's name and got a pass and came out to California, because I figured in Hollywood I'd be able to get a start singing. But it was hard to get a job here in 1939 if you were black. Not to be paranoid about it, the only jobs blacks could get in California were as chauffeurs, busboys, or maids. It was hard. I used to walk all the way from 42nd and Central to 5th Street downtown, just to try to get a job. Finally, I got a job washing dishes at the Owl Drugstore, 8th and Broadway, for seventeen dollars a week. I worked there for a long time and worked up from dishwasher to cook.

"While I was working at the Owl Drugstore, everybody used to think I was a singer. I used to go to Little Harlem, and that was the first place they let me sing. T-Bone Walker had a white drummer from Texas, named Jimmy, Big Six playing tenor saxophone, and Norman Bouton on trumpet. Bouton was going with a girl from my hometown, and he asked them to let me sing. 'Let Toots sing,' he said; and I might as well confess that 'Toots' was my nickname then. From then on, whenever T-Bone would call me, I'd get up and sing.

"I was too young to run around with T-Bone at that time. He was the biggest thing on the West Coast, the biggest name in the black area. He used to do a radio show with Al Jarvis, one of the first blacks to do that. He had recorded with Les Hite by then, and also with Freddie Slack on a tune called *Riffette*. Not too many people seem to know about that, but I know it, and I remember it. A lot of people recognized T-Bone's great talent, but they didn't give him the chance he should have had. He never had it, even until his death. But T-Bone didn't have regrets. He lived a good life, and he made a lot of money. He had a lot of hits and he gambled. He also gave plenty of money away. He never did say no, even when he wasn't doing too good at the end. He helped everybody, but he was an artist who could never get stranded anywhere in America, because there'd always be somebody to help T-Bone.

"Besides Little Harlem, I also used to go to Lovejoy's and stay up all night long with Slam Stewart and Art Tatum, who played in the hallway there. They all thought I was entertaining, even Tatum. Lovejoy's was a big after-hours joint, a chicken place upstairs at Vernon and Central Avenue. Ivie Anderson's Chicken Shack was right across the street.

"For a time I was also a cook on the Union Pacific, and when I was in Omaha I used to sing with Johnny Otis. I always claim that I'm the one responsible for him coming to California. I used to hang out with Jesse Price and Harlan Weatherford, and I told Jesse about Johnny. So when Jesse was getting ready to leave, he told Harlan what I had said, and Harlan told me that when I went back to Omaha I was to tell Johnny Otis that if he came here he could have Jesse Price's job.

"What Johnny loved in those days was Basie and big-band stuff, and when he came out here he got a good big band himself. He dug musicians, but he didn't dig blues then. It was later that he saw the way the wind was blowing with rhythm and blues and found out how popular the blues were in Europe and Japan.

"I was still at the Owl Drugstore when war broke out, and they wanted me to go in the army. When they sent me job papers, I had my landlady tell 'em I'd gone to Richmond to see my mother. When I got there, I went over to the Maritime Commission, told 'em I was a cook, and they gave me a bar and a half as chief steward and cook in the Merchant Marine. I just didn't want to go in the army!

"I was in the Merchant Marine when I sang with Teddy Weatherford (the pianist) in Calcutta. That was the first blues I ever sang in my life! We were unloading ammunition and stuff for the CBI theater—China, Burma, India—where they were fighting the Japanese.

"Teddy Weatherford had gone to China with Buck Clayton. When war broke out there, they all went home except him, but he couldn't stay in China so he went to India and married an Indian lady. He had a family, and he died in 1945; but when I was there he had a big band in the Winter Gardens and was doing well. He played great jazz piano, and also violin. He had Caughey Roberts, who Lester Young had brought to Count Basie. He's a good alto player, and he's still playing in town. Teddy also had a tenor saxophone player out of Chicago. Anyway, when they asked me to sing, I sang with 'em!

"When I got back to California, my mother was living in Vallejo, and that's where I joined Jay McShann. Walter Brown had left Jay in San Francisco, and then he had a little light fellow who used to pattern after Wynonie Harris, but he quit, too. Anyway, everybody in Vallejo was asking Jay to let me sing. Eventually, I sang a Joe Turner tune, *Wee Baby Blues*, and Jay McShann hired me that night. I was about twenty; and I really never had to scuffle like a lot of people did.

"I liked Jay right away. We went to Stockton next day, and then on up to Seattle. We had to ride trains at that time because of the gas shortage, and on the way he told me he wanted me to sing conventional blues, as close to Walter Brown as I could. For the rest of the tunes, he said for me to go for myself. I admired him for that. Where so many other bandleaders would have been telling you, 'You got to do what I tell you,' he said, 'Go for yourself!'

"Jay taught me a lot, and I stayed with him. I would ask what to do, and he told me. He took a liking to me because I would listen. He's only about a couple of years older than I am, and he's not as old as a lot of people think he is. He came to Kansas City *young*. He taught me a lot of moral things. Drinking was his worst enemy at that time, but contrary to what a lot of people thought, Hootie was one of the most wonderful persons. He was much misused at that period. He was just starting to make money, and a lot of people got to him. Managers are a necessary evil, but there was no protection in those days. The army had taken him right in the prime of his career, but with his flat feet he couldn't stand around in the army long. When he got out, he put another big band together, and that was when I joined him. He was carrying sixteen pieces, and he had great musicians like Paul Quinichette, Jesse Price, and Benny Bailey during '44, '45, and '46.

"I never forget the first theater date I played. I had been looking forward to it for a year and a half. It was at the Regal Theater in Chicago, and Dinah Washington and the Ravens were also on the bill. They went to the manager and said there was too much singing, so they cut me off the show. That hurt me worse than anything in my whole life. It was the biggest disappointment, and Jay couldn't do anything about it. All I'd been doing was opening the show; and Dinah was the star.

"Years later, when I'd gone out on my own, I had the pleasure of working on the same bill with her in Chicago. I called Jay McShann in Kansas City and said, 'Jay, this is the first time I ever had any vindictive thoughts about an entertainer, and I'm going to stop this show cold if I have to crawl on my knees!'

" 'Who is the entertainer?' he asked.

" 'Dinah, and I'm opening up in front of her.'

" 'Good,' he said. 'Go ahead.'

"She was a great talent, and I never did mention that she'd been responsible for one of the biggest hurts I ever had; but I think she sensed how I felt. She introduced me in the second show by saying, 'Ladies and gentlemen, now the male star of our show . . . !'

"McShann had taught me how to go on the stage. He had also taught me never to worry about where they put you on the bill. I still use that knowledge today, and it pays. It may be a big responsibility closing a show, but I don't want it. I'd as soon open as close; because I know whoever's following me is going to have to be good, and that makes the whole show good.

"I guess I was with McShann about three years. We used to drive everywhere together, and he took me into his confidence. He was married then and living in South Bend, and I knew a lot of his private, personal business. It was all *great* experience. You could be mad at

Jay, but he'd have you laughing twenty minutes after you hit the bandstand because he'd be so involved in his music. After a while, he had to reduce the band from sixteen pieces to five or six. Times were rough for big bands then. We kept Benny Bailey. We had Addison Farmer on bass, and Pete McShann, Jay's cousin, was on drums. On alto we had a guy we called Floatin' Booty, but his real name was Bill Barnet. We played all over, including here in Hollywood. I asked Jay to play on the session with me when I made *Ain't Nobody's Business*, the one that sold all the records. A lot of people didn't know he was on it.

"Art Tatum loved Jay McShann, idolized him. He said he was the greatest blues player he ever heard in his life. One day I never forget, we were down at Mike Jackson's, a bar on Central Avenue, and Tatum was drinking a beer.

" 'Would you like to sing one?' he asked.

" 'Yeah,' I said.

" 'What key?'

" 'Put it in B-flat.'

"He started in B-flat, but after that he went to every key in the ladder, and I didn't know what key he was in. Jay had told me what he would do, so I paid no attention to Art and his chord structures, kept my mind on B-flat, and sang right through.

" 'Spoon,' he said, hitting me on the shoulder and laughing, 'nobody in the world can do that. I put you through so many keys.'

"He had a sense of mischief and loved to do things like that.

"Jay and I never had a falling out—*never!* People like to tell how he'll go in his pocket and pull out a dollar if somebody needs money. He's the greatest in the world for that. He can have $5,000 in his pocket, but out will come a one-dollar bill! He pleads poverty all the time, but if you press him he'll say, 'You're about to kill the old man,' and out will come two dollars! I don't know, but I guess when you're hiring sixteen men you have to use tactics like that.

"At the time I'm speaking of, we were staying at the Mom's Hotel on 5th and Central, here in Los Angeles. All the bands stayed there—Lionel Hampton's, everybody's. The manager of the hotel took a liking to me and said I should stay out here in California and further my career. I didn't think much about it until we went to Omaha and some of my things were stolen out of the truck. From there we went on to Chicago, where I told Jay I was thinking of going back to California to try something on my own.

" 'Aw, he just had a nightmare!' was what Jay's manager, Johnny Tumino, said when he heard I was leaving. But I did quit, because I knew I could stay at the hotel. That kept me going till I got straightened out; but I had it rough for a time."

(1978)

Jimmy Witherspoon was much more versatile than the average blues singer, and his career subsequently burgeoned. He toured frequently in Europe, where records had made him popular. He had his own radio show in Los Angeles, starred in a film entitled *Black Godfather*, appeared often on television, scored a big success at the Monterey Jazz Festival, went to Japan in 1973, and sang in clubs throughout the United States.

Eddie Barefield

(ALTO AND TENOR SAXOPHONES AND CLARINET)

"I was born in a little coal town called Skandia, right out of Des Moines, Iowa. All my people were coal miners—my father, his father, and grandfather's father. They all worked in the pits, and they'd go from one town to another in the Des Moines area. My father died when he was thirty-five. They had to bring him out of the mine for an emergency appendix operation. I was eleven.

"My mother played some piano and my father played guitar around the neighborhood. They used to sing in two-part harmony, songs like *Sweet Adeline,* and I'd join in with third harmony when I was just a little tyke. I was the first child born in the family [December 12, 1909], and I used to spend half my time with my grandparents and half with my father and mother. I always wanted to be a fighter, and my father taught me. I had a punching bag in a barn in my backyard, and I'd be out there punching and training myself to be a fighter all day. When I started school, the big boys used to put pennies in a hat to see me box older kids 'cause I was very good with my dukes. I had a hundred and twenty amateur contests, fighting for the Des Moines newsboys at Tommy Ryan's.

"A friend of mine, Merle Williams, lived across the street and was learning to play piano with a lady named Josephine Guy. 'Boxing's a rough game,' he said, 'Why don't you learn to play music?' So I started studying with his teacher, and practicing on his piano. After about a year I quit, because the fellows thought Merle was a sissy and they began to call me one, too. I didn't want to be a sissy, so I went back to boxing! But Merle was persistent, and one day he came over and persuaded me to go to a rehearsal of a community band they were organizing. 'The girls will like you better if you go to music,' he said. When we got to the rehearsal, an old man was playing tenor saxophone. I had never seen one before, and I immediately decided that that was what I wanted. I found out that with the C-melody sax you didn't have to transpose, and I begged my mother to get me one. When Christmas morning came, there was a York alto saxophone under the tree. 'Santa Claus didn't have any C-melody saxophones left,' my mother said.

"The first thing I did was to get a screwdriver and take that alto apart! I wanted to see how it worked, but when I couldn't put it together again, my mother put all the pieces in a bag and took it back to the store. She wouldn't let me have it again until she found a teacher for me, a fellow named Charles Bushman. I took one lesson from him and he taught me the preliminary scale. From then on, when my mother gave me a dollar for a lesson, I put my horn in a drugstore and went to the movie. But I was practicing every day, practicing with records. We always had records in the house—Fletcher Henderson's, Sidney Bechet's, Boyd Senter's, and Rudy Wiedoeft's. In those days, even Senter wasn't *too* corny. I learned all Coleman Hawkins's solos, all Sidney Bechet's, and some of them I still play, like *Wild Cat Blues*. I used to listen to Joe Smith's trumpet, too, on the records by the blues singers.

"Merle Williams and I got a little group together, the Jimtown Rounders, with Melvin Saunders on drums—just a trio. We used to rehearse, and people got to like what we were doing. My mother always believed in lodges and social groups, and she had joined me to a junior lodge. We used to have a turnout on a certain day of the year, and we'd all be dressed up with red socks and everything. I was standing watching the parade when a lanky kid came running by, and he yelled, 'Look at the sissy with the red socks on!' I couldn't break the line, but as soon as the parade stopped I was going to go out and punch him in the nose. We started fighting, but after they pulled us apart he told me he was a trumpet player. 'Well, I'm a saxophone player,' I said. His family lived in Perry, Iowa, and his father knew mine and was a coal miner, too. That's how I met Leroy White, later known as 'Snake' White.

"He joined the Jimtown Rounders, but he and Merle didn't get along. Snake was a tall, handsome guy and he had all the girls, but Merle was short and jealous of him. However, we started playing little school dances for kids and we became quite popular and began to get all the jobs around. Older musicians would come down and turn up their noses at us, and I guess we made some pretty horrible sounds.

, "One day I was downtown buying the music of *Aggravatin' Papa*. (Snake was the only guy in our group who could really read. Merle could read a little, but all pianists did in those days was *oompahs*. I was playing by ear, although I was like the star.) They were building the Capitol Theater on 6th and Grand Avenue in Des Moines at that time, and as I passed by a guy way up on the scaffolding hollered down to me.

" 'Hey, kid, where you going?'

" 'I'm going home.'

"He came down and saw the music in my hand.

" 'What you got there?'

" 'Some music.'

" 'Let me look at it.'

"Then he wanted the trumpet part, but I told him we already had a trumpet player. He came and heard the group, said he would play tuba, and got him an E-flat. His name was Edgar Pillows, and he was in his twenties, while we were all under fifteen. He took over and we became the Edgar Pillows Night Owls. He started booking us and we began to play homecomings, country clubs, and all kinds of dances. In 1926, he got a job in Omaha for us to go to Galveston, Texas, on a train with Miss Nebraska for a beauty contest. They took the seats out of one coach so people could dance, and we played the whole trip. We stopped off in Hot Springs and several places in Arkansas, and stayed ten days in New Orleans. Alphonso Trent's band was playing at the Hotel Galveston. That was when he had Snub Mosely on trombone, James Jeter on sax, Lester Clark on trumpet, and A. G. Godley on drums. When we were not playing, we hung out with them and had a good time. We were in Galveston nearly a couple of weeks and it was great experience for a boy of sixteen!"

This was the real beginning of Barefield's extraordinarily varied professional career. Pillows next got the band work with a carnival, where they played for a minstrel show led by Rastus Jones. After traveling through Missouri, Arkansas, and Texas, Barefield arrived in

Kansas City on Labor Day, 1926, when he should have been home and getting ready for school. He heard all the bands in the area, including those of Bennie Moten and George E. Lee, and was preparing to go to California with a bunch of youngsters from Pittsburgh led by Syd Valentine, when detectives, acting on his mother's behalf, found and returned him to Des Moines—and school.

After playing with pianist Ace Oliver and groups in the Des Moines area, he went to Chicago by train at the instigation of his friend, Bill Fulton, riding the blinds hobo fashion. "I soon found out," he said, "that I wasn't as great a player as I thought I was." While looking for jobs, he went to work in the Hammond stockyards so that he could send money each week to his mother. He lived with Fulton, a chef, who always kept a big pot cooking for friends from Des Moines. In return, Barefield taught him saxophone.

Barefield met Louis Armstrong for the first time on Easter Sunday at the Warwick Ballroom. "He didn't mean too much to *any*body then," he recalled. "People used to laugh and make fun of him. 'What does he think he's doing, singing?' In those days, if you didn't sound like Caruso you weren't singing! But when those records like *Heebie Jeebies* and *Cornet Shop Suey* came out, musicians began to take notice."

After Barefield was hired by a group called the Society Syncopators, the leader soon discovered he could not read and recommended him to Bill Frye, a pianist who played house-rent parties and chitterling struts on weekends. Working with Frye, Barefield made a living until a telegram came from a group called the Virginia Ravens, who had heard of him in Des Moines. He joined them in Genesco, Illinois, playing tenor saxophone, and soon became an attraction with his slap-tonguing and antics modeled on those of Slim Freeman, "a big, long, tall guy" who was featured with the Midnight Ramblers. The Virginia Ravens were led by Lee Lancaster, a singer and something of a disciplinarian. When he in turn found out that Barefield could not read, he fired him, but the band's sponsors, a Mr. and Mrs. Fath, insisted that Barefield remain. Ill feeling ensued, and the saxophonist scornfully rejected Lancaster's offer to teach him to read. Then one day he realized that he was being foolish, so he went to Lancaster and apologized. The singer thereupon taught him for an hour a day, and in a few weeks he was able to switch from tenor to alto and play lead saxophone. This led to a job at the Broadway Gardens in Madison, Wisconsin, with a band led by pianist Don Pilips. The pay was sixty dollars a week, very good for the time, and he enjoyed his stay in Madison, but the engagement ended with the summer. He went to stay with a cousin in Milwaukee, where he again encountered the Virginia Ravens. The group was reorganized with the addition of Merle Williams on piano, Edgar Pillows on bass, Snake White on trumpet, and Joe Thomas [Walter 'Foots' Thomas's brother] on alto saxophone. They worked the Wisconsin territory sucessfully until one night at a resort on Sharon Lake, Barefield had too much applejack and took out his .38 automatic on stage and fired it off, scaring everybody in the ballroom. ("Most of the musicians who went on the road had guns," Barefield said, "because we were carrying money and needed protection.") This incident provoked a split in the band. Five of the musicians elected to stay with Barefield, among them Pillows, White, and a "terrific" piano player named Frank Hines, who had replaced Merle Williams.

On their way to Minneapolis, they ran into Red Curry, a gangster from St. Louis. He got them to play on the train, collected money for them, and then took them in a truck to a gangsters' convention on Grandview Island. It was late when they arrived and the hotel was dark, but Curry had them open up from the truck with *Hail, Hail, the Gang's All Here*. Lights went on and startled heads popped out of windows.

In Minneapolis, the musicians organized a group they called the Ethiopian Symphonians, and it was here that Barefield taught himself to write arrangements, copying from Fletcher Henderson records. "Everything was written from the alto saxophone," he said, "and after I'd learned the part I'd write the harmony parts. Frank Hines got me interested in chord progressions, so I got a McNeil banjo book and really started studying chords."

That winter of 1927–1928 was a hard one and work was scarce, but Minneapolis was then a wide-open city with a flourishing red-light district. Barefield used to play at Royal Langford's, where the prostitutes congregated after work, and often he would end up with a saxophone bell full of money. Eventually, pianist Clarence Johnson— "known as Mr. Five by Five, because he was short and wide"— secured a job at the Spencer Hotel in Bismarck, North Dakota, and Barefield and Snake White went with him.

The Young Family Band was in Bismarck and it was there Barefield first met Lester Young, who was playing alto saxophone. Their hotel rooms were near together, and one day Young knocked on the door and introduced himself. He had heard the records Barefield was playing, among them *Singin' the Blues* and others by Frankie Trumbauer, whom he always referred to as a strong early influence.

After they had all returned to Minneapolis, the Fletcher Henderson band came to town. Barefield remembered that Benny Carter heard Young jamming there "and flipped over his playing." The Trumbauer style was translated to tenor saxophone when Young changed to that instrument in Minneapolis, and he became "the first tenor player to play different from Coleman Hawkins." Barefield himself cited Coleman Hawkins as a major influence, along with Sidney Bechet and Johnny Hodges. The latter's soloing on Ellington's *It's a Glory* made a powerful impression on him.

"The Do Dads from Diddy Wa Diddy" was the picturesque name, derived from a comic strip, of a seven-piece group Barefield and his friends, Snake White and Merle Williams, formed to play at the Nest Club. When bandleader Eli Rice came through the city, he heard and liked the group and persuaded Barefield to join him in Milwaukee, where he was required to play clarinet for the first time. Ed Inge, who was there with Bernie Young's band, gave him his first lesson. Earl Keith was more responsible for his subsequent proficiency. "Earl was one of the finest musicians, on saxophone and clarinet, I ever played with in my life," Barefield said warmly. "He had a great ear, he could sight-read, and he played a little piano too, but he never went far away from Minneapolis. His parents were good to him, and I think he had a bunch of kids. He was a better jazz man than Chauncey Haughton, another underrated musician. Chauncey could have been a virtuoso, but he was out of place in Duke Ellington's band." Keith played lead in the Rice band, Willard Brown tenor, and Barefield third saxophone. Others in the band who were to make big names in jazz were Joe Thomas and Eddie Tompkins on trumpet, and Keg Johnson on trombone.

After a short period with Grant Moore's ten-piece band, Barefield took Ed Inge's place with Bernie Young, whose group went into Chicago's Savoy Ballroom in the fall of 1929 for the winter. Young's group featured Barefield as the "Child Wonder" (he was nineteen) and trumpet player Raymond "Syd" Valentine as the "Patent Leather Kid." Valentine was "a very tall, handsome fellow, and vain, but he'd amaze you when he played. He was very fast and didn't care nothing about Louis Armstrong or anybody. Louis and his band played opposite us at the Savoy in 1930 when he was doing his fifty high Cs, but Raymond still stood them on their ears." Also in the band was Cassino Simpson, the one pianist in the city who could challenge Earl Hines. Unfortunately, he became addicted to heroin and ended his days in a mental home. Omer Simeon was playing in the Metropolitan Theater with Erskine Tate's band. "I used to go over just to hear him," Barefield remembered. "He was a great saxophone player as well as a clarinetist, but he never had the credit he deserved. His record of *Beau-Koo Jack* had just come out."

At the beginning of the summer, 1930, the Bernie Young band went to Tulsa, where Barefield met the Alphonso Trent band again, this time with violinist Stuff Smith in its ranks. Tulsa, an oil town, he recalled as being full of "pavilions and dance halls" at that time. Returning to Chicago, he rejoined Grant Moore and went to Sioux City, Iowa. When he was late getting to the bus one day, Moore drove off and left him.

Next he went back to Eli Rice and Minneapolis, where he found Lester Young again, playing at the Nest Club with Frank Hines. After a short stay with Rice, Barefield joined Frank Terry's Chicago Nightingales in Toledo for an engagement at the Recreation Ballroom, where he heard Art Tatum for the first time. "Somebody led this little blind guy up on the bandstand, and Frank Terry said we ought to hear him play at intermission," Barefield said. "Well, I'd heard Earl Hines and Frank Hines, and I was on my way out of the hall when I heard this *Brrrrrrmmmm!* on the piano. That was Art, and he stood me on my ear. He lived across the street from me with his parents, and we became friends. Teddy Wilson was in Toledo, too, so we had a little gang that used to hang out together—Art, Teddy, George White [a saxophone player], and me. We'd go around to the houses and jam in the barns. Art played at a club called Noble's, and he also had a job on the radio, so he got a chauffeur. One night we were down at Noble's wondering where he was. We found out that he went out for juice, got in his new Ford, and ran into a telephone pole. I don't think he could see so well then as he did later."

From Toledo, Barefield returned to Minneapolis, where Ralph Cooper, "a promoting type of character," sent for him to join the band at the Regal Theater in Chicago. But the union intervened and took the whole band off the job because Cooper had imported an out-of-town musician. "So there I was," Barefield said, "stuck in the Hotel Trenier with Ralph Cooper and Reginald Foresythe as roommates. Reginald was from England and he was writing arrangements for Earl Hines at the Grand Terrace. Earl told me to bring some of mine over, but I had only written for one trombone and when I added another trombone part I wrote it wrong. It sounded horrible, so then Reginald showed me how to voice for the brass.

"Luckily for me, Bennie Moten's band came to work at a theater on the North Side, and they stayed at the Trenier, too. Ben Webster had left Blanche Calloway and was with them, because they were planning to reorganize the band. I was always jamming in those days, and my reputation had gotten around. So Ben took me out to the theater and I jammed with Basie and all of them. The result was that they took me back to Kansas City with them. We had three saxes, two altos, and a tenor, because Jack Washington was playing alto then.

They got Hot Lips Page and Joe Smith—Pops Smith's brother—on trumpets. Joe had married a Kansas City girl and wanted to live there, but he didn't stay too long. He drank a little, but nobody could play like him. He had been in that show, *Shuffle Along*, and everybody knew him through his records. He was a quiet, moody guy, and I liked him, but he was quite independent, too. They got Dee Stewart in his place, so we had Dee, Lips, and Joe Keyes for a trumpet section.

"I was the lead man in the reed section and we cooked up a lot of 'head' arrangements. If somebody knew the melody, we'd play that first. Then Ben would take a solo, and I might take one. Lips Page would come down next and play ten, fifteen, or twenty choruses, while we set up riffs behind, a different riff for each chorus. That's how riffing started. Lester Young and I used to play a dance for kids in Minneapolis, just two alto saxophones, no piano, bass, or drums. We'd pat our feet, take solos, and riff together. Of course, it could get repetitious, but the reason the Moten band was so much looser was because it had so little written material. The playing was freer, but we didn't just grab a bunch of notes and play 'em without any division. No matter how many notes you play, you divide them into some kind of form. The music has to be divided and accented. Hawk started double-timing, but he still swung, even on a slow tune. Parker, Dizzy, and all of 'em double-timed, but when you start getting away from that and playing a group of five or a group of seven, then the swing leaves. When we were playing by ear, jazz was limited by what the ear could hear. Then we utilized chords, up and down, and Dizzy and the boppers embellished it a bit more by using the scales. But I never did go along with all the talk about a Kansas City style, a Chicago style, a West Coast style. Styles are individual things, and at one time everybody had his own different, distinguishing style.

"We played around Kansas City and down in Oklahoma. Sometimes, to make ends meet, I had to play with other bands, but then Moten decided to go east once more. He was established, but it was a hazardous trip, especially since someone was stealing the money. It was quite a band we had, with Lips, Dee, and Joe Keyes on trumpet; Eddie Durham and Dan Minor on trombone; Jack Washington, Ben Webster, and myself on saxophones; Basie and Walter Page in the rhythm section, with Leroy Berry on guitar and Pete McWashington on drums; and Jimmy Rushing as vocalist. Bennie Moten played piano, too, but Basie played most of the time and Buster Moten conducted.

"We were stranded in nearly every city on our way to New York—in Columbus, Ohio, in Zanesville, Ohio, and in Cincinnati. In Zanesville I stayed in Sy Oliver's mother's house. I didn't know Sy then, but I met his mother, his sister, and his little brother. We were all young in the Moten band and we didn't care. We just hung around the town until they got another raggedy bus. And those buses were always breaking down! One time in Virginia we were coming down one of those steep hills and the brakes refused to work. The handbrake came out in the driver's hand, and the bus went careening down through a town at about sixty miles an hour. We were frightened to death and we were just lucky we didn't run into anybody.

"Being stranded meant that you were in a town without work or money. You had to eat and sleep, but you couldn't get out. Bennie might hustle up enough to get us a meal ticket. We would eat *anything*. Mostly it was hot dogs and chili, with booze. We weren't alarmed, because it was a common thing, and finally, somehow, we got to the Pearl Theater in Philadelphia. We knew we were going to work for a week and get a week's salary, so everybody could have some money in his pocket. We were all whooping it up, juicing, and taking the chorus girls out. When payday came, we all lined up to get our money. When I saw Bennie send a guy out to get a plate of beans and some whiskey, I felt something was wrong. Then he told us that the bus and the box office receipts had been attached to pay for uniforms he'd bought on his previous engagement at the theater, when he borrowed the money from Mr. Steiffel, the theater owner. So there we were, standing out in front of the theater with our bags and horns—and no bus! The man had booked us for a whole week only to get his money back. Now we couldn't pay our rent, our tabs, or anything. But Bennie finally met a little, fat colored guy named Archie Robinson, who was an agent, and they went off together in Archie's car. They came back with a great big old raggedy bus, and we all piled in to go to Camden to record for Victor, something they'd cooked up at the last minute.

"Now we were all very hungry, but somewhere or other Archie found a rabbit. We pulled off the highway to a pool hall, where they made a big tub of stew with this one rabbit. I always figured it was a cat, because I couldn't understand where he'd find a rabbit in Philadelphia or Camden. Take the head off and you wouldn't be able to tell the difference. I always made a joke of it and kidded Basie about having had some cat stew. Anyway, it tasted very good. We stood around the pool table sopping up the gravy and stuff with bread until the tub was empty, and then we got in the bus again and went over to the church they used as a studio. That was my first record date.

"We recorded ten sides: *Toby, Moten Swing, The Blue Room, Imagination, New Orleans, The Only Girl I Ever Loved, Milenberg Joys,*

Lafayette, Prince of Wales, and Two Times. We never got paid for them to this day. *Toby* was a tune I wrote, and when I later signed a new release on it a woman gave me fifty dollars and said I'd be getting further checks. But I never got any more checks, and in '41 or '42 I instituted a suit against Victor. Ben Webster talked to my lawyer and they advised me to drop it, because Victor might one day be able to help me. I never got any help nor any money, not even when *Toby* was reissued. I don't know whether Moten originally got money. We were just young, stupid kids at the time.

"The way we played on those records, with those fast tempos, was the way we used to play every night. We didn't have any music, but we sure used to swing! The people used to do the Peabody to those fast numbers. In the old days they called it the one-step. It was white dancers who named it the Peabody.

"I think the secret of swinging comes from the drummer's foot. Why don't drum teachers teach the drummers now to play the bass drum today? They all have fast hands, but no foot. Buddy Rich can swing because he's got a good foot, but most of them can't keep the beat going without rushing the tempo. Willie McWashington didn't do anything on those Moten records but just keep time. In those days that was *important*. Of course, Walter Page's bass was the big thing, and working with him was the making of Freddie Green. He's not an outstanding soloist, but for time. . . . The different sections of the band rehearsed separately, so the piano, guitar, bass, and drums were *together*, but today everybody has his own time. Even the horn players played in time in the old days, but nowadays guys think they're too good to pat their feet! When I teach now, I encourage guys to do that, because it helps get a body rhythm that helps their playing.

"After the Camden session, we set out again and were stranded in Newport News, Virginia. Eventually we got back to Kansas City. There were a lot of musicians there, but not much *regular* work, despite what they say. The work was around, out on the road, and K.C. served as a center. There were jam sessions, but they were nearly all freebies. Piney Brown was like a numbers man and he owned the Subway Gardens. He liked musicians and took care of them, so all the guys hung out in his place. Hot Lips Page's man was Ellis Burton, who ran the Yellow Front Café. But there were no places where a big band could keep working steady except Fairyland Park, where Thamon Hayes had the band.

"So I left and joined Zack Whyte's band in Columbus. Sy Oliver, Snake White, Ben Richardson, Vic Dickenson, Eli Robinson, and a boy named Benson on drums were in it. So was Gus Wilson, who played trombone and was Teddy's brother. He was writing, too. He made fifty arrangements on the same tune, *Clementine*. Every night he would come in with a new one and tear up the old one! I was playing lead alto and I often wish I hadn't. I'd have gotten more solos and more recognition if I'd been a tenor player. Hawk was the cause of that. His work from the early twenties onwards meant that the arrangers favored the tenor. Basie was a tenor freak, not only for Lester Young but for Herschel Evans, too. I first heard Herschel when I was in San Anton' with Bennie Moten. I got him to come up from Texas to Milwaukee once. He didn't stay long. He hadn't seen snow before, and the first day it snowed he went back to Texas!

"I stayed with Zack Whyte till I got pneumonia in Chattanooga, and I had to spend a couple of months there recuperating. Then I got an offer to join McKinney's Cotton Pickers in Erie, Pennsylvania. We went out on the road from there with Billy Bowen conducting, and they finally fired McKinney! We went down to Carlin Park in Baltimore and played there all summer. Roy Eldridge and his brother Joe joined us there. We already had Buddy Lee on trumpet, Prince Robinson on tenor and clarinet, Ed Cuffee on trombone, and Cuba Austin on drums, but the band was really going downhill then and we were making only thirty dollars a week.

"In the fall of 1933, the Cab Calloway band came to the Hippodrome Theater in Baltimore. We used to go out jamming every night till daybreak in our red Eton jackets, and one night Cab was out drinking and heard me blowing in some little club. He invited me down to the theater to hear his band, but I thought he was drunk and didn't go. Then I ran into Doc Cheatham and Walter 'Foots' Thomas, who knew me by reputation, and they said Cab had looked for me to go by.

"I went down the next day and went backstage. Baltimore was segregated then and the doorman stopped me and said Mr. Calloway was busy. (The Hippodrome was for whites, but the Royal was a black theater.) Cab was just coming downstairs and saw me. 'Yeah, let him in,' he said. So I stood backstage and watched the show. Afterwards, I borrowed an alto and we had a little jam session. Cab called Irving Mills and told him to come on down from New York. 'I've got Johnny Hodges and Benny Carter all wrapped up in one guy!' he said.

"Cab hired me as an addition to the three saxes he already had, but I went back to the Cotton Pickers that night. It was payday, and when I said I was leaving they said I couldn't without giving two weeks' notice. They refused to pay me and we had a big fight right on the bandstand. I had been using Billy Bowen's clarinet and I said, 'If you don't pay me, I'll keep it.' When he grabbed at it, I hit him. Then three or four of them jumped on my back, and I threw all of them up against the wall. The only guys that didn't jump on me were Roy Eldridge and Prince Robinson. We fought all the way to the hotel, but I didn't get my money, and when I went down to Cab the next day I had a black eye. He asked what had happened, and after I explained he put a hundred dollars in my hand right away so I could go and pay all my bills.

"Right after that, we played a week at the Capitol Theater in New York, and then we went into the Cotton Club. The following year we went to Europe, but before we left we had a record session where I was featured on an instrumental version of *Moonglow*. Cab always sang on his records, but after we'd made three titles that day he found he hadn't any lyrics for a fourth, so we made *Moonglow* in one take to complete the date. After we got back from Europe, we were playing a dance in Texas and heard this record on a jukebox. I was always crazy about Benny Carter, and when I heard the saxophone chorus I thought it was him. I asked the manager of the place who it was playing, and he said, 'Don't you know your own record?'

"Cab was one of the best bandleaders I ever worked with. One thing I specially liked was that he would always let bygones be bygones. He periodically threw a party for the fellows, and he always gave lavish Christmas presents. When payday came, you never had to go and ask for your money. The road manager was there to hand it to you. Everything was done first-class—traveling, playing, and accommodations. He wouldn't work unless the accommodations were suitable for all the men. He was so hot then he could dictate his terms. The kids used to come to the theater, bring their lunches, dance in the aisles, and pull his clothes off him. Often, when I dream in my sleep, it's about Cab, and I'm always rushing, trying to get to the job on time, but I never get there.

"I left Cab in California in 1936, not that I was dissatisfied, but I was always a bit of a vagabond and this was the first time I'd been in such a beautiful climate. Also, I was sick with ulcers and I decided I'd settle there. I thought I was a pretty carefree guy, but later I found out I was a worrier. I still am, although I think I'm more relaxed now. I worry about not being able to play like I want to play, and I still practice two or three hours a day."

Barefield formed a band of his own that included such musicians as Don Byas, Tyree Glenn, Dudley Brooks, and Lee Young. His old friend, Snake White, came out to join him. The union raised the customary objections to out-of-town musicians, but Barefield got around this by adding the secretary of the union to his personnel. He also wrote a book of arrangements for the band, which soon secured a coveted engagement at Frank Sebastian's Cotton Club. The band was a success, played up and down the West Coast, and appeared in a movie called *Every Day's a Holiday* with Louis Armstrong.

When the attractions of Los Angeles began to pall, Barefield disbanded and took the opportunity of going back east as a member of Fletcher Henderson's band for an engagement at the Grand Terrace in Chicago. Because Hilton Jefferson was playing first alto, Barefield played third and inherited the role of clarinetist, previously the responsibility of first Buster Bailey and then Jerry Blake. The keys of Henderson's arrangements made the clarinet solos difficult, and after a week he indicated his intention of quitting. "Aw, man, don't worry," Henderson said. "I'm satisfied. Just stay in there." Barefield did that, took his parts home each night, practiced, and after a while got them under his fingers.

From Chicago he went to Don Redman's band at the Savoy Ballroom in New York. (*"Down Beat* credited the alto solo on the record we made of *Milenberg Joys* to Don, but it was me.") From that time on, New York was Barefield's base. He had more bands of his own. After Chick Webb's death, he led the Webb band for Ella Fitzgerald. He auditioned for a job on ABC's Blue network, got it, and stayed four years, working with leaders like Paul Whiteman and Paul Laval. For two years he conducted the band in *A Streetcar Named Desire.* After touring South America with Cab Calloway in 1951, he became involved, like so many musicians of his generation, in the Dixieland revival and often played with Sidney Bechet at Ryan's. ("When Sidney got drunk he'd say, 'You got it the rest of the night!.' Then he'd go home.") The big-band business had deteriorated as a result of wartime taxes and other restrictions.

"For about ten years," Barefield said, "people forgot to dance. The music became listening music, and the bands began to stop swinging. When you have to get the people to dance, you have to swing!

"For me, the greatest alto player who ever lived is Benny Carter. Charlie Parker brought a whole new and fresh thing to saxophone playing, but there was no comparison in terms of sound. Benny's fitted him for playing lead *and* solo work. Charlie's led to solo work only. It wasn't right for a lead sax, but he was one of the most talented musicians. Today, all these young white kids have got a Charlie Parker school going. And not all the bop tones were bad. For instance, Clifford Brown, the trumpet player, played all the stuff and had a big, fat sound with it.

"I think there is a misunderstanding among the younger musicians.

There's a time for a straight sound and a time for vibrato. A musician like Benny Carter can play with or without vibrato, as all good saxophone players can. When you play in harmony together, and everybody has a different part, vibrato should be used, but when you play in unison and everybody's playing the same thing, then you need the straight tone. People who rehearse bands, and a lot of musicians, don't always know this.

"Basie's band *sounds* better rehearsed than all the other bands I know of today. I give the credit to one man, Marshall Royal. He's a thorough, trained musician, good on both alto and clarinet, and he turned out to be one of the greatest lead men. He and Bobby Plater are both from the Benny Carter school. I don't agree with people who said Marshall played too loud. Benny played strong like that, too, and he could take a bunch of mediocre saxophone players and make them sound good. When Marshall wanted to come down, he'd bring that whole section to a whisper, but when he came on strong, I don't think the rest of 'em had the technique to come up with him, especially on fast numbers."

A hardy survivor, Barefield continues to play with enthusiasm and conviction in all kinds of contexts, but he is not blind to the realities of his profession: "The record companies have played God and changed the whole trend. The first thing they ask is, 'What's your gimmick?' There's no gimmick in just playing good music."

(1972)

Leo "Snub" Mosley

(TROMBONE AND SLIDE SAXOPHONE)

"I was born in Little Rock, Arkansas, December 29, 1910. I used to be a clown in school, and that's where I got my nickname, after a popular comedian called Snub Pollard. The high school band was my first step. My parents weren't musical and I had no tuition at all. I got different trombone books and just studied and practiced. The books tell you the positions, and you go from there to chords and things like that. The first real lessons I ever had were years later in New York with David Gornston.

"I was inspired by a trombone player in Little Rock called Slats. He played with Sterling Todd and His Rose City Orchestra. Todd played piano and had about ten pieces. Alphonso Trent got his inspiration from that band.

"Trent formed a band in Fort Smith and came down to Little Rock. He had James Peter and Hayes Pillars playing saxophones. They looked a bit like Mexicans, and so did Trent. He was a beautiful piano player, and he always kept the style he started out with. His band could swing, but it also played pretty music. I was fifteen when I joined,

326

and my father, who was a drayman with wagons and trucks, didn't want me to leave home.

"There wasn't much work around Little Rock, apart from hotels one or two nights a week. Sometimes we'd go to Brinkley or Memphis, for a short engagement. Eventually we decided we were going into Texas. That's why I believe in predestination. It was one of those things that determined our destiny.

"We called Trent 'Foney,' short for Alphonso. He was wealthy and his parents were considered to be among the few Negro millionaires at that time. Real estate was their game. Trent didn't need to worry. He was Grand Master of a couple of lodges, and he really got into music for kicks, but nevertheless we found out about hunger on our travels.

"We played three or four towns on the way to Texas. I remember we played a show right in front of Sale's Drugstore in Helena. One day we made only six dollars, out of which we had to buy sandwiches and pay for our night's lodging. We were nine pieces and we traveled in three cars. The great A. G. Godley was on drums and Britt Sparks on tuba. A bit later we got Peanuts Holland on trumpet.

"The section we went into was very bad, racially speaking. We played a place called McKinney and they advertised us on the front page of the newspaper: FAMOUS NIGGER BAND HERE TONIGHT. Nigger, not Negro! I kept that paper for years. It was insulting talk, but a lot of them had used the term for years and forgotten its significance. There were intelligent and quite nice white people in Texas who had become so accustomed to using it that they wouldn't think of apologizing.

"When we got to Dallas, we played a curb dance out at a park. We didn't have many people, but the guys just felt like playing. In the meantime, a bellhop at the Adolphus Hotel had told the manager about our band, and at intermission he took Trent over and introduced him to Mr. Ellifritz and a bunch of people sitting over on the side.

" 'I think we might just try you fellows out for a couple of weeks at the hotel,' they said.

"In the Southwest, where I was born, it was not unusual to play in big hotels for white dances, but we were the first colored band to play for a white audience in the state of Texas. Not only that, we were playing in the Adolphus Hotel, *the* biggest hotel in Texas at that time. The Goulds, the Rockefellers, they all came to that hotel. I never forget when Paul Whiteman came and stayed there in 1926. His band was nationally famous, and when Henry Busse, his trumpet player, came up to me and said, 'Young fellow, I like what you're doing,' I thought it was a heck of a compliment.

"We went in there for two weeks and stayed a year and two months.

The difference between then and now was that we had to go in and
out by the back elevator, although inside we had every compliment
and respect. No such thing as using the front door, even though we
were artists! Management couldn't do anything about that then, and
they took a big gamble when they got us in there. It was a big step
forward, and the Ku Klux Klan planned to tar and feather us, just
because we were playing for the white people. That wasn't the feeling
of the majority, especially not of the big, rich people, but only of the
lower element, the crackers.

"There was some opposition, too, from the biggest white band around
there, the Jimmy Joy band that played hotels in Dallas and the
Muehlebach Hotel in Kansas City. Later on, we played the Muehlebach, too.

"After we left the Adolphus, we were at the Gunter Hotel in San
Antonio for six or eight months. I met Buddy Rogers and Clara Bow
there. It was big time! When we started broadcasting over one of the
biggest stations in the nation, WFFA in Dallas, we used to get an
enormous number of letters from all over, even from Canada. We
became so famous in Texas, Arkansas, and Oklahoma that we used to
make even more money when we went on tour than at the hotel engagements. To make ten dollars then was like making fifty nowadays,
and often we'd make as much as seventy-five apiece a night. If it had
all been organized with agents as in New York, we wouldn't have
made as much, but we didn't have agents to contend with. Everybody
was writing about the band in those days, because it had done what
they called the impossible. All the men were upright guys. They dressed
beautifully, carried themselves and behaved well—and they played! I
really got my schooling in that band.

"Trent was a happy-go-lucky guy, but he knew what he wanted.
As I said, we used stocks, but we also had great head arrangements.
When he brought Sy Oliver in, Sy changed the band somewhat, but
we didn't let him change it too much! He was a better arranger than
he was a trumpet player, but he was only in the band, I would say,
about six months.

"I did the writing on *I Found a New Baby*, and it was a hit when
the record came out. I think Gus Wilson did *Clementine*, which was on
the back. He was Teddy Wilson's brother and a very good arranger.
I'll tell you why *Clementine* sounds like Lunceford to you. Trent was
Lunceford's inspiration.

"When we first got famous, we went to Memphis to play a dance,
and Jimmie Lunceford came to it. In fact, I gave him his first arrangement. I don't remember what it was, but I sneaked it out of our book
and let him copy it, and then put it back. Willie Smith was playing in

a local school band that Jimmie was teaching, and Sy Oliver was still
with Zach Whyte. By the time Sy joined us, we had three trumpets, two
trombones, and four saxophones. He was quite enthused about the
band and the fine musicians in it, and we were quite enthused about
his arranging.

"I took most of the trombone solos, but Gus Wilson took some.
I never have been influenced by other trombone players, and I always
had my own style. Sometimes people say, 'Doggone, you sound like
Tyree Glenn!' That's because I gave him his first lessons. He used to
come to Dallas when he was a little boy, and I used to slip him into
the dances.

"The guy that impressed me most was Jack Teagarden. He was with
Mal Hallett when we played a battle of music in a restaurant in Cleveland. He impressed me greatly and we exchanged compliments.
Jimmy Harrison I heard only on records, but I don't believe what
people say about Teagarden getting his stuff from Jimmy.

"Tommy Dorsey wasn't a jazz soloist, but he could play beautiful,
melodic music. I like both Dicky Wells and J. C. Higginbotham, as
friends and trombonists. They came up about the same time as I did,
but they didn't influence me. I always stressed tone, and no matter
how fast I played I always tried to keep my tone going.

"Going back to the Trent band, I should say that a lot of the time Sy
Oliver stood up and conducted. It was when he left that we got George
Hudson. We also got Stuff Smith. We'd heard of him, and he used to
stand in front of a little group and direct it. He played a helluva jazz
violin, as you know. He was one of the greatest I ever heard. I've
heard other guys who were sweeter, but for swing and all-round band
work, jazz, and everything, he was *it*. He sang and danced, too, and
so did I. We made a record for Gennett where Stuff, Hayes Pillars,
and I were the vocal trio. It was on *Gilded Kisses*, the first number I
ever wrote.

"We played in different sections of the Adolphus. One day we'd be
in a place called The Spa, where there was no dancing at all. Bamboo-
land was another place that was just for listening. In both of them,
besides jazz and sweet, we'd play silly classics like *William Tell*, but
not in the Junior Ballroom. Besides Stuff on violin, we had Wendell
Hayman, who doubled on alto and violin.

"We went back to the Adolphus Hotel twice, each time for three or
four weeks. It's still a fine hotel, and my biggest ambition is to go
back there with my own group. It's owned by the Busch family, and
money is no object.

"The second time we played San Antonio, we were at the Plaza Hotel
for six months. It was in San Antonio that I picked up the slide

saxophone. I heard a guy there who had something that was almost like mine, but more like a whistle. Anyway, it gave me the idea. It's altogether different from the trombone. The positions are smaller, and it slides up and down, which was awkward for me at first. It's not a real complicated instrument, but you've got to play the exact positions because they're close together. Nobody who set his mind on it would have much trouble. Very few of these instruments have been made, because there has never been any promotion. But I've had mine stolen twice. The second time I had to buy my own instrument back! I used to use a trombone mouthpiece, but now I use a sax mouthpiece on what is basically a soprano sax.

"The Trent band broke up in Albany, in 1932, I think. We'd just finished playing the Kenmore Hotel there. That's when the original Ink Spots came into being. Charlie Fuqua was singing with Trent, and the guitar player was up in front of the band. We'd picked them up in Indianapolis where they had an act. When we broke up, we decided to drive to Cleveland, and there I introduced them to Deek Watson, the original owner of the Ink Spots. The three of them got together in the Majestic Hotel, and then they went to Cincinnati and got Hoppy, the fourth Ink Spot.

"I started working around Cleveland in little dumps with small groups. I worked in one place where I made about twelve dollars a week. With tips, you might end up with thirty dollars. You couldn't save any money, but you could live fairly well on that. Then Claude Hopkins told me they needed a band in St. Louis, and I turned that over to Jeter and Pillars. I went down and played with them about a week, until they got straight, and then I came back and joined Claude Hopkins.

"I was with Claude about a year. That was some rhythm section he had—Claude on piano, Henry Turner on bass, Pete Jacobs on drums. They were really swinging.

"Ethel Waters came to Little Rock with Johnny Dunn and His Jazz Hounds when I was still in school. That was when I first became aware of jazz and a lover of it. Back in the early thirties, when we said a guy took a 'hot' solo, we meant he was jumping and swinging. Of course, Louis Armstrong started a lot of that. I think we were all influenced by him, no matter what instrument we played. When I went with him after I left Claude Hopkins, that was the biggest thrill of all.

"I joined without a rehearsal, but I'd had my schooling with Trent and could sight-read anything, so I had no trouble at all. Although I hadn't had a teacher, all the studying, practicing, and playing with first-class musicians—that paid off. I guess if I had had teachers they would have told me not to get my tone the way I did. But to my mind the best way for a man to get his tone or notes is the way he knows how to get 'em. You take Dizzy Gillespie—I don't see how he does it. I was always determined to play my horn right, and I tried to be original. My chops are as strong today as when I was twenty-five. I massage my gums, all my teeth are strong, and I practice as much today as I ever did.

"Louis Armstrong had taken over Luis Russell's band. It was just a background for Louis, really, but there were musicians in it, like Louis Bacon, Harry White, J. C. Higginbotham, Charlie Holmes, Pops Foster, and Paul Barbarin. I wrote a song called *Man with a Funny Horn*, meaning my slide saxophone, and they did it on just one show at the Earle Theater in Philly. It wasn't very good, so they took it out and I never got a chance to do much of anything after that.

"I was with Louis a bit over a year, and it made headlines in the *Amsterdam News* when I left: *Mosley Quits Armstrong*. I quit because I didn't get a chance to play anything of my own. I went out on a tour with Fletcher Henderson for a few weeks, playing a lot of college dates in New England at places like Yale and Harvard. Chu Berry was in the band. They had some of the damnedest music, in keys like B-natural. You're supposed to be able to play in any key, but . . .

"Then I went with Fats Waller's big band for a few months. The first engagement was at the Howard Theater in Washington, and after that we had a lot more theater dates. It was better, but I still couldn't play like I wanted to play.

"When I left Fats I organized my own band of six pieces. We used to broadcast on that *'Round the Town* program over WNEW. My first job as a bandleader was at Maury's Tavern up in the Bronx. I had Sheets Tolbert on alto and he was very good. He's teaching down in Texas now. Freddie Jefferson was on piano, Carl Smith on trumpet. We went from the Bronx to the Famous Door on 52nd Street for about three months, in 1938, and then over to the Onyx. I was at Leon and Eddie's for a couple of weeks, singing and entertaining. Then we went to the Queens Terrace on Long Island, in 1939, when Alan King and Jackie Gleason worked downstairs. I was with the William Morris Agency by this time, and they put me in the roof garden of the Wisconsin Hotel in Boston in 1940. From there we went to Hollywood, playing places in between like the Beachcomber in Omaha. We were in Billy Berg's Swing Club a couple of months, broadcasting coast to coast. Ken Murray heard us, came down and caught us one night, and put us into his show, *Ken Murray's Blackout*, a great hit. That

would be about 1942. We started recording for Decca in 1940. *Amen*
was really improvised at a 1941 session. It sold well, but Woody
Herman's version sold even better.

"In 1945, I went overseas on a USO tour. It was during the war and
they needed entertainment. We were gone nearly a year, in New
Guinea, the Philippines, the East Indies, the Bismarck Sea—all those
areas. I had Bill Johnson, who used to be with Erskine Hawkins, on
alto, Bob Carroll on trumpet, and A. G. Godley on drums. He's still
around, in Seattle. He used to drink very heavily, but he was one of
the greatest drummers I ever listened to. I think Jo Jones would agree
with me about him, although their styles are different. I think A.G.
may have started that bit where everybody jumps off the bandstand and
leaves the drummer to work out by himself up there.

"It's been small groups for me since then, all the time. Around 1945
I got Keg Purnell, a big asset, on drums. We were at the Hundred
Club in New York for about eight months, and on the ABC network.
I went in the Follies on Broadway in 1955 or 1956 and stayed until
1961, all the time playing both instruments. Then I was out at The
Sands at Needle Beach for six seasons, and The Sands in Las Vegas
isn't any finer.

"I keep thinking the trend is away from rock toward jazz and melody,
but you know the guys promoting rock are not going to take that lying
down. So they call it the 'now' sound. When I went back to visit my
father in Little Rock, I was going to play with a rock group there until
one guy began screaming at the top of his lungs over a powerful mike.
The group knew three chords, but not very well. Times sure do
change."

(1971)

Sir Charles Thompson

(PIANO)

"Hey, Chase," Illinois Jacquet called, "ain't you got one of those tunes, man?"

"Yes, here's one!" Sir Charles Thompson answered.

It was May 21, 1947, and the record session had not been fruitful until that moment, when Thompson took charge. "I want you to play this soft, fellows," he said. "Joe, I want you to use a mute. You play the melody. I'll answer on the piano. Illinois, you take the middle." There were two takes and a new jazz standard was born.

"So far as I was concerned," Thompson said, "I didn't care if they called it *Mud in the Hole,* but Fred Robbins was a big disc jockey then and I could see the possibilities when they named it *Robbins' Nest.* Jacquet's managers were under the impression it was his tune and they arranged for all kinds of people to record it. Claude Thornhill made one of the best versions, a classic, and I think he and I have a similar conception of piano playing. Later on, after Ella Fitzgerald had made her record of it, they brought in someone else to write words, so

now there are three names on the song and it is no longer *Robbins'*
Nest but *Why Have a Falling Out Just When We're Falling In Love?*

"It's surprising how many ditties come out of the backgrounds of
arrangements. The riffs you set behind ad lib solos can often become
songs, and that was just what happened with *Robbins' Nest*. It was one
of many tunes I had in my head, and I had been writing music and
lyrics since I was sixteen. Singers, for instance, have always been crazy
about a song called *Wishing Well* I wrote on a bus between Philly and
Washington, but, like a lot of others, it has never been published or
recorded. After *Robbins' Nest*, I wore out many pairs of shoes going
up and down Broadway trying to place my songs. They would want to
change the words to make them sound like other songs, and they had
all kinds of other unoriginal ideas. So many of these guys in the publishing business imagine they are in a position to say what will or will not
be a hit. If they are such geniuses, why don't they write hits themselves? I never would go in with my hat in my hand and one knee on
the floor, so some doors were closed in my face because of that, and
word got around that I was pretty hard to deal with. Well, I had spent
a lot of time learning to play, but I had also picked up some ideas about
music.

"Today, you may have talent, but it isn't necessarily accepted, because you have competition from rock 'n' roll and what is known as
'progressive' music, a term which in my opinion is just a lot of
baloney. It's not progressive music. It's just another style. I don't know
anyone in the world who plays more alto than Buster Smith, and he's
thirty years older than Vaseline. When they start telling me someone
like Ornette Coleman is a genius, I don't go along with that at all. What
word are they going to use for musicians like Coleman Hawkins, Duke
Ellington, and Art Tatum? Music is made by musicians and singers,
but critics and a. and r. men have taken the front seat instead of the
back seat. Rock 'n' roll is nothing but a manufactured product. They
take the very least of jazz and build it up to where people accept it.
Anyone can play it, if he has the nerve—and very little pride! The
musicians who play rock 'n' roll *best* are musicians who can't play anything else. When I talk about rock 'n' roll I'm mad, and I don't try to
hide the fact.

"As far as I'm concerned, the guys who made big-band jazz too
complicated are as bad as those responsible for rock 'n' roll. I remember
when you could hear 'progressive' musicians along the street saying,
'Count Basie isn't playing anything,' because he wasn't playing what
they were playing. If you're too far over the people's heads, no one
understands it. If it's beneath the people, you're underestimating their
intelligence. I hope the day will soon come when we musicians can

play as we feel, as we did when I started in the game. And if you didn't play well, you couldn't get on the same bandstand with those who could. You have to have qualifications. But the way rock 'n' roll has it now, it makes a man with no qualifications stand up and fill his chest out, just as though he were a real artist. That isn't fair to musicians or the public."

The son of a Methodist minister, Thompson was born in Springfield, Ohio. The whole family was musical. Although his mother played piano, and his sister, a schoolteacher, taught the same instrument, he began his musical career at school on violin. He took instruction for three years and found it interesting until he realized how few were the opportunities in classical music. "There was," he said, "even less opportunity for violin in jazz. I don't think I heard any jazz on the fiddle until well into the thirties, and that was by a guy who played around Chicago.

"I became interested in jazz because it was a way of expressing myself freely. I understand nonmusicians who say they envy us, because we have this way of expressing moods and emotion that they haven't. I can be very disgusted with life and the business, but if I can play piano, I can lose myself in the music completely. It's like medicine to me, or golf.

"Golf was my real first love, and indirectly it led me back to music. You have many interests as a child, but from the age of twelve on I've been very definitely interested in golf. I caddied for Jimmy Thompson at that time in Broadmoor, Colorado. We were only allowed to play in the early hours of Monday, but I soon became good at the game. We used to practice with one club, a niblick, back and forth in a field, a hole at each end. Now I'm lucky if I shoot under ninety. But it's surprising how much a child sees, and hears. I didn't like the tone of voice or the names some of those players would use when I was shagging balls for them, and the restricted opportunities for playing made me think about music again. Everybody wanted to hear music, no matter who you were or what you looked like. They would accept you if you played good jazz, because there were not too many who could.

"Very few people recognize the similarity between golf and jazz. There are almost identical conditions in both. There's a fundamental way of playing, but there's no set pattern for doing it the same way twice. You're always trying to improve your game and there's always a challenge. It's the challenge that makes you lose yourself and give off your emotions. You can get mad, you can explode, or you can be happy because you made a terrific shot. Even if your ball falls in the exact spot it fell in yesterday, your shot isn't going to be the same. To get that ball on the green depends on how the wind is blowing, and you have to consider how damp it is, or how the ball's going to roll when it hits the green.

"When you play piano or organ, you're thinking all the time of the chord changes that go with the piece, but simultaneously you disregard the chords to an extent to play what you feel. In golf, there are certain ways you make a shot, to make it go high or low, or maybe curve to the left or right, and it requires quick thinking as in music, because you can never stand around long figuring what kind of shot to make. For instance, when you make a shot out of the trap, you're taught to 'explode' it, which means hitting the sand about a couple of inches behind the ball and following through, but plenty of times the shot requires you to hit the ball itself. You have to size this up in a moment. Sometimes you play music softly for expression, sometimes loudly. Sometimes you hit a golf ball soft and easy, sometimes hard. You look the course over like a map, and what's more like a map than an arrangement?"

"My family wasn't poor, but there was always a certain economic strain. So I've done many things, none of which I'm ashamed of. I've shined shoes and washed cars; I've been a bellhop, an elevator operator, and a hotel clerk; but as a caddy I learnt lessons in psychology that have been invaluable.

"The very Christian background I had didn't fit jazz, but my father wasn't critical. In fact, he always told me the important thing was to do *well* whatever I was interested in, but I knew it wasn't too good for him to have a son playing jazz in nightclubs when he might be in the pulpit preaching against that kind of life. So I joined a Franklin D. Roosevelt project, the Civilian Conservation Corps, which had to do with clearing land and forest. I was sixteen, but I put my age up to eighteen to get in, and I went to Cape Girardeau, Missouri, near St. Louis. It was from there I branched out into bands. I had gone through two or three piano books while learning violin, and I had had good teachers. I became the company clerk, played piano in the mess and then with local bands. They were not very good, but I was *heard*.

"I got an administrative discharge to better myself and joined Cecil Scott, who had one of the best bands in the Midwest then. This wasn't the same Cecil who came to New York in the twenties, but the band included the late Eddy Byrd, an outstanding drummer from my hometown. The other great band in St. Louis at that time was Jeter-Pilars's. Alphonso Trent's was another fine outfit operating in the area which included St. Louis, Memphis, Dallas, Oklahoma City, and Kansas City.

"I was too young and inexperienced to keep up the pace with Scott. Eventually, I was stranded and had to return to my family, which was then in Parsons, Kansas. That was the hometown of Buck Clayton, whose father was also a minister, although of another denomination. It was then I really got my inspiration to stay in the music field. Buck had just returned from China and was about to join Count Basie. In a small town like that, he was a kind of idol. He paid me a couple of compliments which encouraged me to believe I might make it some day. So I went off again with the first band that came along, a small one, what you might call a carnival band, and this time against my father's wishes. He didn't like the look of the little ragged bus we traveled in. I left that band in Omaha, Nebraska, because they weren't making any money at all. The guy would give you thirty-five cents for food, and though you take chances when you're young, I got tired of eating only one meal a day.

"Lloyd Hunter had had a good band long before I joined him and I was very happy when he came after me with a job. Gus Johnson was in that band, but he was playing bass fiddle. I remember one time it was so cold in North and South Dakota that he played with his gloves on! Debo Mills was on drums and he was compared with Jo Jones, they were so much alike. Debo was with Horace Henderson for a while later on, but he never got a chance to branch out in the East.

"As a pianist, I had originally been influenced by Claude Hopkins. I heard him in broadcasts from New York while we were living in Columbia, Missouri. Then I heard Fats Waller, and he influenced me, too. Another real inspiration was Duke Ellington. I was impressed not only by his music, but by his diction, his choice of words, his manner of dressing, and his suave personality. I'm sure he gets a bang out of words and it's original in our field. There are plenty of people who dress themselves up in tails, but then when they speak the words don't coincide with the clothes they're wearing. Of course, Art Tatum had the greatest of all influences on me, as he had on most pianists of his time, because of his ingenious imagination, his creativity, his speed, and his flawless performances. He's a subject I could talk about all night.

"By the time I left Lloyd Hunter to join Nat Towles, I was reading music well enough for a jazz pianist. In the normal stock arrangement you can cut a corner, because the chords are written above the notes in the staff. I had remained limited for a time through reading the chords and ignoring the notes. You hardly ever got to read sheet music, but I had been doing that, working over popular songs, out of my own ambition. Now I began to study arranging, for the men in the Towles band were an inspired bunch and very competitive in their thinking. They felt they were waiting for the chance to get to New York to compete with Basie, Lunceford, and Duke Ellington. John Hammond tried his best to get them there, but Nat couldn't see where it would be to his advantage, and he was afraid of big offers attracting his men away. Buddy Tate was a spark in the tenor department. On trombone we had the late Fred Beckett, and Henry Coker, who, in my estimation, is unrecognized as one of the greatest trombones in the world. There was C. Q. Price on alto, a fine musician and arranger. 'Little Nat,' a cousin of Nat Towles, was on drums. He kept good time and wasn't in the way.

"C.Q. and a couple of the other fellows had had more experience in arranging and I got quite a few tips from them. I studied all the great bands and when I wanted further information I would take a regular lesson. I was influenced by what I heard, but I often didn't know who had written the arrangements I liked. I became aware of what Andy Gibson was doing for Count Basie and Charlie Barnet, realized he was a great arranger, and grew very interested in the way he voiced. Then I was attracted to Fletcher Henderson. He was so very valuable to Benny Goodman because he would write those swinging ideas with simple voicing that could be played and understood easily. Until Nat Towles broke up the big band a few years ago, he still used some of the arrangements we wrote then. I believe Neal Hefti played in that band after I left and picked up quite a few ideas about arranging from the book.

"I drifted to California in another very good band, Floyd Ray's, but it was having booking troubles and was on the verge of breaking up. It had one of the greatest trumpets of the day in Charlie Jacobs. He played the same as Dizzy Gillespie, but he was killed in a freakish case of mistaken identity. Eddy Byrd was on drums. Count Basie's band was in California at the time and Buddy Tate—a good friend of mine—and all its members seemed very congenial people, and they were very inspiring to young musicians who were trying, as far as possible, to stay within the realm of normalcy. I played in some pictures while I was in Hollywood and eventually joined Lionel Hampton's first big band.

"I came East with Lionel and I have respect for him as a person and an artist, but the music wasn't to my taste and I felt uncomfortable. He wanted the drummers to play a back beat all the time, and that was bad for a pianist. Shadow Wilson joined and he wouldn't be influenced. He had a lot of will power. One time there was a move to fire him, but all the fellows liked Shadow so well and their sentiment was so strong that Lionel had to keep him. After Shadow left, there were never any great drummers with Lionel.

"I quit the band in Chicago and worked with George Clark in Buffalo until John Hammond persuaded me to come to New York in 1940 to join the Lee and Lester Young band at Café Society Downtown. That was where I got my title. There was an Earl, a Duke, and a Count, so I guess they thought they'd have a knight as well. It was a great little group. Besides Lee and Lester, there was Paul Campbell on trumpet, Bumps Myers on tenor, Red Callender on bass, and a wonderful guitar player, Louis Gonzales. After that, Red, Gonzales, and I played a little stint as the Red Callender Trio. Red's a terrific musician, a strongly built, soft-spoken man with a gentle personality. He has a big warm sound and he's one of the very few I ever heard play with Art Tatum and meld with him perfectly.

"I was with Lucky Millinder a couple of years, and although he wasn't a musician he was good to work for. He had a natural ability for directing music and he knew every part of the arrangements. He was a great favorite at the Savoy, but unfortunately the best bands he ever had never recorded owing to some recording ban. He had an alto player called William Swindell who was one of the greatest I ever heard. I wrote one or two arrangements for Lucky. By this time I had also contributed to Basie's book (did you ever hear *My, What a Fry?*), to Hampton's, Horace Henderson's, and Jimmy Dorsey's, but now I was concentrating on playing. You have to play to play well, but writing is something you can pick up as long as you can hold a pencil in your hand.

"Next, I decided I wanted to participate in the 52nd Street scene. This was the time when Roy Eldridge and Lips Page were supreme, before Dizzy Gillespie became famous. I played with them, with Don Byas, and Coleman Hawkins. I went to California in 1944 with Hawk and made some records and a picture. He was another great inspiration to me and I found the recording very exciting. My solo on *Stuffy* was the first that ever sounded good to me. When the group broke up, I ran into Illinois Jacquet. We had been in Hamp's band together and had remained friends. Knowing his Texas background, and what he and I have both been subjected to, makes me understand him. He, his brother Russell, and I became partners in a band, but it didn't do too well until we started recording in the East. Illinois was suddenly hot, and it was because he had the opportunity to showcase songs that I made him co-composer of *Robbins' Nest*. *Strange Hour* was in a similar vein, but it was in a key similar to *Body and Soul* and I think the middle changes were a little too complicated for the average ear.

"Jacquet had made a lot of noise with Jazz at the Philharmonic, but he made the greatest impression with that little band he had in 1947. I remember once we played a battle of music against Dizzy's big band over in Jersey. When we got through it sounded as though we had fourteen pieces and he had eight. We were Shadow Wilson, Al Lucas, Joe Newman, Russell Jacquet, J. J. Johnson, Leo Parker, Illinois, and myself, so that gives an idea of what was happening musically. Leo Parker had great talent. He had a tone like Harry Carney—and there are very few baritone players who have that full sound—and he played fast with all the modern figures and designs of Charlie Parker, and he knew his instrument.

"Eventually, I got discouraged and went back to California. I was away from music for quite a time. Jobs out there were very scarce and the only pianist working regularly was one of my favorites, Hampton Hawes, a terrific musician. He's an improvement on Bud Powell, plays as fast and intricate as anybody, but has a very beautiful and soft approach to ballads. What brought me back to music was a shortage of organ players. I never cared too much for organ. Although it was a novelty, and I liked to hear Fats Waller play it, I didn't care for the sound. A fellow hired me because he couldn't get anyone else to play it. So I studied the organ, stayed out there three years, decided to give New York another chance, and have been here ever since."

During this period, Thompson played at Count Basie's Bar on Seventh Avenue, and recorded for Columbia, Prestige, and the British Lansdowne Series. He went to Europe for the first time as pianist with Buck Clayton's band in 1961. "If my mother had not fallen sick," he said, "I'd still be in Europe. I enjoyed playing over there more than I enjoyed playing any time in my life, because the people were receptive and so sincere in their liking for music."

(1961)

33. *Richard Boone at the Newport Jazz Festival, 1968.* (Stanley Dance collection)

34. *Bobby Plater.* (Courtesy RCA Records)

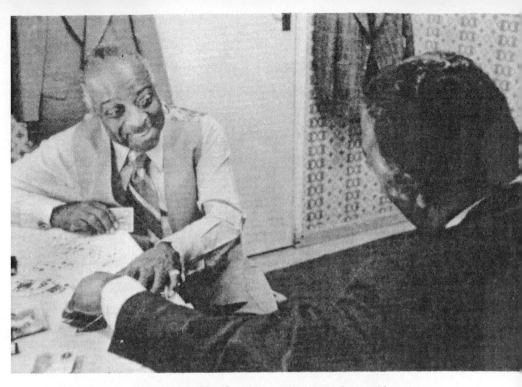

35. Basie backstage in England, 1977. (Courtesy Valerie Wilmer)

36. Count Basie and Jay McShann. (Stanley Dance collection)

37. *Jay McShann at the piano.* (Courtesy Jay McShann)

38. *Jay McShann's Orchestra, McShann at the piano.* Left to right: *Bill Nolan, Walter Brown, Charlie Parker, Bob Mabane, Bernard Anderson, Harold Bruce, John Jackson, Harold Ferguson, Orville Minor, Joe Baird, Gus Johnson, Gene Ramey.* (Courtesy Gene Ramey)

39. *Jay McShann's Orchestra, early 1940.* Left to right: *(front)* McShann *(standing)*, Bob Mabane, Earl Jackson, Lester Taylor, William Scott, Joe Coleman; *(rear)* Gus Johnson, Lucky Enois, Gene Ramey, Orville Minor, Harold Bruce, Buddy Anderson, unknown. (Courtesy Gene Ramey)

40. *Jay McShann's Orchestra at the Savoy Ballroom, 1941.* Left to right: *(front)* McShann, Lucky Enois, Gene Ramey, Walter Brown, Bob Mabane, Charlie Parker, John Jackson, Freddie Culliver, Lawrence Anderson, Joe Taswell; *(rear)* Gus Johnson, Harold Bruce, Bernard Anderson, Orville Minor. (Courtesy Gene Ramey)

41. *Gene Ramey and Count Basie.* (Courtesy Jack Bradley)

42. Left to right: *Earle Warren, Teddy Wilson, Jimmy Rushing, and Sir Charles Thompson.* (Courtesy Earle Warren)

43. *Gus Johnson sings at Colorado Springs.* Left to right: *Milt Hinton (bass; partially hidden), Clark Terry, Johnson, Zoot Sims, Frank Rosolino, Benny Carter.* (Courtesy Gus Johnson)

44. *Alphonso Trent's Orchestra.* Left to right: *A. G. Godley, T. Holder, Chester Clark, Snub Mosley, Gene Crook, Alphonso Trent, James Jeter, Brent Sparks, John Fielding (vocal), Bill Holloway.* (Courtesy Gene Crook)

45. Left to right: *Joe Newman, Paul Quinichette, and Buddy Tate recording.* (Courtesy Atlantic Records)

46. *Jimmy Witherspoon* (left) *and Chico Hamilton* (right) *at a Los Angeles concert.* (Stanley Dance collection)

47. *The Virginia Ravens on tour. Eddie Barefield, tenor saxophone, is at left center.* (Courtesy Eddie Barefield)

48. *Eddie Barefield's California Band—Barefield, alto saxophone, conducting. Pianist unknown; Buddy Harper (guitar); Al Morgan (bass); Lee Young (drums); "Country," Tyree Glenn (trombones); (left to right, front) Jack McVea, Hugo Dandridge, Paul Howard, Don Byas (reeds); (rear) Red Mack, Freddie Traynor, "Pee Wee" (trumpets).* (Courtesy Eddie Barefield)

Melvin Moore

(VOCALIST)

"Nobody in the family, so far back as I can remember, was musical, but although she didn't sing professionally, my mom had a marvelous voice. I was born in Oklahoma City and I got my formal training in high school there—cantatas, operettas, and so forth. I think Miss Zelia M. Brough was one of the great music teachers of all time, and she turned out some wonderful musicians. But Charlie Christian was like Peck's bad boy then. He wouldn't go to school, although he used to be on the school grounds sometimes with his banjo-uke. Charlie would be swinging and Professor Page, the principal, would have a hard time running the kids inside.

"I played valve trombone in the school band, and our music was mostly standard pieces. When I found out I could make four or five dollars a night singing, that was the end of the instrument. I had started in the church, of course, where all black people who sing start with spirituals and gospel songs. Then at school I began singing things like *Trees* and *Jeannie with the Light Brown Hair*, but I actually got known around Oklahoma City first as a blues singer, because

Jimmy Rushing was a dear friend of mine. Only my voice was more mellow than his, and I *liked* ballads, and eventually I became known as a ballad singer.

"I started out with Charlie Christian's brother, Eddie. He played piano and bass, and he was a good musician. The whole family was musical and they had a family band like Oscar Pettiford's people had. Eddie's father played bass, his mother piano, and another brother played a little fiddle. This brother's real name was Clarence, but we called him 'It.'

"The first date with Eddie was what we called a 'pig stand,' one where his little group and bandstand were set up in the middle of a barbecue. After I'd sung my song, I'd take my box and go out and collect some money! I enjoyed that first night, and from then on that's where we'd be weekends. The five of us would make sixteen or seventeen dollars a night. Then Charlie got so it was a case of three-for-me-and-one-for-you, and everybody got mad. So we broke it up for a time, but we got together again and worked in a little place called the Rhythm Club. That's where I became like the toast of Oklahoma City and everybody was talking about Melvin Moore.

"I first heard T-Bone Walker at the Boga ballroom in 1935. He was in tails, playing the guitar behind his neck, and doing the splits! He was out of Dallas, Texas, and he was the only black guy in a band led by Count Balaski. He was the star, and he used to set the people on fire. There was even a big write-up about him in the white paper. He was about four years older than me, and I was sixty at Halloween [1977]. Being a musician, he came down to Second Street, where Charlie Christian and everybody hung out. He and Charlie used to cut heads. The guy that taught Charlie everything on guitar was Chuck Richardson. He was a big man with big hands, and he could read music. He used to show Charlie things, and I think he showed T-Bone about chords, too. Charlie was nearly a genius and it seemed as though he could do whatever he wanted to do. He was one of the best pool players around, and he could dance as good as anybody.

"Andy Kirk's band came to town and played and broadcast from the same Boga Ballroom. His singer, Pha Terrell, came in the club where we were playing, and I was into my big song. Everybody turned around immediately, telling each other, 'Pha Terrell's in the house!' I died. That was my first feeling of the green thing, so I slipped out the back door. But Pha had heard about me, and two weeks later he came by my house with Willie Perry, a friend of mine and a saxophonist.

" 'I know how you felt, man,' Pha said, laying it on, ' 'cause the same thing happened to me.'

"He ran it down, and from then we were the best of friends. He was a jack-of-all-trades and, like Charlie Christian, it seemed he could do whatever he wanted to do. He'd been a boxer. Then he was a dancer, and when his feet went bad on him, he just started singing. He taught me everything I know about shortcuts in singing and how to do things. He was a sweetheart. After he left Andy Kirk, he went out to California about 1944, and died. When I heard about it, it just tore me up, because he was such a good friend.

"Andy Kirk's band stayed in Oklahoma City a long time, and that was when Mary Lou Williams heard Charlie Christian, who was playing so good and so differently from everyone else. Just on Mary Lou's say-so, Benny Goodman had to hear him. When Charlie first came to New York, he came by train. I was living at the Woodside Hotel at that time, and I went down to meet him. Gigs were very, very short then, but my hometown boy arrived with six or seven hundred dollars in his pocket. He gave me a hundred, and I was rich! Charlie went all over town cutting heads. I remember that Fred Waring was in New York and he had Les Paul, the guitar player, with him. Les used to come uptown and cut everybody's head—until he ran into Charlie, and Charlie dusted it.

"I had first left Oklahoma City in 1936. I ran away from home! I needed about three credits to finish high school. What happened was that Don Albert and his band—out of New Orleans—heard me sing when they came through, and they wanted me to join them. I couldn't wait to do that! They were based on San Antonio, Texas, and in October, right before my birthday, I got on a bus and went down there. My old man like to died about that: 'Three credits and don't want to finish high school, blah, blah, blah.'

"Don had one of the best bands in the Southwest. I stayed with him about a year and a half. Sometimes we worked right on the Mexican line in towns like McAllen, Harlingen, and Brownsville, where it was always nice and warm. I remember once we came out of Amarillo through a howling snowstorm in the panhandle, and the next day we were pulling oranges off the trees in McAllen. It was gorgeous, and I'd never seen anything like that before. I also made my first trip to New York with Don. I was doing mostly ballads with him, but when they made the records in San Antonio for Vocalion, they had a wonderful singer named Merle Turner, so I didn't get to record till I joined Ernie Fields.

"Don Albert's and Alphonso Trent's bands were about the best in that area, although there was a bunch of nothing-but-good, fifteen-piece bands around. Every city had one. There was Eli Rice's out of Minneapolis. Clarence Love had a nice little band. And there were about five good bands in Kansas City alone. Nearly all of them were trying to sound like Jimmie Lunceford's. They couldn't get to Duke, but they would get as close as they could to Lunceford. To come to New York was *everybody's* dream then. That was *it!* Some of 'em made it and some of 'em didn't. And there were *some* musicians out there! Henry Bridges, a saxophone player out in Oklahoma, could play as good as anybody. There was John Hardee out of Texas. Arnett Cobb, Buddy Tate, Illinois Jacquet, and Budd Johnson—they all came out of Texas, and good bands. Milton Larkins had one of those bands and I just heard he's left New York, bag and baggage, and gone back home to Houston, to some kind of music job on the radio.

"I left Don Albert because of my dad. He kept leaning on it: 'Why don't you come home and finish high school?' So I went back and did that, and during the Christmas holidays I was talking to Ernie Fields. He had a band in Tulsa, which was about a hundred-and-twenty miles away. He'd heard about me, because my name got around when I was traveling with Don Albert, and he wanted me to work with him. I was supposed to go to Langston University, but I told my dad, 'Man, I've been out, I've seen what life's about, and you'd only be throwing your money away, because I don't think I could stand that school.' He understood how I felt, and I played some good gigs with Ernie during those Christmas holidays, and joined his band right afterwards.

"I was with Ernie Fields from 1938 to 1949. We were all over the country, coast to coast. We played the Apollo every year. In fact, Ernie's band was the only one Frank Schiffman allowed in there twice a year at that time. We played the Savoy, we played everywhere. One of the outstanding musicians in the band was René Hall, who played guitar and trombone, and was the arranger. Another was Luther West, a very good saxophonist who had gone to school in Tulsa with Earl Bostic. Tulsa was where we were established, our base. We even had a little old hit called *T-Town Blues*, and I sang on it: '*Goin' back to Tulsa to get my women in line . . .*' I'll tell you who produced that record—Ahmet Ertegun, who went on to much bigger things with Atlantic. We were successful, but we didn't really get the breaks. John Hammond was the key to the whole thing then. He brought a bunch of good bands into New York, but Basie's was his preference, and he put all his energy behind it.

"I had offers from other leaders while I was with Ernie, but I stayed because it was like home, and comfortable. Everybody thought I was making a lot of money with him, but I was barely living. All I wanted to do was sing, and maybe I never knew how good I was. But after being ten years with one guy, other leaders thought they couldn't afford me! When I did leave, I was supposed to work with Louis Jordan. I had given Ernie a couple of weeks' notice in advance at the Apollo, and I went to Louis in Philadelphia.

" 'Come on in, man,' Louis said. 'I've got some bad news.'

" 'What's happened?'

" 'Ernie's got a contract on you that can't be broken.'

" 'I know better. There's no contract like that!'

" 'Well, I'd rather not go through this thing.'

"He gave me a hundred dollars to go back to New York and rejoin Ernie, but I'd made my commitment and I wasn't going to do that. I spent a couple of weeks in New York, went to Chicago to see my mother's people, and then went back to Tulsa where my family was. (I was married by this time.) I got a little five-piece band together and started rehearsing. A man in the numbers business had some nice money, so he backed me and we worked for ourselves for a while. Then Diz [Gillespie] came through and played a dance in Tulsa.

" 'Man, why don't you come on with the band,' he said, 'because Johnny Hartman's leaving?'

" 'I'll think about it,' I said.

"That was in 1949. He kept bugging me, and finally he called and said, 'We're going in the Howard Theatre in two weeks. Come on! And that was my first gig with them, along with Sammy Davis and the Will Mastin Trio. *Everybody* was in that band! The piano player was John Lewis. Al McKibbon was on bass. Paul Gonsalves and John Coltrane were in the reed section. Melba Liston was on trombone. It was just a super band, but it broke up after I'd been with them about six months. I decided I was going to stay in New York and not go back to Tulsa.

"One day I was walking the streets and ran into René Hall. He had been writing for Earl Hines, but now he had also come to New York to stay.

" 'Hey, man, what're you doing?'

" 'Nothing too much,' I said.

" 'Look, they're having a rehearsal at the Savoy with Fletcher Henderson.'

"So I went up there. Lee Richardson and a lot of others were trying to get the gig. Lucky Thompson was on the band, and when he saw me he walked me over to Smack [Henderson].

" 'Hey, Smack,' he said, 'here's your singer!'

"I worked with Fletcher at the Savoy about six months. It was really a pick-up band. I remember Joe Benjamin and Don Lamond were in it. That must have been about 1950, and thanks to Joe Benjamin I next got a job with Lucky Millinder. Lee Richardson was with Lucky at the time. He had been with Luis Russell and *The Very*

Thought of You was his big song. He got in trouble, got a habit, and Lucky couldn't deal with it. So then I worked with Lucky nearly two years, and we made some pretty nice sides, too. Anisteen Allen and I were the singers and I had to do some of the songs Trevor Bacon had done earlier on. Trevor had gone with Bull Moose Jackson and His Buffalo Bearcats, and he was killed in an automobile accident down South.

"Lucky kept a good book and he always had good bands. Everybody liked him because he paid everybody well. Jimmy Mundy was writing for him at the time, and although I sang mostly ballads, I did a little bit of everything, whatever they wanted me to do, even things like *Chew Tobacco Rag*, which we recorded for King. Lucky and I would also go and make those big transcription records for the army, which is how I came to record with people like Earl Hines and Erroll Garner. I don't know what they ever did with some of those things.

"After Lucky, it was tough going till I ran into Billy Bowen, who was with the Ink Spots. Bill Kenny had just given up the quartet, and we were like the second Ink Spots group, because Charlie Fuqua had one, too. I worked with Billy Bowen for fourteen years. He played sax and flute, and another guy played guitar. Besides singing, I played drums. I had done a little of that at school. We went to Europe, to the South Pacific, all over the world. In fact, we were on a round-the-world tour when we broke up. We were in Bangkok, three months on the way, and everybody got homesick. We were all married, we had money in our pockets, and we were just tired of being away from home. Billy was crying the blues then!

"I was going to get me a little trio and work around New York, because I was tired of the road. Then I ran into Joe Medlin, a good friend of mine from way back. He used to sing with Buddy Johnson's band. Joe put me in the record business, where I've been ever since. He introduced me to the boss at Decca and we got successful over there with Jackie Wilson and a few others. The first time I ever recorded had been in the Decca studio where they had that Indian on the wall with his arms stretched out, asking the question, 'Where's the melody?' What I got into was more or less promotion, not a. and r. work. All my life I'd been communicating with people, and I felt I was very lucky to come out of one phase into another that was related to it. Music has been my whole life, and I was just telling a fellow today how it all revolves around the thirteen notes to a scale, the chromatics and the majors. In forty years, I've heard it all, and the same notes are still there. The only thing that really changes in the music is the rhythms. But so much of the music today you wouldn't even have listened to when I was a kid. Everybody would have said it was junk!

"What they call 'soul' now is nothing but a word. It's been there all the time. The blues, all the music, is based on the gospel thing. Basically, all of it comes from the church. Soul is nothing but blacks singing the way they feel. Some guys sing now so you can see their veins standing out! James Brown, for example, hollering and screaming with no inhibitions—I guess that's soul. But the people I sang to enjoyed the way I did my songs. The first time I heard B. B. King, he was a ballad singer, singing pretty songs, and scuffling with a little four-piece band. It took the white college kids about thirty-five years to discover him!

"Now I'm with Prelude Records, but I'm not optimistic about the record business. The way the big companies are combining, they're going to put all the little ones out of business. If you're not part of a conglomerate, forget it! They're into everything—shoes, food, films, clothing, books, everything. I just don't understand what's happening, or why it's allowed to happen."

(1977)

Melvin Moore returned to his old role briefly when drummer Panama Francis organized the presentation of "Music of the Savoy Ballroom" at Carnegie Hall in 1975. The bands of Lucky Millinder and the Savoy Sultans were recreated by musicians of the New York Jazz Repertory Company, and Moore's vocals with the "Millinder" band, in which Panama Francis had also played, impressed with their professional authority.

APPENDICES

Some Basie Itineraries

There are repeated references in this book to arduous tours of one-nighters back and forth across the country. These tours became a necessity in prolonging the existence of big bands. In the beginning, each band would travel in several automobiles, but as buses became more comfortable and reliable, the rented bus became the primary means of transportation. Fuel shortages compelled the use of trains during World War II, and after the war the proliferation of airlines opened up the possibility of international one-nighters—particularly in Europe and Latin America—but today the bus remains the most common and economical form of band transportation within the United States.

The following itineraries of Count Basie and his orchestra will give some idea of what is involved in terms of travel and distances covered. But besides traveling, to perform at night, the musicians of course have to check in and out of hotels each day, pack and unpack bags, get meals as and when they can. It is a way of life with which men like Count Basie and Freddie Green have been familiar for over forty years—and that says much for their temperament and physical durability.

Right into the 1960s, there were clubs where big bands could occasionally sit down for engagements of two or more weeks, but these places have almost become a thing of the past. Clubs such as Birdland, Basin Street East, the Cotton Club, and Grand Terrace, and Connie's Inn are long gone, and so are ballrooms such as the Savoy. Theaters that once employed bands as part of their stage shows no longer do so. What remain for big bands, essentially, are single concert and dance dates, usually in a different venue—when not in a different city—each night. An agent's commission for such bookings is customarily 15 percent, instead of the 10 percent for longer engagements. Transportation costs continually rise, as do the musicians' hotel and living expenses, and these together lead to higher salaries. . . . All of which attests to a measure of the heroic in the way Count Basie has for so long maintained a band of superior quality.

Itinerary for the period March 1–30, 1965

March   1   University of South Florida, Tampa, Florida
           2   Schrafft's Carriage House, Cocoa Beach, Florida
           3   Officers' Club, Charleston Air Force Base, Charleston, South Carolina
           4   Bennett College, Greensboro, North Carolina
           5   Rutgers University, New Brunswick, New Jersey
           6   Aronimink Country Club, Newtown Square, Pennsylvania
           7   NCO Club, Bolling Air Force Base, Washington, D.C.
           8   Frostburg State College, Frostburg, Maryland
           9   Downtown Motor Lodge, Mansfield, Ohio
         10   Meldwood Lounge, Brynon, Pennsylvania
         11   Macero's Tavern, Glens Falls, New York
         12   Gouverneur Morris Hotel, Morristown, New Jersey
         13   Open date
         14   Academy of Music, Philadelphia, Pennsylvania
         15   E. M. Club, Navy Training Station, Bainbridge, Maryland
         16   Hammond High School, Alexandria, Virginia
         17   Palace Theatre, Lorain, Ohio
         18   Open date
         19   Kiel Auditorium, St. Louis, Missouri
         20   Sheraton-Chicago Hotel, Chicago, Illinois

21 Holiday Ballroom, Chicago, Illinois
22 IBCW Hall, Local 1031, 5247 W. Madison, Chicago, Illinois
23 Club Laurel, Chicago, Illinois
24 Prom Ballroom, St. Paul, Minnesota
25 Civic Auditorium, Fargo, North Dakota
26 Open date
27 Sioux City, Iowa
28 Municipal Auditorium, Kansas City, Missouri
29 Hotel Savory, Des Moines, Iowa
30 WGN-TV, Chicago, Illinois

Itinerary for the period August 30–October 12, 1968

August 30 Century Plaza Hotel, Los Angeles, California
31 Recording date, Los Angeles, California
September 1 Factory Nite Club, North Hollywood, California
2 Jazz Suite, Beverly Hills, California
3–4 Recording dates, Los Angeles, California
5–14 Basin Street West, San Francisco, California
15 Friars Club, Beverly Hills, California
16 Hollywood, California
17–18 Sebastian's Hotel Eldorado, Sacramento, California
19 Chabot College, Hayward, California
20 Monterey Jazz Festival, Monterey, California
21 High Chapperal Ballroom, Chicago, Illinois
22 Laurel Club, Chicago Illinois
23 Miami Club, Miamiville, Ohio
24 Elks Lodge, Rochester, Michigan
25 Central Michigan College, Mt. Pleasant, Michigan
26 Rooser Tail, Detroit, Michigan
27 Chase Park Plaza Hotel, St. Louis, Missouri
28 St. Louis, Missouri
29 Orchestra Hall, Chicago, Illinois
30 Chicago, Illinois
October 1 Norfolk, Virginia
2 Jolly Roger, Brookfield, Connecticut
3 Steak Pit, Route 4, Paramus, New Jersey
4 Huntington Town House, Huntington, New York
5 Riviera, Port Washington, New York
6 Shannopinn Country Club, Pittsburgh, Pennsylvania

7	Royal York Hotel, Canadian Room, Toronto, Ontario, Canada
8	Coda Restaurant, Syracuse, New York
9–11	Paul's Mall, Boston, Massachusetts
12	Providence, Rhode Island

Itinerary for the period June 18–August 26, 1973

June	18	Steamer Admiral, St. Louis, Missouri
	19	Pfister Hotel, Grand Ballroom, Milwaukee, Wisconsin
	20	Place des Arts, Montreal, Quebec, Canada
	21	Crossroads, Moira, New York
	22	Leisure Lodge, Preston, Ontario, Canada
	23	Richmond Hill Arena, Richmond Hill, Ontario, Canada
	24	Centennial Hall, London, Ontario, Canada
	25	The Grand Theatre, Kingston, Ontario, Canada
	26	Eduardo's Supper Club, Buffalo, New York
	27	Off
	28–29	Ramada Inn, Louisville, Kentucky
	30	Indianapolis Museum of Art, Indianapolis, Indiana
July	1	Parkway Ramada Inn, Ballroom, Niagara Falls, New York
	2	Roseland Ballroom, New York, New York
	3	Carnegie Hall, Newport Jazz Festival, New York, New York
	4	Hopkins Plaza, Baltimore, Maryland
	5	Baynard Stadium, Wilmington, Delaware
	6	Stokesay Castle, Reading, Pennsylvania
	7	York Country Club, York, Pennsylvania
	8	Sheraton-Cleveland Hotel, Cleveland, Ohio
	9	Edinboro State College, Edinboro, Pennsylvania
	10–26	Off
	27	Eisenhower Park, East Meadow, New York
	28	St. Regis Hotel, New York, New York
	29	Watchung View Inn, Somerville, New Jersey
	30	Off
	31	Bethlehem, Pennsylvania
August	1	High School Stadium, Clarkston, New York
	2	Ole Barn, Inlet, New York
	3	Brockton High School, Brockton, Massachsetts

4	Off
5	Jug End Resort, South Egremont, Massachusetts
6	Brothers Two, Smithtown, New York
7	Robin Hood Dell, North Philadelphia, Pennsylvania
8	Rain date for August 7
9–11	Colonie Hill, Hauppage, New York
12	Wisconsin State Fair, Milwaukee, Wisconsin
13	Eastland Shopping Center, Harper Woods, Michigan
14	River Oaks Shopping Center, Calumet City, Illinois
16	Denver, Colorado
17	Los Angeles, California
18	Vancouver, British Columbia, Canada
19	Seattle, Washington
20–26	Mr. Kelley's, Chicago, Illinois

Selected Discography

Many of the records in this discography, although no longer in catalog, can be found in specialist stores or on the mailing lists of secondhand dealers who advertise in such magazines as *Cadence* and *Coda*. The designation (E) after the record's number indicates an English release, (F) a French.

Count Basie
All records in this section are by Count Basie and His Orchestra unless otherwise noted.

BENNIE MOTEN'S KANSAS CITY ORCHESTRA, 1929–32	Victor LPV-514
THE BEST OF COUNT BASIE, 1937–39 (two discs)	Decca DXSB-7170
GOOD MORNING BLUES, 1937–39 (two discs)	MCA 2-4108
THE COUNT AT THE CHATTERBOX, 1937	Jazz Archives 16

COUNT BASIE AT THE FAMOUS DOOR, 1938–39	Jazz Archives 41
THE COMPLETE COUNT BASIE, VOLS. I to X, 1936–41 (ten discs)	CBS 66101 (F)
THE COMPLETE COUNT BASIE, VOLS. XI to XX, 1941–51 (ten discs)	CBS 66102 (F)

(The above two sets contain everything Basie recorded for the company, including previously unissued titles and alternative takes.)

SUPER CHIEF, 1936–42 (two discs)	Columbia G-31224
THE COUNT, 1939	Columbia P-14355

(The two comprehensive French sets contain everything on these U.S. releases, although SUPER CHIEF includes, oddly enough, several items on which Basie does not play! THE COUNT complements Columbia's Lester Young albums, q.v., and is notable for the total absence of Young as a soloist—despite which it remains a valuable collection.)

ONE O'CLOCK JUMP, 1942–50	Columbia JCL-997
THE V-DISCS, VOLS. I and II, 1943–45	Jazz Society (Sweden) AA-505, AA-506
COUNT BASIE, 1947–49 (three discs)	RCA FXM 3-7053 (F)

(All the essentials from Basie's underrated Victor period are included in this handsomely boxed set. Illogical groupings on single Victor and Camden LPs have been made from time to time. They may still be obtained occasionally, from specialist dealers.)

BASIE JAZZ (Count Basie Sextet), 1952	Clef 633
DANCE SESSION, 1953	Clef 626
DANCE SESSION #2, 1954	Clef 647
SIXTEEN MEN SWINGING, 1953–54 (two discs)	Verve 2-2517

(Many titles from the two DANCE SESSION albums are included in this reissue.)

BASIE, 1954	Clef 666
COUNT BASIE SWINGS, JOE WILLIAMS SINGS, 1955	Clef 678
APRIL IN PARIS, 1955	Verve 8012

HALL OF FAME, 1956	Verve 8291
AT NEWPORT, 1957	Verve 8243
THE ATOMIC MR. BASIE, 1957	Roulette 52003
BASIE PLAYS HEFTI, 1958	Roulette 52011
EVERY DAY I HAVE THE BLUES, 1959	Roulette 52033
BREAKFAST DANCE & BARBECUE, 1959	Roulette 52028
ONE MORE TIME, 1959	Roulette 52024
CHAIRMAN OF THE BOARD, 1959	Roulette 52032
NOT NOW, I'LL TELL YOU WHEN, 1960	Roulette 52064
KANSAS CITY SUITE, 1960	Roulette 52056
JUST THE BLUES, 1960	Roulette 52054
EASIN' IT, 1960–62	Roulette 52106
THE COUNT BASIE STORY, 1960 (two discs)	Roulette RB-1

(This is an interesting collection of Basie's hits from the thirties and forties as remade by the 1960 band, the soloists chiefly featured being Frank Foster, Billy Mitchell, Frank Wess, and Joe Newman. An excellent accompanying booklet by Leonard Feather is illustrated with a number of rare photographs, some from Mrs. Basie's personal collection.)

THE LEGEND, 1961	Roulette 52086
BASIE AT BIRDLAND, 1961	Roulette 52065
FIRST TIME (The Count Basie and Duke Ellington Orchestras together), 1961	1961 Columbia CL 1715
ON MY WAY AND SHOUTIN' AGAIN, 1962	Verve V6-8511
COUNT BASIE & HIS KANSAS CITY SEVEN, 1962	Impulse AS-15
LI'L OLD GROOVEMAKER, 1963	Verve V6-8549
BASIE'S BEAT, 1967	Verve V6-8687
STRAIGHT AHEAD, 1969	Dot 25902
STANDING OVATION, 1969	Dot 25938
BASIE JAM (nonet), 1973	Pablo 2310-718
FOR THE FIRST TIME (trio), 1974	Pablo 2310-712
BASIE JAM, #2 (octet), 1976	Pablo 2310-786

BASIE JAM, #3 (octet), 1976	Pablo 2310-840
A PERFECT MATCH (with Ella Fitzgerald), 1979	Pablo D2312110
ON THE ROAD, 1979	Pablo D2312112

Several of the Roulette sets listed above have been incorporated in a two-record series entitled ECHOES OF AN ERA, the relevant numbers being RE-102, RE-118, and RE-124. The Impulse album by the Kansas City Seven and STANDING OVATION on Dot have been united in another two-record set, Impulse IA-9351/2.

The Basie band has provided expert accompaniment.to most of the popular singers of the past three decades, such as Ella Fitzgerald, Billy Eckstine, Frank Sinatra, Sarah Vaughan, Tony Bennett, Sammy Davis, Jr., Arthur Prysock, Jackie Wilson, Kay Starr, Teresa Brewer, and the Mills Brothers. Generally, these do not fall within the scope of this book, but details of those records still available can be found readily in the Schwann Catalog.

Jimmy Rushing

GOIN' TO CHICAGO, 1954	Vanguard 8518
LISTEN TO THE BLUES, 1955	Vanguard 8505
THE JAZZ ODYSSEY OF JAMES RUSHING, ESQ., 1956	Columbia CL 1152
IF THIS AIN'T THE BLUES, 1957	Vanguard 8513
LITTLE JIMMY RUSHING & THE BIG BRASS, 1958	Columbia CL 1152
RUSHING LULLABIES, 1959	Columbia CL 1401
THE SMITH GIRLS, 1960	Columbia CL 1605
FIVE FEET OF SOUL, 1963	Colpix 446
BLUES & THINGS (with Earl Hines), 1967	Master Jazz 8101
GEE, BABY, AIN'T I GOOD TO YOU?, 1967	Master Jazz 8104
WHO WAS IT SANG THAT SONG?, 1967	Master Jazz 8120
EVERY DAY I HAVE THE BLUES, 1967	Bluesway 6005
LIVIN' THE BLUES, 1968	Bluesway 6017

THE YOU AND ME THAT   Victor LSP 4566
USED TO BE, 1970

Lester "Prez" Young

THE LESTER YOUNG STORY,   Columbia CC 33502
VOL. I, 1936–37, (two discs)
THE LESTER YOUNG STORY,   Columbia JG 34837
VOL. II, 1937–38 (two discs)
THE LESTER YOUNG STORY,   Columbia JG 34840
VOL. III, 1938–39 (two discs)
THE LESTER YOUNG STORY,   Columbia JG 34843
VOL. IV, 1939–40 (two discs)
LESTER YOUNG & CHARLIE   Jazz Archives 42
CHRISTIAN, 1939–40
PREZ AT HIS VERY BEST,   Trip 5509
1943–44
LESTER YOUNG & THE   Commodore 15352
KANSAS CITY SIX, 1944
THE COMPLETE SAVOY   Savoy 2202
SESSIONS, 1944–49 (two
discs)
THE ALADDIN SESSIONS,   Blue Note LA456-H2
1945–48 (two discs)
LESTER SWINGS, 1945, 1950,   Verve 2-2516
1951 (two discs)
MEAN TO ME, 1954 & 1955   Verve 2-2538
(two discs)
PREZ & TEDDY & OSCAR, 1952   Verve 2-2502
& 1956 (two discs)
THE JAZZ GIANTS '56, 1956   Verve 1-2527
LAUGHIN' TO KEEP FROM
CRYIN' 1956   Verve 8316
LESTER YOUNG AT OLIVIA   Pablo 2308-219
DAVIS' PATIO LOUNGE,
1956

Buck Clayton

CLASSIC SWING OF BUCK   Riverside 142
CLAYTON, 1946
JAM SESSION: THE HUCKLE   Columbia CL 546
BUCK & ROBBINS' NEST,
1953

HOW HI THE FI, 1953–54	Columbia CL 567
ALL THE CATS JOIN IN, 1953–55	Columbia CL 882
BUCK CLAYTON JAMS BENNY GOODMAN FAVORITES, 1953–54	Columbia CL 614
BUCK MEETS RUBY, 1954	Vanguard 8517
JUMPIN' AT THE WOODSIDE, 1954	Columbia CL 701
CAT MEETS CHICK, 1955	Columbia CL 778
BUCK CLAYTON SPECIAL, 1957	Philips BBL 7217
BUCKIN' THE BLUES, 1957	Vanguard 8514
SONGS FOR SWINGERS, 1958	Columbia CL 1320
COPENHAGEN CONCERT, 1959 (two discs)	Steeple Chase 6006/7
BUCK & BUDDY, 1960	Swingville 2017
ONE FOR BUCK, 1961	English Columbia 33SX1390
ALL STAR PERFORMANCE, 1961	French Vogue LD 544-30
PASSPORT TO PARADISE, 1961	Inner City 7009
BUCK & BUDDY BLOW THE BLUES, 1961	Swingville 2030
ME & BUCK (with Humphrey Lyttelton), 1963	World Record Club T324
LE VRAI BUCK CLAYTON, VOLS. I & II, 1964	77 LEU 12/11 & LEU 12/18
JAM SESSION, VOL. I, 1974	Chiaroscuro 132
JAM SESSION, VOL. II, 1975	Chiaroscuro 143
JAM SESSION, VOL. III, JAZZ PARTY TIME, 1976	Chiaroscuro 152
JAM SESSION, VOL. IV, JAY HAWK, 1974–75	Chiaroscuro 163

Swingville 2017 and 2030 have been reissued together as KANSAS CITY NIGHTS, Prestige 24040. Similarly, THE GOLDEN DAYS OF JAZZ, CBS JC2L-614, contains Columbia CL 614 and CL 701.

Jo Jones

THE ESSENTIAL JO JONES, 1955–58 (two discs)	Vanguard VSD 101/02

JO JONES TRIO, 1958	Everest 5023
VAMP 'TIL READY, 1960	Everest 5099
PERCUSSION & BASS (with Milt Hinton), 1960	Everest 5110
DRUMS ODYSSEY, 1972	Jazz Odyssey 010 (F)
THE DRUMS, 1973 (two discs)	Jazz Odyssey 008 (F)
THE MAIN MAN, 1976	Pablo 2310-799

Eddie Durham

| EDDIE DURHAM, 1973–74 | RCA LPLI 5029 (E) |

Earle Warren

| EARLE WARREN, 1974 | RCA LPLI 5066 (E) |

Dicky Wells

DICKY WELLS IN PARIS, 1937	Prestige 7593
BONES FOR THE KING, 1958	Felsted 2006
TROMBONE FOUR-IN-HAND, 1959	Master Jazz 8118

Harry "Sweets" Edison

SWEETS AT THE HAIG, 1953	Pacific Jazz 11
SWEETS, 1956	American Record Society 430
GEE, BABY, AIN'T I GOOD TO YOU?, 1957	Verve 8211
THE SWINGER, 1958	Verve 8295
HARRY EDISON SWINGS BUCK CLAYTON, 1958	Verve 8293
MR. SWING, 1958	Verve 8353
SWEETENINGS, 1958	Roulette R-52023
JAWBREAKERS (with Lockjaw Davis), 1962	Riverside RLP 430
OSCAR PETERSON & HARRY EDISON, 1974	Pablo 2310.741
JUST FRIENDS, 1975	Black & Blue 33.106 (F)
EDISON'S LIGHTS, 1976	Pablo 2310.780
SIMPLY SWEETS (with Lockjaw Davis), 1977	Pablo 2310.806
EARL MEETS HARRY (with Earl Hines), 1978	Black & Blue 33.131 (F)

Buddy Tate

JUMPIN' ON THE WEST COAST, 1947	Black Lion 172 (E)
ROCK 'N' ROLL, 1954	Baton 1201
BUDDY TATE & HIS CELEBRITY CLUB ORCHESTRA, VOL. I, 1954	Black & Blue 33.006 (F)
ALL STAR JAZZ, 1955–56	Allegro 1741
SWINGING LIKE TATE, 1958	Bittersweet 827
TATE'S DATE, 1960	Swingville 2003
TATE-A-TATE with Clark Terry, 1960	Swingville 2014
GROOVIN', 1961	Swingville, 2029
BUDDY TATE (with Milt Buckner), 1967	Black & Blue 33.014 (F)
BUDDY TATE & HIS CELEBRITY CLUB ORCHESTRA, VOL. II, 1968	Black & Blue 33.020 (F)
UNBROKEN, 1970	Pausa 7030
BUDDY TATE (with Wild Bill Davis), 1972	Black & Blue 33.045 (F)
BUDDY TATE & EARLE WARREN, 1973	RCA LFLI 5034 (E)
MIDNIGHT SLOWS (with Wild Bill Davis), 1973	Black & Blue 33.054 (F)
KANSAS CITY WOMAN (with Humphrey Lyttelton), 1974	Black Lion 312 (E)
THE TEXAS TWISTER, 1975	Master Jazz 8128
JIVE AT FIVE, 1975	Mahogany 558.103 (F)
LOVE AND SLOWS (with Harry Edison), 1976	Barclay 900.550 (F)
BACK TO BACK (with Scott Hamilton), 1979	Concord CJ. 85

Helen Humes

HELEN HUMES, 1947–48	Trip 5588
HELEN HUMES, 1959	Contemporary 3571
SONGS I LIKE TO SING, 1960	Contemporary 3582
SWINGIN' WITH HUMES, 1961	Contemporary 3598
HELEN COMES BACK, 1973	Black & Blue 33.050 (F)

SNEAKIN' AROUND, 1974	Black & Blue 33.083 (F)
THE TALK OF THE TOWN, 1975	Columbia PC 33488
ON THE SUNNY SIDE OF THE STREET, 1975	Black Lion 30167 (E)
HELEN HUMES & THE MUSE ALL STARS, 1979	Muse MR 5217

Snooky Young

THE BOYS FROM DAYTON, 1971	Master Jazz 8130
SNOOKY & MARSHALL'S ALBUM, 1978	Concord CJ-55
HORN OF PLENTY, 1979	Concord CJ-91

Joe Newman

JOE NEWMAN & HIS BAND, 1954	Vanguard VRS 8007
JOE NEWMAN & THE BOYS IN THE BAND, 1954	Storyville 318
THE COUNT'S MEN, 1955	Jazztone 1220
LOCKING HORNS, 1957	Roulette R-52009
JIVE AT FIVE (with Frank Wess), 1960	Swingville 2011
JOE NEWMAN'S QUINTET AT COUNT BASIE'S, 1961	Trip 5546
GOOD 'N' GROOVY, 1961	Swingville 2019

Marshall Royal

ALTO ALTITUDE (three tracks), 1953	EmArcy 36018
BLUE PRELUDE (Gordon Jenkins Orchestra), 1960	Sunset 50011
FIRST CHAIR, 1978	Concord CJ-88

Lockjaw Davis

KICKIN' & WAILIN', 1947–48	Continental 16001
MODERN JAZZ EXPRESSIONS, 1955–56	King 506
BIG BEAT JAZZ, 1955–57	King 599
UPTOWN, 1955–57	King 606

JAZZ WITH A HORN, 1956	King 526
EDDIE'S FUNCTION, 1956–57	Bethlehem 6035
COUNT BASIE PRESENTS (with Joe Newman), 1957	Roulette 52007
THE COOKBOOK, 1958 (two discs)	Prestige 24039

(The above set contains albums originally issued as Prestige 7141 and 7161.)

VERY SAXY (with Coleman Hawkins, Arnett Cobb, and Buddy Tate), 1959	Prestige 7167
HAWK EYES (with Coleman Hawkins), 1960	Swingville 2016
STOLEN MOMENTS, 1960	Prestige 7834
TRACKIN', 1962	Prestige 7271
LOCK THE FOX, 1966	Victor LSP-3652
THE FOX AND THE HOUNDS, 1967	Victor LSP-3741
LOVE CALLS (with Paul Gonsalves), 1967	Victor LSP-3882
LEAPIN' ON LENOX, 1974	Black & Blue 33.072 (F)
CHEWIN' THE FAT (with George Arvanitas), 1975	Spotlite 15 (E)
SWEET & LOVELY, 1976	Classic Jazz 116
EDDIE "LOCKJAW" DAVIS & HARRY "SWEETS" EDISON, 1976	Storyville 4004
STRAIGHT AHEAD, 1976	Pablo 2310-778

Frank Wess

THE AWARD WINNER, 1954	Mainstream 56033
KENNY CLARKE (with Kenny Clarke), 1955	Savoy 12006
NORTH, SOUTH, EAST . . . WESS, 1956	Savoy 12072
FRANK WESS QUARTET, 1960	Moodsville 8
WHEELIN' & DEALIN', 1962	Prestige 7231

Frank Foster

JAZZ STUDIO ONE (studio group), 1953	Decca DL 8058

FRANK FOSTER QUARTET   Vogue 209 (F)
  (with Henri Renaud), 1954
NO COUNT, 1956   Savoy 12078
BASIE IS OUR BOSS, 1963   Argo 717

Joe Williams

TOGETHER (with Harry   Roulette 52069
  "Sweets" Edison), 1961
JOE WILLIAMS AT   Victor LSP-2762
  NEWPORT, 1963
ME & THE BLUES, 1963   Victor LSP-2879
PRESENTING JOE   Solid State SS 18008
  WILLIAMS (with the Thad
  Jones–Mel Lewis Orchestra),
  1966
JAZZ GALA '79 (with the
  Claude Bolling Orchestra),   Personal Choice PC 51001
  1979 (two discs)
PREZ & JOE, 1979   GNP/Crescendo 2124

Al Grey

THE LAST OF THE BIG   Argo 653
  PLUNGERS, 1959
THE THINKING MAN'S   Argo 677
  TROMBONE, 1960
AL GREY–BILLY MITCHELL   Argo 689
  SEXTET, 1961
SNAP YOUR FINGERS (with   Argo 700
  Billy Mitchell), 1962
NIGHT SONG, 1962   Argo 711
SHADES OF GREY, 1965   Tangerine 1504
GREY'S MOOD, 1973–75   Classic Jazz 118
LIVE AT RICK'S (with Jimmy   Aviva 6002
  Forrest), 1978

Eric Dixon

ERIC'S EDGE (with Sonny
  Cohn), 1974   Master Jazz 8124

Richard Boone

I'VE GOT A RIGHT TO SING,   Nocturne 703
  1969

Nat Pierce

KANSAS CITY MEMORIES (with Joe Newman & Jo Jones), 1956	Coral 57091
BIG BAND AT THE SAVOY BALLROOM (with Buck Clayton), 1957	Victor LPM 2543
JUGGERNAUT (Frankie Capp & Nat Pierce Orchestra), 1977	Concord CJ 40
LIVE AT THE CENTURY PLAZA (Frankie Capp & Nat Pierce Orchestra), 1978	Concord CJ 72

Jay McShann

EARLY BIRD (with Charlie Parker), 1940–43	Spotlite 120 (E)
KANSAS CITY PIANO (three tracks), 1941	Decca DL 9226
NEW YORK—1208 MILES, 1941–43	Decca DL 9236
K.C. IN THE '30s (McShann, Julia Lee, and other K.C. favorites), 1944–47	Capitol T1057
KANSAS CITY JUMP, 1947	Fontana SFJL-917 (E)
JAY McSHANN, 1947–49	Polydor 423.245 (E)
THE BAND THAT JUMPS THE BLUES, 1947–49	Black Lion 2460.201 (E)
McSHANN'S PIANO, 1966	Capitol T.2645
CONFESSIN' THE BLUES, 1969	Black & Blue 33.022 (F)
JUMPIN' THE BLUES, 1970	Black & Blue 33.039 (F)
GOIN' TO KANSAS CITY, 1972	Master Jazz 8113
THE MAN FROM MUSKOGEE, 1972	Sackville 3005
KANSAS CITY MEMORIES, 1973	Black & Blue 33.057 (F)
KANSAS CITY JOYS (with Buddy Tate and Paul Quinichette), 1976	Sonet 716
CRAZY LEGS & FRIDAY STRUT (with Buddy Tate), 1976	Sackville 3011

THE LAST OF THE BLUE DEVILS, 1977	Atlantic SD 8800
A TRIBUTE TO FATS WALLER, 1978	Sackville 3019
KANSAS CITY HUSTLE, 1978	Sackville 3021

Paul Quinichette

THE VICE PRESIDENT, 1952–53	Trip 5542
MOODS, 1954	Trip 5579
BORDERLINE (with Mel Powell), 1954	Vanguard VRS 8501
ON THE SUNNY SIDE, 1957	Prestige 7103
FOR BASIE, 1957	Prestige 7127
THE KID FROM DENVER, 1958	Biograph 12066
BASIE REUNION, 1958	Prestige 7147
LIKE BASIE, 1959	United Artists 4024
PREVUE (with Brooks Kerr), 1974	Famous Door HL-106

Jimmy Witherspoon

SPOON CALLS HOOTIE (with Jay McShann), 1947–48	Polydor 423.241 (E)
JIMMY WITHERSPOON, 1948–49	Crown CLP 5156
JIMMY WITHERSPOON SINGS THE BLUES, 1952	Crown CLP 5192
GOIN' TO KANSAS CITY BLUES (with Jay McShann), 1957	Victor LPM 1639
THERE'S GOOD ROCKIN' TONIGHT (with Harry Edison), 1958	World Pacific 1402
THE 'SPOON CONCERTS (with Roy Eldridge, Ben Webster, and Earl Hines), 1959 (two discs)	Fantasy 24701
IN PERSON (with Buck Clayton, Dicky Wells, and Buddy Tate), 1961	Vogue 456-30 (F)

ROOTS (with Ben Webster),   Reprise 6057
  1962
EVENIN' BLUES (with T-Bone   Prestige 7300
  Walker), 1963

Eddie Barefield
EDDIE BAREFIELD PLAYS   Cosmopolitan 500
  THE WORKS OF EDGAR
  BATTLE, 1962
EDDIE BAREFIELD, 1973–74   RCA LFLI 5035 (E)
THE INDESTRUCTIBLE   Famous Door HL 113
  E.B., 1977

Leo "Snub" Mosley
CASCADE OF QUARTETS,   Columbia 33sx1191/1218 (E)
  VOLS. I & II (one track in
  each), 1959

Sir Charles Thompson
SIR CHARLES THOMPSON   Apollo 103
  ALL STARS (with Charlie
  Parker), 1945–47
SIR CHARLES THOMPSON   Vanguard VRS 8003
  SEXTET, 1953
SIR CHARLES THOMPSON   Vanguard VRS 8006
  QUARTET, 1954
SIR CHARLES THOMPSON   Vanguard VRS 8009
  & HIS BAND (with Coleman
  Hawkins), 1954
SIR CHARLES THOMPSON   Vanguard VRS 8018
  TRIO, 1955
SIR CHARLES & THE SWING   Columbia CL 1364
  ORGAN, 1960
ROCKIN' RHYTHM, 1961   Columbia CS 8463
HEY, THERE!, 1973   Black & Blue 33.073 (F)

Bibliography

Books

Panassié, Hugues. *The Real Jazz*. New York: Smith & Durrell, 1942.

Ellison, Ralph. *Shadow and Act*. New York: Random House, 1953. (See Part II, "Sound and the Mainstream.")

Shapiro, Nat, and Nat Hentoff, eds. *Hear Me Talkin' to You*. New York: Rinehart, 1955.

Horricks, Raymond. *Count Basie and His Orchestra*. London: Gollancz, 1957.

Shapiro, Nat, and Nat Hentoff, eds. *The Jazz Makers*. New York: Rinehart, 1957. (See Nat Shapiro on "William 'Count' Basie.")

Hentoff, Nat, and Albert McCarthy, eds. *Jazz*. New York: Rinehart, 1959. (See Frank Driggs on "Kansas City and the Southwest.")

Williams, Martin, ed. *The Art of Jazz*. New York: Oxford University, 1959. (See "The Parent Style and Lester Young," by Ross Russell.)

Traill, Sinclair, and the Hon. Gerald Lascelles, eds. *Just Jazz, Volume IV*. London: Souvenir Press, 1960. (See Count Basie on "This Band.")

Hentoff, Nat. *The Jazz Life*. New York: Dial, 1961. (See "Count Basie.")

Hodeir, André. *Toward Jazz*. New York: Grove Press, 1962.

James, Burnett. *Essays on Jazz*. London: Sidgwick & Jackson, 1962. (See "Lester Young.")

Reisner, Robert George. *Bird*. Secaucus, N.J.: Citadel, 1962.

Green, Benny. *The Reluctant Art*. New York: Horizon Press, 1963. (See "Lester Young.")

Dexter, Dave. *The Jazz Story*. Englewood Cliffs, N.J.: Prentice-Hall, 1964.

Simon, George T. *The Big Bands*. New York: Macmillan, 1967.

Schuller, Gunther. *Early Jazz*. New York: Oxford University, 1968. (See "The Southwest.")

Dance, Stanley. *The World of Duke Ellington*. New York: Scribners, 1970. (See "Paul Gonsalves," "Clark Terry," and "Booty Wood.")

Williams, Martin. *The Jazz Tradition*. New York: Oxford University, 1970.

Wilmer, Valerie. *Jazz People*. London: Allison & Busby, 1970. (See "Lock the Fox" and "Buck Clayton.")

Blesh, Rudi. *Combo U.S.A.* Philadelphia: Chilton, 1971. (See "The Prez.")

Russell, Ross. *Jazz Style in Kansas City and the Southwest*. Berkeley and Los Angeles: University of California Press, 1971.

Simon, George T. *Simon Says*. New Rochelle, N.Y.: Arlington, 1971.

Wells, Dicky (with Stanley Dance). *The Night People*. Boston: Crescendo, 1971.

Feather, Leonard. *From Satchmo to Miles*. Briarcliff Manor, N.Y.: Stein & Day, 1972. (See "Swing and Basie" and "Prez.")

Russell, Ross. *Bird Lives!* New York: Charterhouse, 1973.

Dance, Stanley. *The World of Swing*. New York: Scribners, 1974. (See "Andy Gibson," "Vic Dickenson," "Quentin Jackson," and "Benny Morton.")

McCarthy, Albert. *Big Band Jazz*. New York: Putnam's, 1974.

Morgenstern, Dan, and Jack Bradley, eds. *Count Basie and His Bands*. New York: New York Jazz Museum, 1975.

Brask, Ole, and Dan Morgenstern. *Jazz People*. New York: Abrams, 1976.

Dexter, Dave. *Playback*. New York: Billboard Publications, 1976.

Murray, Albert. *Stomping the Blues*. New York: McGraw-Hill, 1976.

Dance, Stanley. *The World of Earl Hines*. New York: Scribners, 1977. (See "Budd Johnson," "Dicky Wells," and "Charlie Carpenter.")

Hammond, John (with Irving Townsend). *John Hammond on Record*. New York: Ridge Press, 1977.

Gridley, Mark C. *Jazz Styles*. Englewood Cliffs, N.J.: Prentice-Hall, 1978. (See "The Count Basie Bands.")

Giddins, Gary. *Riding on a Blue Note*. New York: Oxford University, 1981.

Besides the standard references by John Chilton, Hugues Panassié, and Leonard Feather, and the general discographies of Brian Rust and Jorgen Grunnet Jepsen, the following are particularly relevant:

Count Basie, 1929–1950. A discography compiled by Bo Scherman and Carl A. Hallstrom. Copenhagen: Knudsen, 1969.
Count Basie, 1951–1968. A discography compiled by Jorgen Grunnet Jepsen. Copenhagen: Knudsen, 1969.

Magazines

The best and most detailed research on jazz in the Southwest has been done by Frank Driggs, whose own book on the subject is long overdue. His many interviews include:

"Jay McShann." *Jazz Monthly,* March 1958.
"Elmer Crumbley." *Coda,* August 1958.
"Walter Page." *Jazz Review,* November 1958.
"Buddy Tate." *Jazz Review,* December 1958.
"Milt Larkins." *Jazz Monthly,* December 1958.
"Andy Kirk." *Jazz Review,* February 1959.
"Ed Lewis, I and II." *Jazz Review,* May and October, 1959.
"Don Albert." *Jazz Monthly,* July 1959.
"Clarence Love." *Jazz Monthly,* December 1959.
"Ben Smith." *Record Research,* March 1960.
"Tommy Douglas." *Jazz Monthly,* April 1960.
"Eddie Barefield." *Jazz Review,* July 1960.
"Budd Johnson, I and II." *Jazz Review,* November 1960 and January 1961.
"Harlan Leonard." *Jazz Journal,* October 1963.
"Red Perkins, I and II." *Jazz Journal,* November and December 1964.

Other articles that can be profitably consulted are:

Dance, Stanley. "New York Impressions." *Jazz Hot,* no. 17, 1937.
Simon, George. "Up for the Count." *Metronome,* November 1948.
Gleason, Ralph. "Count Basie: Bouquets for the Living." *Down Beat,* November 17, 1950.
Williams, Mary Lou, with Max Jones. "Mary Lou Williams: Life Story." *Melody Maker,* April 3 to June 12, 1954 (eleven consecutive issues).
Hammond, John. "Count Basie: A 20th Anniversary." *Down Beat,* November 2, 1955.
Freeman, Don. "Count Basie" (interview). *Down Beat,* May 16, 1956.
Panassié, Hugues. "Reminiscing About the Count." *Jazz Journal,* April 1957.

Dance, Stanley. "The Conquering Count." *Jazz Journal,* December 1957.

Dance, Stanley. "Skip Hall and Eli Robinson." *Jazz Monthly,* September 1958.

"Relaxin' with the Count." *Down Beat,* September 18, 1958.

Hodeir, André. "Du Côte de Chez Basie." *Jazz Review,* December 1958.

Panassié, Hugues. "Lester Young." *Bulletin H.C.F.,* April 1959.

Panassié, Hugues. "Lips Page." *Bulletin H.C.F.,* December 1959.

Gazzaway, Don. "Conversations with Buster Smith." *Jazz Review,* December 1959, January and February, 1960.

Gazzaway, Don. "Before Bird—Buster." *Jazz Monthly,* January 1962.

Feather, Leonard. "Basie." *Swank,* May 1963.

Gelly, Dave. "The Count Basie Octet." *Jazz Monthly,* July 1963.

Lambert, G. E. "Count Basie: The Middle Years." *Jazz Monthly,* September 1963.

Panassié, Hugues. "Herschel Evans." *Bulletin H.C.F.,* April 1964.

"Why Count Basie Keeps Swinging." *Sepia,* May 1965.

Holroyd, Steve. "Four Decades of Basie, I and II." *Melody Maker,* August 17 and August 24, 1968.

"Count Basie: Press Conference." *Asbury Park Evening Press,* August 17, 1969.

Giddins, Gary. "On the Road with the Super Chief." *New York,* May 12, 1975.

Postif, François. "Goodbye, Pork Pie Hat." *Jazz Hot,* nos. 362 and 363, 1979.

Index

Song titles are in *italics*.

375

Detroit Perspectives

Glorious architecture of the 1920s: the Michigan Theater, now doing
service as a parking structure. (Courtesy of Bob McKeown, 1986.)

Detroit
Perspectives

Crossroads and Turning Points

Edited by Wilma Wood Henrickson

Wayne State University Press   Detroit

03   02   01   6   5   4

Library of Congress Cataloging-in-Publication Data
Detroit perspectives : crossroads and turning points / edited by Wilma Wood
Henrickson.
        p.   cm. — (Great Lakes books)
    Includes bibliographical references and index.
    ISBN 0–8143–2013–9 (alk. paper). — ISBN 0–8143–2014–7 (pbk. :
alk. paper)
    1. Detroit (Mich.)—History—Sources.   2. Detroit (Mich.)—
History.   I. Henrickson, Wilma Wood, 1915–   .   II. Series.
F574.D457D5   1991
977.4'34—dc20   90–37064
                                                                     CIP

GREAT LAKES BOOKS

Contents

Acknowledgments

The compiler of an anthology has many reasons to be grateful and many people to thank. One can only hope not to miss too many of those to whom gratitude is due.

Without good friends over many years, this work, of whatever worth it has, would not have been possible. First, to Philip Mason, head of the Walter Reuther Archives and Library of Urban Affairs, I owe a debt of untold measurement for his ready sympathy, warm encouragement, and demanding standards. I am also grateful to JoEllen Vinyard, of Eastern Michigan University, for being a strong supportive editor at *Detroit in Perspective: A Journal of Regional History.* I am thankful that for some years the Detroit Historical Society made *Detroit in Perspective* possible. Like most area history buffs, I shall continue to mourn its passing. Tom Jones, of the Historical Society of Michigan, has been helpful both currently and in the past.

Early encouragement was given by Jean Owen, former editor at the Wayne State University Press. Alice Nigoghosian, Anne Adamus, and editor Robin DuBlanc at Wayne State University Press have not only been unfailingly patient in the many stages of this work, but were able to secure rights to reprint several selections originally published by the press.

I thank the editors of the *New Republic* and Bill Newlin of New Republic Books for several acts of generosity. I feel an especially warm gratitude to old friend Bill Grant, not only for his brief history of a school crisis, "Integration's Last Hurrah," for the *New Republic*, but also for his encouragement in the early stages of this effort.

Among contributors there are many old friends. There is Jack Widick, who has written much great stuff, but is here represented by a single chapter of *Detroit: City of Race and Class Vio-*

lence, now reissued by Wayne State University Press, chosen because it describes the essence of Detroit's Camelot years under Mayor Jerome Cavanagh, years which have been so quickly forgotten by so many. I thank Kenneth Cockrel for his willing gift of material he had written for the Detroit Alliance for a Rational Economy (DARE), and mourn with many that his untimely death will make it impossible for him to add to service given his city.

There is Marie Oresti, of the Catholic Interracial Council. Our shared memories go back to wartime years with the Detroit Housing Commission, an experience also shared with Bette Jenkins (Downs). Both women shared a quiet fury at the obvious institutional racism of those years. Others, who are of course credited with their writings but whose personal help beyond that is gratefully acknowledged, include James Bell, Councilwoman Maryann Mahaffey, Harold Norris, the Reverend David Gracie, and Ernest Dillard.

Then there are Arthur Johnson, Victor Reuther, Jack Russell, Dan Luria, and Kathryn Kozora. Ron Williams also encouraged me through several appearances in that journalistic gadfly, *Metro Times*. Nor can one forget the gracious generosity of John Hersey in giving permission to use two telling chapters of *The Algiers Motel Incident*.

Special thanks go to David Lawrence along with Vivian Guilmette and Editor Neal Shine of the *Detroit Free Press* for patient and friendly help in arranging rights to reprint, and also for an introduction to Barbara Stanton, who made several helpful comments on the treatment of the 1967 riot.

At the *Detroit News*, Publisher Robert S. Giles willingly granted permission for the reprinting of several items, including the *News*-owned copyright of the *Detroit Times's* romantic story on the suicide of Janet MacDonald in 1939.

Thoughtful suggestions came from Steve Babson and Ron Alpern. Two other friends, Councilman Mel Ravitz and Carol Campbell, part-time poet and full-time assistant to Mayor Coleman Young, both graciously offered help and corrective advice during the course of this work.

Some who have taken on the painful task of reading some piles of manuscript include JoEllen Vinyard, Dale Vinyard, of Wayne State University, Philip Mason, and the Reverend Hugh White, urban affairs consultant to Bishop Coleman McGehee of the Episcopal Diocese of Michigan. Louis Goldstein, AIA, currently serving as Michigan coordinator of the AIA's Committee on Historic Resources, found time to read several sections pertaining to housing and planning. Stanley Solvick of Wayne State University read some material with a cautious, friendly eye, but not he nor any of these others should be blamed for surviving errors.

For access to good material in good libraries, I thank the entire staff at the Burton Library, most especially Alice Dalligan, retired director, Mary Karshner, Judy Barmatoski, and Deborah Evans, as well as Margaret Ward, now retired. Edward Weber, of the Labadie Collection at the University of Michigan, and Francis X. Blouin, director of the Bentley Library, have gone out of their respective ways to be helpful with troublesome requests. The Bentley Library provided reading access to the papers of an old friend, the late Josephine Gomon. None of this material is reproduced or quoted here, but it shed fresh perspectives on the trial of Dr. Ossian Sweet as well as Detroit life in the twenties. The very helpful staff at the Walter Reuther Archives and Library of Urban Affairs included Warner Pflug, Michael Smith, Kathleen Schmeling, and Tom Featherstone.

Access to materials not easily available has been made easier by Bill Lynch, bookseller and collector, who lent me several rare editions of books. I also wish to thank Anne Hinchman Berry for permission to include Theodore Hinchman's letter from the manuscript collections of the Burton Library.

Let us mention now those absent friends of long ago, believers in history, diggers of truth. In the thirties the history department at Detroit City College, which grew to become Wayne State University, was a more formal and completely masculine department. It was 1970 before I had the courage to call old friend William J. Bossenbrook "Bill." Among the faculty with whom I studied were historians Sidney Glazer, Raymond C. Miller, Alfred Kelly, Milo M. Quaife, and Winfred Harbison, as well as folklore specialist Thelma James and sociologist Donald C. Marsh.

Very especially I value the memory of Mary Ritter Beard, whom I first met through the help of Dr. Bossenbrook, who urged me to send her a copy of my thesis on Eleanor Roosevelt. Mary became my mentor, which lasted for some years—until I foolishly decided that five children and the writing of history did not mix. Even then, she sustained and encouraged me, never failing to remind me that I would be a historian yet. To her and her work every American woman historian of a later vintage owes gratitude.

I am grateful to Bob McKeown, whose photographic insight into the city's dark corners is well known, and whose talent is to be credited for a number of the photographs in this book. One or two of these also appeared in *Metro Times*, whose editor and publisher, Ron Williams, should also be thanked. Some illustrations are credited to the Reuther or Burton collections. Credits are noted with each, though not the gracious searching help so freely given at each institution.

To Cameron Waterman I am indebted not only for his gift of a family photograph of the *Uarda*, but also for the sharing of his insights about one period in the life of old Detroit.

I thank Norman McRae, director of the social studies department of the Detroit Public Schools, not only for the material he has written but also for the informal information over the years and his perceptions of the black condition in Detroit.

My most continuing obligation is to my husband, Merle Henrickson, some of whose writings, spanning almost fifty years, appear here, and who, as a reader, can be counted on to be unfailingly critical. To our gently sharp-tongued daughter, Kirsten Brainard, I owe the comment that she had never realized while growing up in Detroit that she and her family occupied the center of the local universe. I can think of no more accurate, though embarrassing, perception of her mother's ego. It is clearly ego that has allowed me to make choices as to which events, decisions, and turning points in this city to include in the book. I am sure many of my readers will question my choices, and they have the clear right to do so.

My own hope is that this book will not only give some pleasure to those who care about history and cities and some insight to students, but also that it will open up areas that still need further questioning. Younger historians should find many dark corners worth exploring, and citizens some things worth fighting for.

Introduction

This is the story of 150 years of change in a city and its environs. Detroit was the capital of the huge area termed the Michigan Territory, the major trading center of the entire Northwest, and its oldest settlement. "A small city," Mr. and Mrs. William Woodbridge called it—with some contempt—in 1822, but in 1837, the year Michigan became a state, it was already more than 130 years old. Detroit's story is told here through a selection of readings focused on moments of change. Those cited in this work fall into several patterns, most of which have recurred several times in the years between 1837 and the present.

Perhaps the earliest, as well as one of the most persistent, of these turning points is the deterioration of the city's natural environment as Detroiters—sometimes mindlessly, more often under the direct pressure of making a living—marred the area's original beauty.

Other major changes in the life of the city came about through raw physical growth, growth that accelerated during an early land boom and three wars. At these times newcomers could hardly be absorbed, much less welcomed. They were times of unplanned urban sprawl, with further depletion of both physical and human resources.

Today there is a frightening shrinkage of the once-proud city, a shrinkage that is combined with a lopsided growth at the outer edges and in the half-dozen counties which make up the "Detroit Metropolitan Area," as the census-takers term it.

Some shifts in the direction of the city's life have been tied to the attractions of wealth. All too often the fat years have coincided with wars. Still, there has been money in Detroit. Dollars earned in Michigan created a local Gilded Age long before the automobile industry became the symbol of Detroit wealth.

Decisions that affect civil liberties or civil rights account for quite a few of the documents cited. Several relate to the care, or lack of it, given to children in the public schools, and others to those civic actions loosely termed "urban planning," which tend to lock us into living patterns we have not chosen.

Some accidental decisions have compelled the city to take new directions, closing off some options, opening others. Many major changes have been allowed to be made by simple drift. All too often a decision is arrived at by the few with no participation, perhaps even no awareness, by the many.

I assume, for instance, that in spite of the wide publicity given to the new City Charter Commission and its many study groups, during the 1970s, few realized fully what the new "strong mayor" government would mean in the political life of the city. In the years since the adoption of the charter, it has become the habit of both ordinary citizens and the daily press to deride the city council for its supposed personal weakness and lack of action. The coincidence of the election of a mayor, Coleman Young, whose own personal political style was that of the strong mayor, has helped to personalize the issue for the past fifteen years.

There have been trade-offs in the growth of the city, prices paid for decisions taken. Samuel Zug was a good businessman, given to religious and charitable works, an abolitionist, and a worker in the Underground Railroad. After the Civil War he bought a wooded island in the Detroit River. I suspect, but cannot prove, that its marshy inlets may have been useful earlier when he was helping in the escape of slaves to Canada. When the damp fogs of Zug Island made it seem an unpleasant place to retire, Zug sold the property to a group of developers. In later years Zug Island became synonymous with one of the ugliest features of industrial growth—the blight near the mouth of the Rouge River—where during times of full employment strange clouds arise to block the view of the riverfront from the decks of the Boblo boats cruising by. (This is not to mention what the same clouds of pollution do to the workers' families of southwest Detroit.) Pollution was long considered a necessary price to be paid for industrial growth, which of course meant jobs.

Trade-offs may involve changes other than physical: a number of those I have cited in documents are set primarily in human terms. The geometric expansion of Detroit's suburbs in the years following World War II did not just change maps dramatically or force the extension of utilities. There were many subtle human trade-offs made by the people moving outward. Most home buyers were tools of real estate developers and had little choice. With home financing sources and the Federal Housing Administration (FHA) working on the side of blandness, the new neighborhoods turned out to be as homogenized as to the age and income of their residents as they frequently were in design. It is also possible to pinpoint a turning point during the late 1940s and the 1950s when, by a fairly conscious decision, at least some Detroiters turned their backs on living among neighbors of other races. The process also destroyed many old ethnic neighborhoods, leaving children of the next generation dependent on the artificial support systems of "ethnic festivals" or the International Institute for a knowledge of other cultures. A series of local elections in the late forties, especially the 1949 choice of Mayor Albert Cobo, marked not only the acceptance of a segregated society, but also an outreach toward one.

Yet during those same years, there was at work a crosscurrent of change, triggered by the United Auto Workers (UAW). To labor's credit, the union was usually at odds with the trends developing toward a closed society. I have included some material on labor-sponsored housing and on a program for rescuing the schools from the dull straitjacket of "the System."

I am not trying to establish an anthology of the best-known writings on Detroit history, nor am I trying to ignore the classics in this field. A few selections from some of the early scholarship should encourage a further look into materials that are receding far enough into the past to become "endangered species" for most readers. There are selections from Silas Farmer, historian and son of the mapmaker John Farmer, and from Clarence M. Burton, who earned his living by authenticating abstracts and titles for real estate but whose massive personal historical collections became the basis of the department of the Detroit Public Library that bears his name. Along with historian-journalists Robert B. Ross and George Catlin, these are the early greats. I have omitted Francis Parkman's tale of the conspiracy of Pontiac to confine myself as much as possible to the years immediately before Michigan's statehood and the period of statehood itself— approximately the time from 1830 to the present.

Another sort of endangered species is the document written long ago in a style that now seems cumbersome and archaic. Few of today's readers would stand in line for a chance to read Lewis Cass's entire position paper on Indian removal—for such it was, a political document, probably aimed at getting the attention of the newly elected president, Andrew Jackson. Yet many of us have become sensitized to the experience of the Native American and are at least curious about the displacement of an entire people. Cass provides a statement of the rationalizations used by thoughtful white men to justify the actions of the times.

I have used both sources and secondary materials, whichever seemed to tell the story most effectively. There are included a number of newspaper articles and other fugitive materials. A good many of these are used simply because of the directness of the material, however incomplete, or tinged with its own bias, it may be. (Witness Mayor John Smith, basically a good man, challenging the Ku Klux Klan in 1925, yet somehow sure that the city's problems would go away if Negroes would just restrict themselves to neighborhoods where they were "welcome!")

I have also included as secondary accounts of events, some hard-won research by people who cared. It is a delight to bring to attention such superb research as that done by Alexandra Mc-Coy on the wealthy elite of the years before and after the Civil War and Jack Elenbaas's examination of the arrest of Alderman Tom Glinnan in 1912. Jorge Castellanos's article, "Black Slavery in Detroit," is one that deserves a more general public than it is likely to have. Few except scholars read scholarly journals, and one of the best of them in this area, *Detroit in Perspective*, is now dead. Castellanos's article appeared in the final issue of that periodical.

The Sojourner Truth housing riots of 1942 are cloudy in Detroit memories, dwarfed as they were by the troubles of 1943. I have included here a section of Bette Jenkins's courageous thesis on the role of her employer, the Detroit Housing Commission. Jenkins traces the thread of confusion running through the news reports of wartime violence by whites that many Detroiters ignored at the time.

Sometimes a style of writing is so evocative of the period that style alone does much to account for the document's inclusion, as with the obituary of Clara Ward. There is a sly, chuckling style behind the surface formality that John Lodge, a venerable Detroit politician, shared with his collaborator, Milo M. Quaife, which imparts a special flavor to Lodge's revelations of 1912 Detroit.

Walter Pitkin, onetime professor of journalism at Columbia University, was best known for his depression best seller, *Life Begins at Forty*, and is little remembered for his rambling, somewhat opinionated autobiography, *On My Own*. Long out of print, but with irreplaceable material on the Detroit of a century ago, this too is an endangered species among books.

One further criterion comes to mind: there still seems to be justification for making certain that materials by or about women or minorities are included. Over the years, such materials have not automatically gotten into print. Also, the writing of black local history by black scholars is a relatively recent, though growing, development. One of these scholars, Norman McRae, has worked in the field for a quarter of a century, and I am pleased to be able to include a selection from an unpublished manuscript by him.

This has not been an attempt to set forth a list of documents included, but rather to clarify the reasons for choice: interest to the reader, probability that it will not be easily found elsewhere, appropriateness to the themes involved, sometimes by a style or mood illuminating that theme, and, "other things being equal," the inclusion of women and minorities as both writers and actors. Preference has been given to direct source material, except when the historian's skill is needed to clarify the intentions of a somewhat murky original document. Given the frailties of historians, that does not happen often.

Part I

The River We Lost

The River We Lost

From the moment when the French first came to that nameless place on the narrows and called it "D'étroit," they were bewitched by the astonishing beauty of the river. The description given by the voyageurs is simply not believable in today's world. Was it ever really like that? Of course such paradise could not survive.

In exploring the Detroit River, we shall begin with the river of Cadillac's report, handed down to us through Silas Farmer, that tireless nineteenth-century historian. Then we shall move to the tale of the first major riverfront developer, the Cass Farm Company, organized by Detroit's leading citizens during the boom times of the 1830s. Its hopes and final failure are recorded by Clarence M. Burton, who remains the all-time expert on land titles and real estate transactions in early Detroit. This section will conclude with a modern evaluation of the old east side riverfront, prepared several years ago for the Detroit Recreation Department by historian Kathryn Kozora. The material used from her work covers the early and mid nineteenth century and shows the uses Detroiters made of their riverfront during the years of early commercial growth.

1. Cadillac's Account of Detroit

as reported by Silas Farmer

Since you [King Louis XIV of France] have directed me to render an account of it, I will do so, premising that Detroit is actually but a channel or river of medium breadth and twenty-five leagues in length, according to my estimate, . . . through which flows and escapes slowly and with sufficiently moderate current, the living and crystal waters of Lake Superior, Michigan, and Huron (which are so many seas of sweet water) into Lake Erie, Lake Ontario, or Frontenac, and which finally, together with the waters of the St. Lawrence, mingle with those of the ocean.

Its borders are so many vast prairies, and the freshness of the Beautiful waters keeps the banks always green. The prairies are

Silas Farmer, *History of Detroit and Wayne County and Early Michigan*, 3d ed. (Detroit: Farmer & Co., 1890; Detroit: Gale Research Company, 1969), 11.

bordered by long and broad rows of fruit trees which have never felt the careful hand of the vigilant gardener. Here, also, orchards, young and old, soften and bend their branches, under the weight and quantity of their fruit, towards the mother earth, which has produced them. It is in this land, so fertile, that the ambitious vine, which has never wept under the knife of the vine-dresser, builds a thick roof with its large leaves and heavy clusters, weighing down the top of the tree which receives it, and often stifling it with its embrace.

Under these broad walks one sees assembled by hundreds the timid deer and faun, also the squirrel bounding in his eagerness to collect the apples and plums with which the earth is covered. Here the cautious turkey calls and conducts her numerous brood to gather the grapes, and here also their mates come to fill their large and gluttonous crops. Golden pheasants, the quail, the partridge, woodcock, and numerous doves swarm in the woods and cover the country, which is dotted and broken with thickets and high forests of full-grown trees, forming a charming perspective, which sweetens the sad lonesomeness of the solitude. The hand of the pitiless reaper has never mown the luxurious grass upon which fatten woolly buffaloes, of magnificent size and proportion.

There are ten species of forest trees, among them are the walnut, white oak, red oak, the ash, the pine, white-wood and cotton-wood; straight as arrows, without knots, and almost without branches, except at the very top, and of prodigious size. Here the courageous eagle looks fiercely at the sun, with sufficient at his feet to satisfy his boldly armed claws. The fish are here nourished and bathed by living water of crystal clearness, and their great abundance renders them none the less delicious. Swans are so numerous that one would take for lilies the reeds in which they are crowded together. The gabbling goose, the duck, the widgeon, and the bustard are so abundant that to give an idea of their numbers I must use the expression of a savage whom I asked before arriving if there was much game. "So much," he said, "that they draw up in lines to let the boats pass through." . . . In a word, the climate is temperate, and the air purified through the day and night by a gentle breeze. The skies are always serene and spread sweet and fresh influences which makes one enjoy a tranquil sleep.

If the situation is agreeable, it is none the less important because it opens and closes the door of passage to the most distant nations which are situated upon the borders of the vast seas of sweet water. None but the enemies of truth could be enemies to this establishment so necessary to the increase of the glory of the king.

2.   The Cass Farm Company of 1835

Clarence M. Burton

One of the largest real estate enterprises that flourished at that period [1835–36] was what was known as the Cass Farm Company. This organization was similar to the corporations of our time, though in fact it was a copartnership. It was organized June 18, 1835. The organizers were the foremost business men of the city, ten in number: Edmund A. Brush, Charles C. Trowbridge, Eurotas P. Hastings, DeGarmo Jones, Shubael Conant, Elon Farnsworth, Oliver Newberry [and Henry Whiting, Augustus S. Porter, and Henry Cole].

. . . The company at first purchased all of the Cass farm south of Larned Street from Gov. Lewis Cass for $100,000 and they gave

Clarence M. Burton, "The Cass Farm Company of 1835," in *The City of Detroit, Michigan, 1701–1922*, ed. Clarence M. Burton, William Stocking, and Gordon K. Miller (Chicago: S. J. Clarke, 1922), 1: 341–43.

him a mortgage for the full amount. The additional security was the obligation of the purchasers and the moneys they expended in improving the property. Before we go further into the history of this company we will ascertain what the Cass farm was. It was a large farm of more than five hundred acres, reaching from Cass Avenue to Third Avenue of the present city and extending from the Detroit River three miles in depth to the railroads on the north. It had originally consisted of three farms and the origin of record title reaches back to the time when this country was under the French Dominion. . . . The property subsequently came to be owned by the estate of William Macomb and by the terms of his will passed on his three sons, David, William and John. Lewis Cass purchased the property from these heirs about the year 1816 for $12,000. It was practically unproductive, for aside from the small portion he wanted for the use of himself and family, it was leased for farm purposes at a small rental. But the times changed so completely between 1830 and 1835 that the front portion of the farm was now needed for business and dwelling purposes. The front, below Larned Street, was mostly covered with the waters of the Detroit River and this had to be all filled in to make it of any use. The work of filling in was begun in 1835. A contract was given to Abraham Smolk to do this work for the company. The entire tract was conveyed by the owners to Augustus S. Porter, August 17, 1835. Mr. Porter was to act as trustee for the company and make conveyances of the property as it was sold in parcels. Porter appointed Charles C. Trowbridge his successor to act in case of his death or disability. The formation of this company and the enterprise it demonstrated is thus referred to in the Free Press of March, 23, 1836:

City Improvements: We are highly gratified to learn from authentic sources that our enterprising fellow citizens Messrs. Newberry, Conant, Jones and others, proprietors for the Cass front, are making preparations for the erection of a splendid hotel on the site of Governor Cass' old residence. It is a subject of congratulation that our citizens are becoming alive to the importance of an addition to the comforts and convenience of travelers. It is true that we have two commodious and excellent hotels and a host of others good enough in their way but it is a subject of public notoriety that hundreds of passengers were compelled last season to remain over night on board the steamboats, or leave the city, for want of lodgings and even now at this inclement season when navigation is closed, applicants are daily dismissed from public houses for want of accommodations. . . .

We predict that the month of May will flood Detroit with persons seeking a temporary or permanent abode. The rapid growth of this city, its situation on the great chain of lakes at the very center of Michigan and the important public improvements by railroads now being constructed, have attracted the attention of foreign capitalists and thousands of men will seek an abiding place among us. The construction of the Cass Hotel on the liberal scale intended, will remedy many of those evils of which complaints have justly been made, and its beautiful situation, commanding a lofty view up and down the river, cannot fail to secure to it a large share of public patronage. . . .

A year of work in filling in, building wharves and selling took place before we find any report of their sales. The demand for lots had been good and there were plenty of sales and many buildings were erected. On October 20, 1836, the trustees reported that they had expended $53,388.27 in improvements and had sold lots on contract and for cash to the amount of $191,936.37. Of these sales $113,552.90 was considered good. Not enough money had been received to warrant any payments either to Cass on his mortgage or to the members of the company. Before this sale took place the following notice of it appeared in the daily press:

GREAT SALE OF THE FRONT OF CASS FARM, DETROIT

The owners of this splendid property, comprising from 15 to 20 acres, having a front of wharfing on the ship channel of the Detroit River of 1400 feet in length, well laid out in lots to suit the purpose of warehousing and commerce, will be offered for sale at public auction at the Michigan Exchange in the City of Detroit on Tuesday the 20th day of September next. The improvements made by the owners in wharfing this front and in reducing the high bank on which the Mansion House of Governor Cass stood, to an easy and convenient grade from Larned Street to the channel of the river, is one of the most important and extensive that has been undertaken by individuals in the west. . . . The proprietors have been engaged in this work for about a year and are rapidly completing it, having from 60 to 100 men constantly employed. . . .

The great financial depression that swept over the entire country in 1837 was not felt at once in Detroit and the sale of the Cass front went on at high speed. Messrs. Porter and Conant made an inventory of the property of the company on October 12, 1837, and found that they had in unsold lots $307,307.50 and in good contracts $113,552.90, making a total of $420,860.40. The times of depression had come, however, and it was not only impossible to sell more lots, but the contracts already made were being forfeited and the lands were falling back upon the company. The matter was a failure and it only remained now to make the best of it and get out with as little loss as possible. Nothing whatever on the principal had been paid to General Cass on his mortgage and the interest was paid only until January 1, 1837.

In 1839 Mr. Brush visited Cass in Paris, where he was living as the minister to France, and in the interest of the company made a proposition to him which was accepted. By this agreement the remaining lots were divided into ten portions and one portion allotted to each member of the company. The mortgage to Cass was discharged and in 1840 he took a new mortgage from each member for $10,000, covering the share of each. The ten members gave their unsecured bond for $17,500, the interest unpaid on the original mortgage. In November, 1840, Trowbridge gave up his interest to Henry R. Schoolcraft, John Hulbert and the Reverend William McMurray. These men had purchased interests under Mr. Trowbridge sometime before this, but now he stepped out of the company completely and turned over his shares to his successors completely without any further compensation. Affairs remained in this way for some years. The times were getting harder and harder and as no sales could be made the partners could not pay their mortgages. Their money was gone and to force payment for the mortgages would have compelled them to seek the court of bankruptcy. Farnsworth, Porter, the executors of the Cole estate, Whiting, Hastings, Brush and Conant all surrendered their interests to Cass in 1843. Oliver Newberry and Mrs. Catherine H. Jones [widow of DeGarmo] only retained their interests in the estate.

Thus ended in disaster one of the greatest real estate transactions that ever took place in Detroit. It started out on the wave of prosperity that swept over the country in 1835, and ended in the gulf of disaster and despair that followed in the wake of the financial crisis brought about by rotten wild cat banks and the depreciated currency of 1837.[1]

Editor's Note

1. As Mr. Burton indicates, the outcome of the Cass Farm deal was disaster for the partners. Historian Milo M. Quaife, in lectures given in 1936, said that while two or three partners escaped long term damage, August Porter handed over all his assets and died a poor man, and that only C. C. Trowbridge landed "butter side up." Trowbridge's escape involved the sale of his share to Henry Schoolcraft and two of Schoolcraft's associates at a time when land prices had begun to drop. Trowbridge also gave up to Cass a number of other land parcels in order to maintain his credit. Cass was a hard taskmaster. The partners, in varying degrees, had been close associates and friends of his before the venture. The Michigan legislature later outlawed the old practice of strict foreclosure that made it possible for mortgage holders to collect far more than the original investment.

The lasting effects were not on some important Detroit pocketbooks but on the river's edge. This was the first clear loss of the shape of the shoreline and the extent of the river to industry and development. The Cass Company also seems to have made no effort to provide general public access to the water's edge. Access to the Detroit River is still something of a key bargaining point between public advocates and real estate developers.

As for the land that Abraham Smolk once dredged and filled, it now lies firmly under a series of steel-fenced parking lots near the Joe Louis Arena.

3. Detroit's East Riverfront: People and Places of Yesterday

Kathryn Kozora

With the opening of the Erie Canal, the early 1800s brought steam navigation and the beginning of the settlement of the west. The Detroit River, now a water pathway connecting Detroit to the eastern seaboard and the Atlantic Ocean, put the city on the migratory route. The completion of a canal at Sault Ste. Marie connecting Lake Superior and Lake Huron joined Detroit to the Upper Peninsula of Michigan where accessibility to its lumber and mineral resources lured business and laborers to the north as well as industry to locations along the Detroit River. The changing land use patterns on the east riverfront reflected these new business interests as the heirs of the original French farm owners sold their land to those implementing the new economy.

Kathryn Kozora, *Detroit's East Riverfront: People and Places of Yesterday*. (Detroit: Detroit Recreation Department, 1982), 1–20.

In addition to the abundance of raw materials for industry—copper, iron ore, and coal—building materials were also plentiful. These included sand, plaster, and a large supply of brick clay and limestone. At this time, Michigan also produced more lumber than any other state. All these resources can be traced to activities on the east riverfront. The Hart Map of Detroit in 1853 shows a dozen saw mills with accompanying lumber yards, a shipyard and dry dock on the river between Riopelle and Dequindre, a large lime kiln located at the foot of DeQuindre and the city's Hydraulic works and reservoir at the foot of Orleans. . . .

From the early 1880s, various railroad companies had huge land holdings on both the east and west riverfront which provided lines for the movement of raw materials, finished products and people. The first of these companies on the east riverfront was the Pontiac and Detroit Railroad which occupied the land from Randolph to Beaubien and later to Riopelle. The Detroit and Milwaukee, the Great Western and the Detroit, Grand Haven and Milwaukee were some of the numerous companies that were associated with this section of the riverfront, often two or three companies at a time. A vast railroad complex was formed that became the center of much freight and passenger activity.

Shipbuilding became a successful early industry on the east riverfront which retained its importance until the early 1900s. At this time, new technology began to make wooden ships obsolete and the shortage of space on the riverfront property made it impossible to expand the facilities. In 1852, the first large vessel, a wooden propeller steamer designed to carry passengers and freight, was launched from what was to become the Detroit Dry Dock Company located at the foot of Orleans. As the center of wooden shipbuilding in Detroit, the Detroit Dry Dock Company supported numerous related industries. Among these were the Frontier Iron Works at 210 Chene which produced marine engines, the East End Boiler Works at 255 St. Aubin, the Taylor Water Tube Boiler Company at 1440 Franklin and the Murphy Iron Works at 3198 Guoin, manufacturers of marine and stationary engines. Under the leadership of Frank E. Kirby, one of the owners of the Detroit Dry Dock Company and a naval architect, many innovative vessels were developed including the "Lansdowne" a Detroit River railroad car ferry that was the largest ship on the lakes when launched in 1881. It is still in existence and there are plans to restore it as a floating restaurant. The Detroit Dry Dock Company was to become known for its major advances in wooden shipbuilding and enjoyed a nationwide reputation.

Other early industry on the east river front included the Schulte Brothers Soap Factory at Franklin and Rivard, one of the oldest establishments in Detroit. "German," "German Laundry" and "Indian Chief" were some of the soap varieties produced. The American Eagle Tobacco Company at 45–53 Woodbridge was started in 1848 and was one of a growing number of firms that created a viable industry around tobacco in Detroit. The Berry Brothers Varnish Manufactury opened in 1858 on the corner of Leib and Wight. Scattered around the area were a number of foundries and tanneries. These smaller industrial firms usually employed just one or two people and had apprentices training.

Next to Detroit Dry Dock Company was the reservoir of the City of Detroit. With increasing numbers of people in the city, supplying water became a problem. In the days of the French farms, planks had been extended into the river and water was drawn with buckets. Later, several wells were dug near the river and in 1824 a wharf was erected at the foot of Randolph Street where the Peter Berthelet family was in charge of the operation of the round house. . . . The plan for the hydraulic works was copied from the Old Manhattan works of New York City and had a 50-foot tower topped by a wooden tank that was 20 feet high. A narrow, winding stairway led to the top of the tower where "in olden times, a visit was one of the things to be enjoyed by all visitors." This system was in use until 1860 when another larger complex was built farther east on the river. . . .

Away from the main stream of commercial and financial activities which took place west of Woodward, the east riverfront took on an identity of its own. From a hodge-podge of mixed use starting with the mansions on Jefferson to the variety of industry found on the water's edge, neighborhoods emerged producing a kaleidoscope of activity. The resident population lived in small one and two story frame houses built along unpaved streets. Homes were clustered on Franklin, Woodbridge, Wight Streets or scattered throughout the area and interspersed with stores, shops and buildings of craft and industry. A myriad of small business and other services emerged—blacksmiths, barbers, bakers and butchers; shoemakers, saloon keepers, along with a seamstress or two. Grocery, drygoods, notion and drug stores provided for resident needs. Meat markets, machine shops and warehouses were side by side.

Boarding houses and a number of small hotels provided the housing for the transient population—sailors, travelers and the countless hangers-on of an immense new industry based on the world-wide movement of people and goods. . . .

There were fifty taverns and saloons listed in the 1855 Detroit Directory and a large number of them were located on the east riverfront, evenly divided between German and Irish ownership.

An editorial written in the 1885 Detroit Directory deplores the condition of the three mile Detroit riverfront. The writer observes that the various owners are protecting, improving or neglecting their property at will, "and in some instances have wholly barred the passage of the public from the water's edge." He states that the docks, with few exceptions, were in disrepair with "accidents and loss of life not uncommon." Also reported are a new line of docks being constructed from Orleans to the west side. Historically, there had been a continuous fill-in and expansion of the river's edge. As early as 1804, city officials approved the building of wooden cribs at the edge of the river that were to be filled with rubbish and other materials to create more land. In 1819, while giving permission for the building of a wharf at the foot of Randolph Street, it was noted that "as the city grew, an increasing amount of rubbish and refuse was deposited on the low grounds at the river's edge. This created an almost constant nuisance."

In 1826, permanent improvement of the riverfront was begun by depositing earth from the embankment of Ft. Shelby along the edge of the riverfront. This work continued until 1834. By 1889 an international agreement was made ending all further expansion of the river's edge.[1]

Editor's Note

1. This is one instance among many of Detroiters not taking seriously their agreements with Canada, whether about shorelines or air and water pollution. About five years after the 1889 agreement, Hazen

Pingree was urging a large extension of shoreline near the site of to-day's Cobo Hall.

The great expansions of the modern riverfront began in the late 1940s at the urging of the U.S. Army Engineers, with the cooperation of the Detroit City Plan Commission. Later river's-edge expansions made possible the building of Cobo Hall.

Part II

The Land

The Land

Land from the Indians: By Treaty and Expulsion

When the United States of America became a new nation, the Native Americans, whom other Americans universally spoke of as Indians, were in possession of the land and were not planning to go away. From the moment of the Europeans' arrival in North America, it was clear that the key to the newcomers' existence was land ownership. Clear, too, that the Indian's *use* of land, while it might include a private garden spot or a tribal claim to a hunting area, was not at all like the white man's concept of land *ownership*, with deeds, mortgages, and inheritance rights on paper. To the European, Indian land use was negligent, indolent, and inefficient. To the Indian, land and water were life-sustaining. It follows that the formalization of Indian treaties came about as an invention of the white man. Step by step, the land would pass from Indian hands to those of the white settler.

Early U.S. treaties were military in nature and had the purpose of establishing the sovereignty of the United States, making sure that the British could neither control the land nor the Indian tribes. As William Hull's negotiators put it to the "Chippewas, Ottawas, Pattawatamas [sic] and Wyandots" gathered at Detroit in 1807: "The said nations of Indians acknowledge themselves to be under the protection of the United States, and no other power, and will prove by their conduct that they are worthy of so great a blessing."

41

A considerable number of Michigan land gains were already made by the Americans under treaties drawn up before statehood. There were twenty-one treaties signed with the Chippewas alone, from 1785 to 1836, and many of these included Michigan lands.[1]

Some of the major land cessions made by treaty in the Northwest were:

1. *1785*, a treaty signed at Fort McIntosh. Much of the land deeded was in Ohio, but there were specific guarantees for Detroit, as well as Michilimackinac, from the "Wyandots, Delawares, Chippewas, and Ottawas." These were repeated in 1789, in a treaty made by General Arthur St. Clair.[2]

2. *1795*, Treaty of Greenville. Here General Anthony Wayne negotiated the cession of northern Ohio, northern Indiana, and "six miles square at the mouth of Chikago river, emptying into the southwest end of lake Michigan." This treaty repeats, with additions, the cessions of Michilimackinac and Detroit and the surrounding area, described as "The post of Detroit, and all the land to the north, the west and the south of it, of which the Indian title has been extinguished by gifts or grants to the French or English governments: and so much more land to be annexed to the district of Detroit, as shall be comprehended between the river Rosine [Raisin], on the south, lake St. Clair on the north, and a line, the general course whereof shall be six miles distant from the west end of lake Erie and Detroit river."

The treaty of Greenville was signed by representatives of the "Wyandots, Delawares, Shawnees, Ottawas, Chippewas, Pattawatimas, Miamis, Eel Rivers, Weas, Kickapoos, Piankeshaws, and Kaskaskias," in itself a good listing of Indian tribes who had at least some members in the old Northwest. With his accustomed and well-known pride, General Anthony Wayne declared, "Henceforth all hostilities shall cease; peace is hereby established and shall be perpetual."[3]

3. *1819*, Treaty of Saginaw. This treaty essentially covered the entire eastern half of the Lower Peninsula; it might better be described as involving the drainage areas of the Saginaw, the Rifle, the Au Sable, and Thunder Bay rivers in the eastern half of Michigan. The soft wetlands in the west central part of the state did not yet interest settlers. It was negotiated by Lewis Cass, governor of Michigan Territory and treaty-maker extraordinary. The

long-range result of this treaty was to open eastern Michigan for lumbering. This was a treaty marked by elaborate preparations and a hidden agenda for Indian removal that did not yet succeed.[1]

4. *1821, Treaty of Chicago.* Cass and Solomon Sibley obtained title to western Michigan south of the Grand River in a treaty negotiated with Potawatomis and Ottawas. Intended to make western Michigan—as well as the territories of Indiana and Illinois—more accessible to migrants, it was not popular with the Potawatomis when they had thought it over. It probably laid the groundwork for further hostilities in the West.

5. *1836, Treaty of Washington.* Change and distortion were the key factors in this treaty. In its final form, the treaty ceded to the United States all the remaining lands not included in tribal reservations in the Lower Peninsula and drastically cut those reserved lands. Extensive cessions were also made in the Upper Peninsula. Many individually owned areas that had belonged to Indian families of traders or Indian Agency employees were phased out. At this point, the government instituted a "buy-out" program on these, in the interest of what would today be termed cost efficiency. Among the signers for the government were a number of traders and officials who accepted cash payments "on behalf of their Indian families": John Holiday, John Drew, Rix Robinson, Leonard Slater, Louis Moran, Augustin Hamelin, and William Lasley.

The men and women who had owned these lands were often related to both the chiefs and the white negotiators across the table. Prominent Detroit families whose Indian children received early land grants included Rivard, Cicotte, Moran, Godfroy, and Beaubien, among others. Nor were there only French names. Sophia Biddle, given 640 acres near Mackinac, was an educated spinster and a welcome guest at the home of her relatives, the Biddles of Wyandotte. Her letters, in the Bentley library at the University of Michigan, show thoughtfulness and self-possession.

A major component in the 1836 treaty was the goal of Indian removal. Previously in the background, it was now accomplished by that harsh realist, Andrew Jackson. President Jackson's secretary of war and man in charge was Lewis Cass. They used as negotiator of the treaty Henry Schoolcraft, a scholar of Indian lore whose wife, Jane, was the daughter of the famed Ojibway chief Waub-Ojeeg. Schoolcraft was reportedly the official who was closer to understanding and caring about the Indians than any other prominent American of his time. Yet it fell to him to negotiate the treaty that set the wheels in motion for Indian removal. Both the removal of the Indians and the settlement of the Michigan-Ohio boundary were conditions that had to be met before Congress would grant statehood to the Michigan Territory.

The treaty was negotiated in Washington, subject to intense administration pressures. Even had he chosen to try, Schoolcraft could not have stopped the official urge to move the Indians westward and clear the land.[5] When the treaty was finally ratified by the U.S. Senate two months after it had been signed, it had been amended drastically. All the large tracts, for instance, in the areas of the Traverse and Père Marquette rivers that had been reserved for Indian use were now to belong to the Indians for a maximum of five years only. Worst of all, the Indians were no longer to have the option of relocating among the Chippewa of the Wisconsin and Minnesota regions. These changes and others made by amendment will be outlined in a section that will deal specifically with the Treaty of Washington.

To secure Native American agreement to the treaty, Ottawa and Ojibway treaty-signers remained in Washington at government expense for the two months it took Congress to ratify the treaty. Gifts were given. President Andrew Jackson took a personal interest; Jackson indeed had his own suit copied for one of the chiefs who admired it.

By May 27, when the revised treaty was ratified by Congress, the Ottawas and Ojibway had given up permanent title to almost all the reservation lands granted them in March. We cannot help but wonder how the phrase "Indian giver," used to describe a person who first gives and then takes away, crept into our language. Something is terribly wrong here.

Section readings begin with Lewis Cass's statement on Indian removal, written shortly before he became Andrew Jackson's secretary of war, responsible for carrying out that policy. Possibly meant as a "position paper" aimed at the president, it is a reasoned argument for Indian removal by the man who for years held power over Indian affairs in the Northwest. As such it represents the best rationalizations of the day.

I include sections of the Treaty of Washington, along with the significant distortions introduced by amendment. The section concludes with a speech given by a young Ojibway chief at Saginaw in 1819 and directed at Lewis Cass, who was negotiating the treaty with the Ojibway.

Editor's Notes

1. "Chippewas," in *Treaties between the United States of America, and the Several Indian Tribes from 1778 to 1837*. . . (Washington, D.C.: Commissioner of Indian Affairs, 1837; Millwood, N.Y.: Kraus Reprint Company, 1975), 650–58.
2. Some of the confusions and, perhaps, repetitions might have been wiped out if the advice of Henry Schoolcraft had been taken:

   A DEFECT IN MAKING INDIAN TREATIES
   "The cession of lands by Indians should invariably be made by a map drawn by them & appended to the original treaty. Countries are sometimes bartered by a wave of the hand. A bad or careless interpreter, who is explaining a written treaty, points his finger wrong in defining a boundary, leads a tribe to suppose they have not ceded, accessory to this wave of the hand. Millions of acres are thus, sometimes, put in dispute. Treaties are made to explain treaties, & purchases to cover purchases. All resulting from a bad interpreter, or the want of a line of a ms. or sketch map."

   The quotation appears in Schoolcraft's literary journal, the *Literary Voyager, or Muzzeniegun*, which he edited with his Ojibway wife. In his modern edition of Schoolcraft's Periodical (East Lansing: Michigan State University, 1962), Philip P. Mason described it as a "manuscript magazine produced by Schoolcraft during the winter of 1826–27." It is a tremendous source of material by and about Indians, including many Ojibway (Chippewa) folktales and beliefs.
3. *Treaties*, 54. An Indian view of General Wayne is reported in the *Literary Voyager* of December, 1826, under the heading "Conundrums" on p. 33: "When did a wagon crush the Western Indians? Ans. When Gen. Wayne drove over them at Maumee."
4. See the reminiscences of Ephraim S. Williams, "The Treaty of Saginaw in the Year 1819," *Michigan Pioneer and Historical Society* (hereafter referred to as *MPHS*) (1884): 262–70.
5. In a recent, rather unfriendly, biography, Richard C. Bremer states that by 1836 Schoolcraft had swung away from his earlier opposition

to Indian removal, probably under the influence of Cass, and was now dedicated to the effort to Christianize the Indians, with removal as a means of accomplishing this. See *Indian Agent and Wilderness Scholar; The Life of Henry Rowe Schoolcraft* (Mount Pleasant: Clarke Historical Library, Central Michigan University, 1987), 158–90.

1. Considerations on the Present State of the Indians and Their Removal to the West of the Mississippi

Lewis Cass[1]

The destiny of the Indians, who inhabit the cultivated portions of the territory of the United States, or who occupy positions immediately upon their borders, has long been a subject of deep solicitude to the American government and people. Time, while it adds to the embarrassment and distress of this part of our population, adds also to the interest which their condition excites, and to the difficulties attending a satisfactory solution of the question of their eventual disposal. . . . That the Indians have diminished, and are diminishing, is known to all who have directed their attention to the subject. . . .

The Indians have gradually decreased since they became first known to the Europeans. . . . There is no just reason to believe

Lewis Cass, *Considerations on the Present State of the Indians and Their Removal to the West of the Mississippi* (Boston: Gray and Bowen, 1928), 1–66.

that any of the tribes, within the whole extent of our boundary, has been increasing in numbers at any period since they have been known to us. This opinion is expressed by the Superintendents of Indian Affairs in the report submitted to Congress at its last session, by the war department; and from the favorable opportunities possessed by those officers, of acquiring correct information upon this subject, their opinion must carry with it considerable authority. The whole amount of Indian population, within the United States, east of the Mississippi, is estimated in this report at 105,060. . . .

In the same report, the number of Indians west of the Mississippi is thus estimated . . . making a general aggregate of 313,130, within the United States. . . . And these are the remnants of the primitive people, who, only two centuries ago, possessed this vast country; who found in the sea, the lakes, the rivers, and forests, means of subsistence sufficient for their wants.

It would be miserable affectation to regret the progress of civilization and improvement, the triumph of industry and art, by which these regions have been reclaimed, and over which freedom, religion, and science are extending their sway. But we may indulge the wish, that these blessings had been attained at a smaller sacrifice; that the aboriginal population had accommodated themselves to the inevitable change of their condition, produced by the access and progress of the new race of men, before whom the hunter and his game were destined to disappear. But such a wish is vain. A barbarous people, depending for subsistence upon the scanty and precarious supplies furnished by the chase, cannot live in contact with a civilized community. As the cultivated border approaches the haunts of the animals, which are valuable for food or furs, they recede and seek shelter in less accessible situations. The number of these animals may be diminished, but cannot be increased, by the interference of men; and when the people, whom they supply with the means of subsistence, have become sufficiently numerous to consume the excess annually added to the stock, it is evident that the population must become stationary, or, resorting to the principal instead of the interest, must, like other prodigals, satisfy the wants of to-day at the expense of to-morrow.

. . . Whether the tribes upon this continent had attained the maximum of their population before the discovery, we have not now the means of ascertaining. It is certain, however, as well as from a consideration of their mode of life, as from a careful examination of the earlier narratives, that, greatly as they exceeded their present numbers, they were yet thinly scattered over the country. There is no reason to believe that vegetable productions were ever cultivated to any considerable extent by the Indians, or formed an important part of their food. Corn, and beans, and pumpkins were indigenous to the country, and were probably raised in small quantities around each Indian village. But they were left to the labor of the women, whose only instrument of agriculture was a clam-shell, or the shoulder-blade of a buffalo, tied to a stick. Their habits of life were then what they now are. They returned from their hunting grounds in the spring, and assembled in their villages. Here their few vegetables were planted. But although the seed-time came, no harvest followed; for before their corn was ripe, it was generally consumed, with that utter recklessness of the future, which forms so prominent and unaccountable a feature in their character. As the autumn approached, they separated and repaired to their *wintering* grounds, where, during eight months of the year, they were engaged alternately in the chase, and in those relaxations and amusements, peculiar to the condition of the hunter. This was the annual round of aboriginal life.

. . . Other circumstances cooperated in the work of [Indian] destruction. Fire-arms were introduced, and greatly facilitated the operations of the hunter. Articles of European merchandise were offered to the Indians, and they were taught the value of their furs, and encouraged to procure them. New wants arose among them. The rifle was found a more efficient instrument than the bow and arrow; blankets were more comfortable than buffalo robes; and cloth, than dressed skins. The exchange was altogether unfavorable to them. The goods they received were dear, and the peltry they furnished was cheap. A greater number of animals was necessary for the support of each family, and increased exertion was necessary to procure them. . . .

Herds of buffaloes were once found upon the shore of Lake Erie, and at the base of the Allegany mountains. They have now receded to the plains beyond the Mississippi, and are now migrating still further west. A few years since, they were unknown in the Rocky Mountains. They have now passed that barrier, and will ere long reach the Pacific. The beaver has nearly disappeared upon all our borders, and hunters and trappers have followed them to the waters of the Columbia. Even the common red deer, once so abundant, is rarely found east of the Allegany, and is becoming scarce in the western regions.

But a still more powerful cause has operated to produce this diminution in the number of the Indians. Ardent spirits have been the bane of their improvement; one of the principal agents in their declension and degradation. . . . [In areas close to white settlers it] has been found impracticable to prevent the sale of spirituous liquors. . . . The most judicious laws are eluded or openly violated. The love of spirits, and the love of gain, conspire to bring together the buyer and the seller. As the penalties become heavier, and the probability of detection and punishment stronger, the prohibited article becomes dearer, and the sacrifice to obtain it greater. We shall not attempt to investigate the cause of the inordinate attachment displayed by the Indians to ardent spirits. It is probably without a parallel in all the history of man. . . . This predisposition was the subject of observation and regret two centuries ago; and the earlier historians and travellers, while they furnish the record of its existence, furnish also the evidence of its overpowering influence and destructive consequences. . . . [2]

To the operation of the physical causes, which we have described, must be added the moral causes connected with their mode of life, and their peculiar opinions. Distress could not teach them providence, nor want industry. As animal food decreased, their vegetable productions were not increased. Their habits were stationary and unbending; never changing with the change of circumstances. How far the prospect around them, which appears to us so dreary, may have depressed and discouraged them, it is difficult to ascertain, as it is also to estimate the effect upon them of that superiority which we have assumed, and they have acknowledged. There is a principle . . . operating through all their institutions, which prevents them from appreciating or adopting any other modes of life, or any other habits of thought or action, but those which have descended to them from their ancestors. . . .

Many of [the Indians] were carefully taught at our seminaries of education, in the hope that principles of morality and habits of industry would be acquired, and that they might stimulate their countrymen by precept and example to a better course of life. Missionary stations were established among various tribes, where zealous and pious men devoted themselves with generous ardor to the task of instruction, as well in agriculture and the mechanic arts, as in the principles of morality and religion. The Roman Catholic Church preceded the Protestant in this labor of charity; and the *Lettres Edifiantes* are monuments of her zeal and liberality. Unfortunately, they are monuments also of unsuccessful and unproductive efforts. What tribe has been civilized by all this expenditure of treasure, and labor, and care? From the martyrdom of Le Père Brebeuf, in 1649, upon the shore of Lake Huron, to the death of the last missionary, who sacrificed himself in a cause as holy as it has proved hopeless, what permanent effect has been produced? Year after year sanguine anticipations have been formed, to be succeeded by disappointment and despondency. We are flattered with accounts of success, with explanations for the past and hopes for the future; and this, without the slightest intention to deceive. But the subject itself is calculated to excite these expectations. There are always individuals attending these establishments, who give fair promise of permanent improvement and usefulness. And as these prospects are blighted, others succeed to excite the same hopes, and to end in the same disappointment. . . .

The Wyandots, who occupied so much of the care of the Roman Catholic missionaries, have dwindled to about 700 individuals, who are seated upon a *reservation*, near the centre of the state of Ohio. Serious divisions of opinion exist among them, and a sedentary life begins to be irksome. Already their attention is directed to the trans-Mississippian regions. The Delawares, to whom the Moravians so long and faithfully devoted themselves, have already passed over the Mississippi, where they are resuming their pristine habits. A small society yet exists in Upper Canada; but they are diminishing, and certainly their appearance indicates neither prosperity nor improvement.[3] The Iroquois or Six Nations, the Shawnese, the Miamies, the Potawotamies, and the Ottawas, all of whom have engaged the care and attention of individuals and societies devoted to this object, furnish no evidence of any melioration in their condition, which has resulted from the prosecution of these efforts.

The cause of the total failure cannot be attributed to the nature of the experiment, nor to the character, qualifications, or conduct, of those who have directed it. The process and the persons have varied. . . . But there seems to be some insurmountable obstacle in the habits or temperaments of the Indians, which has heretofore prevented, and yet prevents, the success of these labors. . . .

Experience has shown, that the Indians are steadily and rapidly diminishing. And the causes of this diminution, which we have endeavored to investigate, are yet in constant and active operation. It has also been shown that our efforts to stand between the living and the dead, to stay this tide which is spreading around them and over them, have long been fruitless, and are now hopeless. And equally fruitless and hopeless are the attempts to impart to them, in their present situation, the blessings of religion, the benefits of science and the arts, and the advantages of an efficient and stable government. The time seems to have arrived, when a change in our principle and practice is necessary; when some new effort must be made to meliorate the condition of the Indians, if we would not be left with a living monument of their misfortunes. . . .

But after all, it cannot be denied, and ought not to be concealed, that in this transplantation from the soil of their ancestors to the plains of the Mississippi, some mental and corporeal sufferings await the emigrants. These are inseparable from the measure itself. But by an appropriation liberally made, and prudently applied, the journey may be rendered as easy for them, as for an equal number of our own people. By a continuation of the same liberality, arrangements may be made for their comfortable support, after their arrival in the land of refuge, and until they can accommodate themselves to the circumstances of their situation; until they can secure from the earth or the forests, that means of subsistence, as they may devote themselves to the pursuits of agriculture or of the chase.

The amount of the expenditure necessary for their migration and establishment is not a subject for serious consideration. All should be given, and no doubt will be given, that can be reasonably employed in their comfortable support. It is not a question of profit or loss, but a great question of national policy, involving the rights and feelings of those, from whom we have obtained much, and for whom we have done little.

Although the Indians are migratory in their habits, yet their local attachments are strong and enduring. *The sepulchers of their fathers are as* dear to them as they ever were to the nations of the East. . . . Now, when the time of severance has approached, we owe it to them, to ourselves, to the opinion of the world, that the process should be conducted with kindness, with liberality, and above all, with patience. The assurance of the Secretary of War[4] "that nothing of a compulsory nature to effect the removal of this unfortunate race of people has ever been thought of by the President, although it has been so asserted," is honorable to the government, and consolatory to those who are looking with most solicitude to the condition of the Indians. The intimation of the Secretary that the object of the President was "to explain fully to them and to the country, the actual ground on which it was believed they were rightly entitled to stand," is equally in accordance with justice, policy, and the public feeling.

Let the whole subject be fully explained to the Indians. Let them know that the establishment of an independent government is a hopeless project; which cannot be permitted, and which, if it could be permitted, would lead to their inevitable ruin. Let the offer of a new country be made to them, with ample means to reach it and to subsist in it, with ample security for its peaceful and perpetual possession, and with a pledge, in the words of the Secretary of War, "that the most enlarged and generous efforts, by the government, will be made to improve their minds, better their condition and aid them in their efforts of self-government." Let them distinctly understand, that those who are not disposed to remove, but wish to remain and submit to our laws, will, as the President has told the Creeks, "have land laid off for them and their families, in fee." When all this is done, no consequences can affect the character of the government, or occasion regret to the nation. The Indians would go, and go speedily and with satisfaction. A few perhaps might linger around the site of their council-fires; but . . . soon . . . they would dispose of their possessions and rejoin their countrymen. And even should these prefer ancient associations to future prospects, and finally melt away before our people and institutions, the result must be attributed to causes, which we can neither stay nor control.

Editor's Notes

1. The title page of the original document does not name Lewis Cass as author, yet the attribution to him is so accepted that all libraries fortunate enough to have a copy list him as such. Cass was in the habit of writing for literary journals using a pseudonym. The timing here suggests that the 1830 edition was indeed a "position paper" intended to catch the attention of the new president, Andrew Jackson. An Arno Press reprint (New York, 1975) is generally available in libraries.

2. Cass, who was personally a teetotaller, did not hesitate, when negotiating with the Ojibway at Saginaw in 1819, to have barrels of brandy available to speed the settlement, according to Ephraim Williams, trader in that area. Williams tells of the treaty in "The Treaty of Saginaw in the Year 1819," *MPHS* 7(1884): 262–70.

3. Cass himself had been a general during the War of 1812, which had led to the misfortunes of the Delawares in Upper Canada, and of the Moravian missionaries who lived among them. To his credit, he had at least arranged a pass for the refugees from a destroyed village to go to Ohio, where a number of them relocated in the area north of Columbus. For an extensive account of the little-known Moravians and the Delawares among whom they lived, see Elma Cray and Leslie Robb Cray, *Wilderness Christians* (Toronto: MacMillan, 1956).

4. Presumably Major John Eaton, Andrew Jackson's first appointee to this post, which Cass later inherited.

2. Change and Distortion: The Treaty of Washington, 1836

Commissioner of Indian Affairs

Reprinted here are major sections of the original treaty and the final revisions of those sections made by Congress before ratification. The amendments, which appeared at the end of the treaty in the original document, are rearranged here to follow directly the articles to which they apply, so that the reader may more easily follow the basic changes negotiated by the government after the Indians signed the original treaty.

I have kept the spelling and format of the original document intact.

OTTAWAS AND CHIPPEWAS
Concluded March 28, 1836—Ratified May 27, 1836.
Articles of a treaty made and concluded at the city of Washington, in the District of Columbia, between Henry R. Schoolcraft, commissioner on the part of the United States, and the Ottawa and Chippewa nation of Indians, by their chiefs and delegates.

[Article 2, omitted here, described the boundaries involved in northern Michigan and a part of Wisconsin and was not amended.]

ART. 2. From the cession aforesaid the tribes reserve for their own use, to be held in common, the following tracts, namely-:One tract of fifty thousand acres, to be located on Little Traverse

Commissioner of Indian Affairs, *Treaties between the United States of America and the Several Indian Tribes from 1778 to 1837* (Washington, D.C.: Commissioner of Indian Affairs, 1837; Millwood, N.Y.: Kraus, 1975), 650–58.

bay; one tract of twenty thousand acres, to be located on the north shore of Grand Traverse bay; one tract of seventy thousand acres, to be located on or north of the Pierre Marquetta river; one tract of one thousand acres to be located by Chingassanoo, or the Big Sail, on the Cheboigan; one tract of one thousand acres, to be located by Mujeekewis, on Thunder-bay river.

[AMENDMENT to] ART. 2. Line two, after the word "tracts," insert the following words, to wit: *"For the term of five years from the date of ratification of this treaty, and no longer;* unless the United States grant them permission to remain on said lands for a longer period" [Italics mine][1].

ART. 3. There shall also be reserved for the use of the Chippewas living north of the straits of Michilimackinac, the following tracts, that is to say: Two tracts of three miles square each, on the north shores of the said straits, between Point-au-Barbe and Mille Coquin river, including the fishing grounds in front of such reservations, to be located by a council of the chiefs; the Beaver islands of lake Michigan for the use of the Beaver island Indians, Round island, opposite Michilimackinac, as a place of encampment for the Indians, to be under the charge of the Indian department; the islands of the Chenos . . . Sugar island, with its islets in the river of St. Mary's; six hundred and forty acres at the mission of the Little rapids; a tract commencing at the mouth of the Pissisowining river, south of point Iroquois; thence, running up said streams to its forks; thence westward, in a direct line to the Red water lakes; thence, across the portage to the Tacqimenon river, and down the same to its mouth, including the small islands and fishing grounds in front of this reservation; six hundred and forty acres on Grand island, and two thousand acres on the main land south of it; two sections on the northern extremity of Green bay, to be located by a council of the chiefs. . . .

[AMENDMENT to] ART. 3. After the word "tracts," in the second line, insert the following words, to wit: "For the term of five years from the date of the ratification of this treaty, and no longer, unless the United States grant them permission to remain on said lands for a longer period." . . . It is understood that a place for fishing and encampment, made under the treaty of St. Mary's, of the 16th of June, 1820, remains unaffected by this treaty.[2]

ART. 4. In consideration of the foregoing cessions, the United States engage to pay to the Ottawa and Chippewa nations the following sums, namely: 1st. An annuity of thirty thousand dollars per annum, in specie, for twenty years; eighteen thousand dollars to be paid to the Indians between Grand river and the Cheboigan; three thousand six hundred dollars to the Indians on the Huron shore, between the Cheboigan and Thunder-bay river; and seven thousand four hundred dollars to the Chippewas north of the straits, as far as the cession extends; . . . Five thousand dollars per annum for the purposes of education, teachers, school-houses, and books in their own language, to be continued twenty years, and as long thereafter as Congress may appropriate for the object. . . . Three thousand dollars for missions. . . . Ten thousand dollars for agricultural implements, cattle, mechanics' tools, and such other objects as the President may deem proper. 5th. Three hundred dollars per annum for vaccine matter, medicines, and the services of physicians, to be continued while the Indians remain on their reservations . . . six thousand five hundred pounds of tobacco; one hundred barrels of salt; and five hundred fish barrels, annually, for twenty years. . . . One hundred and fifty thousand dollars, in goods and provisions, on the ratification of this treaty, to be delivered at Michilimackinac.

[AMENDMENT to] ART. 4. At the close thereof insert these words: "and also the sum of two hundred thousand dollars in consideration of changing the permanent reservations in articles two and three to reservations for five years only, to be paid whenever their reservations shall be surrendered, and until that time the interest on said two hundred thousand dollars shall be paid annually to the Indians. . . . "

[It is interesting to note how many of the obligations of the white man set out in Article 4 hinged on the continued Indian occupation of the reservation lands, a right that Article 4 in its final form denied.]

ART. 8. [italics mine]. *It is agreed that as soon as the said Indians desire it, a deputation shall be sent to the west of the Mississippi, and the country between lake Superior and the Mississippi, and a suitable location shall be provided for them, among the Chippewas, if they desire*

it and if it can be purchased upon reasonable terms, and, if not, then in
some portion of the country west of the Mississippi, which is at the dis-
posal of the United States. . . . When the Indians wish it, the
United States will remove them . . . provide them a year's subsistence in the country to which they wish to go. . . .

[AMENDMENT to] ART. 8. Strike out after the word "the,"
where it first occurs in line two, to the words "States," in the
eighth line, and insert in lieu thereof these words: "Southwest of
the Mississippi river, there to select a final place for the settlement of said Indians, which country, so selected, and of reasonable extent, the United States will forever guaranty and secure to
said Indians. . . ."[3]

ART. 12. All expenses attending the journeys of the Indians
from, and to their homes, and their visit at the seat of Government, together with the expenses of the treaty, including a
proper quantity of clothing to be given them, will be paid by the
United States.

ART. 13. The Indians stipulate for the right of hunting on the
lands ceded . . . until the land is required for settlement.[4]

In testimony whereof, the said Henry R. Schoolcraft, commissioner, on the part of the United States, and the chiefs and delegates of the Ottawa and Chippewa nation of Indians, have
hereunto set their hands, at Washington, the seat of Government, this twenty-eighth day of March, in the year one thousand, eight hundred and thirty-six.

Henry R. Schoolcraft
John Hulbert, *Secretary.*

Oroun Aishkum, of Maskigo,	his x mark
Wassangaze, of do [*sic,* ditto]	his x mark
Wabi Windego, of Grand river,	his x mark
Ainse, of Michilimackinac,	his x mark
Chabowaywa, of do	his x mark
Jawba Wadiek, of Sault Ste. Marie	his x mark
Waub Ogeeg, of do	his x mark
Apawkozigun, of L'Arbre Croche	his x mark
Keminitchagun, of do	his x mark
Mukuday Benais, of do	his x mark

Aishquagonabee, of Grand Traverse   his x mark
Akosa, of   do   his x mark

  [Witnessed by:]

Lucius Lyon,   Leonard Slater
R. P. Parrott, Capt.U.S. Army   Louis Moran
W. P. Zantzinger, Purser, U.S. Navy   Augustin Hamelin, jr.,
                                                     Henry A. Lenake . . .[5]

Editor's Notes

1. This effectively removed Indian claims to five reservation areas which amounted, in total, to 142,000 acres. The five-year limit, as opposed to perpetual ownership, would just represent time to pack up and move.
2. This not only has the same effect on many northern islands and spots in the Upper Peninsula, but would seem to account for some of the later legal confusions as to Indian fishing rights.
3. The key phrase seems to be *"Southwest* of the Mississippi." The original option of northwest lands would have allowed, though in a more restricted area, the continuation of traditional patterns of hunting and fishing. None of this would ever be possible, in the same way, "southwest of the Mississippi."
4. No changes are indicated here, but note that the final termination of the privilege is left completely in the hands of the U.S. government.
5. Signing for the government were John Holiday, John Drew, Rix Robinson, Leonard Slater, Louis Moran, Augustin Hamelin, and William Lasley, each of whom had agreed in the original treaty to cash settlements for land which had been owned by them on behalf of their Indian families, a trust relationship that was not always honored by the guardians.

3.   You Do Not Know Our Wishes

Chief Oge-Maw-Keke-too

You do not know our wishes. Our people wonder what has brought you so far from your homes. Your young men have invited us to come and light the council fire. We are here to smoke the pipe of peace, but not to sell our lands. Our American father wants them. Our English father treats us better; he has never asked for them. Your people trespass upon our hunting grounds. You flock to our shores. Our waters grow warm; our land melts like a cake of ice; our possessions grow smaller and smaller; the warm wave of the white man rolls in upon us and melts us away. Our women reproach us. Our children want homes; shall we sell from under them the spot where they spread their blankets? We have not called you here. We smoke with you the pipe of peace.

Chief Oge-Maw-Keke-too, addressing Lewis Cass, as reported by Ephraim Williams, "The Treaty of Saginaw in the Year 1819," *MPHS* 7 (1884): 264.

The Land

Who Got the Land?

One of the political war cries in modern Michigan has been "Jobs, jobs, jobs!" We should translate this into "Land, land, land!" for understanding the past. No existence in Michigan Territory or in the new state of Michigan would have been possible without land as the basic commodity. Often the decision as to who got the land went to the one who had the swiftest horse to take him to the land office or the most force in facing down squatters and other claimants. Lumberman Dan Ward boasted in his autobiography of having beaten the *"landlookers"* of the St. Mary's Ship Canal Company to the land office to register the claim.

After the original people of the region—Chippewa or Ojibway, Potawatomis, Ottawas, and others—were forced out of their lands, the next project was the measurement and logical organization of land on which, of course, many settlers were already living.

Neat, square townships were formed, working out from a baseline road (called Eight Mile Road in the Detroit area). The charting of the new Territory of Michigan became a model for how such things ought to be done. Of course, occasional errors occurred on some of the maps, and some resurveying had to be done. Still, the work of John Mullett, William Burt, and Lucius Lyon, among others, was amazingly accurate given the hard conditions under which it had to be done. Descriptions of the planning process of those days and how it was accomplished are from a Detroit City Plan Commission document of 1954, *Trafficways for Three Million People.*

Order and straight-lined efficiency ended as one entered the city limits. Detroit, which once consisted only of military fort, parade ground, a few narrow farms on the river's edge, and common pasture, was becoming a town. Inevitably, the transition was accompanied by confusion and delay, argument and countercharges. There were lost records and auctions where it seemed almost everyone wanted their money back. The fire of 1805 that wiped out the town just as it was to make its first start at living under American rule did not help. Judge Augustus Woodward, friend of President Jefferson, provided elegant plans modeled on the work that famed engineer and city planner Pierre Charles L'Enfant and Benjamin Banneker, black mathematician, had done for Washington, D.C. Unfortunately, Woodward also came equipped with secretiveness and a disregard for anyone who asked for explanations. Practical home owners, according to Silas Farmer, looked at the Grand Circus that Woodward planned to be the hub of future parks and boulevards—and used it as a dumping ground for dead cats.

That land was of the greatest importance in the Michigan economy was shown in the boom years just before 1837 and in the tremendous crash in land values that followed. Both the madness of the boom and the later troubles are told of in the selection "U.S. Land Office" from Silas Farmer.

The biggest of all land acquisitions, scorned by many at the time, was the Upper Peninsula. Michigan got it by yielding seven miles across her southern border, including Toledo, to Ohio. A brief letter Senator Lucius Lyon wrote a Detroit friend does not detail either the transaction or the military skirmishes that surrounded it but does convey a sense of the machinations necessary for Michigan to achieve statehood.

This material on how the land was obtained and distributed just begins to cover the surface. There is the whole question of what became of the "school sections," those grants in each township for education, as mentioned in *Trafficways.* Some vanished in the early 1840s after bank failures, and especially that of the Michigan Bank, had wiped out both the state's credit and its cash. More public land went into grants to railroads—good lands, given as a reward to men who engaged in that most prosperous business. The grants seemed necessary at the time, but harder to understand later. Other entrepreneurs, such as canal builders, toll road builders, and lumbermen, found ways to get land for their efforts. Their rewards were based on the extent to which they provided access to the land. Land had to be easily available, and land too heavily wooded, swampy, or without roads would not attract the new immigrants who meant prosperity for all.

I will consider the matter of accessibility further in Part IV. For now I am more concerned with the distribution of the land itself. Still, it is clear that the rewards of providing access to land were frequently paid in the coin of land itself. The St. Mary's Ship Canal Company's membership of prominent Detroiters received hundreds of thousands of acres of good pine land for constructing the first of the locks at Sault Sainte Marie.

I recommend the exploration of land acquisition in Michigan for extensive further study for anyone interested in how grants were made, guidelines set, and rules broken, in Michigan lands.

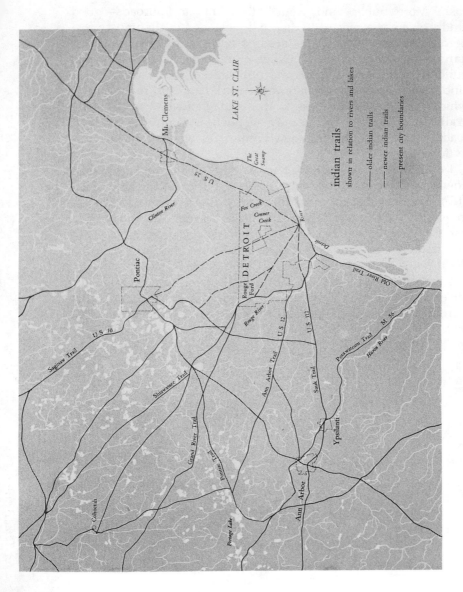

Indian trails created the routes of Michigan's later highways. (From *Trafficways for Three Million People*, Detroit City Plan Commission, 1949. Used with permission.)

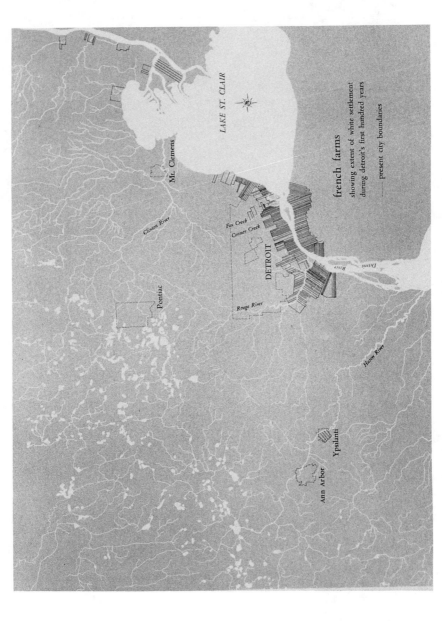

french farms

showing extent of white settlement
during detroit's first hundred years

—— present city boundaries

LAKE ST. CLAIR

Clinton River

Mt. Clemens

Fox Creek

Conner Creek

DETROIT

Pontiac

Rouge River

Detroit River

Huron River

Ypsilanti

Ann Arbor

The French farms, in narrow strips, gave every man his own bit of waterfront. (From *Trafficways for Three Million People*, Detroit City Plan Commission, 1949. Used with permission.)

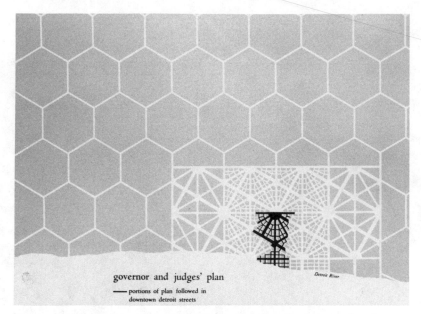

The core of Judge Woodward's plan set the growth patterns for the city. (From *Trafficways for Three Million People,* Detroit City Plan Commission, 1949. Used with permission.)

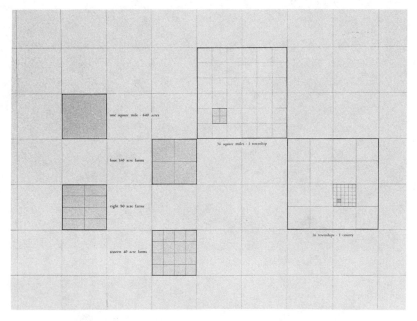

How Michigan land was surveyed and platted after the Land Ordinance of 1785. (From *Trafficways for Three Million People,* Detroit City Plan Commission, 1949. Used with permission.)

1. Trafficways for Three Million People

Detroit City Plan Commission

French Farms

. . . The main French settlement was along the Detroit River where the French houses stood in a row all along the bank all the way from the mouth of the Rouge east to the great swamp just east of Belle Isle. As more French came they lined the shores of Lake St. Clair and the Detroit River to Lake Erie.

Settlements of the French moved up the Ecorse and Rouge Rivers at the time of the American Revolution from 1776 to 1783. Farms lined the Rouge River about eight miles to what is now the northern boundary of Dearborn. . . . In the years following the

Detroit City Plan Commission, *Trafficways for Three Million People*, text by Merle Henrickson, design and drawings by William Kessler, maps by Frederick Pryor (Detroit: Detroit City Plan Commission, 1949), 5–18.

American Revolution, French settlers began to fill in the banks along the Raisin and Clinton Rivers, and other smaller creeks. . . .

As the French settled along the rivers, each farm had a narrow frontage 400 to 900 feet wide on the river, and extended inland as much as three miles.

When more people came to Detroit to settle in later years, these old French farms were subdivided separately as each owner saw fit. Each subdivider laid out his farm according to his own notions of what would make good lots and good streets. Most of the owners laid out straight streets running back from the river for the length of their farms but very few of them bothered to provide continuous streets running parallel to the river. Jefferson Avenue already existed as an Indian trail. Harper Avenue runs along the northern boundary of the French farms. However, other east-west streets had offsets wherever some farmer disagreed with his neighbors about where the road should run.

Jefferson's Land Plan of 1785

When people from Michigan travel in Kentucky, Tennessee, Virginia, Missouri, or for that matter almost anywhere through eastern or southern states, they are often puzzled why the roads do not run straight north and south or east and west. Neither are there any square or rectangular farms.

Roads wind around following streams, and all the farms are irregularly shaped pieces of land with boundaries marked by big boulders, tall trees, or other landmarks.

When plans were being discussed for settling the Northwest Territory, including Michigan, Wisconsin, Illinois, Indiana, and Ohio, Jefferson suggested that there should be a more orderly way of measuring and dividing the land than had been followed before. His plan was to divide all the unsurveyed land into mile square pieces by running parallel roads one mile apart north and south, and east and west. Each mile square or section would contain 640 acres which could be divided again into four 160-acre farms, or eight 80-acre farms, or sixteen 40-acre farms.

By joining these square pieces of land together, Jefferson proposed to form the small divisions of government. Thirty-six one-mile squares, or a square six miles in each direction would be a township. Sixteen townships joined together, or a big square 24 miles in each direction would make a county.

The Land Ordinance of 1785 established this system as the basic pattern for surveying the land in the Northwest Territory which became the states of Ohio, Michigan, Indiana, Illinois, and Wisconsin. The same pattern was later followed in other states of the west.

Of course, many of the actual township and county boundaries were set up and changed several times by the territorial government as more people came to settle in this new territory. As a result the final boundaries adopted did not all match up as orderly squares. Oakland County, for example was five townships wide and five high, while Livingston County next to it was four wide and four high. Both follow the same basic square mile grid pattern, however.

The plan for dividing land also established a system of roads. The roads follow the survey lines which divided the land of the state into square miles. Eight Mile Road is called Base Line Road as it runs across the state because it is the east-west base line from which the rest of the state was measured. All across the state the roads follow these survey lines except where lakes, swamps, or high hills forced people to wind the roads around them.

Within Detroit we know the survey lines today as Livernois, Wyoming, Schaefer, Greenfield, Southfield, Fullerton, Fenkell, McNichols, Seven Mile and Eight Mile. These survey line roads form much of the network of main roads or thoroughfares for Detroit today.

Governor and Judges' Plan of 1807

Grand Circus Park, Washington and Madison Boulevards, Cadillac Square, and several small triangular parks in downtown Detroit make the city almost unique in American cities in having a street system in its central business area which departs from the rectangular pattern.

Viewed from an airplane, downtown streets converge on Grand Circus Park forming half of a six-sided block in the pattern of bathroom tile or a honeycomb.

69

The unusual plan of streets was drawn by Judge Augustus Brevoort Woodward after the town was destroyed by fire in 1805. Judge Woodward's plan was originally drawn to cover a much larger area than what exists today in downtown Detroit. Grand Circus Park is only half of the park originally drawn by Judge Woodward. Other boulevards were supposed to run northeast and northwest to other "circuses" and "campuses" about a half mile apart in all directions.

The owners whose buildings had been destroyed by the fire were given new lots in exchange for their old lots on narrow streets. Governor Hull and Judges Woodward and Bates would not permit people to rebuild their houses until the new plan had been drawn and approved.

The plan seemed so fanciful that Judge Woodward could not get people to follow it beyond the area affected by the fire. The Woodward plan extends to Cass Avenue on the west and Randolph on the east which were the boundaries of farms not yet subdivided when Woodward laid out the plan for the land between. On the north side the plan was stopped in the middle of what was to be a larger circular Grand Circus Park.[1]

Editor's Note

1. Several major expressways whose construction was begun in the fifties overlaid the remainder of the judge's handiwork.

2. United States Land Office

Silas Farmer

From 1825 to 1837, the immigration from the Eastern States increased so rapidly that business flourished, and by the purchase and clearing of lands large sums of money were brought into and scattered about the Territory. As early as 1833 capitalists began to come from New York to invest in wild lands. In 1836 the number of immigrants amazed everyone; the steamers and sailing vessels were literally loaded down with people who came to settle in Michigan and the West. From five hundred to seven hundred frequently arrived on a single boat. During the month of May public lands were entered so rapidly that on Monday, May 9, the register [sic] had to close his door and receive applications through the window, and the receipts at the Land Office between the 1st and the 25th of the month were $278,000.

"United States Land Office," in Farmer, *History of Detroit*, 37–38.

The total amount received at the three Michigan land offices, namely Detroit, Kalamazoo, and Monroe, was over $1,000,000. During the year the total sales in Michigan amounted to the enormous sum of $7,000,000. Numerous associations were formed for the purchase of wild lands and embryo city sites, and at the mouth of every western river, and almost every township corner, towns were laid out. "On paper" creeks were magnified into streams, and comparatively insignificant streams were transformed into large rivers floating steamboats and other watercraft, while on the land the speculator's dreams took form in imaginary hotels, churches, schools, and railroads. Absolute forests were in imagination transformed into cities, and sold at ten thousand per cent advance. The laying out and making maps of these "paper cities" kept the few draughtsmen then in Detroit busy all day long and far into the night. Hundreds of dollars in the "wildcat" currency of the times, were frequently paid for a draughtsman's services for a single day. Leading men of both parties formed pools with fifty or a hundred thousand dollars, and committed the amounts to the discretion of agents who were to be compensated by a share of the profits in the lands purchased.

The details of some of these enterprises are so ludicrous as to be hardly credible. There remain to this day survivors of the crowds which, in the height of the season, occupied the entire width of Jefferson Avenue in front of the Land Office, each individual awaiting his turn to enter and secure his prize. Sometimes large sums were given to secure the services of the fortunate man at the head of the column by another who was far in the rear. Horses were mercilessly driven and killed in the race to reach the Land Office. In one instance, at midday, two men on horseback were seen turning the corner of Woodward and Jefferson Avenues, hastening at full speed to the Land Office. It turned out that they were victims of a cruel joker in Genesee County. Each of them had ridden all night, breaking down two horses apiece in the seventy-mile race, in order to be the first to enter a certain tract of land. The sequel showed that they wished to purchase entirely different parcels. . . .

It is utterly impossible to describe . . . the actual condition of the public mind at that period. This abnormal activity began to show itself in 1834, grew rapidly in 1835, and culminated in 1836; and when the panic came, the sites of many "paper cities" could be bought for less than the price of wild land, and to this day [1890] are owned and assessed as farm lands.

3. The Biggest Land Deal of All

Lucius Lyon

In 1836 Lucius Lyon, a surveyor and friend of Cass and Schoolcraft, had already been named senator by the territorial legislature but could not take office until Michigan became a state. Ohio had the power in Congress to block statehood until it could have Toledo. Lyon waited in Washington and attended the boundary discussions. He claimed throughout that he was not part of any compromise or deal but insisted that if Ohio got its way, Michigan should make sure it benefited in the north. Michigan accepted a new southern boundary, seven miles north of the Ohio line, and received millions of acres in the Upper Peninsula. The arrangement was unpopular at home, and Lyon's enemies considered him what would today be called a "wimp." The fact that Lyon had been actively involved in setting up the 1836 treaty negotiations that wiped out most Indian claims in the Upper Peninsula meant little to Michiganders, who saw the whole thing as a defeat by Ohio. Lyon won statehood for Michigan but lost any chance of remaining a U.S. senator.

Excerpts from two of Lyon's letters revealing his anger and frustration are given here.

To Edward Mundy, Lieutenant Governor, Michigan, Feb. 26, 1836— I am awaiting with anxiety and impatience to see the report of the committee on the judiciary of the house of representatives on our boundary question and admission into the union. The report will be made in a day or two and on the boundary will be against us. All political parties here are courting the favor of Ohio, Indiana and Illinois and there no longer remains any doubt that the interests of Michigan are to be sacri-

"Letters of Lucius Lyon," *MPHS* 27 (1896): nos. 73, 52.

ficed. Our admission will be made to depend on the assent of the legislature to the boundary claimed by Ohio and Indiana. . . . Under this state of things there remains for Michigan no hope of redress. She will be compelled either to submit to the grossest wrong or make an attempt at revolution. . . .

To Col. D. Goodwin, Detroit, Feb. 4 [1836]— I thank you for the suggestions contained in yours of the 22d ult., relative to an addition to the state of Michigan on the west, provided Congress should break up our boundary on the south . . . which I yet hope will not be done. It if should be however, I for one, shall go in for all the country Congress will give us west of the lakes. It will only require the consent of the legislature to receive it, according to the doctrine which maintains that Congress can cut and carve the territory as they choose, and if that doctrine is to prevail, we will take advantage of it and let the "Devil take the hindmost" as gamesters say; for on this principle, all the legislation of Congress in relation to the boundaries of the states formed in the territory northwest of the river Ohio has been and is a mere bullying, and gambling operation where power and interest and artifice combine to insult and rob and cheat the weak and defenseless of their just rights.

Part III

The People
of Early Michigan

The People of Early Michigan

It is most unfair to ignore those who were here long before statehood, but that is what we must do for the most part. Native Americans appear in the accounts of travelers and in the treaties they were compelled to sign. For the rest, we defer to the growing scholarship of Native Americans about their people in Michigan.[1]

Of the French there is also a good deal left unsaid. The earliest French were trappers and traders, less likely to have family with them than the British, and therefore most likely to find spouses among the Ojibway, Wyandot, and Ottawa women. These men who followed the fur trade into the northern woods were here before Cadillac, who was greeted by a Pelletier.

By the 1830s, the business emigrants from New York State and New England had closed their minds as to any French capacity in matters of importance. As they saw it, the French opposed sensible road expansions to help the city grow simply because the new roads divided their farms, sometimes even separated them from the river—which was the Frenchman's preferred method of transportation. To the Yankees, French families seemed always on the go, by boat or pony cart, to dances, weddings, and christening parties. Soon the French found themselves outvoted by the newcomers, but still Campaus and Beaubiens refused to sell their land, even when offered many times market value.

Slowly the French were backed into corners, and always accused of being thriftless. Yet there were still Morans in banking. A Marantette broker struggles with the current ills of the stock market and it was a Pelletier who helped found and direct one of Michigan's largest credit unions. One branch of a Ford family—banking more than automotive—is descended from the French wives of Elijah Brush and his father-in-law, John Askin. The genealogy of the French shows that a number of them, accused by the newcomers of too much love of parties, married into those respectable and sober families, and their descendants are now found on corporate boards of directors. As Alexandra McCoy suggests in her study of mid-nineteenth-century wealth excerpted in Part V, it is never wise to overlook the people who were here first.

The British came early to control Detroit after their victory in 1763. They left most reluctantly, having to be reminded several times that they had lost the war of 1812, even though they had forced Detroit's surrender in 1813. Among all British colonials of the old British Empire, one imperialist deserves to be remembered locally: John Askin, merchant and wheeler-dealer. When Askin finally prepared himself to leave for Canada, he insisted that a respectable government would honor his land claims. These claims numbered millions of acres, and included more than half of the lower peninsula of Michigan. Fortunately Askin was forced to leave the United States with his claims denied.[2]

Others who sometimes arrived with the earliest of settlers were black: slaves, usually, of the French or British, or captured by Americans or by Native American raiding parties. Because of their early arrival, even though in very small numbers, it seems appropriate to include blacks early in our discussion of the people of early Michigan during the years between statehood and the Civil War.

In a study of slavery in Detroit, Jorge Castellanos has set out three periods: the French, 1701–60; the British, 1760–96; and the American, 1796–1837. Here I quote from his introduction, then include one or two items from the French and British periods, following these with the section "Slavery in American Detroit."

Castellanos's work reflects a breadth of scholarship that is unusual in its use of both Canadian and United States sources. The interrelatedness of blacks in Canadian and American history of the early nineteenth century makes this a good area to explore.

Racism was in the Detroit area early, though it often appeared in that subtle, unaware form by which the master assumes the slave is happy, as Friend Palmer did when he wrote: "As a class the negroes were esteemed by our early time population . . . little cruelty was practiced by their owners . . . the negro was satisfied with his position . . . and was ever ready to help . . . against the treacherous Indians."[3]

Though it is possible to trust General Palmer much of the time, more credible accounts of blacks in Detroit's early days have been provided by Jorge Castellanos and Norman McRae. McRae contributes "The Thornton Blackburn Affair" from his Civil War Centennial study for the Michigan Historical Department. This was a case of escaped slaves that served to crystallize the fears of both races in Detroit during the 1830s.

On reading McCrae and Castellanos it becomes possible to believe, if not fully understand, that the promise of freedom wrapped into the Northwest Ordinance could be denied and postponed for almost a century. That is, of course, for blacks. Young Native American scholars insist that for their people, there was never even a meaningful promise in the ordinance.

By 1837, the balance of power had fallen into the hands of the New Yorkers and New Englanders because of the rapid increase in population that came after 1825, with the opening of the Erie Canal. These newcomers quickly formed the majority. They were mostly male, young, single, and geared to the expectation of early success. Lucius Lyon, born in Vermont, was just thirty-six when he took his seat as the first United States senator from Michigan and had already served two terms in Congress representing Michigan Territory. Michigan's most famous citizen, Lewis Cass, had served as federal marshal and state legislator in Ohio before coming to Michigan as territorial governor in 1813, at age twenty-nine.[4] Stevens Thomson Mason, the "boy governor" at barely twenty-one, was not too unusual against the backdrop of his times.

The places from which the young men came put their imprint on them and on their trades and politics. There were New York State men, canny and commercial; there were New Englanders who were no less interested in personal survival, but who were determined to import a measure of culture and morality as well.

New Englanders arrived first, bringing to Detroit the lyceum, the debating society, and the "reading circles" for leisure entertainment. Like the New York State people, they also brought account books and the Protestant church. They established Michigan's free public schools, surveyed lands, set up local governments. Unlike the soldiers and fur traders, they brought their women with them or sent home for them as soon as possible.

The feminine minority had its own problems on the frontier. New England men, with their cultural baggage of thrift, morality, and a tendency to elevate women, were apt to wound them in strange ways, never more so than when they were at their most well-meaning. When Mrs. William Woodbridge for a time received no invitations to the "Reading Circle" due to a supposed slight to Mrs. Cass, Woodbridge and Cass overreacted in many letters as they tried unsuccessfully to arbitrate a quarrel among ladies.

Then there was Zachariah Chandler, born in Vermont, up-and-coming young merchant in 1841—certainly one of Detroit's most eligible bachelors. A friend, attorney James F. Joy, introduced him into the home of one of the area's prominent families, the Stephen Trowbridges, who lived in rural Oakland County. Chandler was quickly attracted to twenty-two-year-old Elizabeth Trowbridge and began calling regularly. Her parents liked him and were not disturbed to learn that an understanding for their future had been reached between them.

One Saturday afternoon, Chandler arrived at the country home and the couple went horseback riding together. When they returned she was crying, and Chandler left immediately. In a tearful scene, she told her family that Mr. Chandler had broken off their engagement abruptly, saying only that he was not in love.

While the Trowbridge family was fuming with justified anger, Chandler worsened the situation by writing Charles C. Trowbridge, the girl's uncle, sending a check for three thousand dollars while trying to acknowledge that no "reparation" would make up for the destruction he had caused, or wipe out his sense of guilt for the broken promise. In 1841, a year of bank closings and failed land deals, three thousand dollars was no small sum.

Zachariah Chandler's idea was given a family veto through Charles Trowbridge and no money was allowed to change hands. Instead Miss Trowbridge survived grief and embarrassment to find her own solution. The following January she married a New Yorker and went to live, we hope happily ever after, in Brooklyn. Chandler became a United States senator and a millionaire but kept a certain aura of the outsider among the society of old Detroit.

As for the New York State men, a witty letter by Theodore Hinchman, written during the financial disasters of the 1840s and included here, shows that skillful interest in money which seems to have been in the baggage New Yorkers brought on the canal boats.

Among the next arrivals were the Irish, at least some of whom arrived well before the potato famine, which is usually thought of as the main cause for Irish migration. Their life in nineteenth century Detroit has been ably chronicled by JoEllen Vinyard in her extensive and sympathetic study, *The Irish on the Urban Frontier*, from which is reprinted a section on the working life of these newcomers.

The last of the major ethnic groups to arrive in sizable numbers before the Civil War were the Germans, who by the 1870s represented the very largest foreign-born population group in Detroit. Although not written until many years after the arrival of the early Germans, Walter Pitkin's study of the home and family of the prosperous miller Rickel during the 1880s is the best description I have found of the German culture in Detroit.

Another vital group in Detroit and southeastern Michigan comprised those German immigrants who were also Jews. Irving I. Katz points out that there were Jews among the early traders and trappers, and that one of them may well have furnished the inspiration for Stephen Vincent Benet's famous short story, "Jacob and the Indians." Their arrival in significant numbers, however, occurs at about 1850.

From *The Beth El Story*, I have selected a section that not only tells of some of the early arrivals but puts into sharp focus the state of Central Europe at that time, when Germans, Hungarians, and Austrians came to America to avoid the shadows of repression. The section will serve not only to sketch in the background particular to German Jews, but also to add to our understanding of other Germans, such as the socialist Dr. Herman Kiefer, who pioneered in public health, the farmers of Frankenmuth and Saline, and the storekeepers, craftsmen, and brewers (over fifty of them by 1860) of Detroit's East Side. From various sources we gain the impression that there were many cheerful social blendings among Jews and Gentiles in this early period. Anti-Semitism came later to the area, though it definitely came.

Editor's Notes

1. See for instance George Cornell, James M. McGlurken, and James A. Clifton, *People of the Three Fires: The Ottawa, Potawatomi and Ojibway of Michigan* (Grand Rapids, Mich.: Grand Rapids Inter-Tribal Council, 1986).
2. The late Milo M. Quaife, editor of Askin's voluminous papers in the Burton Historical Collection (BHC) at the Detroit Public Library, maintained in discussing the power of John Askin in dealing with both British and United States government officials that it was "a near thing" that Michigan was not lost to that fabulous entrepreneur.
3. General Friend Palmer, *Early Days in Detroit* (Detroit: Hunt & June, 1906), 104. A highly personalized and anecdotal collection of old memories, this is a good source for old locations and old families.
4. See Frank B. Woodford, *Lewis Cass: the Last Jeffersonian* (New Brunswick, N.J.: Rutgers University Press, 1950), 37.

1.   Black Slavery in Detroit

Jorge Castellanos

Slavery in Detroit differed in many ways from the "peculiar institution" of the American South. It was introduced by the French and not by the British, and it developed initially under the influence of French law and custom as they were reinterpreted in colonial New France. Basically domestic in character, slavery never played a role in the economic life of the frontier town. It proved to be, however, extremely persistent and tenacious: it was retained by the British when they occupied Detroit in 1760; it survived when the city became part of Michigan Territory in 1796, in open violation of the anti-slavery provisions of the Northwest Ordinance of 1787; and it was not finally abolished until 1837 by the first constitution of the state of Michigan.

Jorge Castellanos, "Black Slavery in Detroit," *Detroit in Perspective: A Journal of Regional History* 7, no. 2, (Fall 1983): 42–57.

Slavery in French Detroit

. . . According to one source, there were 45 slaves in Detroit in 1706, when the total population of the city (excluding soldiers, but including the slaves themselves) had arrived at 563. Slaves represented then 7.99% of the total population. Most, if not all of them, were Indians or *Panis*, as they were called from the Indian tribe name Pawnee. The conversion of Indian slavery into Black slavery proceeded very slowly during the French period and was not completed until the British period, i.e., after 1760. At any rate, the population of Detroit and the number of slaves increased at a very slow pace under French rule. There were only 62 slaves in the city in November, 1760, when it was surrendered to a British force under the command of ranger Major Robert Rogers. There is no doubt that by then some of them were Black. . . .

Most of the first Black slaves in Detroit were obtained from the Indians who captured them in their raids against slave plantations in the South. Later some were brought to the city and its surrounding area by Southerners who moved in with their chattels. . . .

. . . Although relatively marginal in character, slavery was solidly entrenched in French Detroit society when the transfer of Detroit from France to Great Britain took place in 1763, after the Treaty of Paris officially ended the French and Indian War. . . .

Slavery in British Detroit

Paraphrasing a Gallic proverb it may be said that the more Detroit changed the more it remained the same. A new sovereignty meant a new power structure and new laws and regulations, particularly for control of the fur trade . . . but the post remained a small frontier town of fur traders and small farmers. . . .

Slowly, but continually, however, the city prospered under the new regime. Population increased. . . .

In March, 1779, by order of the commanding officer of Fort Ponchartrain, Captain R. B. Lernoult, a census of the settlement of Detroit was taken. . . . The census showed there were 294 households in Detroit in 1779. About 23% of them held slaves. [In 1782] the census showed there were 321 households in Detroit. Now 25.8% of them held slaves. . . . slaveowners represented about one-fourth of the number of households in Detroit, a respectable figure, indeed. And even more, the slaveowners tended to be the most influential members of the community. Slavery had become an important status symbol in the small frontier town. Although secondary in its economic influence, it was vital in many other respects. And that explained why it survived so long.

Black slavery increased in the British period, reinforcing itself numerically through several channels. After the occupation of the city, the economic system remained the same except that systematically British merchants took over the fur trade from the French until they controlled it absolutely by the 1780's. A number of Irish, Scotch and English traders, and also a few farmers, settled in the Detroit area. . . . A number of them were slaveowners and brought their chattels with them. A few residents also introduced slaves acquired in the American South.

. . . But [during the American Revolution] by far the most important sources of increase were the Detroit-based Indian raids against American settlements in the valley of the Ohio River and in Illinois. In those raids, the Indians often killed the whites whom they could not sell, but kept the Black slaves whom they could exchange for guns, ammunition and liquor. In 1780, a mixed force of whites and Indians, under the command of Henry Bird, attacked several forts in Kentucky. Some Black slaves were taken . . . some [were] sold in Detroit. For several years afterward, one of the owners of those slaves, Mrs. Agnes Le Force, tried in vain to repossess 13 of them who were in the hands of very prominent Detroiters. . . .

Generally speaking, the treatment given to the slaves did not differ substantially from that prevailing under French rule. Manumissions were not uncommon. . . . A few slaves received an elementary education and were placed in charge of activities requiring a certain level of culture. . . . Mullett, one of the ten Negroes owned by Joseph Campeau, acted as his master's clerk and earned the respect of the community for his integrity and shrewdness in business matters. Hector, who belonged to Gen. John R. Williams, was put in charge of the *Oakland Chronicle* plant. Crimes committed by white residents against slaves did not go unpunished. But sometimes the punishment dispensed to slaves for relatively minor felonies was disproportionately brutal, as in the case of Ann Wyley, who was condemned to death and executed for having stolen six guineas from the firm Abbott and Finchley. . . .

In 1793 the legislature of Upper Canada (to which Detroit was incorporated) passed a law providing for gradual abolition of slavery, thus setting a precedent within the British Empire. But that law freed not one slave this side of the Detroit River. When Great Britain evacuated the Detroit post on July 11, 1796, in conformity with the Jay Treaty, slavery in the city was at its historical peak numerically as well as institutionally.

Slavery in American Detroit

Under the new American regime, slavery abruptly declined. A large number of British residents moved to Upper Canada, settling about Windsor, Sandwich, Lake St. Clair, etc., and taking their slaves with them. So serious was this emigration flow that the population dwindled to about 500 in a few months. It was to take almost a decade for the Detroit population to reach the 2,000 plateau again. The abolitionist law in 1793 in Upper Canada was not really too radical. No slaves could be imported, and the children born to slave mothers after the act was passed would become free at age twenty-five, but those who were legally enslaved in 1793 would remain as such until death. Apart from patriotic feelings, the British slaveholders decided to leave because the antislavery provisions of the Canadian law seemed more promising to them than the abolitionist clause in the Northwest Ordinance of 1787, which they expected would become operative immediately after the occupation of the city by General Wayne's troops. Article VI of the Ordinance read:

There shall be neither slavery nor involuntary servitude in the said (Northwest) Territory, otherwise than in the punishment of crimes whereof the party shall be duly convicted: provided always that any person escaping into the same, from whom labour or service is lawfully claimed in any one of the original states, such fugitive may be lawfully reclaimed and conveyed to the person claiming his or her labour or service as aforesaid.

The Ordinance, however, did not put an end to slavery in Detroit. Slave owners petitioned Congress in 1802 to suspend it for ten years. Congress refused. But after a period of haggling with the slaveholders remaining in the city, Governor St. Clair interpreted Article VI as meaning that the extension of slavery was prohibited in the Territory (no slaves could be brought in), but those already in the Wayne County would remain indefinitely in their masters' possession. As so often happens in those cases, the struggle between freedom and property was decided in favor of the latter, that is, in favor of the privileged interests. The purgation of slavery from the lands becoming ready to enter the Union, which Thomas Jefferson considered essential for the future of the country, suffered a delay in Michigan Territory.

The slaves reacted to these disappointing events with massive desertions and with appeals to the courts for their freedom. A curious situation developed, due to the peculiar legal status of slavery in the adjacent territories of Michigan and Upper Canada. Since the introduction of new slaves was prohibited in both, any slave escaping from one side to the other was considered free. There were so many Canadian runaways in Detroit that soon after becoming the first Governor of Michigan Territory in 1805, William Hull gave them permission to organize themselves into a militia. However, Judge Woodward immediately brought charges of misgovernment against Hull, claiming that arming the Blacks was injurious to proprietors of slaves both in Detroit and in Canada. The Governor defended himself against the charges but the military club was disbanded.

A few slaves used the *habeas corpus* proceedings in attempts to obtain their freedom. In 1809 a Black woman called Hanna and "a mulatto boy" called Thomas were declared "free persons and not slaves." But most of the cases were decided in favor of the owners. The most famous of these decisions was *In the matter of Elizabeth Denison et al.*, issued in 1807 by Justice Woodward. It is so typical of the ambiguities of abolitionist legislation that it deserves detailed attention. In his conclusions, Judge Woodward begins by accepting without qualifications that "in this Territory slavery is absolutely and peremptorily forbidden." But immediately the question of property rights challenged the "absolute" principle of freedom. Woodward asked himself whether the provisions of the Ordinance were not nullified by that clause in the Jay Treaty of November 19, 1794, which established: "All settlers and traders shall continue to enjoy unmolested, all their property of every kind. It shall be free to them to sell their lands, houses or effects, or to retain the property thereof at their discretion."

The real issue, of course, was whether "property" included "slavery." Judge Woodward said yes. "Property" was used in the Treaty "with a latitude the most extensive of which it can possibly be made susceptible." Spain and Great Britain accepted the institution in their colonies, and even the United States of America, who claimed "the foremost rank of the world in protecting and maintaining the liberties of mankind," still recognized slavery. Since the Canadian slave law of 1793 confirmed the slave status for life for those who lived in the Detroit area at that time, all slaves in the possession of settlers on July 11, 1796 were the legitimate property of their holders. Therefore, Judge Woodward concluded, "I consider the return of the writ of *habeas corpus* sufficient, and I order Elizabeth Denison, James Denison, Scipio Denison and Peter Denison, Junior to be restored to the possession of Catherine Ineker Tucker." And so, the logic of class privilege defeated that of human justice, a treaty was made to prevail over an act of Congress, and the life of a moribund institution was legally prolonged for several years.

Meanwhile, the slaveholders—who were desperately in need of labor—tried to revitalize the declining system of indentured servitude. In 1803, John Reed, a runaway slave from Kentucky, appeared in Detroit during the summer. According to F. C. Bald: "Daniel Ransom provided bond for the Negro's release and had Solomon Sibley write to (Reed's owner) Colonel Grant, offering to buy the man. Sibley explained that he could not be held in Detroit as a slave, but that Ransom could probably persuade him to indent himself for a term of years." *Engagés* were employed side by side with slaves in Detroit at the turn of the century. John Askin had a gang of them working in a pinery close to the St. Clair River cutting timber. In 1799, Askin begged the McGills from Montreal to send him six or eight *engagés* in the spring. If more came than he could use it would be easy for him to sell their services at a very good price. The Detroit merchant wanted young men. He wrote: "Smart young boys does (sic) nearly as well as men and are much cheaper and easier managed."

The number of slaves continued to drop. The 1810 census enumerated 17 slaves in the city of Detroit, although the number at the time was probably higher; some slaveholders simply failed to report them. The 1820 census, for the first time, recorded none. But since slaves were made taxable property as late as 1818 it is doubtful that the 1820 figure was right. However, for all practical purposes, by 1830 slavery could be considered extinguished in Michigan. Simultaneously, the number of free Blacks increased from 67 in 1820, to 126 in 1830, and 138 in 1834. In 1837 there were 222 Blacks in Wayne County. The free Blacks were relatively few in numbers but extremely active in the defense of their rights and those of the fugitive slaves who happened to arrive in Detroit. In 1806, 1828 and 1833 angry demonstrations defeated the slave-hunters' intentions of using the fugitive slave law against runaways living in the city. The 1833 incident almost became a riot when the Blackburn family was freed from their captors and smuggled into Canada.

Slavery was legally abolished in Detroit by the provisions of the first Constitution of the state of Michigan. The Constitutional Convention met at the territorial capital of Detroit on May 11, 1835. On May 18, the leader of the Democrats, John Norvell, a delegate for Wayne County, proposed and the assembly unanimously accepted that a committee of seven be appointed to draft an article abolishing slavery in the future state. The committee reported two days later that it was in favor of the prohibition of the "peculiar institution" and proposed the adoption of the following article: "Neither slavery nor involuntary servitude shall ever be introduced into this state, except for the punishment of crimes, of which the party shall have been duly convicted." Norvell took the floor and said he was anxious that this article should be the first one adopted into the Constitution. By a vote of 81 to none, the assembly concurred.

The elimination of slavery, however, did not bring equality to the Black community. On May 22, the Convention committee on elective franchise proposed that the right to vote be restricted to "the white male inhabitants." Only the delegates, Joseph H. Patterson, Darius Comstock and Ross Wilkins, raised their voices against the discriminatory constriction. Wilkins was particularly vocal in his protest: "If . . . all men are free and equal, and we want to confine ourselves to the principles of the Declaration of Independence, where is the propriety of confining the right of voting exclusively to white male inhabitants?" He insisted that he was for allowing the "Negro to vote if he be intelligent and worthy of the privilege." His words were received with sneers by some and Wilkins insisted: "I see [some] gentlemen smile. . . . But I know many Negroes, or men of colour if the distinction be preferable, who are sober, industrious, intelligent, worthy members of society."

These good intentions were killed by John Norvell's intervention in the debate. The man who had urged the Convention to abolish slavery now demanded the limitation of the political and civil rights of the free Blacks. The right to vote, he argued, was not entirely a natural right, but a question of expediency. "Why, then," he asked, "should we invite within our limits; why hold out inducements to the migration hither, of a description of population confessedly injurious, confessedly a nuisance, to the community? It would not be denied that the Negro belonged to a degraded cast of mankind. We did not take them as equals to our homes, to our tables, to our bosoms. . . . Nature has marked the distinction. Society has, in all ages, recognized and sanctioned it." Norvell wanted to record his "solemn protest" against the "admission of the black to any association of equality, at the polls or elsewhere. . . . " In other words, slavery (which was dead anyhow), no; but segregation, which was very much alive, yes. The Convention once more agreed.

It was not the first time in Detroit's history that a piece of legislation purportedly designed to defend the Blacks was used against them. Only eight years before, in 1827, the infamous *Act to regulate Blacks and Mulattoes, and to Punish the Kidnapping of such Persons* was passed. Although pretending to protect the Black population, in practice it was an attempt to exclude them from the city and from the rest of Michigan Territory. Now the same Constitution that legalized their freedom, disfranchised them, deprived them of jury duty (a privilege only of electors) and closed the doors of the militia to them. Soon a statute was to prohibit inter-racial marriages in the state. It has taken more than a century of bitter struggles to correct some of those wrongs. Slavery was certainly scratched from the books in 1837, but racism proved to be much more stubborn than slavery had ever been.[1]

Editor's Note

1. Professor Castellanos's notes are extensive and include for the French period several references to *Liste du habitants du Détroit*, in the Burton Historical Collection, items in the John *Askin Papers*, vol. 1, edited by M. M. Quaife, also BHC. William R. Riddell is cited for "The Slave in Canada," *Journal of Negro History* 5 (1920): 267, and for his *Life of William Dummer Powell* (Lansing: Michigan Historical Commission, 1924).

The source for several of the anecdotes of the British period is the anonymous but useful typescript, "Negroes in Detroit," BHC.

2. The Thornton Blackburn Affair

Norman McRae

One of the ironies of Michigan history is that most of the American settlers in Michigan had come from the East and had brought along many of the New England values and ideas about education and human rights. Nevertheless, their relations with Negroes in Michigan were unduly influenced by the "black codes" of their sister states. "Black codes" were laws enacted by states to limit Negroes from participating in the full privileges and responsibilities of citizenship. These laws generally prohibited Negroes from voting, attending schools with whites, entering and using public facilities such as hotels, theatres, and restaurants, and in some cases, it forced them to post a bond

Norman McRae, *Negroes in Michigan during the Civil War*, ed. Sidney Glazer (Lansing: Michigan Civil War Centennial Observance Commission, 1966), 4–7.

with the local government to insure good behavior and to guard against indigency. . . .

On April 13, 1827, a law was passed which required all "black people to register at the county clerk's office after May 1, 1827." Those Negroes who did not have their "free papers" would not be permitted to reside in the territory. In addition, those Negroes who met all other requirements for residence had to post a five hundred dollar bond to insure their continuous "good behavior." All Negroes who could not meet the requirements were forced to leave the territory. Many merely crossed the river and entered Canada. Thus the Negro population of Detroit was reduced to sixty-six free Negroes.

This restrictive law of 1827 did not hinder Negroes from coming to Detroit on their way to Canada. Since the law of 1827 was never strictly enforced, many stayed here. Whenever their qualifications for residence were too closely checked, they merely crossed the river. One couple who stopped in Detroit rather than go into Canada was Mr. and Mrs. Thornton Blackburn. . . .

In 1831, Thornton Blackburn and his wife escaped from Louisville, Kentucky. They became members of the Negro community and were apparently well liked. In 1833, they were apprehended by their owner who invoked the Fugitive Slave Law of 1793, and had Sheriff Wilson place them in the city jail until they could leave on the steamer *Ohio* for Louisville. For this service the sheriff and his deputy received fifty dollars each. Meanwhile the Negro community was angered by the arrest which in their point of view was a miscarriage of justice.

The steamer *Ohio* was to leave on Monday. On Sunday, Mrs. Madison Lightfoot and Mrs. George French, two of Detroit's most prominent colored matrons were allowed to visit Mrs. Blackburn in the city jail. Mrs. Blackburn exchanged clothing with Mrs. French and in this disguise was quickly taken across the Detroit River to Amherstburg, Ontario. When Sheriff Wilson discovered the hoax, Mrs. French was threatened with the fate of permanently taking Mrs. Blackburn's place and this entailed being taken back to Kentucky where she would be sold into slavery to compensate the owner for the loss of one female slave. Later that day, however, Mrs. French was allowed to leave the jail.

The following day when Mr. Blackburn was to leave the jail to be returned to slavery a crowd of Negroes gathered outside the jail. They were angry, and the situation was rife with danger. As the sheriff, his deputy, the slave owner, and his slave approached the prison coach, the crowd drew closer. Blackburn asked the sheriff if he might speak to the crowd in order to allay their fears and to appease their anger. As the people crowded in to hear Blackburn, someone slipped him a pistol which he brandished and ran into the coach where he locked himself in, and promised to kill whoever attempted to recapture him. . . .

The group of white people who had been looking on immediately came to the rescue of Sheriff Wilson. In the melee that followed, Blackburn was slipped from the coach by Sleepy Polly, and Daddy Walker [a local black citizen] whisked him away to Canada. Sheriff Wilson was fatally wounded by an unknown assailant. The prison coach was disabled so that the pursuit of Blackburn was impossible. Daddy Walker threw any possible pursuers off the trail by going out Gratiot and then doubling back to River Rouge where he and Blackburn escaped by boat to Sandwich, Ontario. We have seen this particular scene played out in countless motion pictures. The only missing element is the man who said, "They went thata way."

Meanwhile back in Detroit a full scale race riot was in progress. In the subsequent examination, those persons involved were fined and sentenced to work on the street repair gang. Mr. Lightfoot was jailed for allegedly slipping the gun to Blackburn. Mr. and Mrs. French fled to Canada.

Many Negroes who had not been involved in the Blackburn affair planned a march in order to protest mob brutality and various injustices. Mayor Chapin issued a proclamation which silenced the planners of this demonstration. The proclamation stated that all Negroes who could not prove that they were free would be expelled from Michigan. And once more there was an exodus to Canada. Thus ended what the white citizenry of Detroit termed "The First Negro Insurrection."

3. A Young New Yorker in Detroit, 1841

Theodore Hinchman

During the winter of 1841, when Theodore Hinchman wrote the following letter to his brother in New York, Detroit was in the depth of the depression that followed the collapse of the land boom and the failures of local banks. Hinchman was working as a bookkeeper for John Owen, a businessman of varied interests: wholesale groceries, ship chandlery, and brewing. Still a bachelor who had not yet persuaded a certain teenaged Miss Chapin to come to Michigan, Hinchman was a careful observer of the local scene.

Dear Brother John

Having an opportunity to send you a line by Mr. Doremus who leaves here tomorrow for New York I will not let it pass.

Our state is in a great confusion and excitement in consequence of the failure of the Bank of Michigan to redeem its liability. The suspension law expired on the first. . . . [1] Since then the bank instead of giving six month Drafts, as it had previously, gives nothing. More than 80 suits have been commenced against it. Our circulation is composed almost entirely of its notes. Everybody became alarmed and lost confidence and endeavored to dispose of the bills they had on hand. The Detroit merchants,

Theodore Hinchman to John Hinchman, 19 February 1841, Hinchman Papers, BHC.

consequently, did a very good business. Instead of trying to sell goods as usual, it was our object to avoid it.

The legislature, which could have granted relief, refused to do anything, each party fearing to move in the matter.

The Merchants have held meetings, passed resolutions—and expended their breath & wisdom in discussing the matter, adopted resolutions & a memorial to the legislature praying them to loan the bank $750,000 state stocks. . . . The legislature have at least appointed a committee to examine the banks. They went into the bank, and wished to examine the items, which the bank refused to allow, so the investigation stands—

Some of the merchants, ourselves among the rest, have at last stopped taking the money in order to save from risk; and to bring the members of the legislature to terms, as all of the state funds are in the Bank of Michigan and the members will not get their pay at all if the money does not pass.

The Bank says they can pay give them time, and a loan, but if they do not get these, they will *wind up*. If so the money will fall 50 per cent immediately. We do a very small business in consequence. Mr. O. [Owen] has the *blues some*. I am on hand—as usual—will have more time to devote to reading & for Societies and Society—

The Young Men's Society have had excellent lectures by lernd [*sic*] and talented men this winter. A course of chemical lectures commenced the evenings. Our *Athenian Club* prospers. You ought to look in and see six egotistical *wise* young men, all ready to thrust their opinions on the club, all full of eloquence and self-esteem. Whether it be special talent, or only the character of a Wolverine, I leave you to judge.

Parties are all the rage, one almost every evening. The members of the legislature are almost always invited. They are beautiful monuments to politeness.

They afford some amusement to our city people. It is not uncommon for them to walk into the rooms, among the ladies, with their hats and cloaks on. Wisdom—unpolished! Unpresuming! 300 & 400 invitations are often sent out. Instead of dancing, we find only a crowd of people. I have been invited to three or four large ones lately. I don't enjoy myself very much, however, as I never flourish very extensively in a large crowd. . . .

Yr Brother Theodore

Editor's Note

1. Refers to the Currency Act passed by the Michigan Legislature a year earlier. This had given the bank power to issue drafts by which the state could pay the cost of internal improvements such as railways or canals. When the legislature did not renew the law, much of the program collapsed.

4. The Irish on the Urban Frontier

JoEllen Vinyard

By midcentury Detroit housed Irish who had left their native land with education and resources, Irish who had left with nothing but managed to parlay work and chance into wealth and position, and Irish whose disadvantages of a lifetime continued to weight them down. There was work to be done in the city on top, in the middle, and at the bottom. The range of opportunities accommodated the spectrum of Irish abilities, if not always in precise proportion to the newcomers themselves. Like the children's nursery rhyme, the Detroit Irish community in 1850 had its "rich man, poor man, beggar man, thief."

At midcentury, while the Irish were the largest immigrant group, they had not arrived in numbers so overwhelming as to

JoEllen Vinyard, *The Irish on the Urban Frontier: Nineteenth Century Detroit, 1850–1880* (New York: Arno Press, 1976), 48–79.

disorganize the existing economy or undermine their own position. In Detroit, with opportunity considerable and religious prejudice negligible, assets or liabilities of background most often determined the work that Irish immigrants could get.

Early in the nineteenth century, years when the prosperous eastern counties were contributing the most steady flow of emigrants, Detroit fell heir to several of that small number of Irishmen with resources of wealth and talents. Those who arrived in America with a profession or a skill had high aspirations; sharpened perceptions made them more critical of inadequacies in the seaboard cities where they landed. . . . Some made several shifts in the course of their continuing search and many such immigrants leapfrogging westward, began to arrive in Detroit by the late 1820's. . . . According to some reports the westward bound Irish usually had resources of at least $100 a family and some had as much as $5,000.[1]

Indeed, the act of getting to Detroit took some money. Coming from New York City before midcentury the traveler had to pay twenty-five to fifty cents for the Hudson River trip to Albany, then $5 for the railroad fare to Buffalo unless he endured the cheaper but longer canal trip. Finally $1.50 to $5 for a steamboat ticket from Buffalo to Detroit. . . . [2]

The Irish who had collected in Detroit by 1840 were prospering. That year the parish roster for the Irish Catholic church, Most Holy Trinity, bore witness. Of the 189 male pew holders, 59 were businessmen, 52 were in skilled occupations such as carpentry and masonry, 44 were laborers, and 16 were tailors or shoemakers. Four men were clerks, one was a collector for the United States customs, four were farmers. The Irish church had three judges, two medical doctors, two teachers and an architect.[3]

A number of these early arrivals stayed on in the city. In 1850 at least 267 of the 647 families headed by Irish men had been in the country for five years or more, many of them in Detroit for some time. There was, by then, a sizeable contingent among the Irish that had accumulated a stability of residence that stretched back 10 to 25 years.

Within the decade of the 1840's, however, the Detroit Irish community had expanded to include increasing numbers of poor and uneducated, the men and women who were more representative of the overwhelming peasant masses in Ireland. Like his wealthier countrymen, the Irish farmer-turned-American laborer often arrived in Detroit after a series of moves; moves made gradual by straitened means and stops marked always by a sameness of low-paying, unskilled work. Occasional immigrants arrived without luggage. Finding themselves unable to afford the whole passage to Detroit, they had to promise it as security along the way. . . .

In 1846 Detroit began to accumulate still another group of Irish immigrants: the fugitives from the failure of the potato crops. At midcentury at least 52 Irish families in the city had crossed the ocean within the preceding four years along with the famine migration. These were the years when peasants from the poorest areas from the South and West were cleared from the land with little or no reimbursement; when droves of subsistence cotters finally resigned themselves to emigration; when jobless townsmen from the cabin districts crowded into the steerage sections of departing ships.

The most destitute of the desperate famine refugees were not likely to make their way at once to Detroit unless they had contacts in the city who offered encouragement, aid, and comfort. Over four-fifths of the Irish family heads who came to Detroit between 1845 and 1850 were credited with the ability to read and write, a rate almost the same as that of the earlier arrivals. This suggests that Detroit did not gather in many from the lowest levels of Irish society even during the famine years. . . .

Longer residents jibed that on a Saturday night one could spot an Irishman just off the boat by his beaver hat, "high water" trousers, and short clay pipe. The reality of the maladjustment bit deeper. While the number of newly arrived Irish who fell upon charity was not staggering, the number who managed quickly to get good jobs was not impressive. At midcentury the Irish who had arrived in the United States after 1846 differed significantly in occupation from those who had come earlier. Among the pre-famine immigrants, 40% worked as laborers, whereas 79% of those who had come after 1846 were in that category.

Irishmen compelled to make their way as common laborers often preferred the jobs considered in Ireland to be more manly. Occupations that called for physical strength and prowess were greatly admired. In the 1850's, over 400 men were regularly employed by the 43 sawmills along the Detroit river front and many Irish were among the number. Others found work in the iron furnaces and related industries. By 1858 there were five iron furnaces in the county. Production had increased tenfold since 1840 and jobs had grown apace. Allied to the smelting works had come factories that manufactured cars, wheels, axles, locomotives, boilers, steam engines and stoves. In 1854 Captain Eber Brock Ward built the Eureka Iron and Steel works. Soon after the Wyandotte Rolling Mills located nearby. [Both plants, according to Vinyard, had deliberately located in Ecorse township on the edge of one of Michigan's finest remaining forest tracts, where charcoal supplies were still available.[4]] The two factories were the largest industrial employers in Wayne County in the 1850's. Jobs were available there for the unskilled, for those willing to do the hauling and heaving. Scores of Irishmen hired on. There were scores of unskilled jobs to be had on the roads being built on all sides of Detroit. . . .

In keeping with the entrepreneurial organization of the city, dozens of Irish laborers were self-employed. Over fifty of the more than 300 Irish laborers were draymen. Several owned their team and wagon and many worked along with their sons or brothers. The fleet of draymen hauled wood, coal and freight to and from the docks and railroad yards.

The pushcart or backpack with assorted household wares provided another means of self-employment. Here was a chance to work when, where and if one chose. In Ireland, however, hawkers were regarded contemptuously as the lowest outcasts of society, along with the tinkers, wanderers and itinerant beggars. Because of the old stigma, the poor profits to be accrued, or both, a scant five Irish family men and five single men fell back on this way of making a living. . . .

Chronic unemployment among the Detroit Irish population was confined to only a few, according to census reports. In 1850 eight Irish family men and 15 single men had been without work for at least six months. An additional 5% of the male family heads did not list any occupation; this too was a small number even if most were potentially employable but out of work. The low rate of unemployment attested to the job possibilities of the city, and perhaps to the assets and efforts of the Irish who selected Detroit as a home. . . .

Countless men worked only sporadically, separated from the chronically unemployed neither by state of mind nor state of being. For most families the way of life provided by a breadwinner who was a casual day laborer was one of privation and economic insecurity. . . .

The average daily earnings of a common laborer in Michigan in 1850 amounted to $.88. . . . Over the decade of the 1850's, along with a general trend, workers in Michigan increased their daily earnings to a level of $1.04. By 1860 draymen in Michigan averaged about $1.34 a day.[5]

Whatever day work a man did, money came uncertainly and often seasonally. The amount was small recompense for work that, however manly, was predictably hard and frequently dangerous. The laborer's continued strength and good health meant everything to his family, but the odds were not favorable. With less chance to accumulate savings, family crises, whether continuing or sudden, fell especially hard upon the laborer and his family. To a considerable extent the frontier economy and the culture of Detroit, much like the agricultural society from which the Irish came, viewed the family as a work unit. It was a matter of course and of honor that the family members were mutually self-sustaining.

Notes

1. Robert Ernst, *Immigrant Life in New York City* (New York: King's Crown Press, 1949), 62, quoting *The Irish-American* (26 August 1849).
2. Edward H. Thomson, *Emigrant's Guide to the State of Michigan* (New York: State of Michigan Emigration Department), 45.
3. Richard R. Elliott, "First Irish Catholic Parochial Organization Established in the Western States, Trinity Church, Detroit, 1835," *American Catholic Historical Researches*, no. 12 (January-October 1895): 134–37.
4. Vinyard, *Irish on the Urban Frontier*, 96.
5. Stanley Lebergott, *Manpower in Economic Growth* (New York: McGraw Hill, 1964), 541, 219.

5.   Germans

Walter Pitkin

One day Harry Rickel asked me to come over to his house. I went. And that simple act was one of the three or four main turning points of my life. It brought me into a new culture which was complete and exciting. It was the first one I had entered, next to the one I grew up in. . . .

It was our second high school year when I met Harry. He was different. He had a certain serious interest in things that few other students showed. At the same time he was hail-fellow-well-met. He was utterly unlike the Germans around us in Fourteenth Street. I soon learned how and why.

The Rickels lived in a big brick house on the north side of Adelaide Street. To us of Fourteenth Street it was a king's palace. Yet it was only a comfortable dwelling with high ceilings and many rooms, all furnished well but plainly.

One by one, the family appeared. First the mother, a sweet, simple woman who reminded me in some ways of my own mother. Then the two oldest brothers, both so much older than I that to them I was just a kid. They heeded me little. Then Martha and Armin, the two youngest. Martha was a darling of eight or nine years; I quite fell in love with her. Armin was a clever boy with a bright smile. He won me, too, on the spot. All was well. Yes, but what was that noise outside?

A harsh noise. A loud noise. A noise from a human throat. A noise indicating anger. And so in came Mr. Rickel, lord of the manor. A small, slightly bent man, with thin, tight lips, he was trying to shake off a bad temper. Somebody who had come up the walk with him had enraged him, and he did not try to suppress his fury.

The family hushed. Mr. Rickel rumbled and bumbled around, uttering something in German. Then Mama Rickel said something to him in German. Then the older sons. I fell out of the parade.

When we sat down for supper, the old man had subsided. Then he said to me, in excellent, crisp English: "If you want to be around here much, you must learn German."

Thenceforth he was sprightly, told stories, poked fun at the boys and girls, was altogether charming.

"You study Greek, under Sherrard?" he lifted his brows. "Now, see here, you fool!—" this to Harry. "You should learn Greek. But you are too lazy." And then into a rasping diatribe against the unambitious Rickel children.

The victims sat mute throughout it. That was the custom. How different from us Yankees! We'd have talked back. And not too sweetly, under criticism.

What was this? A tall, slender bottle of Rhine wine being poured into glasses around the table. Wine! None of that wicked stuff in our Prohibitionist home. When Uncle Walter craved wine, he sneaked off with me to Put-In-Bay. Here the family drank it unashamed. Yes, this was a new culture indeed.

Such wine! Put-In-Bay never grew its equal. Old man Rickel grinned, and poured me another glass, and then another. Oh, yum! Incidentally I ate like two pigs too. And such food! A potato salad the like of which had never hypnotized my tongue. Cold cuts of every sort, all the finest. Black rye bread. Heaps of strong cheese. . . . But enough! I must get back to trivial matters.

Did Harry and I sit on the porch? Did we lie on the lawn? Did we go upstairs? Did we fall asleep at the table? Who knows? Not I. All I recall is my wandering home late that night, vowing that German pumpernickel was the best pumpernickel to be had for a nickel, and that some day I must go to Germany where that wine came from. Hooray!

I took to dropping in once a week, then twice.

"You must take German lessons from Hermann," Mr. Rickel insisted. "It is a shame you do not understand us half the time. Yes, you go see Hermann, tomorrow."

So to Hermann I went. The teacher dwelt along the railroad tracks on the east side. He was a hulk of beery fat through which two merry little eyes peered, for all the world like a little pig looking under a fence . . . or something.

"We begin now," he said and set a stein of beer in front of me. He uttered sundry short sentences having to do with beer and drinking in company. He began with *"Prosit"* and worked up. After an hour of this, he brought in a china coffee pot which we drained while I babbled at my best.

My best was bad. Sherrard was getting my best. I didn't have genius enough for two bests. So I gave Hermann my second best and made a fair start. And before winter set in, I had caught my stride. Hermann was pleased. But old man Rickel was delighted, although he was stingy with compliments.

Harry began taking me around to the *Harmonie Verein*, the best German club within many hundred miles. There I met the grand old Germans, the Marxhausens, the Carstens, the Muellers, the Breitmeyers and a score more. There too I began to discover that my German was a wretched blend of the real stuff and second-generation American German. The latter was what I heard and used with boys and girls of my own age. It enraged old man Rickel. He used to berate Harry by the hour for getting words out of order or using the wrong gender. But little did that help anybody. The second generation was growing up American. The larger background of culture that made German what it was no longer existed in Detroit. But the German elders didn't understand that one must have the total situation in order to develop habits suited to it.

As this was the first alien culture into which I moved, I observed it closely and came to many conclusions about it. Some of these came much later, of course; but they may be stated here, without ruining my story. I liked enormously the willingness to work hard, the eagerness to learn everything about a subject, the almost brutal frankness, the neatness and the marvelous plain food. I could not understand the mania for singing and for games. And I powerfully disliked the power of the elders over the young. This marked the widest breach between our old Yankee world and the German.

The older men puzzled me for a long time. They worshipped Abe Lincoln. Old man Rickel would speak of Abe as if Abe were God. I never could do that, though I too admired Abe in my own way. Other men of the passing generation then would praise America and our democracy more fervently in private talks than any Fourth-of-July orator could. At length this grew clear.

Old man Rickel was a little boy back in Germany when in 1848 Carl Schurz and his band joined the revolution, to overthrow the old regime. Failing, Schurz and the others fled to America, where they were received with hurrahs by our own patriots. Many of them grew rich, famous and powerful here. Our people took them in warmly. These revolutionists later joined the Union Army and fought to preserve the Union. Abe was their Commander-in-Chief.

Alert, ambitious German boys followed the blazed trail. Between 1850 and 1880 thousands of the keenest, most democratic among the youth of the Fatherland came over here. And out of their number grew up the German community centering around the *Harmonie Verein*. . . .

Merchants, manufacturers, chemists, engineers, physicians, professors,—of such was the group made up. No wonder that I came to dislike the French and Irish and Poles and other groups out our way! I did not understand at the time that I was making an unfair comparison. I was setting over against the cultured, prosperous upper class Germans our own rabble of poor, struggling toilers, not one of whom had ever enjoyed what we today call a high school education.

Thus are our prejudices formed.

Old man Rickel shaped my life as much as anybody else. He never knew it. I wish I might have told him before he died. He would have been pleased.

He had a fanatical love of German learning. Germans knew best, Germans studied hardest. Germans made the greatest discoveries. The only thing wrong with Germans in the old country was that they were political morons. They allowed the Hohenzollerns to kick them around.

"Philosophy and psychology?" said he many a time. "If you ever wish to amount to anything in those fields, you must study at Berlin."

"Arabic?" said he again. "If you don't go to an Arab country to learn it, you must go to Berlin."

In this he was supported by his son-in-law, Dr. Osius, a keen physician lately arrived from Germany. Osius was German of the Germans. In time I found out how and why. He laughed softly when anyone mentioned Johns Hopkins Medical or Harvard Medical.

"In time, I am sure," he would say, "these will become great institutions. But as yet—" And then a polite and devastating shrug . . .

6. German-Jewish Immigrants

Irving I. Katz

There were Jewish fur traders and trappers in Michigan from shortly after the arrival of Cadillac. However, this selection is about those late-comers from Germany who came to the area in the years after 1837.

Mid-century brought a new influx of Jews to American shores immediately before and after the abortive European revolutions of 1848. The revolutionary fire which swept across Europe in the 40's fed on many fuels—nationalism, socialism and liberalism. Within the multi-national Austrian Empire especially, political, social and economic dissent raged high. The Austrian Empire was a hodgepodge of national and ethnic groups—Germans, Slavs, Magyars and Italians. It extended into Bohemia, Hungary, Italy and the Germanies, all spliced together by the Hapsburg monarchs into a motley and loose-jointed empire.

The rising currents of liberal and nationalist sentiment in Europe in the 30's and 40's lifted these people to rebellion against

Irving I. Katz, *The Beth El Story; with a History of the Jews in Michigan before 1850* (Detroit: Wayne University Press, 1955), 50–58.

the aristocratic government of Prince Metternich and the monarchy. Throughout most of the Germanies, led by independent Prussia, there was a clamor for liberal reform and the formation of a German federation which would exclude Austria. In Germany, it was largely a middle class movement which drew its recruits from the ranks of university professors, students and literati as well as from merchants and some workers. In 1848 revolutions erupted throughout the Austrian Empire and in almost every continental country but Russia. Liberals and nationalists, often allied, fought for the independence of subject nationalities and for governmental reforms. Socialists also joined in the general revolt.

Within a year, however, those new revolutionary governments which had been formed either failed or were snuffed out by the Hapsburgs as quickly as they were established. The elements of idealism and optimism of the pre-1848 years gave way to those of reaction and bitterness. Nationalism became a militant and aggressive religion. The age of "Blood and Iron" was being ushered in.

During these years, there began the early exodus of many central and southern Europeans to the United States. Among them were Jews from Germany and Hungary, where nationalist and racist feelings were on the rise. A number of these Jews, particularly from Bohemia, Silesia, Bavaria and Hungary finally settled in Michigan.

Michigan was now attached to the East by a transportation network of water and rail lines. The Michigan Central Railway provided a number of commercial opportunities to merchants and peddlers. Many Jews continued west from the Atlantic seaboard to Buffalo, then on to Michigan, settling in Detroit and those cities linked to Detroit by rail. Many German Jews settled in Ann Arbor, where there was already a large German-speaking population.

Ann Arbor and Ypsilanti were among the first communities where Jews settled in the 1840's. In 1850, the entire population of Washtenaw County totaled 28,567. Ann Arbor counted something less than 5,000 citizens; Ypsilanti only about 3,000. In the decade from 1840 to 1850 Detroit had increased its population from 9,102 to 21,019. Michigan itself had grown from about 212,000 to almost 400,000 by 1850. Saginaw was a mere village with about 900 citizens. . . . Grand Rapids and Kalamazoo both ran about 2,500. . . .

Ann Arbor and Ypsilanti were chosen by the new Jewish immigrants for two principal reasons: first, because in the 1840's Washtenaw County was the best county for farm stock, wool and hides; second, because many of the farmers in this county were recent German immigrants themselves and the Jewish arrivals found here the language of their native land and a place where they could earn a living, mostly as peddlers, until they could establish themselves as merchants, manufacturers or craftsmen.

Among the first to come to Ann Arbor from Bohemia were the five Weil brothers, who arrived as follows: Solomon in 1843, Moses and his wife in 1844, Leopold in 1845, Marcus in 1846 and Jacob in 1848. The Weil brothers formed a nucleus of a colony of Jews and their home became the headquarters of all German-Jewish arrivals. Here the humblest peddler always found a hospitable welcome. The brothers were orthodox in their religious observances, maintained a kosher household, and conducted the first *Minyanim* (services) held in Michigan. The first Sabbath and festival services were held, in 1845, in a house in the lower town of Ann Arbor which was jointly occupied by Leopold Weil and his brother-in-law, Judah Sittig, who came to Ann Arbor about 1845. Later they gathered at the home of Leopold and Moses on Washington Street, or at that of Solomon and Marcus on Huron Street. After their parents arrived in 1850, services were held uniformly at the parents' home, a brick house on Washington Street, near their tannery.

For the rites which followed the birth of Solomon Weil's eldest son, in 1848, a *mohel* (circumcizer) was brought all the way from Cleveland, Ohio, and it is said that when, in 1850, the parents of these brothers were sent for, the father, at their request, purchased a *Sefer Torah* in Prague and piously bore the Scroll of the Law in his arms all the way to Ann Arbor.

. . . Leopold Weil and Judah Sittig attempted farming in Lima Township, as did Moses Weil, together with one Weidel, a Bohemian Jew, in South Lyon Township, but all gave it up after a year or so because of the wildness of the locality and the rampage of the savage beasts of the forest.

Other German-Jewish immigrants who came to Ann Arbor and Ypsilanti before 1850 were: Charles, Adolph, and Louis

Bresler with their father, Leo Bresler; Charles, Henry, and Emanuel Lederer; Moses Rindskoff, Charles Fantle, Solomon Bendit, David Weidenfeld and brother, Adam Hersch, Isaac Altman, Simon Sloman, the Fantes brothers, one Hayman, one Feder, and possibly Alex and Martin Guiterman, Solomon Sondheim and Benjamin Goodkind. Many of these later moved to Detroit, when the city began its commercial rise.

Lewis F. Leopold, whose name was Freudenthaler in his native Baden, Germany, his wife Babette, who was a member of the Oesterreicher (Austrian) family, their infant son, Lewis' sister, Hannah, and Lewis' brother, Samuel, were located on the island of Mackinac in 1845. The brothers became the first pioneers in this locality in the fishery business and were soon shipping a thousand barrels of salted fish to Cleveland each season. This business, together with the sale of supplies to fishermen, Indian trading, and the purchase of furs, laid the foundation for an extensive business and they became prominent as owners of Lake Michigan vessels and merchants in the ports of the Great Lakes. . . .

Within a few years after 1850, the Leopolds and Austrians established leading stores in Michigan, at Eagle River, Eagle Harbor, the Cliff Mine, Calumet, and at Hancock, Joseph Austrian having selected the latter place as the site for his first store and warehouse.

Edward Kanter, a native of Breslau, Germany, who came to Detroit in 1844, was a resident of Mackinac in 1845, where he was employed by the American Fur Company. In 1846, he worked for the Leopolds and Austrians mentioned above. He remained in Mackinac until 1852 when he moved to Detroit. Kanter became the first Jewish banker in the city by founding the German-American Bank. He was a very colorful personality and the first Detroit Jew to be active in politics, having been elected among other offices a member of the state legislature in 1857. He was also a great friend of the Indians and because of his bustling activity was named by them "Bosh-Bish'gay-bish-gon-sen," meaning "Fire Cracker." The Indians always had a great liking for Kanter; they never missed an opportunity to call on him in Detroit or to send greetings to him. The merchants of Detroit in the early 1860's were at a loss one day to account for a circle of Indians gravely squatted in front of Kanter's store on the main business street, Kanter making one of the circle, the whole company smoking and maintaining a strong silence until they (the merchants) were informed that the Indians were a delegation of chiefs on their way to see the Great White Father at Washington, who would not pass through Detroit without smoking a pipe of peace with "Firecracker". . . .

A study of the city directories of Detroit published before 1850 disclosed the following:

The 1837 *Directory*, the first to be published, contains 1,330 names, but not one that can be safely claimed as Jewish.

In the second *Directory*, issued in 1845 and containing 2,800 names, we find Solomon Bendit and Company, dry goods; Goodkind and Freedman, fancy and dry goods; and Moses Rendskopf (later Rindskof).

In the third City *Directory*, published in 1846 and containing 3,238 names, the following known Jews are listed: S. Bendit and Company, dry goods; Frederick Cohen, portrait painter; Solomon Freedman, fancy and staple dry goods; Adam Hersch, cigar maker; Moses Rendskopf; Jacob Silberman. The *Directory* also contains an advertisement by Frederick E. Cohen. . . .

In the 1850 *Directory*, the fourth, in spite of the large increase in the population, which then numbered 20,019, only the following Jewish firms and individuals are listed: A. Amberg and Company, merchant tailors; S. & H. Bendit and Company, dry goods; F. E. Cohen, portrait painter; Solomon Cohen, peddler; S. Freedman and Brothers, dry goods dealers; Alexander Grunwald, clothing store; Adam Hersch, firm of Silberman and Hersch; Leopold Pappenkeimer (later Pappenheimer), fancy store; Silberman and Hersch, cigar manufacturers; Jacob Silberman, firm of Silberman and Hersch. . . .

The list of Jews in the 1850 *Directory* is not complete, however, for we know that several other Jews resided in the city. By the fall of 1850, there were in Detroit more than the traditionally required *minyan* (ten males over the age of thirteen), to start a congregation, and on September 22, 1850, the little band of Jews in Detroit organized the Bet El Society (now Temple Beth El), Michigan's first Jewish congregation, thus founding the first Jewish community in the state of Michigan.

Part IV

Getting Around in Michigan: Problems of Internal Improvements

Getting Around in Michigan: Problems of Internal Improvements

In the beginning Michigan traveled by foot or canoe, later on horseback. Those with means might secure an Indian guide. Soon the growing daily business of Michigan made these devices impractical. The Erie Canal, opening in 1825, brought newcomers by the thousands, but it did not solve the problem of how they would move about in Michigan. Swamps and rumors of swamps kept many settlers out of the interior.

Silas Farmer remarks that in the boom days of 1834 there was great excitement because of a new stagecoach line. "The entire distance from Detroit to Chicago," exulted a newspaper editor, "may be performed in less than five days."

"A Fortnight in the Wilderness" is a report by Alexis de Tocqueville of a trip from Detroit to Saginaw in 1831. That most urbane of foreign travelers conveys a sense of beauty and loneliness in a strange land.

Neither land nor water assured safety for the traveler. Getting from place to place soon became not only an inconvenience but a major political issue for the area. The internal improvements program has often been labeled a political pork barrel, a view still standard in many textbooks of American history. The alternatives are rarely considered: mud above wagon wheels, ships lost in lake storms, without lighthouses, the isolation of families in the wilderness.

Senator Zachariah Chandler begged Congress for roads, lighthouses, channel dredging, and railroads from the time of his first election to Congress in 1856. The internal improvements issue was to him a case of North versus South from his first day in Congress. Later known for his strong antislavery views and his sponsorship of the Reconstruction Amendments, he should also be remembered for his fight to unlock the Northwest.

1.   A Fortnight in the Wilderness

Alexis de Tocqueville

We reached Detroit at three o'clock. It is a little town of between 2,000 and 3,000 inhabitants. . . . We had crossed the State of New York, and steamed 400 miles on Lake Erie; we now were on the frontier of civilization. Still we did not know what course to take. To cross almost impenetrable forests; to swim deep rivers; to encounter pestilential marshes; to sleep exposed to the damp air of the woods;—these are efforts which an American easily conceives, if a dollar is to be gained by them—that is the point. But that a man should take such journeys from curiosity he cannot understand. Besides, dwelling in a wilderness, he prizes only man's work. He sends you to visit a road, a bridge, a pretty village; but that you should admire large trees, or wild

Alexis de Tocqueville, "A Fortnight in the Wilderness," in *Memoir, Letters, and Remains of Alexis de Tocqueville* (Cambridge and London: MacMillan, 1861), 140–207.

scenery, is to him incomprehensible. We could make no one understand us. . . .

We soon saw that it would be impossible to obtain the truth from them in a straightforward manner, and that we must manoeuvre.

We therefore went to the United States' Agent for the sale of wild land, of which there is much in the district of Michigan. We presented ourselves to him as persons who, without having quite made up our minds to establish ourselves in the country, were interested to know the price and situation of the Government lands.

Major Biddle, the officer, now understood perfectly what we wanted, and entered into a number of details to which we eagerly listened. "This part," he said, (showing us on the map the river of St. Joseph, which, after many windings, discharges itself into Lake Michigan), "seems to me to be the best suited to your purpose. The land is good, and large villages are already founded there; the road is so well kept up that public conveyances run every day." Well, we said to ourselves, now we know where not to go, unless we intend to travel post over the wilderness.

We thanked Major Biddle for his advice, and asked him, with an air of indifference bordering on contempt, towards which side of the district the current of emigration had, up to the present time, least tended. "This way, . . . towards the northwest. About Pontiac and its neighborhood some pretty fair establishments have lately been commenced. But you must not think of fixing yourselves farther off; the country is covered by an almost impenetrable forest . . . towards the northwest, full of nothing but wild beasts and Indians. The United States propose to open a way through it immediately; but the road is only just begun, and stops at Pontiac. I repeat, that there is nothing to be thought of in that quarter."

We again thanked Major Biddle for his good advice, and determined to take it in a contrary sense. We were beside ourselves with joy at the prospect of at length finding a place which the torrent of European civilization had not yet invaded.

On the next day (the 23rd of July) we hired two horses. . . . Having bought a compass, and some provisions, we set off with our guns over our shoulders, and our hearts as light as if we had been two school-boys going home for the holidays.

Our hosts at Detroit were right in telling us that we need not go far to see woods, for a mile from the town the road enters the forest, and never leaves it. The ground is perfectly flat, and often marshy. Now and then we met with newly-cleared lands. As these settlements are all exactly alike, whether they be on the outskirts of Michigan or of New York, I shall try to describe them once for all.

The little bell which the pioneer takes care to hang around the necks of his cattle, that he may find them in the dense forest, announces from a great distance the approach to the clearing. Soon you hear the stroke of the axe; as you proceed traces of destruction prove the presence of man. Lopped branches cover the road; trunks half calcined by fire, or maimed by steel, are still standing in the path. You go on, and reach a wood, which seems to have been maimed by sudden death. Even in the middle of summer the withered branches look wintry. On nearer examination a deep gash is discovered around the bark of each tree, which, preventing the circulation of sap, quickly kills it. This is generally the planter's first measure. As he cannot in the first year cut down all the trees on his new property, he kills them to prevent their leaves overshadowing the Indian corn which he has sowed under their branches.

Next to this incomplete attempt at a field, the first step of civilization in the wilderness, you come suddenly upon the owner's dwelling. . . . Here the trees have been cut down, but not uprooted, and they still encumber with their stumps the ground that they formerly shaded; round these withered remnants, corn, oak saplings, plants, and weeds of every kind spring pell-mell, and grow side by side in the stubborn and half-wild soil. Like the field around it, this rustic dwelling is evidently a new and hasty work. . . .

We did not reach Pontiac till after sunset. Twenty very neat and pretty houses, forming so many well-provided shops, a transparent brook, a clearing of about a square half-mile surrounded by the boundless forest: this is an exact picture of Pontiac, which in twenty years may be a city. . . .

We were taken to the best inn in Pontiac (for there are two), and as usual we were introduced into the barroom; here all, from the most opulent to the humblest shop-keeper, assemble to smoke, think, and talk politics on the footing of the most perfect equality. The owner of the house, or rather the landlord, was, I must not say a burly peasant, for there are no peasants in America, but at any rate a very stout gentleman, whose face had about as much frankness and simplicity as that of a Norman horse-dealer. . . . [He] never looked you in the face when he spoke, but waited till you were engaged in talking with someone else to consider you at his leisure. . . . .

We said to him, "Before fixing in your country, my dear landlord, we intend to visit Saginaw, and we wish to consult you on this point." At the name of Saginaw, a remarkable change came over his features. It seemed as if he had been suddenly snatched from real life and transported to a land of wonders. His eyes dilated, his mouth fell open, and the most complete astonishment pervaded his countenance.

"You want to go to Saginaw!" exclaimed he; "to Saginaw Bay! Two foreign gentlemen, two rational gentlemen, want to go to Saginaw Bay! It is scarcely credible." "And why not?" we replied. "But are you well aware," continued our host, "what you undertake? Do you know that Saginaw is the last inhabited spot towards the Pacific; that between this place and Saginaw lies an uncleared wilderness? Do you know that the forest is full of Indians and musquitoes; that you must sleep, at least for one night, under the damp trees? Have you thought about the fever? Will you be able to get on in the wilderness, and to find your way in the labyrinth of our forests?"

After this tirade, he paused, in order to judge of the effect which he had produced. We replied, "All that may be true, but we start tomorrow for Saginaw Bay. . . . "

He asked us: "Perhaps you are sent by the Canadian fur company to establish relations with the Indian tribes on the frontier?"

We maintain our silence.

Our host said no more; but he continued to muse on the strangeness of our scheme.

"Have you never been to Saginaw?" we resumed. "I," he answered, "I have been so unlucky as to go there five or six times, but I had a motive for doing it, and you do not appear to have any." "But you forget, my worthy host, that we do not ask you if we had better go to Saginaw, but only how we can get there most easily."

Brought back thus to the matter in hand, our American recovered his presence of mind and the precision of his ideas. He explained to us in a few words and with excellent practical good sense how we should set about our journey through the wilderness. . . . He took the candle, showed us a bedroom, and after giving us a truly democratic shake of the hand, went to finish his evening in the common room.

On the next day we rose with the dawn, and prepared to start. . . .

We had been advised to apply to a Mr. Williams, who, as he had long dealt with the Chippeway Indians, and had a son established at Saginaw, might give us useful information. After riding some miles in the forest, . . . we saw an old man working in a little garden. We spoke to him, and found out that he was Mr. Williams.

He received us with much kindness and gave us a letter to his son. We asked him if we had anything to fear from the Indian tribes through whose territories we were about to pass. Mr. Williams rejected this idea with a sort of indignation. "No, no," he said, "you may proceed without fear. For my part, I sleep more fearlessly among Indians than among white people."

I note this, as the first favorable impression given to me of the Indians since my arrival in America. In the thickly-peopled districts, they are always spoken of with a mixture of fear and contempt; and I think that in those places they deserve both. . . . If the reader, however, will go on with this journal, and follow me among the European settlers on the frontier, as well as among the Indian tribes, he will form a higher, and at the same time a juster idea of the aborigines of America.

After we left Mr. Williams, we pursued our road through the woods. From time to time a little lake (this district is full of them) shines like a white tablecloth under the green branches. . . .

Still travelling on, we reached a country of a different aspect. The ground was no longer flat, but thrown into hills and valleys. Nothing can be wilder than the appearance of some of these hills.

In one of these picturesque passes, we turned suddenly to contemplate the magnificent scene which we were leaving behind, and, to our great surprise, we saw close to us, and apparently following us step by step, a red Indian. He was a man of about thirty, tall, and admirably proportioned. His black and shining hair fell down upon his shoulders, with the exception of two tresses, which were fastened on the top of his head. His face was smeared with black and red paint. He wore a sort of very short blue blouse. His legs were covered with red *mittas*, a sort of pantaloon which reaches only to the top of the thigh, and his feet were defended by mocassins. At his side hung a knife. In his right hand he held a long rifle, and in his left two birds that he had just killed.

The first sight of this Indian made on us a far from agreeable impression. The spot was ill-suited for resisting an attack. On our right a forest of lofty pines; on our left a deep ravine, at the bottom of which a stream brawled along the rocks, hidden by the thick foliage, so that we approached it, as it were, blindfold! To seize our guns, turn round and face the Indian in the midst of the path was the affair of an instant. . . . He halted in the same manner, and for half a minute we were all silent. . . .

I said, that when we turned round, arms in hand, the Indian stopped short. He stood our rapid scrutiny with perfect calmness, and with steady and unflinching eye. When he saw that we had no hostile intentions, he smiled: probably he perceived that we had been alarmed. I never before had remarked how completely a mirthful expression changes the savage physiognomy. . . . An Indian grave and an Indian smiling are different men. . . .

Making signs, we asked him for the birds which he carried; he gave them to us for a little piece of money. Having made acquaintance, we bid him adieu, and trotted off.

At the end of half an hour of rapid riding, on turning round, once more I was astonished by seeing the Indian still at my horse's heels. He ran with the agility of a wild animal, without speaking a single word or seeming to hurry himself. We stopped; he stopped; we went on; he went on. We darted on at full speed; our horses, natives of the wilderness, leapt easily every obstacle: the Indian doubled his pace: I saw him, sometimes on the right, sometimes on the left of my horse, jumping over the brushwood and alighting on the ground without the slightest noise. He was like one of the wolves of the North, which are said to follow horsemen in hope of their falling and thus becoming a more easy prey.

The sight of this strange figure, now lost in the darkness of the by our side, became at last an annoyance. . . . It occurred to us that he was leading us into an ambush.

We were full of these thoughts, when we discovered, right in front of us in the wood, the end of another rifle; we soon came alongside of the bearer. We took him at first for an Indian. He wore a kind of short frock-coat, tight at the waist, showing an upright and well-made figure. His neck was bare, and his feet covered by mocassins. When we were close to him, he raised his head; we saw at once he was an European, and we stopped short. He came to us, shook us cordially by the hand, and we entered into conversation.

"Do you live in the desert [forest]?" "Yes; here is my house." And he showed us among the trees, a hut even more miserable than the ordinary log-house. "Alone?" "Alone." "And what do you do with yourself here?" "I roam about the woods, and I kill right and left the game which comes in my way, but the shooting is not good here now." "And do you like this sort of life?" "Better than any other." "But are you not afraid of the Indians?" "Afraid of the Indians! I had rather live among them than in the society of white men. No, no; I am not afraid of the Indians; they are better people than we are, unless we have brutalized them with strong liquors, poor creatures!"

We then showed to our new acquaintance the man who followed us so obstinately, and who at that moment was standing stock still, a few paces off. "He is a Chippeway," said our friend, "or, as the French would call him, a *sauteur*. I would lay a wager that he is returning from Canada, where he has received the annual presents from the English. His family cannot be far off."

So speaking, the American signed to the Indian to approach, and began to talk to him in his language with great fluency. The pleasure that these two men, so different in race and in habits, took in exchanging their ideas, was a striking sight. . . . After examining carefully the rifle of the savage, the white man said to us,—"This is an excellent musket; the English no doubt gave it to him, that he might use it against us, and he will certainly do so, in the first war. This is how the Indians call down upon their heads their own misfortunes,—but they know no better, poor things!" "Are the Indians skilful in the use of these long heavy guns?" "There are no shots like the Indians," replied our new friend, in tone of the greatest admiration. "Look at the little birds which he sold you, sir; there is but one shot in each, and I am sure that he fired at them only twice. There is no man so happy as an Indian in the districts whence we have not yet frightened away the game; but the larger sorts scent our approach at a distance of more than 300 miles; and, as they retire, they leave the country before us a waste, incapable of supporting any longer the poor Indians, unless they cultivate the ground.". . .

We proceeded on our way. We maintained the same rapid pace, and in half-an-hour reached the house of a pioneer. Before the door of the hut an Indian family had encamped. An old woman, two young girls, and several children, were crouching round a fire to the heat of which were exposed the still palpitating limbs of a whole kid. A few steps off an Indian was lying quite naked on the grass, basking in the sun, whilst a little child was rolling about in the dust by his side. Here our silent companion stopped: he left us without bidding us adieu, and sat down gravely among his countrymen.

What could have induced this man to follow our horses for five miles? We never could guess.

After breakfasting in this spot, we remounted, and pursued our journey through a wood of thinly scattered lofty trees. The underwood had been burnt away. . . . The ground was covered with fern, extending under the trees as far as the eye could reach.

Some miles further on, my horse lost a shoe. . . . Not far off, happily, we met a planter, who succeeded in putting it on again. [He] advised us to make haste, as the daylight was beginning to fail, and we were at least five miles from Flint River, where we intended to sleep.

Soon, indeed, we were enveloped in perfect darkness. We were forced to push on. The night was fine, but intensely cold. The silence of the forest was so deep, the calm so complete, that the forces of nature seemed paralysed. No sound was heard but the annoying hum of the musquitoes, and the stamp of our horses' feet. Now and then we saw the distant gleam of a fire, against which we could trace, through the smoke, the stern and motionless profile of an Indian.

At the end of an hour we reached a spot where the roads separated; two paths opened out in different directions—which should we take?. . . . One led to a stream we did not know how deep; the other to a clearing. The moon just rising showed us a valley full of fallen trees: further on, we descried two houses. . . .

We determined to take advice before proceeding My companion remained to take of the horses, whilst I, with my gun over my shoulder, descended into the valley.

Soon I perceived that I was entering a new settlement. Immense trunks of trees, their branches as yet unlopped, covered the ground. By jumping from one to another, I soon was near the houses. But the stream separated me from them. Happily, its course was impeded in this place by some huge oaks that the pioneer's axe had no doubt thrown down. I succeeded in crawling along these trees, and at last reached the opposite side.

I warily approached the two houses which I could see but indistinctly. I feared they might prove Indian wigwams. They were unfinished. The doors were open, and no voice answered mine. I returned to the edge of the stream whence I could not help admiring for a few minutes the awful grandeur of the scene. . . . The moonlight played upon the shattered remnants of the forest, creating a thousand fantastic shapes. No sound of any kind, no murmur of life was audible.

At last I remembered my companion, and called loudly to tell him . . . to cross the rivulet and join me. The echo repeated my voice over and over again in the solitary woods, but I got no answer. I shouted again, and listened again. The same death-like silence reigned.

I became uneasy, and I ran by the side of the stream till I reached the place lower down where it was fordable.

When I got there, I heard in the distance the sound of horses' feet, and soon after Beaumont himself appeared. Surprised by my long absence, he had proceeded towards the rivulet. He was already in the shallow when I called him. The sound of my voice, therefore, had not reached him. He told me that he, too, had tried by every means to make himself heard, and, as well as I, had been alarmed at obtaining no answer. If it had not been for this ford which served as a meeting place, we should perhaps have been looking for each other half the night.

We resumed our journey with the full resolution of not again separating, and in three quarters of an hour we at last came upon a settlement, consisting of two or three huts and, what was still more satisfactory, a light. A violet-coloured line of water in the hollow of the valley proved that we had arrived at Flint River. Soon,indeed, a loud barking echoed in the woods, and we found ourselves close to a log-house, separated from us only by a fence. As we were preparing to climb over it, we saw in the moonlight a great black bear, that standing on his hind-legs, and at the very extremity of his chain, showed as clearly as he could his intention to give us a fraternal embrace.

"What an infernal country is this," said I, "where they keep bears for watchdogs.". . .

We halloed at the top of our voices and with such success that at last a man appeared at the window. After examining us by the light of the moon: "Enter, gentlemen," he said, "Trink, go to bed! To the kennel, I say, they are not robbers."

The bear waddled off, and we got in. We were half dead with fatigue. We asked our host, if we could have oats for our horses. "Certainly," he replied, and began to mow the nearest field with American *sangfroid*, and as if it were noon-day. Meanwhile we unsaddled our horses. . . .

. . . There was but one bed in the house; it was allotted to Beaumont. I wrapped myself in my cloak, and lying down on the floor, slept as soundly as a man does who has ridden forty miles.

On the next day (July 25th) our first care was to inquire for a guide.

A wilderness of forty miles separates Flint River from Saginaw, and the road is a narrow pathway. . . . Our host approved of our plan, and shortly brought us two Indians whom he assured us we could perfectly trust. One was a boy of twelve or fourteen; the other was a young man of eighteen . . . [who had] taken care to paint his face with black and red in symmetrical lines; a ring was passed through his nose, and a necklace and earrings completed his attire. His weapons were no less remarkable. At one side hung the celebrated tomahawk; on the other, a long sharp knife, with which the savages scalp their victims. Round his neck hung a cow-horn containing his powder; and in his right hand he held a rifle. . . . his eye was wild, and his smile benevolent. . . .

. . . We asked him his price for the service he was about to render to us. The Indian replied in a few words of his native

128

tongue; and the American immediately informed us that what he asked was about equivalent to two dollars.

"As these poor Indians," charitably added our host, "do not understand the value of money, you will give the dollars to me, and I will willingly give him what they represent."

I was curious to see what this worthy man considered to be equal to two dollars, and I followed him quietly to the place where the bargain was struck. I saw him give to our guide a pair of mocassins and a pocket-handerkerchief, that certainly together did not amount to half the sum. . . .

However, the Indians are not the only dupes of the American pioneers. Every day we were ourselves victims to their extreme cupidity. It is true that they do not steal. They are too intelligent to commit any dangerous breach of the law; but I never saw an innkeeper in a large town overcharge so impudently as these tenants of the wilderness, among whom I fancied I should find primitive honesty and patriarchal simplicity.

All was ready: we mounted our horses, and wading across the rivulet (Flint River) which forms the boundary of civilization, we entered the real desert. Our two guides ran, or rather leapt like wild cats across the impediments of the road. When we came to a fallen tree, a stream, or a bog, they pointed to the right path, but did not even turn to see us get out of the difficulty. Accustomed to trust only to himself, the Indian can scarcely understand that others need help. . . .

From time to time our Indians halted. They placed their fingers on their lips in token of silence, and signed us to dismount. Guided by them, we reached the spot whence we could see the bird for which we were searching. It was amusing to observe the contemptuous smile with which they led us by the hand like children. . . . . .

As we proceeded, we gradually lost sight of the traces of man. . . . Before us was the scene that we had been so long seeking—a virgin forest.

Growing in the middle of the thin brushwood . . . was a single clump of full-grown trees, almost all pines or oaks. Confined to so narrow a space, and deprived of sunshine, each of these trees had run up rapidly, in search of air and light. As straight as the mast of a ship, the most rapid grower had overtopped every surrounding object. . . .

But it is time to return to our journey to Saginaw. We had been riding for five hours in complete ignorance of our whereabouts, when our Indians stopped short, and the elder, whose name was Sagan-Cuisco, traced a line in the sand. He showed us one end, exclaiming, *Michi, Conte-ouinque* (the Indian name for Flint River), and pointing to the other, pronounced the name of *Saginaw*. Then, marking a point in the middle, he signed to us that we had achieved half the distance, and that we must rest a little.

The sun was already high, and we should gladly have accepted his invitation, if we could have seen water within reach; . . . we motioned to the Indian that we wished to halt where we could eat and drink. He understood us directly, and set off with the same rapidity as before. An hour later he stopped again, and showed us a spot where we might find water about thirty paces off in the forest.

Without waiting for us to answer, or helping us to unsaddle our horses, he went to it himself; we followed as fast as we could. A little while before the wind had thrown down a large tree in this place; in the hollow that had been filled by the root was a little reservoir of rain water. This was the fountain to which our guide conducted us, without . . . [it] having occurred to him that we should hesitate to partake of such a draught. We opened our bag. Another misfortune! The heat had entirely spoilt our provisions, and we found our dinner reduced to the small piece of bread, which was all we had been able to procure at Flint River.

Add to this a cloud of musquitoes, attracted by the vicinity of water, which we were forced to fight with one hand while we carried our bread to our mouths with the other, and an idea may be formed of a rustic dinner in a virgin forest. . . .

We soon began to think of starting, but we were dismayed to find that our horses had disappeared. Goaded, no doubt, by hunger, they had strayed from the road in which we had left them, and it was not without trouble that we succeeded in tracing them; we blessed the musquitoes that had forced us to continue our journey.

The path soon became more and more difficult to follow. Every moment our horses had to force their way through thick brushwood, or to leap over the large fallen trees that barred our progress.

At the end of two hours of an extremely toilsome ride we at length reached a stream. . . . We waded across it, and from the opposite side we saw a field of maize and two huts that looked like log-houses. As we approached, we found that we were in a little Indian settlement, and that the log-houses were wigwams. The solitude was no less perfect than in the surrounding forest.

When we reached the first of these abandoned dwellings, Sagan-Cuisco stopped. . . . He again traced a line in the sand and showed us by the same method as before that we had accomplished only two-thirds of the road; then he rose and pointing to the sun, signed that it was quickly sinking into the west, next he looked at the wigwam and shut his eyes. . . . He wished us to sleep in this place. I own that the proposal astonished us as much as it annoyed us. It was long since we had eaten, and we were but moderately inclined to sleep without supper. The sombre savage grandeur of scene that we had been contemplating ever since the morning, our utter loneliness, the wild faces of our guides, and the difficulty of communicating with them, all conspired to take away our confidence.

There was a strangeness too in the conduct of the Indians. Our road for the last two hours had been even more untrodden than at the beginning. No one had told us that we should pass through an Indian village, and everyone had assured us that we could go in one day from Flint River to Saginaw. We could not therefore imagine why our guides wanted to keep us all night in the desert.

We insisted upon going on. . . . Sagan-Cuisco had paid particular attention to a little wicker bottle that hung by my side. A bottle that could not be broken. . . . I signed to him that I would give him the bottle if he would take us immediately to Saginaw. He then seemed to undergo a violent struggle. He looked again at the sun, then on the ground. At last he came to a decision, seized his rifle, exclaimed twice, with his hand on his mouth, *Ouh! Ouh!* and rushed off before us through the bushes.

We followed him at a quick pace, and we soon lost sight of the Indian settlement. Our guides continued to run for two hours, faster than before.

Still, night was coming on, and the last rays of the sun had disappeared behind the trees, when Sagan-Cuisco was stopped by a violent bleeding at the nose. . . . It was evident that fatigue and want of food had exhausted their strength. We began to fear lest our guides should renounce the undertaking, and insist on sleeping under a tree. We therefore proposed to mount them in turns on our horses.

They accepted our offer without surprise or shame. It was curious to see these half-naked men gravely seated on English saddles, carrying our game-bags and guns slung over their shoulders, while we were toiling on before them.

At last night came. The air under the trees became damp, and icy cold. In the dark the forest assumed a new and terrible aspect. Our eyes could distinguish nothing but confused masses without shape or order; strange and disproportioned forms; the sort of fantastic images which haunt the imagination in fever. The echo of our steps had never seemed so loud, nor the silence of the forest so awful. The only sign of life in this sleeping world was the humming of the musquito.

As we advanced the gloom became still deeper. Now and then a fire-fly traced a luminous line upon the darkness. Too late we acknowledged the wisdom of the Indian's advice; but it was no longer possible to recede.

We therefore pushed on as rapidly as our strength and the night permitted. At the end of an hour, we left the woods, and entered a vast prairie. Our guides uttered three times a savage cry, that vibrated like the discordant notes of the *tam-tam*. It was answered in the distance. Five minutes afterward we reached a stream; but it was too dark to see the opposite bank.

The Indians halted here. They wrapped their blankets round them, to escape the stings of the musquitoes; and hiding in the long grass, looked like balls of wool, that one might pass by without remarking, and could not possibly suppose to be men. . . .

In a few minutes we heard a faint noise, and something approached the bank. It was an Indian canoe, about ten feet long, formed out of a single tree. The man who was curled up in this frail bark wore the dress and had the appearance of an Indian. He spoke to our guides, who, by his direction, took the saddles from our horses, and placed them in the canoe.

As I was preparing to get into it, the supposed Indian touched me on the shoulder, and said, with a Norman accent which made me start,

"Ah, you come from old France! . . . stop—don't be in a hurry—people sometimes get drowned here."

If my horse had addressed me, I should not, I think, have been more astonished.

I looked at the speaker, whose face shone in the moonlight like a copper ball. "Who are you, then?" I said. "You speak French, but you look like an Indian." He replied that he was a "Bois-brulé," which means the son of a Canadian and an Indian woman. . . .

Following the advice of my countryman, the savage, I seated myself in the bottom of the canoe, and kept as steady as possible; my horse, whose bridle I held, plunged into the water, and swam by my side, meanwhile the Canadian sculled the bark, singing in an undertone to an old French tune some verses, of which I caught only the first couplet,—"Between Paris & St. Denis, there lived a maid,"&c.

We reached the opposite bank without accident; the canoe immediately returned to bring over my companion. All my life I shall remember the second time that it neared the shore. The moon, which was full, was just then rising over the prairie behind us, half the disk only appeared above the horizon. . . . Its rays were reflected in the stream, and touched the place where I stood. Along the line of their pale, tremulous light, the Indian canoe was advancing. We could not see any sculls, or hear the sound of rullocks [rowlocks]. The bark glided rapidly and smoothly—long, narrow, and black, resembling an alligator in pursuit of his prey. Crouching at the prow, Sagan-Cuisco, with his head between his knees, showed only his shiny tresses. Further back, the Canadian was silently sculling, while behind followed Beaumont's horse, with his powerful chest throwing up the waters of the Saginaw in glittering streams. . . .

[We proceeded to a house] about a hundred yards from the river. . . . we should probably have repaired our strength by a sound sleep if we could have gotten rid of the myriads of musquitoes that filled the house; but this was impossible. . . .

These insects are the curse of the American wilderness. They render a long stay unendurable. I never felt torments such as those which I suffered from during the whole of this expedition, and especially at Saginaw.

We went out very early, and the first objects that struck us were our Indians, rolled up in their blankets near the door, and sleeping by the side of their dogs.

This was our first daylight view of the village of Saginaw, which we had come so far to see. A small, cultivated plain, bounded on the south by a beautiful and gently flowing river; on the east, west, and north by the forest; constitutes at present the territory of the embryo city. . . .

The village of Saginaw is the furthest point inhabited by Europeans to the north-west of the vast peninsula of Michigan. It may be considered as an advanced post; a sort of watch-tower, placed by the whites in the midst of the Indian nations. . . .

After breakfast we went to see the richest landowner in the village, Mr. Williams. We found him in his shop engaged in selling to the Indians a number of little articles of small value, such as knives, glass necklaces, earrings &c. It was sad to see how these poor creatures were treated by their civilized brother from Europe.

All however, whom we saw there were ready to do justice to the savages. They were kind, inoffensive; a thousand times less given to stealing than the whites. It was only a pity that they were beginning to understand the value of things. But why a pity? "Because trade with them became every day less profitable." Is not the superiority of civilized man apparent in this remark? The Indian in his ignorant simplicity would have said that he found it every day more difficult to cheat his neighbour; but the white man finds in the refinement of language, a shade which expresses the fact, and yet saves his conscience.

On our return from Mr. Williams' we went a short way up the Saginaw to shoot wild ducks. . . . The report of a gun in the woods roused us from our dream. At first it sounded like an explosion on both sides of the river; the roar then grew fainter, till it was lost in the depth of the surrounding forest. It sounded like the prolonged and fearful war-cry of advancing civilization. . . .

The facts are as certain as if they had already taken place. In a few years these impenetrable forests will have fallen; the sons of civilization and industry will break the silence of the Saginaw; its echoes will cease; the banks will be imprisoned by quays; its current, which flows on unnoticed and tranquil through a nameless waste, will be stemmed by the prows of vessels. More than 100 miles sever this solitude from the great European settlements; and we were, perhaps, the last travellers allowed to see its primitive grandeur. . . .

It is this idea of destruction, with the accompanying thought of near and inevitable change, that gives to the solitudes of America their peculiar character, and their touching loveliness. You look at them with a mournful pleasure. You feel that you must not delay admiring them. The impression of wild and natural greatness so soon to expire, mingles with the lofty thoughts to which the progress of civilization gives rise—you are proud of being a man; and yet you reflect almost with remorse, on the dominion which Providence allots to you over nature. . . .

We wished to quit Saginaw on the next day, the 27th July, but one of our horses was galled by the saddle, and we resolved to remain a day longer. . . . At five A.M. we resolved to start [the return journey to Detroit]. . . . In three hours we reached a deserted wigwam on the lonely banks of the river Cass. . . .

On leaving the wigwam we found several paths. . . . After due examination and discussion, we could think of nothing better to do than to throw the bridle on our horses' necks to leave them to solve the difficulty. In this way we forded the river as well as we could, and were carried in rapidly in a southwesterly direction. More than once the roads became nearly invisible in the brushwood. . . we were not completely reassured till we reached the spot where we had dined three days before.

We knew it again by a giant pine, whose trunk, shattered by the wind, we had before admired. Still we rode on with undiminished speed, for the sun was getting low. . . . As night was coming on, we came in sight of the river Flint; half-an-hour later we were at the door of our house. This time the bear received us as old friends, and rose upon his hind legs to greet our happy return.

During the whole day we had not met a single human face; the animals, too, had disappeared. No doubt they had retired from the heat. All that we saw, and that at rare intervals, was now and then, on the bare top of a withered tree, a solitary hawk standing motionless on one leg, and sleeping quietly in the sun, as if cut out of the wood on which he was resting.

THE CHEAP, PLEASANT & EXPEDITIOUS ROUTE.

BETWEEN THE

EAST AND WEST

IS NOW BY THE

Detroit & Milwaukee R. R.

Fare $3.00 less than by any other Route.

1871.   **1872.**

Two Express Trains Leave Detroit Daily with Passengers for

PONTIAC, HOLLY, FENTONVILLE, FLINT, SAGINAW, OWOSSO, ST. JOHNS,

Lansing, Grand Rapids, Grand Haven,

MUSKEGON, MILWAUKEE, CHICAGO, ST. PAUL, ST. ANTHONY,

AND ALL POINTS ON THE MISSISSIPPI RIVER.

First Class Staunch Steamships

Built expressly for this Line, ply on the Lakes to and from each Train.

CLOSE CONNECTION MADE AT DETROIT WITH THE

GREAT WESTERN RAILWAY

OF CANADA,

For Buffalo, Rochester, Boston, New York, Philadelphia, Toronto, and with Grand Trunk Railway f
Montreal, Quebec, and with Cleveland and Lake Superior Line of Steamers.

For Emigrants this Line offers Cheap and Comfortable Transit.

For particulars see Company's Time Table to be had at any of the Stations on application.

THOS. BELL, Gen'l Supt.

D. M. R. R. Office, Detroit, 1871.

"Getting around" in Michigan gradually became easier. Clark's *Detroit City Directory* of 1871 advertised the combination of lake and rail travel that came to serve the public. (Courtesy of Bill Lynch.)

2. Zachariah Chandler's Fight for Internal Improvements

Detroit Post and Tribune

Upon the day following that on which Mr. Chandler first took his seat in the Senate Judah P. Benjamin of Louisiana[1] offered a resolution providing that thereafter the standing committee of that body should be appointed at the commencement of each session of Congress. The Committee on Commerce then consisted of seven members . . . composed of Messrs. Clay of Alabama, chairman, Benjamin of Louisiana, Bigler of Pennsylvania, Toombs of Georgia, Reid of North Carolina, Bright of Indiana, and Hamlin of Maine. Mr. Chandler was assigned to the committee on the District of Columbia. . . . Mr. Hamlin was also appointed to this inferior committee, giving it two Republican members, where the Committee on Commerce had but one. The

"Zachariah Chandler: An Outline Sketch of His Life and Public Services," *Detroit Post and Tribune* (1880): 164–181.

general assignments of places to the minority was so inadequate and unfair that a Republican caucus (the first Mr. Chandler had attended) had been called to consider the matter. Mr. Chandler, although a new member, was one of its speakers and gave strong expression to his sense of the injustice with which both his party and the Northwest had been treated. It was decided to make a formal protest. There was but one [Republican] member to represent the country of the Great Lakes and the whole of New England and New York. . . . But the Republican protest, well-grounded as it was, proved then unavailing.

In his first speech before the entire Senate, Chandler commented:

> I rise, sir, to protest against this list of committees as presented here. Never before, in the whole course of my observation, have I seen a large minority virtually ignored in a legislative body upon important committees. This is the first time that I have ever witnessed such a total, or almost total, ignoring of a large and influential minority. But, sir, whom and what does this minority represent? It represents—I believe I am correct in saying—more than half—certainly nearly one-half—of all of the free white inhabitants of these United States; and yet this minority, representing the commerce and revenues of the nation, is expected to be satisfied with one place on the tail end of a committee on Commerce. I may almost say that that committee is of more importance to the Northwest than all the other committees of this body; but the great Northwest is totally ignored upon a committee in which it takes so deep an interest. Not a solitary member of this body from that portion of the country is honored with a position on that committee, and yet you have been told of the hundreds of millions of dollars' worth of commerce which is there looking to protection from this body. . . .

Before Mr. Chandler entered the Senate there had been some work done by the United States upon the most serious natural obstacle to the navigation of the Great Lakes, the tortuous channels and extensive shoals at the mouth of the St. Clair river, known as the "St. Clair Flats." Largely through Senator Cass's efforts an appropriation of $45,000 had been made in the Thirty-Fourth Congress (it was passed over Franklin Pierce's veto) for this work, and this sum had been expended under the supervision of Major Whipple in the clearing out of a channel through the shoals of about 6,000 feet in length, 150 feet in width, and nine feet in depth at low water. This improvement, valuable as it was, did not prove at all adequate, and was made much less useful in the few following years by a lessening in the depth of the waters of Lake St. Clair. The rapidly growing commerce of the lakes manifestly demanded the early construction and permanent maintenance through these shoals of a first-class ship canal, which could be safely used in all conditions of water and weather by vessels of the largest class. Mr. Chandler. . . commenced at once his attack on the great obstacles in its way—namely the disposition of the older States to undervalue the commercial importance of the Northwest, and the traditional hostility of the Democracy [sic] to all internal improvements. The first measure . . . was a bill "making an additional appropriation for deepening the channel of the St. Clair Flats;" when it was introduced it was referred to the Committee on Commerce. There an effort was made to strangle it by persistent inaction. Accordingly, on April 24, Mr. Chandler introduced in the Senate a resolution instructing the Committee on Commerce to report back this bill, for action in the Senate. This resolution not receiving immediate consideration, on May 3 he called it up and demanded a vote. Mr. Clay, the chairman of the committee, opposed it with much temper, and moved to lay it on the table, but this motion was lost by one vote. Mr. Clay then attacked Mr. Chandler's resolution as insulting to the Committee on Commerce. . . . Mr. Hamlin, the sole Republican member [on the Committee] expressed his gratification at the fact that the Senator from Michigan (Mr. Chandler) had offered this resolution; he thought that it was appropriate and that the action of the committee called for such instructions. . . . Mr. Benjamin . . . moved as a substitute for the pending resolution, a general order to the committee to report on all public works on which there had been any expenditure, and this motion prevailed. Mr. Chandler, who was after a specific point and not a mere generality, accepted this as a defeat, and began anew by giving notice on the spot that he should ask leave at a subsequent day to introduce a bill for the improvement of the St. Clair River Flats, making an appropriation of $55,000, this being the amount estimated by the United States Engineers as being necessary at that time. On May 10 he presented this bill, but the

Senate refused to refer, and adopted a motion to lay it upon the table. Mr. Chandler met this second defeat without discouragement, and later in the session did succeed after two efforts in procuring the addition of this item of $55,000 to the civil appropriation bill. But the threat of an executive veto of the whole measure, if this appropriation was not omitted, proved potent with the Senate, and it was ultimately stricken out. Mr. Chandler closed his last speech on this measure at that session, with a demand for a vote by yeas and nays, and these words: "I want to see who is friendly to the great Northwest and who is not—for we are about making our last prayer here. The time is not far distant when, instead of coming here and begging for our rights, we shall extend our hands and *take* the blessing. After 1860 we shall not be here as beggars."

Mr. Chandler said in an address at St. Johns, in Michigan, October 17, 1858:

> When I took my seat in the Senate I supposed every section of the country would be fairly heard in the details of business. There were twenty Republican Senators representing two-thirds the revenue, business, and wealth of the country. How were they placed on committees? Out of seven on the Committee on Commerce they had one. I call attention to this fact. It bears the mark of design. How does this work? . . . I introduced at an early date a bill appropriating money for the St. Clair Flats, and it went to this Southern Committee on Commerce. I procured all the necessary plans and maps and estimates and gave them into their charge. One hundred days rolled away and they had not deigned to examine them. I then introduced a resolution, instructing them to report. Subsequently I introduced a bill myself which was laid on the table. By the most untiring efforts I succeeded in getting the desired appropriation tacked upon a appropriation bill and passed. But the President's friends threatened a veto of the whole bill unless this was stricken out—and that was done. Thus committees were packed against us and we were thwarted at every turn. Thousands of dollars can be obtained for almost any creek in the South, while the inland seas of the North are denied a dollar, and we are left to take care of ourselves the best we can.

The second session of the Thirty-Fifth Congress began in December, 1858. . . . Mr. Chandler moved to take his St. Clair Flats bill from the table. This time it was passed by a vote of 29 to 22, and sent to the House, . . . [where it] was finally passed, its introducer working for it with the utmost energy in the committee-rooms, on the floor, and by private solicitation. It reached Mr. Buchanan in the last days of that Congress, and he killed it by withholding his signature but without a formal veto. The Thirty-Sixth Congress met in December, 1859, and on the 4th of January Mr. Chandler's bill to deepen the St. Clair Flats Channel made its appearance. On February 2 Mr. Buchanan informed Congress, in a special message, of his reasons for "pocketing" the measure at the last session. This veto took the position that the improvement of harbors and the deepening of rivers should be done by the. . . . States, and Michigan . . . with Upper Canada should provide the necessary means. . . . Mr. Chandler reviewed this message at length. . . . Jefferson Davis at once came to the defense of the veto on constitutional grounds and a running debate followed, on the subject, between Messrs. Chandler and Bingham of Michigan, Hamlin, Crittenden, Davis, Toombs, Wigfall and others. Mr. Crittenden condemned the veto, while Toombs and Wigfall joined Davis in its defense. Thus the plotters of rebellion assumed a hypocritical attitude as defenders of the constitution. . . as they assumed a virtue that they never had, that of being patriots with a deep regard for the the fundamental law of the land. No action followed this debate, but on February 20 Mr. Chandler moved that his bill be made the special order for the 23d. . . . when that day arrived the Senate refused to proceed . . . no action was taken before adjournment. The second session of this Congress commenced in December, 1861, with civil war imminent and no chance for the consideration of any project for internal improvement. At the meeting of the next Congress the Democracy found itself in a petty minority, and remained powerless at Washington for many years. As soon as it became plain that rebellion could not destroy the life of the nation, Mr. Chandler brought forward again his bill for the improvement of the channels at the head of Lake St. Clair, and with the powerful support of his colleagues and the commercial interests of the Northwest obtained without difficulty from Republican Congresses such appropriations as were required for the construction of a great ship-canal. . . . [2]

Mr. Chandler was the firm friend of an intelligently-planned and general system of internal improvements. His labors, and those of men like him, have borne fruit in manifold aids to commerce scattered over river, lake and ocean—light-houses, breakwater, harbors of refuge, straightened and deepened channels and improved natural highways. He was prompt to recognize the claims of all sections, but was especially vigilant in regard to the necessities of the Northwest, and his memory will long be cherished throughout the region of the Great Lakes as that of the most ardent and efficient champion of its commercial development.

Editor's Notes

1. Judah Benjamin is better known for his role as treasurer of the Confederacy than as senator from Louisiana.
2. The "great ship-canal" was, of course, the St. Marys River at Sault Sainte Marie.

Part V

Detroit and the Civil War: Glory and Ambivalence

Detroit and the Civil War: Glory and Ambivalence

At first the men of Michigan went off bravely and hopefully to the Civil War. The spirit of those early days is well captured by Frank B. Woodford's essay, "Thank God for Michigan!" But the war years were tangled, unhappy ones for many Detroiters; many men from Detroit did not return from Spottsylvania, from Wilderness, from Andersonville. Some Michigan men were ordered by General George Custer to accompany him to the West at the war's end when they thought the war was over and they would be coming home.

Not everyone of importance favored the war. Some saw it only as disunity. The handsome, socialite Episcopal Bishop McCoskry could not bring himself to encourage his own chaplains in the field. Late in 1860, Democrat Lewis Cass resigned his cabinet post as secretary of the interior in disgust when he saw he was powerless to stop the drift of United States armaments to Southern forts. President Buchanan, a Southerner, was clearly less than interested in the problem of the rapid depletion of Northern arsenals. Yet Cass remained, for all that, a Democrat. Never a copperhead, Cass was simply one who believed in the Union, thought of abolitionists as single-issue men who spoiled good politics, and felt his life work was draining away. The elderly widower sat out the war years at the home of his daughter, Mrs.

Canfield, widowed by the Mexican War, while Detroit changed around him.

Perhaps the most significant change was one of attitude. As the war progressed, the joy that had attended the first departing militia was gone, replaced by a new ambivalence. In this city—where once black and white abolitionists had contrived escape to Canada for hundreds of slaves, where once Sojourner Truth and Frederick Douglass had spoken—the average citizen had somehow changed sides.

Abolitionism was no longer embraced. The *Detroit Free Press*, never in favor of a war it thought unnecessary, allowed its most sensation-seeking reporter to write an incendiary account of the trial of "the Negro Faulkner." Faulkner, a black man of conservative, non-integrationist views, was falsely accused of sexual improprieties involving two young girls. A would-be lynch mob formed at the jail following his trial, and the militia was called out. One of the white rioters was shot by a soldier, and in the rioting that followed over two hundred black family homes were destroyed by fire. Most of the homes were on the near east side, in the Brush-Beaubien area now known as Greektown. Some reports of the riot from the *Detroit Advertiser and Tribune*—the *Free Press*'s ideological rival—are included in this section. One probable factor in the white working-class anger was that this was during the time of the draft quotas. In 1863, the war appeared to be going badly for the North, and men were advertising for substitutes to serve in their stead, offering steadily growing bounties.

Detroit stubbornly retained "Colored School #1," "Colored School #2," and "Colored School #3." These nameless schools were officially held by the board of education to be equal to other schools; the board claimed that a majority of white parents and children were so prejudiced that it dare not permit black and white children to attend school together. Yet, to many parents of the time, and to black teachers such as Fannie Richards and Delia Pelham, the segregated solution was no longer acceptable.

Five years after the Faulkner riot, Detroiters had a clear chance to choose direction. A proposed new state constitution included a provision for black male suffrage. Every ward of the city voted it down, with working-class precincts defeating it by the widest margins.

The Thirteenth, Fourteenth, and Fifteenth Amendments on which Senator Chandler had labored were needed nowhere more than in his home state of Michigan. Because of them, the state could no longer deny the vote to any of its male citizens, and Justice Cooley of the Michigan Supreme Court ruled in an opinion reprinted here that Detroit's "colored schools" were unacceptable as well. Justice Cooley had a certain advantage over Thurgood Marshall a century later. In chiding Detroit for racism that might damage children, Cooley was writing the majority, not the minority, opinion of his court.

Last in the Civil War documents is Alexandra McCoy's account of the changes in wealth that occurred between the 1840s and the end of the Civil War. Though many of Michigan's prewar leaders, or their families, were still among the wealthy, there were newcomers, and new industries as well. The stage was clearly set for the Gilded Age that was to follow.[1]

Editor's Note

1. Friend Palmer states that when Peter Henkel heard Chandler remark that the war would be a long one, he promptly bought up pork and storage space. John Bagley stored pipe tobacco and other men stocked up on "high wines" (i.e., port and sherry) before new special revenue taxes pushed up the prices. Palmer observed that he heard and saw it all, but had no money to invest. Palmer, Scrapbook no. 28, BHC.

1. "Thank God for Michigan!"

Frank B. Woodford

William H. Withington went to war, but on the way he stopped long enough to buy a corset for his wife at Mrs. Mc-Adam's shop in Jackson, Michigan. To remind himself of what he had to purchase—a "No. 28, fasten in front with strap, $2"—he jotted down the essential information and specifications in his little pocket notebook. On the opposite page, he registered the number of his service revolver. It was 1107. Withington was a careful man; a written record was much more reliable than a frail memory.

Having done his errand at Mrs. McAdam's, Withington boarded the Detroit train. The date was April 16, 1861. He made

Frank B. Woodford, *Father Abraham's Children* (Detroit: Wayne State University Press, 1963), 25–35.

the journey, in all probability, with his fellow townsman, Governor Austin Blair, whose business in Detroit was urgent.

Besides being an up-and-coming businessman, of whom everyone in Jackson expected great things, the twenty-six-year-old Withington was captain of the local militia company, the Jackson Greys. It was in his capacity as a military man that the governor might have wished his company. Governor Blair was embarking on a fateful journey. He was on his way to meet his advisors and see what could be done about raising an infantry regiment to fill Michigan's quota under President Lincoln's call for 75,000 volunteers for three months service.

The call to arms came as no great surprise to Captain Withington. He had been expecting it, and, with the thoroughness which was typical of everything he did, he started early to get ready for war. A native of Dorchester, Massachusetts, there was enough Yankee in him to make him methodical and precise. The entries in his notebook reveal a good deal about him. A careful man with a dollar, as every young man on his way up should be, he noted every penny he spent.

The following week Withington paid his dues to the Jackson Greys—another twenty-five cents. It was a sound investment, because on February 15 he was elected captain of the company.

What Withington had been anticipating happened April 15. When the news of Fort Sumter's surrender was announced, the Jackson Greys assembled immediately in their armory and voted to offer their services, which, their captain proudly recorded, "were tendered by me to the Gov. this day." It was with satisfaction that he pointed out that in the aye-and-nay voting on the question all thirty-one votes were ayes. . . .

When it came to raising a company of volunteers or buying a corset, Withington gave the matter at hand his close personal attention.

The enthusiasm with which the Jackson Greys embraced the goddess of war was duplicated all over Michigan in every town which had a militia company. Each unit was as eager as Withington's to offer its services. Each began to fill up its ranks to the authorized strength of seventy-eight men with a spirit which was as competitive as it was patriotic. Orders were that the first ten companies ready would be accepted; the laggards would have to wait until they were needed.

First of all, though, there were certain necessary preliminary steps which had to be taken before a regiment could be put in the field. There had to be a staff. Governor Blair took care of that by appointing one while he was in Detroit on April 16. Alpheus S. Williams, or "Pap" Williams, as his men called him, a fatherly veteran of the Mexican War, was made brigadier general. . . .

Captain Whittlesey, his pockets stuffed with the money that Treasurer John Owen had been able to borrow or beg, set off to New York to purchase cloth for uniforms.

The week following Governor Blair's call for troops was one of feverish activity and excitement. In the preparations to go to war, the experiences of the Detroit Light Guard were typical of what all the militia companies went through.

The Light Guard was a venerable military association which traced its origins back to the Black Hawk War when it was organized as the Brady Guard. Prior to the outbreak of the Civil War it was primarily a social organization which attracted gentlemen of standing in the community as members. Military training consisted of occasional drills and parades, but much more frequently there were dances and banquets. Now and then, the Light Guard journeyed to another city to fraternize with some other militia company, playing host in turn, and trying to outshine the other in a display of hospitality. Several militia companies occasionally joined in a summer encampment for three or four days, and vied for prizes in drill competition.

An encampment was held for three days in Jackson in August, 1860, and the Light Guard attracted "much attention by their uniform step and easy line." . . . Each man received a bouquet from the belles of Jackson, a token which fired the Detroiters up to such a pitch that they handily won the competitive drill prize—thirty-five dollars. Most of the money, unfortunately, had to be paid to farmers to reimburse them for fences torn down to supply firewood. . . .

Being a member of the peacetime militia was something like belonging to a uniformed lodge or fraternity.

Then came April, 1861, and everything changed!

The Light Guard met in its armory on Woodbridge Street the evening of April 17 and, as Withington's Jackson Greys had done two days earlier, voted to "tender our services as a company to the commander-in-chief of the Michigan Militia, and ask to be enrolled in the regiment called for in his proclamation of the 17th inst."

Several of the members, substantial business and family men, some well on towards middle age, had to resign because of their personal circumstances. . . .

The rolls were filled by April 19 with seventy-five of the most promising applicants from the throng which clamored to join.

"Recruits came in by the hundreds, and many were so anxious to enlist with the famed Light Guard that money was liberally offered for the honor and privilege." So said Frederick Isham, a Detroit newspaperman who later went to the front as a war correspondent.

Of those accepted, almost all were Detroit residents. The average age of the company was twenty-three. Columbus Starkweather, Otis Cook, and Irving Garrison, at eighteen, were the "babies" of the company. Eventually, twelve men were dropped, but for every vacancy thus created there was a score of eager applicants.

Training began immediately, and on April 20 rookies with two left feet were learning the rudiments of squad drill in the open spaces of Campus Martius, the plaza adjoining City Hall. . . . Recruits who considered themselves as seasoned veterans after two or three days in the awkward squad became impatient. They had expected to be off for the front within a few hours after enlisting. . . .

Old campaigners, watching the preparations and recalling their experiences in former wars, were free with suggestions to the recruits about how to survive the rigors of the field. . . . The *Free Press* (April 25, 1861) printed the following sound advice from an "Old Soldier."

1. Remember that in a campaign more men die from sickness than by the bullet.

2. Line your blanket with one thickness of brown drilling. This adds by four ounces in weight and doubles the warmth.

3. Buy a small India rubber blanket (only $1.50) to lay on the ground or to throw over your shoulders when on guard duty during a rainstorm.

4. The best military hat in use is the light colored soft felt; the crown being sufficiently high for air to stir over the brain.

5. Let your beard grow, so as to protect the throat and lungs.

6. Keep your entire person clean; this prevents fevers and bowel complaints in warm climates. Wash your body each day if possible. Avoid strong coffee and oily meat.

7. A sudden check of perspiration by chilly or night air often causes fever and death. When thus exposed do not forget your blankets.

April 24 brought the awaited general order forming the regiment—the 1st Michigan Infantry—and listing the companies which had been selected, giving them their designations. . . .

"The makeup of the companies," said the state adjutant-general, "was composed of young men from all the professions and trades, and really embraced a class of the most respectable of the community." He might have added that for most part the members of the 1st were from the first families, and socially elect, of their various towns.

From April 18 to 24, all drilling was in company armories, but after the formation of the regiment, a shift was made from the companies' home bases to Fort Wayne, the army base on the Detroit River near the western limits of the town. . . . [By Monday, April 29] all companies had reported in and Colonel Willcox [Orlando B. Willcox of Detroit] took command of the regiment. Later the same day a detail of regular troops which had been stationed at Mackinac joined the 1st Michigan at Fort Wayne. Their arrival was delayed by their transport running aground on Belle Isle. Several hours were required to free the vessel.

Willcox and his officers had a problem of discipline on their hands from the outset. The light-hearted rankers, fresh from their roles as store clerks, bookkeepers, students, and young gentlemen about town, weren't accustomed to the restrictions of military life. They regarded their induction as the beginning of a glorious, carefree outing which would reach an exciting climax some afternoon when they would smash the rebellion with one blow.

Companies A and F discovered they didn't have much to do at the Fort before the rest of the regiment arrived. Playing cards and reading soon palled, and the men saw no reason for not returning to town for an evening of pleasure. Strict orders had been given that no one was to leave the Fort without a written pass. That posed no problem. The men simply wrote out their own. A stop was put to that after twenty men had passed the guard, but others discovered a convenient exit through an unwatched sally port. Most of them spent the night in Detroit, but all of them were on hand in the morning for reveille.

The first few days were devoted to giving the recruits the outward appearance of soldiers. On May 1, the first consignment of rifles arrived and was distributed. The arms which the men had brought with them were turned over to the home guards. The new weapons, described only as "minie guns", were probably Springfield 1855 muzzle-loading rifles of .58 caliber. This assumption is based on the statement that the regiment was equipped with the most up-to-date weapons. The records fail to show where they came from . . . the rifles of the 1st Michigan may have been Federal issue, sent down from the United States Arsenal at Dearborn.

It was time to put away the fancy uniforms of the independent companies which the men had been wearing since they moved into the Fort. The colorful trappings of hussars, dragoons, and zouaves, were shipped home and the new uniforms were donned.

Captain Whittlesey had returned to Detroit with $20,000 worth of cloth which he had purchased from the A. T. Stewart Department Store in New York. Detroit tailors, working on contract, made up to each man's individual measure the uniforms, which were described as "gray petershams for overcoats, navy blue for coats, and navy flannel for pants." The headgear was the familiar kepi, or forage cap, and the ladies of Detroit held sewing bees at which they made havelocks [attached head and neck scarfs] for the men. These, it was said, would be most useful as protection against sunstroke when the regiment marched victoriously through the hot, sunny South. . . .

About a thousand troops were crowded into space [at Fort Wayne] which lacked facilities for that many. To relieve the overcrowding, the passenger steamer *Mississippi* was borrowed from the Michigan Central Railroad and moored alongside the Fort. It was used to quarter four companies, and provided a mess hall for the entire regiment.

At first the mess was catered by a hotel man, Hiram R. Johnson. It came as something of a shock to the young gentlemen to discover that they were expected to eat at bare pine tables "with tin cups and plates, with iron spoons and cutlery." The menu was described as similar to that served in the average dollar-a-day hotel. Apparently it did not compare favorably with mother's cooking. The soldier's indignation exploded into a small riot one day when their dessert consisted of rice pudding instead of pie!

Gradually, however, the regiment began to shake down. Squad drill gave way to company and battalion exercises, and the 1st Michigan began to feel very soldierly. The Fort was visited daily by hordes of admiring civilians—friends, relatives, and plain sightseers who were impressed by the progress the troops were making. The easiest access to the Fort from the city was by boat, and the Windsor ferry line scheduled regular trips, with hourly sailings on Sunday. One day alone it was estimated that ten thousand people visited the Fort. . . .

The daily routine was strenuous. Reveille sounded at sunrise; sick call was at 6:30, and breakfast at 7. The guard was mounted at 8; dinner call came at 1 p.m., and the evening parade was held one hour before sunset. Tattoo was blown at 9, and all hands were expected to be in their straw-stuffed pallets half an hour later.

On May 1, the regiment was mustered into Federal service. That required new physical examinations, and there was a weeding out of the unfit and the under-aged—some of the recruits having lied about how old they were. There were also opportunities, before induction, for second thoughts, and those who wished to do so were permitted to resign. Few availed themselves of that privilege. . . .

After three weeks of preparation, the 1st Michigan was deemed ready. Orders were issued to start for Washington on May 13, and go by way of Cleveland, Harrisburg and Baltimore. . . . Friends and relatives came in droves for final good-byes, and on the night of departure, it was said, the "pillows of their sisters and sweethearts were wet with tears."

Departure time was late afternoon. At 5 p.m. two Michigan Central steamships, the *Illinois* and the *May Queen*, drew alongside the Fort, and the 1st Michigan, 798 strong, went aboard. Slowly the two vessels moved up-river to Woodward Avenue, where a brilliant fireworks display was touched off as a civic farewell. Then . . . with the regimental band stationed in the bow of one of the ships, playing "The Girl I Left Behind Me," the two vessels turned their prows downstream.

The 1st Michigan was off to war!

The self-esteem which the regiment carried with it was not lessened during its trip East. . . . People lined the railroad tracks through Ohio and Pennsylvania to see them pass. At every stop delegations brought food to the men; young ladies presented locks of their hair and occasional kisses to the gallant-looking fellows from the Wolverine state, who, in turn, were feeling more heroic by the minute.

At Harrisburg the regiment was issued rations and for the first time was told to do its own cooking. This was a new and baffling experience, and the results were something less than a gourmet's delight. Despite orders not to leave camp, many of the men chucked underdone beef and scorched coffee into the bushes and lit out for the restaurants in town.

Colonel Willcox and staff were being entertained by Governor Curtin of Pennsylvania at a late dinner in a fashionable Harrisburg hotel. During the course of the festivities Willcox did a little boasting about the firm discipline with which he controlled his men. As proof he declared that the regiment was caged up in camp, strictly observing his orders to remain there. The colonel was in the midst of this self congratulatory dissertation when its effect was completely spoiled. For at that moment about twenty privates of the 1st Michigan filed into the dining room and sat down. The Colonel's face "when his eye fell on us—was a sight for the gods!", one of the men recalled later. . . .

It was 10 o'clock the night of May 16 when the Michigan regiment arrived in Washington, but even at that late hour it was warmly welcomed. In those uncertain days Washington was in a state of perpetual jitters. Rebel flags could be observed from time to time on Arlington Heights across the Potomac. Many Washingtonians sympathized openly with the South. There was no assurance that enough loyal Union troops could be assembled to hold the city against a Confederate coup or attack.

Then, out of the night, came those fine, soldierly-looking men from Michigan, the first Western regiment to reach Washington. Loyal citizens breathed easier.

"The Michigan Rifle Regt. came into town last night about 10 o'clock, marching from the depot up the Avenue to Eleventh Street," the Washington correspondent of the *New York Evening Post* informed his newspaper. "They were preceded by a splendid band of music which soon aroused our citizens, and long before they had reached the quarters assigned to them, hundreds of people were out to give them welcome. The enthusiasm of the crowd was irrepressible, for this was the first Western regiment which had arrived at the capital."

To a lonely, burdened man in the White House, the band's blare and the tramp of feet brought the answer to a question which had bothered him: Would the Western states remain loyal to the Union and support it with men and resources?

Now he knew.

"Thank God," said Abraham Lincoln, "for Michigan!"

2.   The Faulkner Riot

Detroit Advertiser and Tribune

The headlines below graced the front page of the Detroit Advertiser and Tribune *on Saturday, March 7, 1863. In themselves they formed a synopsis of the horror story that followed. William Faulkner, a downtown saloon-keeper, who happened to be black, had been accused of sexual assault by two nine-year-old girls, Ellen Hoover, black, and Mary Brown, white. He was bound over for trial and was then found guilty by a jury on March 6.*

The wave of violence that swept over the city is chronicled here. After seven years in Jackson prison, Faulkner was proven to have never committed a crime. Mary Brown confessed that the girls had made up the tale to avoid being punished for coming home late.

CASE OF THE NEGRO FAULKNER
He is Convicted and Sent to the State Prison for Life
Attempt to Lynch Him on his Way to Jail
He is Protected by the Military
The Soldiers Assailed by the Mob Fire Upon it and Kill One Man
General Assault Upon the Negroes Throughout the City
Several Negroes Believed to be Murdered
A Large Number Horribly Beaten
Great Destruction of Property by Arson
Several Fires Under Way at the Same Time
Military Called on from Ypsilanti and Fort Wayne

"Case of the Negro Faulkner," *Detroit Advertiser and Tribune* (7 March 1863): 1–2.

Scenes, Incidents, &c.
Full Particulars Up to Two O'Clock this Morning

What Transpired in the Court Room

This (Friday) afternoon the Court assembled, and the jury were promptly in their seats, the Courtroom being densely crowded. Judge Witherell charged the jury in the only manner which the law seemed to justify. The jury retired, and after an absence of about ten minutes, brought in a verdict of guilty. His Honor then told the prisoner to stand up, and asked him if there was any reason why the sentence of the law should not be pronounced in his case, to which the prisoner replied that there was. He was then told to come forward and give his reasons, which he did. He said that the saloon which he keeps is a place of public resort; that the girls Mary Brown and Ellen Hoover, for reasons which he could not at the time comprehend, were—and had been for several days—in the habit of calling into the saloon; that he remonstrated against it and on several occasions, in the presence of one or two of his customers, he told them to leave. He was satisfied, since this crime had been laid against him, that they were accessories to a plot to get him removed from the building he occupies. He said that he had no time to get testimony, his principal witness being a tall young man who boards somewhere near the Michigan Central Depot, and he believed he was a map peddler, who came frequently to the saloon to get a lunch or dinner. He again expressed his belief that this was a plot got up by his enemies to injure his character and drive him from his place.[1]

His Honor, the judge, replied that if his statements were true, or had been established in evidence during the trial, this would have mitigated his case to some extent; but as there was no evidence to that effect, and as the jury after a careful hearing of the testimony, and a full knowledge of the law, had pronounced him guilty of one of the highest crimes known on the statute book, it only remained for him to pronounce the sentence. "You are therefore," said the Judge, "sentenced to the State Prison at Jackson, there to be confined during your natural life." The sentence was highly applauded by the crowd present. . . .

The Scene in Front of the City Hall and Vicinity

An order was then issued that the Courtroom be immediately cleared. A large concourse had already assembled in front of the City Hall and was constantly increasing, and violent threats were made to take the life of the prisoner. The officers were firm and resolute in their determination to convey him safely to the jail and, as a precaution, a detachment of the Provost Guard from the Barracks, under the Lieutenant Van Stam, was called to aid. When the troops arrived at the Campus Martius, they were hooted at and assailed with a variety of offensive weapons, but they behaved coolly and prudently. The prisoner was brought down from the Courtroom, and proceeded, escorted by several of the police and the soldiers up Monroe avenue and Randolph street to Gratiot street, followed by several thousand people, many of them bent upon seizing the prisoner. . . . Stones, brick-bats, mud and sticks were hurled against the soldiers, in a perfect shower. . . .

Upon reaching Gratiot street, the crowd had largely increased, and became more violent, until the officers reached the intersection of Gratiot and Clinton, when several of the soldiers were seriously injured by bricks and stones . . . an order was given to fire. The first volley was probably composed of blank cartridges. . . .

In Front of the Jail—A Man Killed

When the crowd had reached the front of the jail on Beaubien street, brickbats, stones, mud, and every available missile was thrown at the soldiers. . . . The soldiers were again ordered to fire a second volley, which they did, with fatal effect. One man, Charles Langer, daguerrotype artist, . . . was shot dead, the ball striking in the pit of his stomach. . . .

The authorities succeeded in securing the prisoner in jail, and the soldiers passed on to the Barracks. . . . The mob then seemed determined to wreak their vengeance upon Negroes that could be found in the street. A portion of the crowd then passed down Beaubien street, and assailed several Negro houses on the way. Some of them took a turn up East Lafayette, and stoned every

159

house known to be occupied by negroes, and broke in windows, tore down fences, and committed many other outrages. . . .

Morris Horan, blacksmith, who keeps shop on the corner of Larned and Wayne, was shot from the inside of a house occupied by negroes, next to the cooper shop on Beaubien street, near East Fort.

Soon after this the cooper shop was fired by the mob, which together with the dwelling house adjoining it, and a barn nearby, were completely destroyed.[2]

A dwelling house belonging to colored people, on the corner of Beaubien and Lafayette streets, was completely riddled. Almost the entire floor of the house was torn out, and the furniture piled up in the street in front and burned. . . .

The mob was composed, to a large extent, of young fellows brought up in the "street school"—rowdies and vagabonds, ignorant, unreasoning, and crazy with whisky and prejudice. Their spirit and their shouts were full of bitter and violent hatred for the negro. "Kill the nigger!" "D——n the nigger!" "Butcher all niggers!" "Stone that nigger house!" "Tear down that nigger dive!" "Every d——n nigger ought to be hung!" We will do the mob the justice to suppose that but few of them could read, and that they despised, above all things, the free school and the church. They are exactly the fittest material for political demagogues to work with. . . .

Nearly every respectable person in the crowd, and there were many present, from that pardonable motive, curiosity— condemned the rioters and endeavored to quiet them.[3] But arguing with the rioters was useless. . . . The mob had caught the political slang, and fiercely demanded the lynching of some "d——d Abolitionists," seeing the negroes had mostly hidden themselves. We saw fellows plunge across the muddy streets and dash along the sidewalks—in their insane fury to "kill a nigger,"—at a rate of speed that a loafer of their style was never known to practice except when running from an officer.

Occurrences in the Evening

A number of small wooden buildings on Lafayette street between Beaubien and St. Antoine were fired, and six of them with their furniture, were entirely destroyed. In one of the tenements, the inmates were locked in, and were threatened with death if they attempted to escape. But even the mob spirit relented when the wretches begged for mercy and burst the doors open to escape from being burned to death.

Robert Bennett, a molatoo [sic], was badly cut and rushed to the Biddle House. . . . Dr. Steward, a respectable colored Physician, residing on Clinton street, opposite the jail, an old grey headed negro, was fearfully beaten. . . .

While the main body of rioters were engaged in the destruction of the houses on Lafayette street, a large crowd of boys and men, probably forty in number, discovered an inoffensive colored man in an alley in the rear, and immediately assailed him with bricks, stones, and clubs, knocking him down in the ditch. Boys from eight to ten years of age seized bricks and stones and with the most fearful imprecations, such as "Pray, you d——n nigger, we will kill you!" rushed upon him. The negro was beaten very badly and has probably since died. We have not learned his name.[4]

Editor's Notes

1. It would be satisfying to have more information as to whether there was some basis in fact for Faulkner's fears. However, William Faulkner's name and address are not listed in any city directions, even in the later years when he had a market stall provided for him by an embarrassed citizenry.
2. The cooper was Whitney Reynolds. He lost seven hundred dollars and his tools.
3. Among the "respectable persons" involved was John J. Bagley, later governor of Michigan, and a worker for school equality and Catholic Bishop Lefèbvre. Most praise went to a courageous Irish police officer, Daniel Sullivan.

   Not so good as people went was the fire marshal, W. M. Champ, who admitted he had not allowed the fire hoses to be turned on the black homes while they were in flames because the mob had threatened to cut them if he did so. He saw his duty as protecting city property. He ordered adjacent white homes to be hosed down, however, "for the greatest good of the greatest number."

4. The victim, Joshua Boyd, was featured in later news accounts. Boyd was an escaped slave who had come north to "freedom" a few years earlier.

Other riot incidents were reported in the *Advertiser* during the following days, several due to research by the Reverend S. S. Hunting, Unitarian minister. Families with small children were forced to spend the rainy weekend in the woods east of town. Many went to Canada, as people had following the Blackburn incident a generation earlier.

3. A Northern Victory Does Not Create Equality

Detroit Advertiser and Gazette

The Detroit Advertiser and Gazette *worked persistently but without success for the passage of a new Michigan constitution that would give the vote to black males. I quote from two editorials, one published immediately before and the other immediately after the special election.*

Our readers will bear in mind that but a few days remain before they will be called upon to vote upon the new Constitution. We have very thoroughly discussed the provisions of this instrument, and if we have at all succeeded in our purpose, we have shown that it is superior to the present organic law. That it has no defects we have not pretended. . . . There is no such thing as unanimity to be attained in the support of the Constitution of a State. If on the whole, a Constitution is a good one, and we shall have future opportunity of remedying by amendment the more salient objections, it ought to secure the support of all good citizens. . . . The proposition for revision originally came from the Democratic press, the *Free Press* of this city, leading off

"Close Up the Column," *Detroit Advertiser and Gazette* (3 April 1868): 2.
"Election Results," *Detroit Advertiser and Gazette* (7 April 1863): 2.

163

in the discussion. Democrats, in common with Republicans, felt that we had outgrown our organic law, and were it not that the new Constitution secures Equal Suffrage, a large number of Democrats would vote for it. Leading Democrats in the State helped make it, and voted in detail for all of its principal provisions. It is opposed by the Democratic party now, not because they wish to defeat the Constitution as a whole but because they wish to defeat negro suffrage in it. . . .

We earnestly appeal to Republicans who for any cause, are meditating a vote against the Constitution, to temperately weigh the considerations we present. To defeat Equal Suffrage after liberating a race and pledging ourselves to their protection, is to prove recreant to our principles and to deny our record. To defeat Equal suffrage in Michigan, where there are about a thousand colored voters, and to establish it in South Carolina where the newly enfranchised colored citizens actually constitute a majority of the people—to enforce possible negro government in another state, while we will not permit one colored man when offset by one hundred white men, to vote in our own State, is disgraceful inconsistency and hypocrisy. . . .

[In commenting on the election results, the editors make their disappointment clear.]

The new Constitution is badly defeated. It was opposed by all the enemies of Impartial Suffrage in this region, and in many sections of the interior by the Prohibitionists, who feared the success of the revised instrument without the Prohibitory clause. It also encountered every adverse vote in the Republican party on the ground of its increased salaries, its exemption clauses, the railroad question, the agricultural college location, and other points involved in the various sections. These questions invited the scattering fire of thousands in the aggregate, all over the State. . . . We labored to the best of our ability to secure its adoption, we deeply regret its defeat, and in giving our last kick as its advocate we console ourselves with the reflection that we died game.[1]

Editor's Note

1. The constitution lost in every one of Detroit's ten wards, and most heavily in the working-class neighborhoods, where blacks may have been seen as potential job competitors.

   At the Fourth Ward voting place, August Thiele's grocery store at Hastings and Croghan (now Monroe), the vote was 93 for and 584 against the constitution. This was the neighborhood most affected by the brutal house burnings during the Faulkner riot five years earlier. In no other ward did voting rights do quite so badly, though in the Michigan Avenue home of John Kiely, "cigar maker," the measure was defeated by 729 to 133, and in William Wunsch's home-and-saloon polling place on Clinton Street, there were 149 votes for to 527 against.

   Among the business and professional voters, things were somewhat better, though there were no victories for black suffrage there, either. Voters from the great houses downtown voted at City Hall, and 144 of them favored the constitution, with 171 against. The votes from the elegant homes along Cass, Woodward, and Second north of Grand Circus Park were tallied at Steam Engine House No. 3 on Clifford Street. There were 508 for, with only 613 against.

   These statistics appeared in the late edition of the *Advertiser* of April 7.

4.   School Desegregation and the Workman Case

Supreme Court of Michigan

Joseph Workman was listed in the city directory as "porter (col'd) [colored]." He was also the father of a ten-year-old son on whose behalf he brought suit to force the admission of his son to the school nearest his home, the Duffield, rather than the nearest "colored school." The Detroit Board of Education fought the case all the way to the Michigan Supreme Court—and lost.

Reprinted here is an abridged version of The People ex. rel. Joseph Workman v. The Board of Education of Detroit, *including the arguments before the Michigan Supreme Court and the majority opinion in favor of Workman, delivered May 12, 1869, by Chief Justice Cooley.*

H. M. & W. E. Cheever, for relator [argument for Workman]:

The board of education of the city are a body corporate, . . . to them is committed the direction and regulation of the free schools of the city. . . . Section one of the act of 1842 provided that "the city of Detroit shall be considered as one school district, and hereafter all schools organized therein, . . . shall . . . be public and free to all children residing within the limits thereof, between the age of five and seventeen years, inclusive." . . .

[The legislature's] intention clearly was to commit the care and custody of the free schools of the city of Detroit to the respondents . . . to be by them carried on as nearly as possible in accor-

Supreme Court of Michigan, Workman v. Board of Education, *Michigan Reports* (April Term 1869): 399–499.

dance with the general state law, not to be "regulated" in such a way as to be virtually closed against one class of citizens, while open to others.

. . . By the law of the state, children must attend in the district where they reside . . . .

A "regulation" requiring children to go from the tenth ward to the ninth, a distance of over two miles, and pass other schools on their way, becomes virtually a prohibition of the benefits of the school system.

Again, the Duffield has its grades; the colored school is a primary school only; and the exclusion of the colored child from the union school is an absolute prohibition of an enjoyment of the higher grades of the free schools.

The power to regulate is not the power to prohibit. . . . The primary intention of the act is to give free schools to all children in the city. . . .

D. B. and H. M. Duffield, for respondents[1] [summing up for the board]:

Respondents insist that the [Workman child] is not entitled to the *mandamus* [the right to attend Duffield School], prayed for the following reasons:

1. Because it is at this time impossible for the respondents to comply with it on account of the lack of room in the schools. . . .

2. Because the relator has no such interest in the matter as entitles him to ask for a *mandamus*.

The petition should be made by the child excluded, by its next friend: . . .

3. Because the resolution of respondents requiring colored children to attend separate schools, established and maintained exclusively for them, is:

First. Authorized by statute.

Second. An exercise of their discretion, with which this court will not interfere; and,

Third. A reasonable regulation "for the good government and prosperity of the free schools of said city." . . .

There has been no exclusion of relator's child from the public schools of said city. The return expressly avers that the relator's child can, at any time, upon proper application, be admitted to the colored schools. . . .

This power to regulate the classification and distribution of the school children must be placed somewhere outside the scholars. . . .

Can it be said to be unreasonable for respondents to separate colored from white children in the public schools as long as stated? Comp. L. [Compiled Laws of Michigan] p. 950 . . . forbids intermarriage between them. . . .

. . . The fact is averred and admitted that there exists among a large majority of the white population of Detroit a strong prejudice or animosity against colored people, which is largely transmitted to the children in the schools, and that this feeling would engender quarrels and contention if colored children were admitted to the white schools.

Whether the association together of black and white children in the same schools would not equally foster and engender this prejudice may well be doubted. . . .

We submit that both upon principle and authority the *mandamus* should be denied.

COOLEY CH. J. [Chief Justice]:
. . . The legislature of 1867 passed an act amendatory of the primary school law, one section of which is as follows: "All residents of any district shall have an equal right to attend any school therein. Provided that this shall not prevent the grading of schools according to the intellectual progress of the pupils, to be taught in separate places when deemed expedient." . . .

It cannot be seriously urged that with this provision in force, the school board of any district which is subject to it may make regulations which would exclude any resident of the district from any of its schools, because of race or color, or religious belief, or personal peculiarities. It is too plain for argument that an equal right to all the schools, irrespective of all such distinctions, was meant to be established.

Does this provision apply to the city of Detroit? That city, as we have seen, is expressly declared to be "one school district", and is, therefore, within the words of the act of 1867. That the legislature seriously intended their declaration of equal rights in the schools to be partial in its operation, is hardly probable. . . .

The declaration is incorporated in the general primary school law. I am not aware that there is any organized portion of the state that does not come under some of the provisions of that law. The specially created union school districts [the larger towns and cities] are subject to it, except so far as the special legislation creating or governing them is inconsistent. The declaration in the Detroit free school act that the city shall constitute one school district, is idle for any other purpose than to connect the city with the primary school system which the general law establishes. . . . It is not true, therefore, that the primary school law has no application in the city of Detroit, or that we may say of any of its provisions respecting districts that Detroit is exempt from them. . . .

. . . And as all other portions of that law not inconsistent with the free school act apply to the city of Detroit, so must the section establishing equality of right in the schools apply also, unless it can be shown to be inconsistent. No inconsistency was pointed out on the argument, nor was any reason suggested as likely to have influenced the legislature to make that city an exception. . . .

. . . Yet, if we were to look outside the act of 1867 for the occasion of its passage, we should probably find that occasion to exist only in the city of Detroit, and in some two or three of the union or graded districts where distinctions based on color were kept up, which were unknown in other portions of the state. . . .

. . . We do not discover that there is anything in any of those statutes—and we include particularly in this statement the Detroit free school act—that overrules or modifies the requirement of the general law, that the right to attend the schools shall be possessed equally and impartially by all classes of residents.

The conclusion is inevitable that the legislature designed the impartial rule they established to be of universal application.

It remains to be seen whether there are any formal objections to the writ prayed for. It was suggested by the respondents that the father, as such, could not apply for a *mandamus* on behalf of his infant child, but that the child should apply by guardian. . . . The father is the natural guardian of the child. . . . Although the proceeding is for the benefit of the child, the duty of placing him in school is the parent's, and the father is entitled . . . to appeal to the courts for the removal of any unlawful impediments. It was also urged that the application for the writ did not show affirmatively that the child possessed the necessary qualifications for admission to the school. It shows, however, that the father applied for his admission, and offered to submit him to all the rules, examinations and regulations of the board with regard thereto, and was refused because of the child's color. . . .

As the statute of 1867 is found to be applicable to the case, it does not become important to consider what would otherwise have been the law [italics mine].[2]

Editor's Notes

1. For the Workman case the board of education hired the attorneys Henry and Divie Bethune Duffield, sons of the prominent minister for whom the school was named.

    Among their many arguments the Duffield brothers claimed "that there is a strong prejudice against the colored people among the majority of the population of the said city, and among many of the children in said schools, . . . and that the abolition of said colored schools, and the indiscriminate union and mingling of colored with white children in all the public schools, would be greatly prejudicial to the best interests of said public schools, and would engender strife and discord among the scholars thereof."

2. Ruling in favor of Joseph Workman, the court, speaking through Justice Cooley, held that the Detroit Board of Education was required to give equal access to education to Workman's son. Although Justice Cooley's other decisions have been widely studied in law schools for a century, this one apparently never reached the state's colleges of education. Though the labor-backed reform coalition of 1955–70 went far in removing the evils of discrimination, it was from a belief that "quality integrated education," the phrase of the late UAW attorney and board member Abe Zwerdling, was a good in itself. The statute of 1867 on which Cooley based his opinion was clearly essential if Michigan was to conform to the provisions of the new Fourteenth Amendment, which forbade the states to legislate inequality. It is still amazing that the Detroit Board and its lawyers tried so stubbornly to ignore its validity.

    Historians concerned with the history of Michigan blacks are well aware that racial integration has been late in coming to the schools—if indeed one believes that it has! However, few Michigan scholars or educational administrators have been aware how completely Cooley's decision on behalf of Joseph Workman and his son made innumerable, persistent actions of discrimination by the Detroit Board of Education over many years (and no doubt actions by some other Michigan boards of education) simply outside the law.

5. A New Power Structure: Wealth before and after the Civil War

Alexandra Ueland McCoy

To Alexandra McCoy we owe a specific knowledge of who were the wealthy of Detroit and Wayne County before and after the Civil War, as well as significant factors that may have helped determine their good fortune. For this story of wealth and power, I have chosen excerpts from McCoy's work describing the economic elite of 1844 and that of 1860 through 1866.

The research methods used for tracing the wealthy are thorough and innovative. For the 1860s group there were the extra resources of the federal census and the records of a special federal income tax levied during the Civil War. Information from the latter is referred to under the title "tax rolls" in Table 2.

The Economic Elite of 1844

Ninety-seven individuals made up the economic elite of Wayne County, Michigan, in 1844. These men were selected primarily on the basis of their known wealth with important economic roles as a secondary consideration. Tax assessment rolls for real and personal property for the city of Detroit and Wayne County provided the comprehensive measurement by which the men were ranked.[1] Wealth figures were based on the assessment formula then in operation, which was to rate property at 30% of actual cash value.[2] Therefore, Lewis Cass, whose real and per-

Alexandra Ueland McCoy, "Political Affiliations of American Economic Elites: Wayne County, Michigan, 1844, 1860, as a Test Case" (Ph.D. diss., Wayne State University, 1965), 55–92.

sonal property was assessed at $73,383, appears on Table 1, as being worth $244,365. . . .

Property in Wayne County was, of course, not as precise a measurement of wealth as an income tax would have been. It left out extensive ventures into land in other Michigan counties and in other states.[3] Personal wealth did not reveal itself entirely on the tax rolls where personal property was usually itemized as horses, carriages and furniture. Farmers and Mechanics Bank was assessed for $20,000 worth of stock, but nowhere does individual ownership of bank stock show up.

Nor is there any evidence of the investments of twenty-three men known to be involved in burgeoning copper companies.[4] Robert Stuart, a former American Fur Company official, who negotiated a treaty of sale of copper lands with the Indians, owned 125 shares "given gratis". Charles Moran, a leading landowner, held fifty shares in the Eagle Harbor Mining Company, along with Charles Howard, John Hurlburt, Shadrach Gillett and Fred Wetmore.

The predominance of realty in the tax rolls, while undoubtedly reflecting the major source of wealth, obscures the relative liquidity of individuals. Elon Farnsworth's plea for ten dollars from Solomon Sibley (valued at $19,330 and $33,093, respectively) suggests an occasional dire lack of cash as late as five years after the crash of 1837: "I am obliged to raise some money today and take the liberty to ask you for the ten dollars for which I gave you a receipt and was credited to your account in the Henry estate. I would not trouble you, but I suppose this fund is lying in the bank and I find it impossible to collect any old debts".

Indebtedness undoubtedly plagued many of these men. . . . The affairs of C. C. Trowbridge reveal the long struggles of a debtor struggling to pay off the obligations incurred when the banks went under after 1837. Trowbridge complained: . . . "the failure of the bank brought down upon my head the consequences of acts with which I had no more connection than the Grand Turk himself. I lost by this and another bank $25,000 which added to my other losses left me almost hopelessly in debt".

Trowbridge was probably sounding poor to Olcutt, his creditor, because in 1845 he was buying property worth over $1,000 in Allegan County, and in 1846 his friend Robert Stuart congratulated him on his expanding opportunities: "I am truly gratified at the good state of your affairs. Will you make anything out of the railroad? . . . "

Other evidence of economic standing to complement known wealth was sought for two reasons: first, to sustain the selection of men at the lower ranks, worth less than $15,000, and second, to include people in key positions who simply did not turn up on the tax rolls. Thus, nine individuals worth between $10,000 and $15,000 holding key positions were added to these seventy-two over $15,000 who were clearly of the top elite on the basis of wealth alone. The positions were members of the Board of Trade, officers in banks or corporations or manufacturers of concerns employing more than twenty hands. Sixteen who did not appear on the tax rolls were selected if they were officers or manufacturers of large concerns. . . . George Russel, for example, owned ferry boats and an iron foundry and engaged in land speculation but did not appear on the tax rolls.

Key positions were shown to be reliable indicators when careers were followed beyond 1844. Many of the men at the lower ranks had the enterprising qualities which would make them men of great wealth in 1860. Though not rich in 1844, H. P. Baldwin, Christian H. and Frederick Buhl, and James F. Joy showed their abilities by buying up the stock of the Michigan State Bank for 15% of face value before it re-opened in 1845.[5] It was the enterprise of these men which gave them a foothold, because during the early forties most of the capital for railroads and banks came from eastern sources. James F. Joy's promotion of the sale of the Michigan Central brought him out of the limited scope of debt-collecting for banks into the large sphere where he was to make his fortune.

Manufacturers were identified from a study of Detroit industry made in 1848. This list [from the *Detroit Daily Advertiser* June 16 and August 22, 1848] was of inestimable value because it described the 139 establishments then operating either as to number of employees, annual value of product, or in the case of lumber, total [board] produced.[6]

Once selected, the elite was divided as to economic role, degree of wealth and time of arrival in Wayne County. . . .

The attempt was to assign roles according to probable major source of income. All men chosen from the tax rolls were land-

Industry in old Detroit. *Detroit City Directory* of 1859. (Courtesy of Bill Lynch.)

owners, for example, but only men who had no other apparent major source of income were identified as landowners. To recognize its importance to a frontier economy, fur was listed where it represented rise to wealth, even though the actual trade had passed its peak. . . Classified as non-specialized entrepreneurs were men who had interests diversified beyond one business and a directorship. Josiah L. Dorr, for example, was a merchant, part owner of the Detroit Iron Company, and a director both in a copper company and a bank. Bankers were often lawyers; they are classified solely on their active officership in 1844. Thus, Elon Farnsworth, a lawyer in 1844, became a banker in 1860.

The wide divergence in wealth suggested an investigation of the relationship of economic roles to wealth. Landowners and fur fortunes were almost exclusively concentrated among the top (above $50,000) and medium ($25,000 to $50,000) brackets. . . .

All other roles were concentrated in the low bracket, with lawyers, bankers and manufacturers conspicuously lacking among the highest incomes. This division, favoring roles natural to a frontier economy, suggests that early arrival was also a key factor. It is therefore not surprising to note that 72% of the men at the top of the wealth scale were in Wayne County before 1820, in contrast to the majority of the lower ranks who came after 1830.

The value of arriving early might seem to suggest that the top members of the elite were self-made men. Quite the contrary was true. Out of a total of thirty-two well-to-do fathers known for the entire ninety-seven [members of the elite], twelve of these belonged to the eighteen men worth more than $50,000.

The likelihood is that a much larger number of these men enjoyed an advantaged early environment to enable them to start a business in the West, where $5,000 or $6,000 was required to purchase a good stock.

. . . There was an easy manner, a democratic stance among the economic elite in the early days. Jacob Farrand recalled: "The people here in the earlier days of Detroit went along just about as they were; men of business lived along in a conservative sort of way, one year and another, devoid of any aristocracy. All the old inhabitants were people of a social nature inviting to each others houses and lived along in an enjoyable way".[7]

[Some merchants who retired] . . . became capitalists or bankers. These were the men who saw the new avenues for making great fortunes. They became the leaders of the group designated as the economic elite of 1860.

Table 1
The Economic Elite of 1844—Bases for Selection and Economic Role

Listed According to Wealth		To Detroit	Economic Role
Lewis Cass	$244,365	1813	Landowner
Oliver Newberry	$179,553	1820	Shipping
DeGarmo Jones	$116,150	1818	Non-Specialized
Shubael Conant	$110,882	Born	Merchant
John R. Williams	$117,459	Born	Landowner
James Abbott	$116,523	Born	Fur, copper
John Biddle	$116,207	1820's	Fur
Joseph Campau	$111,791	Born	Fur
Barnabas Campau	$103,672	Born	Fur
Peter Desnoyers	$ 92,241	Before 1820	Merchant
Josiah R. Dorr	$ 79,144	1825	Non-Specialized
Edmund A. Brush	$ 77,704	1802	Landowner
Antoine Beaubien	$ 75,124	Born	Landowner
William Brewster	$ 71,878	1815	Fur
Franklin Moore	$ 58,308	1833	Merchant
Zachariah Chandler	$ 58,275	1833	Merchant
Charles Moran	$ 56,809	Born	Landowner
John Drew	$ 51,521		Merchant
Jonathan Kearsley	$ 48,151	1819	Landowner
John Hurlburt	$ 47,892		Fur
Robert Stuart	$ 46,959	Before 1820	Fur
Thomas C. Sheldon	$ 46,786	1817	Landowner
Jonathon L. King	$ 43,872	1829	Merchant, Mfr.
Francis Eldred	$ 39,294	1816	Merchant, Mfr.
Dominique Riopelle	$ 39,160	Born	Landowner
John McDonnell	$ 37,395	1812	Landowner
David Cooper	$ 35,407	1799	Merchant
Darius Lamson	$ 34,132	1830's	Merchant
John Owen	$ 34,054		Merchant
John Palmer	$ 33,699	1818	Merchant

Table 1 (cont.)

Listed According to Wealth		To Detroit	Economic Role
Solomon Sibley	$ 33,093	Before 1810	Mfr., Quarry
Thomas Rowland	$ 32,733	1812	Landowner
Pierre Teller	$ 29,304	Before 1830	Merchant
Chas. C. Trowbridge	$ 27,579	1819	Banker
Alex C. McGraw	$ 26,640	1809	Merchant, Mfr.
Theodore Romeyn	$ 25,363	1835	Lawyer
Levi Cook	$ 25,557	1815	Merchant
Louis Davenport	$ 25,041	1830's	Shipping
William Woodbridge	$ 24,718	1812	Lawyer
Douglass Houghton	$ 24,598	1830	Banker
David Thompson	$ 23,829		Landowner
Shadrach Gillet	$ 23,676	1815	Non-Specialized
John Watson	$ 23,476		Merchant
Moses L. Dickinson	$ 23,176	1831	Merchant, Mfr.
Eustache Chapoton	$ 23,026	Born	Builder
Charles Desnoyers	$ 22,693	Born	Merchant
Henry N. Walker	$ 22,680	1834	Banker, Lawyer
Eurotas P. Hastings	$ 21,934	1825	Merchant
Frederick Wetmore	$ 21,811	1841	Merchant
Richard H. Hall	$ 21,645	1836	Merchant
Alanson Sheley	$ 21,534	1831	Builder
W. N. Carpenter	$ 21,328	1826	Merchant
Charles Brush	$ 21,078	Born	Landowner
Harmon DeGraff	$ 20,313	1837	Merchant, Mfr.
Buckminster Wight	$ 20,273	1832	Sawmill
George F. Porter	$ 20,855	1829	Banker, Lawyer
Thomas Coquillard	$ 19,906	Born	Mason
Elon Farnsworth	$ 19,330	1822	Lawyer
Alexander Newbould	$ 19,064		Merchant
Lewis Goddard	$ 18,697		Banker
James F. Joy	$ 18,564	1836	Mich. State Bank, Lawyer
James A. Van Dyke	$ 18,691	1834	Copper, Lawyer
John Scott	$ 17,649	1829	Builder
Peter DesNoyers	$ 17,629	Born	Merchant
William Chittenden	$ 17,149	1835	Central R.R.
J. Nicolson Elbert	$ 16,899	1840	Non-Specialized
John Roberts	$ 16,816	1820	Merchant, Mfr.

Table 1 (cont.)

Listed According to Wealth		To Detroit	Economic Role
Alpheus S. Williams	$ 16,533	1836	Non-Specialized
Francis Cicotte	$ 16,317	Born	Landowner
Alexander D. Fraser	$ 16,137	1823	Lawyer
John G. Atterbury	$ 15,984	1830's	Lawyer
Alvah Ewers	$ 14,418	1829	Merchant
Samuel Pitts	$ 14,069	1831	Mfr., Lumber
Theodore Williams	$ 13,852	Born	Merchant
Henry P. Baldwin	$ 12,820	1838	Manufacturer
Chauncey Hurlbut	$ 12,654	1825	Merchant
Benjamin Kercheval	$ 12,097	1821	Merchant
Orville Dibble	$ 11,655	1830's	Hotel Prop.
Alfred Dwight	$ 11,655	1833	Non-Specialized
George Bates	$ 10,000	1834	Copper, Lawyer, Banker

[Most of the following names on the list have only sources of wealth indicated, sometimes judged by number of employees. There are also more gaps in the information available about this group. "Non-specialized" includes such mixtures as ferry boats and foundries, or newspapers and copper. Robert Banks used his "25 hands" in the manufacture of clothing and is the only black who was wealthy enough to make the list.]

Table 1 (cont.)

Listed According to Wealth		To Detroit	Economic Role
Robert Banks	25 hands		Merchant, Mfr.
William Barclay	45 hands		Mfr., Iron
Christian Buhl	25 hands	1833	Mfr., Merchant, Banker
Frederick Buhl	25 hands	1833	Mfr., Merchant, Banker
Charles Howard	Banker	1840	Non-Specialized, Copper
Oliver Hyde	56 hands	1832	Mfr., Foundry

Table 1 (cont.)

Listed According to Wealth		To Detroit	Economic Role
Silas Kendrick	64 hands	1837	Mfr., Foundry
George B. Russel	Ferry	1836	Non-Specialized, Iron, Builder
William F. Smith	Sawmill	1841	Manufacturer
George B. Throop	Bank Pres.	1832	Banker, Lawyer
Wesley Truesdail	Non-Spec.	1836	Banker, Copper Sawmill
John Welles	Bank Cashier		Banker
Gurdon Williams	Railroad		R. R. Pres.
Charles Jackson	$15,700	1816	Builder
Horace Hallock	60 hands	1831	Merchant, Mfr.
Francis Raymond	60 hands	1832	Mfr. (with Hallock)
William Gooding	120 hands		Mfr., Steamboats

Notes: [The first] eighteen men having property over $50,000 are classified as "High".
[The next] twenty men, representing approximate wealth of between $25,000 and $50,000, are classified as "Medium".
The next [group of men] with wealth over $25,000 are classified as "Low".
[Throughout the table, gaps occur when the information was not available. Some interesting "economic indicators" have been deleted, such as membership in the Board of Trade, or additional directorships held, but all information given for the basic categories has been included.]

The Economic Elite Of 1860

. . . One hundred and thirty-five men worth more than $50,000 made up the economic elite. In 1844 there were only eighteen individuals who surpassed this qualifying lower limit and more than half of the elite were worth less than $25,000. Wealth therefore was a sufficient basis for selection without regard to economic role. Selection was buttressed by the existence of two sources listing property, the Detroit tax rolls and the census of 1860.[8] Income was also used as an indicator of wealth. Thanks to the Civil War income tax and the custom of printing lists of taxpayers in the local papers, the top Detroit incomes for 1864 could be identified.

The formula worked out for combining income and property as criteria was as follows: Only the thirty-four incomes over

$10,000 were used as a basis for selection because the figures were for 1864 rather than 1860. Since anyone in 1860 with an income between $5,000 and $10,000 was accounted among the "rich", those over $10,000 would seem to be economic leaders, even interpolating back to 1860. Furthermore, these high incomes undoubtedly concealed greater wealth. The tax of 1864 excluded [such] income as dividends or interest received from banks, trust companies, railroads, canals or turnpike companies, or gains from the sale of real estate held more than one year. Thus the $91,037 received by millionaire E. B. Ward did not reflect his extensive property in steamboats, railroads, plank roads and banks.

With property evaluations ranging from $50,000 to $1,000,000, only those worth over $200,000 were ranked "High", bracketed with men having incomes over $10,000. . . . The existence of two sources for 1860 on real and personal property provided an excellent check on the identity of the elite. Although the Census evaluation and local property value did not always coincide, the existence of two records showed unmistakably who the rich men were. The great majority show up as men of considerable property on both lists. Those who appeared on one list with property between $100,000 and $200,000 were ranked "Medium" and those between $50,000 and $100,000, "Low. . . . "

The rise in the value of rich men's holdings since 1844 appears more striking when one considers that 1860 was not a boom period—prices had remained depressed since the crisis of 1857 with only a slight improvement in the middle of 1860. . . . Although Detroit was far from matching New York City's seventy-nine men who reported incomes of $100,000 or more in 1864, 315 incomes over $2,000 was not a bad showing next to New York's 10,900 in 1863. Compared against the incomes of the general population of New York, the wealth of Detroit's elite stands out sharply: in the 1860's only about 1% of the population of New York received incomes of $842 or more. When it is also remembered that burgeoning dividends were omitted from income calculations, the wealth of the Wayne County elite supports Rufus Tucker's conclusion that during the Civil War period "the wealthy were wealthier in relation to the mass than now, although there were fewer of them".

A breakdown of the composition of the 1860 elite according to economic roles shows significant changes in the economy. The non-specialized entrepreneur gives way to the capitalist. Instead of engaging in banking, selling, and small manufacturing, the successful merchant now invests the proceeds of his successful business in other firms and becomes the director of several. The Buhl brothers are good examples of the merchant turned capitalist, although Frederick Buhl modestly referred to himself in the 1860 Census as "hatter". Their early venture as fur merchants and hat manufacturers came to a profitable close in 1853. C. H. Buhl bought out a hardware firm, invested extensively in railroads and by 1863 had enough to put one million dollars into iron manufacturing in Pennsylvania.

Despite industrial growth, landowners were the leading group, representing 26% of the 1860 elite. Their predominance reflects the vital role land values played in the growth of American fortunes. . . . Eight were heirs of large landowners and six were retired merchants. Others were actually modern real estate operators. Partners William B. Wesson and Albert Crane dominated the field and made fortunes as pioneers in land-dividing. They were the first to sell lots on time with only a small down payment. That these men did differentiate their roles is seen by their designations in the 1860 Census. While Crane and J. W. Johnston referred to themselves as "real estate dealers", David Thompson and Alexander Newbould were "speculators", Wesson called himself a "landowner", and seven put themselves as "gentlemen". John C. Williams was a "farmer". George Duffield was actually a leading Presbyterian clergyman, but since this role would hardly have been the direct route to a fortune worth $50,000, he has been called a landowner. Like other landowners, he was alert to the possibility of making money elsewhere. . . .

Quite predictably, manufacturers also outnumber the merchants among the elite. . . . Eleven of these "industrialists" were in lumber manufacturing, typically combined with large operations in lumber lands. Samuel Pitts and Buckminster Wight continued from profitable beginnings in the forties, surpassed, however, by New England lumbermen, F. Adams, N. W. Brooks, Charles Merrill and Henry Benson, who came to Detroit in the fifties. New men and earlier starters shared other fields. E. B. Ward, who made a fortune in the forties as a vessel owner, began his enormously successful career as iron manufacturer when he established the Wyandotte Rolling Mill in 1853. D. M. Richardson built the first match factory in 1856 and two others got rich with tobacco: K. C. Barker and Company was built in 1848, John J. Bagley's firm in 1853. Alexander McGraw and Henry P. Baldwin had expanded their shoe manufacturing and merchanting operations—Baldwin's income was next to Ward's in 1864 at $33,647. Other basic products which supported the elite were beer (William C. Duncan and Richard Hawley), meat (John Hull), and leather (George Curtis and George Kirby).

An interesting type was the doctor turned capitalist. Doctors, who required only the most rudimentary training to practice, were attracted to growing towns where the opportunities in non-medical pursuits engaged them to such an extent that it was "often difficult to differentiate between their merchandising activities and professional practice". Dr. George Russel abandoned his practice as early as 1837 to begin his career as a manufacturer in the construction of ferry boats. Dr. Eliphalet M. Clark's medical practice was so subservient to his industrial pursuits that even a medical source considered only his "first grain elevator at the foot of Fort Street and his enterprise to manufacture locomotives in 1855". There is no available evidence of Dr. Samuel Truedell's activities as a businessman, but it is doubtful that he could have accumulated his estate on the basis of medical practice alone. With professional man William Woodbridge, whose sky-rocketing wealth had placed him fourth among the elite, Truedell has been called a landowner.

A man's economic activity did not seem to have as great a bearing on his relative wealth as it did in 1844 when landowners and fur fortunes monopolized the higher ranks. . . . Capitalists and manufacturers had the greatest likelihood of attaining the high and medium brackets of the wealthy. Bankers and lawyers were, predictably, still in the low brackets.

Mobility, seen as the achievement of wealth by men of lower class origins, was difficult to determine. Evidence was too scanty to determine with any certainty to what extent the elite of 1860 were self-made men. The forty-one men known to have well-to-do fathers divided among the various ranks as follows: High 18; Medium 12; Low 11.

There was, however, a marked persistence in holding on to wealth once gained. The carry-over from the elite of 1844 was pronounced. Taking into consideration those known to have died or moved away, only one-fifth of the 1844 elite failed to qualify in 1860. The old elite divided themselves in the different ranks as follows: High 27%; Medium 27%; Low 46%. Those who were at the top in 1844 tended to stay there. Only one took a fall. John Drew, who had been worth more than $50,000 in 1844 as a merchant, had become a retired "gentleman" with a modest estate of $22,000.

As a postscript to the discovery that wealth tended to multiply and perpetuate itself, seventeen of the men of 1860 or their inheriting descendants were listed among Detroit's forty-two millionaires in 1892.[9] [Those names included on the earlier list are indicated by asterisks.]

Table 2
The Economic Elite of 1860—Bases for Selection and Economic Role

High: Property worth over $200,000 and / or income over $10,000

	Property (Census)	Property (Tax Roll)	Income (1864)	Economic Role
Joseph Campau*	$3,400,000	$ 380,653		Landowner
Lewis Cass*		$1,189,725	$22,700	Landowner
E. B. Ward	$1,007,000	$ 89,743	$91,037	Capitalist
Wm. Woodbridge*	$ 330,000	$ 599,916		Landowner
Albert Crane	$ 210,000	$ 474,704		Landowner
Charles Merrill	$ 210,000	$ 409,923	$11,026	Lumber
Z. Chandler*	$ 300,000	$ 433,288	$56,236	Merchant
E. A. Brush*		$ 392,646		Landowner
James F. Joy*		$ 365,584	$19,918	Capitalist
William Hale		$ 354,228		Landowner
George B. Russel*		$ 333,166		Capitalist
Wm. B. Wesson	$ 105,000	$ 313,592		Landowner
C. H. Buhl*	$ 250,000	$ 217,682	$33,400	Capitalist
J. C. D. Williams	$ 125,000	$ 249,750		Landowner
John Owen*	$ 180,000	$ 245,254	$19,522	Capitalist
Alex M. Campau		$ 232,184		Landowner
Luther Beecher		$ 221,944		Merchant
David Cooper*	$ 93,000	$ 208,500		Landowner
H. P. Baldwin	$ 115,000	$ 208,291	$33,647	Capitalist
Henry E. Benson		$ 141,774	$30,480	Lumber
David Whitney			$30,000	Lumber

Table 2 (cont.)

High: Property worth over $200,000 and / or income over $10,000

	Property (Census)	Property (Tax Roll)	Income (1864)	Economic Role
K. C. Barker		$ 48,285	$29,611	Manufacturer
Chas. DuCharme	$ 55,000	$ 50,449	$29,400	Merchant
Allen Shelden		$ 40,950	$27,500	Merchant
Reuben Town		$ 49,950	$27,500	Merchant
Edward Orr			$27,498	Merchant
N. W. Brooks		$ 38,000	$24,100	Lumber
E. Ward	$ 18,000	$ 52,558	$24,508	Shipping
J. J. Bagley			$23,180	Manufacturer
Richard Hawley		$167,998	$22,205	Manufacturer
Francis Adams		$ 38,661	$18,803	Lumber
Franklin Moore*	$ 41,000	$ 74,259	$19,181	Merchant
F. Buhl*	$ 83,000	$ 82,750	$16,280	Capitalist
S. Pitts*		$140,526	$19,829	Lumber
John Stephens	$140,000	$143,134	$18,730	Merchant
Ira Davis	$ 65,000	$ 27,072	$14,777	Shipping
D. M. Richardson			$14,650	Manufacturer
George Curtis			$14,500	Manufacturer
C. W. Jackson	$ 32,300	$ 77,439	$14,226	Manufacturer
J. Wiley		$ 66,200	$14,179	Manufacturer
George Kirby	$ 45,000	$ 66,933	$12,708	Manufacturer
G. F. Bagley			$11,326	Merchant
George Peck			$10,913	Capitalist
S. Mandelbaum		$ 50,782	$10,000	Capitalist
Francis Palms*		$ 25,641		Landowner [lumber]

Medium: Property worth between $100,000 and $200,000

	Property (Census)	Property (Tax Roll)	Economic Role
Charles Moran*	$101,000	$198,468	Landowner
Alexander McGraw	$135,000	$192,773	Merchant, Mfr.
Wm. S. Biddle	$120,000	$191,308	Landowner
J. Mott Williams	$ 52,000	$163,236	Landowner
John P. Clark	$162,600	$ 62,637	Shipping
Jacob Beeson	$160,000	$ 29,304	Banker

Table 2 (cont.)

Medium: Property worth between $100,000 and $200,000

	Property (Census)	Property (Tax Roll)	Economic Role
John Hull	$156,000	$129,397	Merchant
Jacob S. Farrand	$145,000	$ 59,440	Banker
Henry Haigh	$154,000	$ 17,482	Merchant
Richard H. Hall*		$155,993	Merchant
Samuel Lewis	$ 77,500	$144,062	Capitalist
N. P. Stewart	$ 60,000	$142,357	Banker
Theodore Eaton	$ 95,000	$141,247	Capitalist
J. W. Johnston	$110,000	$140,397	Landowner
H. H. Emmons	$140,000	$102,064	Landowner
William A. Butler	$ 42,000	$139,860	Banker
Shubael Conant*	$121,500	$134,348	Capitalist
Moses Dickinson*	$ 35,000	$130,039	Landowner
Alanson Sheley*		$124,125	Capitalist
W. C. Duncan	$ 55,000	$121,794	Manufacturer
David Thompson*	$120,000	$100,982	Landowner
O. M. Hyde*	$120,000	$ 62,271	Capitalist
Eustache Chapoton*	$ 24,000	$112,809	Builder
Ebenezer Penniman	$112,500		Merchant
E. M. Clark	$ 76,000	$111,205	Capitalist
Jonathon L. King		$110,556	Merchant, Mfr.
Peter Desnoyers*	$ 36,000	$107,026	Landowner
W. N. Carpenter*	$105,000	$ 61,605	Landowner
Albert Ives	$100,000	$104,678	Banker
Francis Eldred*	$ 50,000	$102,897	Merchant, Mfr.
Samuel P. Brady		$101,614	Merchant
John C. Williams	$101,000	$ 94,155	Landowner
Gabriel Chene	$ 53,000	$101,731	Landowner
C. C. Trowbridge*	$100,000	$ 62,853	Banker
H. N. Strong	$146,000	$101,481	Shipping

Low: Property worth between $50,000 and $100,000

	Property (Census)	Property (Tax Roll)	Economic Role
A. D. Fraser*		$99,067	Lawyer
Buckminster Wight*	$33,000	$99,594	Lumber

Table 2 (cont.)

Low: Property worth between $50,000 and $100,000

	Property (Census)	Property (Tax Roll)	Economic Role
Ashael S. Bagg	$80,000	$99,733	Hotel Prop.
Henry T. Backus	$80,000	$18,731	Lawyer
Alex. H. Newbould*	$66,000	$94,738	Landowner
Dominique Riopelle, Jr.		$94,821	Landowner
Hugh Moffat	$50,000	$92,407	Lumber
William Barclay*	$66,800	$91,575	Manufacturer
George F. Porter*		$91,297	Banker
Gurdon Williams	$90,000	$43,883	Capitalist
George Foote	$87,000	$53,280	Merchant
Chauncey Hurlbut*		$86,945	Merchant
James Burns		$86,746	Merchant
Theodore Williams*		$84,781	Landowner
Oliver Bourke	$85,000	$21,395	Merchant
Caleb Ives		$85,364	Banker
Ransom Gardner	$75,000	$83,333	Merchant
C. A. Trowbridge	$75,000	$79,920	Manufacturer
Henry A. Wight	$35,000	$79,254	Lumber
Stanley G. Wight	$33,000	$79,254	Lumber
Francis Raymond*	$20,000	$76,590	Merchant
F. B. Sibley	$60,000	$75,880	Manufacturer
S. B. Scott	$75,000		Merchant
Caleb Van Husan	$70,000	$73,593	Capitalist
George Duffield	$50,000	$70,096	Landowner
Alexander Stowell	$70,000	$11,655	Landowner
Henry N. Walker*	$70,000		Banker
John Palmer*	$12,000	$67,832	Landowner
Alexander Chapoton	$40,000	$67,732	Builder
Jared C. Warner	$66,000		Landowner
George B. Truax	$60,000	$65,054	Lumber
Eugene St. Amour	$65,000	$94,821	Builder
William Ten Eyck	$64,130	$61,921	Landowner
Charles Jackson*	$64,000	$50,749	Builder
Colin Campbell	$23,000	$63,603	Merchant
William Kieft Coyl	$60,000	$62,637	Landowner
Giles B. Slocum		$61,921	Merchant
Frederick Wetmore*		$61,671	Merchant
Levi Cook*	$60,000	$60,772	Banker

Table 2 (cont.)

Low: Property worth between $50,000 and $100,000

	Property (Census)	Property (Tax Roll)	Economic Role
Samuel Truedell	$60,200	$60,106	Landowner
Darius Lamson*		$60,106	Landowner
Thomas Lockwood	$60,000	$26,007	Lawyer
Elon Farnsworth*	$50,000	$58,774	Banker
Thomas F. Abbott	$55,000		Merchant
Geroge W. Bissell	$50,000	$48,701	Merchant
F. J. B. Crane	$50,000	$49,726	Landowner

Other members of previous elite [1844]

Horace Hallock	$30,000	$44,788	Merchant, Mfr.
A. S. Williams	$39,000		Gentleman
Thomas Coquillard	$13,520	$33,300	Builder
George C. Bates		$22,105	Lawyer
John A. Welles	$25,000		Lawyer
John Drew	$22,000		Capitalist
John Roberts	$14,000	$15,251	Retired
Theodore Romeyn	$15,000		Lawyer
J. N. Elbert	$16,500		Postoffice Clk.

Notes

1. "Detroit Real and Personal Property Tax Assessment Roll, 1844," Burton Historical Collection, (hereinafter referred to as BHC); "Wayne County and Personal Property Tax Assessment Roll, 1844", BHC. "Springwells Real and Personal Tax, Assessment Roll, 1845", in William Woodbridge Papers, BHC. The existence of more than one record provided a good check. The Detroit records were more complete and therefore the main source. A few individuals qualified on the basis of land owned in the townships outside the city.
2. Michigan Historical Records Survey Project, Division of Professional and Service Projects, Works Progress Administration, *Inventory of the*

Municipal Archives of Michigan, City of Detroit, No. 10, City Treasurer (Detroit: The Survey, 1940), 18.

3. Abbott Papers, BHC; E. P. Hastings Papers, BHC; C. C. Trowbridge Papers, BHC; "Land Book of Alfred Dwight", A. A. Dwight Papers, BHC; Robert Stuart Papers, BHC.

4. Jacob Houghton, Jr. and T. W. Bristol, *Reports of Wm. A. Burt and Bela Hubbard, Esqs. on the Geography, Topography, and Geology of the U.S. Survey of the Mineral Region of the South Shore of Lake Superior for 1845* (Detroit: C. Wilcox, 1846, 92–102). Officers of working companies: Degarmo Jones, Gurdon Williams, Charles Howard, John Owen, George E. Bates, Wesley Truesdail, A. H. Newbould, Pierre Teller, James A. Van Dyke. Officers of organized companies: C. M. Hyde, A. S. Williams, James Abbott, James Van Dyke, Peter Desnoyers, F. Cicotte, John Drew, Theodore Williams, George C. Bates.

5. Also George F. Porter, Z. Chandler, C. C. Trowbridge, President, Alex H. Adams, Cashier, Burton, *Wayne [County]*, II, 1224.

6. *Detroit Daily Advertiser*, June 16, 1848, August 22, 1848. . . . The twenty-two largest firms—employing more than 25 hands, doing annual business worth $50,000 or more or producing more than 2,000,000 [board feet] of lumber were: S. N. Kendrick, Machine Shop, 64 hands, $70,000 per annum; H. (Wm.) Barclay, Michigan Foundry, 45 hands, $70,000 per annum; William Gooding, Ship and Steamboat Building, 120 hands; William Smith, Eagle Steam Saw Mill, 36 hands (partner Alfred Dwight); Robert Banks, Clothing Manufacturer, 25 hands; Hallock and Raymond (Horace Hallock and Francis Raymond Clothing), 60 hands, $50,000 per annum; O. M. Hyde, Hydraulic Foundry and Machine Shop, 56 hands; F. and C. H. Buhl, Hat Manufacturers, 25 hands, $30,000 per annum; Wight's Steam Saw Mill, 2,000,000 feet (Buckminster Wight); Moore's Lumber Yard, 2,600,000 feet (Franklin Moore); Black River Lumber Yard, 2,500,000 feet (Alanson Sheley, manager). . . .

7. "Detroit in History", Palmer Scrapbooks, IV, BHC, 210.

8. "Finance City Treasurer Tax Roll Real and Personal Property, 1860", BHC; Eighth Census of the United States, 1860. Michigan. Microfilm Copy, BHC.

9. E. Alfred Brush and Lillie Thompson (son and granddaughter of E. A. Brush), Christian H. Buhl, Mrs. Dr. Book and Francis Palms (daughter and son of Francis Palms), Estate of John J. Bagley, Theodore H. Eaton, Estate of Jacob S. Farrand, James F. Joy, William B. Moran (real estate inherited in part from Charles Moran), Mrs. T. W. Palmer (daughter of Charles Merrill, inherited), Allan Shelden, Alanson Sheley, Estate of William B. Wesson, David Whitney, Jr., Luther Beecher, William Butler.

Editor's Note

Government record sources listed under notes 1, 2, and 5 should be of considerable value to other scholars, especially the inventory of municipal archives conducted by the Works Progress Administration, listed in note 2. I have deleted a number of McCoy's notes for reasons of length. I have also renumbered the second data table (Table 5 in original work) for clarity.

Part VI

The Gilded Age Comes to Detroit

The Gilded Age Comes to Detroit

The period we know as the Gilded Age appears abruptly after the Civil War, and somehow it is surprising to find it occurring in Detroit. We are used to tales of the great fortunes of New York and Philadelphia, or of the California railroad barons. In Detroit, however, that midwestern port city, a supply center for the backcountry, the changes were profound. Industrialization seemed to be almost concurrent with the war. Of course, this was a Northern city and, more than that, a city in the state that claimed the Republican party as its own—winning people on a winning side. The war economy and party loyalty helped to create new wealth.

We have noted from Alexandra McCoy's list of the wealthy of 1866 a number who had been wealthy in 1844. Some of those names will continue to occur in any discussion of Detroit's elite through the next years: Buhl, Joy, and Ward, among others. But the base for wealth had already begun to shift from land ownership or "merchant" to other means of getting or keeping wealth. There were newcomers. 1866 is a bit too early for either Strohs or Fords. Yet a Henkel daughter married a Stroh, even if neither family was a part of the Gilded Age. Industrial growth would add new names and new industries for those who became, or remained, wealthy. The McMillans produced railroad cars but had been lumbermen. Lumber and railroading were strongly linked together from 1865 on. Senator McMillan was said to have the largest yacht on the Great Lakes and one of the more opulent mansions in Washington.

Even more lavish was the home of Congressman Hale of Maine. Hale was described as a "bon vivant" who had his money by way of his wife, the only child of Senator Zachariah Chandler. Eber Ward, as Vinyard informed us, moved from shipping to heavy industry. Industries expanded to include others, usually related, and the banks and insurance structures that strengthened them. The interlocking directorships of these firms were held by the new wealthy and, always, some of the old. The scope of Detroit's wealth and its far-flung ambitions is illustrated by the fact that before and after the Spanish-American War several prominent Detroiters had land investments in Cuba. Homer Warren, Detroit's preeminent realtor, even opened an office in Havana for a time.

In general, land ownership remained important but became an auxiliary, rather than a main source, to major wealth until the real estate expansion of the 1920s. Some land within the city of Detroit, however, was useful as homesites. On East Jefferson, beginning to crowd out the old French homes, and on downtown Lafayette, Fort, and Washington streets (later Washington Boulevard), rose the new mansions of the wealthy, complete with carriage houses. In a few years they would extend northward out Woodward Avenue, to be followed by luxurious apartments. By the turn of the century a rental in the Palms on East Jefferson or the Addison on Woodward (now a check-cashing center for the poor) was enough to guarantee a young couple a place in the social register.

In the homes, managed by women, even more than in the clubs dominated by men, we catch the flavor of Detroit's Gilded Age. Downtown, on West Lafayette Street, the ladies were "at home" on Tuesdays, with flowers and music in the drawing rooms. Other streets chose other afternoons when the lady of the house waited at home for callers. The evenings saw still more music, as well as cards, dinners, or supper parties after the guests returned from a play at one of several downtown theaters.

Included in this section is an account of summers on a small (compared to Senator McMillan's) ninety-five-foot yacht. It was possible, however, to operate even a yacht with informal intimacy. That was the case with the steam-and-sail *Uarda*. Steam-and-sail yachts were of relatively short duration on the Great Lakes, but to Cameron D. Waterman, the *Uarda*'s owner, steam seemed the only rational way to get to the north shore of Lake Superior or Georgian Bay. Sailing, along with fishing of course, was the most fun when you got there.

With any size of boat, it was possible to run up to the "Old Club" at Harsen's Island, where a large informal dining room welcomed members. At other times many of the same crowd might be found enjoying simple foods and good fun at Harbor Springs, several hundred miles northwest on the eastern shore of Lake Michigan. A still smaller section of this elite might be found a long way from home at the Huron Mountain Club, which was—and remains—a remote wilderness area in the Upper Peninsula.

The Gilded Age was the age of the gentleman's club. Clubs served as an escape from the niceties of home. There were dozens of clubs, lodges, and "secret societies" listed in the city directories. There was something for everyone. There was the "Order of Chosen Friends," the "United Ancient Order of Druids," the "Centennial Boating and Athletic Association," which shared a dock at the foot of MacDougal Street with the Detroit Yacht Club. The Detroit Boat Club took the foot of Joseph Campau for its boat house and demonstrated its considerable status by holding its winter meetings in the Russell House, at Woodward and Campus Martius. There were three curling clubs for Scotsmen. The German community had a choice of Turnverein for gymnasts and the Harmonie for singers and musicians. Hunting and fishing clubs included the Lake Ste. Claire Fishing and Shooting, already called the Old Club and already elite. There were the Detroit Club and the Yondotega, the Prismatic and the Witenagemote. In the latter two, members took turns presenting a learned topic for discussion. There is a legend of a Witenagemote member who, unable to afford a horse and carriage, walked seven miles to meetings because "the talk was good."

A final indicator of Detroit's Gilded Age was the ability of its wealthy daughters to marry titled Europeans. This midwestern city had its full share of countesses, baronesses, and princesses. They came from such Detroit families as Cass, Lothrop, Palms, Walker, McMillan; daughters and granddaughters of politicians, distillers, lumbermen, landowners, and Indian traders.

First was Isabelle Cass, who became the Baroness von Limbourg in 1858. Most famous was her niece, Maude Ledyard, the granddaughter of Lewis Cass who became Baroness von Ketteler. The baron, who was Germany's ambassador to China, managed with foolhardy bravery to get himself shot down early in the Boxer Rebellion. His young, widowed bride spent the next year or two sewing rare old silks into sandbags for defense from Chinese gunfire.

It was left, however, to the daughter of one of Michigan's wealthiest and most tough-minded capitalists to exploit to the fullest the possibilities of foreign marriage and a life that included any number of mistakes. Clara Ward, daughter of Captain Eber Brock Ward, became in 1890 the Princess Chimay. Her obituary is included here.

From this we move to an account by Walter Pitkin on how the "rest of us" lived during the Gilded Age. In "Castle Garden Days," Pitkin describes several widely differing Detroit neighborhoods of the 1890s, but he is mainly oriented to the near West Side, the Grand River-Trumbull area, not too far from the ballpark.

1.   Summer Escapes: Life on the Steam Yacht *Uarda*

Wilma Wood Henrickson

From 1891 through 1893, the crew of the easy-going steam yacht *Uarda*, skippered by its owner, Cameron Davenport Waterman, included as cabin-boy and all purpose deckhand, Will Wood, the editor's father. Will was 16 when he came to Grosse Ile to work on the *Uarda*, but he had already formed the habit of keeping a diary.

Saturday, June 17 [1891]. . . . Between 12 & 1 we started on her [*Uarda*] for Detroit, landed at M.C.R.R. [Michigan Central Railroad] dock and took on a party of about 20 men. . . . Started down the American channel and crossed Lake Erie to Kingsville.

Wilma Wood Henrickson, "Summer Escapes: Life on the Steam Yacht *Uarda*," *Chronicle of Michigan History* (Fall 1984): 6–9.

By now Will had learned that Mr. Waterman expected to pay for all food his crew consumed on shore. There would be no skipping dinner or economizing for the sixteen year old boy: " . . . had roast beef, sliced potatoes, spring lamb, mint sauce, string beans, peach pie, and tutti-fruitti ice cream."

> Sun. 19. Done all the work and went to breakfast. Had mutton-chops, baked potatoes, omelet, French rolls, and chocolate. Started away at 11. Landed the party in Detroit. Before this one of the men went around and then handed me a handful of change, amounting to $1.80.
>
> Mon. 20. . . . Went out at 2:30. Took on a party of 31 at Detroit, mostly ladies. The waiter was on board and we served French pineapple ice-cream (in small bricks), raspberries, and cake. Came down the main channel a little below the stock farm and up the Canadian. . . .

On August 2, the *Uarda* began her first northern cruise of the year with an overnight stay at the Old Club, at the "Flats," the delta of Lake St. Clair on the American side.

> I have hardly anything to do after morning work is done. We have two regular meals a day: breakfast between 7 & 8 and dinner between 6 & 10 p.m. Can help ourselves to lunch at any time. Landed Campbell at Somerville [near Marysville, south of Port Huron] and Douglas and Russel at Port Huron. Reached Lake Huron at noon. Squall came up during the afternoon. The wind blew and the water looked black, but here was very little rain. Had the foresail up. Are lying at a long pier a mile long, forming a harbor of refuge [Sand Beach Harbor, now known as Harbor Beach]. Run 100 mi.

The next day's sailing followed a favorite pattern of Captain Waterman's: they left at 4:20 in the morning and sailed until 6:30 in the evening, to reach Detour at the edge of the Upper Peninsula.

> Crossed Saginaw Bay—75 mis. by noon. Out of sight of land for three hours. Detour is a mile above Point Detour, the entrance to St. Mary's River. A straggling village of one street, one store, and two hotels. People fish in summer and lumber during winter. Run 161 miles.

During the next few days, Will saw "the hole for the new lock," the sunken S. S. Pontiac, and "the finest scenery yet. Rock covered with trees," in the North Passage. Then "Let Douglas off at Point Detour. He gave me 50 cents."

From Algomah Mills, Ontario, on the North Channel's north side, they were headed for home. At Goderich, the diary records:

> Left Kilarney 4:30 a.m. Arrived 8 p.m. Crossed the mouth of Georgian Bay. Out of sight of land. Steered while they were at dinner. Run 168 miles. This beats the record. Went uptown. 161 steps up the hill. The business part of the town is around the courthouse in a 16 sided polygon. Geo. and I went around it and had started on the second trip before finding it out.

George White, cook on the *Uarda*, was the first black Will Wood came to know. He was to appear frequently in the diary over the next three summers. An entertaining raconteur, at home in the ship's galley, he was also able to build a fire on land in the rain to grill Lake Superior whitefish for a party depressed by a damaged boat. He bargained with Indians for berries and maple syrup that went with the blueberry flapjacks and fried perch. He had a talent for making friends quickly in faraway ports, which eased the loneliness of the uncertain adolescent who served as cabin boy.

The *Uarda* reached home on August 31, and fall chores began on both yacht and farm. The yacht remained in use all fall. On October 7, the Watermans watched the race between the yachts *City of the Straits* and the *Papoose*, from their boat deck in Lake St. Clair.

On December 13, Will was paid off for the season. His check that day for $84.75 covered the past four months at $20 wages per month and $4.75 for out-of-pocket expenses. He had received $20 earlier. With the help of Mr. Pitman, owner of a coal company and drydock, and a frequent passenger on the *Uarda*, he opened an account at the Mechanic's Bank, and then enrolled at the Detroit College of Commerce, paying $22.50 for three month's tuition, $6.15 for books. "They socket [sic] to one for everything." On Sundays that winter he wore his "new red tie and derby" to St. Thomas Episcopal Church in Trenton. The Watermans, following their custom, sailed on a passenger liner for Europe, where Mrs. Waterman and the children would spend most of the winter in France while Mr. Waterman returned for a businessman's winter in Detroit.

An anxious spring without work after finishing business college ended when Will was rehired to help get the *Uarda* ready for summer. On July 27th: "Went to Detroit with the yacht. Got a new carpet for the cabin and had the compasses adjusted." On August 1 the *Uarda* docked at Pitman's for taking on supplies and the next evening the Watermans again started their August cruise with a night at the Old Club on Harsen's Island. "We have eleven on board and the same cook as last year."

The *Uarda* resting on a beach near Tobermory, Ontario, c. 1895.
(Courtesy of Cameron Waterman, grandson of the steam yacht's owner, Cameron Davenport Waterman.)

This year they went west from Mackinac to Charlevoix and Northport on Lake Michigan, then to North Manitou Island where Will lost a quarter to the lake, but "talked with several nice young Chicago Minnehahas summering here."

There followed several stops along the south shore of Georgian Bay and the shores of the Bruce Peninsula, then called the Saugeen.

Sun. 28, Meaford, Ont. Stood watch at breakfast time about an hour. Arrived here 7 p.m. Ran nearly the entire length of Georgian Bay—110 miles. Had trouble keeping kids off [at the dock]. . . .

Tues. 30, Owen Sound. . . . Went up-town after dinner. Met a young fellow outside the Methodist church and went to Epworth League with him and afterwards around town. Went abroad the *Pacific, Baltic, Marine Hearse, City of Midland* and *Athabasca.* The last has twice as much brass on her engine as we have on the whole yacht. Saw two steam shovels unloading her cargo of wheat. . . .

A storm in Georgian Bay forced them off their route, and made the trip home difficult:

With every pitch the water would spout up the hawse-pipes and the propeller wheel would come half out of the water. In turning around we gave such a roll that half the dishes were smashed. . . . Was so rough that we could have no tables set for breakfast, but we are bound to reach Detroit by Sunday. . . . The *Western Reserve* broke in two, ten miles off Whitefish Point in last Thursday's gale, and all but a wheelman were drowned. . . .

Will worked that winter at the Detroit Club, but the following June he was once again on Grosse Ile, doing farm chores while waiting for the *Uarda* to get under way. There was hay to be loaded, currants and cherries picked, and then on June 30, the *Uarda* went to Detroit "to see the Spanish caravels going to Chicago." This was one of the early excitements leading up to the Columbian Exposition that fall. The *Uarda* "had small flags up. Great tooting of steam vessels in the river. The new fire tug *Detroiter* was out showing off."

Will was more sophisticated now. The "trip to 'Mettawas' " is noted mainly for a $2 tip from Mr. Waterman's guests. He tries to be casual about his day off on the Fourth of July:

Spent the "Glorious" at Grosse Ile until 10 a.m. Then to Slocum's Island [later known as Elizabeth Park]. . . . Over sixty gallons of ice-cream sold. $155 made by the K.L.M. [Knights of Labor Marching Band]. Dancing, racing, boat racing, girling as usual. . . . Was introduced to Miss Pearl—of whom I have heard ever since coming to Grosse Ile. Her reputation as a flirt is unequalled. . . . I was in her company for three hours. Went for a row uptown and back. She wished me to come down next Sunday afternoon.

On July 10, a minor disaster struck. "*Uarda* refused inspection on account of boilers." The "new Almy tubular" purchased the previous year had never lived up to expectations.

> Thurs. 13. Started about 8:30 with a special permit to go to the dry-dock. Mr. Waterman had appealed to Supervising Inspector Westcott and he inspected and passed the boat today. Went in dry-dock p.m. Got part of bottom scrubbed. . . .
>
> Friday, August 4, Thessalon, Ont. North shore of the Northern Passage of Georgian Bay. . . . Run through the beautiful North Passage & the Devil's Gap to this small town. A great ice jam in April carried away part of the dock and sank a tug. Temperance camp meeting in progress.

There followed several days of crisscrossing paths in an effort to locate supplies which had been due to arrive on the *S.S. Telegram*. Trips to Kilarney, "Dog River," and Pilot Harbor proved useless but not uneventful. On Monday they saw the boiler of the *City of Montreal*, "lost eight years ago. Just raised from Bonner's Bay. . . . Scaled a bluff for huckleberries . . . 150 feet."

On a Tuesday which ended at Otter Cove, there were more adventures.

> Ran twenty miles to Gravel River. Too windy to anchor. Back 15 miles to cove. Anchored. George and I went to the falls on the side of the bluff. I never saw anything like it before. A shallow fall of water—150 ft. zig-zagging down. In ascending we crossed six times. Ira [Waterman child] fell in.

The party now planned to relax and enjoy fishing in Lake Superior, but the diary entry of Saturday, August 19, is headed ominously: "Sunk at Bachawamung."

The *Uarda* lived again, after expensive and ingenious repairs. With a style appropriate to Detroit in those times—perhaps the best of the Gilded Age, the Watermans continued to enjoy cards and charades on the boat, good fishing and the company of friends. Let Newport and Manhattan have their monstrous occasions. Let Senators Zach Chandler or James McMillan imitate the eastern style. Some Detroiters could—and did—live well.

2.   The Age of the Gentleman's Club

Detroit Free Press

Recognizing the importance of clubs on Detroit's social scene, the Free Press undertook a survey of a wide range of them in 1893. They found the Detroit Club to be an all-around leader. Though its membership frequently overlapped with the "thinking men's" or the "sporting men's" clubs, it combined substantial prestige with a willingness to have business deals made over its linen tablecloths.

This is a series of excerpts from their survey.

DETROIT AS A CLUB CITY
Some of the Places Where Men Do Congregate
And Where They Follow the Bent of Their Inclination

Of the social clubs the Detroit Club, with a beautiful modern home at the corner of Cass and Fort streets, is the richest and most influential. It is just 11 years old, and has erected a home at a cost of something like $120,000. Clergymen, lawyers, army and navy officers, professors, doctors, merchants, hotel proprietors, editors, manufacturers, bank presidents, railroad presidents, architects, contractors, real estate dealers, and men of leisure are the component parts of the contented family that calls this club its intermediate home. The dullest understanding can comprehend the advantages resultant to the welfare of the city from the interchange of ideas between these men of affairs.

"Detroit as a Club City," *Detroit Free Press* (2 July 1893): 25.

203

Money has not been spared to make of this club a resort to fill the most exacting with a sense of satisfaction. There is a reception room unsurpassed in the west, a library of valuable books and a wealth of interesting current literature; a large fully-equipped dining-room, several smaller dining-rooms for private use, a cafe, a billiard and pool room, bowling alley, card rooms, barber shop, complete toilet facilities in every part of the building. Members may escort their wives, daughters and sweethearts to the club with the knowledge that what they see there will be only of the purest and best. The reception room set aside for the use of the gentler sex is a bower of beauty, and by a large and constant attendance they show their appreciation of what has been done for them. The dinners and suppers held within its walls are marvels of completeness and elegance.

Celebrities who favor Detroit with their presence are invariably, when not too difficult of access, escorted to this social circle, which shines all the brighter for the introduction of a new gem. Upon its registers may be seen the names of men whose achievements ring out from across the ocean. Others there are, now dead, remembered and revered because of their deeds.

The man of business has found the club an invaluable convenience in one respect. He is frequently visited by patrons who have come to negotiate a sale or a purchase of goods, or a piece of land or an interest in somebody's business. It is desirable that he treat these visitors as guests, and show them courtesies not demanded in the routine of life. What is more inviting than a visit to the club, where a luncheon is partaken and an hour is spent in the company of our foremost men of affairs?

The Harmonie Society

This club is a forty-niner. Detroit was a muddy little village in those days, but it had within its borders a gathering of honest, fun-loving Germans who thought to strengthen their friendships in social organization. Then was born the Harmonie Society. . . . It has seen Detroit grow from a swamp-fringed village to a prosperous metropolis, and it has taken pride in that growth because its own members have individually assisted in it.

It has been progressive, too, has grown with the city, kept pace with advanced ideas and shown its liberalism in every action. . . . The club has primarily a large hall, with stage and roomy gallery, and, secondarily, a basement containing a bar, billiard and pool tables, and a long, roomy dining-room with kitchen. With very simple accessories the mind and the stomach are amply provided for.

Though the society is famous for its musical strength as evidenced in its concerts, the principal feature is its yearly masquerade, which is given in February. . . . Appropriate costumes of the richest material are secured, and the young men and women excite their minds with pleasurable anticipation. A series of tableaux, well staged and costumed with historical accuracy are prepared, and orchestras are provided. When the night of pleasure arrives, the singers contribute of their talent to these harmonies, and it is talent that even a New York audience could with pleasure listen to. . . .

The Germans are by nature an amusement-seeking, sociable race. They enter into their sports with a heartiness and a zest that add cent per cent to their effectiveness. Drop into the building any evening in the winter season and you will see knots of men gathered here and there, usually around a table, discussing news and current topics and playing dominos, whist, skat and kindred games or telling yarns and singing fatherland songs. They have their beer, too; one must admit there would be something lacking without it. . . .

The Phoenix Club

This club is well along in its teens. It has a series of large well-furnished rooms above the drug store at the corner of Woodward avenue and Duffield street. It was organized by Hebrews, and is composed mainly of members of this race, though a few of the most prominent Gentiles also take an interest in its doings. No class in Detroit more heartily enjoy themselves than do these same Phoenixers when gathered at their club. They are fond of cards and light wines, dances and private theatricals. When you see these rooms ablaze with lights and a crowd of well-dressed people leaving carriages to pass through a canvas hallway stretched across the walk and leading up to the entrance, you may infer that a young Jewish man and woman have been married but an hour before and that a reception at the Phoenix Club is to follow.

The Prismatic Club

But little is known of the Prismatic Club. Its members abhor publicity and talk about their club affairs but little.

The members are all men of responsibility and culture, discuss the latest religious controversy, the new navy, the financial situation, the world's fair and kindred topics, and, as they are all readers and students as well, an evening in their society is equal to a month of close perusal of the magazines and newspapers.

There are no young men in this society, or, more properly speaking, fraternity, and the attractions necessary to hold them are missing. A few rooms, tables, chairs, and standard books answer all demands. The cigars and other good things may be brought, if necessary, to meeting. Sometimes the members are disposed to poke fun at each other, after the manner of Philadelphia's famous Clover Club, and it is surprising how much wit, humor, and sarcasm can be showered forth upon the unfortunate who happens, for the moment, to be the butt. They are genial, congenial, spirits, these, and they can select the best things intellectual with a discriminating judgment that nets a high standard of excellence. Though it has been said they discuss questions of vital interest, yet they have about them an originality that permits of license of a different character. There is not, perhaps, one man among them who has not seen life in its sterner aspects, whether in early privation or in war, who has not traveled somewhere in America or Europe or Asia or South America, and absorbed material for future use. There is not, moreover, a dull man in the Prismatic Club. An author, a historian, a journalist, might sit out two or three sessions of the club and every magazine or newspaper in the land would eagerly publish to the world those tales of adventure and observation as retold by himself. That's the Prismatic Club. . . .

The Witenagemotes

They are a choice lot of spirits—young and middle-aged men, every one of whom is well-known in Detroit. But their movements at Witenagemote are deep, dark, mysterious as the grave. Somebody asks why, but nobody has found out enough about them to answer. They have a banquet at the Russell House once a year, at which time they get back in the ordinary, in full evening dress, with a clown's high pointed white hat in addition, lock the doors and sing, drink champagne, make addresses, drink champagne, tell stories, and drink champagne. Of course, they are not adverse to good imported cigars. It is said the wit and humor that emanates from this banquet is plentiful enough to be cut into slabs and finish the Woodward avenue paving. . . . [1]

Editor's Note

1. The Detroit Club maintained its magnificence, like other clubs of its time, because there was a working class willing to serve its needs, even if this meant long hours and split shifts. One of these workers was the same Will Wood who had worked on the yacht *Uarda*. Through Charles Rathbone, a property manager who had been a frequent guest of the Watermans on the *Uarda*, Will was able to secure a job at the Detroit Club. Will started work in December of 1892, just as its "new building" was opened. The same building at the corner of Cass and Fort streets still serves as the home of the Detroit Club, almost a century later. Extracts from Will's diary follow.

> December, 1892 Tues. 13. Went up to Detroit and saw Charles Rathbone. He told me to meet him at the Det. Club house at 12:30. I went there and he got me a job as "door-boy" at $15 a month and board but not lodging. Am to commence Friday. . . .
>
> Friday 16. Came up on 9:35 train [from Trenton] to Detroit and went to the club-house. Went to Hudson's and was measured for a uniform. Worked until 6 carrying from the old to the new house corner of Fort and Cass sts. Hard work climbing upstairs. Hired a room at 156 3rd st. at $1 per week.
>
> Sat. 17. Moving all day. Had supper to-night in new house. They had an informal opening to members to-night. We live very plain here. Just meat, potatoes and bread. 18 yrs. old today.
>
> Sun. 18. Went to work in my new uniform as door-boy. Worked until six. My hours will be from seven to six every-days and from twelve to six Sundays. . . .

Mon. 19. From 12:30 to 2:30 there was such a rush (about 80) that I thought I could never stand it.

Thur. 22. Cold. Had a grand reception this evening. Had a fine orchestra. We used the bowling-alley for a coat-room, and it looked like a railroad collision and an earthquake. The things were checked without order and we had to look all over for any certain number, unless the owner remembered where it was put. Came away at 12:10. Seventeen hours on duty! . . .

Sun. 25 Snow nearly all day. The most lonesome Christmas I ever spent. Went to work at 12:15. . . .

3.　Clara Ward, Detroit's Prodigal Princess of Chimay

Detroit News

Clara Ward, daughter of Captain Eber Brock Ward, the Great Lakes shipper, lumberman, and industrialist, became the Princess Chimay in 1890. Self-proclaimed mistress of King Leopold of Belgium, she is best defined by her flowery, romantic obituary in the Detroit News *of December 19, 1916. It summarizes for us one aspect of the Gilded Age.*

A score of years ago, Clara Ward was the idol of Detroit young womanhood. Wealthy and beautiful, she left her native Detroit to marry the Prince de Chimay and Caraman, a Belgian nobleman closely allied to the royal family. Her light burned brightly in the capitals of Europe. She was favored of kings, the leading figure in many startling escapades, the toast of Paris. She was a princess, an American princess, who had captured the old world by her wit and her daring as much as by her lovely face.

Today she lies dead in her home in Padua, Italy—a prodigal daughter spurned by her mother, shunned by her former companions, her life ended, if not in poverty, as least in unlovely cir-

"Clara Ward, Detroit's Prodigal Princess of Chimay," *Detroit News* (19 December 1916): 1–2.

cumstances. She died a woman without illusions. She had gone the pace. She had lived intensely, a slave of her desires; she died an outcast, an old woman of 43 years, just when she should have been in her prime. . . .

The story of Clara Ward reads like a romance of the Duchess. At the age of 17, in 1890, when the country was stormed by impecunious noblemen of Europe, seeking gold for their damaged titles and equally damaged selves, Miss Ward, daughter of a multi-millionaire lumberman, was married in Paris to the prince. . . . A papal nuncio officiated, and the witnesses were the British and American ambassadors. . . . She had a yearly income of $50,000 from the estate of her father, and besides the fortunes of her mother and uncle were hers to draw on. . . .

For several years the prince and his American wife lived contentedly in Belgium. Two children were born to them. . . . But beneath the surface the fires that were later to consume her were burning fiercely. At last they burst out and the princess began to go on trips to Paris incognito. Once there, making the rounds of the gayest cafes and music halls, she squandered money riotously, everywhere dazzling with her beauty and startling with her prodigality. On one of these unbridled tours of the French capital, she met in a restaurant a Gipsy fiddler. He was—and is— a man of unprepossessing appearance physically. He is short and slender, his shoulders stooped. He wears a black moustache, and his black hair sweeps romantically back from his forehead. And in his eyes burn searing lights. These eyes kindled anew the tempestuous fires within the girl. These eyes won the princess from her husband and made her for years the slave of the Gipsy, [Jancsy] Rigo. . . .

Just as she had climbed up from a Detroit schoolgirl to a princess, so now she put aside her coronet and made the descent. And a turbulent time it was! In 1901, her uncle, Thomas R. Lyons, who was appointed conservator of her estate, showed that in seven years his niece had spent nearly a million dollars, $750,000, and most of it frittered away in company with the sparkling-eyed Rigo. Two years in Egypt cost $150,000; six weeks in Paris $32,000. She paid $35,000 for a pair of diamond earrings and then, tiring of them, pawned them for $4,000. . . . Shortly after her marriage to Rigo she gave a frank interview:

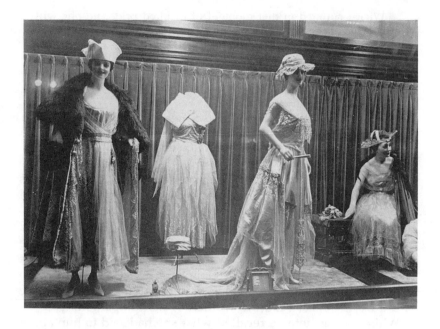

A final flare-up of Gilded Age elegance: J. L. Hudson display window, November, 1916. (From J. L. Hudson File, BHC. Used with permission.)

The true cause of my elopement with Rigo lies at the king's door [Leopold of Belgium]. I did not leave home from caprice, but because I had lost my position and was too proud to remain anywhere under sufferance. From the very first moment that I arrived in Brussels King Leopold showered me with attentions. At last came the celebrated garden party at the palace at Laeken.

The king neglected his guests for me. By his favoritism, the jealousy and hatred of the entire court was aroused against me. I defied them, as I have all my life defied everyone. The attentions of the king were pleasing to me, and I encouraged them. . . .

At last, at a certain fete, during a moment which will live in my memory till I die, I stood alone on one of the steps of the great staircase leading to the palace conservatories.

As I entered the great hall every woman there turned her back on me, or gazed at me contemptuously.

What I suffered in that moment of insulted pride, no one will ever know. Then it was that I broke the strictest law of court etiquette, which demands that no one shall retire from the assembly until the queen has left.

An officer stood near me. I turned and asked him to give me his arm out of the palace. He refused. I left alone, banishing myself from the court forever.

I am done with it all. I wanted to be free. I am at least out of the rotten atmosphere in which modern society lives. It does not want me, and I do not want it—so we are quits.

The last chapter in her life, as far as Detroit is concerned was written two years ago, when Rigo, her gipsy lover, was engaged by a local cafe to feature its cabaret. Relatives of Clara Ward— there are many of them living in the city and vicinity—could have seen her fiddler husband jauntily stepping about the smoke-filled cafe, ogling the women and playing his sensuous Hungarian airs on his eloquent violin.

Here is a man who cut a wide swath through Europe with one of the world's most beautiful women as his companion. . . .

While he was here he recalled what she had said to him about her home. "Once we thought we would go back to her native city together," he described the incident, "and she said, 'Ah, Jancsy, la belle Paris is not more beautiful than Detroit when the lights are shining on the river.' "[1]

Editor's Note

1. Clara Ward married four times; the obituary writer seems particularly shocked that one husband was an Italian railroad porter. Rigo divorced Clara, as had the Prince of Caraman and Chimay earlier. The prince was a cousin of King Leopold of Belgium, and there are some implications that he might have divorced Clara earlier, except for the social impossibility of naming his kinsman the king as corespondent.

   Clara was not allowed to see her children after the divorce, and her mother, although she herself had been a target of gossip when she had displaced the first Mrs. Eber Ward some years earlier, turned off all attempts Clara made at reconciliation.

4.   Castle Garden Days

Walter Pitkin

Not everyone lived in luxury during the Gilded Age. Then, as now, ordinary folks outnumbered the elite. Walter Pitkin, who was born in 1878, describes the working-class neighborhood of his childhood. Ethnic and racial groups were less defined by neighborhood than they would be in another decade or two. Pitkin also contrasts his own neighborhood with some others in late-nineteenth-century Detroit.

For years I carelessly assumed that I grew up in old Detroit. But I didn't. I lived west of Trumbull Avenue and south of Grand River Avenue. What's more to the point, I was one of the first inhabitants of this area. But old Detroit lay east of Trumbull Avenue and north of Grand River Avenue. It differed from my Detroit as greatly as Park Avenue differs from First Avenue, in New York City. Look first at my Detroit—and laugh, if you want to.

We Connecticut Yankees were first to arrive in what later became our neighborhood. And we were one of the first families to settle the great triangle enclosed by Grand River Avenue, Poplar

Street and the Belt Line Railway. Who followed us? Everybody except Yankees. Those were Castle Garden Days. Our Detroit became an annex and an outlet for Castle Garden.

You don't know what that means. Why should you? There was no Ellis Island until I was thirteen years old. That mighty immigration station did not open up for business until New Year's Day of 1891. Before then aliens came in through Castle Garden, at the foot of Manhattan Island, now called the Battery.

During the decade before Ellis Island the stream of newcomers became a torrent. . . . A heavy leakage from that stream reached us. It came all of a sudden, shortly after 1886.

First came the Bergers, from Holland. Then the Stanleys, originally out of England. Then the mighty swarm of Scots—the Murrays and McKees and Maddoxes and Kerrs, mostly from Edinburgh. Then the mightier swarm of Considines and Magees and Shaughnessys and Donohues and Coxes and Hughes out of Ireland. Then the tidal waves of Poles, who moved in half a mile west of us and became a little Poland once and for all time. Then a thin scattering of Germans, Danes, Norwegians and Belgians: the Zimmermans, the Sorensons, and others.

Along with these folks from Castle Garden came two lesser streams out of Canada. One was old French Canadian, the other was freshly out of France but by way of Montreal and Quebec; the Fontaines, Labadies, and a few others. Finally came a mere spatter of English and old-stock Americans from many sources; the Grinnells, the Hudsons, the Edgecombes and others.

By 1890 almost every lot had a house on it. Everybody worked hard, stuck to his own job, held fast to his own culture, and left everybody else free to do the same. We had no paupers, no rich; no loafers except Charley, the tramp; and no society folks.

At the time I failed completely to understand my environment. I missed the significance of my easy contacts with people of many races, religions, nationalities, and crafts. No boy in a New York slum could have enjoyed the wide variety of acquaintances I did. The later immigrant groups kept to themselves, created colonies, clung to their languages and cultures, and sought no outside connections. Not until the children of these immigrants grew up did the old colonies break down a little. But in my Detroit, every family had broken away from its sources. We had no Scotch quarter, no Irish quarter, no German quarter, no

French quarter. There was a Polish quarter, but it lay far outside of our neighborhood.

Nor was there any one business, trade, or craft that overshadowed the others. Starting at Grand River and working down one side of Fourteenth Street and then back up on the other side, I recall a druggist, a carpenter, a fisherman, a civil engineer, a ship carpenter, a school teacher, a printer, a livery stable man, a tug boat captain, a mason, a cattleman, a newspaper editor, a candy maker, a customs officer . . . as far up and down the street as memory's mare pulls me through the dust. Then up a side street, Joe Labadie, the writer of dime novels, a saloonkeeper, a carpenter. . . .

Some were Catholics, most were Protestants, but several were Free Thinkers and atheists. Some were drunkards, while others were rabid Prohibitionists. Some were thugs and thieves, but most were honest and hard working. Neither Republicans nor Democrats claimed many, for these newcomers had as yet formed no strong political convictions. They had to work too hard. For politics they had little time.

As yet there was no true community. The group was purely arithmetical, a mere sum of its parts, and all the parts stood out alone, free, unfused. The place was likewise crude. Through most of our early years there the road was dirt, the ditches just deep holes, the sidewalks made of rough pine boards nailed to two frame timbers. . . . Many of us kept a few chickens and let them forage for themselves half of the year.

. . . About five hundred feet west of Trumbull Avenue, as you go down Grand River Avenue, you smell something not too good. You see a huge red building on an alley. You walk around to the rear and look in. Two huge men are slaughtering steers hung from high tackles. The floor runs deep in warm blood. The men are blood from head to foot. The warm carcasses hang on hooks, covered with a million flies. A few small boys loiter around to get certain cuts for their home kitchens. The Magees sold these cheaply on the spot.

This, the Magee slaughterhouse was—as I say—a scant five hundred feet from one of the most charming mansions and gardens of old Detroit, the home of James E. Scripps, the great newspaper publisher. And this propinquity, in a far from poetic fashion, symbolizes the two Detroits, the world of difference be-

215

tween two cultures. Our Detroit came right up to the steps of the Scripps fence. The stenches from the slaughter house breezed in upon the Scripps family when the wind took a certain turn.

Scripps had transplanted a fairy fragment of old Surrey to the back door of Donnybrook Fair. He had copied a fine old English manor house and set it about with a delightful garden. He had cut off the world with a fancy fence which cost more than any house in our block. He kept a gardener. He installed an art gallery. . . .

This frontier of frills and fashion, the east side of Trumbull Avenue north of Grand River Avenue, lay far beyond the mass of Quality Folks. There were blocks and blocks of plain folks between Scripps and Woodward Avenue; but these plain folks were not like those of Fourteenth Street. They were Yankees out of Massachusetts, Yankees out of the Western Reserve, alias Ohio; a medley of middle-class lawyers, doctors, dentists, engineers. . . . Finally you reach Quality Street, which some would have said was Cass Avenue and others Second. There began one of the two areas that made up the heart and soul of old Detroit. It spread out irregularly on both sides of Grand Circus Park about to Willis Avenue, then faded out into green fields and dirt roads.

The other area was Jefferson Avenue, roughly from Chene Street out to Belle Isle Bridge, the end of the old Boulevard. Here dwelt many of the old French families, some in shabby genteel fashion, but most of them in a quiet, unstudied magnificence hard to equal anywhere else on earth, then or now. Row upon row of elms, maples, and oaks. Immense, dreamy lawns, stretching from the front gates clear down to the river; little boat houses on the shore, sheltering canoes and launches and sail boats and a few launches; mansions of brick, rather plain on the outside, but luxurious inside. . . .

[Old Detroit] was the most leisurely of American cities. Off the beaten tracks of westbound pioneers, it was not backwash, for it had more old wealth and old culture by far than did any of the cities in the great line of march between the Atlantic and the Pacific. Beside it, Buffalo was a mere outhouse. . . . Beside it, Chicago was a dung heap. Bostonians declared it was more like Boston than any other place. Yet it was no more Boston than I am Lillian Russell. It was, in truth, Detroit and nothing else.

In the Eighties I saw it as wide, cool streets, as brick houses set far back in soft lawns; as a riverside refreshed with breezes out of every quarter and down from every cloud; as a place where prominent citizens chatted by the hour with one another on park seats and at street corners; as a place where nobody hurried except to fires; as a place where people read important books and discussed them endlessly; as a place where a well read man was more welcome to dinner than a rude lumber baron who had just made another million by cheating homesteaders up back of Alpena.

All this I saw even when young. But never was I a part of it. Nor did I even taste it until after 1892. So you see it is only by a legal fiction that I call myself a citizen of old Detroit. True, our neighborhood had been recently taken into the city. We were, officially speaking, in the Tenth Ward. But we might as well have been called the Violent Ward, so far as old Detroit was concerned. Judged by Detroit's standard, we were violent. In 1885 we were living in 1865. We were the laggards in the cultural lag.[1]

Editor's Note

1. Though ethnic and racial groups have changed more than once since Pitkin's time, this near West Side area still retains its reputation for diversity and takes pride in violence. The mansion of James Scripps was razed some years ago, but part of his garden is occupied by the Frederick Douglass Library. Across Grand River Avenue the square tower of Trinity Episcopal, the very British church Scripps built, dominates the skyline, dwarfing even the golden arches of a nearby MacDonald's.

Part VII

The Progressives and Other Reformers

The Progressives and
Other Reformers

Detroit venerates strong mayors. In the line that
stretches from Solomon Sibley to Coleman Young, there have not
been many. Among the dozens of mayors, Zina Pitcher, Hazen
Pingree, James Couzens, Jerome Cavanagh, and Frank Murphy
come to mind, with, of course, the current incumbent, Mayor
Coleman Young. Of them all, Pingree stands the tests of history
as well as any.[1] In Detroit he also served as an advance guard for
the Progressive movement that sprang up in other cities.

Though Pingree dominates Detroit's Progressive period, he
could not have succeeded had the climate of the times not shifted
to reform. Some of the shift is to be found in the columns of the
Detroit Evening News under the editorship of James Scripps, who
was dedicated to producing a newspaper for the working class.
His stance is reflected in the very first document of this section:
two editorials from his paper on Belle Isle, which he termed the
"People's Park." Militant support was given to the purchase of
Belle Isle by ordinary people. Clearly the time was ripe for reformers, Mayor Pingree among them.

Best known for his "potato patches"—land made available to
the unemployed for growing food—Pingree showed that he was
a reformer in many other, more significant, ways. Like Franklin
Delano Roosevelt later, he came from a secure financial position
to befriend workers and was therefore considered "a traitor to his

221

class." His ultrarespectable church refused to renew the family's reserved pew after Pingree's first term in office.

The mayor sided with strikers when their picket lines were attacked by the police. He fought diligently, though with only minimal success, against the combine controlled by the McMillans and Hendries that owned the franchise of the Detroit City Railway. He fought for the establishment of the Public Lighting Commission and urged public ownership of all utilities.[2] He demanded an end to the toll road contracts, which he believed were a device to rob Detroiters whenever they left the city limits. He cut government costs, installed tax reforms, opened the assessment process, and encouraged citizen appeals.

Pingree is also notable for his championing of both riverfront development and park improvements, arguing that a good way for the city to make money was by preserving and developing its aesthetic advantages. His idea of extending outward the river shoreline downtown in order to build a large assembly hall and convention center has, of course, been a feature of Mayor Coleman Young's administration, almost a century later.

Believing that state government stymied his reform efforts in Detroit, Pingree ran for governor to correct the ills of his beloved city. He was elected governor while continuing to serve as mayor of Detroit, apparently believing that he could hold both offices at the same time. The Michigan Supreme Court thought otherwise. Pingree's abrupt resignation as mayor, early in 1897, was forced by that body.

There were weak spots in Pingree's reform efforts. They grew directly out of his anxiety to provide good, cheap government for the workingman, but sometimes the odds were just too great. His long battle with the transport monopoly headed by the McMillans was not finally settled until a quarter of a century after his term of office.

In dealing with public education, his concern with what he believed to be workers' interests led him astray. Pingree was certain that in the Detroit Board of Education he had found the center of corruption. He was not content with sending angry veto messages, several relating to the new high school building, whose location and cost he heartily distrusted. Later it would become "Old Main" to generations of Wayne State University students.[3] One summer evening in 1894, Pingree arrived at a board of education meeting with several policemen and had four board members arrested on the spot for receiving bribes from a furniture company. The mayor failed to win his court case, partly because the furniture salesman needed as a witness had opportunely left town, but also because his sweeping attack was too general. It incurred, for instance, a libel suit brought by one innocent board member who was not arrested but who resented the mayor's inclusive tirade.[4]

I have included two of the mayor's typical veto messages, both addressed to the board of education.

Pingree's cause was less just when he tangled with the growing forces of progressive education represented among the board's employees. In what now seems a total misunderstanding of the facts, Pingree believed that the liberal educators, and particularly their spokesperson, Assistant Superintendent Mathilde Coffin, were proposing an elitist curriculum that sidestepped the needs of the children of the working poor. Coffin was a formidable reformer in her own right, and the broad curriculum she proposed was in a number of ways more clearly related to young people and jobs in Detroit than Pingree ever realized. However, Coffin never had the mayor's support, and on one occasion he vetoed the budget line item that represented her salary.

I have included my own article on Coffin from the late journal *Detroit in Perspective*.

There were several other reformers who showed a casual disregard for standard opinion in their pursuit of ideas. Sketches appear here of Jo Labadie and Eliza Burt Gamble. There could have been others, such as D. Farrand Henry, scientist; Carrie Van Oostdyke, suffragist; Judson Grennell, single-tax economist; the lawyer and journalist Mary Stuart Coffin (no relation to Mathilde); the Pelham brothers, who were publishers of a black newspaper before they were government servants; and any number of others. All of them carried on a variety of crusades in casual disregard of standard opinion. All of them, in a less kind age, would be termed eccentrics.

Blacks were largely left out of the Progressive period. For them, the achievements of Reconstruction had not come easily, and the triumphs did not last long. Mayor Pingree failed to help. We think it was only a sad coincidence, rather than any purposeful effort. When his own commitment to eliminating patronage got in the way of blacks who had achieved through machine politics the offices for which many were thoroughly qualified, but could never have hoped to win by election, this does not seem to have been a fact that he noticed. His first concern was the effort to avoid deal-making and special favors. Forrester Washington calls the period one of "recrudescence" for blacks and in a telling historical essay tells us why.

Editor's Notes

1. Though Melvin G. Holli's *Reform in Detroit: Hazen S. Pingree and Urban Politics* (New York: Oxford University Press, 1969) is the outstanding biography of Pingree, much personal information about the Pingree family and their life-style is to be found in the unpublished typescript "Pingree," by Cyril Arthur Player, BHC.
2. Detroiters lost interest in public ownership after the Progressive period. When, in the 1970s, someone suggested selling the Public Lighting Commission Pingree had established to Detroit Edison, the rationale for public ownership seemed to be understood by only one or two city officials. Fortunately, Councilman Kenneth Cockrel was able to carry the day for maintaining the yardstick function of PLC.
3. Although Pingree himself lived at Woodward and Farnsworth, sharing what is now the site of the Detroit Institute of Arts with D. M. Ferry, he felt that the neighborhood was too elite to be welcoming to high school students. The site chosen at Cass and Warren was a part of the Cass estate and was being marketed under the name of the Cass Farm Company.
4. Emma Fox Papers, BHC. Fox, a clubwoman and parliamentarian, served a single term on the Detroit Board of Education as one of two women members during a period when the Michigan Legislature permitted women to run for that office as well as to vote in local school elections. (Eliza Gamble was particularly scornful of this small sop to motherhood.)

1.   Belle Isle: The People's Park

Detroit Evening News

When the city, after much debate, purchased Belle Isle in 1879, there remained stormy political discussion about its maintenance costs. Ten years later the arguments reached a climax as a bond proposal for the park conflicted with rival efforts to secure bonding for Grand Boulevard, which was to circle the city three miles from downtown. The Evening News *took up the fight for Belle Isle, calling it the "People's Park." Two of its many editorials on the park are reprinted here.*

Boodlers Hate the Park

"We love him for the enemies he has made", said Gen. Bragg at the democratic convention of 1884 when eulogizing Governor Cleveland. Belle Isle Park does not need such a commendation as that, for the people love it for its own sake, and for its own beauties; but the same words might be used of it, whenever its interests come up in the common council. It is an enterprise solely for the people's benefit; it has catered to no private interests. . . .

"Boodlers Hate the Park," *Detroit Evening News* (16 February 1889): 2.
"Shallow Politics," *Detroit Evening News* (18 February 1889): 2.
Both are also in Randall Scrapbook, no. 23: 22, 29, BHC.

At one time, not long ago, a well-organized conspiracy was hatched in the council, led by a leading boulevard alderman,[1] to get rid of it altogether by selling it, and this was only defeated by an angry manifestation of popular feeling, which subsequently swept the proposer out of office. The report of the committee on parks last night, favoring the recommendation of the mayor for park improvement bonds, was the signal for another uprising of the enemies of the park. Every man of them is tarred with the same stick. For years past, they have been the constant source of scandals in the city government, and some of them have escaped indictment and prison only on legal technicalities. Every man of this sort opposes bonding the city for the improvement of the People's Park,[2] but warmly endorses the scheme for handing the resources of the city over to the Speculator's Boulevard.

Shallow Politics

If the story be true that the Republican aldermen propose, as a measure of party politics, to resist the bonding of the city for the improvement of the island park, they will commit a very foolish political blunder. It is said that taking advantage of the mayor's recommendation of bonds for the park and for sewers, some political Smart Alecks among them imagine they see an opportunity to place their party in the attitude of the champion of municipal economy by resisting all bonds for whatsoever purpose and put the local democracy in a hole at the same time, as the champion of extravagance, and that they have suddenly seized upon this program for use in the next municipal election. . . .

The same [as of sewers] may be said of the island park. The rich do not need it. Their own dooryards are in many cases beautiful parks. In summer they go to the seaside, and if they wish an airing without going away, their fine horses and carriages can whirl them off to their villas at Grosse Pointe. They will probably take little comfort in the island park even when it is completed, for the poor will be there in their homely garments, and with their homely ways, to offend the eyes and ears of my lord and my lady. But the council will make a mistake to accept this indifference of the rich towards the park as an index of popular opinion. The masses of the people want it. It is seaside, villa, air,

226

Young women sketching on Belle Isle, 1905. (From BHC. Used with permission.)

water—everything in the way of rest and comfort—to which they can escape from the squalid and often unwholesome surroundings of their homes. They are frightfully in earnest about it. They have watched its progress and marked its enemies, and they will mark for destruction any political party which will place itself in the way of its speedy completion.

It cannot be completed by the niggardly annual appropriations which the council doles out to it. They are eaten up by the cost of maintenance; nothing is left for the work of improvement. . . .

Editor's Notes

1. This reference is very likely to James Randall, politician and developer, who was nicknamed "Boulevard Randall." He also kept the scrapbook that provides the sources noted here.

227

2. The role of Belle Isle as a "people's park" began early. Thorough histories of Belle Isle, formerly Isle au Cochons, or Hog Island, appear in Farmer, *History of Detroit*, 75–79 and Burton, *City of Detroit*, vol. 1, 438–62. The island was originally bought from the Ottawa and Chippewa Indians by a British lieutenant, George MacDougall, in 1768 for "5 barrels of rum, 3 rolls of tobacco, 3 lbs. of vermilion, a belt of wampum and 3 lbs. of paint." Extra rum and paint were given on possession.

   According to an unidentified news clipping in a Burton scrapbook, sometime in 1912 two enterprising members of the Chippewa group, Rising Sun and Oscar Beaver, tried to have the property returned to their nation, stating that the original bargain was obviously unfair. See Burton Scrapbook, no. 72:195, BHC.

2. Excerpts from the Mayor's Annual Messages, 1891 and 1896

Hazen Pingree

As early as January, 1891, in his second annual message to the Detroit Common Council, the mayor was casting wistful eyes at New York's Central Park and urging Detroit to take it as an example. By the time of his seventh and final annual message, in 1896, Pingree was able to focus his plans on the riverfront. Both messages are lengthy and are excerpted here.

A Central Park

Those who have kept track of the growth of Detroit in the past 25 years, have noticed that the city has scattered like a large village, spread out over much more territory than has been necessary for its real size, as indicated by its population. The result has been that there is property within a block or two of the City hall, which is as valuable as much that is two or three miles away. This central property has not been desired for residence purposes, it is too high in price for factories, and it is being gradually abandoned by wholesale houses. No state is better located

Hazen Pingree, Annual Message of the Mayor, *Journal of the Common Council*, City of Detroit (13 January 1891): 2–9.
Hazen Pingree, Annual Message of the Mayor, *Journal of the Common Council*, City of Detroit (20 January 1896): 2–14.

229

than Michigan, and no city than Detroit for building up and conducting large manufacturing interests. Neither is there any city in the country that could be made to draw so many outsiders within its limits, by its beauties, as Detroit. In other words, it can be made a great manufacturing city, and a great place of resort for strangers, both winter and summer. By taking advantage of its location, its climate, and its natural beauties, it could be made a veritable Paris of America. And this means a good deal, when it is considered that fully one-half the population of Paris, is supported by strangers attracted to that city by the reputation of its parks and boulevards.

A large park, in the center of the city, would boom Detroit more than the establishment of half a dozen Union Depots or of 18 or 20 factories. The Grand Circus Park was wisely designed by the governor and judges who replatted Detroit after the fire as the hub of a park system, consisting of broad avenues radiating from it as a common center.

The only mistake which they made was in not making this Central Park large enough for the subsequent growth of the city. They undoubtedly had the same thing in mind as those who laid out Boston, who reserved for the perpetual common use, that magnificent Central Park now known the world over as "Boston Commons". Bostonians regard it as of such great advantage to them that no sum of money would induce them to part with it; and they have of late years added to it, by purchase, another Central Park of nearly equal size, known as the "Public Gardens". It is a well-known fact that after the purchase and improvement of Central Park in New York City, the rapid rise in the taxable value of the land near it more than met the interest on its cost.

A glance at the map of the city will show that the spaces, southeasterly and southwesterly from the Grand Circus are so cut up into small parks, avenues and alleys, that private property is less than one-half of the whole. And that property, from its irregularity, and for reasons before mentioned is held at comparatively low figures. It could be obtained by the city either by purchase or condemnation, for a reasonable amount. The space south of Elizabeth east to Brush or Beaubien streets; south to Gratiot avenue; up Miami [later Broadway] avenue, crossing Woodward avenue at Park street, down Washington to Grand River, and up to its intersection with Elizabeth street, if made into a common or central park would be of untold advantage to every other part of the city, and to the country in general. Such a magnificent space of 82 acres, of which only 43 acres would have to be purchased, would be a lasting monument to the wisdom of the city fathers who procured it, and would justly entitle all who aided in the cause to the gratitude, not only of this generation, but of generations yet unborn.

Waterfront Improvement

Among our public spirited citizens there have been discussions from time to time during the past year looking to the formulation of some plan whereby Detroit can extend its reputation as one of the most beautiful cities of the United States and add to the volume of the steadily increasing stream of visitors.

Already Detroit has become a favorite resort for visitors from the Southern States during the summer months, and an attractive city for the conventions of the various State and inter-State organizations for the promotion of private enterprises.

But although the city has attained to the dignity of the first class in point of population, and of public improvement in nearly all lines, there is a lack of facilities for the accommodation of conventions of the first class, such, for example, as the national conventions of the political parties.

During the discussions alluded to, attention has been chiefly directed to the waterfront of the city along a river unsurpassed for volume and excellence of water in the world. It is a magnificent stream, worthy of any expense of ornamentation and of works of utility, yet the entire sweep of the river front is without that character of improvement in docks, buildings and breathing places for citizens in any way worthy of the great river, or of the business presenting itself.

While it cannot be expected that Detroit, like New York, can adopt the policy of acquiring the entire water front, as New York City did in 1871, and enter into the construction of piers, roadways and parked spaces, and meeting the expenses of construction and the employment of an army of men by the rental of piers and the receptacles for freight, it is not impossible that Detroit can afford to . . . select some section of the water front for improvement.

My attention has been directed to the acquiring by the city through condemnation proceedings, or ordinary purchase of the property along this front bounded by the river, Woodbridge street and Third street, upon which I find the total assessed valuation to be $1,496,030, and I present this matter to your honorable body for your consideration, and also for the consideration of the general public, and this special section of the water front is put forward as much for its general suggestiveness as for making it a possible objective point with which to start the project of water front improvement.

I would recommend that your honorable body refer this important subject to some committee that can afford the time for the consideration of it, and that such committee invite the cooperation of the Manufacturer's club.[1]

Editor's Note

1. We note that Pingree's plans for the riverfront included an extension into the river to provide a great assembly hall for national political conventions. There is a surprising similarity to the dreams of Mayor Coleman Young a century later. Both men saw the river as a political and economic asset to the city, and, as with his championship of a greatly expanded Grand Circus Park, Pingree shared the later mayor's dream of Detroit as a traveler's paradise.

3. Board of Education Vetoes, 1893–94

Hazen Pingree

Mayor Hazen Pingree could be quick to anger, and often used his veto power. There was a particularly harsh quality in his relations with the board of education, which he identified with corruption. After all, it was their meeting he once invaded with policemen and arrest warrants for four members.

The following two letters from Pingree to the board are less sensational than that action, but give the flavor of his annoyance and are typical of his routine expressions of displeasure.

January 26, 1893

To the Board of Education:

GENTLEMEN:—I am informed that it has been the custom of your Committee on Real Estate and School Buildings to open bids for construction of school buildings, heating, ventilation, etc., in the Secretary's office, behind closed doors, to which the representatives of the various newspapers and the bidders themselves are denied admission. This plan may be pursued from the purest of motives and the opening conducted with the most absolute impartiality and fairdealing. But the fact that this important work is done in secret, when it should be open to public

Hazen Pingree to the Detroit Board of Education, 26 January 1893 and 8 October 1894, *Proceedings of the Detroit Board of Education, 1893–1894* (Detroit: James H. Stone & Co.).

233

scrutiny as the sunlight of Heaven, engenders suspicion of wrong-doing, where perhaps none actually exists. Your board is handling the public money, and a large amount of it; and not only your actions, but also those of all your committees, should at all times be open to public inspection. As Mayor of the city, and as an ex officio member of your board, I would respectfully advise the adoption of a resolution directing that hereafter the opening of bids for any kind of public work in charge of the Board of Education be open and public, instead of private and secret, as at present.

Very respectfully,
H. S. PINGREE,
Mayor

Detroit, October 8, 1894.

To the Board of Education:

I herewith return to you without my approval so much of the proceedings of your honorable body by which you have selected as a High School site the block bounded by Warren, Hancock, Cass and Second Avenues.

My reasons for this action are as follows: The building of a High School is a matter in which almost every citizen of Detroit is deeply interested. I have endeavored to get an expression of opinion upon the question of this location and find that while there is a great diversity of sentiment, the majority of the citizens who take an interest in the matter are opposed to a location so far north. The selection of a site within the mile circle would be more satisfactory. . . .

Very respectfully,
H. S. PINGREE,
Mayor

4. "Too Bright for the Schools?" —Assistant Superintendent Mathilde Coffin

Wilma Wood Henrickson

> The schools have been going to the dogs . . . for nearly a generation. . . . Rooms are crowded with children who should have been educated in the essentials in a few short years and permitted to go out in the world and assist their parents to earn bread. . . .
>
> People who can afford it and have a grain of sense no longer send their children to the public schools, which are becoming more incompetent every day—and more costly to the taxpayer.
>
> —*Detroit Evening News*[1]

So what else is new? The year was 1896, and the angry quotations are from the *Detroit Evening News*, forerunner of to-day's *Detroit News*. . . . Detroit was entering a third year of major depression. This would not be the first, nor the last time that hard-up Detroiters would ask to have Detroit's children educated cheaply, for entry-level, even dead-end jobs.[2] Yet most were proud of their schools. Throughout the nineties Detroit's public

Wilma Wood Henrickson, " 'Too Bright for the Schools?'—Assistant Superintendent Mathilde Coffin," *Detroit in Perspective: A Journal of Regional History* 7, no. 2 (Fall 1983): 26–39.

schools had been making exciting gains. Natural science, physical education, a school for the deaf had all been added, kindergarten re-introduced, music and art strengthened. New schools had been built: the elite and controversial new high school out in the country at Cass and Warren, plus the Poe, the Harris, the Campbell, the Columbian. Even her enemies agreed that many, perhaps most, of the educational changes within the new buildings were due to the resourcefulness of one woman—Assistant Superintendent Mathilde Coffin.

Under the friendly, hands-off leadership of Superintendent William Robinson, Coffin had reduced class size which in some cases had reached as many as 75 students, and revised the entire elementary school curriculum. . . .

Coffin was determined to break with rote learning and drill. "Too much of just such work in the past is what has helped produce so many stupid people," she wrote tartly. To avoid teachers being "enslaved by a single textbook," she brought a range of texts and newspapers into the classroom. Children were to be urged to check varied references and prove the truth of their statements. Teachers were urged to get rid of the printed "Plan Books" which contained canned lessons and bulletin board ideas for the year ahead. Fresh work, related to today's world, would be the thing.

Times were hard in the spring of 1896, but Coffin was at the height of her powers. She had been effectively serving as Assistant Superintendent of Schools for five years, though not always with that title. Her $250 a month salary made her one of the more highly paid women executives in the country. It meant that she could live at a good address, . . . on Woodward Avenue, between Charlotte, and Peterboro, it meant that she could be one of the few Detroiters to have a telephone. . . .

Less than a year after Coffin was at her peak of influence, however, she would be jobless, "released from her duties for the good of the schools," struck off the payroll, and forced to go to court for her salary.

On Saturday evening, March 14, 1896, Miss Coffin returned from a Teachers' Institute in Monroe County. She told her audience there of her latest experiment—the introduction of the newspaper in the form of a sample abridged edition of the *Evening News* into the classrooms of Detroit. Coffin opened her own copy of the *Evening News* to find her ideas the subject of sharp attack under the headline: "EDUCATION FADS RUN MAD":

> God help the poor children. . . . This new fad is not proposed for the purpose of making them better readers, but solely to stuff their poor brains with the press of rubbish that is called the news of the day. . . . Wise fathers and mothers, while their children are still at school, try to keep the newspapers out of their hands. . . .
>
> It is astonishing that anyone in authority in the schools would have the impertinent audacity to propose forcing into the child's hands reading matter which his father or his mother would shrink from giving him access to at home.

Coffin immediately, and recklessly, took up the challenge. In one of many letters to the editors of the *Evening News* she undertook a serious defense of the courses her critics had labelled "fads":

> Your free use of the word "fad" prompts me to ask what you mean by it. . . . Are drawing, physical culture, and nature study fads? . . . You plead for the three R's. Nature study furnishes something to read and write about. We do not find that the presence of something to say "dissipates the minds of the children" in writing. If our children are allowed to continue this study of nature and history, they are in danger of forming the habit of saying something when they write.[3]

The *Evening News* did not back away, but continued to argue for traditional methods, such as arithmetic drill, rather than the individual problems Coffin urged. One editor openly stated that employers would prefer not to hire young bookkeepers whose training in mathematics might cause them to raise awkward questions.

Coffin retorted, "A boy is more than an adding machine." In a direct challenge to the editor of the *Evening News* [James Scripps], she stated:

> A man's prejudice against the public schools may be so strong as to paralyze his thought power in that direction and render him incapable of making judgments based upon facts. Your loose writ-

ing about educational matters shows a lack of acquaintance with the schools and the work which is doing in them at the present time. One purpose of education is to develop responsibility to truth; this, I take it, is even more important than the three R's.

The behind-the-scenes uproar was sufficient to cause Coffin to offer her resignation. The Board refused to accept it, but the genie was out of the bottle now. . . .

Coffin had strong defenders, among them Mrs. Carrie Oost-dyke, president of the Independent Voters' Association and Attorney D. Augustus Straker, a leader in Detroit's black community.

School Inspector Marr, who would later fall by the wayside, went so far as to say: "Miss Coffin stands for the main question, whether we are to go ahead or to turn back. . . . There are two classes among the teachers, those who are in favor of Miss Coffin and those who are opposed and they can be divided by the measure of their skill and enthusiasm in their work. The better teachers are unanimously for Miss Coffin. . . . "

However, stories on Coffin's progressivism would soon be obscured in all the papers by the Board's actions in the growing fiscal crisis.

. . . During this period, control was vested in sixteen Board members termed "School Inspectors," one elected from each of the city's sixteen wards, with eight to be chosen in each biennial election. The Board of Estimates, in part appointed by the mayor, had substantial power over the budget, though, within the framework outlined, the Board of Education could maneuver to rearrange expenditures within categories. The mayor himself had veto power, and Mayor Pingree often used it. He clearly felt his vetoes were necessary to curb extravagance which could hurt working taxpayers. . . . He fought the plans for the new high school, for instance, every inch of the way. . . .

In March the *Evening News* carried a small item congratulating Inspector Hall [a west side dentist], for his shrewdness in making friends with the Board of Estimates in his efforts to get the "fads" out of the school budget. Inspector Hall seems to have felt he had a mandate to return the curriculum to the three R's. He was probably an enemy of Coffin's even before she made a stinging remark that children would continue to sing whether or no Inspector Hall succeeded in eliminating music in the schools. Until now most of the Board had been united in its warm support of Robinson and Coffin. Always members stood together against the Board of Estimates, their natural enemy at budget time.

In April, the Board of Estimates, certainly with the approval of Mayor Pingree, slashed the education budget mercilessly. Building funds, cut severely in previous years, were now all but gone. No matter that many of Detroit's school children could not have a full day of school because there was no place to put them, or that . . . the average child stayed in school only five years, [or that] . . . Detroit's school age population during the nineties was one of the fastest growing in the country.

The Board of Estimates not only slashed the salary category, but made it clear that they expected some of the savings to come through the elimination of the "special teachers"; this meant Coffin and the supervisors of the various departments who were working under her.

. . . The Board of Education determined to make a number of budget decisions on its own. . . . Two weeks were abruptly slashed from the remainder of the school year; there was discussion of an even shorter year for 1896–97, and general salary cuts were put into immediate effect. Coffin's pay would now be reduced to $235 a month. The pensions of retired teachers . . . would be cut $5 a month, leaving them with $30. . . . Teachers of many years seniority, including well-known kindergarten specialist Fannie Richards [the first black woman hired by the Detroit Public Schools], were cut from $72.50 to $70 a month.

When the schools reopened in the fall, everything that could go wrong for Coffin did. . . . Someone with an eye for small economies suggested that teachers pay a dollar fee to cover the costs of . . . the monthly teachers' meetings arranged by Coffin; letters of protest appeared in the papers. The writers pointed out that a dollar was a lot of money when you had taken a pay cut above the lost time in June. . . . One writer noted also that the speakers Miss Coffin chose always seemed to want teachers to read more and to work much more, with the idea of constantly changing the lesson plans to fit the children. Teachers had little enough free time as it was. . . .

Coffin invited even more public notice by her active part in a women's group that championed educational reform. . . . Coffin seems to have enjoyed the full confidence of Robinson, and the warm support of most of the Board. The Women's Educational Union would change all that.

The first mention of this group occurs in the fall of 1896. Feminist, radical, and mushrooming in growth, in sixty days it had gained the support and membership of the top staff of the public schools. Coffin was elected vice-president, and the Superintendent's wife served as treasurer. George Brown, labor editor of the *Evening News*, writing in its Sunday edition, the *News-Tribune*, predicted that membership might easily go to 10,000 and that the political strength of Detroit women, who were allowed by Michigan law to vote in local school board elections, could lead to sweeping changes in the schools.[4]

The Union was the brain-child of feminist author Mrs. Eliza Burt Gamble, described by one school inspector as a "man-hater . . . on a rampage." For over two months, the Union, meeting constantly in the schools after hours, seemed on the edge of power. Coffin . . . addressed over four thousand mothers at its various meetings during the fall. What happened between October, when school officials, including Board President Caleb Pitkin [father of Walter Pitkin], had warmly endorsed the Women's Union, and December when it was a major factor in Coffin's firing?

From the outset, meetings were held at a feverish pace, at first in Mrs. Gamble's home, then, after the Board with some hesitation approved, in the schools after classes. Soon major meetings of the organization were scheduled in the Board of Education building on Miami Avenue—later Broadway. . . . Conflict surfaced with the prospectus of the main message the Union would deliver to mothers. . . . Harriet Scott, principal of the Normal School, understood that she had been chosen to write it. Gamble, a published writer, without prior consultation, used her own skills to prepare a separate document directed at the mothers of Detroit's school children. This was a surprise to everyone, but most of all to Mrs. Scott, and that particular meeting was a disaster. . . .

The Superintendent's wife . . . believed there were secret meetings to which she was not invited. . . . [Mrs. Robinson] quickly came to believe that the whole group represented a plot against her husband's best interests. She decided that Coffin herself really wanted to be Superintendent of Schools. With apparent naivete, she blurted out at a committee meeting of the Union that her husband had told her he didn't enjoy working with women's groups, and planned to have as little as possible to do with the Women's Educational Union. . . .

Coffin then tried to discuss the role of the Union directly with Robinson. On Saturday morning, October 24, meeting with him in his office, she asked him to assure the principals that the group had his firm support. She stated that he then became "very angry," "paced the floor," and finally said, "There's too much of this female business. I'm tired of it." Coffin reports, "I rolled up my coat collar and left the office. Afterwards, . . . he explained to a friend of mine that he made no reference to myself, which, however, did not lessen the indignity."

During November, Gamble had a open, angry break with Robinson and called a press conference in which she accused him of "throwing cold water" on the Women's Union. Unfortunately, Coffin was again present, and Robinson later suggested to her that she was over-tired because of the long hours she had put in doing organizing work with the group, and that it was time to get back to her regular duties. Coffin was angry enough at this that she went over Robinson's head to Inspector Marr, as chairman of the board's Committee on Schools and Teachers, and asked him to seek a definition of her responsibilities as Assistant Superintendent. The reply came from Robinson early in December in a written memo. The memo listed routine jobs and managed to seem both derogatory and hostile.

Coffin was to report each Friday exactly what she had done during the week, to provide efficiency ratings on teachers in any buildings she visited, and to be available in her office every afternoon between four and five, Monday through Friday. The sting was in the last requirement. This was precisely the time that the Women's Educational Union was conducting its meetings. . . .

Coffin only had to live by the new rules a short time before the game was over. "IT'S OUT! *That Dark Secret the Board of Education Would Keep: The Women Can't Be Muzzled, And Here It All Is; Breach Between Superintendent Robinson and Miss Coffin*" were the headlines the *Detroit Free Press* used on its page one story on December 18, covering the rift between Coffin and Robinson.

On December 17, apparently obsessed with the public's right to know, Coffin released to all Detroit papers the story of her troubles on the job over the past two months. Just a day later she also announced her candidacy for the position of Superintendent of Schools. Jokingly, she told reporters that she had been "nominated" by Mrs. Robinson. Before the Superintendent's wife spread those rumors, it had not occurred to her to try to displace him. However—when the issue had been raised, it had suddenly occurred to her that she had been doing the major share of Robinson's work for several years now; his contract would expire in July—and why not?[5]

It was on December 17, too, that Gamble proposed the dissolution of the Women's Union, at an angry meeting at which she was booed by a faction of women principals. . . .

That same evening the Committee on Schools and Teachers of the Detroit Board of Education recommended that the full Board "relieve Miss Coffin of her duties." The Board made it official at its next meeting on Tuesday, December 22. "DECAPITATED" said the *Evening News*.

When the vote was taken [to fire Coffin] only long-time Board member Dr. Lucien Ellis dissented. . . . He explained to reporters that no one could give a reason for the board action. He seems quite correct. The official board minutes remain abrupt and sketchy, referring only to "the good of the schools."

If the Board was not saying much officially, much was being said by the press. . . . the *Journal* sadly urged her to resign. In both the *Evening News* and the *Free Press*, Coffin almost knocked the Cuban revolution out of the headlines. Coffin was accused of claiming to have written most of Robinson's reports and speeches, a point which may have been true. . . . She was accused of having schemed to get Robinson's job for herself. (Her version of her decision to seek the appointment, inept as it sounds, is probably the true one.) She was accused of being influenced, even "spoiled" by a mysterious male friend. She was accused of bewitching Robinson. Always she was accused of making too much money.

William Voigt, Jr., a brewer and former Board member, was candid above all others: "She is a very bright woman. In fact, she is too bright for the good of the Detroit schools. In her ambition and exploiting of scientific education, she has overshot her mark."

On Christmas Eve the *Evening News* carried its second mention by name of Franklin Ford, the mystery man accused by some of giving her ideas and urging her on to covet the Superinten-dency. . . . In the words of the men interviewed: "He has some great ideas, but they are too deep for me" . . . "A dreamer. He wants to correlate everything" . . . "I do not understand just what his interest is in our schools" . . . "I believe he has been an itinerant newspaperman. I understand that at one time he was connected with Bradstreet's " . . . "In fact, he is a sort of conun-drum to me, as he is to everyone else."

Ford had, in fact, been an editor with Bradstreet's, predecessor to Dun and Bradstreet's, for the ten years prior to 1887. He was an investigative journalist with a special interest in banking and credit; he tried to persuade the University of Michigan to estab-lish a school of journalism. . . . "Conundrum of the day," the *Evening News* summarized Ford, and seemed to forget him.[6]

In its angry meeting of December 22, Board Attorney William Baubie had offered his legal opinion on breach of contract to a Board which refused to listen. Baubie angrily, and as it turned out accurately, predicted, "You'll ask me for an opinion when she takes you to court!"

On January 28, 1897, the Board, in a notably chiseling effort to save money, voted not to pay Coffin her January salary, with Lu-cien Ellis and a few others dissenting. Miss Coffin sued. She asked for the balance due on her contract and $5,000 damages. She was represented by . . . former judge John J. Speed, Master in Chancery, one-time Corporation Counsel, codifier of the City Charter. The Board remained stubborn in its refusal to pay and was summoned to Circuit Court in April.

From the start, Coffin dominated the trial and charmed the jury. . . . Board members who appeared as witnesses against her . . . were unable to substantiate their allegations. They could prove she was in the Van Dyke School one afternoon instead of in her office, but they were forced to admit she was there on of-ficial business. They could prove she was active in the Women's Educational Union, but no one could remember ever ordering her not to be. Circuit Court ruled in her favor, and the Board promptly voted to appeal to the Michigan Supreme court, which refused the appeal, seeing no evidence that Coffin had either vi-olated directions or refused to perform her duties.

Judge Carpenter, of Circuit Court, handed down his decision favoring Coffin on Friday, April 30. Three days later, on Monday,

May 3, 1897, Mathilde Coffin and her "excellent friend," Franklin Ford, were married at the Church of the Transfiguration on Park Avenue in New York. William Livingstone's friendly *Detroit Journal* headlined the event "NEEDS NO SCHOOL!" and announced that the Fords would live in New York.

What happened after in the schools? Most of the new work remained in place. True, Miss McGrath was now able to sell the Board her arithmetic drill book, which epitomized the methods to which Coffin had objected. The political and economic geography researched and promoted by Coffin, with its emphasis on Great Lakes shipping and Detroit resources and industry, slowly sank without a trace. But when the principals petitioned that natural science be kept in the elementary schools, it was. Kindergarten, after a brief cut-back, appeared again. Physical education, art, music, shop, homemaking, and a special school for the deaf were here to stay. After a one year lapse, new schools would be built again. Coffin and Robinson had set in place the notion that the public schools must make room for a full day's schooling for every child. Never again would Detroit teachers be proud to say out loud that they were still using their unchanged lesson plan book left over from college days. Certainly never again would a Detroit newspaper claim that its own pages were too immoral for classroom use.

As the *Free Press* had correctly predicted in December, the Women's Educational Union would show no political clout whatever in the spring elections. Or ever.

Superintendent Robinson, a victim of the controversy, would fail to keep his contract after the Board's annual meeting in July, and retire to sell insurance. Popular and politic young-man-in-a-hurry Wales Martindale would succeed him.[7] Among the new schools built by Martindale, one of the very first would be appropriately named the James Scripps, for the publisher of the *Detroit Evening News*.

Hazen Pingree, who had believed that the new methods were not in the interest of the worker's children, became Governor of Michigan in January, 1897. A school would be named for Pingree in 1902, as there would be, in time, for many of Coffin's one-time women subordinates: the Myra Jones, the Isabel Thirkell, the Ella Fitzgerald, the Fannie Wingert, the Jennie Fleming. No statues with pigeon droppings are dedicated to Mathilde Coffin in any park, nor would any school be named for her—nor, for that matter, for black educator Fannie Richards, who was another genuine pioneer of the era.

In December, 1897, attorney Speed was able to force out of the Board a belated paycheck for Coffin's services from her December release to the date of her wedding—$993.62, plus $21 costs, for a total of $1014.62. [The Board first went to the Michigan Supreme Court, which refused to overturn the Circuit Court's decision in favor of Coffin.]

The woman who wouldn't appear in Detroit's history books left the schools with a progressive statement of how—and why—history should be taught:

> You [the editor of the *Evening News*] believe history should be taught in the schools, but you would have the past taught as something separated from the present. Is it thus separated in fact, or would you simply teach it so? . . . Is it your idea that the best preparation a child can have for living in this world is to know nothing about it? . . . Is the living, growing, moving, wonderful world about us to be excluded from the schools? . . . Are we to have only the past—a dead past torn from the present? Some day, regardless of obstacles, the school will connect with life. . . . [8]

Notes

[For the convenience of the reader, no attempt has been made to reproduce here the full notes that accompanied the original article in *Detroit in Perspective*.]

1. *Detroit Evening News* (14 March 1896): 3.
2. The earliest was the Lancastrian experiment 1818–1824, a system whose aim was to teach up to 1,000 students, with one teacher. Sister Mary Rosalita, educational historian, called it "a system under which education was superficial, and discipline a negative quality. . . . it could not long be upheld simply because it was cheap . . . a scheme in which the memorizing and reciting of lessons glibly was the be-all and end-all, . . . a makeshift for genuine education." *Education in Detroit Prior to 1850* (Michigan Historical Commission, 1928), pp. 187–204. See also Moehlman, *History of the Detroit Public Schools*, (Bloomington, Ill., Public Schools Publishing, 1925), pp. 45–57.

3. Coffin, Mathilde, "The School and the Newspaper, Letter of Mathilde Coffin to the Detroit Evening News, Replying to the Editorial of March 14," March 17, 1896. Excerpts and Miscellania File, BHC.
4. *Sunday News-Tribune*, Nov. 22, 1896.
5. *Detroit Free Press*, Dec. 17, 1896. All local papers carried some of this material, or made reference to it over the next few days.
6. *Detroit Evening News*, Dec. 24, 1896. Ford's own statement of his goals for himself and U. of M. are outlined in *Draft of Action*, Ann Arbor, 1892, (E & M Files, BHC.)
7. In December 23, 1896, the *News* had termed Martindale a "pushing man" who had been criticized for "having a political turn." Times had changed by July!
8. Coffin, Mathilde, Reading Room File, BHC.

5.   The General Strike

Jo Labadie

The capitalists don't like the general strike. Do you know why? Because it is the most effective weapon the workers have thought of. Capitalists don't want to do the hard work themselves, and what are they to do with their capital if their slaves refuse to use it? If it isn't used, there is no profit for the idler. There is no income for the mere owner. Capital deteriorates from want of use. The life of capitalism depends upon the use of capital for usury's sake. Usury is the heart of capitalism, and when this stops the thing is a dead one.

The general strike is not an invasion of anyone's rights or freedom. If you refuse to work for any reason whatever, how is this an invasion of anyone's rights? . . . If one has not the right and freedom to quit work when he wants to then is he slave indeed.

Jo Labadie, "The General Strike," in *Essays by Jo Labadie*, The Labadie Shop, 1911, 38–43, BHC.

The traitorous workers who act as shooters and beaters of strikers and [as] strikebreakers are impotent against a general strike that embraces even a quarter or a third of the workers in fundamental industries. The general strike is direct. You don't need to depend on someone else to do your striking for you. It is an old saying that if you want a thing done, do it yourself. This is a thing you must do for yourself if it is to be done. No politician or agent or middleman comes between you and what you want done. The politician is eliminated from the problem. That is why the politicians, good, bad, and indifferent, are against it.

The ballot isn't a comparison [*sic*] the general strike in effectiveness. For nearly a century and a half the working men of this country have voted. What have they accomplished by it? During all this time the grafter, the skin brigand, the industrial, commercial, and political pirates have absorbed the land, the machinery, the money and everything else necessary for the production and distribution of the material comforts of life.

And how about the bullet? Why hasn't the killing of man by man during the hundreds and thousands and possibly millions of years settled these questions of men's relations to the rest of their kind if war and violence can do it? Is it time the old ways are discarded and new and less destructive, less violent and invasive ones be tried? . . . There is only one thing that can defeat the general strike. Hunger is a powerful taskmaster. It will drive men back to industrial slavery if their loved ones come within reach of its lash. But the general strike need not last long. It ought to be so general and complete as to stop the wheels of commerce and industry in the wink of an eye. It should be so universal as to paralyze the arm raised against it. It can do it. It will prevent violence if it be widespread enough. It is more effective than guns. It is less noisy and dangerous than powder and dynamite. It is the ultimate manifestation of the worker's self-ownership. . . . [1]

Editor's Note

1. An excellent brief account of Labadie's pampleteering and labor activities, written by his granddaughter, Carlotta Anderson, is to be found in "Jo Labadie, Detroit's Gentle Anarchist," *Michigan History* (June–July 1986): 32–39.

6.   The Sexes in Science and History

Eliza Burt Gamble

> With the progress of civilization and since
> women as sexual and economic slaves have become depen-
> dent upon men for their support, no male biped has been
> too stupid, too ugly, or too vicious to take to himself a mate
> and perpetuate his imperfections.
>
> —*Eliza Burt Gamble*

I had reached the conclusion, as early as the year 1882, that the female organism is in no wise inferior to that of the male. For some time, however, I was unable to find any detailed proof that could consistently be employed to substantiate the correctness of this hypothesis.

In the year 1885, with no special object in view other than a desire for information, I began a systematized investigation of the facts which at that time had been established by naturalists relative to the development of mankind from lower orders of life. It was not, however, until the year 1886, after a careful reading of *The Descent of Man*, by Mr. Darwin, that I first became impressed with the belief that the theory of evolution, as enunciated by scientists, furnishes much evidence going to show that the female among all the orders of life, man included, represents a higher stage of development than the male.

Notwithstanding the superior degree of development, which according to the facts elaborated by scientists, must belong to the female in all the orders of life below mankind, Mr. Darwin would have us believe that so soon as the human species appeared on the earth, the processes which for untold ages had been in operation were reversed, and that through courage and perseverance, or patience, qualities which were the result of extreme selfishness, or which were acquired while in pursuit of animal gratification, man finally became superior to woman. . . .

. . . Although women are still in possession of their natural inheritance, a finer and more complex organism comparatively free from imperfections, and although, as a result of this inheritance, their intuitions are still quicker, their perceptions keener, and their endurance greater, the drain on their physical energies, caused by the abnormal development of the reproductive energies in the opposite sex, has, during the ages of man's dominion over her, been sufficient to preclude the idea of success in competing with men for the prizes of life. Although an era of progress has begun, ages will no doubt be required to eradicate abuses which are the result of constitutional defects, and especially so as the prejudices and feelings of mankind are for the most part in harmony with such abuses. . . .

If we examine the subject of female apparel, at the present time, we shall observe how difficult it is to uproot long-established prejudices which are deeply rooted in sensuality and superstition; and this is true notwithstanding the fact that such prejudices may involve the comfort and even the health of half the people, and seriously affect the welfare of unborn generations. . . .

Although the female of the human species, like the female among the lower orders of life, is capable of appreciating fine colouring, and to a considerable extent, the beautiful in form, the style of dress adopted by women is not an expression of their natural ideas of taste and harmony. On the contrary, it is to Sexual Selection that we must look for an explanation of the incongruities and absurdities presented by the so-called female fashions of the past and present. The processes of Sexual Selection, which, so long as the female was the controlling agency in courtship, worked on the male, have in these later ages been reversed.

For the reason that the female of the human species has so long been under subjection to the male, the styles of dress and adornment which have been adopted, and which are still in vogue, are largely the result of masculine taste. Woman's business in life has been to marry, or at least it has been necessary for her, in order to gain her support, to win the favour of the opposite sex. She must, therefore, by her charms, captivate the male.

. . . It is not singular that in the struggle for life to which they [women] have been subjected they should have adopted the styles of dress which would be likely to secure to them the greatest degree of success. When we remember that the present ideas of becomingness or propriety in woman's apparel are the result of ages of sensuality or servitude, it is not remarkable that they are difficult to uproot, and especially so as many of the most pernicious and health-destroying styles involve questions of female decorum as understood by a sensualized age. . . .

Ever since the dominion of man over woman began, a strict censorship over her dress has been maintained. Although in very recent times women are beginning to exercise a slight degree of independence in the matter of clothes, still, because of existing prejudices and customs they have not yet been able to adopt a style of dress which admits of the free and unrestricted use of the body and limbs. It is believed that woman, the natural tempter of man, if left to her own sinful devices, would again as of old attempt to destroy that inherent purity of heart and cleanliness of life which characterizes the male constitution. Woman's ankles and throat seem to be the most formidable foes against which innocent man has to contend, so the concealment of these offending members is deemed absolutely necessary for his protection and safety. . . .

When we consider that apparel is but one, and a minor one, of the strictures under which women have laboured during the latter era of human existence and when we consider all the ignoble and degrading uses to which womanhood has been subjected, the wonder is not that women have failed in the past to distinguish themselves in the various fields of intellectual labour in which men have achieved a limited degree of success, but that they have had sufficient energy and courage left to enable them even to attempt anything so far outside the boundary of their prescribed "sphere." . . . [1]

Editor's Note

1. Very little is known about the personal life of Gamble. In spite of the bitterness attributed to her by the press, there are no recorded objections from Mr. Gamble to his wife's outspoken feminism. John Gamble was a real estate developer with considerable property at Orchard Lake. The couple had two children. In a 1912 letter to Jo Labadie, in which she states that she has "always thought of herself as a socialist," she complains of the colds and bronchial trouble she suffered at Orchard Lake, where Mr. Gamble's work took them in the summers. It all sounds amazingly docile for a woman whose historical scholarship has set the tone for much later research. Mary Ritter Beard, in 1945, praised her work in early history. Beard also hunted in vain for Detroit traces of Gamble's work for the Women's Archives on which she was working.

7.   Progressivism Skips
Detroit Blacks

Forrester Washington

While the Progressive reformers came more and more to identify good government with the curtailment of ethnic variation, one group, as usual, suffered more than others. Looking back on this period in 1920, sociologist Forrester Washington called it a time of "recrudescence" and loss of power. He was describing the same period that a later historian, Rayford Logan, would term nationally the "nadir" of hopes raised during the Reconstruction period.

Period of Political, Social, and Economic Recrudescence—1895 to 1915

A. Loss of Occupational Status

Beginning with 1895, Negroes gradually lost their hold on the good paying positions in the hotels. Some hotels, even some of the larger establishments, have retained Negro waiters down until today. But the majority of the larger ones, as well as many of the smaller ones, supplanted their Negro employees with white foreigners, chiefly Greeks, in the late 90's.

Forrester Washington, "History," in *The Negro in Detroit: A Survey of the Conditions of a Negro Group in a Northern Industrial Center during the War Prosperity Period* (Detroit: Associated Charities, 1920).

About the same time, there began a gradual replacing of Negro barbers with white barbers in the better shops.

In other occupations, also, Negroes began to lose the monopoly of employment which they had possessed for years. There was a notable decrease in the number of Negro coachmen, butlers, gardeners, etc.

The chief reason given for these changes was the craze at that time on the part of the fashionable classes to copy the styles of Europe. Hence, the supplanting of Negro coachman with English coachman; Negro hotel cooks with French cooks, etc. It is also said that the change in the class of personal service workers was due to the large immigration from Europe at that time which enabled employers to obtain highly trained servants at a lower wage than they had been paying Negroes.

One result of this loss of status in the personal services field was the attempt of Negroes to get a footing in the manufacturing and mechanical field. In 1897, a committee of Negroes, among whom were Albert Johnson, William Ernst, and Robert Williams, was formed for the express purpose of obtaining jobs in industry for Negroes who were losing out in hotels and domestic service.

This committee took as its premise the fact that the Negro constituted one-fifteenth of the population, and that, therefore, one-fifteenth of the employees in any establishment having at least fifteen workers, should be Negroes. The committee was not successful in creating a large number of openings for the Negro but it was responsible for the introduction of Negro conductors and motormen on the street railways[1] and for the introduction of a few Negro laborers into one of the stove companies.

The occupational status of the Negro continued to retrogress down to the year 1915.

B. Loss of Political Power

The change from the convention system of nominating candidates to the primary system of nominating candidates which occurred about 1895, acted as a blight on the Negro politically. Up until that year, Negroes had held many important municipal, county and state appointive and elective position. One Negro had been elected to the City Council.[2] Four Negroes had been elected to the State Legislature. One Negro had been elected Circuit Court Commissioner. But since the year 1894, when William Ferguson was re-elected Estimator of the City of Detroit, no Negro had been elected to public office.

C. Loss of Social Privilege

Beginning with 1890, there developed an increasing rift in the cordial relations which had existed in the white and colored races in Detroit. Evidence of this was the "Ferguson suit against Geiss" [sic; Geis] a prominent restaurateur, for discrimination in a public restaurant. Ferguson's suit against Geiss was only the beginning of similar acts of discrimination in theatres and restaurants. Few of the suits after the Ferguson-Geiss case ended as satisfactorily as did that case for the colored people. In many cases judgment was awarded to the Negro when he had been refused admission or set aside in public places but the judgment was usually from one to six cents, so that the offending parties were encouraged to repeat their acts of separation.

Among the reasons given for this development of racial antipathy was the increasing number of Negroes in the state and, secondly, an undesirable migration of race-track followers that began before 1890.

This undesirable migration began shortly after 1885, when race-tracks were established at the 8-mi. Road and Grosse Point. Most of the track followers were undesirable elements of both races from the South. Both of these elements went into the quiet restaurants and amusement places of Detroit and conducted themselves in such a boisterous manner that their patronage became very undesirable. However, the colored "sports" were the chiefest sufferers, as they were the only ones discriminated against.

In 1895, the betting feature of horse-racing was eliminated all over the United States. Consequently, the race-tracks were abolished in Detroit but almost simultaneously other tracks were established at Windsor, Ontario, on Canadian soil, just across the river from Detroit. The proximity of Windsor attracted the touts, gamblers, book-makers and the undesirable followers of the race-track from all over the country, so that down until the present day Detroit has had to suffer from the behavior of this race-horse class.

Soon after the abolition of race-track betting the famous "Reform Wave" struck Chicago and eliminated at least a large part of the colored "red light" district. A great many proprietors of disorderly resorts in that city and their hangers-on, came to Detroit because it had the reputation of being a "wide open town".

Whatever the reasons for the declining of the old friendly relationship between the white and colored people of Detroit, the fact remains that policies of separation have grown gradually more common since 1895.[3]

Editor's Notes

1. This was a battle that had to be fought all over again by the NAACP and others when it was discovered in 1940–41 that blacks were systematically being screened from employment as conductors, motormen, or bus drivers for the Detroit Streets and Railways Commission (DSR). The usual device was an apparent failure of preliminary health examinations; it was widely reported that at least one doctor would insist that any black applicant coming before him had failed the Wasserman test.

2. The position was actually one with the Board of Estimates, comparable in power but not the same as that of alderman. William Patrick was the first black elected to the Detroit Common Council.

3. It is likely that some of Washington's information came to him from older Detroiters during the years of 1917–18, when he served as executive secretary of the fledgling Detroit Urban League. It is probable that families such as the Coles, the Lamberts, the Johnsons, the Swans, and the Pelhams instructed the newcomer in area history. However, Washington brought to the local history of his people a young man's anger.

Part VIII

July, 1912: Business
Dominates Reform

July, 1912: Business Dominates Reform

After the exit of Pingree from local and state politics, it was downhill all the way for Detroit as far as the Progressives went. Some of the uglier aspects of petty election fraud reasserted themselves but, more importantly, the aims of the reform movement underwent a distortion.

As the automobile became an industrial force to be reckoned with, so did the former makers of wagon wheels, or marine engines, or bicycles, who were now making cars. Their drive toward Americanism came at the very moment when whole new groups of foreigners were arriving, mostly from southeastern Europe. Long-defined political neighborhoods and enclaves of the foreign-born received diminished respect, as people were encouraged to identify them with corruption, saloons, vote-buying, and mysterious radicalism.

The city hoped for responsible and efficient government, the kind that Mayor Pingree had tried for and almost achieved. It was willing to pay by devaluing its ethnicity.

There were relatively few blacks in Detroit until the very end of this period; they were not a particular target of the reformers of 1912. However, their rapid increase during the labor shortages of World War I made the group more visible by 1918, when the new city charter was adopted. By then it was clear that the reformers looked forward to a millennium of good government,

259

preferably controlled by white Anglo-Saxons. All in all, to gain a superficially clean city government, the first steps were taken in an effort to homogenize the people.

All Detroit was stunned by the newspaper headlines of July 26 and 27, 1912. Not since Mayor Hazen Pingree's school board arrests almost twenty years earlier had there been such a demonstration that politics was, indeed, a dirty business. In all, twenty-six of the city's thirty-six aldermen were arrested for allegedly taking bribes. Many would, in fact, shortly be released, and the prosecution's case would finally revolve around Tom Glinnan, an alderman—comparable to a member of today's city council—from the city's newest ward, the eighteenth, in southwest Detroit. That Glinnan would eventually escape all charges would be regarded as either a triumph of civil liberties or proof that a new system of urban government was needed, depending on point of view.

The new system did indeed come to pass with the charter of 1918, which replaced the board of aldermen, elected by wards, with a nine-member council elected at large, a system that survives today.

I have chosen two interesting, differing accounts of the incident. One version comes from the memoirs of elder statesman John C. Lodge, who served many years as alderman, councilman, and mayor. Lodge's memoirs, *I Remember Detroit*, were dictated by him in 1948 and published by Wayne University Press the following year. The other account is by Jack Elenbaas, urban and political historian of the Progressive period. His analysis in *Michigan History* (Winter, 1970) shows an awareness of the civil liberties issue that is generally lacking from the contemporary accounts.

1.   I Enter Politics

John C. Lodge, with
Milo M. Quaife

Henry M. Leland was an able engineer who at the beginning of the century designed the Cadillac automobile. He rose to prominence as President of the Company and in later years created the Lincoln automobile. For practically a third of a century he was one of Detroit's foremost industrial and civic leaders. He was an earnest advocate of good government, who believed the city was "going to the demnition bowwows."

Pliny W. Marsh was a young lawyer who had served as attorney for the Prohibition party of Michigan . . . in 1909 Mr. Leland brought him to Detroit and with the cooperation of Divie B. Duffield and a few others they created a little organization with a name which nearly killed it—the Detroit Civic Uplift League.

John C. Lodge, with Milo M. Quaife, "I Enter Politics," in *I Remember Detroit* (Detroit: Wayne University Press, 1949), 84–88.

Imagine, if you can, trying to accomplish anything in politics with a name like that. By the man in the street it was dubbed the "Goo-goo League." When Mr. Leland came to seem me about the organization I told him that the first thing they should do was change its name. "It is rather difficult to uplift people," I said. "Just call it the Detroit Citizen's League." This change was made, and the name, Detroit Citizen's League, was adopted. . . . a couple of years passed before it was able to exert any material influence upon the city government, which continued to be dominated by the Wets.

Then came the blowout of 1912. Early in the spring a resolution was introduced to the Board of Aldermen requesting the President of the Board to appoint a committee to go to Pittsburgh and interview the officials of the Pennsylvania Railroad on the possibility of extending its services to Detroit. [Lodge, Mayor Thompson, and a number of others went to Pittsburgh without effect.] . . .

It was just at the beginning of the era automobile men like to refer to as "the game", and our output of automobiles was rapidly becoming tremendous. We who were on the ground knew what was happening to our city, but the officials of the Pennsylvania Railroad at Pittsburgh could not see it. . . .

Although I was a member of the Board of Aldermen, I had no knowledge of the wholesale bribery that was going on until I read the exposure of it printed in the late afternoon edition of the *News* on July 26, 1912. That was a tremendous newspaper scoop. About two weeks prior to this, Homer Warren [Detroit postmaster, who was also serving as president of the board of commerce] telephoned me one morning to ask if I could come to his office, as he wanted me to meet a couple of gentlemen who were coming in at eleven o'clock.

So I went over to the post office, where Mr. Warren introduced me to Walter Brennan, a real estate man from the Wabash Railroad. With him was Rufus Lathrop, who was the local attorney for the Wabash. They proceeded to say that they wished to have Seventh Street closed from Fort to West Jefferson (then called River Road), and Mr. Warren asked me what I thought of the project.

I replied that I had gone to Pittsburgh two or three weeks before that to offer every possible aid to the Pennsylvania Road if it would come into Detroit, and that I did not see how I could consistently oppose the Wabash proposition, a road that was already here. I then said to Mr. Brennan that I hoped nothing would happen between then and the time the Aldermen acted to make me change my mind, any boodling on this, and I would be off the reservation.

I said this because I had some suspicion concerning the action of certain Aldermen in the past. But the proposal seemed to be entirely proper, and it received the vote of the entire Board with the exception of one Alderman from the ward which contained the local opposition to the measure. It subsequently appeared that Andrew H. Green, Manager of the Solvay Company, and a group of associates had raised the sum of $10,000 with which to employ the Burns Detective Agency of New York in an attempt to smoke out the whole bunch of saloon grafters, and that Brennan, who was in fact Walter Burns [of the Burns Detective Agency, an early security company], had been sent to Detroit to trap them.

This brings me to the point of narrating the handiwork of Edward R. Schreiter. At that time an Alderman could draft an ordinance for submission to the Board. Now this has to be done by the Corporation Counsel, or at least must be approved by him. Schreiter, who was a clever fixer, had promoted an ordinance creating the office of Secretary of the Board of Aldermen, to be filled, of course, by himself. Thereafter he had about half of the Aldermen eating out of his hand. He provided them with free theater tickets, tickets to the race track over in Windsor, and I don't know what else, until the matter of the Seventh Street closing came up.

Although I knew nothing of the bribery in this connection, the existence of a smelly situation generally was publicly suspected, and in fact all through the arraignment and trial that followed, the *Journal* kept saying: "You haven't attacked the wart on the face of city politics—Ed Schreiter." So I concluded it was time to get rid of him, and although Bert Allen, another Alderman whose name wasn't in the list of bribe-takers, objected that I was prejudging the case, we had more than a quorum, and my ordinance to abolish the office of Secretary to the Board was passed by unanimous vote, which disposed of Mr. Schreiter.

Seeing that he was through, I supposed he figured that he had better play the rat, and he went to Brennan with a printed list of the Board of Aldermen which I still have, on which he had inserted the sums—ranging from $1,000 downward—which each of the bribe takers would accept, and one by one they trooped into Brennan's office in the Ford Building, where they were paid the sums Schreiter had indicated. Highest on the list was Thomas E. Glinnan, bellwether of the flock, who received $1,000. Most of the others were given sums ranging from $100 to $300. Brennan had installed a dictaphone in his office to record the transactions and when the men came out policemen waiting in the corridor arrested them and took them over to headquarters.

This was the story the *News* published that afternoon of July 26. The scandal was a stench in the nostrils of the whole city, but it had the incidental benefit of ridding us of Schreiter, who had provided the brains for the dishonest Aldermen who stupidly followed his leadership. Bad as their conduct was, however, there was some extenuation for it. The enactment of the ordinance for the closing of the street-end was wholly proper. Their fault lay in the acceptance of pay as a reward for their votes. Yet, although I have never indulged in it, the acceptance of theater passes and other favors by public officials is commonplace. Of course, the only motive for such gifts is the desire to influence the action of the recipients.

Thomas E. Glinnan, who was an Alderman from the Eighteenth Ward, in which Green's business was located, was the only one of the bribe-takers who was ever brought to trial, and he was acquitted. Although he admitted that he had received the money, his attorney, James MacNamara, argued successfully that it had been forced upon him by Brennan without his consent. He was the big boss, and following his acquittal there seemed to be no point in prosecuting the other Aldermen. The Eighteenth Ward extended westward from about Military Avenue to the City Limits. It was an industrial section inhabited largely by railroad and working men.

Glinnan had been elected Alderman of the Eighteenth Ward twice. Subsequently the city created three new wards—increasing the number from eighteen to twenty-one—by making the Nineteenth and Twenty-first wards out of the Seventeenth, and taking the southwesterly part of the Eighteenth Ward to make the Twentieth. After the debacle of 1912, Glinnan was re-elected to the Board of Aldermen three times, once from the Eighteenth and twice from the Twentieth Ward. He was a strong-minded man, and though he had but little or no formal education, he had a great deal of native force and ability. Evidently he was the kind of representative the people down there wanted. In 1918 he filed his petition for the new City Council, but in the election he ran number 18, the lowest in the list of nominees.

2. The Excesses of Reform: The Day the Detroit Mayor Arrested the City Council

Jack D. Elenbaas

As I have suggested in the introduction to this section, Elenbaas sees different villains in his look at urban politics.

The 1912 Detroit city council scandal and trial of Alderman Tom Glinnan revealed the dark side of that zealous reformer who worked out his strategy during the Progressive Era. Ambitious politicians on the outside looking in, brutally competitive newspapers fighting for survival, plus influential businessmen with a desire for more political influence over city hall, all came together in that summer in 1912 to create one of the most sensational scandals in the history of American municipal government, and all of it was done in the name of reform. . . .

[Long before the trial] . . . all of the Detroit papers agreed that the case against Tom Glinnan was especially airtight. The prosecutor's office had the marked money, it had witnesses, it had a

Jack D. Elenbaas, "The Excesses of Reform: The Day the Detroit Mayor Arrested the City Council," *Michigan History* 54, no. 1 (Winter 1970): 1–18.

confession, and it had recordings of the conversation that had taken place between Glinnan and Detective Brennan at the time the bribe was made. The Burns Agency prided itself on being scientific, which included the latest in wire tapping devices. Detective Brennan declared: "Mayor Thompson, I want to congratulate you. It is refreshing to come to a city like Detroit and find a man big enough and willing to go out and clean up grafters not for the sake of putting them in prison but for the good of the municipality. . . . "

The plight of the arrested aldermen, however, continued to remain uncertain long after the 1912 mayoral election was over. It was not until the spring of 1915, over two and a half years later, that their fate was finally decided.

After two months of examination, during which time seven of the seventeen aldermen arrested August 9 were released, the court bound over for trial the remaining ten. The Prosecuting Attorney, Hugh Shepherd, then announced that he would try the case of Thomas Glinnan first. He believed that the case against the alderman was a strong one and that the prosecution could with certainty count on a conviction.

Glinnan's defense council was headed by James A. MacNamara, a successful Detroit attorney. . . . For the next nineteen months Shepherd and MacNamara engaged in a series of legal maneuvers that included two requests for changes of venue and the challenging of hundreds of prospective jurors. . . .

The selection of a jury proved to be a never-ending task, as the defense successfully challenged whole lists of names of prospective jurors. In his challenges MacNamara charged that the jury commissioners, whose job it was to submit the list of names for jury duty, had been quite selective in carrying out their task; so selective, in fact, argued the defense, as to insure the conviction of Tom Glinnan. On the stand Pontius Wood, one of the jury commissioners, admitted that no names were selected from the defendant's ward. He also testified that the commissioners had agreed to exclude from the list politicians, saloonkeepers, and Negroes. Judge Phelan asked: "Do you mean that you would not put the name of a good law-abiding citizen upon the jury list because his color happened to be different from yours? Why if we allowed that it would be easy to take the next step and bar citizens on account of their nationality or religion."

"Well, we barred saloonkeepers," replied Wood.

It was also revealed by the defense in the examination of the jury commissioners that the prestigious Detroit Board of Commerce had secretly submitted to the commissioners a list of names of men that it would like to see serve on the Glinnan jury. With this kind of evidence and this kind of aggressive defense, Tom Glinnan's attorneys were able to challenge 750 names and to delay the start of the trial nineteen months.

Finally on July 6, 1914, the last juror was seated, and Alderman Glinnan was brought to trial. The prosecution's case rested on its witnesses which included Detectives Brennan and Burns, Andrew H. Green, Jr., and the two arresting officers. The prosecution also claimed that it had the roll of marked bills taken from Glinnan at the time of the arrest and the recordings of the conversation that took place between Glinnan and Brennan at the time the bribe was received. The final piece of evidence that filled out the prosecution's case was the alleged statement made by Glinnan after his arrest.

The defense, seemingly faced with an impossible task, attempted to develop three lines of argument in the hope of freeing the alderman. The first approach of the defense was to destroy the credibility of the prosecution's witnesses. A second approach was to establish reasons why some men wanted Glinnan out of the way. And finally, a third line of argument used was to disprove the charge that a conspiracy had ever existed between the alderman and the detective who posed as a Wabash Railroad official. If it could be proved that at no time before the vote on the petition did Glinnan agree to accept money from Brennan, then of course, the prosecution did not have a case.

Two of the prosecution's major witnesses, Detectives Burns and Brennan, received very rough handling by Defense Attorney MacNamara. In the cross-examinations the defense established the fact that the detectives had been invited by Mayor Thompson and had been financed by Andrew H. Green to "test the integrity" of certain aldermen believed to be corruptible. The defense charged that in effect the Burns Agency came to Detroit to encourage aldermen to commit a crime which, MacNamara argued, was a crime in itself.

The past record of the Burns Agency was gone over thoroughly by the defense, and the two detectives were forced to admit that their organization had gotten into trouble in various cities such as Omaha, Atlanta, and New York. Some of the detectives employed by Burns Agency, it was revealed, were still under indictment for perjury in some of the cities mentioned. The record also showed that William J. Burns, the head of the agency, had been removed as an officer of the Association of Police Chiefs for "unprofessional conduct." MacNamara described Burns as an "assassin of character deadlier than a cobra" who engaged in reckless and lawless methods. On a number of occasions the defense managed to get the two detectives to contradict one another. . . . The defense charged that these men were simply hired witnesses brought to Detroit to do a job using any means necessary and that they had used illegal means in the past and were using them again. In their treatment of the defendant, argued the defense, they had used the whole gambit including bribery, perjury, and the third degree.

Another star witness of the prosecution was Andrew Green. He also received a severe grilling at the hands of the defense. Mr. Green was a prominent Detroit businessman with a record of civic involvement. He had provided the money to finance the investigation as well as the bribes, and he had been present in the room where Glinnan was alleged to have made the confession. During the cross-examination Green estimated that the whole affair had cost him around ten thousand dollars, more or less. . . . Green did admit that he had promised Glinnan a job in his company, the Solvay Process Company, if the alderman would confess. . . .

Other witnesses for the prosecution included the county detectives, the stenographer, and the dictograph operators. All claimed to have been in the room where Glinnan had produced the money and had made the alleged confession. In the cross-examination the defense established that Detective Burns had shouted at Glinnan and had threatened him. They also testified that Burns had ordered Glinnan to remove the money from his left-hand coat pocket immediately after his arrest. The question then posed by the defense was, how did Mr. Burns know which pocket the money was in, unless he had schemed with his cohort Brennan to have it planted there?

As for the recordings of the conversation between Glinnan and the bribe-offering Detective Brennan, the defense brought in as expert Fred Ireland, the chief stenographer for the United States Congress, who testified that the dictograph machine could not have operated effectively under the conditions present in that office at the time of the arrest. The witnesses also disagreed as to whether or not Glinnan had confessed, and as a result the court refused to allow any statement made by Glinnan at the time of the arrest to be used as evidence, because it obviously had been obtained by threats and because its contents could not be substantiated. When Glinnan's defense counsel had finished with the prosecutor's witnesses, not one left the stand with his credibility intact.

A second line of argument developed with great care by the defense counsel was the establishment of motives for the arrest of Alderman Glinnan. In the testimony of the two detectives, Burns and Brennan, it was revealed that they had received large sums of money from both Green and from the county treasurer. The defense concluded that the detectives had been hired to "get Glinnan" and that the amount of money they received depended on how successful they were.

As far as the motives of Andrew Green were concerned the defense promised that: "We shall show you . . . it was a scheme to assassinate the character of a fellow citizen by hired crooks masquerading as private detectives . . . to make a political holiday for Andrew Green and to make a pay-day for the Burns Detective Agency."

Green's role in this whole affair was shrouded in mystery. He had a reputation for contributing money to various causes, and on one occasion he had posted bail for two labor organizers who had been arrested in connection with an alleged dynamiting conspiracy. More recently he had contributed money and effort in the fight to get the Thompson-Hally [street railway] ordinance passed. After its defeat, there was talk about Green becoming the Democratic candidate for mayor in the upcoming local election. Glinnan and Green had recently locked horns over the Thompson-Hally proposal, and it was quite evident that a certain amount of antagonism and political rivalry had built up between the two men.

On the stand Green testified that after the defeat of the Thompson proposal, he had met with the mayor to discuss why it was so difficult to get necessary reforms passed. The mayor explained, said Green, that too many aldermen in the city council had to be paid before anything was done. Green then suggested to the mayor that they devise a plan that would expose the bribe-takers. In a letter to Thompson dated February 14, 1912, Green wrote. "I wish to say that I will undertake whatever you wish me to do in regard to this matter." By that time Thompson had already conferred with Burns, the price had been set, and now Green had agreed to foot the bill.

Green admitted that he had decided to run for mayor but then withdrew his name on July 24, 1912, which was just two days before the first arrests were made. He explained that his decision to withdraw was caused by his employer's refusal to continue his salary during his term as mayor. The defense offered another explanation, claiming that Green, who at first thought that his financial backing of the investigation of the aldermen would help him to win votes, suddenly realized that the detectives had no evidence against the aldermen, but were going to frame them. Green then . . . decided to drop out of the mayor's race before the whole thing blew up in his face.

The motives of Mayor Thompson in this case were also explored by the defense although the ex-mayor never took the stand. . . . Brennan testified that Thompson had indicated to him that, "if you reach Glinnan you reach them all." The conclusion drawn by the defense was that Thompson had hoped to salvage his sagging political career by posing as a "graft-hunting" mayor and that he had called in private detectives to trap in any way they could his opponents in the city council, especially the "Boss of the Common Council" Tom Glinnan.

All of the prosecution's witnesses had reason to want Alderman Glinnan out of the way, reasoned the defense. For the Burns Agency it was simply money as it had been at other places across the country where they had operated. For Andrew Green it was a combination of a desire for reform, plus public recognition and possible political opportunity. And for Mayor Thompson it was a chance to escape political defeat and at the same time bring down upon his political tormentor, Tom Glinnan, the righteous wrath of vengeance in the disguise of reform.

After having raised serious doubts concerning the credibility of the prosecution's witnesses and after having established certain underlying causes for Glinnan's arrest, the defense now moved to discredit the charge that a conspiracy had existed between Detective Brennan and the defendant before the final vote on the Wabash petition had been taken. The key to the prosecution's and the defense's case on this point was the testimony of Detective Brennan. . . .

Brennan arrived in Detroit February 23, 1912, and a few days later he met with Van Dyke and Thompson in Van Dyke's office. At this meeting Brennan received instructions to "test the integrity" of certain aldermen mentioned by Van Dyke and by the mayor. Among those mentioned was Tom Glinnan. . . .

Brennan's testimony further showed that for the next two months he had nosed about the saloons and hotels that were located around city hall, hoping to uncover information about the illegal activities of those aldermen mentioned by Mayor Thompson. . . . Finally they [Brennan, Burns, Thompson, Green, and Van Dyke] hit upon the idea of submitting a bogus petition to the city council and then seeing which aldermen would sell their votes. The Wabash Railroad Company was contacted and it consented to allow the name of the company to be used on the petition, and on May 7, Glinnan as a member of the Street Opening Committee introduced it to the council. The first vote on the petition came July 9, and all the councilmen except one voted in favor of it. . . . On July 11, two days after Glinnan had recorded a vote in favor of the petition, the defense pointed out, Brennan stated that he met with Glinnan at the phony Wabash office and offered him $750 for his vote. Glinnan testified at this point that Brennan did not offer him any money but had invited him to the Wabash office to discuss a possible position on the railroad. Here the case rested on the word of Brennan or Glinnan, and the jury had to decide which to believe.

A few days after the July 11 meeting between Glinnan and Brennan, a final vote on the Wabash petition was taken and it passed. On July 24 Brennan met Alderman Glinnan on the street and invited him to drop by his office on the 26th and pick up his money. Glinnan testified on the stand that Brennan had said nothing about money but instead had suggested that he come to his office on the 26th with letters of recommendation for the job they had discussed earlier. . . . Glinnan's story was that . . . he had turned over the letters of recommendation to Brennan, and then he was ushered out the door into the hands of the waiting detectives who immediately placed him under arrest. Following his arrest he was hurried into an adjoining office where Detective Burns demanded that the harried alderman turn over the roll of money he had in his coat pocket. Then Glinnan was subjected to a three hour ordeal in which Burns threatened, Green pleaded, and the assistant prosecutor waited for a confession which Glinnan insisted he never made.

The defense concluded its case by maintaining that the whole incident was a frame-up to get Glinnan. Glinnan had never at any time, argued the defense, agreed to accept money nor in fact did he take any money. Instead Burns and Brennan, after having failed to come up with any proof of wrongdoing on the part of the alderman, had gone to Thompson and Green and had concocted this desperate scheme as a last resort. Glinnan, stated the defense, had favored the railroad's petition before his discussion with Brennan on July 11 when the detective alleged he had offered Glinnan the money. As a matter of record, Glinnan had supported the petition on the first vote taken on July 9. The defense also maintained that on the day of the arrest, the alderman was lured to the Wabash office with the promise of a job and then had marked money planted in his outside coat pocket. After the plant was made, . . . the hapless Glinnan was then subjected to the third degree for three hours in a futile attempt to get a confession out of him. It all boiled down to one fact, declared the defense, and that is do you take the word of Brennan, a "hired witness," or the word of Tom Glinnan, a "dedicated public servant?"

The jury deliberated forty-five minutes and returned a verdict of not guilty. The courtroom went wild. The following spring the Wayne County prosecutor's office asked that charges be dropped on the remaining nine aldermen still waiting to be tried. . . . The court agreed and the cases of the other nine aldermen were dropped.

It has been stated that the arrest of the ten aldermen and the trial of Thomas Glinnan helped move Detroit closer to the new charter she finally received in 1918. The new city charter abolished the board of aldermen and the partisan system of ward representation and in its place established a nonpartisan, highly centralized system of local government designed to be more efficient and less corrupt. Although no convictions had been obtained, the board of aldermen had been disgraced, and now reform organizations such as the Detroit Citizen's League and the Board of Commerce used this scandal to good advantage in bringing about the changes in Detroit's government that would give these groups more control than they had had under the old ward system. This was all done, of course in the name of reform. The partisan ward system of government which had based its strength on an intricate relationship between aldermen, ward bosses, and organized blocs of voters was done away with in the new 1918 charter. In its place a more centralized nine-man council elected at large was established which would be out of the hands of the ward bosses and in many cases out of touch with the needs of the wards. City council elections would now be susceptible to well-financed campaigns in which the newspapers and organized civic groups would have a much greater degree of influence.[1]

Editor's Note

1. In the preparation of this article, Elenbaas made extensive use of Wayne County Court records and the Scallen Papers, BHC, as well as the newspapers of the time. Other scholars working within this period during the last few years have made use of the insights shown here.

Part IX

**Agents of Change:
The Automobile and
World War I**

Agents of Change: The Automobile and World War I

Detroit's trademark, the automobile, arrived well before 1900. Manufacturers of products that characterized Detroit industry during the second half of the nineteenth century—marine motors and steam engines, bicycles, carriages, wagons, and farm implements—were led naturally to attempts at production of the automobile, the newest excitement spreading through the business world.

Throughout the early 1900s, several imaginative automotive inventors were eliminated by the competition. Automotive history is a whole separate field for the historian. I will only comment that the scope of those early deletions, long before the "Big Three," can be seen in the panorama of unfamiliar car names. Just a few of those that no longer exist are: the Maxwell, the Detroit Electric, the Dort, the King, the Huber, the Herreshoff, the Sommer, the Aerocar, the Welch, the Peerless, the Leland, Reo, and Durant. Other names, such as Packard and Olds, were absorbed into new management and financing structures, and there is, of course, an Oldsmobile today. Just one early inventor, the first Henry Ford, would head the greatest individually owned auto plant of them all.

The world war brought no cessation in automobile manufacturing; in addition there were government contracts for armaments and for a time even airplanes.

As industry grew, so did the responsibilities its leaders took on. There came to be a unity of stance. When the President of the "Good Citizens League," a Negro organization, wrote angrily to the chamber of commerce, "when it comes to the Negro you have just one opinion"; he was speaking only a part of the truth. More and more industrialists shared one opinion about not only the Negro, but a great many matters—the Industrial Workers of the World (IWW), the open shop, "Americanism" programs for factories and schools . . .

While World War I speeded up industrial development and helped to channel its direction into automotive and auto-related areas, it did not fundamentally change the direction toward Americanism in which the city's leadership had been moving since 1912.

The businessmen reformers of 1912 brought into the war years their notion of the ideal worker for the new factories. If he (and it was usually "he") were not born an American he would be taught to become a good imitation of one. Thrift and temperance were important, too. Liquor went with political corruption, even rebellious anarchism. (After the Russian Revolution in October, 1917, "Bolshevism" came to be the new term used to disparage those "outside agitators" who carried on the struggles of labor.)

Employers pointed out, with reason, that intemperance, which they often associated with foreigners, could lead to factory accidents. Yet a careful reading of state labor inspectors' reports, with their urgings to cover a wheel, repair electrical equipment, or install guards on punch presses, does make one wonder what priority was really given to accident prevention.

A fear of being thought German or pro-German pervaded the ordinary people of the city. Carl Schmidt, leather tanner, head of the house of Traugott Schmidt, was besieged by questions about why he continued his business trips to Germany until America entered the war. He defended himself by endowing an entire field hospital unit in France for Harper Hospital. Schmidt's choice of a humanitarian cause could have been no coincidence. He was, after all, a Socialist and a pacifist as well. He continued to attend meetings in aid of the Socialist presidential candidate Eugene Debs, and it was during this period that he bought a retirement home for his old friend Jo Labadie. It was a time when lesser Schmidts changed their names to Smith. There was little *gemütlichkeit* among Detroit's very large German-American community as they dutifully bought Liberty bonds.[1]

Twenty-five thousand blacks came to Detroit to find work. They slept on the floor of the railroad station and, till rousted by the police, in parks. They stretched five to a bed in the rooming houses of the east side. Luckiest of all were those met by friends or relatives. They might be just as crowded, of course, but the fear of a strange town, with strange customs, would be less.

The Urban League, to its everlasting credit, tried to meet the need. It was considerably misunderstood at times, by whites and blacks alike. The early Urban League was a benevolent creation of industrialists and social leaders, mainly white. They hired a young man fresh from Harvard as executive-secretary, then questioned his phone bills and the cost of office supplies. Despite this lack of trust, Forrester Washington went on with the job. He instituted a questionnaire for employers in an effort to find factory openings for blacks. Instead, he found any number of managers who felt they should be thanked for hiring a "colored night man" or a janitor among a work force of several hundred. The future dean of the Atlanta University School of Social Work got his basic training in heartbreak and disappointment in wartime Detroit.

Washington left for a federal post in 1918 and was replaced by John Dancy. Dancy continued Washington's efforts to get the newcomers to conform to urban habits. Women were told not to appear in public wearing housedresses and dustcaps or bandanas, men not to gather in large groups talking loudly at street corners. All were urged to cultivate the white man's definition of good manners to gain his respect. These warnings naturally caused annoyance among some local blacks.[2]

For a first look at the changes brought about during this period of concentrated industry before and during the first world war, we return to the river and use it as a measure for what was happening. This time we look at a particular spot on the Detroit River, Sam Zug's old island, sold by him long ago, which industry was distorting beyond recognition.[3]

By 1914 people were coming to Detroit from all over the country. One reason was Henry Ford's widely advertised Five Dollar Day. A news account from the *Detroit Journal* indicates that the start of the Five Dollar Day was not Ford's greatest moment.

Later workers would learn that for a variety of reasons the five dollar day often did not amount to five dollars. Also, strings attached to the money repelled many workers not used to personal intrusion in their lives.[4]

Then in "Detroit—A City Awake," we take a first look at what the influx of workers was already doing to the shape of the city as early as 1911. The need of housing for workers' families was already acute. Yet Myron Adams, writing for *Survey*, found there were still green trees, fresh air, and open space in much of the city. Adams also saw factories creating a ring of blight at the city's edge, and a sad lack of planning to prevent further troubles.[5]

There were crosscurrents, of course, amid the general conformity demanded by industry. Businessmen began to welcome some women workers during World War I, but with a startling lack of response to their needs. In a report of the state labor inspectors, Mary Girardin and her colleagues recorded again and again, "Immediately provide a separate lavatory for your women workers," or "Readjust the working hours of your female employees to conform to state law," as well as serious safety violations.

Editor's Notes

1. Carl Schmidt's war years are described in a scrapbook of clippings and miscellany (Schmidt Collection, Bentley Library, University of Michigan).

   Another person who suffered from ties to Germany was Rebecca Shelley, a young pacifist who spent some time in Detroit as one of a group persuading Henry Ford to finance a peace ship in an effort to ward off war in Europe. Shelley lost her U.S. citizenship upon marrying a German citizen because of a restrictive wartime law. Though she spent much of her life in the Battle Creek area, her Detroit ties at the time of World War I have been documented in a recent monograph by Beverly Fish of Wayne State University. Shelley lived to be an active pacifist during the Vietnam War.

2. Detroit Urban League Papers, Bentley Library, Box 1. See also *Sand against the Wind: The Memoirs of John C. Dancy* (Detroit: Wayne State University Press, 1966). Dancy made a determined effort to befriend

all who could help his people and served for many years as executive secretary of the Detroit Urban League, following Forrester Washington.

3. Sam Zug has been blamed too often for downriver industrial pollution. Zug was a furniture maker, businessman, and philanthropist He was also an abolitionist and spent large sums to buy farmland in Canada for those who came by the Underground Railway. It is entirely possible, though not proven, that Zug Island, at the narrowest point of the Detroit River, was a way station on the route to Amherstburg—and freedom.

4. The beer and wine served as a matter of course in the homes of many ethnic groups had investigators from Ford's "Sociological Department" opening the doors of the workingman's icebox to check his habits.

5. Myron Adams's 1911 article was followed by another look at housing in Detroit published by *Survey* just five years later. John Ihlders, writing in 1916, was shocked at the preventable troubles that had come to the city's working poor. No one had cared enough to prevent inflationary high rents, the progressive dilapidation of homes, and even homelessness itself.

1. Industry and the River: The Fate of Zug Island

Detroit Free Press

On July 14, 1891, the business pages of the Free Press *carried the headline, "SALE OF ZUG ISLAND." This was news indeed, and just the beginning. The next fifteen years of rapid growth in Detroit heavy industry, especially automotive, would bring many changes to the marshy bog that thrust out into the Detroit River at the mouth of the Rouge.*

The sale mentioned here was of property that had been known as Brady Island since Sam Zug had sold it to George Brady and Charles Noble. In detailing the current sale, the writer gives us much island history and captures the ongoing process of change.

Brady Island can hardly be called an island at all, it being that peninsula of Ecorse Township that fronts on the Detroit River just below the Exposition Building, while a bend of the Rouge affords water frontage to one side and the rear. A swale known as Mud Run cuts it off from the mainland, but as Mud Run is only five feet deep, it doesn't count as an island maker.

The property includes 4,000 feet of Detroit River frontage from the mouth of the Rouge to the big coaling trestle of S. B. Smith & Co. and 8,000 feet of River Rouge frontage. . . .

[The island] was orginally the property of Lewis Cass, who sold it to the late Samuel Zug, who in turn sold undivided inter-

"Sale of Zug Island," *Detroit Free Press* (14 July 1891): 7.

Zug Island in later days: Ford works and shipping at the mouth of the Rouge River, 1970. (From UAW International. Used with permission of Reuther Archives.)

ests to George N. Brady and the late Charles W. Noble. . . . Messrs. Russell and Bourke will proceed at once to the improvement of the property by dyking the island, dredging slips for factory frontages into the interior of the island and the construction of railroad side tracks. The whole property will be made available for manufacturing purposes as soon as possible. It is altogether likely that in 1892 a railroad trestle, and a coal dock, similar to that of S. B. Smith & Co., will be constructed at the mouth of the Rouge River. A sulphur spring on the island that bubbles up 1,200 barrels of mineral water per day may be put to earning its living by the new owners.

This deal insures the completion of the work of reclamation of the marshes that formerly extended from Fort Wayne down to

Ecorse. The exposition property is a piece of reclaimed marsh. The Rouge River Improvement Company, composed of Michigan Central Railway people, has reclaimed 500 acres with a mile of frontage on the Detroit river.[1] Another mile of frontage, including 245 acres, is in process of reclamation, by Messrs. Russell and Dee, adjoining the Rouge River property, and the remaining three-fourths of a mile, the property of George A. Dupuis and William Blay, will be attacked just as soon as Mr. Dupuis' dredges are disengaged from work already contracted for in the same district. The home of the duck, the muskrat, and the mud hen seems to be doomed to destruction.

Editor's Note

1. At the time of these transactions, the "Michigan Central Railway people" were headed by president and general manager Henry Brockholst Ledyard, eldest grandson of Lewis Cass. Cass was not only the original owner of Zug Island but of much of the other area property— that is, of course, if we disregard the Indians, for whom the mouth of the Rouge had been a traditional gathering place.

2.　　The Five Dollar Day

Detroit Journal

ICY FIRE-HOSE DELUGE
STOPS 1,200 IN RIOTOUS
RUSH FOR FORD'S JOBS

Five Men Arrested and Three Thousand Soaked With
Water in Zero Cold When Crowd
Tries to Enter Works.
SMASH WINDOWS; WRECK STANDS
Crowd Irritated at Douche Hurls Stones at Factory
Then Angrily Attacks Street Venders' Places—
14,000 Applications By Mail.

A deluge of ice cold water, playing from two fire hoses in the hands of Highland Park policemen, stopped the rush of 12,000 men for jobs at the Ford Motor Co. plant Monday morning and caused a near-riot in Manchester avenue, on which the factory entrances to the Ford shops are located.

Three thousand men were soaked with water, it is estimated. With the temperature hovering close to the zero mark, and a biting blast coming across the fields from the northwest, they were an unenviable lot as they hurried away to find some place in which to thaw out. Their clothing froze a moment after they encountered the business end of the hose.

"Icy Fire Hose Deluge Stops 1,200 in Riotous Rush for Ford's Jobs," *Detroit Journal* (13 December 1913): 1.

285

Five of the job-seekers were arrested. Chief of Police Seymour, of the Highland Park department, was inclined to blame the slowness of Ford factory heads for the necessity of turning the hose on the crowd.

Only One Door

"Only one door into the factory was open at 8 o'clock," said Chief Seymour. "Had several been open, the Ford employes could have entered without trouble. But they all were heading for the single door and the job-seekers were mingled with them inextricably. We could not reason with the Ford employes or with the others. The Ford men were going to work later than usual, owing to the new eight-hour shift going into effect today, and were afraid they might lose their jobs if they were late. So they kept pressing forward. Had there been several doors open, we could have kept the crowd back while they went in, as we did afterwards when some of the officials arrived and threw the other entrances open."

As early as 10 o'clock Sunday night, when a gale was blowing and the mercury steadily falling, with a promise of zero weather in the air, men began to congregate about the Ford plant. Monday was the day when the $5 minimum for laborers went into effect, and the thought of it was sufficient incentive to the gathering men to brave the elements by an all-night vigil. By midnight a line of the job-seekers was extended to Oakland Avenue from near Woodward. As the hours passed, the shivering, stamping crowd increased little by little until at daybreak records of last week for men seeking jobs went by the boards.

Crowd Angry

The crowd was not as good-natured as last week's gatherings. The weather had its effect, of course, but hope of success was not as great Monday as before. The temper of some in the crowd was shown late Sunday evening, when some men attacked Patrolman Smith and tore his uniform, snatched away his revolver, club and handcuffs, and were fighting hard when help arrived for Smith.

Chief Seymour said Monday that the officer's assailants were Turks, and that they did not belong in the job-seeking crowd.

Disorders have been feared daily and Chief Seymour each day has detailed his entire forces to the Ford district. Up to Monday, however, inconsequential battles between men seeking vantage points in the crowd were the only disturbances.

Monday morning the scene appeared to be about as normal as any day last week until close to 8 o'clock. Then the Ford employes began to appear in large numbers to go to work. They found the street so congested that entrance was difficult. The police were holding back the job-seekers so as to leave a lane for employes, but the latter arrived so rapidly that they soon filled all the space left and soon the job-holders and job-seekers were thoroughly mingled.

The Ford employes wore little badges, but as the dense crowd jammed toward the single door that was open the police found it difficult to see just who got in. Soon there was such a congestion that no one could move. The police shouted orders until they were hoarse, but without effect. Then they threatened the crowd with the fire hose, but the crowd would not listen. The jobholders kept pressing forward and the job-seekers clung to them. Many could not do otherwise because of the enormous pressure on them from behind.

Then the police turned on the water, and employes, job-seekers and police officers themselves were drenched in short order. Scrambling backward, the mob overturned the "hot dog" lunch, cigar, and other stands across Manchester avenue. Some men, drenched and angry, picked up bricks, stones and bottles and hurled them at the hose users. Many of these missiles went through the factory windows.

When the crowd had backed off to a safe distance the Ford workers were permitted to come up again and other doors to the factories were opened, so that they soon were at work. Then the jobless ones began to move away. By 10 o'clock there were only a few hundred left walking about in the cold, wind-swept streets.

3.   Detroit—A City Awake

Myron E. Adams

During the Progressive period, many cities took a fresh look at the homes of their newcomers and poor. Detroit was experiencing unprecedented growth in 1911 when the magazine Survey, *a guidebook for the profession of social work, published a series on housing. Writer Myron Adams was perhaps too hopeful of positive action in Detroit. Devastated by wartime in-migration, the city lacked homes for thirty thousand families by 1920.*

The completion of a comprehensive building code, the reorganization of the department of buildings, and the establishment of a housing commission under the direction of the Board of Commerce are indications of an awakened interest in protecting the city of Detroit from the evils attending its constantly increasing housing problem.

The census shows one of the causes of a housing problem in Detroit. In 1870 the population was 77,599; in 1880, 116,340; in 1900, 285,754, and by 1910, it had increased to 465,766, without unusual gain by annexation. Through all these years Detroit has ranked among the first cities in the number of houses owned by residents. Its position at the crossroads of interstate and international commerce, its varied industries, the conditions under

Myron E. Adams, "Detroit—A City Awake," Survey (5 August 1911): 666–71.

which men have labored, as well as the unusual recreational opportunities on river and lake, have made a strong appeal to the home-builder and have been among the most obvious causes of its growth.

The city was well planned. From the civic center, the Campus Martius, which is located some blocks from the river front, radiate a series of avenues, while the streets run parallel and perpendicular to the river. Thus Detroit resembles an open fan with the river for outer edge. Three miles to the east and the west, the Grand Boulevard Parkway commences at the river and extends around the city, enclosing the most thickly built part in a square. Outside this parkway are the best residential and an increasing number of factory districts.

Congestion has been retarded, notwithstanding the rapid growth of the population, in a number of ways. The land is without hills or valleys to raise natural obstacles to normal expansion, and there have been many open spaces, some of them large farms held for a rise in value. Of late, however, improved transportation facilities and the tendency to build farther out have forced the sale of these lands, and they are fast building up. Other obstacles to congestion were the diffusion of population in special industrial districts along the river front, with its twelve miles of factories, the Parkway and its factory districts, and the routes by which the railroads have entered and completely encircled the city. Not only are foreign groups separated from one another, but the groups themselves are divided, and we have two Polish, two Hungarian, and two Italian settlements.

To these hindrances to congestion must be added the possibility of almost unlimited expansion, with easy access to places of labor. It is significant that practically all the automobile factories, which have been built within the last five years, are located in the outskirts, where before there were great tracts of vacant land.

The census shows that the population of Detroit increased by 180,000 during the last ten years. The question immediately suggests itself as to what provision has been made for housing these people. The answer is unsatisfactory because of insufficient statistics, except for the last three years . . . .

Thus in three years 63,493 people were housed in new buildings, independent of alterations and additions. . . . Despite all this Detroit has felt the pressure of incoming population, and shows evidences of overcrowding. There are two chief causes of this in two distinct classes of districts.

The first is the steady exodus to the suburbs of people whose homes once formed the downtown portion of the city, and whose places are taken by renters and roomers with little interest in the property they occupy and still less in the neighborhood. On the east side, and within a radius of three-quarters of a mile from the center of the city, this old district with its cheap boarding houses, many in bad repair, and its men's lodging houses, combined with the infrequent homes of long-time property holders, forms the border of the dreary district of houses of prostitution and their kind. On the west side is a similar district where these conditions are being duplicated. The disintegration goes on, without perceptible opposition. The number of people who crowd into smaller quarters constantly increases.

The second cause is the rapid growth of foreign-born colonies. Ten years ago the first evidences of congestion became evident in the Jewish quarter. Practically every family lived then in its own house, with grass and flowers in the yard. But with rapid growth, rents increased, and the occupation of the same house by two families began. The demand for more rooms continued; landlords raised the roofs of their cottages to admit another story and extended the buildings so that they covered the whole lot; some moved the house to the rear and put another in front of it, others attached it to the barn by a connecting apartment, or remodeled the barn to house more than one family.

If the process of remodelling which has been going on for the last five years is to continue without interference, the whole Jewish quarter will become one great district of overcrowded tenements, some of a very bad type. In the center of the district is the largest public school in Michigan. . . . The city has appropriated $65,000 for a recreation park, which will in some measure compensate for the loss of open spaces for children, who are found here in great numbers. But it will not change housing conditions nor prevent congestion.

The Hungarian colony lies in the Delray district, an industrial section some four miles from the center of the city. The Hungarian has a racial magnetism that attracts all friends and relatives from the other side. Admission is denied to none who can crowd in. Cottages built for four or five people house thirty and thirty-five. Every corner is used, and there is little furniture but beds and kitchen utensils. Sometimes the cellar or back yard is made into a primitive refuge for boarders.

The Polish district on the west side is by far the best of the sections inhabited by foreign-born residents. Industrial advantages have divided the Poles into two distinct communities. They are thrifty homemakers, owning 90 percent of the houses in the district. They seem to prefer the one or two-story dwelling with a yard, and seldom occupy the two-family flat or the tenement, as their Jewish and Servian neighbors do.

The Italians, rapidly increasing in number to 15,000 or 20,000, occupy a large district within the inner mile circle. There are few homemakers among them, and the boarders roam from city to city and from section to section. Many live in houses once among the most desirable in the city. These bring high rents, with consequent overcrowding. Repairs are lacking and disorder prevails.

The Servians, the Dalmatians, and the Bulgarians form a colony of about 5,000 near the car shops. Here under the "boarding boss" system familiar in most industrial cities, there are few houses with fewer than six boarders, besides the boss and his family. When the shops are busy this number is doubled, and the beds are used day and night. In one tenement on a rear lot, which had four separate flats with twelve rooms, were seven women, five boarding bosses, and fifty-two boarders—and that in a slack season. Inspectors of the Board of Health, who have power to prevent overcrowding, have cut down the number of boarders and improved the general sanitary condition of the neighborhood. One of the serious problems is the number of dark rooms created by the building of new houses and tenements on the lot line. These shut off all light from one side of the building. In addition to positive causes of concentration of population and increasing congestion, there was a lack of proper building legislation for prevention, regulation, and inspection. It is fair to say that until last February there were no ordinances which could keep conditions from growing more serious. Methods of building were practically unrestricted. Tenements could be built to cover the entire lot. A building could be so erected as to shut off the light and air, and even to prevent access to another building on an adjoining lot. Practically the only restrictive provisions were within limited fire districts, and they covered only the construction of side walls and roofs. In certain respects, where the condition of the house actually created a public nuisance, the Board of Health had authority to bring the matter before the courts, and from time to time some of the most unsightly and unsanitary places were reached in this way. The Board of Building Inspectors created in 1885 and the fire marshal's office created in 1887 lacked jurisdiction over dwellings.

But in 1907 the Legislature empowered the mayor to appoint a building commission of five men, which was instructed by the Common Council to formulate a building code. The commission completed the code in the spring of 1910, and for almost a year the Common Council gave it serious consideration. . . . [The code enacted for the construction of dwellings and tenement houses seems] adequate to remedy defects already apparent and to prevent prospective building operations which might lead to congestion. . . .

. . . [The cooperation of] the Board of Commerce and the Central Council of Charities resulted in the organization of the Detroit Housing commission, composed of representative men who intend to reinforce and supplement at every point the work of the Department of Buildings. . . .

There is every reason to believe that this commission will eventually approach the problem on the constructive side, and lead the movement to increase the number of houses that can be secured at small rents, or be purchased by men earning moderate wages. This combination of public administration reinforced by private support and approval will do much to keep the problem of congestion out of the increasing list of conditions that prevent natural and healthy living in a city which has always been a city of homes.[1]

Editor's Note

1. The Adams study is valuable for its clear descriptions of the shape of the city's growth and the special nature of its housing. Most material on housing needs of that period refers to "tenements" and "walk-up apartments." This was never the Detroit pattern, and the problems of New York were not those here. Detroit had its own.

4. Women Workers: A Surprise to Industry

Michigan Department of Labor

In every American war, women and minorities have been drawn into performing new sorts of work. World War I was no exception. Detroit employers had some problems in getting used to women workers. Some of these are revealed in the introduction to the Thirty-Fifth Annual Report of the Michigan Department of Labor, followed by a few typical citations made by labor inspectors of Detroit companies where women were part of the 1917 work force.

The most important question that the Labor Department has to deal with is that to do with women wage earners. The world war has brought about a revolution in women's work. Woman's tendency to venture more and more into traditional occupations of men received an enormous acceleration when the first soldiers were called to the colors abroad. Thousands of women are now working in occupations that not even the most advanced suffragist asked to be thrown open to them. There is literally not a thing that man has done that women are not now doing. This is not only true of manufacturing work and the

Michigan Department of Labor, "Women Wage Earners" and "Factory Orders Issued, 1917," in *Michigan Department of Labor, Thirty-Fifth Annual Report* (Lansing: Michigan Department of Labor, 1918), 9–10, 365–93.

293

professional and business occupations, but it is also true of the hardest kind of mechanical and laboring work.

So there has arisen the most vital problem that has ever faced the Department and the State. Women have been employed in some occupations in which men only were formerly employed, and for which little or no protection was provided by law. Again in some cases new dangers have developed for which former laws made no specific provisions.

In 1916 there was employed in the work shops and factories in Michigan 72,613 women, 14 years of age and over pursuing gainful occupations, of whom 72,063 were over 16 years of age.

In all groups of occupations the number of women to each man has increased, or the number of men to the number of women has decreased since the beginning of the war. The change in some instances has been remarkably abrupt, and must continue to be increasingly so.

The specific question asked: What will be the reactions between the excessive and abrupt employment of women, the diminuation in the number of working men, and the effect upon labor conditions generally throughout the State?

A great number of industries throughout the State have sought to break down the standards regarding the hours of labor women and children are permitted to work in gainful occupations. . . .

The engagement of women in the manufacturing of war materials . . . presents many features of outstanding interest. There, workers include dressmakers, laundry workers, textile workers, domestic servants, electrical workers, shop assistants, women and girls of every social grade and of no previous wage earning experiences. The danger of industrial employment to these workers include not only the risk of injury from accident but also the risk to health arising from the conditions under which an industry may be conducted. . . .

Factory Orders Issued, 1917 [Detroit] September 17, 1917

DODGE BROTHERS MOTOR CAR CO.—At once guard pulleys on machines 5871–5872, Dept. 17. Guard all lower pulleys. Guard wheel running machine 5022, Dept. 40. . . . Place signs opposite all stairways where women are working on third floor, and also on fourth floor directing way to fire escape.

September 6, 1917

HUPP MOTOR CAR CO.—At once box all lower belts and pulleys throughout plant. Box belt and wheel on machines 147–148–149. Box large belt machine 143. Guard all electric switches lower than 6 feet from floor. Guard emery wheel, Dept. XX. Put fire escape on fourth floor where women are employed.

September 4, 1917

JONES-REGAN CO.—At once place a higher hood on meat chopper machine to prevent one operating the machine from getting their hand in knife while machine is in operation. Do not permit males under eighteen years of age to operate dangerous machinery.

December 6, 1917

KROGER GROCERY AND BAKING CO.—At once provide separate toilets for use of your men and women employes at 394 Grand River Ave. Provide stools for use of women in their leisure time. Keep store heated to at least 70 degrees. Drain and keep basement in a sanitary condition.

August 28–29–30–31, 1917

PACKARD MOTOR CAR CO.—[among some sixty-five citations] . . . At once in Department C cover gears on lathe 2668. Box lower pulley on machine 4118. Put hood on all enameling tanks. . . . Guard all belts and pulleys where women are working. . . .

March 21, 1917

POSTAL TELEGRAPH CO.—At once arrange the hours of your female employes to conform to the 54–hour law and procure and keep on file permits for all employees under 16 years of age.

November 2, 1917

WABASH RAILWAY COMPANY—At once provide at least two or three additional toilets for female employes, and about three more for male employes. Provide another door or exit in rear of offices, second floor, leading to freight house, as a means of exit in case of fire.

December 28, 1917

WOLVERINE CREAMERY PRODUCTS CO.—At once provide a sanitary, properly designated toilet for the use of your female employes.

Part X

The Twenties: Decade of Contradictions

The Twenties: Decade of Contradictions

On New Year's Day, 1920, the new Federal Bureau of Investigation, under the direction of Attorney General A. Mitchell Palmer, who was rumored to have presidential ambitions, arrested several thousand persons in cities across the country, more than three hundred of them in Detroit. All were suspected of being "Bolsheviks."

The drive for Americanism did not stop at the war's end. Like other aspects of American life in the twenties, it carried with it its own contradiction or crosscurrent. There was an anti-Bolshevik drive, but there were also dissenters and fighters for civil liberties. The twenties have often been portrayed as carefree and prosperous, the happy-go-lucky days of the flapper. But Detroit, which had seen sharp rises in employment and inflation during the war years, now suffered sharp depression. Many small businesses failed during the postwar slump. Merciless layoffs occurred at the larger ones.

Never were the twenties as prosperous for all as the myth would have us believe. In part this was because the continuing Americanism drive was accompanied by a drive against labor unions. Industrial Detroit was proud of its strong "open shop" policy. Even the craft unions of skilled tradesmen were on the defensive. Still there remained throughout the decade a sharp discrepancy in pay between the organized worker and his more numerous unorganized brothers and sisters. The thousands of autoworkers, the best known and most conspicuous part of Detroit's work force, were almost completely unorganized. They were subject to extremes of seasonsal unemployment, often working only five or six months a year. Since this situation caused many to leave town, the city was subject to a constantly shifting population.

As for clerical employees, these, usually female, were consistently and notoriously underpaid during that period of high living costs. Even before the depression years, both embezzlement and suicide were known among Detroit's middle class. Meanwhile, the drive for Americanism was tied in with an increasing social pressure for conformity that, perhaps for the first time, was clearly beamed at the consumer as well as the worker.

Nowhere were contradictions more apparent than in civic and moral questions. Huge churches were built and filled with worshippers, yet many claimed liquor was surpassing automobiles as the town's largest industry. There was no real proof of this, but it sounded well, and certainly the demand for alcohol increased, and the industry was resourceful and inventive. The river traffic between Detroit, Walkerville, Sandwich, Ecorse, and Amherstburg was phenomenal.

Detroit's geographic location on the Canadian border certainly helped organized crime to get a foothold. There was the Purple Gang, involved in labor racketeering and extortion, targeting small businessmen. There was the Sugar Hill gang. There were gamblers galore, though the widespread policy, or "numbers," racket did not become a growth industry until the end of Prohibition in the early thirties. The Detroit Police Department had established what it called its "Italian Squad" well before the twenties. Now it was said to be needed because of the Mafia. Certainly Detroit had its own coalition of definable Italian families believed to be affiliated with organized crime. The situation was a great embarrassment to autoworkers, small storekeepers, and fine craftsmen of Italian heritage. The names of the families suspected by the community, sometimes unjustly, of being unduly rich may still be read on the gravestones of the downtown Church of the Holy Family. It is less certain whether the "Italian Squad" of the Detroit Police Department was at all effective in pinning down this sector of organized crime.

Sometimes it seemed as if everyone wanted the glamor of being part of the "liquor racket," and certainly many of the town's journalists, politicians, and, unfortunately, police were. Even in the relatively arid stretches of northwest Detroit, there was a legend that a fern or other large plant in the window of any small business meant "booze served here."

The first urgent problem Detroiters acknowledged was the housing shortage. The war years had brought uncontrolled inflation of rents and an acute shortage of physical space. The postwar years led to the creation of new "subdivisions" at the edge of town. These new fringe areas for workers were distinctly segregated. An example was Brightmoor, developed by B. E. Taylor for a working-class clientele. Brightmoor was strictly white and in its early days a focal point for Ku Klux Klan agitation.[1]

In the mid-twenties the Eight Mile-Wyoming area was opened to blacks—some said in part because of the anger of a white developer against a former colleague who owned adjacent land. Brightmoor, Eight Mile-Wyoming, and a number of other subdivisions catered to the poorest workingman's wish to own a little place in the country where he could sustain himself and his family during layoffs with a few chickens and a garden. Just a few years later, as Detroit's city limits would stretch out to engulf those new communities, those chickens and the occasional pig would come to seem inappropriate.

The housing crisis came to a head with the Ossian Sweet case. A young, black doctor who had lived through the bloody wartime riots in East St. Louis, Sweet was faced with the hostility of new neighbors on Detroit's east side. He made the decision to barricade himself, his family, and several friends in his new home. The evening ended with the besieged firing guns over the heads of rock throwers who had clustered around the house; one man across the street died in the gunfire, and Dr. Sweet and his companions were tried for murder. The Sweet trial forced at least some Detroiters to recognize that there were factors here that they did not understand and led to open acknowledgment that the Ku Klux Klan was a force in the city. It also led to the first official attempt to examine race relations in Detroit.

The selections for the twenties begin with the Red Scare, as it was viewed in U.S. Senate Judiciary Committee hearings held in 1921, two years after the Detroit arrests. There was another crosscurrent here in the events of the winter of 1920. A number of local business and government leaders, including the former Ford executive, Mayor James Couzens, were repelled by the outside invasion by the fledgling FBI. Whatever they had bargained for, to their credit, it wasn't this. The Red Scare story itself, as it appears in testimony given by a local reporter to the Senate committee, is self-explanatory.

Several documents follow that are related to the Ossian Sweet case, beginning with the news story itself with its revealing headlines. John Smith was mayor at the time and tried manfully to work through his own confusions on race problems to a realization that the Klan was active and that injustices were occurring. His open letter to his police chief immediately after the shooting is revealing social history of the times.

A far more sophisticated view than the mayor's is that taken by a young observer at the trial, David E. Lilienthal, later to be appointed director of the Tennessee Valley Authority (TVA) by Franklin Roosevelt. Lilienthal's praise for the fairness of Judge Frank Murphy sharpens one's perception of the state of justice received by blacks in other courtrooms across the country.

An important view of another major problem in the city of the twenties—police brutality—is revealed in a report by an interracial commission appointed by Mayor Smith. The report was prepared under the auspices of the Detroit Bureau of Governmental Research, now the Citizens' Research Council, and the director of the study was the same Forrester Washington who had been the first executive secretary of the Detroit Urban League in 1917. The material that appears here is a segment dealing with the killings of black civilians by Detroit police within a period of less than one year. It is important to remember that this entire study was a by-product of the mayor's concern and bewilderment over the Sweet case. There is no reason to suppose that official Detroit would have taken any notice of police brutality directed against blacks, or their housing, employment, recreation, and other problems if the city had not been upset by the actions of Dr. Sweet.

The murder of a crusading radio journalist in the lobby of his downtown hotel ties together various threads of gangsterism, civic corruption, and the Ku Klux Klan. Cyril A. Player, a local journalist aiming at a nationwide liberal audience through the

New Republic in 1930, did his best to show the pattern of an increasingly troubled Detroit.

Detroit of the twenties was suffering simultaneously from organized crime, the Klan, bitter racial and ethnic prejudice, auto layoffs every summer, and constant hardship among its respectable poor. Yet all of it was played against a backdrop of reported wealth, glamor, and excitement.

No one can fault that backdrop. The stage setting of the twenties has left magnificent architectural remainders: the Union Guardian Building, the Fisher Theater, the gilded movie palaces of downtown, and a string of mammoth churches along Woodward Avenue. Carrara marble, Tiffany windows, and Detroit's own irridescent Pewabic tiles: those were the glittering hallmarks of the twenties. Today the Pewabic formula is gone and no one can find the gilded frogs that once served as ashtrays in the ladies' rest room of the Fisher Theater. Too bad the reality never matched the backdrop.

Editor's Note

1. John W. Carey, "The Growth of Brightmoor," *Brightmoor: A Community in Action* (Detroit: Brightmoor Community Center, 1940), 1–2.

1.   The Red Scare of 1919

U.S. Senate Judiciary Committee

The pattern of "Americanization" and its identification with a distrust of organized labor was firmly set by Detroit employers by the war's end. When Attorney General A. Mitchell Palmer ordered the mass arrest and possible deportation of "enemy aliens" in Detroit, the effort was massive, overextended, and, in all, sloppy.

In a town where the business community was committed to the open shop, Palmer had clearly gone too far. Mayor James Couzens, (later a United States senator) was among the city's leaders shocked into protest. Detroit leaders would be among those to appear later at the hearings of the Senate Judiciary Committee when it investigated the conduct of the Justice Department.[1]

The most substantive Detroit testimony was given on March 20, 1921, by a Detroit News reporter, Frederick Barkley, whose employers had apparently given him a free hand in investigation and reporting.

Statement of Mr. Frederick R. Barkley

Senator STERLING. Will you state your full name and your occupation?

Mr. BARKLEY. Frederick R. Barkley. I am a writer on the Detroit News, and I have lived in Detroit the last four years.

Senator STERLING. Have you been connected with the Detroit News during that period?

Senate Judiciary Committee, *Hearings on Charges of Illegal Practices of Department of Justice*, 66th Cong., 1 March 1921, U.S. Cong. Hearings, 41st–73d Cong., 1869–1934, 169: 709–23.

Mr. BARKLEY. I have been connected with the Detroit Free Press during the first year of those four years and with the Detroit News the other three years.

Senator STERLING. What do you know, if anything, about these arrests?

Mr. BARKLEY. . . . On January 3 I was sent by my paper to the Federal Building to write a story or make a report—to find out what the conditions were there, which we had heard of indirectly.

I went up there and found great confusion among the department agents. . . . It was very difficult to get any information from them. . . . I think the figures show, as they have been collected, and as they have been published from time to time, that they made around 1,000 arrests altogether, so that that would account for the fact that they only reached 800, because they had been able to release some by the time they had made the last raid.

As I said, they did not have the names; they had no name lists available of the men. Their women, of course, having missed them and having heard about this, came in and went into the lower corridors and tried to get information about whether their husbands were there or not, and it was difficult to get up to the top of the stairs, and, even if they did, it would be very difficult to find them. Sometimes, as a man would be rushing back and forth attending to his work, one of these women would get hold of him and ask if such and such a man was there, and then he would shout the name up, and these officers would shout through and ask if Mike So-and-so was there.

Senator STERLING. Do you know of any instances where an answer to the question as to whether a certain man was there or not was denied to those who went there?

Mr. BARKLEY. Not deliberately; but on account of the general circumstances it was apparently impossible to pay any attention to these friends and relatives. They had too big a crowd to take care of the men themselves.

Senator WALSH of Montana. [Senator Walsh will be referred to hereafter as Senator Walsh.] You spoke about when these raids were made in dance houses, and study halls, and restaurants.

Mr. BARKLEY. Yes. Of course, I did not witness the raids myself, but at the House of the Masses or Shore Hall [sic, Schiller

Hall] was, I understood, where they got the most. That was the headquarters of the Socialist Party. It was a big, 3-story building, and they had a restaurant on the ground floor, which I understand, they ran cooperatively by an association, I think, with the Workers' Educational Society.

Senator STERLING. They had rooms there where the Socialist Party came and held their meetings?

Mr. BARKLEY. Yes, the whole building had been owned by the Socialist Party. When they were thrown out by the Socialist Party at the convention, they joined the Communist Party as a body, and the same group just transferred their membership, and the hall went over to the Communist Party; and it has been the subject of litigation ever since. And as I have been informed, they were having a dance in this hall the night of January 2, when the raid occurred. We were told that they arrested all the members of the orchestra that was playing there, which plays at all the high-class entertainments in Detroit.

They also arrested all the men who were eating in the restaurant on the ground floor, which, so far as I could tell from the outside, resembles any short-order restaurant. There is nothing to indicate that it is different from any other restaurant.

Senator STERLING. Do you know whether they cater to anybody except their own members?

Mr. BARKLEY. . . . I know that a girl I talked to down in a lower corridor said that her brother had belonged to the Socialist Party, and when the switch to the Communist Party was made he did not join the Communist Party because he did not believe in force; but he continued to patronize the restaurant, and he was eating his dinner there that day; and he had been confined there for three days because he was caught in the restaurant getting his dinner. She seemed an intelligent girl, more Americanized than most of those who were arrested.

Senator WALSH. They found both men and women in the place?

Mr. BARKLEY. Yes.

Senator WALSH. Did they arrest women also?

Mr. BARKLEY. No, they did not arrest the women. This girl was at dance this night in the hall. She said they were holding classes in the anterooms and the side rooms there, and they broke up the classes.

Senator STERLING. Do you know whether or not, aside from the dance hall, there are rooms or halls which are used for the purposes of societies, socialist and communist?

Mr. BARKLEY. Oh, yes; I assume the whole building was owned by the Communist Party at that time and operated by them.

Senator WALSH. Was it your understanding that the members of that orchestra were identified with those societies?

Mr. BARKLEY. No, it was just a professional orchestra, which played for balls and dances and all sorts of affairs.

Senator WALSH. Did you say they were arrested?

Mr. BARKLEY. I was so informed. I would not say that at first hand, but I was informed that they were arrested, the whole thing; that they took in every man they found.

What I started to say was that these women would come up there looking for their husbands. As they transferred the men to the various precinct police stations and other places, they had no record kept of where the men went. A woman might come up there, looking for her husband, and he might have been transferred by that time to a police precinct station. Some of the women told me that it was five or six days before they found where their husbands were. In one case in particular I remember the woman had no money, and she had to beg her food from the neighbors, and it was five or six days before she found her husband. I think she got some cash from him then. . . .

There were nine precinct police stations in Detroit, and so far as I know they were sent to all of those. In the outlying sections it would be difficult, if a person did not know which one of them a relative was at, to find him. They might have to make the whole round.

Senator WALSH. Some reference was made to some of them going to the Municipal Court Building.

Mr. BARKLEY. Yes; I will go into that now. I have some figures on that here. In the first place, about 400 men were released out of this group as soon as they could get to them, possibly within a day, and sometimes two, or three or four or five days, as they came along, and were examined. Some of them were found to be citizens who had been picked up accidentally. I was told of one man who was going past this building when the raid took place, and he just got swept along with the crowd.

They took 128 of them to what is known as the "bull pen" at the municipal court. That is a room that is designed to hold prisoners awaiting trial for petty offenses—to hold people for two or three hours. They bring people up from the jail and hold them there until their cases are called. It is a room 24 feet by 30 in size, I was informed by officials in the building. They had 128 men in there. That had a stone floor, with some flat benches with no backs—just room for perhaps 20 men to sit on those benches. In that room they were held for seven days. This was a cellar room with one window. It had a little toilet off it, and one door, a grated door; and that was the condition that led the health commissioner upon the complaint of the municipal court judges, and the threat of the employees in the restaurant in that building to strike if those men were not removed, to make recommendations and recommend again to the mayor, and that led to the action that was read to you that the council later took. I went down there and looked in. They were packed in there just about as close as you could get them. One man had an infected hand and he had not had any treatment for it, that was the second day, and his hand was all swelled up and purple; and I think that was one of the conditions that led these men, the employees in the restaurant, to threaten to strike.

They told me they had been fed one cup of coffee and two biscuits twice a day. That was the only food they had had.

Senator WALSH. Did you try to verify that?

Mr. BARKLEY. . . . I was not able at that time to verify it. . . . It was similar to the action that had taken place in the Federal building where Barkey [Arthur Barkey, chief agent for the Justice Department at Detroit] said that they had brought in coffee and doughnuts.

Senator WALSH. Was there any systematic effort on the part of the officials to feed them?

Mr. BARKLEY. No. Barkey said, "We brought them in coffee and doughnuts; but," he said, "they have all got good food from their homes, and boxes of oranges, and," he said, "we did not have time to bother with it; and they are being fed now anyway. Their friends are bringing in food." . . . Of course, I assume probably their friends did furnish them with food. This is what they told me they got from the Government.

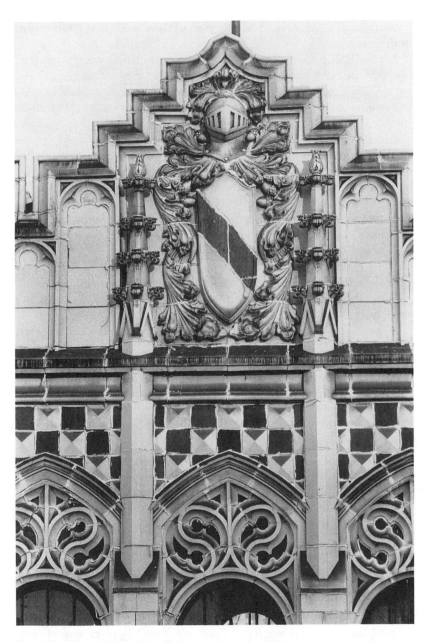

The Twenties—Detroit's Golden Age of architecture. Facade of the Metropolitan Building, John R. Street. (Courtesy of Bob McKeown, 1987.)

Senator STERLING. You do not understand that they were limited to that?

Mr. BARKLEY. No, I do not; but the conditions were such that Mayor Couzens said, in his report to the city council: "These conditions are intolerable in a civilized city." . . .

Senator WALSH. . . . What publicity was given to this condition of things?

Mr. BARKLEY. On the day I made the inquiries and the investigation in the Federal building I wrote a story which was printed on the front page of the News, about a column and a half—it was given rather striking publicity—just outlining conditions there as stated by Mr. Barkey. When that story appeared, The Detroit Free Press, which was friendly to Mr. Barkey and never criticized his actions or appeared to criticize him, quoted Mr. Barkey as follows:

"The public should bear in mind that this is not a picnic, and the Department of Justice is not providing settees for criminals."

Three hundred and fifty of them were later released for lack of evidence.

"They have to sleep on the floor. That is right. But a stone bed in the post office probably isn't any harder than a board bed in the jail. The majority of them are getting better than in their five-sleep-in-a-bed homes, and they have more food than they can eat. Relatives and friends have brought in whole boiled hams, boxes of oranges, and other delicacies."

Senator WALSH. Was the Detroit Free Press quoting Mr. Barkey there?

Mr. BARKLEY. They were quoting Mr. Barkey to that effect.

I believe that covers pretty nearly the situation, as far as the detention is concerned. Of course of these 800 that were held for varying periods from a day up to three or four days, many of them were released. I am told that many of them were former servicemen, who had gone to a dance at the House of the Masses, and that they had managed to get in a body early next morning and announce who they were, and they were let out right away. . . .

. . .They brought one man in to me on April 12. . . . I wrote down the story he told me. . . . this man's name was Walter B. Reps. I do not know what the final outcome of his case was. . . . He was born in Poland 34 years ago, and married there and came

310

to the United States in 1913. He was a small man, neatly dressed and sturdy, with work-calloused hands and an intelligent, kindly expression. He had been an industrious workman. He had learned his trade as a cabinetmaker in Poland, and when he reached the United States he came to Detroit and went to work at once in a furniture factory. Later [Reps] left this factory to work for the Ford Motor Company, where he was employed at the time of his arrest. In order to become more expert in mechanics and English, he attended a school conducted four nights a week in a Polish educational society's hall.

In 1917 he bought a little house, paying $1,000 down and $75 every two months. He continued to go to night school and placed his children, now 5 and 7 years old, respectively, in the public schools. He had been a member of the Socialist Party in Poland, and as all his associates in Detroit were members of the Detroit Polish branch of the same party in this country he also joined here.

When the Detroit Polish branch switched its allegiance from the Socialist Party to the Communist Party last fall, he believed, as did his fellow members, that the switch meant merely a change in name, inasmuch as the membership group remained the same. That was the basis or ground for his arrest. He told me that he was arrested on the evening of January 2 when he and a dozen others were studying an English lesson at their hall, No. 1648 Central Avenue.

Senator WALSH. Is that the House of the Masses?

Mr. BARKLEY. No; this hall is the social center for the Polish workmen of the neighborhood, where they held their dances, their classes, and political meetings. He said that was all there was going on that night; they were studying an English lesson when the Department of Justice agents broke in. He said that as far as he could understand there was no presentation of warrants. They did not tell them what they were wanted for, but just took them out and bundled them into the automobiles and took them down and put them in this Federal building cage. . . .

Senator STERLING. You do not know just what he meant by "political meetings?"

Mr. BARKLEY. No, I do not know. I remember he said he wanted to live in this country and wanted to pay for his home; and he seemed to be inoffensive and have no idea of violence.

Senator STERLING. I do not know whether or not you stated when he came to this country.

Mr. BARKLEY. In 1913. Reps's wife did not find him until Monday. I think January 2 was Friday. She was allowed to talk to him through the bars long enough for him to tell her to bring him some food. Soon after she left, his turn to appear before the examiners came. This was when they asked him, according to what Reps said, his name, age, and nativity, whether he was a citizen or an alien, and whether he belonged to the Communist Party; and on his assertion that he did, and without any questions to learn whether he knew what the party platform was or whether he believed in it, he was set down presumably as a "dangerous alien" and was taken with others to a cell in police headquarters. He was there two days, he said, in very crowded conditions. When his wife again sought him at the Federal Building where he had been, she was unable to find out where he was. . . .

Two days later Reps and others were again transferred, this time to the "bull pen" of the Municipal Court Building, and later he was taken to Fort Wayne. He was kept at Fort Wayne until February 1.

On January 26th he was subjected to a second examination, which was a duplicate of the first. In neither instance was he informed of the charge against him. He had had no counsel, nor had he had an opportunity to be judged by a jury.

At the time of his second examination, he was told to make ready for deportation in two or three days. . . .

Three days later, when desperate pleas from his wife had induced Dr. P. L. Prentis, the chief immigration officer, to reduce his bail from $10,000 to $1,000, Reps was released on bail, which his wife had been able to borrow in various small amounts from neighbors and acquaintances. In the month he had been held, Mrs. Reps had only $25 from his last pay at Ford's on which to live.

He expected deportation orders at any hour, and he sold his house, getting $200 less than he had paid for it. He also sold his furniture, for $170, and he spent considerable money buying heavy winter clothing for the expected trip to Russia.

He waited two weeks for the deportation order. It did not come. The purchasers of his house demanded occupancy and moved in, leaving Reps and his family one room in which to live.

Then he got another job with the Cadillac Motor Car Co., and was working there in April.

On April 10 he received from Dr. Prentis a second order, telling him, "The order of deportation in your case has issued, You are directed to have all your affairs straightened up so that you will be ready for conveyance to port of departure within a short period." On inquiry of Dr. Prentis, Reps was told that his wife and children could not accompany him; that the "Government had no money to deport wives and children," and that inasmuch as his orders from Washington directed deportation of men only Reps would have to go alone.

That was the status of this poor man at the time I questioned him. He had lost considerable money selling his home and his wife had been under a period of uncertainty and was at that time.

Senator WALSH. What I was really desirous of getting was what impression they made upon you as a body.

Mr. BARKLEY. They seemed simple men, not perhaps very highly educated. They were clean. Most of them were fairly well dressed for workingmen, not dirty-looking fellows. They did not look like what we have been led to believe bolsheviks look like—that is, when they were taken in there. After four or five days, of course, they had all grown a pretty good crop of beard. They were not permitted to shave, and they slept in their clothes.

Senator WALSH. Did they look like good, decent, reputable dressed workingmen, or did they look like what you might call tramps or general rounders?

Mr. BARKLEY. No; they were reputable workingmen. Their families were very well clothed. In fact, one of the papers stated about some well dressed women who had incited these men. It was their wives and families who had come in there. Some of them were making good money, up to $10 and $12 a day. They were skilled workmen. . . .

Senator WALSH. Were you permitted to talk to any of them?

Mr. BARKLEY. No; not while they were in the Federal building corridor. It was impossible to talk to them. There were police at this one door where you could go up there.

When I went to the municipal building I talked to them there through the gates.

Senator WALSH. Were they allowed to see their attorneys?

Mr. BARKLEY. They were not allowed to see any attorneys, as I was told, while they were in the Federal building. Whether they were after that, I do not know. . . .

Editor's Note

1. Mayor Couzen's actions included calling on the common council for a resolution of protest to the federal government for the manner in which the arrests were made and the prisoners confined. He insisted that the Department of Justice remove its prisoners from any city-owned facilities. He had his health commissioner protest the fact that men were held in buildings with hopelessly inadequate sanitary facilities, little food, and no medical care. He was joined in his efforts by attorney Fred Butzel, chemical company president Frederick Stearns, and Sebastian S. Kresge. These men secured bail, attorneys, and funds for the men's families.

Two young lawyers, who were less known in 1920–21 than they would become later, involved themselves in the defense efforts. One was Walter Nelson, who was active in the Sweet trial as one of the attorneys assisting Clarence Darrow. Nelson became a widely respected lawyer, specializing in labor and civil rights issues.

The other was Solomon Paperno, who courageously wrote the Justice Department in Washington with questions on behalf of arrested clients. Perhaps it shows something of the nature of the new FBI that Paperno, who had been born in Russia, became an immediate suspect because of his immigrant status in spite of his American citizenship.

2. Dr. Ossian Sweet Defends His Home

Detroit Free Press

ONE SLAIN AND 1 SHOT BY NEGROES
VICTIM'S WIFE IN COLLAPSE, IS NEAR DEATH. . . .
Home at 2905 Garland Avenue, In White Neighborhood, Is Scene;
12 Jailed

At 3:30 o'clock this morning, it was announced that Assistant Prosecutor Edward H. Kennedy, Jr. would recommend warrants charging murder against the 11 negroes now under arrest in connection with the outbreak last night at 2905 Garland Avenue. . . .

Shots poured without warning and seemingly without provocation last night at 8:30 o'clock from the second story windows of 2905 Garland Avenue, into which Dr. and Mrs. Ossian M. Sweet, a Negro couple, had moved Tuesday, cost one man's life, put another in the hospital with a bullet in his leg, and called out 200 heavily armed police reserves, detectives, and regular policemen from every precinct, as well as an armored car.

"One Slain and 1 Shot by Negroes," *Detroit Free Press* (10 September 1925): 1.

A police Inspector, a Lieutenant, and a patrolman had been standing within 25 feet of the house which was lighted only in the upper windows. They had been talking over the potential trouble that might emerge from Negroes moving into the white neighborhood.

A rain of bullets ended the conversation. As if the triggers of a dozen guns were being pulled simultaneously, the firing started. It stopped with the same suddenness that it began. While the police ran up the steps and hammered at the door of the house, the gathering throng counted the casualties.

Father Killed Instantly

Leon Breiner, 3063 Garland avenue, father of two children, who was walking on the east side of Garland, across the street from the house, was killed instantly, a bullet entering his head. Erik Hofberg 52 years old, 2918 Garland avenue, ran out of his house when he heard the shooting and was just in time to receive one of the last bullets fired. He was taken to Receiving Hospital, shot in the leg. . . .

Thousands of angry residents surged down the streets, and these were joined by hundreds of other people. . . . It was estimated 5,000 persons gathered.

When inspector Norton M. Schuknecht, of the McClellan avenue station, leaped to the veranda, and hammered in the door, Dr. Sweet, an interne at Dunbar Hospital, a Negro institution, answered at once.

Weapons Are Seized

People outside were throwing stones through the windows, Sweet asserted.

The house was sparsely furnished. There were so many Negroes in it that there were not enough chairs for them to sit on. All apparently had gathered on the upper floor, and all, according to the police, were armed. The police seized six revolvers, two rifles and a shotgun. The kitchen was well stocked with provisions, however, and there were several trunks in the place.

In a corner of the front upstairs room there was a black traveling bag. It was tagged with a card which read "Madame O. H. Sweet, Paris", and there were various other labels of transatlantic travel. Inside were several varieties of ammunition, shells, and cartridges.

12 Taken To Headquarters

Sweet, his wife, and their 10 guests were taken to police headquarters. Then the police began the difficult task of maintaining order.

About an hour after police had quieted the crowd, a car filled with Negroes drove up two blocks away from the scene of the shooting and stopped. When a score of persons started toward it, police fliers escorted the Negroes out of danger.

In describing the start of the shooting, Inspector Schuknecht said there had been no demonstration previously. . . .

Residents of the district today will ask why the neighborhood was not informed by police that a special police guard had been stationed in the vicinity of 2905 Garland avenue and a riot squad maintained at the McClellan avenue station. . . .

3.   Mayor John Smith Accuses the Ku Klux Klan

John W. Smith

The gunfire in front of Dr. Sweet's home had hardly died away before the city's mayor laid the blame for this and other incidents on the Ku Klux Klan. The Detroit Free Press, *on the morning of September 13, headlined an open letter from Mayor John W. Smith to Police Commissioner Frank Croul.*

Dear Commissioner:

The outrage of Wednesday evening, in which one man was killed and another seriously injured, deals with the province of government under the direct jurisdiction of the department of police. . . .

[It has been] the custom, not only in this city, but in all communities of the northern part of this country,—to treat for political purposes—jealousies and prejudices existing between different races as non-existent. I believe that the present crisis in Detroit must put an end to such criminal delicacy.

My duty, which is your duty and your officers' duty, is laid down by law. The constitution of the United States, the constitution of Michigan, the charter of the city of Detroit, and the laws

John W. Smith, "Mayor's Open Letter," *Detroit Free Press* (13 September 1925): 1–2.

of all those governmental agencies fix clearly the legal relationships which may exist regarding life and property. And they affect all races the same.

When any person moves into a new neighborhood, it becomes
by law the duty of the police agencies to protect that man or
woman in his life and property. . . . A mayor, police commissioner, or police officer, who fails in any particular in extending
legal protection to all persons, regardless of creed or color, would
be subject to removal from office. . . .

But the duties which are ours legally, differ materially from
what we, as sensible men, know are the causes which resulted in
the recent murder, and which, if they are unchecked, may cause
equally shameful incidents in Detroit's future history.

In that connection I must say that I deprecate most strongly
the moving of Negroes or other persons into districts in which
they know their presence may cause riot or bloodshed. I express
this personal feeling, which is perhaps beyond the proper province of an executive officer, sworn to enforce legal policies which
are different, but I do it in the hope that some official expression
can prevent a recurrence of the tragedy of Wednesday evening.

. . . In all these years there was no such incident as that which has
blackened our city's name within the past few days. These colored men and women who were long residents of this city, decided their own problems, with the realizations of their legal
rights, modified by their own common sense. It does not always
do for any man to demand, to its fullest, the right which the law
gives him. Sometimes by doing so he works irremediable harm
to himself and his fellows.

The first sign of a feeling, which resulted fatally Wednesday,
came with the revival of the Ku Klux Klan. The evidence is clear
that the unfortunate incidents which recently happened in the
northwest section of the city and the tragedy on Garland avenue
came from the activities of that organization. . . . for months, the
men and women of whom I have spoken before, have been going
from house to house conducting a cowardly campaign which
they would not dare suggest in public. These men and women
have gone to homes where resentment is strongest against members of the Negro race and have whispered their criminal propa-
ganda. They have stated that the mayor of the city, who happens
to be me, has placed 500 Negroes in the fire department. They

319

have reported that the mayor of the city has filled the police department with Negroes. They have stated that every department of the city government is overrun with Negroes. They have stated further that it was I who inspired and fostered the movement of colored citizens into districts inhabited previously entirely by white persons. . . . Every one of these charges is untrue.

And on the other hand, a similar campaign by the same people was conducted to arouse the resentment of the Negro population against the present government. There the story told was exactly the opposite to that told to the white persons. It was that no Negroes were being employed in the city government; that no police protection required by law was being given to Negro residents. . . .

For months, during the course of this criminal campaign, a constant procession of colored persons has been moving in and out of the headquarters of a candidate for Mayor [Charles Bowles] favored by the Ku Klux Klan. I have evidence that certain colored persons are on the payroll of the Ku Klux Klan, with the aim of influencing members of their race against the present government. . . .

I have said that I deprecate the moving by colored persons into districts in which their presence would cause disturbances. I shall go further. I believe that any colored person who endangers life and property, simply to gratify his personal pride, is an enemy of his race as well as an incitant of riot and murder. These men who have permitted themselves to be the tools of the Ku Klux Klan in its efforts to fan the flames of racial hatred into murderous fire, have hurt the cause of their race in a degree that cannot be measured. I feel that it lies with the real leaders of the colored race in Detroit to dissipate their murderous pride. This seems to exist chiefly in a very few colored persons who are unwilling to live in sections of the city where members of their race predominate, but who are willing to rely on the natural racial pride of the rest of their people to protect them when they move into districts where their presence may be resented. . . .

It lies with you and members of your department to protect fully life and property of all persons without regard to creed or color. And in addition to those laws, there are laws against inciting to riot. There are those in this community—some who think themselves in positions of security, who have been deliberately and maliciously arousing the people of both races against each other, driving [the] less cowardly to defy the law, and as we have seen, to murder and death. . . . [1]

Editor's Note

1. Mayor Smith won reelection two months later, after a bitter campaign against Klan-endorsed Charles Bowles. Though more open-minded than many other politicians of his time, he was not able to divest himself of the confusions shown in this letter. Like most white Detroiters then and for some years later, he did not comprehend the extent of the need for housing for Negroes. He conceded that the law was clearly on the side of the Negro who wished freedom to choose his neighborhood, yet appealed to him to forgo his legal rights.

4. Has the Negro the Right of Self-Defense?

David E. Lilienthal

Few criminal cases have combined the dramatic intensity, the forensic brilliance, and the deep social significance present in the trial just concluded at Detroit of Dr. Ossian Sweet and ten other Negroes charged with the murder of a white man. For more than a month all the efforts of the prosecutor and the police were bent towards securing a verdict of life imprisonment from the white jury. Fighting for the right of the defendants and all other Negroes to defend themselves against assault was the ablest criminal advocate who ever faced an American jury, Clarence Darrow, and with him Arthur Garfield Hays of New York, Walter M. Nelson of Detroit, and Herbert Friedman of Chicago. The jury, after deliberating for forty-six hours, was unable to

David E. Lilienthal, "Has the Negro the Right of Self-Defense?" *The Nation* (23 December 1925): 724–25. Reprinted by permission of The Nation Company, Inc.

agree, and on November 27 was discharged. Perhaps it was only to be expected that there would be no agreement among twelve men selected at random from a community—or a nation for that matter—in which there is so little agreement upon the difficult problem really at the bottom of the case.

For this was no ordinary murder trial. Back of it all was the whole sensitive problem of race relations, intensified a thousand-fold by the recent Northern migration of the Negro; hovering over and touching the whole proceeding was the somber cloud of race prejudice.

. . .It is a tribute to the capacity of Clarence Darrow to rouse the best in common men, and to the fairness of the extraordinary young judge [Frank Murphy] who presided, that seven jurors held out for two days for acquittal and thus prevented their fellows from sending the defendants to the penitentiary.

The theory upon which the prosecution sought to send these eleven Negroes to prison for life—the extreme penalty in Michigan—is an interesting phase of this memorable case. No evidence of who fired the shot which killed Leon Breiner was available; he was struck by one bullet, whereas eight or ten were fired from within the house. It was therefore impossible to charge one defendant as the murderer and the others as co-principals, aiding and abetting. The charge of a conspiracy to kill would have been less severe than first-degree murder. The state accordingly charged each of the eleven with murder, alleging that all eleven acted under an *agreement* to kill anyone committing even the slightest trespass, regardless of the necessity for defense, so that each was equally responsible for the shooting done by one. No effort to prove such an agreement was made either by words or conduct, but the killing itself was regarded both as the crime and proof of the murderous agreement! Trade unionists who have suffered for generations by reason of the legal sleight-of-hand known as "conspiracy" will do well to keep their eyes open upon this latest refinement upon that doctrine of oppression.

Proceeding upon this ingenious theory, the state, after proving that there was a killing, sought to anticipate and defeat the defendants' plea of self-defense. Witness after witness, chiefly white residents of the neighborhood, took the stand and insisted that the crowds which gathered about Dr. Sweet's home were

323

small, orderly, and even "neighborly." Some were sorry specta-
cles under Darrow's pitiless cross-questioning and biting sarcasm, but for the most part they clung to the story that although
it was necessary to have on duty sixteen policemen, in charge of
a deputy chief, the neighborhood was a veritable vale of peace.
One witness, asked by the prosecutor how many people he saw
about the Sweet house, replied: "There was a great crowd . . .
no, I won't say a great crowd . . . a large crowd . . . well, there
were a few people there and the officers were keeping them moving." The cross-examination was illuminating:

> Q. Have you talked to anyone about the case?
> A. Lieutenant Johnson (the police detective in charge).
> Q. And when you started to answer the question you forgot to
>   say "a few people," didn't you?
> A. Yes, sir.

Those state witnesses who could be induced to admit that
stones had been thrown amused the courtroom by referring to
them as "pebbles," the "pebbles" introduced into evidence being
chunks of cement, some of them the size of one's fist. The testimony of the police detailed to guard the house corroborated that
of the residents of the vicinity in every respect.

The defense first produced witnesses, most of them Negroes,
who gave a wholly different picture of conditions just before the
shooting—a picture of an angry, threatening crowd, determined
"to run the niggers out." It was further established that shortly
after Dr. Sweet's purchase of a house in this white neighborhood,
some seven hundred residents of the community held an over-
flow mass meeting, and organized an "Improvement Association." That the "improvement" intended was keeping Negroes
out of the district was clear.

The principal defendant, Dr. Sweet, was put on the stand and
stated the circumstances surrounding the shooting, as they appeared from within the beleaguered house. He told of the crowds
on September 8 when he moved in, of the police detailed because
of the known temper of the vicinity, of the threats and the stoning, of the massing of the crowd, and of the shooting. Then followed one of the most remarkable direct examinations to be
found in all the records of criminal cases: a vivid picture of the

fear-ridden mind of a black man, terrified by a hostile crowd of whites outside his home. The testimony was particularly effective because it came from the lips of a highly educated man, a graduate of two universities, just returned from research in Vienna, and a highly skilled physician. To show that Dr. Sweet believed his life was in danger Mr. Hays questioned him upon his mental life and emotional experience in so far as they touched upon his fear of mob violence. The examination brought out that the witness had seen the brutalities of the Washington race riots, had read accounts of the Chicago cruelties, of those at East St. Louis, Tulsa, and Omaha. He had talked with Detroit Negroes who had been driven from their new homes by white neighbors: in one case a fellow-physician whose house but three months before had been sacked by a mob, and who had been forced to convey away his newly-purchased home while policemen looked on approvingly. Much of his information concerning the way his people had been abused and tyrannized by whites came from a reading of *The Nation*, and a number of issues were introduced into evidence. Thus the whole sordid panorama of bestiality was unrolled before the jury, in an effort to convey to the white men an understanding of the fear that gripped those eleven barricaded blacks. When finally the witness was asked his state of mind at the time of the shooting, he answered: "When I opened the door I saw the mob and I realized I was facing that same mob that has hounded my people throughout its entire history. . . . "

The climax of the trial was reached when Clarence Darrow walked slowly to the jury box and began his closing argument. A deep silence fell over the crowded noisy courtroom. The old man with the unutterably sad face and the great stooped shoulders seemed no mere lawyer pleading for hire. He seemed, instead, a patriarch out of another age. . . . Quietly and sadly he besought these twelve men to inflict no further hatred and injustice upon a race that has known nothing but hatred and injustice. He seemed to be pleading more that the white man might be just than that the black be free, more for the spirit of the master than the body of the slave. . . .

And then suddenly the voice of the lawyer rang out like a brass gong, his eyes became hard and grim, every muscle of his huge body was tense and strained. Darrow was no longer the patriarch, the philosopher. Now he had become the warrior, the

More architecture of the 1920s, much of it neglected and in disarray. United Artists Theater. (Courtesy of Bob McKeown, 1987.)

veteran of a hundred battles for human freedom—battles against the greed of the strong, the cruelty of the many, the bigotry of the ignorant. . . . his head lowered like a fighter coming out of his corner, he turned upon the prosecutors, his arms swinging, eyes narrowed and pitiless, the brass gong clanging an alarm and a challenge. . . . John Brown before the Arsenal at Harper's Ferry. Owen Lovejoy defying the mob at Alton.

. . .There are no more underground railroads or fugitive-slave laws or whipping-posts. But there are mobs and torches and trees hideous with swinging black shapes, and there is suspicion, prejudice, hatred. And on the new battlefield, fighting a subtler foe, and one that perhaps may never be wholly defeated, is Clarence Darrow, son of the Abolitionists.

The story told in that courtroom was undoubtedly a sordid and disheartening one, but not wholly so. Has the white man of today advanced beyond his brother of two hundred years ago who traded slaves for rum? No one can answer with any assurance. But that the black man is making headway is clear beyond doubt. Of this, the young defendants themselves are striking evidence. Most of them are either graduates or students of colleges and professional schools; their grandparents were slaves who could neither read nor write! At the press table sat two colored newspapermen the match of any correspondent there. The factories seen from the courtroom windows are employing more and more Negroes every week. And there is encouragment, too, in the fact that Negroes can command so fair a trial in a land where most trials of Negroes have been mob-dominated travesties. For this trial was probably the fairest ever accorded a Negro in this country; had it been otherwise the defendants would now be on their way to a life in prison.

5. Police Brutality

Forrester Washington

Mayor Smith's almost immediate reaction to what he and the police saw as the September, 1925, murder of a presumably innocent white bystander by violent blacks was to appoint a committee to discover what had gone wrong in the city's race relations. To head the staff he brought back to Detroit the sociologist Forrester Washington, who had been executive secretary of the Detroit Urban League during its opening days.

The study itself was in twelve parts. Among them were included sections on housing, police brutality, employment opportunities, discrimination, the refusal of some labor unions to accept Negro members, and comparable health conditions for Negro and white families. I have reproduced here several of the cases from the police brutality section of the report.

Each of the cases presented here ends in the death of a civilian.

Negroes Killed by the Police

The homicide reports show that during the period from Jany. 1, 1925 to June 30, 1926, 25 Negroes, as compared with 24 whites were killed by the police. The following are case studies of samples of these killings, beginning with June 30, 1926 and working back through 1925. The names were selected according to date. Only those cases whose families could be located are included. The method followed is to submit for each case 1) the

Forrester Washington, "Police Brutality," in *The Negro in Detroit, 1926*, report of the Mayor's Interracial Commission (Detroit: Bureau of Governmental Research, 1926).

findings of the Survey Staff 2) the verbatim police reports 3) Negro Newspaper Reports and Comment.

Henry Noble

Survey Findings

Henry Noble was born in Fort Valley, Georgia in 1898. When he was around fifteen years old his family migrated to Steubenville, Ohio. . . .

Because of the high wages which can be obtained in Detroit, Henry and his brother came here for the purpose of accumulating sufficient money to purchase their mother a home. When they first arrived he and his brother resided in the same home, but in October, 1925, he moved to 972 Lafayette Avenue, because of his continual connections with petty theft charges. Here his landlady informed him on the first of December that he would have to vacate his room. While there he did not work but spent a great deal of his time in pool rooms and gambling joints.

He was absolutely illiterate. His landlady had to read and write his letters.

He was married, but separated before coming to Detroit.

At the time of his death Henry did not own any property nor did he have a bank account. He was insured, however, in the Metropolitan and National Benefit. These policies provided enough money for his burial and left a surplus for the family.

The Police Report

"About 3:25 A.M., March 31, 1926, Henry Noble, Frank Foster and Jack Griskell were breaking into the Congress Pharmacy at 901 E. Congress Street. Frank Foster and Jack Griskell were arrested by Patrolmen W. Burkuhl and H. Bartlett. Henry Noble was inside the Drug Store, and when he saw the officers he ran out of the side door. The officers commanded him to stop, but he kept running, so they fired several shots, which struck him in the head and chest. He was taken to Receiving Hospital in subconscious condition in #1 Auto where he died shortly after arrival. Patrolmen Burkuhl and Bartlett were exonerated by Assistant Prosecutor Oscar Kaufman. Inquest pending."

The Detroit Independent (Negro Newspaper)

"Henry Noble, 22 years old, who resides at 972 E. Lafayette was shot and killed by Patrolman Burkuhl of the Central Station. The killing took place at the Congress pharmacy, 901 E. Congress Street, where Patrolmen Burkuhl and Harry Bartlett went in response to an alarm that the store was being robbed. On reaching the scene the officers are said to have found and arrested two colored lookouts stationed outside the building. After handcuffing the two men to their automobile wheels, they returned to the store, where it is reported they saw a third man on the inside busily engaged in plundering the place. Burkuhl then fired at the man through the window, at the same time calling him to halt, and as the latter fled through the door, Patrolman Burkuhl fired four shots in his body. Noble died before he reached the Receiving Hospital. Officer Burkuhl has the reputation of being one of the crack shooters of the local police department, having to his record the killing of three other alleged bandits."

Bertram Johnson

Survey Findings

Bertram Johnson . . . came to Detroit about eleven years ago and was married six months after his arrival. Since coming to Detroit the family has resided at 4179 Beaubien Street for the last seven years.

Johnson has worked steadily since his arrival in Detroit. For the last four years he had been operating a tailor shop at 4181 Beaubien. He worked with the D&C Navigation Company for five years and for three years as captain of waiters at the Charlevoix Hotel.

His chief recreation outside of home was race horses. The greater part of his spare time was spent attending the race tracks. He was not especially interested in any other sport.

Johnson was an intelligent man. He took advantage of the educational opportunities offered in New York and completed three years of high school work there.

His educational training enabled him to take part in much of the Negro community life of Detroit. He was a member of the Catholic Church and was associated with a number of fraternal organizations, among which were the Elks and Moose. Johnson was a voter and was interested in political issues.

The Police Report

"Bert Johnson, colored, age 25, 4181 Beaubien Street, about 6:15 P.M. February 17, 1926. Bert Johnson, colored, while resisting arrest for violating the prohibition law and attempting to attack Patrolmen Cornelius Everdyke, Harold McNinch, and Paul Perdew with a large knife in his blind pig at 3725 St. Antoine Street. He was shot in the neck by Patrolman Everdyke. Bert Johnson was taken to Receiving Hospital in #1 auto where he died shortly after arrival. February 23, 1926, Patrolman Everdyke exonerated by coroner's jury in charge of Coroner Albert L. French."

The Owl (Negro Newspaper)

"Bertram Johnson was murdered when he tried to compel Patrolmen Everdyke and Perdew to respect the legal rights of another Negro, Roland Hicks. These Patrolmen were invading Mr. Hick's place of business without search warrant, and without any other right under the law, to proceed. Johnson demanded that they leave—this so wrought up these policemen who were acting, seemingly, under the old adage of the South, that the black man had no rights that needed to be respected—that they began to assault Bertram Johnson and when he resisted Patrolman Everdyke shot at him.

"Investigation discloses that on the first shot Johnson stopped dead still with his hands down, and his head erect, looking at the policeman, at which time, Patrolman Perdew grabbed Johnson from the back, held him, while Everdyke, taking aim, shot Johnson through the neck—murdering him in cold blood."

Gertrude Russian

Survey Findings

Gertrude Russian was born in Arkansas in 1892. Because of the poor educational opportunities offered, she was unable to go any further than the third grade.

She spent her childhood and practically her entire womanhood in Arkansas. It was not until the fall of 1924 that she and her husband migrated to Detroit. While in Detroit she was not engaged in any work outside of the home. Mrs. Russian had not taken much part in the community life of Detroit. . . .

Police Report

"Gertrude Russian (colored) age 31 years, 2494 Beaubien Street. About 11:40 P.M. November 25, 1925, Patrolmen Joseph MacManus, James Dooley and John Nee, while walking in plain clothes and when in front of 2494 Beaubien Street Joseph MacManus was accosted by Gertrude Russian (colored). The patrolman placed her under arrest for accosting men on the street. They placed her in a Ford police car near by and Patrolman MacManus sat alongside her, while Patrolman James Dooley and John Nee were taking care of a disturbance across the street. Gertrude Russian drew a knife and stabbed Patrolman MacManus in the abdomen and right side of back. Patrolman MacManus drew his gun and shot Gertrude Russian in the neck, killing her instantly. Patrolman MacManus was taken to Receiving Hospital. Inquest pending."

Detroit Independent (Negro Newspaper)

"Gertrude Russian was shot and killed on Thanksgiving Eve, November 25, 1925 at the corner of Beaubien and Winder. She was arrested for soliciting and thrown into scout car No. 320–015 by three policemen. There was a disturbance a few yards away on Beaubien Street and two of the officers who made the arrest were called away from the car. The officer remaining got into a heated dispute with his arrested victim and was seen in the act of striking her with his blackjack.

"The woman made desperate by the blows pulled out her knife and began slashing the officer across the stomach; the officer fired, the bullet making a gunshot wound in the leg. As the two officers who were called away approached the car, the wounded officer in charge of the woman yelled to them, 'She cut me'. 'He shot me', the woman answered.

"The other two officers jumped into the car and drove away, but when only a few yards, two other shots were heard fired into the body of the woman, and she died instantly."

Marcus Lawhorn

Survey Findings

Marcus Lawhorn was recognized by neighbors as an outstanding character in [the] Negro Underworld. It was said that he was both a user and peddler of narcotics.

Because of the absence of relatives there is not very much known about his early life. It is said, however, that he had only a meagre amount of education.

He was not lawfully married, but at various intervals, had several women in his apartment.

Lawhorn was not a member of a church nor was he associated with any of the constructive forces of the city. He was buried by the Welfare Department.

Police Report

"Marcus Lawhorn, alias George Williams, alias Wilson, alias Markus de Horn, colored, 45 years, of 550 Watson, about 12:50 P.M. January 20, 1926, Patrolman Alfred Letourneau, Roy Rollyson and Clarence Mayo of the 13th Precinct, went to 550 Watson Street to serve a warrant for assault and battery on a Mrs. W. Smith. Patrolman Letourneau was searching the house for Mrs. W. Smith when he found Marcus Lawhorn, alias Marcus De Horn, alias George Williams, alias Wilson, lying on a bed in the house smoking an opium pipe. Marcus Lawhorn, alias De Horn, offered Patrolman Letourneau some money if he would not arrest

333

him on a dope charge. The officer upset the money, Marcus Lawhorn then ran out of the house. Patrolman Roy Rollyson chased him and commanded Lawhorn to stop. He refused and when in the rear of 534 Erskine Street, Lawhorn reached for his hip pocket and Patrolman Rollyson drew his gun and shot, striking Lawhorn in the left side of the back, killing him instantly, January 26, [sic] 1926. Patrolman Roy Rollyson was exonerated by coroner's jury in charge of Coroner J. E. Burgess."

The Detroit Independent (Negro Newspaper)

"Marcus Lawhorn, 550 Watson Street, was shot in the back and killed here, January 20, 1926 by Patrolman Roy Rollyson.

"It is reported that a squad of officers, of which Rollyson was a member, went to the Watson Street house in answer to a telephone call informing them that there was a disturbance in the house. They found Lawhorn in his apartment where it is said a quantity of narcotics was thought to be concealed. It is alleged that when the officers attempted to arrest Lawhorn, he ran from the house. He was followed by Patrolman Rollyson through the back door and out into the alley at the rear of 534 Erskine, where Lawhorn and the officer stopped. The officer shot him in the chest. Death came instantaneously. Rollyson was brought before the police trial board and exonerated. Lawhorn did not have any weapons on his body."

Steve Tompkins

Survey Findings

Steven Tompkins was born May 25, 1885 at Parsville, S.C. Tompkins attended the public school at Parsville until he reached the fourth grade. He and his wife came to Detroit in 1917 to answer the great demands for Negro labor. During the eight years he spent here, he was employed as a laborer at Ford Motor Company. He was not a member of a church here nor did he take an active part in the community life of Detroit. Tompkins was not associated with any of the fraternal organizations, but held several policies in insurance companies.

Police Report

"Steve Tompkins (colored) age 42 years, 7727 Russell Street, about 12:20 P.M. August 20, 1925, Patrolman Proctor Pruitt was serving a summons on Steve Tompkins at his home at 7727 Russell Street for violating the Prohibition Law. Steve Tompkins is the colored man that shot Patrolman Proctor Pruitt back in April, 1923 and Judge Jeffries discharged Tompkins. When Patrolman Pruitt tried to serve Steve Tompkins with the summons he recognized the officer and ran to his bedroom. Patrolman Pruitt followed Tompkins into the bedroom and, when the officer saw Tompkins reaching into the dresser drawer and drawing a gun, Patrolman Pruitt shot Steve Tompkins in the left temple, killing him instantly. Inquest pending."

The Owl (Negro Newspaper)

"Steven Tompkins, colored, was peacefully residing in his home at 7727 Russell Street when Patrolman Proctor Pruitt knocked on his door. He was admitted by his wife. The officer served a summons on Steven Tompkins, and investigation disclosed the fact that while Tompkins was reading the summons Patrolman Pruitt pulled out his gun and deliberately, in cold blood with malice aforethought, killed and murdered Tompkins in his own home on the pretext that Tompkins, a few years before had shot him."

Mrs. Lillie Smith

Survey Findings

Mrs. Lillie Smith was born in 1900 in Charleston, S.C. The meagre amount of education she had was received in the public schools of that city. She completed the third grade.

Mrs. Smith was a church member but was not allied with any of the fraternal organizations of Detroit. She was insured with several insurance companies.

Police Report

"Lillie Smith, colored, age 25 years, 1545 Alger Avenue. About 7:25 P.M., February 1, 1925, Patrolman Fred Williams, while walking his beat at Russell near Brewster Street, heard two shots fired in rapid succession and then saw an International Truck, No. 95–485, driving at a rapid speed north on Russell near Brewster Street with James Smith driving and Lillie Smith, his wife, beside him. The Patrolman went out into the street, flashed his light and called to them to stop. They refused and the patrolman fired two shots, one bullet striking Lillie Smith in the left jaw. She was taken to Receiving Hospital in No. 3 Auto where she died February 8, 1925 at 5:00 P.M. Patrolman Fred Williams arrested and now awaiting trial (February 28, 1926)."

The Detroit Independent's Report
(Negro Newspaper)

"Fred Williams, a policeman, deliberately murdered Mrs. Lillie Smith, expectant mother, by shooting at the truck driven by her husband, February 1, 1925, near the corner of Alfred and Russell Streets, striking her directly in the neck, was freed in five minutes by a jury. Mrs. Smith was taken to the Receiving Hospital after the shooting, where she died a double death, by giving birth to an infant who still lives. Mrs. Smith died as a result of the wound."

George Sims

Survey Findings

George Sims was born in Knoxville, Tennessee in 1893. . . . he successfully completed three years of high school work.

In 1915 he married and the following year he and his wife migrated to Detroit in response to the great demand for Negro labor. At the time he was killed, he was employed at Ford's River Rouge Plant. He supplemented his payroll by peddling coal because at this time Ford's plants were only working four days a week. Sims was a member of the St. John's Methodist Church.

The Police Report

"George Sims, colored, age 38, 1985 Mullett Street. About 1:10
A.M. February 25, 1926, Patrolman Peter Scalley and Kenneth
Lawrence while patrolling in a scout car, they saw a man in the
alley between Hastings and Rivard, Clinton and Macomb Streets.
The officers approached this man and ordered him to throw up
his hands. He immediately reached for his pocket. Patrolman
Scalley, thinking the man was reaching for a gun, shot him in the
chest and below the heart. He was taken to Receiving Hospital,
where he died shortly after arrival. This man was later identified
as George Sims, colored, and has the reputation of being a
strong-arm man. Inquest pending."

The Owl's Report (Negro Newspaper)

"Last Thursday morning about one A.M. George Sims, a Ford
worker, was killed by Patrolman Peter Scalley, in cold blood.

"Sims, a Ford worker working four days a week, has a wife
and two daughters and lived at 1985 Mullett Street, called at a
friend's house who lives in the alley off Russell between Clinton
and Macomb Streets, to borrow his wagon, to peddle coal with,
in order to make extra money for his family, due to the loss of
two days in the factory.

"He was standing in the alley talking with this friend from the
window, with a thermos bottle under his arm, when officers Scalley and Kennedy drove up. Scalley ordered Sims to 'throw up his
hands' which he did. The thermos bottle he was carrying under
his arm fell on the pavement and Scalley fired and killed Sims in
cold blood. Sims had no weapons on his body."

. . .The explanation given rather generally by the police especially by the inspector of the homicide and Italian squads as to
why there are so many killings of Negroes is that the Negro is a
desperate criminal and officers have to shoot first. The Inspector
of the Italian Squad and others have spoken of the number of
brutal killings of police by Negroes. The reports of the homicide
squad, however, show that during the eighteen months from January 1, 1925 to June 30, 1926, policemen were killed by four Negroes. In one case, that of Edward Jordon, the policeman
received a bullet which was intended for another Negro with

whom Jordon had been fighting. This other Negro ran out of the hotel and Jordon firing after him killed the officer who was standing on the corner. In the other two [sic] cases the officers were killed by men whom they had cornered.

During the same period seven white men killed officers and in six of these cases the murder was committed by a hold-up man who turned on the officer when he interfered. In other words, as far as killings are concerned, the records do not show the Negroes to be hunters of policemen.

As an example of what may be done by a different method of handling there is a case of a lieutenant of the Italian Squad who is in general charge of that Department dealing with Negroes. He has not shot a man in fifteen years yet the Inspector of the Squad says that he can go into a den and arrest any man he chooses with perfect impunity. The general situation may be inferred from a comparison with the statistics for New York, which has the largest Negro population in the country (183,248). The Secretary of the Police Department of New York City says that in 1925 there were three Negroes killed by policemen. In the same year 14 Negroes were killed by policemen in Detroit with its Negro population of 82,000 in 1925.

As a complication of the situation it is commonly believed among colored people that a large number of Southern policemen are employed in Negro districts, having been recruited for the specific purpose and that they come with deep-seated prejudices against the Negroes which make it impossible for them to give them fair treatment. At any rate Detroit has not followed to any great extent the policy adopted by some cities of using colored policemen and on the local force there are only 14 colored men out of 3000. . . . [1]

Editor's Note

1. Minor errors and inconsistencies in the staff or police reports have not been corrected or noted unless they raise questions as to content. It might also be mentioned that the victims included all sorts of men and women, not only the innocent or well-behaved.

     There were many areas of police administration and performance targeted for criticism in the report; among these was the bland assumption of the police that the Negro district and the "vice" district shared the same boundaries. Given police willingness to believe that any black neighborhood was at best a potential crime area, the net result was that one group of Detroiters—about eight percent of all citizens at that time—was essentially powerless to determine its own life-style.

6. Gangsters and Politicians in Detroit: The Buckley Murder

Cyril Arthur Player

Radio was still new in 1930, and the election night murder of popular radio announcer Jerry Buckley stunned the city. Buckley had been stalwart in his opposition to both the Klan and organized crime. His large popular audience included many who had not responded to the tragedy of the Sweet case. The Buckley mystery is recounted here from an article by journalist Cyril Arthur Player written for the New Republic.

Detroit is paying the penalty for its negligence. The tomb of Gerald E. Buckley, whither tens of thousands have tramped to share their conviction of his martyrdom, is the melancholy monument to a citizenship that fell asleep.

The obvious facts are these: In November, 1929, Detroit elected a mayor, Charles Bowles. On July 22 last, Detroit recalled Mr. Bowles from that office. Within an hour or so after the last returns had been announced—in fact, at half past one in the morning—Jerry Buckley, "political commentator" for a local radio station, a champion of the recall and foe of the underworld, was shot to death as he sat in the lobby of a hotel.

Cyril Arthur Player, "Gangsters and Politicians in Detroit: The Buckley Murder," *The New Republic* (13 August 1930): 361–63.

The Buckley murder was the eleventh so-called gangster killing in Detroit within two weeks, but he was also the first "white man" to be "put on the spot." Previous murders, excepting the attempt last January on the life of a police inspector, have been confined to an Italian group and may have been due to an imported Sicilian domestic feud. Buckley's murder marked the added and anticipated step of the paid-killer era, which troubles the land, and proved also the unsoundness of the "dog eat dog" policy which police authorities say spells eventual self-extermination of the gangster.

Probably 100,000 persons passed through the modest Buckley home to view the slain man. Almost as many attended the funeral, which was the largest seen in Detroit since that [of] the celebrated mayor and governor, Hazen Pingree. The newspapers have not columns enough to express the popular horror and indignation . . . in tribute to a man who fought energetically for old-age pensions, for jobs for needy families, and for every form of humanitarian relief. . . .

But the significant fact is that the Buckley slaying was the logical climax of preceding events, although it arrived after the tide of Detroit's political fortune had turned. The shots of the slayers were almost a dramatic necessity as the "curtain" for the campaign that was waged here, and for such a piece of lawlessness as had been read into local history. But the tremendous demoralization of city government caused by looseness, ignorance, incapacity and selfishness had already been recognized by an alarmed citizenship. The offending regime, so young in months, already was doomed.

Charles Bowles is one of those inadequate men whom destiny occasionally chooses for tragi-comic relief. He . . . came into local politics from nowhere. Twice defeated for mayor, though ardently supported by the Ku Klux Klan, he obtained a place on the bench of the recorder's [criminal] court. He was reelected to this position but resigned it to make the race for mayor in a three-sided primary. The incumbent, John C. Lodge, was eliminated, and Bowles defeated a former mayor, John W. Smith.

As soon as he became mayor it became apparent that Mr. Bowles, sipping at the sweets of power, was cradling large ambitions. Under the charter, the mayor's office is non-partisan. Mr. Bowles began to build up a branch Republican machine, and in that process the well integrated units of public service began to fall apart. He made his chief blunder at the very start. He chose for commissioner of public works a man whose previous activity in public office had left him thoroughly distrusted by the public, a man who had been obliged to resign the police commissionership in a former administration to save his chief, the mayor, from defeat in a reelection.

This man who, meanwhile, had built up a substantial fortune in business, was John Gillespie. From the very day he took office until the day he abruptly resigned, following the recall, Gillespie was known as "commissioner of the works." He was the administration, and all those who knew their way around waited at his door.

The town, moreover, was running pretty much as it liked. Mayor Bowles had campaigned on the platform that the police department needed a shaking up. . . . A well-known lawyer, Harold H. Emmons, was named commissioner. The Emmons appointment was the only one made by Bowles which really commanded public respect. It was made at the request of an informal committee of citizens and before the advent of "the Gillespie" to power.

Police Commissioner Emmons returned from a business trip to meet the rising anger of a community that was fast preparing to take drastic measures. Mayor Bowles went to the Kentucky derby with a party organized by "the Gillespie". Emmons promptly launched his raids on the gamblers, and the familiar haunts began to "go dark." But when Bowles and Mr. Gillespie returned from the races, the mayor promptly fired Commissioner Emmons, replacing him with Thomas C. Wilcox, as futile a man as was Bowles himself.

Mr. Wilcox . . . was prompt to warn the gangster world that "Detroit is going to get the best blankety blank cleaning of its life."

Nevertheless, things went on as before. The *News* and *The Free Press* continued to call attention to open law violations and unsavoury conditions. Former supporters of Mr. Bowles drew away, non-political well-wishers became shocked and the voice of indignant criticism became a loud and swelling chorus. But somewhere out of that chorus, at first vague and shifting, then suddenly firm and positive, there emerged the word "Recall."

. . .The [recall] campaign itself set a record, probably nation-wide, not only for its bitterness, but for the lavish employment of the radio, and for the mud two of the opposing speakers slung at each other over the air. . . . Mr. Gillespie [acting as Bowles' cam-paign manager] hired an army of workers and a squadron of au-tomobiles was marshalled to carry voters. When Mr. Gillespie came to pay up, after the battle was lost, the amount of the bill for defending Mayor Bowles and himself, nearly reached, it is said, the sum of $100,000. He then suddenly resigned, with the words that he was "sick and tired of the whole mess." . . .

But the news of the recall count, exciting though it was, was drowned out by the noise of the shots that killed Jerry Buck-ley, who had just finished his night's work of announcing the returns.

Buckley was born in Detroit. He was the son of a horseshoer, who became editor of the *Horseshoers' Journal*. He worked his way through college . . . and in time graduated from a law school. He sold real estate, became interested in government work and was engaged by the bureau of intelligence of the Internal Revenue Department. At one time he did social service work for the Ford Motor Company, and often told friends that the knowledge he gained in that work made him the relentless enemy of racketeers and gamblers.

He certainly went after them when his radio announcing de-veloped into editorial comment on affairs. During the recall cam-paign his speeches were the most pungent and devastating of any that were on the air. Several times his life was threatened, and on election night it is said that he had three bodyguards standing near him while he was at work.

His work done, he returned to the lobby of the hotel where he was staying, and took his seat in one of two chairs placed pecu-liarly and conspicuously together. The other chair was occupied. He chatted a few minutes and then began to read a paper. Three men entered. One stood aside while the other two went behind Buckley and pumped a stream of lead into him.

This dramatic climax to a notorious situation brought the Gov-ernor of the State and the Adjutant-General hurrying by airplane to Detroit. Commissioner Wilcox, when he was offered state aid, reported to the newspapermen that he told the Governor:

"We are doing very nicely."

Then happened one of the most inscrutable things in the whole queer story. The Hearst-owned *Times*, which had stood on the fence during the campaign, took occasion to say in its issue reporting the tragedy:

"Buckley also was known as an associate of underworld racketeers and had been accused many times of using the radio for blackmail."

Doubtless *The Times* has since regretted this unjustified attack on a dead man, for the public rose in wrath and pilloried Buckley's defamers. But Commissioner Wilcox obviously was impressed, and had an idea. He announced that he was the fortunate possessor of an affidavit declaring Buckley had shaken down a man in the whiskey racket. Closely pressed by a News reporter, and asked to submit the affidavit to a judge to establish its validity, Wilcox admitted that the document had no signature as yet. The following day he proclaimed he had obtained a signature. And the next day the signer, a self-confessed bootlegger, made a second affidavit in which he declared that he could not read English, except very slowly, that he did not know the contents of the first affidavit, that he had signed it at the instigation of the commissioner, and at a time when he, the signer, thought he would be imprisoned if he did not sign. He added that personally he thought very highly of Buckley.

The evil genius which had accompanied Mr. Bowles all through his administration, managed to stay with him to the end. Arrests have been made. The centralized vice squad has been abolished and, as a consequence, hundreds of blind pigs were raided—proving, of course, that they had been in existence all the time and that the police knew where to find them. But neither the affidavit which Commissioner Wilcox worked so hard to obtain in order to destroy Buckley's character, nor the raiding of the blind pigs, has any relationship whatever to the capture of Buckley's slayers who, presumably, were imported killers and promptly disappeared. . . .

The reasons for Buckley's slaying still remain as much a mystery as the identity of the man or men who hired the killers. . . . Buckley's character scarcely is the issue, however, and the majority of Detroit's citizens believe profoundly in his integrity. . . .

Detroit seeks today a big man to take up the burden. . . .

Part XI

Hunger Comes Early to Detroit: A Decade of Depression

Hunger Comes Early to Detroit: A Decade of Depression

The depression of the 1930s has been the remembered war of older Americans for some years now. Its memories were ground into later generations as an unattainable standard of human suffering. Now only older grandparents have the dubious privilege of passing on the oral traditions of the depression. Among blacks with family roots in Paradise Valley, there are tales of rent parties. The music v·as never better than when "the man" would serve a final eviction notice in the morning, unless friends could raise the money tonight. In one west side Polish neighborhood there is a memory of lard sandwiches in the lunch bucket.

During the forties and fifties, Mary West Jorgenson, social worker at the Brightmoor Community Center, heard from several families the story of "the roast that went around the block." Half a dozen families on one street had worked out an ingenious method to preserve the tradition of beef on the table. One family, chosen by lot the first time, was obligated to buy the first roast on Saturday and enjoy their own Sunday dinner—but no more—from it. The remainder went next door to be reheated on Monday, to another house on Tuesday, and then on down the street, becoming progressively stew, then hash, until there was a final bare bone at the home of the last family for a watery soup at the end of the week. That family then scraped up the funds for a good twelve-cents-a-pound roast on the following day, which in turn began its own wanderings down the block.

The legend was wonderful. It included the self-discipline needed not to steal for your own child, and the housewifely resourcefulness of gravy on day-old bread, or the stew that was almost totally carrot and onion, with lots of water. The heartbreaking end of the story for Mary Jorgenson, teller of the folktale, came some years later when she spoke of the story in front of some of the women who had told it to her, thinking of it as a proud recollection for those who had lived it. One woman in the room abruptly began to scream, "We never did anything like that at all on X Street. We were never, ever that poor. Someone just made that up! It's a filthy, disgusting lie!" The other women, including several original narrators, kept shamefaced silence.

But that, too, was part of Detroit's depression. Lots of pride and a constant self-questioning stalked all adults who lived through those years. It was hard on those with middle-class beliefs and habits. Depression legends were filled with tales of the wealthy who were reported to have jumped out of office building windows or off the decks of cruise ships. There were also clerks and small businessmen and unemployed autoworkers who had hunting rifles. But most people survived as best they could.

The women stayed at home, confined by poverty to bitter loneliness and isolation. Detroit was a tradition-oriented society as far as men's and women's roles went—a "lunch-bucket town," some said. It was hard for the nonworking woman to comprehend the size of the problem destroying her life, or the new ways of perceiving it. Lucky were the men whom tradition allowed to play catch, or horseshoes, or even kick-the-can in the alleys, and who filled the public libraries to bursting, reading till closing time.

There were several legacies of the depression. Even before the full impact of the New Deal and its message of hope, there was a joining of issues over that very basic question of blame and self-blame. The Ford Hunger March demonstrated openly to many that Big Business didn't care. To some, the depression began to point the way to radical solutions as surely as had the bank failures that had preceded President Roosevelt's bank holiday. Honorable men went into chain groceries (this was before the supermarket) and stripped the food from the shelves for their families. Solemn, hard-faced men asked the librarian to find them a copy of this Karl Marx they had heard so much about. Both Mayor Frank Murphy and the president proclaimed that there was a right not to go hungry—and both made enemies who came to be seen as the people's enemies. Could the poor be blamed for poverty when it was so universal and openly acknowledged? Some did blame them, of course. When a bureaucrat in the welfare department embezzled, there were those to whom it proved only that the welfare clients themselves were cheaters who created an atmosphere that infected the respectable persons who dealt with them.

For most Detroiters the mutual acknowledgment of poverty led to a belief in the need for changes in society. One of these was the rapid growth of cooperative associations. A rural idea brought into town, it spread into many fields: buying clubs which expanded into grocery stores, a dairy with milk delivery routes, several housing efforts, and an optometrist's clinic. The expanding cooperative movement faded with the later transitions brought about by World War II, but while it lasted it provided exciting alternatives.

If some of the depression perceptions did not last long, the union movement, growing at first in secret, had at last come to stay. There came with it, for some, a lively interest in radical solutions of many sorts. It was an interest bred in those crowded libraries, but also in church halls, in "penny restaurants," in bars, on park benches, and in back alleys where grown men played kick-the-can.

Against this grim backdrop I reprint several articles portraying Detroit in the thirties. The first demonstrates that the depression really did begin early in Detroit. No one waited for the October, 1929 stock market crash. When Ford discarded the Model T for a new Model A, thousands were out of work. Paul U. Kellogg described the times for *Survey* magazine in October, 1928.

Next, "Detroit in Black and White," a wide-ranging account of the condition of blacks during the years before and during the depression, from a unpublished manuscript on the Michigan Civil Rights Federation by Norman McRae.

"Labor Spies and the Black Legion," by Forrest Davis, appeared in the *New Republic*. It can be regarded as a fairly accurate account of some horrible events, and shows some evidence that Davis probably talked with attorney Maurice Sugar during its preparation. There is considerable documentation for both its facts and its analysis of them in the Maurice Sugar Collection at the Reuther Library.

A significant crosscurrent was beginning as unorganized, unskilled workers began to fight back. One chapter from Steve Babson's *Working Detroit*, "The Tide Turns," tells of the moment when the UAW sit-down strikes created a new order of things.

The Reuther brothers knew to their sorrow that life was dangerous for union leaders. I include Victor Reuther's account of intruders at a family birthday party to illustrate this.

At the end of the decade, there came another political upheaval. Mayor Reading, the apparently innocuous choice of the outer sections of the city, was revealed as guilty of large-scale corruption and went to jail. Other changes were on the way. Mayor Reading was almost crowded off the front pages by the outbreak of war in Europe.

1. Ford Motor Company's Changeover from the Model T

Paul U. Kellogg

Acres of modern glass and steel construction, huge cement works, high lines and ore bins, blast furnace stacks and towering ovens form the matrix of the ocean-going port Henry Ford has dug out of the River Rouge. This is his Fordson plant at Detroit—"home" to Model A; and in one of the swift new Fords I was swung along a concrete road that led into it. . . . But the broken hopes, the plans gone wrong, the households wrenched apart, the children [removed] from schooling, as results of such a lay-off as that of the Ford plants in 1927 are not so easily visualized. They are there, nonetheless, as Detroit knows to its cost. . . .

Statistics given me by the company show 82,890 on the payroll last June as against 99,739 for June, 1926—a spread of 17,000; but

Paul U. Kellogg, "When Mass Production Stalls," *Survey* (1 March 1928): 683–728.

as against 120,275 for January, 1926—a spread of 37,000. These totals take no account of local companies supplying Ford parts, some of which shut down entirely. A social worker put the figure between maximum and minimum production at the Ford plants and those serving them at 60,000. A lay-off of 25,000 people at $6 a day, means a loss in wages for one month of $3,750,000, a lay-off of 60,000 means $9,000,000 a month less income for men and families.

The situation was mitigated by the fact that several other cars manufactured in Detroit, with Ford getting off the market, had a boom year in 1927—Hudson, Essex, Chrysler, Cadillac. There were no signals of panic. Bank deposits were up. New skyscrapers were going up. Merchandising in the big downtown stores was satisfactory. But that of the outlying stores that serve the residence neighborhoods of factory people was poor. Home buyers and real-estate operators were in trouble all down the line. The leniency of banks in tiding people over was not alone due to considerateness; it would have been disastrous to foreclose. Doctors were hard hit, and there was scarcely a trade or profession that did not feel the pinch. The municipality was confronted with a pyramiding load of relief. In its money-raising campaign last fall, the Community Fund appealed to well-to-do Detroiters for $600,000 more than the year before (and they responded)— $300,000 to make good the loss in collections from wage-earning families, $300,000 to carry on the greater burden of work thrown upon the private medical and charitable agencies of the city.

The Ford family was one of those to respond, giving $175,000 in all. Yet I do not gather that Mr. Ford thought through his relations to his employes in a way that would altogether distinguish between their households and his idle coal seams and his timber reserves or the unused water that ran over his spillways. Since his comparatively short-lived foray in paternalism, he has hewn to the line of paying high for work and letting the workers take care of themselves. "Put it all in the pay envelope." Ford dealers had lean months after the fat of the years also; and I imagine Ford lumped dealers and workers together in his mind. . . .

$72,539 was given in relief [by the Detroit Department of Welfare] in December, 1925; $150,950 in December, 1926; $248,187 in December, 1927. By November, 1926, the department was giving relief to 8,000 individuals as against 5,523 in November, 1925; by January, 1927, the figure had gone up to 21,750 as against 8,559 twelve months before; by March it had reached 24,117, continued around 15,000 throughout last spring and summer, and stood at 19,245 November last.

In these comparisons it should be borne in mind that 1925 was a fairly normal year. In 1926, employment, . . . was at its peak during the first half year, but by December twice as many families were on the books of the department as the year before; throughout the winter months of 1927 they were treble. . . . As time went on, the plants of the Detroit firms making screws, springs, cushions, bodies, etc., of whom Ford was the biggest customer, closed down. Their employes were out entirely, as were many of Ford's production men, after last May.

In the earlier period, Ford men were laid off and on in shifts, but Commissioner Dolan [Thomas A. Dolan, of the Detroit Welfare Department] told me that for over a year the department had found it necessary to supplement the wages of men thus staggered by the Ford Motor Company. Among them were men who had worked there for ten and twelve years, but could not support their families on the part-time pay. . . . The Ford commissary, which sells at cost, on a cash basis, offered no credit to help them along. The city department strengthened the hands of the little neighborhood merchants who were carrying them, by giving out (food) orders on these stores. The emptying of shops on the main thoroughfares of the west side of town was illuminating as to the failure of the pay envelopes. Meat markets closed, drug stores, moving picture houses. In a thousand ways the lay-off ravelled the fortunes of households. Help was needed to keep children in school. . . .

The crowded waiting rooms of free clinics registered the inability of people to meet their ordinary doctor's bills. The numbers coming to Harper Hospital's clinic last October were a third more than in October, 1925; to the Children's Hospital, a half more; to the North End Clinic, double; to Grace Hospital treble. . . .

Of all the sufferers, perhaps the Negroes, as the newest comers to Detroit, were hardest hit. A social worker in a Negro district told me of their predicament, but it was set down in cold figures at the City Department. Of the 4,029 families given relief

353

last November, 1,118 were colored, or 28 per cent. These included 5,137 persons out of the 86,000 colored population in the city. More than one out of twenty, in the old hard phrase, were "on the town". . . .

What the Ford Company did tallies pretty well with what the manufacturers attending the President's Unemployment Conference thought other manufacturers could do in the depression of 1921. It employed men, turn about, two or three weeks at a stretch so as to spread out its reduced payroll into as many pay envelopes as possible. It kept up production on Model T till June and thereafter continued to manufacture parts (as well as trucks and airplanes). It employed large numbers in overhauling the plant, designing and rebuilding machinery. It cut the working week to five days, and some of the time and for some of the departments to two and three days a week. It had reason to believe there was a large margin of floating workers, single men—the suitcase crowd—who could shift for themselves, here today, there tomorrow. And another margin of men from small towns and farms, who had home places to go to, and might welcome a vacation. For the rest, it hoped . . . to keep the cut in its labor force down to 25,000, and with part-time work and the savings which people had had a chance to lay by at the high wages, it assumed that they would make out all right. . . .

[Paul Kellogg compared lay-off programs in other companies, some of which met the 1921 depression with joint worker-management committees to plan the necessary cutbacks; in others, mainly in the Chicago garment industry, the committees were actually *union* management committees, and the company assisted in setting up emergency unemployment funds.]

. . . In contrast at Ford's, while there may have been lively considerateness, man to man, as employes were laid off or taken on during the emergency, they had no participation whatever in dealing with a situation they were in up to their necks. In workshop slang, decisions came down "through the roof." Responsibility was single, and divorced from those who most sorely felt its consequences. Through the roof came the intention to keep discarges down to 25,000; but that did not hold by 10,000 between the maximum for 1926 and the minimum for 1927.

Through the roof came the well-intentioned plan of staggering shifts. . . . Meanwhile, they could not meet expenses at home on the part-time pay. Through the roof came the assumption that high wages in the past had given Ford employes fat they could live on over the lean months. . . . Men who had taken Ford employment in earnest as a means of earning permanent livelihood, who had responded to the Ford policy of encouraging high standards of home life, were among those who were squeezed hardest when the bottom fell out of their earnings and they could not keep up payments on their houses.

If automobile manufacturers or tool makers elsewhere invent anything that plays into the making or the running of a car, the management "on the roof" at Ford's are quick to know of it. But there was nothing to indicate that they had heard of what Hills Brothers or the Dennison Manufacturing Company have done in tackling the problems of broken employment, what has been attempted by pioneers in glass and machinery, what any one of a dozen firms in textiles, clothing, or novelties has tried out. . . . Ford cars have invaded Europe from Ireland to Russia. It is to be doubted if his overseas salesmen have sent back anything on the systems of employment insurance abroad, which are national inventions after their kind. . . .

The baseball diamond outside the employment office at Fordson had been thronged on Monday morning, the week of my visit, with men who wanted to work for Ford. Six or seven thousand men applied for work that week in December, and they were hiring three or four hundred a day. . . . They were picking men for the assembly line, and here it was that the sifting process . . . was at work. They were after intelligence, activity, auto experience if possible; young fellows for the most part, American, Canadian, British; Scandinavians as well and Americanized Poles and Russians. "Everyone wants to work on the new car" said the superintendent.

There was something simple and direct in these hiring and firing negotiations, contrasting as they did with the more elaborate functionings of the employment departments of some of our big industries. Certainly the whole situation, the lure of the pay, the pressure for jobs, tended to create a picture of labor as a foot-loose commodity, welling in like a tide. . . . under such circumstances, many an industrial executive comes to regard the employment reservoir as something to tap today and empty into tomorrow, without thought of its human entourage. That indeed was the crux of the situation when they laid off men at Ford's no less than when they were taking them on.

Then the burden of household support was being lifted from the payroll to some hypothetical base outside the realm of Ford concern. As a Detroit business man put it, the Ford Motor Company is a business not a philanthropy; with sales off, the only source from which wages could have been drawn was past profits. Yet that is the source from which an industrial corporation meets payments on its bonds during a depression. And a whole trade insured against unemployment could shift much of the load from profits to prices.

Meanwhile to cut down a working force is all but like lifting a mortgage and transferring the interest charges by magic to other shoulders. There was a saving, a bonus, if you will, on every man put on part time or lopped off Ford's payroll. The discontinued earnings of Ford employes did not coalesce into any obligation which had to be reckoned with in company plans, any pressure to shorten the lay-off and overlap the two productions; anything even to compare with the administrative concern over throwing out old machines which as tools were worth a dollar a pound and as scrap $9 or $10 a ton. The pressure was all the other way round. And in the general view, it was just the men's hard luck.

With such tenuous security from above, what chances are there of the automobile workers bestirring themselves from below, other than individually, for their protection? . . . . The old craft organizations were long since ironed out of the mechanized industries of Detroit. The United Automobile, Aircraft and Vehicle Workers' Union of America, described to me as an embodiment of the One Big Union Idea, pulled a strike among the body workers at the Fisher plant some years ago which lasted thirty days. A strike last fall at the Briggs' plant was over in a week.

Among the old-line unions in the metal trades, the last strike of any consequence was that of 1920 in the Timken works, engineered by the machinists. Today, an employer told me there are scarcely 300 men in the machinists' local. A trade unionist put the figure at 700. At any rate, in this great center of machine production, it is inconsequential and President Martel of the city labor federation was frank to say that to unionize the 150,000 workers in the machine trades was too large a mouthful for organized labor in Detroit to bite off by itself. . . .

I attended a meeting of the central body in Detroit. . . . The picture I came away with was that of small groups of unionists, who had contrived to build dikes against the undermining tides of non-union workers, employed and unemployed, which surrounded them. Indeed, I could not help but feel that they regarded the semi-skilled workers of the machine shops more as a threat to their security than as a field for missionary effort.

In talking with me, President Martel blasted the employers in the mechanical trades for firing out the unions, cutting wages, installing prison labor methods and what not. He was equally outspoken as to the Communists, a lot of hare-brained people whom it was wise to let talk their heads off. "But if Weisbord can crack open the situation and give the employers the hell they've given us, it's coming to them. They won't get any consolation from us—either way."

His reference was to Albert Weisbord, the young Communist who effectively organized the long drawn-out textile strike in Passaic. There is nothing gumshoe about his presence in Detroit. He has opened an office downtown. . . .

To Weisbord's mind unemployment in Detroit has been due not merely to changes in models but to such mechanization and speeding up of work that men are chronically jobless. And to him the change in models is but a curtain-raiser for the "most intensified competition that has ever taken place" (with the home market saturated, foreign makes and tariff walls abroad) between Ford's vertical trust and General Motors aligned with DuPont and U.S. Steel. He sees business headed for a slump within a year, further and violent market changes, increased competition, greater speeding up, longer hours, more unemployment, attempts to beat down wages—"and this in turn means opportunity to organize and revolutionize the working class. . . ."

Therefore the urgings of party members to join their respective trade unions and bore from within. Therefore the missionary work among clubs, sick and death benefit organizations, fraternal bodies, and what they call "language fragments." Even now Weisbord claims they are the only group strong enough "to jam 3,500 to 4,000 people into some of the largest halls in Detroit—

357

almost entirely auto-workers." Today, his soap-boxers are unmolested, the penny sheets sold at factory gates. This he regards as
temporary, due to "the arrogance of Detroit employers," but—

> To organize here means jail and clubbing. We are organizing for
> struggle. When once the workers begin to move, this city will be
> the center of revolutionary activity. Any large strike here means a
> general strike. Any large strike means a revolutionary situation—
> here at the heart of American capitalism and Ford worshipped
> all over the world. With hundreds of thousands of workmen
> out, 2,500 police are not going to stand in their way. That means
> the militia, the regular army. That means men shot down in the
> streets, and when a government shoots down men, events shape
> themselves.

In other words, if Weisbord is a prophet, Detroit will have
more than an unemployment situation on its hands in case of a
general depression. . . . The general wage-cuts he anticipated
were discounted to me by Detroiters familiar with the industrial
situation; but there was no blinking the maladjustments in employment, for which the big employing corporations are ultimately responsible. . . .

The general front of the Employers' Association is indicated by
a paragraph at the top of one of its folders: " . . . 97 per cent of
Detroit's work people pursue their various callings without let or
hindrance from organized labor domination."

The association stands for the "American plan," which in local
practice in the building trades means that the strongest organized unions work closed shop on the same buildings on which
the weaker trades work open shop. There was a sympathetic
strike to unionize them all on a large theater under construction
last fall. It was met by a muster of builders, owners and bankers
involved in the other great structures going up (one of them announced as the biggest office building in the world). A war chest
of $100,000 was said to have been quickly subscribed, one maver-
ick contractor was made to toe the line and the strike was nipped
in the bud. It was a foretaste of what might happen if the dominant motor industry were confronted with a serious labor
conflict.

In the Detroit factories there is no such hybrid situation. I was
assured at the offices of the Employers' Association that men are

not discharged because of union membership or activity; but was told that there has not been a unionized metal trades plant since the war. And to their minds, Detroit "would never have produced the automobiles it has if the unions were in the saddle". . . .

The complete dominance of the employers must exaggerate the tendency on the part of all to follow the line of least resistance, the tendency on the part of the least scrupulous to disregard the human element utterly, and thus to drag the rest down to their level. . . .

After all, Ford with his initiative and power merely exhibits in advance and on a large drafting board, dynamic trends in modern industry. My feeling is that there is something instinctive and fundamental underlying his ruthless dismissal of executives, his near-sightedness when it came to social by-products while he laid off men and overhauled his tools. What I have in mind is something different from the customary charge of autocracy lodged against him. He has had to buck tradition, business opinion, shop practices; he wants orders obeyed, or his insurgency is short-circuited. There is always the danger that his course will degenerate into the whims of a narrow dictatorship. But on its constructive side, his is an intense desire to have his establishment free to experiment. His is the genius of foraging. . . .

If modern industrial operations are themselves to be kept free from the drag of human commitments, then the men who work at them must find security outside the day's job. Security against such hazards as unemployment. My best guess is that if Ford dropped $100,000,000 of his surplus in 1927, his employers dropped a sum very nearly equaling it in lost wages; but his hundred million was in a sense investment; theirs, in every sense, waste. If Ford, with his abhorrence of waste, should put his mind to work on the problem, something as revolutionary as his scheme of financing might come out of it. If he could visualize the junk of household goods and chattels, of smashed hopes and wrecked endeavors, thrown up by his lay-off, see it as he sees that great pile of war scrap at Fordson, and set his bent for salvaging at work . . . what might not issue?

Much has been written of the monotony of mass production. I have dealt here with its insecurity. . . . Workers have tendrils that have struck roots in the households and schools of a city's life. Of the cases receiving relief from the Detroit Department of Public Welfare in 1926, there were considerable numbers born in Austria, Germany, Italy, Poland, Rumania, Russia, but together they did not make up a third of the total. They were not new immigrants. They averaged five to the family. And more than two-thirds of the total were born in the United States and Canada; over one-third were native white Americans averaging over four to the family. . . .

[The production men's] specialized aptitudes give them no equivalent foothold in other industries; their habit-sets even stood in the way of some of them getting back into the new assembly lines at Ford's. Theirs had been dead-end occupations. They had no equity in their work; no say as to the manner in which they were staggered or laid off. They might have been red iron ore or limestone or coal in the big bins at Fordson. And their footing as members of society was equally shaky. Thrift is a good thing; but is it social thrift for tremendous corporate industries to count on individual savings as the sole protection against their own hazards? A year's savings go under rapidly before the fixed charges in a city where the cost of living is notoriously high. Modern business has developed all manner of credit schemes by which workers mortgage their incomes over long periods of time for equipment for urban living, but little as yet to give security for that income—or any part of it.

Ford has done more than any living man to strengthen the position of the man who would work his livelihood out on the soil. He has helped him master isolation and distance. He has put power at his elbow. But when it comes to the production men who build his cars, the net result of his hiring and firing is the other way round. High pay, fear, the urge of the machine and of the boss have been relied on at Ford's, like a four cylinder engine to keep them at work, and when the gas was shut off they stopped. They were no longer production men and their livelihood was a flat tire.

The security of a city rests on the security of its citizens. Detroit needs to re-examine the underpinnings of democracy in this day of untrammeled industrial enterprises which have drawn such huge accretions to her urban mass—so piled up wealth and tall buildings, but so weakened the normal rootholds of domestic well-being.[1]

Editor's Note

1. The magazine *Survey* (which Paul Kellogg edited for many years) and its partner, *Survey Graphic,* failed to survive the thirties depression and therefore missed the times of modern expansion in the field of social work. Old issues of *Survey* represent an unparalleled source of American social history for the years of the magazine's existence.

2.   Detroit in Black and White

Norman McRae

*In a study dealing primarily with the Michigan Civil Rights Feder-
ation, a radical activist group that reached its peak strength between the late
thirties and 1950, historian Norman McRae sketched a background of events and
emotional overtones that spans years before 1935 and the early years of the automotive unions.*

Although the C.R.F. [Civil Rights Federation] technically serviced all of Michigan, most of its activities took place in
Detroit and Detroit was where the action was. . . .

In the 1920's Detroit's corporate area increased to 137.9 square
miles through annexation. In 1920, its population was 993,687
and a decade later it had grown to 1,568,662 and became America's fourth largest city in terms of population.

In order to provide adequate educational and municipal services for an additional half million citizens, the city fathers increased the bonded debt from $26,682,325 to $255,432,020. The
total municipal debt soared to $378.000,000 . . . and hampered

Norman McRae, "The Michigan Civil Rights Congress and Its Involvement in the
Struggle for Negro Rights, 1935–1945" (Unpublished MS, n.d.): 27–37.

the city's efforts to provide welfare services for their destitute citizens early in the depression.

The city tried to obtain some financial assistance from the automobile giants for their pauperized auto workers, but the automobile industry invoked the Protestant ethic, social Darwinism and their various corollaries to justify their refusal. The relief rolls reached their peak in 1931 when 192,000 people were on welfare.

During the period of 1935 to 1945, there was some hope. . . . From 1935 to its demise, the WPA [Works Progress Administration] supported at least 2,000,000 persons in Michigan. The CCC [Civilian Conservation Corps] was a boon to thousands of young men, seventeen to twenty-eight. When it was discontinued in 1942, there were 103 segregated CCC camps in the state that had given young black and white males work and a sense of dignity. The NYA [National Youth Administration] was another New Deal program that was a bulwark against poverty and anomie.

Some Detroiters were employed and they guarded their jobs just as a lioness guarded its cub. A great deal of energy was expended trying to secure work; men left home at midnight and stood in line all night . . . to see the straw boss who might let them into the plant. It was a *rara avis* who got the worm. Another strategy was the practice of leaving home before dawn and systematically canvassing every business and factory within a given area. This saturation technique was predicated upon luck, but men had to have something to believe in.

Those men who had unskilled jobs in the automobile industry endured all kinds of indignities and privations because they knew they could be fired at any moment and there would be 100 men waiting outside to take their places. They knew that the system was stacked against them, but they endured the dehumanizing aspects of the assembly line, the physical torture of the foundry, the monotony on the speed-ups because they knew that their jobs meant survival.

Detroit had a history of being an open-shop town. . . . A man could be on the job for as long as eighteen hours and get paid for only three or four hours, but he had to be on the job to keep it.

The average automobile worker made seventy-six cents an hour. The average annual wage was $1,150, but forty-five per cent of the auto workers made less than $1,000. During this period, auto workers in Michigan made seventy-five per cent of the mo-

363

tor vehicles in the world and eighty-three per cent of those sold in America.

Production figures did not tell the world how difficult life was for these workers. . . .

On August 26, 1935, the United Automobile Workers of America was organized. It was not the colossus that it is today. It was a "blue baby" that needed great care because it was in danger of dying momentarily.

During this period, Walt Disney produced one of his first full-length extravaganzas, "Snow White and the Seven Dwarfs". In this film the dwarfs sang a rousing song called "Heigh Ho". Some wag changed its lyrics to be sung as follows:

Heigh, Ho, Heigh Ho!
I joined the CIO
Now I get my pay from WPA
Heigh, Ho, Heigh Ho![1]

In many cases this was the fate of those who were brave enough to join the UAW. Large companies spent large sums of money on arms, espionage, and the placing of *agents provocateurs* in positions of leadership within the unions. Large companies also practised the rule of *divide et impera*. . . . This was how they maintained the industrial status quo. . . .

By trying to pull . . . diverse [ethnic] groups together under the banner of fair play and civil rights, the C.R.F. made a noteworthy attempt to develop a *modus operandi* that might have helped to improve race relations in Detroit. During the period upon which we have focused, there was an ethnic, class, and racial pecking order that operated in the following manner: Protestant, nativist, middle class and working class, whites and the foreign born, disparaged each other. All of the above groups vilified Jews, but tended to have a pathological fear and hatred of Negroes. Jews did not ignore these attacks nor did they turn the other cheek. They used their organizations to counter attack. They also managed to manifest some compassion for Negroes, but thanked their God that they were not "Swartzers" because that would have been too much of a burden to bear.

Black was not beautiful to the black people of that era, and they did not see themselves as being black. In those days, one was either colored or Negro. Black was a term of derogation and they rejected the idea of being an ethnic group. Most black Detroiters had laughed at Marcus Garvey's U.N.I.A. [Universal Negro Improvement Association] movement and declared that those initials stood for the "Ugliest Niggers in America". The average black and white southerner had more in common than they dared admit. They were created in the same cultural matrix and nourished from the same umbilical cord. And in more cases than either would dare to admit, they were related by blood, but they were diametrically opposed to one another. . . .

The black community was divided. The colored people who were "old Detroiters", those colored people who lived in Detroit prior to the great northern Negro migration of 1915, had little to do with the newcomers. They were content to withdraw into their elitist enclaves and bemoan the passing of the "cherry orchard". The Afro-American power elite might have prevented . . . erosion of their civil rights if it had used its organizations and institutions as an irrigation system to assist this outpouring of black humanity from the rural south. Instead, they used them as dams and many of their rights were washed away along with their complacency. . . . [2]

Everybody suffered during the depression, but some suffered more than others and blacks in Detroit suffered more than anyone. . . . [The black community] needed more housing, jobs, and better education for its young. Blacks with college degrees found it extremely difficult to obtain jobs commensurate with their education. Many lucky and educated blacks found jobs in the post office, and the post office became the cesspool for Negro talent. During the 1935–1945 period, jobs and housing were the key to their Jim Crow kingdom because a person needed a job to secure the limited, over-priced, and inadequate housing.

The automobile industry in general and the Ford Motor company in particular were the magnets that drew black workers to Detroit. This great migration caused a "backlash". Northern whites became alarmed when Negroes were no longer occasional visitors but had instead become part of the community. . . . Hotels and restaurants started to refuse black patronage. Even some theatres began to segregate their Negro customers.

In the auto plants, racial antagonism increased as competition for jobs increased. Management came up with the idea that pro-

365

ductivity of Negro workers depended upon the selection of foremen who understood "Negro psychology". Although southern
whites resented working with blacks as equals, many of them
jumped at the opportunity to secure positions as foremen and to
reinforce management's conviction that they understood "the
Negro" and could make him produce. This same argument was
advanced to justify the hiring of white southerners as policemen
in Detroit. Blacks were "the last hired and the first fired." They
were not hired at all in some plants. The relationship of blacks to
white workers was that of a sparrow to a horse. [McRae supplies
an example of the truth of this rural saying in his following quotation from Lloyd Bailer, one of the first black economists, and
one who studied the auto industry:]

> I asked if Negroes were not employed anywhere in the plant.
> He said, 'yes, some jobs white folks will not do; so they have to
> take niggers in, particularly in duco work, spraying paint on car
> bodies. This soon kills a white man.' I inquired if it ever killed
> Negroes. 'Oh, yes,' he replied. 'It shortens their lives, it cuts them
> down, but they're just niggers.'[3]

Black workers were short-lived. They had a shorter life expect-
ancy than their white counterparts. Pneumonia, tuberculosis and
other respiratory diseases were their chif killers. These illnesses
caused black workers to drop like flies after an attack of pesticide.
In those harsh days before the advent of penicillin and sulfa,
whenever a black factory worker caught pneumonia his friends
came by to bid him adieu.

The Ford Motor Company hired the largest number of blacks.
Although most of them worked in the foundry and foundry machine shop, some were in other departments as well. In other
auto plants the foundry was called the "black department". A
black man either worked in the foundry or he worked as a janitor. At the Ford Motor Company, there were Negroes in key positions. Willis Ward and Donald Marshall worked in the
Sociological Department and were junior executives with some
power. There were also several black foremen, white collar employees and star men.[4] The Ford Motor Company was the exception, but it did not establish any trends. And furthermore, Henry

Ford's liberalism was really tokenism motivated by his paternalistic approach to black workers.

During the dog days of the depression, many black families were held together by the wife. Long before white women joined the work force as the glamorized "Rosie the Riveter", black women were working in laundries and in the homes of the well-to-do as maids and cooks for two dollars a day plus carfare. Early in the morning, one could see them at transfer points waiting for streetcars and buses to carry them to Northwest Detroit, Highland Park, and Grosse Pointe. Many carried the badge of their profession—a large brown paper bag.

The Detroit Housing Commission inventoried housing in 1938. Its findings revealed that 85 per cent of all housing was closed to blacks. Moreover, 50 percent of all housing inhabited by Negroes was substandard, whereas only 14 per cent of that occupied by whites was in that category. . . .

Throughout the city there were a number of invisible lines over which it was not safe for blacks to move even if they could. In Paradise Valley, it was Woodward Avenue on the west, Russell or Chene Streets on the east, the Detroit River was on the south, and in the north the line of demarcation was flexible, in that it moved a block or two every year. On the west side, Grand Boulevard, Tireman, Epworth and Warren Avenue were the outer breastworks. . . .

Officially, the police department did not defend these boundary lines, but they were sympathetic to whites in the area. Reverend Charles Hill reported that when he protested to the police at McGraw Station on the west side of Detroit about the lack of police protection when blacks moved into a previously all-white neighborhood, the police inspector exploded, "Don't you know we could hire somebody to kill you for going on this way?"[5] Reverend Hill was not killed, but neither did the police department protect blacks who dared to move into white neighborhoods. Mob violence also caused a number of Jewish families to retreat from gentile areas.

Indifferent police protection was a major flaw in the relation between the black community and city hall. This aberration illustrated the fact that blacks had some influence, but no power. Municipal reform and a revision of the city charter that changed the representation on the common council stripped black Republicans of what little power they had had. This loss of power happened before World War I.

During the years of 1935–45, a new sycophantic practice was developed. Mock elections were held to elect mayors from certain black neighborhoods such as Sugar Hill and Brownsville. . . . These pseudo mayors had their pictures taken with the mayors of Detroit, but they had no real influence. The real influence wielders during Mayor Richard Readings's administration were Charles Roxborough, one of Joe Louis' managers, and Ulysses Boykin, editor of the *Detroit Tribune*.[6] Some ministers, doctors, and lawyers had influence with various mayors and public officials in Detroit.

There were a number of feeble attempts to establish a political power base such as the attempt to build the United District Congressional Organization, Inc. This organization tried to organize every precinct where Negroes lived. Its efforts were unsuccessful and its organization was short-lived. The resurgence of black political power in Detroit did not come about until it coalesced with the Democratic Party and the CIO [Committee for Industrial Organization].

Notes

1. A reminiscence from the author's boyhood.
2. Norman McRae, review of John M. Green's *Negroes in Michigan History*; Reprint of Francis H. Warren's *Michigan Manual of Freedmen's Progress, 1915,* in *Michigan History,* LIII (1969), 163–64.
3. Lloyd H. Bailer, "Negro Labor in the Automobile Industry" (unpublished PhD. dissertation, Department of Economics, University of Michigan, 1948), 34.
4. Bailer, 32–117. J. C. Price was a star man in the abrasive stock section. He was the supervisor of an all-white crew. E. J. Collins was a general foreman in the die casting department. He supervised 147 men. This group was racially mixed. C. Mimms supervised 24 men in the tank link section. Mr. Jarvis was a foreman in the steel construction division. There were 30 men in this group. R. Hearst was a foreman in the magnesium foundry. P. Norwood, A. D. Boon, T. Shelton, and Linsey Sheffield were foremen in the foundry. . . . A star man was someone who could only be fired with the consent of

Henry Ford. [In an interview with this editor shortly before his death in 1987, Charles Mimms, one of the star men listed by Bailer, spoke of the importance of this role in his own life.]

5. Oral interview with Reverend Charles Hill, May 8, 1967, Charles Hill Papers, Walter Reuther Archives of Labor History and Urban Affairs, Wayne State University, Detroit, Mich.

6. Letters to Mayor Richard Reading in the Mayor's Papers, 1938, BHC, DPL, Box 6. Correspondents with Mayor Reading include: Reuben J. Patton, Rev. William H. Peck, William Sherrill, M. J. Morrison. The latter was the mayor of "Sugar Hill".

3.   Labor Spies and the Black Legion

Forrest Davis

The Black Legion Murders have exposed the existence of an atavistic Detroit under the smooth, modern hood of the motor metropolis. But the human exhibits lined up in Common Pleas Court for the oathbound murder of a W.P.A. worker declined to look the part of throwbacks. Instead, the row of manacled Black Knights, minus skull-and-crossbones regalia, seemed strikingly familiar as they lounged in the jury box—as if you had seen them somewhere else a little while before, perhaps in the bleachers at Navin Field, where the Tigers play. Excessively typical, if that is possible, the twelve might have been trying Dayton Dean, their compeer, who was on the witness stand, as he reviewed the midnight execution of Charles A. Poole for the ethical

Forrest Davis, "Labor Spies and the Black Legion," *The New Republic* (17 June 1936): 169–71.

deviation of wife-beating. Typical working-class, native Americans, frightened and childlike.

Dean, a pudgy pipe-coverer by day, a degenerated romantic by night with a mania for guns and homicide, discussed in emotionless phrases the last moments of Charles Poole. The Detroit press unanimously dubs him the "trigger man," chief of the "killer band." He behaved more like a small boy who has been called before the faculty for shooting paper wads at teacher. The prosecutor, Duncan C. McCrea, asked Dean what he did after Davis—"Colonel" Harvey Davis yonder in the jury box—stopped upbraiding Poole for his supposed mayhem on Mrs. Poole. Said Dean:

"Well, I—Davis stopped talking—I looked around—I knew I was supposed to shoot him, so I started firing."

The execution of Poole, which awakened Detroit to knowledge that a pathological body of assassins operated just under its day-by-day pattern, was performed as casually as that. Nothing in the witness's tone or demeanor suggested that he understood the unprovoked wantonness of his act. The faces of the twelve reflected no revulsion as . . . they stared reproachfully at the "boy" who was tattling. A row of dreadful children they seemed, too young to realize the enormity of their dream world of guns, dire oaths, midnight powwows and group vengeance.

The defendants, from a beardless youth in the center to two gray-headed men at the ends, had unlined faces. The discipline of thought had not furrowed them. A man on one end, nicknamed "the deacon," might have been listening to a hell-and-damnation sermon in a cabin church in Tennessee; at the other extreme, a dark-skinned defendant of sixty-odd, with rapt, deep-set eyes, looked equally capable of playing the fiddle or prophesying for his mountain neighbors. Native stock Americans from the Midlands, they seemed to be as young as the Detroit in which their fumadiddles came to light.

The city of Detroit was not in the jury box with the Black Knights. It should have been.

Detroit is a new city.[1] Here the utmost in technology, or applied science, has been put magnificently to work. A city where nothing in sight existed yesterday; the last word among twentieth-century communities, in which, one might suppose, the scientific spirit had swept aside such anachronisms as night riders. Detroit is bounded on the west by Fordissimus—by Ford's Rouge plant, where 70,000 workers quickstep to the cadence of the conveyor belt; by Ford's Greenfield Village, . . . by Ford's company town, Dearborn, and by Ford's presence as a disguised feudal monarch. Henry the First, radical newspapers call him, in token of the absolute power he wields. On the north, Detroit is bounded by the Reverend Charles E. Coughlin's pulpit—a triumph of that other modern engine, the microphone. In between these points of interest, Detroit's million and a half souls go through the gestures of moderns.

Yet this brittle new town harbored the Black Legion. The punishing assembly line left enough vigor in native workers transplanted to Detroit for them to take bullet-sealed oaths, swear a pox on Catholics, Jews, Communists and Negroes, drape themselves in black robes and conduct punitive expeditions at all hours of the night. Moreover, the social climate was so unscientifically intolerant that the Legion—patched together out of the broken Ku Klux Klan—thrived, making converts, until it acquired political power. Until, indeed, unnoticed by the majority of citizens, the courts, the police force, the street-car and lighting services were infected with men vowed to murder—no less.

The truth, it would appear, is that there are at least two Detroits—Fordissimus and night riders, side by side. The marvels of industrial production on one hand; on the other, reactionary night skulkers, carrying on an American tradition running from the Know-Nothings of the 1840's through Knights of the Golden Circle, barn-burners and whitecaps to the Klan. Two Detroits apparently far apart but not total strangers. At times, as a closer investigation discloses, they meet. They meet at the contact point of labor strife. The night rider, 1936 style, in Ford's Detroit is likely to be a labor spy as well as a Catholic-baiter. The lash that peaks his dark will may as well be hatred of Communists, *i.e.*, union organizers, as distrust of Jews.

A pair of questions troubles any inquirer who looks into the Black Legion phenomenon in the Michigan automobile towns. Who organized and who directs this disciplined body, so secret that its strength is not yet known; so assured that it continues, by informed reports, to grow during the Poole case hullabaloo? That is number one. The leaders of record will not do. Virgil F. (Bert) Effinger, of Lima, Ohio, Dr. William J. (Shotgun) Shepard, of Bellaire, Ohio, and Arthur F. Lupp, the only revealed Michigan "brigadier general" won't answer. They haven't the iron or the intelligence. So rigid, however is the Legion's obligation that the Detroit authorities are still unaware—or so they profess—of the identity of higher-ups. The second question ties in with the first. How nearly does the Legion's behavior approach fascism?

Henry Ford has acquired fame on two counts at least. In the world at large he receives credit for making the most profitable use of the assembly line. Labor regards his factory spy system, euphemized under the title Service Department, as the tops. The motor car industry is open-shop. Other employers do not lag far behind Ford in opposing unionization, by means secret and open. In such a community one would naturally look for a possible link between an anti-social band of night riders and the extensive anti-union forces of dominant employers. Especially as one remembers that the Detroit area lives, breathes and makes motor cars. Economically, Detroit has no other concern.

The link in not concealed.

George Marchuk, treasurer of the Communist Auto Workers' Union, was found murdered in a ditch in Lincoln Park on December 22, 1933. Lincoln Park, a suburb adjoining Dearborn, is predominantly populated with Ford workers, and is a one-time Ku Klux stronghold. There is reason to believe that the Legion has enrolled Lincoln Park officials there. In March, 1934, the body of John A. Bielak, a member of the Hudson Motor Company local of the A.F. of L. United Automobile Workers, was discovered by a roadside near Monroe, Michigan. He had been beaten. Under Bielak's head. his assassins significantly had placed a stack of applications from other workers for union membership. Bielak hadn't had a chance to turn them in.

The murders were unsolved. Labor leaders vainly besought action. Evidence was clamorously offered by the Communists in the Marchuk case; offered with no takers. But, as an outgrowth of the Legion inquiry, it appears that both homicides may be traced. The name of Isaac (Peg Leg) White, ex-policeman in Detroit, later a "brigadier general" of the Legion and now living on a farm near Lansing, Michigan, recurs through the investigations.

White, although he now denies having led the Legion, came into dubious prominence in the months that followed the fatal Ford "hunger march" of March, 1932. The emotional shock administered to Detroit by the deaths of five hunger marchers, the wounding of others, brought on anti-radical, anti-labor hysteria. White found employment for his talents. . . . The ex-policeman was in the employ of the Citizen's Committee at that time . . . the open-shop, vigilante agency of the Detroit Board of Commerce. . . .

White, in company with two other men, came to [a grand jury witness's] office at the Hudson Motor Company to reveal gratuitously, that Bielak and four other men in the paint shop were agitating for the union; were sabotaging the work, and were Communists. The three visitors disclosed that they belonged to a secret order which had as one of its objectives the suppression of Communists. The witness . . . joined the Legion. He attended a number of meetings, including one at which Lupp was elected to succeed White as "brigadier general." . . .

This witness relates White to Bielak's murder. White, as a matter of record, warned Marchuk twice to mind his business and lay off the "union stuff." Bielak, incidentally, was not a Communist.

All this tends to show—a deduction supported by the State Police—that the brotherhood began its life as a labor-spy organization with skull-and-crossbones trimmings. The Legion continues to figure, by report, in subsequent labor disputes. In the Motor Products strike of last fall, the strike headquarters and the homes of five strikers were bombed with black, smokeless powder—indicating expert work. The United Auto Workers and the Farmer-Labor Party in Detroit attribute the bombings to the Legion. . . . William Green of the A.F. of L. demanded from Attorney General Cummings an investigation into the anti-union aspects of the Legion. . . .

Searchers for the fascistic formula in the Legion must find first that the industrialists of Detroit—specifically Ford, General Motors, and Chrysler—,the "big three"—have consciously backed the movement. An occasional relationship between strike-breaking agencies and Legionnaires is not enough. It is possible that manufacturers, large or small, have paid into the coffers of the Legion. No one in authority seems to know where the money has come from. But, so far as my inquiry goes, the motor magnates have not subsidized the Legion. We shall be clearer on that point if and when the leadership stands exposed.

What then? . . . Is [the Legion] merely a survival of the Klan? Michigan, it may be recalled, had the largest Klan membership of any state—875,000. . . . Do we find in Detroit, and Michigan, the sprouts of a new fascistic enterprise that may sweep the country?

The characteristically open behavior of Hitler and Mussolini's movements is lacking in the Legion. Black Knights are sworn to die before revealing the body's existence. We do have here the catering to innate prejudices, the underdog desire for power, the rallying around a symbol—in the case of the Legion, the bullet. We have a private army, this one, indeed, organized under military terms.

But the Legion has no political program. . . . Its desires appear to be parochial and selfish—acquiring jobs and police immunity. The Legion has expended itself in antagonism toward Catholics and, as an afterthought, Communists. The energies of the Legion, a reading of the record shows, have been diffused in the punishment of private offenses. Did a father mistreat his family?—the Legion, made up of indifferent husbands and fathers, galloped to the rescue. . . .

I would say, if called upon, that the Black Legion was a sort of depraved Ku Klux Klan. The Poole execution unmasked it prematurely, so far as its own welfare was concerned. One may suppose that the reverberations of that senseless murder caught the Legion in an early stage. If that is the case, the whole American public may be grateful, while extending condolences to the widow.

Life in Detroit, according to competent authority, is empty as a dried gourd for the creatures of the assembly line. Empty and insecure. One feels that about Detroit. It is a city of strangers; two-thirds of the residents came here after 1914. The town is not devoid of ferment. An isolated, beleaguered minority holds out. . . . The Methodist communion may preen itself on the presence of Bishop Edgar Blake . . . and the Reverend Frederick Fisher as pastor of a downtown church. Both hate fascism, war and injustice and make no bones about saying so. Maurice Sugar, another of the elect, polled 55,000 votes—one-third of all cast— when he ran for the City Council as a Farmer-Laborite last year. . . .

But the working-class norm is in too large a part represented by the defendants in the jury box. Typical 100-percenters, they detest alike Communists, liberals and labor organizers as well as Catholics and Jews. Let no one make the mistake of thinking that the incarceration of Dean and Davis, the displacing and reprimanding of minor office-holders and the public scorn heaped upon the Black Legion will expunge from this community the backward sentiments dramatized by the Legion. . . .

Editor's Note

1. If it seems unlikely to term one of oldest cities in the Midwest "new," we must note that Davis is quite correct in referring to the massive turnover of population during the twenty years of industrial growth before 1936. We cannot quarrel with his appellation, "city of strangers."

4.   The Tide Turns

Steve Babson, with Ron Alpern, Dave Elsila, and John Revitte

The prospects of a union breakthrough against Detroit's Open Shop seemed impossibly remote the morning of November 25, 1935.

Several thousand workers had gone on strike ten days earlier at the Motor Products Corporation, a manufacturer of automobile frames and body parts on the city's East Side. Demanding higher wages and the removal of company-paid detectives from the plant, the strikers had initially won the backing of all the unions competing for members at Motor Products—MESA [Mechanics' Educational Society of America], AIWA [Automotive Industrial Workers' Association], and the AFL's federal local.

Steve Babson, with Ron Alpern, Dave Elsila, and John Revitte, "The Tide Turns," in *Working Detroit: The Making of a Union Town* (Detroit: Wayne State University Press, 1986), 68–75.

377

But AFL support was grudging. Both AIWA and MESA were winning new members in the plant at the federal local's expense, and AFL leaders called the AIWA-led strike "irresponsible" from the outset. It took only a company promise (never kept) of future union-representation elections to persuade AFL members to break ranks and lead their members back to work.

On November 25, the police escorted hundreds of AFL members and leaders past jeering picket lines on Mack Avenue. AIWA and MESA leaders called the AFL capitulation "the most disgraceful scene ever enacted in Detroit." The company called it the beginning of the end for the remaining strikers. They were right.

Detroit's union movement seemed as fragmented and weak as ever. But even as the AFL's strikebreakers crossed MESA and AIWA picket lines that November morning, the elements of a unified and broad-based union movement were beginning to fall in place. That very month, the AFL's national leadership had split into two openly warring camps—a majority still committed to the Federation's traditional craft unionism, but a growing minority now committed to new forms of industry-wide organization.

The tremors that opened this rift in the AFL's leadership began shaking the organization in 1934. Strikes by dockworkers on the West Coast, truck drivers in Minneapolis, autoworkers in Toledo, and textile workers in New England and the South grew into passionate crusades after police gunfire killed 21 strikers in these four conflicts. Rather than surrender to the fatal violence, tens of thousands of workers joined mass picket lines and general strikes, shutting down San Francisco, Minneapolis, and Toledo. Such tactics won at least partial victories in all but the textile strike.

This groundswell of militancy led to the final breach between craft-union leaders who repudiated the strikers and industrial unionists who saw them as the wave of the future. In November, 1935, a half-dozen of these rebellious leaders formed the Committee for Industrial Organization (CIO) within the AFL. Their chief spokesman was John L. Lewis, President of the United Mine Workers.

Industrial unionism had finally found its voice. "Let him who will, be he economic tyrant or sordid mercenary," Lewis declared over NBC radio in 1936, "pit his strength against this mighty upsurge of human sentiment now being crystallized in the hearts of 30 million workers. . . . He is a madman or a fool who believes that this river of human sentiment can be dammed by the erection of arbitrary barriers of restraint." Lewis, in fact, knew better than most that anti-union employers would not surrender to mere "human sentiment." The CIO needed organizers: hundreds of organizers prepared to take on the biggest corporations in the world in a no-holds-barred campaign. To secure these leaders, Lewis turned to the militants he had expelled from his own union in the 1920's—Adolph Germer, Powers Hapgood—and veteran organizers like Rose Pesotta from the Ladies Garment Workers Union, and Leo Krzycki from the Amalgamated Clothing Workers. Brookwood Labor College, founded in New York in the 1920's by A. J. Muste, also provided CIO unions with organizers, including Roy Reuther, Sophia Goodlavich, Merlin Bishop, and Frank Winn.

These men and women were Socialists, a fact the politically conservative Lewis (he'd endorsed Coolidge and Hoover in the 1920's) certainly was aware of. But he needed industrial organizers of proven ability, and despite the fact that he barred Communists from his own union, he was also willing to work with radicals like Wyndham Mortimer, Bill McKie, and "Big" John Anderson to build the CIO. "In a battle, I make arrows from any wood," Lewis responded when asked about his collaboration with Communists. "Who gets the bird?" he later added, "the hunter or the dog?" There was little doubt which role Lewis saw himself in.

The Communists, for their part, had stopped attacking their Socialist and liberal rivals as "Social Fascists." Such carping had isolated Party members from the labor movement at precisely the point when many workers were joining unions and fighting for recognition. To participate in this upsurge, the Party dissolved the Auto Workers Union late in December, 1934, and proposed a Popular Front with moderates and liberals. Individual Communists thereafter muted their radical politics and harnessed their considerable organizing skills to the CIO bandwagon.

The AFL's top leaders also compromised their views in an effort to salvage some control over events. Local leaders and members of the Federation's federal autoworker unions had long demanded their own national organization—coordinating the unionization of a large corporation's scattered operations was otherwise impossible. In August, 1935, the AFL grudgingly responded to this pressure by chartering the United Automobile Workers (UAW) as an international union within the AFL. But the Federation's cautious leaders initially muzzled the new organization by postponing elections and appointing conservative officers.

When delegates to the UAW's next convention, in April, 1936, finally won the right to elect their leaders, they settled on Homer Martin, a former Baptist minister and one-time autoworker from Kansas. The fledgling organization immediately allied itself with Lewis' Committee for Industrial Organization and invited the independent unions in the industry to join its ranks. MESA's two Detroit locals, led by fellow Scotsmen Bill Stevenson and "Big" John Anderson, split off from their parent organization and merged with the UAW in July. The AIWA and a third independent union, the Associated Automobile Workers of America, joined that same month.

The emergence of the UAW as a unified and democratic union gave a tremendous boost to organizing efforts in Detroit's auto industry. There were signs of new life in other sectors of Detroit's labor movement as well. Rebellious truck drivers in the AFL's Teamster Local 299, a small union of general freight drivers, ousted the local's corrupt leaders and began a recruiting drive with three new organizers—one of them Jimmy Hoffa, former Kroger warehouseman. Waiters and Waitresses Local 705 of the AFL's Hotel and Restaurant Workers also expanded its staff and began an organizing drive in the opening months of 1936.

While many workers opposed joining these unions, or, fearful of losing their jobs, chose to remain neutral, a growing number, particularly among the young, were eager to risk joining a militant union movement for change. Their confidence was buoyed by a growing sense of common interests bonding workers together. That emerging "solidarity" had many long- and short-term causes. Americanization campaigns and steep declines in immigration after the 1921 Immigration Act had diluted the "alien" stigma that isolated many unskilled workers from the rest of the population. The city's workforce had also been sifted through a prolonged process of deskilling and mechanization that blurred the old hierarchy of industrial trades. Craft distinctions had not disappeared, but they had become more fluid and unstable. The Depression narrowed the gap between skilled and unskilled still further, for floundering companies usually found more to cut from the above-average wage of their skilled craftsmen.

Indeed, the Depression had been a relentless leveler. Workers who had defined themselves in terms of their trade, their race, their nationality group, or their ambitions, had been merged, at least temporarily, into a single group: the unemployed. . . .

Unemployment had also partially merged the working worlds of men and women. The steep lay-offs in Detroit's heavy industries idled many men whose wives and daughters still worked in service or retail trades. Unemployment among Michigan's wage-earning women was 30 percent lower in 1935 than among men, and in Detroit, the number of working women actually rose by 10,000 during the 1930's—even as the number of employed men fell 74,000. . . .

By 1936, these Depression experiences had transformed peoples' sense of the future. Storybook tales of upward mobility seemed a little ludicrous in the midst of widespread unemployment and poverty.

. . . In November, 1936, politicians pledging to uphold [the] "Wagner Act" won sweeping victories over conservative and right-wing candidates, paced by President Roosevelt's landslide re-election. "If I worked for a wage," announced Frank Murphy, the former Mayor of Detroit who became, that November, the Governor-Elect of Michigan, "I'd join my union."

On November 27, 1936—one year after [a] fiasco at Motor Products and just three weeks after Murphy's election—the first wave of a flood tide of worker unrest washed over Detroit's Open Shop. At 11:30 a.m., 1200 workers at Detroit's Midland Steel plant sat down and occupied their workplace. . . . the Midland workers refused to budge until management met their key demands: recognition of the UAW as their sole bargaining agent, and a 10¢ an hour wage increase for all departments.

Their "sitdown strike" foreshadowed a dramatic shift in the balance of power between Detroit's employers and workers. In the past, management had always relied on the police to forcibly break through union picket lines and convoy strikebreakers into the plant; once inside, the strikebreakers could then be housed in makeshift dormitories and put to work on the machines left idle by the strikers. But Midland's sitdowners had decisively turned the tables. Now they were on the inside, protecting their jobs and machines, while bewildered policemen trudged the plant in the snow and rain. . . .

Morale among the sitdowners remained unusually high throughout the eight-day occupation. Instead of only periodic and often lonely picket duty, the sitdowners now lived together in a tightly knit, 24-hour strike community. The once alien and dingy plant became the scene of a continuous round of pinochle and poker, calisthenics and even football, played in the plant yard. By the time the occupation ended, most of the sitdowners had also memorized the first verse and chorus of *Solidarity Forever:*

> When the Union's inspiration through the workers' blood shall run,
> There can be no power greater anywhere beneath the sun.
> Yet what force on earth is weaker than the feeble strength of one?
> But the Union makes us strong.
>> Solidarity forever!
>> Solidarity forever!
> For the union makes us strong.

The words were not mere rhetoric. In a city with a long and dismal record of racial conflict, the Midland sitdown stood out as an unprecedented example of racial unity. Scores of black and white workers participated jointly in the occupation, and Oscar Oden, a black assembler, was elected to the strike committee. Unity also prevailed between the Detroit AFL and the UAW-CIO, despite the fact that CIO unions had been expelled from the national AFL that same month. . . .

The 200 women workers who joined the sitdown on its first day were not, however, asked to "Hold Fast." Fearing a scandal if the women stayed overnight in the factory with the men, the UAW asked them to evacuate the plant—but the women did not return to their homes. Under the direction of Dorothy Kraus, they established a strike kitchen in the nearby Slovak Hall on Strong Avenue and organized committees to visit and reassure the wives of men still occupying the plant.

When a shortage of body frames forced Chrysler and Ford to lay off 100,000 workers in early December, the pressure on Midland to settle finally grew irresistible. On December 4, the UAW's chief negotiators, Wyndham Mortimer and Richard Frankensteen, announced the terms of a tentative agreement: abolition of piecework wages as soon as possible; a 10¢ per hour pay raise for all but the higher classifications; and recognition for the UAW's elected grievance committee.

For the first time in the city's history, a major auto company had been forced to come to terms with a union representing all its workers. The example was not lost on UAW organizers centered in Flint and Detroit's West Side.

Flint, less than 60 miles north of Detroit, was the homebase of General Motors, the auto industry's undisputed leader. If the UAW was to organize the industry, it would eventually have to win the allegiance of that city's 50,000 GM workers, concentrated in more than a dozen major engine, body and assembly plants. Detroit's West Side was equally crucial. GM had three major factories on the West Side, and dozens of independent parts suppliers also produced everything from brakes to body trim for Ford's huge River Rouge plant in neighboring Dearborn.

Ranged against these corporate giants was the UAW's West Side Local 174. By all appearances, the companies had little to fear: when the local formed in September, 1936, it had only 78 members, a handful of organizers, and a treasury that frequently dipped below $10. With these meager resources, Local 174's President, a 29-year-old toolmaker named Walter Reuther, set out to organize the more than 150,000 autoworkers in West Detroit and Dearborn.

The first target was the Kelsey-Hayes Wheel Company, a West Side employer of 5,000 that made brakes for Ford. After UAW organizers Victor Reuther (Walter's brother), George Edwards, and Merlin Bishop hired on at the firm's McGraw Avenue plant, the UAW asked the company for a bargaining conference and began building its membership. The chief tactic was to call "quickie" strikes in one department after another. These brief sitdowns gave the union visibility, attracted new members, and put the company on notice that it could not fulfill its supply contract with Ford unless it improved working conditions and bargained with the union.

On December 10, 1936, Victor Reuther called one such strike in Department 49, where foremen were "riding herd" on the men and women in the hub and brake-drum section. "Twenty minutes before the shift was to end, I ran and pulled the main switch and shouted 'Strike! We've had enough of this speed-up!' The call for strike action spread through our whole department . . . , and we soon had an enormous crowd gathering around us." When Reuther explained to the company's personnel director that only his brother could get the workers to return to their jobs, the production-conscious manager agreed to allow Walter inside the plant.

What happened next typified the brashness that became the UAW's trademark. Victor, speaking from atop a large crate, continued to "talk union" to a crowd of 500 workers until company officials returned with his brother. "I stepped off the box," Victor remembered, "and Walter stepped on and continued with the same speech. Danzig [the manager] grabbed his trouser leg: 'What the hell is this? You're supposed to tell them to go back to work.'

'I can't tell them to do anything,' Walter replied, 'until I first get them organized' ". . . .

[Kelsey-Hayes] did not want to negotiate the issues of production speed and overtime pay that won the union such support. After several more quickie strikes brought these issues to the fore, company managers finally retaliated, barring the UAW negotiating committee from the plant and threatening to fire anyone who stayed on company premises after quitting time. Some 300 union supporters defied the company's ultimatum and, following the example of Midland Steel, barricaded themselves inside the plant.

Removing them proved to be more difficult than the company had anticipated. In these opening episodes of Detroit's sitdown wave, no one had yet determined the legality of the sitdown tactic. The company claimed the occupiers were guilty of criminal trespass, but the city and county officials refused to evict the peaceful protesters, particularly since the strikers had originally been invited onto company property by Kelsey-Hayes employees.

While public officials debated the point, the company tried to force the issues by infiltrating twelve professional strikebreakers into the McGraw Avenue complex. Entering on the fourth night of the occupation, their apparent goal was to provoke a violent incident as a pretext for calling in the police. But before the intruders could make their first move, UAW lookouts trapped the men in the plant's infirmary.

"This was a Friday and there were a half-dozen union meetings in town," Sophia Goodlavich Reuther, Local 174's secretary later wrote. "We called all the unions and asked them to come in a body to enforce the picket line. When they did, here were a few thousand strong, yelling, 'Throw the scabs out, throw the scabs out!'" . . .

Five days later, with Ford threatening to find another brake supplier, Kelsey-Hayes signed a truce agreement and the plants were evacuated. As the sitdowners marched out the night before Christmas Eve, 2,000 supporters and a union band helped them celebrate the new 75¢-an-hour minimum wage the company had agreed to for both men and women. . . . Kelsey-Hayes also agreed to premium pay for overtime, seniority rules to protect job security, and a 20 per cent reduction in the speed of the assembly line.

Hours after the strike's settlement, organizers Victor Reuther and Merlin Bishop left for Flint, where both played pivotal roles in the upcoming GM sitdown strike. That historic 44-day occupation, lasting from December 30, 1936 to February 11, 1937, riveted world attention on the UAW and elevated John L. Lewis to national prominence. When Governor Frank Murphy sent 3,000 National Guardsmen into Flint and deployed them between the sitdowners and the Flint police, GM abandoned all hope of forcibly evicting the strikers and eventually conceded victory to the UAW.

The world's largest corporation could be challenged and defeated by unarmed workers. The victory had an electrifying effect in Detroit. "Somebody would call the office," recalled Robert Kantor, an organizer for Local 174, "and say, 'Look, we are sitting down. Send us over some food.'" Local 174 grew at a rapid clip, with sitdowns at Cadillac and Fleetwood during the GM strike, and with sitdowns in dozens of smaller places afterwards. Within ten days of the victory at Kelsey-Hayes, Local 174's membership had jumped to 3,000; by the end of 1937, it had reached 35,000.

5. Dangerous Living for Unionists: The Spoiled Birthday Dinner

Victor G. Reuther

By 1938, Walter and Victor Reuther were trying to organize the Ford workers. This was an effort as unsafe for the organizers as it was for the employees because of the bitter resistance of old Henry Ford and Harry Bennett, whom he had hired especially to keep the UAW out.

[Walter Reuther] was a stubborn fighter, and it was no secret that he was a marked man. This was, unfortunately, proved true in the spring of 1938.

April 9 was Sophie's birthday, and we were celebrating it at Walter and May's apartment instead of our own, because Walter had come down with a cold that day. Roy was there, and Ben Fisher, a steel worker organizer, his wife, Hannah, Lewis Steiger, our old friend Tucker Smith from Brookwood, Frank Marquardt, active unionist at the Briggs plant, and Al King, a rank-and-file member of the UAW. No one was aware that for some weeks the apartment had been under constant surveillance by two of Bennett's hirelings, who had rented an apartment close by. Walter phoned a Chinese restaurant to send up dinner. About an hour after he had called, there was a knock on the door, and Sophie and I, who were the closest, opened it. Instead of the delivery boy, there stood two toughs with drawn revolvers. They pushed their way into the room, shouting, "Okay, back against the wall!" At first it was as unreal as a clip from an old silent movie. The shorter gunman wore a dark hat with the brim turned down to conceal his eyes; he was obviously the trigger man. The other gangster spotted Walter immediately, put his gun in its holster, and drew out of his rear pocket an enormous blackjack with a leather strap, which he twined around his wrist.

"Okay, Red, you're coming with us," he said.

Only gradually did we realize this was no joke. George Edwards muttered, "You're not getting out of here. You may shoot some of us, but you won't get out yourselves."

The attackers were obviously surprised by the presence of so large a group; they would have known, by watching the house, that Walter seldom had meetings in his own home. The shorter gunman kept his .38 pointed at us and toyed with the trigger. Walter, who happened to be standing somewhat apart, slowly maneuvered himself into a corner, where he could best fend off the blows. The bigger of the two hoods broke a glass floor lamp over Walter's head, trying to get him off balance so that he would come within striking distance. That failed to put Walter out of commission, so the thug threw a glass-topped coffee table at him. Walter was then on the floor in the corner, using both feet and arms to keep off the swinging blows of the blackjack, and at some point he managed to grasp the end of the weapon and wrench it loose from its leather thong. He tossed it over the man's head in our direction, yelling, "Catch, George!" Comparing notes later, many of us confessed to a sensation of hot lead going through our guts when that happened, and no one made the slightest motion to catch the blackjack before it fell to the floor with a thud.

"Kill the son of a bitch," the larger bruiser shouted to his companion.

Four or five of us moved a few inches toward the man with the gun; it was the slightest of movements, but it gave meaning to George's earlier threat that they could kill some of us but wouldn't themselves get out alive.

During the commotion, little Al King, who had been standing near the kitchen door, slouched down, backed into the breakfast nook, jumped out an open window into the concrete alleyway two flights below, and started to shout for help. This brave action woke up the neighborhood and broke the deadlock. Sophie, at about the same time, decided to distract the killer; she reached her hand into the kitchen and as Al jumped out the window, a pickle bottle came sailing in the direction of the trigger man. We all felt there would surely be shooting now, but after Al's "Help! Help!" had gathered a group in the street, the two professional hoods decided they had better retreat before they got caught, and abruptly fled the apartment.

May and Roy rushed to Walter to see how seriously he was injured. There were some cuts on his face from the broken glass but he had avoided any direct blow from the blackjack. We all collapsed into giddy hysterical laughter. There was an eerie un-reality about that attempt to take Walter on what would have been his last ride. I can't even remember if the Chinese food ever came. I know we bolted the door and propped furniture against it, and immediately called the police. They took an hour to arrive and we let them in only after they had passed identification cards under the door. As they came in, whom should we see in the doorway but three men dressed in civilian clothes wearing dark hats with wide brims pulled down over their eyes! We told them what had happened, and I shall never forget Sophie's wonder-fully blunt response when they asked for a description of the two thugs. She looked the officers straight in their faces, and said, "They looked very much like you."

That birthday party made a change in our way of life that was to last for years—until Detroit's criminal element, backed by cor-poration money, was removed from power, and the workers could win a measure of security and protection. Walter and I got per-mits to carry revolvers and bought .38s. Neither of us had ever fired a revolver in our lives, though we had hunted a little with rifles in the west Virginia hills. We went for target practice to a firing range operated by the Sheriff of Macomb county; we had no confidence in the Detroit police. The idea of carrying a gun in order to fire at another human being was alien and uncomfortable, and I don't think that Walter wore his every day; I certainly did not carry mine. But the guns gave us some security at home. For quite a while after the birthday party, Sophie carried the revolver under her apron when she took the garbage out to the alley.

The police were not overly anxious to find our attackers, but in the underworld there are always individuals who will squeal for a fee. Within two days, Walter received an anonymous call, met the informer in a bar—filled with husky union men in case the call was a trap—and bought the names of the gunmen: Eddie Percelli, alias Eddie Tall, and Willard "Bud" Holt. Percelli was a former rumrunner who had been held as a suspect in the Harry Millman slaying. Bud Holt had once been a Ford Serviceman, and had recently been employed by John Gillespie.[1] Each one of us who had been at the birthday party, brought in separately to view a police line-up, recognized both men at once.

The trial in September of 1938 was a farce. Over eighty prospective jurors were rejected for one reason or another, and the jury, it was reported, was composed of people chosen at random off the street. From the final verdict, one might surmise that many members of this jury were waiting on certain street corners to be picked "at random." Sherman, the defense lawyer, who had championed many other underworld characters, told the jurors, "We contend that Reuther arranged with Holt to come to his apartment at 13233 La Salle Boulevard and stage a sham battle before witnesses to embarrass Homer Martin, president of the UAW, with whom Reuther was at war." An attorney for the Ford Company, working with Sherman, repeatedly spoke of the "radical background" of all the guests at the birthday party, and implied that Walter and I were sinister revolutionists undermining the American way of life. After all, we had lived and worked in Russia for a year. The state prosecutor mentioned nothing about possible motives for an attack on Walter, though everyone knew he was on Ford's blacklist and that until two weeks before the event Holt had been employed as bodyguard for Ford's Gillespie. I strongly suspect that Judge George B. Murphy was as shocked as we were when the jury acquitted Holt and Percelli.[2]

Editor's Notes

1. The Reuthers and many UAW members believed that some Ford Motor executives had been involved in this scheme to eliminate a major

labor leader. But Harry Bennett, responsible only to Henry Ford the elder, had at that time almost total power over personnel and security matters. Gillespie, whom Ford had hired for duties that overlapped confusedly with Bennett's, was a former Detroit Police Commissioner. Homer Martin, then president of the UAW, was a rival of the Reuthers. Martin allegedly contrived a secret agreement with Bennett to control Ford-UAW negotiations. Martin was removed from office by the UAW Executive Board, and charges against him were filed with the National Labor Relations Board. As Victor Reuther muses, "How was it possible that one of the world's largest industrial firms could have had such a barbaric labor relations policy? Certainly the elder Ford must be held responsible for giving Bennett carte blanche and never questioning his methods. . . . " Approximately three years after the birthday party, Ford Motor at last signed a contract with the UAW. It was the last of the auto giants to do so.

2. The Reuther brothers later faced more serious injuries when each of them was wounded in his own home by gunmen. Victor lost an eye, Walter the partial use of one arm. Once again, the would-be assassins were not punished, and there were strong indications that organized crime was involved. By contrast, the affair of the Chinese carry-out dinner, as retold by Victor Reuther, seems a series of absurdities, though for some there it must have been the first real foreboding of fear. Everyone at the birthday party was young, with a world to be changed just ahead of him.

6. Political Corruption: The Time the Mayor Went to Jail

Detroit Times

Mayor Richard Reading, an affable, well-liked man backed by the Civic Searchlight, filed for reelection on Monday, August 7, 1939. On the same day, page one headlines of the Detroit Times *shouted, "MAYOR HUNTS PO-LICE GRAFT IN SUICIDE MOTHER'S EXPOSÉ." On Sunday Mrs. Janet McDonald had dressed her eleven-year-old daughter, Pearl, in a pink taffeta party dress, then killed the child and herself.*

Mrs. MacDonald left a number of suicide notes to the newspapers and public officials, and one to her estranged lover, William McBride, a low-ranking employee of the gambling interests. She provided photos and a copy of her letter to McBride for the press, and eventually succeeded in overturning local government.

Keep Not Your Kisses
Janet MacDonald to William McBride

. . . In spirit I'll return and curse any woman that you make a friend of. Until the day you die I'll keep returning, then we'll go together, and you'll know we should have been together here.

You couldn't fathom the loneliness and sorrow I've had these last few weeks. Some day you may have a glimpse of it, too.

I must go now. My time is up and I'm just a little frightened.

Janet MacDonald, "Keep Not Your Kisses" and "There is a Good Deal of Vice Going On in Detroit," *Detroit Times* (7 August 1939): 1, 2. Permission given by Robert Giles, publisher of the *Detroit News*, holder of *Times* files.

"Keep not your kisses for my cold, dead brow;
The way is lonely, let me feel them now. . . . "

There is a Good Deal of Vice Going On in Detroit
Janet MacDonald to John Bugas, of the FBI

Dear Sirs:

It seems there is a good deal of vice going on in Detroit, and as long as the police are a part of it, it seems perhaps the government should know something about it in order to do a bit of cleanup work.

I am privileged to know that the so-called G-Men are watching a certain Wm. McBride.

This McBride was a partner in the Great Lakes Number house in Oakland Avenue, which closed down July 1st. While the Great Lakes was in operation, McBride took care of the bribe end. He paid (here she named a Detroit police lieutenant) a neat sum monthly, also a large number of sergeants and officers got their portion each month. As long as a number house or handbook paid off, it was allowed to run.

At present McBride's position is that of a go-between man for the lieutenant and the racketeers. The houses pay the lieutenant through McBride and are therefore permitted to run. In the event a house has to be raided of course the lieutenant leads the raid and makes a beautiful bluff of it. However, before the raid, the lieutenant gets in touch with McBride and consequently McBride informs the house to be raided and the headmen clear out before the raid and take any important evidence with them. This is quite a profitable business for both the police officer and Racketeer McBride.

Occasionally they run across an officer or detective who refuses to accept the money, in a case of this kind the detective or officer promptly gets moved to another district or put down in rank.

For a number of years, although McBride always made a large salary, he evaded paying his income tax, however having to pay social security this year he got frightened and had a certain lawyer (whose name I shall omit), fix up his tax returns as though it had been paid properly for the last three years.

McBride had a bad record during prohibition days for smuggling liquor over from Canada. There was a warrant against him for a length of time, but he now claims witnesses are dead and nothing could be done about it. Until very recently he was afraid to cross the Canadian border.

I am mentioning these facts just to let you know how bad a character McBride is. It seems people of his sort should be clamped down on.

McBride has been arrested many times for owning and operating the wrong type of places, but with the majority of the police working with the racketeers nothing has ever been done to convict the wrong ones.

I trust this information is of value and that it will be put to use.[1]

Editor's Note

1. The purple prose and fury of Janet MacDonald scorned had their political effect. In November, 1939, Reading lost the election to Council President Edward Jeffries, Jr., son of a humanitarian turn-of-the-century judge, the Edward Jeffries for whom some west side public housing apartments were later named. Reading lost two to one to Jeffries, after basing his campaign on charges that Jeffries, who was mildly liberal on union matters, was a Communist, or a "fellow-traveler." Charges of major involvement in gambling and protection rackets came later from the one-man grand jury led by Homer Ferguson. Reading would go to federal prison in broken health. Homer Ferguson would go to the U.S. Senate.

Part XII

Arsenal of Democracy

Arsenal of Democracy

World War II brought Detroit the distinction of being called the "arsenal of democracy," a phrase that was easily and often corrupted to "arsehole" by tired people waiting in lines everywhere—at bus stops, at grocery stores, at newsstands for the first chance at the "home for rent" or even "room for rent" ads.

It was a city of absolutely full employment, with all the discomforts that supposedly good state can bring. The last to be hired were being hired. Qualified blacks were suddenly discovered, with the diplomas and certificates they had held all along. A black R.N. appeared as night supervisor at one of the better hospitals. She would have preferred days, she said, but it had been explained to her that her night shift would give her less contact with the public, to whom her presence might give offense. Home care for the elderly or children was all but impossible to obtain on any terms. Wartime child care programs were discouragingly slow to develop and often inadequate when they arrived. Grandma was still the best choice—if she wasn't already working at the bomber plant at Willow Run.

Jobs in Detroit were tied in with the needs of war. For men they were a substitute for, or an adjunct to, military service. If you were here at all, it was because somebody higher up thought you should be. If civilians became tired of living the war effort a minimum of forty-eight hours a week as part of that total concentration of defense industry, government was also troubled by the concentration. Some aircraft were being manufactured in California, and the FBI rushed to head off a suspected plot to blow up the locks at the Soo. Never again, military planners vowed, would all the eggs be in one basket. "Hitler will come here first," people told each other, only half believing it. One thing everyone agreed on was that nobody, but nobody, knew what was going on at the war front. Another was that money— the best money ever— was little fun when you had no time to spend it, or everything you wanted was cancelled out by shortages.

Movies, restaurants, bowling alleys, union halls, tried to meet the upside down, multishift schedules of the war-workers. If your time for hilarious recreation began at 6:30 A.M. or your time for grocery shopping was 10 P.M., someone would make efforts to accommodate.

The city was unbelievably overcrowded. There was rent control, but large, spacious flats were everywhere being divided into tiny apartments, or "housekeeping rooms," for which the owner might charge the rent that had gone with quarters several times as large a few months earlier.

There was price control, but the quality and availability of twenty-six-cents-a-pound hamburger varied tremendously. Complaint about these persistent but minor league hardships was self-defeating and absurd. "Don't you know there's a war on?" was the ready response. Of course Detroit knew. Detroit was part of it. Besides, everyone had a friend or relative in those frightening and glamorous places in the news. Emotions ran high for those in the "real" war.

Selections include Victor Reuther's "'500 Planes a Day,' " in which he tells of the early rejection by both business and government—short of FDR—of his brother's creative plan for conversion of the auto plants to defense.

During the war years there was a crosscurrent of unreadiness. There were the pacifist conscientious objectors, including a group of young ministerial students from Union Theological Seminary. After a year or two living openly in Detroit, they would be sent to various federal prisons as draft resisters. Other Detroit pacifists served as volunteers in army medical units or tried the camps for conscientious objectors. The "Brooklyn House" group of young ministerial students found the camps too oriented to military life. (They did not object to physical labor or danger; several volunteered as human guinea pigs for medical experimentation while serving in federal prison.) During their time in Detroit, the pacifists supported themselves by the nonwar jobs no one else wanted—driving coal and ice trucks, for instance.

Temporary allegiance to pacifism was found among the small but vigorous group of Communist party members during the time when Germany and Russia were allies. This broke apart abruptly when Hitler invaded the Soviet Union, but while it lasted, many of Detroit's Polish were horrified that their native land had been abandoned by the ideologues. Continuing throughout the war years there were also local Bundists, America Firsters, and respectable isolationists who regarded the war as one of Franklin Roosevelt's stunts of self-promotion.

A few of the war critics took the ugly path of stirring up race hatred. Their traces are to be seen in the Sojourner Truth riots of 1942 described by Bette Smith Jenkins. Bigotry was here aided by government vacillation.

Racism shows again in the scenes of June, 1943, described to us by Walter White and Thurgood Marshall in a report for the NAACP. Their report searched out basic causes for this major riot and found lack of housing, official ineptitude, and the actions of would-be saboteurs to be among them. They did *not* find violence within the auto plants, where the UAW-CIO worked constantly to build a sense of brotherhood among its members. This did not prevent nay-sayers who lived outside of Detroit from telling each other that the rioting was started by "union radicals."

For many, survival came to depend more and more on daydreams of the future. These often centered around a postwar dream house. The red-white- and blue-covered women's magazines were filled with them. Among Detroit's young labor union and professional workers, there came to be a dream book of another sort. A mimeographed pamphlet, "What about Housing Cooperatives?", the spare time work of two young city planners interested in Scandinavian housing, circulated widely. The dream grew into a project that almost became a reality. Part XIII will tell of its demise in the early fifties, but here I reprint selections from the text itself, written by Merle Henrickson. It was accompanied by talented and imaginative architectural drawings by Donald Monson, which are not reproduced here.

As the war years went on, most Detroiters were loyal, patriotic—and bone-tired. They showed their customary lack of curiousity about those whom—rightly or wrongly—they characterized as "kooks." They joked about WAVES and WACS, questioning their motives. They honored, the fighting men, however, and endowed them with glamor.

One night at Orchestra Hall (then the Paradise Music Hall), at a meeting of the Wayne County Council of the AFL-CIO, a group that had a considerable importance of its own, the chairman paused as a young man in uniform—a Tuskegee airman home on leave—ran onstage from the wings. "This young man is one of ours, a union brother—he will be back with us and will go far. Watch him, and remember—Brother Coleman Young!" The crowd leaped to its feet, cheering the unknown young man.

1. "500 Planes a Day"

Victor G. Reuther

Months before Hitler's armies marched east into Poland, Walter and I had a conversation with Ben Blackwood, a
trusted aide in the General Motors Department [of the UAW] and
himself a skilled toolmaker, about Roosevelt's call for aid to Britain and the kind of help America was best equipped to give. Because of the unremitting Luftwaffe offensive, it was obvious that
England needed planes, not only guns and tanks, for her defense. As toolmakers we knew it would be many years before
American industries turning out civilian goods could be tooled to
produce weapons in any quantity. But, as Walter said, we should
not romanticize about the nature of the airplane, though the aircraft industry had for so long made a fetish of the highly special-

From *The Brothers Reuther* by Victor Reuther. Copyright © 1976 by Victor G. Reuther. Reprinted by permission of Houghton Mifflin Company.

ized expertise involved. A plane was made of steel and aluminum, like other vehicles, and its component parts could be manufactured by essentially the same kind of machines and machine tools that stamp and turn out the parts of an automobile. We had seen the conversion of peacetime tools—and helped make it—in the Gorky plant, when Russia was arming itself against the inevitable German invasion.[1]

Of course, the automobile manufacturers, asked to take on enormous defense contracts, assumed that they would gradually close down their automobile plants, keeping them on a standby basis, while the government proceeded to build and put at their disposal spanking new factories, equipped with millions of dollars worth of machine tools, most of which would be duplications of the tools sitting idle, or about to sit idle, in the automobile plants as we moved into an all-out war effort.

A careful survey taken by Ben Blackwood and me in GM plants all over the country corroborated Walter's hypothesis and became the basis of his proposal for a "500 planes a day" program, to be undertaken by the automotive industry. He had informal meetings with R. J. Thomas and Philip Murray about his plan.[2] They were both enthusiastic, and Murray submitted it to President Roosevelt on December 20, 1940. . . .

Roosevelt responded with interest, and sent a memo to Knudsen, co-director with Sidney Hillman of the Office of Production Management. . . .

William Knudsen, though deeply devoted to FDR and to the defense effort, must nevertheless have felt put out that Walter Reuther, the "red-headed upstart" who had so often clashed with him across the General Motors bargaining table, should presume to tell the nation what the automobile industry could do about mass tooling for aircraft production. Yet an editorial in Knudsen's home town newspaper, the Detroit *News*, stated on January 6, 1941, that "no industrial leader has paralleled Reuther's initiative and ingenuity in presenting such a plan for consideration."

There was a meeting of top officials of the OPM [Office of Production Management], the Air Force and the Navy, Knudsen, Hillman, R. J. Thomas and Walter. A courtesy call was paid on the President after the discussion. . . .

Walter had made a public appeal on the radio the week before. It was a long speech and an emotional one. Some of it is well worth remembering:

> In London they are huddled in the subways praying for aid from America. In America we are huddled over blueprints praying that Hitler will be obliging enough to postpone an all-out attack on England for another two years until new plants begin to turn out engines and aircraft.
>
> Packard has just finished pouring the concrete for its new engine factory and Ford may soon be ready to begin digging ditches in which to sink the foundations for his. Not until the fall of nineteen forty-two, almost two years hence, will these bright, shiny new factories actually begin to turn out the engines. This is snail's pace production in the age of lightning war. . . .
>
> We believe that without disturbing present aircraft plant production schedules we can supplement them by turning out five hundred planes a day of a single standard fighting model by the use of idle automotive capacity. We believe that this can be done after six months of preparation as compared to the eighteen months or two years required to get new plane and engine factories into production. . . .
>
> Fortunately, despite the headlines which tell us of unfillable orders and labor shortages, we have a huge reservoir of unused machinery, unused plants, unused skill, and unused labor to fall back upon. . . . The tool and die workers . . . are also partially idle. . . .
>
> The plane, from certain points of view, is only an automobile with wings. Our greatest need is for plane engines. . . . The plane engine is the more delicate and compact combustion engine but it is still a combustion engine, containing the same parts. . . . There stand idle in the Cleveland Fisher Body plant toggle presses huge enough to hold and operate a draw or flange die weighing seventy to eighty tons. Such a machine can stamp out airplane parts as well as automobile parts. . . .
>
> It would take years to install in new aircraft plants the same type of presses which now stand idle fifty percent of the time. . . .
>
> Equipment at the Chevrolet Drop Forge plant in Detroit operates at sixty percent of capacity even at this time, which is a peak period for the automobile industry. The machines and hammers in this plant could produce all the drop forgings required for five hundred planes a day and still supply the Chevrolet Company with sufficient forgings for one million cars during the coming

year. Labor asks: Why not use this equipment instead of duplicating it?

Labor's plan springs from the pooled experience and knowledge of skilled workers in all the automotive plants, the same skilled workers who are called upon year by year in the industry to produce new machine marvels. Each manufacturer has the benefit of his skilled workers. We of the United Automobile workers, CIO, have the benefit of the skilled manpower in all the automotive plants, not just in one of them.

Labor asks only in return that its hard-won rights be preserved . . . only that it be allowed to contribute its own creative experience and knowledge and that it be given a voice in the execution of its program. . . .

No question of policy needs to be settled. The President has laid down the policy. We must have more planes. . . .

Quantity production was achieved in the Reich and is being achieved in England by methods labor now proposes to apply to the automotive industry.

The difference and our opportunity is that we have in the automotive industry the greatest mass-production machine the world has ever seen. Treated as one great production unit, it can in half a year's time turn out planes in unheard-of numbers and swamp the Luftwaffe. This is labor's answer to Hitler aggression, American labor's reply to the cries of its enslaved brothers under the Nazi yoke in Europe.

England's battles, it used to be said, were won on the playing fields of Eton. America's battles can be won on the assembly lines of Detroit.

The swollen wartime bureaucracy, with its myriads of dollar-a-year men jammed into Washington, consigned many proposals to limbo, Walter's among them. It was not, of course, attractive to the automobile manufacturers, but it was both imaginative and timely, and was finally given serious consideration by the War Department. It stirred up debate in the press and even inspired Charles E. Wilson, Knudsen's successor as president of General Motors, to challenge Walter to a face-to-face verbal duel in Detroit. . . .

No one was more outspoken against Walter's plan than the chairman of General Motors, Alfred P. Sloan, who declared categorically on November 20, 1940, that automobile plants were not adaptable to the manufacture of any other products. "Only about ten or fifteen percent of the machinery and equipment in an automobile factory can be utilized for the production of special defense material." He was in effect saying: Leave our plants alone on a standby basis, and build new plants for aircraft and tanks and gun carriages; tool them completely for that sort of specialized work though it may take two years to get them into real production.

The tragedy of this two-year delay was compounded by the insanity of saddling American taxpayers with the enormous cost of building new plants, which the corporations would later argue were "special purpose defense plants unsuited for civilian production" and ask that they be turned over to them, for a token fee, to be converted to their own purposes. The auto industry seemed ready to sacrifice the very life of the nation to its profit interests.

Many American workers paid dearly for this intransigence, which, of course, enriched the owners of industry. Corporate profits and the incomes of auto, steel, and other executives went up considerably during 1941. Eugene Grace of Bethlehem Steel, for instance, enjoyed a salary increase that year, boosting his remuneration from $478,000 in 1940 to $537,000 in 1941. Even the small Willys Overland Corporation provided for its president a 71 percent salary increase. Tom Girdler of Republic Steel had his salary raised by 56 percent, bringing it up to $275,000. When these men advocated business as usual, they knew what they were defending—and it wasn't the nation's survival.

Our UAW survey had indicated that at least 50 percent of auto-producing machinery was suitable for defense production. The refusal of General Motors to put at the disposal of the defense effort even its idle machine tools meant that in the urgent first six months of 1941, a crucial period, GM, out of a total production of $1,350,000,000 worth of goods, delivered only $131,000,000 worth of defense products.

Most American industrialists were trying at that point to make money from civilian *and* military sales. Their continued production of civilian cars and other consumer goods brought them huge profits, to which they intended to add the lucrative cost-plus defense contracts. With all their patriotic protestations and "victory councils," they had, in fact, to be shoved, against their will, into a maximum defense effort.

The final assessment of the merits of the Reuther plan came much later. It could be found in the reports of the auto executives themselves when, at the war's end, they boasted, as did K. T. Keller, Chrysler's head, that 89 percent of their machine tools had been converted to war production and could now be easily reconverted into making civilian cars. . . .

Finally, in December, 1941, there was a decree to cut back by 51.5 percent the passenger car production of the "big three" auto producers and the quotas of the smaller firms like Studebaker, Hudson and Nash, by 15.3 percent. A month before, I had challenged automobile executives to concentrate on fewer models in order to eliminate waste of materials and machinery. When the cutback was made an official order, serious pockets of unemployment appeared, as we had anticipated, lasting for six to eight months, and this at a time when the nation was calling for the labor of every person is a combined defense effort.

Within hours after the Japanese air attack on Pearl Harbor and before declaration of war by Germany against the U.S., I reported to the press: "The President's appeal for increase of production seven days a week in defense industries has received the unanimous support of the UAW-CIO. . . . This will not only speed defense production, but will also provide immediate defense employment for additional thousands of workers displaced by auto curtailment and whose skilled labor would otherwise be unused."

Needless to say, the automobile industry went on dragging its feet and it was urged that the cut-off date for passenger cars should be extended to the middle of February.

The CIO and the UAW began to carry their case to the public by writing an open letter to the OPM:

> Half of the nation's auto plants are today closed down. Virtually all of them will be down by the end of January. Blacked out not by Hitler and Japan. Approximately 25,000 automobile workers, men trained in precision, mass production methods, and highly skilled tool and die workers are now idle. Fully 400,000 will be idle by the end of January. The nation has lost two million man days every week in war production. . . . Only a few plants are turning out the vital materials of war. . . .
>
> The program drafted by Walter P. Reuther and other members of the UAW-CIO was referred to you for study and recommendation.

You did nothing about it. Similar plans for increasing production of steel, aluminum, copper and other materials vital to the war program were proposed. You did nothing about them. Labor is ready and determined to do its part . . . willing to accept the bitter necessities of a righteous war. Labor had the right to expect industry to do its part.

Editor's Notes

1. Victor and Walter Reuther spent a year and a half working in the Soviet Union, commencing in November, 1933. Their very understandable wish to see Soviet life at first hand was misunderstood by conservatives, even though the Reuthers were disillusioned with the Soviet government.
2. R. J. Thomas was then president of the UAW, having succeeded Homer Martin; Philip Murray was national president of the CIO.

2.   Sojourner Truth Housing Riots

Bette Smith Jenkins

Early in 1941—months before Pearl Harbor—the Federal government was becoming increasingly concerned about the necessity for providing housing for workers who were to pour into defense areas in very great numbers. As early as May 28, 1941, mention is made of the defense housing program in the Detroit Housing Commission minutes. . . .

On June 4, 1941 the Detroit Housing Commission approved two sites for defense housing projects, one for Negro occupancy and one for white occupancy. The Negro site, in accordance with local policy prohibiting the change, through construction of public housing, of the racial characteristics of a neighborhood, was located on the northwest corner of the intersection of Dequindre

Bette Smith Jenkins, "The Racial Policies of the Detroit Housing Commission and Their Administration" (master's thesis, Wayne University, 1950), 3: 73–130.

and Modern streets in an area predominantly Negro. The site selected for the white project of from three hundred to five hundred units was located on the northwest corner of Mound Road and Outer Drive. . . .

However, the first in a series of stumbling blocks which was to delay the defense housing program developed at the June 16th meeting. The site for the Negro project selected by Washington authorities was at Nevada and Fenelon Streets adjacent to the Atkinson School. . . . [It was previously considered by the Housing Commission to be a white area.]

The minutes of June 19 show dissatisfaction on the part of Commission members with the action of the Federal government. Commissioner Ed Thal objected to the United States Housing Authority's disregard of Housing Commission recommendations. However Commissioner White [the Reverend Horace White, only black member of the commission] stated that, "As much as I disagree with the site selected for the two hundred unit project, the housing shortage in Detroit is so acute, particularly among Negroes, that I feel we should cooperate." . . .

On September 29, 1941 the project was named Sojourner Truth in memory of the leader and poet of Civil War days.

Construction proceeded but by mid-November the ensuing storm of protest came to the attention of Congress under the leadership of Representative Rudolph G. Tenerowicz, Michigan Democratic Congressman from the First Congressional District, in which Sojourner Truth is located. Congressman Tenerowicz carried on an active campaign to bring about a change from Negro to white occupancy. . . . [On November 17, 1941, the housing commission] entered in its minutes a report from Reverend Horace White that Mr. Tenerowicz was attempting to bring about a change to white occupancy. This was the Commission's first official cognizance of "the brewing storm of neighborhood objections."

The project was completed on December 15, 1941, but was still untenanted on January 20, 1942 in spite of the fact that there was a serious housing shortage in the Detroit area, particularly for Negro war workers. On January 20 the Detroit Housing Commission was informed that Washington had designated Sojourner Truth for white occupancy and that a new site for a project for Negro defense workers would be selected. Later Federal officials reported that there was no site available in Detroit. They therefore recommended that the project be located outside the city limits. . . .

But, as other records show, the matter was not closed. [LeRoi] Ottley describes a day-and-night vigil by white people before Detroit's City Hall.[1] He states that when the Ku Klux Klan entered the picture, the picket lines were shifted to the project—and the racial explosion occurred when the Negroes sought to move into the buildings. He further points out that without government protection, Negroes were blocked from entering the project for months. Meantime, he says, F.B.I. investigation turned up links with Axis agents among the agitators. Soon a large section of the liberal white public took up the issue and supported the Negro's right to live at Sojourner Truth. Pressure by Negroes was again applied to make the Washington officials stand firmly by their decision, and the Sojourner Truth Homes were finally turned over to Negroes. . . .

On the night of February 27, 1942 a fiery cross was burned in a field close to Sojourner Truth Homes. . . . That same night one hundred fifty white pickets patrolled the project with the avowed purpose of preventing occupancy by Negro tenants assigned to the first twenty-eight units. By dawn the crowd of picketers had grown to twelve hundred, many of whom were armed.

The first of the tenants, having already paid his rent and signed a lease, arrived at the project about 9:00 A.M. on the morning of February 28, but left without attempting to move in after viewing the mob. A few minutes later two cars and a moving van tried to enter the project grounds but were stopped by the pickets.

Fighting began around 9:30 A.M. when two Negroes endeavored to run through the picket line in their car. At 10:15 A.M. the first heavy flare-up occurred when bricks began to fly between white and Negro groups lined up on opposite sides of Ryan Road, a street near the project. This clash was brought to an end by sixteen mounted police who drove into the ranks.

The most heated battle of the day occurred shortly after 12:15 P.M. when a truckload of Negro men carrying pipes crossed Ryan Road on the west into Nevada Avenue. White pickets bombarded the truck with bricks. The police brought this incident to an end by placing the Negroes under protective custody. Within fifteen minutes, following a decision of authorities to postpone the moving, street battles began, with Negroes lined up west of Ryan road opposite to four hundred fifty white persons who greatly outnumbered them.

The *New York Times* as well as local Detroit papers carried stories on March 1, 1942 indicating that scores of both Negroes and whites were injured before the fighting quieted down.

Two hundred police were stationed in the area by Mayor Edward J. Jeffries Jr. They tried three different times to disperse the crowd with tear gas. Shots were fired, several passing through the windows of Mrs. Mary Williams, a Negro living near the project. Several persons were slashed. Three policemen and fifteen others, both Negroes and whites, were hospitalized.

The *Detroit News* story of March 1, 1942, states that the disorder resulted from the "determination of a crowd of five hundred whites to prevent fourteen Negro families from moving into Sojourner Truth, one half mile east of the riot scene." The same story indicates that "at 3:30 P.M. three Negroes passed police lines and walked east on Nevada toward the project. At Justine Street, one half block from the project, a crowd of whites halted them and fighting ensued."

In general the *Detroit Free Press* story of March 1 confirms the details of the rioting. It reports that knives and guns were detected among the rioters who were disarmed by the police whenever possible. It had been hoped earlier in the day when police sent the moving vans away on order of Mayor Jeffries that the crowds would dwindle.

According to the *Free Press* version rioting finally was halted when the police forced the factions about two blocks apart and Superintendent Alfred Siska issued an order to "clear the streets in the entire area."

The *New York Times* of March 2, 1942, reports that one hundred four persons were arrested on charges of rioting and carrying concealed weapons as a result of the clash. To prevent further violence after the initial disturbance of February 28, one hundred policemen were stationed in the area on March 1 to keep everyone but residents from entering. Boundaries marked off a section one mile square and traffic was detoured around it. On the second day the trouble was confined to minor skirmishes. The *New York Times* story indicates that of the one hundred four arrests, six were for felonious assault, twenty-three for carrying concealed weapons, and seventy-five for inciting to riot.[2]

The *Detroit News* story confirms this report, adding disturbing the peace to the list of charges. Of the persons arrested, all but two were Negroes.

Aftermath of the Riot

On March 2, two days after the major disturbances had taken place, Judge George Murphy began to hear inciting to riot charges against seventy-eight persons who were said to have participated in the skirmishes of February 28. According to the *Detroit Times* of March 2, 1942, the courtroom was jammed with Negro sympathizers. The first four defendants brought before Judge Murphy, all Negroes, were found to be innocent, it being Judge Murphy's contention that there was insufficient evidence to prove that they had disturbed the peace by inciting to riot.

Attorneys for Negroes held for disturbing the peace testified before Judge Murphy in Recorders Court that white persons were illegally picketing the controversial area at the time the incidents were said to have occurred and that no peace existed for Negroes to disturb. The *Detroit News*, March 2, 1942, reported that picket lines had been maintained intact by whites in the Fenelon-Nevada area for three weeks preceding the riot. They made a point of the fact that all of the defendants but two were Negroes.

Felony warrants based on carrying concealed weapons were sworn out against seventeen Negroes. A felonious assault warrant named a white man.

A *Detroit Times* story of March 2 states that police handling of the disturbance was roundly criticized by twenty Negro and white leaders who "voiced particular resentment against Davison precinct Station." The police were accused of bias and of "siding with an organized conspiracy of the Ku Klux Klan." Although picket lines were resumed on the days immediately following the moving-day clashes which marked February 28, further violence was prevented. When fifty white persons assembled for picketing on March 3, they were dispersed by Inspector Cox of the Davison Station. . . . It is interesting to note the terminology used in the *Detroit News* account of that date. It asserted that police *refused* to permit Negro groups to gather at the project; that Inspector Cox *requested* a picket line of fifty people to disperse and that the whites then set up a "headquarters" on Conley Avenue, one block away.

It was the opinion of police and housing officials that the only thing which could prevent continuation of violence in the Sojourner Truth area was postponement of the move-in date for the Negro families and there was, of course, much discussion as to whether or not they would be permitted to occupy the project at all.

The *Detroit Free Press* of March 2, 1942 reports that: "Ever since high-ranking police officials assayed the temper of the crowds around the project, they have agreed that only a small standing army could get Negro families moved into the project peacefully and they wouldn't try to estimate how many it would take to keep peace after the project was in use."

. . . Although sixty-five units of the project had been ready for occupancy since February 6 and one hundred sixty-five were completed by the time the rioting occurred; although they were seriously needed to house Detroit's war workers, Charles Edgecomb, as the Housing Commission's director-secretary, requested and obtained Common council approval to return $1055 in advance rent payments made by prospective tenants who had already signed leases for their dwellings.

Meanwhile the families, having given up whatever shelter they had in anticipation of their new homes, were left with no place to go and were being temporarily housed at Brewster Homes and in buildings located on the site acquired for a future Housing Commission development, Douglas Homes.

On March 2, 1942, word was received by Mayor Jeffries from Washington that occupancy of Sojourner Truth had been postponed indefinitely.

There were those who continued to point out that, had the police acted differently, postponement might not have been necessary. Commissioner Horace White, who had spent considerable time at the scene of the disturbance, informed the mayor that the police, prior to the fighting, had made no effort to disperse the crowds of whites gathering there. He pointed out that the police had permitted both sides, that is whites and Negroes, to line up along Ryan Road across from each other in what he called "an open invitation to fight." This was the culmination of months of protests against Negro occupancy.

Reverend White and Reverend Charles Hill, a Detroit Negro minister, were leaders of a Citizen's Committee which was working to get adequate police protection for families so that they could move to their homes. . . . The committee demanded the removal from his position of Charles Edgecomb whom they accused of cooperating with those advocating white occupancy of Sojourner Truth. It appears that State Police protection might have been available for the task of achieving Negro occupancy but Governor Murray van Wagoner stated that his troops would be sent only upon official request from City of Detroit officials and no such request was made.

Because Mayor Jeffries estimated that the services of three thousand policemen would be required to move Negro tenants to their units at Sojourner Truth, he issued orders that the project be left vacant until the issue could be settled. Police protection to supplement the city force was available, as Detroit police were asked in a telephone conversation whether Federal troops were wanted. However, Detective Inspector Edward Graff turned down the offer, stating that "the situation was in hand."

As Charles Edgecomb, in his capacity as director-secretary of the Detroit housing commission, made his announcement that money for rent advanced by twenty-four Negro tenants would be returned and their leases cancelled, he also assured members of white groups that there would be "no sneak moves" and that they would be notified in advance of any future attempts to move in Negro families.

. . . Serious charges regarding the handling of the emergency were made by John R. Williams, 1926 St. Antoine, Detroit representative of the *Pittsburgh Courier,* (a national Negro weekly with a Detroit edition), who claimed that "real estate interests" were back of the picketing. Williams' statements were quoted in a *Detroit News* story on March 1, 1942. He said,

> This is not a sincere movement by white citizens. These pickets were introduced by real estate interests.
>
> Seemingly, a deal has been made whereby there is picketing and mob atmosphere. The mob atmosphere has given Edgecomb

an excuse for postponing Negro occupancy. Edgecomb is playing ball with the real estate interests. White citizens as a whole are not opposed to Negro occupancy of the project.

In response to the charge, Mr. Edgecomb said that it was "obviously ridiculous. . . . "

One of the encouraging developments during the riot period was that a number of organizations and individuals whose only interest was an unofficial one, a sincere desire to see the controversy settled equitably and fairly and with a minimum of damage, came forward to offer constructive suggestions and to assist in whatever ways were possible.

. . . John Blandford [National Housing Administrator], in an announcement published in the *Detroit Free Press* of March 7, 1942, designated Sojourner Truth for Negro tenancy. In doing so he made "a patriotic appeal" to white residents in the area. . . .

Although Mr. Blandford expressed the fear that the Detroit situation might set off riots in other cities, there is nothing in later records to show that his fears were substantiated. The most serious and tragic aftermath of the Sojourner Truth affair was the race riot which occurred in Detroit in 1943. It is the opinion of Detroit experts in race relations that there are very definite connections between activities of the Detroit Housing Commission and the riot which occurred on June 20, 1943. . . .

Meanwhile sixty-five policeman were assigned to guard the project . . . white protesters were still not ready to accept the determination that Negro war workers were to live at Sojourner Truth, and a crowd of five hundred of them were again picketing on March 10. Tear gas bombs were used to disperse them. The crowd had been stimulated by Joseph Buffa, described as a real estate dealer, and the man who had been their declared leader all along. . . .

Picketing was resumed the following day, March 11, and [the *Free Press*] . . . stated that there were one thousand white men, women and children on hand to picket Sojourner Truth for two hours in the evening despite cold and rain. There was no disturbance as police were on duty on a twenty-four hour schedule and kept the picketers a distance of two blocks from the project in all directions. Joseph Buffa, who, throughout the controversy, was acting in his capacity as president of the Seven Mile-Fenelon Improvement Association, at no time seemed to feel that he was not acting in the best interest of the community. . . .

When it was announced that [two] special assistants to Attorney General Francis Biddle, were arriving in Detroit on March 10 to initiate a Federal grand jury investigation, Mr. Buffa welcomed the news, stating, "We have done nothing but protect our property rights. I don't think there is any law yet against protesting an action. . . . I welcome the investigation. . . . Maybe they will bring into the open some of the 'pinks' on the other side."

There were some differing opinions, however, as to whether Mr. Buffa and his group had been acting within their rights. District Attorney John C. Lehr announced, as plans were carried out for the investigation, the Federal Grand Jury would look into charges that there was a conspiracy to prevent Negroes from occupying Sojourner Truth. . . . Attorney General Biddle announced simultaneously that if it were found that a conspiracy *had* existed to prevent tenants from occupying a Federal project, prosecution might be brought under the civil rights section of the criminal code.

This investigation continued for some time after the immediate situation was cleared up and no study of it has been made. Inquiries were directed to former government employees who worked on the investigation and it is their opinion that it would be impossible to obtain any detailed information from records of the case. There seems to be no indication that charges were brought against anyone connected with the riot as a result of the investigation and Mr. Buffa and his group are still found to be on hand whenever what they consider their right to maintain an untainted neighborhood defined by their standards of racial purity seems to be threatened.

As the Federal investigation got under way, days passed and still Sojourner Truth stood untenanted. . . . The National Housing Agency finally acted, when on April 17, it sent a wire: "Please proceed as soon as feasible with established program for occupancy of Sojourner Truth. . . . "[On April 30] the first Negro families moved to the project and now, eight years later, many of the tenants are still living there peaceably, having proven that they make good neighbors and do not cause a neighborhood to deteriorate. . . . There is, however, evidence that people living in

416

the area were still being stimulated by an organized pressure group, the Seven Mile-Fenelon Association. At the meeting held by the Housing Commission on July 2, 1942, the director read a letter from this organization requesting that a fence be constructed at the project to prevent children living there from playing on privately-owned property.

Notes

1. LeRoi Ottley, *New World A-Coming,* Boston, Houghton Mifflin, 1943, pp. 219 ff.
2. A study of newspaper accounts of the riot reveals that in most instances the *New York Times* refrained from Negro and white designations while the three metropolitan Detroit papers, *The Detroit Times, The Detroit Free Press* and *The Detroit News* used them.

Editor's Note

Jenkins notes that the groups who worked on behalf of Negro occupancy of Sojourner Truth covered a wide spectrum: labor unions, particularly Local 600 of the UAW, the NAACP and the Detroit Urban League, and many Protestant churches, both black and white as to membership. In spite of the hostility to Negro occupancy shown by several Catholic parishes in the Sojourner Truth area, many liberal Catholics from across the city were drawn in to protest the violence. One civic leader, the Reverend Henry Hitt Crane, pastor of the downtown Central Methodist Church, urged Mayor Jeffries to appoint an interracial committee, a proposal that failed at the time. However, the mayor did appoint such a committee only a little over a year later, following the riot of 1943.

Major sources used by Jenkins were local newspaper accounts. She was an employee of the Tenant Selection Office of the Detroit Housing Commission, and so was daily aware of the events described. As this editor, who was a coworker at the time, remembers, Jenkins (now Mrs. Thomas Downs) showed a quick grasp of the realities and compassionate concern.

3.   June, 1943: A City Split in Two

Walter White and Thurgood Marshall

The riot of June 20, 1943, left most Detroiters as surprised as they had been in 1833, 1863, and at the racial incidents in between. It was first assumed, and the media agreed, that this was a "Negro riot," and that a large part of the violence was being committed by Negroes upon whites. A more reliable source of truth was the analysis circulated from the national office of the NAACP.

The NAACP report was in two parts: the first, by Walter White, national Executive Secretary, set forth the background, including demographics and employment, with some factual material on labor unions, which non-Detroiters found hard to believe. The second section, by Thurgood Marshall, then counsel for the organization, later to become Justice Marshall of the U.S. Supreme Court, detailed the events of the riot, focusing on the actions of the Detroit Police Department.

What Caused the Detroit Riots?

In 1916 there were 8,000 Negroes in Detroit's population of 536,650. In 1925 the number of Negroes in Detroit had been multiplied by ten to a total of 85,000. In 1940, the total had jumped to 149,119. In June, 1943, between 190,000 and 200,000 lived in the Motor City.

According to the War Manpower Commission, approximately 500,000 in-migrants moved to Detroit between June, 1940 and

Walter White and Thurgood Marshall, *What Caused the Detroit Riots? An Analysis* (New York: National Association for the Advancement of Colored People, 1943), 5–37.

June, 1943. . . . The War Manpower Commission failed almost completely to enforce its edict that no in-migration be permitted into any industrial area until all available local labor was utilized. Thus a huge reservoir of Negro labor existed in Detroit, crowded into highly congested slum areas. But they did have housing of a sort and this labor was already in Detroit. The coming of white workers recruited chiefly in the South not only gravely complicated the housing, transportation, educational and recreation facilities of Detroit, but they brought with them the traditional prejudices of Mississippi, Arkansas, Louisiana, and other Deep South states against the Negro. . . .

Here and there among these Southern whites were members of the UAW-CIO and other labor union, churchmen and others who sloughed off whatever racial prejudice they had brought with them from the South. But the overwhelming majority maintained and even increased their hostility to Negroes. . . . During July, 1941, there had been an epidemic of riots allegedly by Polish youths which had terrorized colored residents in Detroit, Hamtramck, and other sections in and about Detroit. Homes of Negroes on Horton, Chippewa, West Grand Boulevard and other streets close to but outside of the so-called Negro areas were attacked by mobs with no police interference.

Detroit's 200,000 Negroes are today largely packed into two segregated areas. The larger of these is on the East Side bounded by Jefferson on the South, John R on the West, East Grand Boulevard on the North, and Russell on the East . . . —approximately 60 square blocks. A somewhat smaller Negro area is on the West Side . . . —an area of approximately 30 square blocks. In addition to these two wholly Negro areas, there are scattered locations throughout Detroit of mixed occupancy in which, significantly, there was during the riot less friction than in any other area. . . .

Meantime, but little public housing was created to meet the tragic need for housing for both whites and Negroes in Detroit. Even this was characterized by shameful vacillation and weakness in Washington which only added fuel to the flames of racial tension in Detroit. The notorious riots revolving about the question of who should occupy the Sojourner Truth Housing project in February, 1942, are an example of this. . . .

From all other public housing projects [except Sojourner Truth and Brewster] erected in Detroit, Negroes were totally excluded, although Negroes and whites had lived in complete amity in some of the areas on which these public housing projects, erected through the taxation of Negro as well as white Americans, were built.

Equally contributory to the explosion which was to come has been the attitude of the Detroit Real Estate Association. . . . meantime, every train, bus, or other public conveyance entering Detroit disgorged an ever increasing torrent of men, women and children demanding places to live while they earned the war wages Detroit factories were paying. . . .

Jobs

Early in June, 1943, 25,000 employees of the Packard Plant, which was making Rolls-Royce engines for American bombers and marine engines for the famous PT boats, ceased work in protest against the upgrading of three Negroes. Subsequent investigation indicated that only a relatively small percentage of the Packard workers actually wanted go on strike. The UAW-CIO bitterly fought the strike. But a handful of agitators charged by R. J. Thomas, president of the UAW-CIO, with being members of the Ku Klux Klan, had whipped up sentiment, particularly among the Southern whites employed by Packard, against the promotion of Negro workers. During the short-lived strike, a thick Southern voice outside the plant harangued a crowd shouting, "I'd rather see Hitler and Hirohito win than work beside a nigger on the assembly line." The strike was broken by the resolute attitude of the union and of Col. George E. Strong, of the United States Aircraft Procurement Division, who refused to yield to the demand that the three Negroes be downgraded. Certain officials of the Packard Company were clearly responsible in part for the strike. . . .

There had been innumerable instances, unpublicized, of work stoppages and slow downs by white workers, chiefly from the South, and of Polish and Italian extraction. Trivial reasons for these stoppages had been given by the workers when in reality they were in protest against employment or promotion of Negroes. A vast number of man hours and of production had been irretrievably lost. . . . John Bugas in charge of the Detroit office of the FBI, states that his investigations prove that the Ku Klux

Klan at no time has had more than 3,000 members in Detroit. Other investigations by officials and private agencies corroborate this fact. But the Klan did not need to be a large organization to cause serious disruption of war production in Detroit, because of . . . the increasing percentage of Southern whites who went to Detroit to work in 1942 and 1943. . . .

Gerald L. K. Smith, former assistant and protege of the late Huey Long, has long been active in stirring up discord and dissension in the Detroit area. His activities in America First, anti-union, and other similar groups have been greatly increased in effectiveness by his also being a Southerner trained in the art of demagoguery by Huey Long. . . . Active also have been the followers of Father Coughlin. . . . Ingrained or stimulated prejudice against the Negro has been used as much against organized labor as it has against the Negro. . . .

Detroit Labor Unions and the Negro

One of the most extraordinary phenomena of the riot was the fact that while mobs attacked Negro victims outside some of the industrial plants of Detroit, there was not only no physical clash inside any plant in Detroit but not as far as could be learned even any verbal clash between white and Negro workers. This can be attributed to two factors: first a firm stand against discrimination and segregation of Negro workers by the UAW-CIO, particularly since the Ford strike of 1941. The second factor is that when the military took over, the armed guards in the plants were ordered by the Army to maintain order at all costs. . . .

The Detroit riot brought into sharp focus one of the most extraordinary labor situations in the United States. Prior to the Ford strike of 1941 many Negroes in Detroit considered Ford their "great white father" because the Detroit plant almost alone of Detroit industries employed Negroes. When the UAW-CIO and the UAW-AFL sought to organize Ford workers, their approach at the beginning was a surreptitious one. The unions felt that the very high percentage of Southern whites in Detroit would refuse to join the Union if Negroes were too obviously participating. But when the strike broke, far-sighted Negro leaders in Detroit took an unequivocal position in behalf of the organization of workers. . . .

During the recent riot, R. J. Thomas, president of the UAW-CIO, proposed an eight-point program which was widely published, and helped to emphasize the basic causes of the riot. These points included: 1) creation of a special grand jury to investigate the causes of the riot and to return justifiable indictments with a competent Negro attorney appointed as an assistant prosecutor to work with the grand jury; 2) immediate construction and opening of adequate park and recreation facilities. Thomas called it "disgraceful that the City's normal, inadequate park space was permitted to be overtaxed further by the influx of hundreds of thousands of new war workers;" 3) immediate and practical plans for rehousing Negro slum dwellers in decent Government-financed housing developments; 4) insistence that plant managements as well as workers recognize the right of Negroes to jobs in line with their skill and seniority; 5) a full investigation by the special grand jury of the conduct of the Police Department during the riots; 6) special care by the courts in dealing with the many persons arrested. Those found guilty should be severely punished, and there must be no discrimination between white and Negro rioters; 7) the loss of homes and small businesses, as well as personal injuries, is the responsibility of the community and the city should create a fund to make good these losses; 8) creation by the Mayor of a special biracial committee of ten persons to make further recommendations looking toward the elimination of racial differences and frictions, this committee to have a special job in connection with high schools "where racial hatred has been permitted to grow and thrive within recent years. . . . "

[White cited several other factors that caused the riot, or affected its timing—among them the ineptness of Mayor Edward J. Jeffries, Jr., though he absolved him from personal racial prejudice. He criticized the role of the major newspapers. (He found the Hearst-controlled *Times* actively racist, the *News* apathetic, and gave only the *Free Press*, under the new ownership of John Knight, a clean bill of health.)

Section II of the report, which follows, relates to the activities of the Detroit police force, and includes charges of both malfeasance and corruption. The demand by the NAACP for a grand jury investigation was never heeded.]

Activities of the Police during the Riots June 21 and 22, 1943

From June 24 to July 9, 1943, we maintained an emergency office at the St. Antoine Branch of the YMCA. In addition to myself, we used the services of two private investigators from New York City, one white and one Negro. During this period we received all complaints that were brought to us and made several independent investigations. All of the material in the following report is supported by affidavits. . . .

One of the important factors in any race riot is the local police. Very often disturbances reach riot proportions as a result of inefficiency on the part of the local police. The affidavits we have taken are more than sufficient to justify the calling of a special grand jury to investigate the nonfeasance and malfeasance of the police as a contributing factor in the Detroit riots. . . .

In the June riots of this year, the Detroit police ran true to form. The trouble reached riot proportions because the Detroit police once again enforced the law under an unequal hand. They used "persuasion" rather than firm action with white rioters while against Negroes they used the ultimate in force: night sticks, revolvers, riot guns, sub-machine guns and deer guns. As a result, 25 of the 34 persons killed were Negroes. Of the 25 Negroes killed, 17 were killed by police. The excuse of the Police Department for the disproportionate number of Negroes killed is that the majority of them were killed while committing felonies: namely, the looting of stores on Hastings Street. On the other hand, the crimes of arson and felonious assault are also felonies. It is true that some Negroes were looting stores on Hastings Street, and were shot while committing these crimes. It is equally true that white persons were turning over and burning automobiles on Woodward Avenue. This is arson. Others were beating Negroes with iron pipes, clubs, and rocks. This is felonious assault. Several Negroes were stabbed. This is assault with intent to murder.

All of these crimes are matters of record; many were committed in the presence of police officers, several on the pavement around the City Hall. Yet, the record remains, Negroes killed by police—17; white persons killed by police—none. Eighty-five percent of the persons arrested were Negroes.

Evidence of tension in Detroit has been apparent for months. The *Detroit Free Press* sent a reporter to the police department. When Commissioner Witherspoon was asked how he was handling the situation, he told the reporter: "We have given orders to handle it with kid gloves. The policemen have taken insults in order to keep trouble from breaking out. I doubt if you or I could put up with it." This weak-kneed policy of the police commissioner coupled with the anti-Negro attitude of many members of the force helped to make a riot inevitable.

Sunday Night on Belle Isle

Belle Isle is a municipally owned recreation park where thousands of white and Negro defense workers and their families go on Sunday for their outings. There had been isolated instances of racial friction in the past. On Sunday night, June 20th, there was trouble between a group of white and Negro people. The disturbance was under control by midnight. During the time of disturbance and after it was under control, the police searched the automobiles of all Negroes and searched the Negroes as well. They did not search the white people. One Negro who was to be inducted into the Army the following week was arrested because another person in the car had a small pen knife. This youth was later sentenced to 90 days in jail before his family could locate him. Many Negroes were arrested during this period and rushed to local police stations. At the very beginning the police demonstrated that they would continue to handle racial disorders by searching, beating and arresting Negroes while using mere persuasion on white people.

The Riot Spreads to Detroit Proper

A short time after midnight disorder broke out in a white neighborhood near the Roxy Theatre on Woodward Avenue. The Roxy is an all night theatre attended by white and Negro patrons. Several Negroes were beaten and others were forced to remain in the theatre for lack of police protection. The rumor spread among the white people that a Negro had raped a white woman on Belle Isle and that the Negroes were rioting.

At about the same time a rumor spread around Hastings and Adams Streets in the Negro area that white sailors had thrown a

Negro woman and her baby into the lake at Belle Isle and that the police were beating Negroes. This rumor was also repeated by an unidentified Negro at one of the Negro night spots. Some Negroes began to attack white persons in the area. The police immediately began to use their sticks and revolvers against these Negroes. The Negroes began to beat out the windows of stores of white merchants on Hastings Street.

The interesting thing is that when the windows in the stores on Hastings Street were first broken, there was no looting. An officer of the Merchants' Association walked the length of Hastings Street starting at 7 o'clock Monday morning and noticed that none of the stores with broken windows had been looted. It is thus clear that the original breaking of windows was not for the purpose of looting. Throughout Monday the Detroit police instead of placing policemen in front of the stores to protect them from looting, contented themselves with driving up and down Hastings Street from time to time and stopping in front of the stores. The usual procedure was to jump out of the squad cars with drawn revolvers and riot guns to shoot whoever might be in the store. The police would then tell the Negro bystanders to "run and not look back." On several occasions, persons running were shot in the back. In other instances, bystanders were clubbed by police. To the Detroit police, all Negroes on Hastings Street were "looters." This included Negroes returning from work. There is no question that some Negroes were guilty of looting. . . .

[On Monday] small groups of white people began to rove up and down Woodward Avenue beating Negroes, stoning cars containing Negroes, stopping street cars and yanking Negroes from them, and stabbing and shooting Negroes. In no case did the police do more than try to "reason" with these mobs, many of which were at this stage quite small. The police did not draw their revolvers or riot guns, and never used any force to disperse these mobs. As a result of this, the mobs got larger and bolder and even attacked Negroes on the pavement of the City Hall in demonstration not only of their contempt for Negroes, but of their contempt for law and order as represented by the municipal government. The use of night sticks or the drawing of revolvers would have dispersed these white groups and saved the lives of many Negroes. It would not have been necessary to shoot, but it

425

would have been sufficient to threaten to shoot into the white mobs. The use of a fire hose would have dispersed many of the groups. None of these things were done, and the disorder took on the proportions of a major riot. The responsibility of this rests with the Detroit police.

At the height of the disorder on Woodward Avenue, Negroes driving north on Brush Street (a Negro street) were stopped at Vernor Highway by a policeman who forced them to detour to Woodard Avenue. Many of these cars are automobiles which appeared in the pictures by several newspapers showing them overturned and burned on Woodward Avenue. While investigating the riot, we obtained many affidavits from Negroes concerning police brutality during the riot. It is impossible to include the facts of all these affidavits. . . .

One Negro, who has been an employee of a bank for the last eighteen years, was on his way to work on a Woodward Avenue streetcar when he was seized by one of the white mobs. In the presence of at least four policemen, he was beaten and stabbed in the side. He also heard several shots fired from the back of the mob. He managed to run to two of the policemen, who proceeded to "protect" him from the mob. The two policemen, followed by two mounted policemen, proceeded down Woodward Avenue. While he was being escorted by these policemen, the Negro was struck in the face by at least eight of the mob, and at no time was any effort made to prevent him from being struck. After a short distance this man noticed a squad car parked on the other side of the street. In sheer desperation, he broke away from the two policemen who claimed to be protecting him and ran to the squad car, begging for protection. The officer in the squad car put him in the back seat and drove off, thereby saving this man's life. During all this time . . . blood was spurting from his side. Despite this obvious felony, committed in the presence of at least four policemen, no effort was made at that time either to protect the victim, or since to arrest the persons guilty of the felony. . . .

Vernor Apartments

On the night of June 21st at about eight o'clock, a Detroit policeman was shot on the two hundred block of Vernor Highway, and his assailant, who was in a vacant lot, was in turn, killed by another policeman. State and city policemen then began to attack the apartment building at 290 E. Vernor Highway, which was fully occupied by tenants. . . . Tenants of the building were forced to fall to the floor and remain there in order to save their lives. Later slugs from machine guns, revolvers, rifles, and deer-guns were dug from the inside walls. Tear gas was shot into the building. . . . The tenants were lined up in the street, the apartments were forcibly entered; locks and doors were broken. All of the apartments were ransacked. . . . Most of the tenants reported that money, jewelry, whisky, and items of personal property were missing when they were permitted to return to their apartments after midnight. State and City police had been in possession of the building during the meantime. . . .

After the raid on the Vernor Apartments, the police used as their excuse the statement that policeman Lawrence A. Adams had been shot by a sniper from the Vernor Apartments, and that for that reason, they attacked the building and its occupants. However, in a story released by the Police Department on July 2, . . . it was reported that "The shot that felled Adams was fired by Homer Edison, 28 years old, of 502 Montcalm from the shadows of a parking lot. . . ."

One member of the white mobs, whose face appeared in at least four violent action pictures which have appeared several times in the daily papers of Detroit, is well known to police and has a police record, yet he was never arrested for his part in the Detroit riots. He has since left town after having seen two of his photographs placed again in the *Detroit Free Press*. This type of deliberate non-action is typical of the Detroit Police Force. . . .

Y.M.C.A.

On the night of June 22nd at about 10 o'clock, some of the residents of the St. Antoine Branch of the Y.M.C.A. were returning to the dormitory. Several were on their way home from the Y.W.C.A. across the street. State Police were searching some other Negroes . . . when two of the Y.M.C.A. residents were stopped and searched for weapons. After none were found they were allowed to proceed to the building. Just as the last of the Y.M.C.A. men was about to enter the building, he heard someone behind him yell what sounded to him like "Hi, Ridley." (Ridley is also a resident of the Y.) Another resident said he heard someone yell what sounded to him like "Heil, Hitler."

A State policeman, Ted Anders, jumped from his car with his revolver out, . . . and fired through the outside door. . . . Julian Witherspoon, who had just entered the building, was shot in the side by the bullet that was fired through the outside door and fell to the floor. There had been no show of violence or weapons of any kind by anyone in or around the Y.M.C.A.

The officers with drawn revolvers ordered all the residents of the Y.M.C.A. who were in the lobby of their building, to raise their hands in the air and line up against the wall like criminals. During all of this time these men were called "black bastards, monkeys" and other vile names by the officers. At least one man was struck, another was forced to throw his lunch on the floor. All of the men in the lobby were searched. . . . Witherspoon was later removed to the hospital and has subsequently been released. . . .

4. What about Housing Cooperatives?

Merle E. Henrickson

The real estate pages are in reaction against modern technology. They have become frightened because people are taking "Postwar Houses" seriously. There are probably two reasons for this campaign: fear that little builders can't turn them out, and fear that if anyone does produce them, people will refuse to pay for the stuff they have now.

When the real estate pages say that the postwar house will have a little more glass and many more gadgets, but will otherwise by much the same, they mean that builders cannot or will not produce a better house. Architects and financing agencies are both frank to admit that the system of home financing has done

Merle E. Henrickson, "What about Housing Cooperatives?" plans and drawings by Donald Monson, 1945, Halbeisen Collection, Reuther Archives, Wayne State University.

much to curb experimental work. There must be not hint of deviation from the mortgage bankers' notion of the average taste, "The mortgage risks a banker will assume must necessarily, for the protection of bank depositors, be predicated on the preference of most of the people in housing."

But unfortunately not most of the people looked at one at a time to see who has children, who has dogs, and who has phonograph records. No! It's most of the people tossed in a hat and come out "average American", with 1.8 children, 0.3 dogs. For a million of these average Americans the mortgage bankers will be happy to build about 50,000 five-room Cape Cod cottages on forty foot lots, with petunias and a white picket fence in the front yard and a garage and bird bath in the back. . . . They will point out that in the interest of individuality they have put one-third of the front doors on the left side, one-third on the right, and one-third square in the middle.

The pressure to keep the house a liquid commodity limits the size and type of all homes, even though the family recognizes that it needs four bedrooms or a special feature to accommodate a hobby; it must eliminate what is unique to its own needs because it would make the house harder to sell. . . .

If people are to get better houses, they must decide what needs improving and organize their own cooperatives to get what they want.

A house is intended first of all for shelter. It must have floors, walls, and a roof suitable for the climate in which it is built, and a heating system capable of maintaining a temperature of 68 degrees in winter. Better heating systems are necessary both to reduce pulmonary diseases, and to cut down the amount of housework. Housekeeping is becoming an increasing ritual of washing, dusting, and vacuum cleaning. As the number of labor-saving devices increases, the amount of time spent in performing the basic cleaning operations is also increased. The first technical job to be done in the home is to make surfaces which are easier to keep clean rather than more powerful machines to get dust out of the deeper rugs. For our bathrooms and kitchens we now try to have walls and floors that can be watered down—if ever so gently. But we have other points of heavy traffic in the house where washable surfaces would be a great improvement. Where are small children to play? Must we continue to build houses in which floors are so cold that they must be covered with dust-catching rugs for children to play on? Recent experiments have studied the adaptability of two ancient heating principles to the home. Radiant heat, extensively used by the Romans, employs the principle of heating surfaces with which people come in contact, rather than heating the air and leaving surfaces cold. Solar heating—that is, proper orientation—exposes rooms to the maximum of winter sun by increasing south window exposure while giving greater protection from prevailing winds.

Whatever heating system may prove most practical for installation in group housing, one factor to be considered is elimination of dirt-producing fuel-burning devices. . . .

Whether the things that all families need are to be secured in the homes of low and middle-income families is now a practical problem of standardizing construction methods and organizing a large-scale market to demand a sound product. . . . There is no reason for the house building industry to go farther in the direction of [the] artificial style obsolescence of the automobile industry. . . .

The cooperative neighborhood is not a utopia, but neither does it need to have those limitations of bourgeois individualism which find fullest expression in the suburban home [which] tries to buy everything of the good life for itself, then surrounds it by four walls, a tight fence and a privet hedge, and finds its security in a bill of sale limiting ownership to "white Caucasians"—whatever they may be. The fences around the back yards which chop up the only open space large enough for a ball diamond and cut off the suburban child from social intercourse in his street, are only symbolic of the fuller isolation of the whole suburban family. These families arranged in nice neat rows don't know their neighbors, and seemingly they don't care how high the hedge grows between them.

Part XIII

The Fifties: The Look of Togetherness

The Fifties: The Look of Togetherness

A leading women's journal used the slogan "the magazine of togetherness." It wasn't far off the mark in describing its own goals or those of the times. Yet a young historian said recently, "It must have been terrible to live through the fifties." He was thinking of McCarthyism. But for many Detroiters the fifties seemed an arrival of the promised land: a single family home of one's own, children, and usually with a mother at home to care for them. Auto production was up, the pay the best ever, and the UAW was removing the seasonal layoffs with guaranteed annual wage clauses in the new contracts.

The city expanded. The Northland shopping mall was one of the earliest in the country, designed by Victor Gruen. It was a place to sit in the gardens under flowering crab trees and treat the children to Sanders ice cream. From its opening year the J. L. Hudson anchor store in the mall outdid the expectations of its owners, and in very few years it surpassed the sales of its parent store downtown. Soon Hudson's took the lead in developing other new malls. Meanwhile Northland performed a second function—it proved the need for a second family car.

Other changes in the social structure of the fifties also pinpointed that need. It is well known that American church membership reached its peak during the fifties. It was been less noted that membership in everything else skyrocketed as well. Girl

Scouts, Boy Scouts, Cub Scouts, Little League baseball, American Legion, Veterans of Foreign Wars, Masonic groups—all grew. The organizations that commanded the most time and energy from their membership did the best. All of them reached out for ever younger members, and mothers became chauffeurs.

With the baby boom, pediatrics caught on. The sick child was driven to the office for the new wonder drug penicillin. Then there were music lessons, dance and baton-twirling lessons, plus the parenting organizations of school and church, with their weekend family get-togethers and camp-outs. In an ultimate effort at organization, there was the "family council" for making democratic choices in the home. It took a lot of time to discuss allowances, chores, and maternal frustration with the food budget. Fathers rarely found time to attend a second meeting, and mothers took grim reports of failure back to the Child Study Club.

Some women had more options, but no more time. Improved washers, then driers, supposedly saved many hours per week. So where did the new time go? It was absorbed into increasingly complex routines and skills. There was more clothing to be washed as upscale diversification set in: sportswear; "coffee coats" replacing housedresses; not just bathing suits, but "beach cover-ups"; sharper differentiations in childrens' clothing; and the introduction of the whole range of separate "teenage" styles. The net result was that the traditional Monday wash day ended up being spread through the entire week.

Women's magazines sponsored an endless variety of needlecrafts and recipes. In all of this there were distinct social gradations. Nancy Williams, the governor's lady, did fine needlepoint work; many other women knitted and sewed. Possibly at the bottom of the social and aesthetic heap was the conversion of plastic bleach bottles to sequin-covered containers for the toilet brush.

On top of it all was added television. "We are destroying childhood—the only time left in our world for imagination and reflection," said a perceptive social worker.

Women were everywhere discouraged from working outside the home, except in minor part-time jobs, assumed to be temporary. A report from a young wife and mother of the fifties who did not think of work as temporary is included here in our interview with Benita Mullins. A peace activist then, as she is today,

436

Benita Mullins represents one of the many crosscurrents in the world of the fifties, when the norm was conformity. An interview with her is included for its insights into the world of the women who did work.

Other changes came about through the rising strength of labor unions. Their growing political strength was shown first by the UAW. There were also changes in the scope of labor's interests. The UAW reflected the family orientation of the fifties with a new excitement about health, recreation, child welfare, and schools. This shift in emphasis began with a few determined women. The role of certain UAW wives and women staff members has never received enough credit. The thinking and drive of May Wolf Reuther, for one, was minimized by her husband Walter's notable role.

A meaningful accomplishment in which labor and parents of the general community joined was the Serve Our Schools Committee. Their joint efforts rescued a moribund school system. We include an early program and membership leaflet of the Serve Our Schools Committee.

Liberal reformers were gradually drawn into concern for civil rights. The most profound contradiction of the good life of the fifties lay in the life of the black community. Nowhere was trouble more sharply revealed than in the nature of the Detroit Police Department in its dealings with blacks. This real world of false arrest and midnight beatings was largely avoided by white Detroiters. It was easy to neither know or understand.

The section "White Police in Black Communities" consists of a factual report by the Detroit chapter of the NAACP in 1956. The survey points the way to the years just ahead when a mayor (Jerome Cavanagh) would be elected principally on his promise to combat police brutality.

To capture the dark side of the conformity that came to represent the decade, we must realize that in Detroit the fifties began in 1949.

A major turning point in Detroit history came with the election of Albert Cobo over George Edwards for mayor. Cobo's victory in the primary came as a surprise to many area politicos and opinion-makers, since Edwards had been the high vote-getter for the council in the previous election and was serving as council president. Both the *Free Press* and the *News* favored

Cobo in the primary, the *News* more actively. When Cobo won the primary the *News* took a more aggressive stance in his favor. The editors assigned one of their top reporters, a man who personally liked and respected Edwards, to write an article stressing the location of black precincts that had voted overwhelmingly for Edwards. It was widely believed that the article had an impact in switching blue-collar worker votes to Cobo in the final election. Few noticed the disappearance of the incumbent mayor, Eugene van Antwerp, in the primary. Probably a critical error of van Antwerp's had been favoring the creation of a dozen public housing sites in the city's outlying areas. This raised the possibility that the city's blacks might have a fair choice in housing location.

Included in the campaign literature prepared for Edwards in 1949 and distributed by COPE (Committee of Political Education), the political action arm of the UAW, was a flyer summarizing the differences in outlook between Edwards and Cobo. It is reproduced here, and it sets out clearly several strong directional choices to be made by citizens.

At the same primary election, the voters agreed to create a Loyalty Commission to investigate the presumed dangerous and Communist ideas of city employees. The body operated for many years, providing a few jobs at taxpayers' expense but failing to uncover any Communists. It did, of course, serve as a constant threat to free expression of opinion.

Liberal groups and individuals who made it through the fifties were hurt by the remnants of divisive factionalism that had split the UAW in the late forties, as much or more than they were by the forays into Detroit of outside investigators, such as HUAC, the House UnAmerican Activities Committee. Few "left-wingers" remained in the UAW hierarchy, and the UAW was still the power source of social and political movements in Detroit and the surrounding area. The controlling Reuther group still included many Socialists and former Socialists. Only its opposition on the left could possibly refer to it as "right-wing," yet the factions were unforgiving. Liberals fell into sad, laughable descriptions of themselves and their fellows as "non-Communist, but not *anti-*Communist," "a non-red-baiting authentic Socialist," or "an Addes fellow-traveler—how un-American can you get?" These varied definitions covered lost friendships and much personal pain. Distrust was contagious and not reached by the new anti-biotics. Both sides added considerably to the distortions of labor history for which younger generations would pay in false perceptions of unionism.

On the surface, labor in Michigan was never healthier than in the fifties. Noticeable political gains were made by workers to accompany the economic ones. Union political leadership became more sophisticated after 1949. No longer did labor's top leaders run for elective office themselves. The days of the forties when several members of the UAW Executive Board ran for city council or mayor—and lost—were gone. Like the leaders of industry, these men were now too busy. New methods worked better anyway. Rank and file union members ran for precinct delegates in the Democratic party, rang doorbells, and passed out literature in their neighborhoods—a "worked precinct" was said to increase its margin of victory by an average of thirty percent. Men and women who might have no direct connection with the labor movement but who did have the skills and background needed for a particular elective office were sought out and put on labor-endorsed slates that carried with them an almost certain victory.

Unions had no monopoly on organizational skills. The campaigns of Congresswoman Martha Griffiths made the most of women staying at home. A house trailer took the candidate through far northwest neighborhoods each weekday. Women volunteers, often in yellow skirts embellished with "Martha" in green stitchery, rang doorbells and begged the housewife to drop her duties for "just a few minutes" to come out to meet Mrs. Griffiths. Fresh coffee, tea, or lemonade and homemade cookies helped to establish rapport with the direct-speaking candidate.

Griffiths served Michigan and her country well. She was the first woman to serve on the House Ways and Means Committee and the author of much substantive legislation.[1] At this moment she continues to speak her mind as Michigan's lieutenant governor.

Labor continued to extend its scope of operation into such fresh areas as recreation, education, and housing, from desegregated bowling leagues to school board elections.[2]

In addition to much lobbying for low- and middle-income housing and better landlord and tenant relations, labor found time to assist with two specific cooperative housing developments. There was the small Schoolcraft Gardens Cooperative, which failed, and the giant Gratiot Redevelopment Project, which did not. In the latter case labor stepped in after years of inaction by the city administration had left a large tract of downtown land unused. A coalition was formed between business and labor that at last got the project in operation.

I include documents relating to both Schoolcraft Gardens and Gratiot Redevelopment, as well as Harold Norris's significant statement on the important failure of the Cobo administration to deal with the problem of finding homes for the previous dwellers in the downtown area.

Although I have attempted to show that in the perception of many Detroiters the fifties were more tiring than terrible, there *were* witch hunts. If the Loyalty Investigating Commission was unsuccessful in its efforts to locate and fire any dangerous subversive among city employees, the Detroit Board of Education did remove—and later rehire—one teacher. She was also compelled to go through a rather absurd session of questioning by the Dies Committee when it visited Detroit in 1951. So, too, was a young dry cleaner whose previous job as a union organizer had come to an end when the State County and Municipal Workers were expelled from the CIO for alleged Communism. Coleman A. Young refused to reveal membership lists of the local chapter of the National Negro Congress to the House UnAmerican Activities Committee. It did not hurt him several years later in his election to the state senate, and certainly not in his subsequent election as mayor of the city of Detroit.

Although New York was the venue rather than Detroit, George Crockett also stood firmly on the Fifth Amendment in defending clients accused of conspiracy against the United States. Again, there were some years of semi-obscurity, but after a distinguished career as judge in the local courts, Crockett is now congressman of the Thirteenth District, and represents Detroit's most inner inner city.[3]

There are other examples: "Edie" Van Horne, an effective union steward at Dodge Main, was run out of the factory one day by a group of men who accused her of Communism. She was promptly welcomed back—with flowers—by the rest of her fellow workers.

Editor's Notes

1. Besides sponsoring the original proposed Equal Rights Amendment, Griffiths until her retirement from Congress was a major figure in exposing cost overruns and other absurdities in military spending.
2. Desegregated bowling was won over the protests of a chain of community newspapers who hinted at orgies at which white women would be "forced to have Negro male bowling partners."
3. Like Coleman Young, George Crockett lost some employment due to labor union struggles. He had served with Maurice Sugar as an attorney for the UAW before Reuther's presidency. It would seem that the right to choose counsel would be a prerogative of a new executive, but the bitterness of the times did not permit Crockett's friends and associates to see the matter in that light.

1. Women Workers in the Fifties: Interview with Benita Mullins

Wilma Wood Henrickson

At the war's end the country expected women to return home from their jobs, and many did. However, many women still had to work, and wanted the better pay that had come with the war years.[1] Benita Mullins, who worked at the now-closed Dodge Main automotive plant in Hamtramck during the late forties and early fifties, recalled this and other working experiences of the period during a March, 1988, interview.

[Let's talk about] Dodge Main. This was during the late forties—early fifties?

It was soon after World War II—the late forties. I was hired into the trim shop, and had several different jobs there. I remember one was on the paste line; I think that was the first one— where the seats are made and there's a carousel goes around. Marianna [a friend of Mullins and a fellow Socialist in those years] was working there then as a tack spitter. It was all women who were doing that paste job and all the tack spitters except Marianna were men. I think it's the tacky little jobs, it's the sticky little jobs, more detailed work, that they would want to have all women doing the job.

Benita Mullins, interview with Wilma Wood Henrickson, March, 1988.

442

On the paste line we had a bucket like a paint bucket and a brush like a paint brush. We worked on a car seat as it came by us on the carousel. We put a paste on the iron frame of the seat and then we had pieces of felt that we put on the back of the frame—that came before the upholstery was put on.

What did they pay an hour back then? I know that earlier, during the war itself, the standard rate was $1.03 an hour for practically every job in town.

At some point there—I guess it was when I had gone through the ninety-day probationary period—I know that it was a great day when I was taking home fifty dollars a week. That would be about $1.25 an hour or a little more than that, by the time you figured out the deductions, but I took home fifty dollars.

You told me a little bit the other day about maternity leave, and I gathered that the company didn't really enjoy [giving] maternity leave, and didn't feel much inclined to go along with it.

No, they expected women to take their leave by three months. I did get a letter from my doctor that was worded in such a way that it didn't say exactly when I had to leave so that I could stay as long as I felt okay. Since it was my first pregnancy and I was still very slender, I was able to go on working until really my sixth month. . . . The last several months I was working in a section—this was afternoons, the afternoon shift—in a section where the women made the arm rests and the headlining. I was on a sewing machine making the armrests for a while, and then when it was getting nearer the time—I was farther along—and I don't know whether she [the floor lady] knew that I was pregnant or not, but she probably did—she put me on the headlining. The headlining was on a very wide belt. The ceiling of the inside of the car is what the headlining is. It was felt with channels sewn into it and into those channels long rods are put, different ones in different channels. There were about six in each—four anyway, and maybe six, depending on the length of the car. They are sewn in each piece, in each single headlining. So you have to pick up these rods and get them in there. According to how many women there were working on it you might have to cover more.

Changing shifts at Dodge Main, Hamtramck, c. 1950. (From UAW International. Used with permission of Reuther Archives.)

Did you have to lift these rods over your head or waist-high or what?

Oh, yeah. The table was up above your waist and you had to lift them above the table. The thing was that you'd be eight hours working, lifting these long rods way above your waist.

How did the rods come to you? Were they on a belt line?

No. They were in stacks, in some sort of bin. I don't remember whether they were on the floor. You have to lift them and slide them in and get the beginning of the rod into this little channel and maybe the smallest ones would be the size of your little finger and the other ones like your other fingers, because they were different thicknesses—and slide them all the way in. . . .

Do you know what sort of metal these rods were?

Oh, iron and steel; in those days they weren't using any light metals.

Well, after Rachel was born I was still nursing her and I had a four month leave of absence. When I was ready to come back, the company doctor was giving a physical to see what condition I was in—if I was okay to be rehired. She was using the stethoscope and so on, and when she came to the part where she's sitting in front of me and I'm standing, she says, "So you're still nursing the baby?" Then she says, "Are you pregnant?" and at the same time when she says the word "pregnant," she takes her fist and whams it right into where there would be a baby if I *were* pregnant, before I could say yes or no. I thought this was a pretty horrible thing to do to anybody who might be pregnant. I hadn't even said "yes" or I hadn't even said "no" before she did that.

It was terrible. It sort of confirms your feeling that the company didn't want the women to have maternity leave.

There must have been a lot of pressure on her as a doctor to keep the women's work force within certain bounds. Her reason for not giving me permission to go back to work was that I was still nursing. So I never did go back.

After that I went to the unemployment office, and I guess there must not have been an opening, but later when I had finished nursing at six or seven months, I went back and they made me take a job and by then I *was* pregnant. . . . The early part of my pregnancy I was over at an automobile supply place. It was at Antoinette on Woodward.

Right then they were making plastic seat covers for Oldsmobiles. It was a seat cover that was only used from the time the car left the assembly line until it got to the new owner. It was to protect those beautiful seats until the new owner got them, so that maximizing the output was the main goal. They had a woman who had been working there seventeen years and she set the pace, and it was piecework, the only time I was on piecework.

The thing I remember about that [job] was that in the same building they were repairing cars on the first floor. They did something or others to cars—but a different crew. Where I was sitting at my sewing machine, the back of my chair was within two or three feet from where they were working on a car, and this was inside a building. The exhaust fumes, when they had the motor running, would be coming right on me and I did not like that at all—breathing these car fumes when I was pregnant. And I went to them and said, "This is a great big building, and can't you move that away?" And they said, "No, that's his work station and that's where he is."

Tell me about how you happened to want to work in the auto industry in the first place? I remember that you wanted to. I know that you didn't particularly want a war-related job during the war, and that you were working in the cooperative movement.[2]

That's right. Well, I had a feeling that I really wanted to know—I wanted to know all the different kinds of working situations, the situations that working people have, and I didn't work in the factory during the war. I worked at other jobs that had nothing to do with the war. I worked places like drugstores, bookshops, selling records, for a number of years. One time I had a job processing unemployment claims at MESC [Michigan Employment Service Commission] and MUCC [Michigan Unemployment Claims Commission].

After the war there were people needed for almost every automobile job in town. That was [because of] the postwar auto production. At the factories you got paid more than at the other places—bookstores, dime stores, selling records. As long as you felt young and healthy, it was a fun thing to do, but any time you weren't young and healthy, or had problems of your own, the forced pace, the exhaustion would all make a difference.

And the attitudes of the men in the union?

Well, there were several units where they had just women working—the job on the paste line where I started out—there was a man running it, and I do remember when we went out to lunch he would take the key and turn the line up. There was a key to the carousel and he would turn it up so it went faster. I thought that was a terrible thing to do. You had a half hour for lunch and you run out and get it and you run back in. That's the time you least feel like working faster than usual, but that's when he would turn it up.

Another [woman's job] was the wire room and only women worked in that place. In both cases there was a woman in charge of that unit, a floor lady. They were there because they were able to get the production out.

The women were accepted when Marianna first started working there during the war. . . . As the war ended the men didn't really want women working. They wanted more of their buddies there. But Dodge Main is in Hamtramck, and the Polish women had been working there for a long time, and you kind of had an ethnic community there. In the union the women were just a very small minority. The men controlled the union. It took a very unusual person to make progress in the union—like Edie van Horne.

During the Chrysler strike—I remember that the union was very glad to have people come in and help. I worked at the union hall for a while, processing requests for assistance, I think. They paid fifteen dollars a week, which was just about enough to pay my rent and get enough food to live on; but you did get a meal while you were working there in the union hall. In many ways women got equal treatment with the men when the war ended, but still certain kinds of jobs were reserved for women.

What were some of the things you hoped the union would accomplish for Detroit workers in general, and did it fail you in any way?

There really was never enough chance to improve working conditions. The Chrysler strike, that went on for more than a hundred days. The demands were always for the money conditions, the amount of money you made, and never for the working conditions. The pay scale was sort of a common denominator. There never was any chance to improve working conditions. The working people never had any control. Of course, all the fringe benefits did not exist at all in the forties or early fifties.

In union meetings there was less participation by women, but there were less women employed of the thousands of people employed. . . .

So that would automatically be a smaller minority?

And women who would attend union meetings, that was a minority too. They had less time to spend in the politicking that would go on in a union hall. They had to maintain the home even if they did work. That's where I first saw parliamentary procedure used as a way of gaining political power,—the uses and abuses of it. . . .

Editor's Notes

1. Of women's work in the auto plants at the war's end, Nancy Gabin, labor historian, says: "Despite efforts of the Fair Practices Department and the Women's Bureau [of the UAW] to challenge prejudice against women on the part of management and the union, there was rampant discrimination against women on the local union level. The discrimination took the form of local union toleration of inequitable hiring practices, layoffs of women workers, discriminatory pay scales and transfers by management. . . ." ("Women Workers and the UAW, 1945–1954," in *The Labor History Reader*, ed. Daniel J. Leab (Urbana: University of Illinois Press, 1985), 407–32.

2. Mullins was actively involved in the Socialist party and the union movement and was then, as she is today, a peace activist. This accounts for her not seeking work in war-related industries, but rather joining the automotive work force during the postwar auto boom.

2. Our Principles, Purpose and Program

Serve Our Schools Committee

In the postwar housing boom—and baby boom—all schools were overcrowded. Serve Our Schools was a coalition of religious, labor, and ethnic groups as well as a number of individuals representing only themselves and their children, formed to meet the pressures. Labor played an important role throughout the group's life, though never the dominant one sometimes attributed to it.

The political strength of the group made it possible to elect first board members, then a majority of the board of education. The board recruited as superintendent of schools Dr. Samuel Miller Brownell, former commissioner of education under President Eisenhower. A copy of the program and platform of Serve Our Schools follows.

Our Principles

To offer each child, each citizen, who goes to our schools the best chance for personal growth, for self-realization, and for a full, good life.

To prepare each child and citizen for a constructive life in the community, in the democratic American tradition.

"Our Principles, Purpose and Program," Serve Our Schools Committee, Mildred Jeffrey Collection, Box 17, folder 11, Reuther Library, Wayne State University.

Our Purpose

—To determine
the real needs of the public schools in Detroit.
—To secure
public understanding of those needs.
public support for a program to meet those needs.
—To find
good candidates for membership on the Board of Education.
—To work
for their election.
and at the same time
—To cooperate
with other groups in Detroit who want similar goals.
with the Board of Education, interpreting school problems to the public, and public views on education to the Board.

3. White Police in Black Communities

National Association for the Advancement of Colored People, Detroit Chapter

Thirty years after Forrester Washington's 1926 study of the Detroit Police Department, the Detroit branch of the NAACP found it necessary to study once again the matter of police brutality. The complaints studied occur in the terms of Mayors Cobo and Miriani.

The study is entitled, An Analysis of Police Brutality Complaints Reported to the Detroit Branch National Association for the Advancement of Colored People in the Period from January 1, 1956 to July 30, 1957.

In August of 1957 the Detroit Branch NAACP began an analysis of police brutality complaints which were reported to the Branch office in the period January 1, 1956 to July 30, 1957. The analysis covered a total of 103 cases and was completed in October, 1957.[1]

The principal objective of the NAACP in making this study was to illuminate some of the basic problems in the area of police-community relations and to find the common factors that might emerge. The results, it was felt, could be used in a further

National Association for the Advancement of Colored People, *An Analysis of Police Brutality Complaints Reported to the Detroit Branch National Association for the Advancement of Colored People in the Period from January 1, 1956 to July 30, 1957* (Detroit: National Association for the Advancement of Colored People, 1957).

effort to inform the public and the appropriate public officials on the extent of the problem of police brutality in the community and some of the factors contributing to it. Such information should also be helpful in bringing about some of the desired corrective measures in police methods and a better climate of goodwill between law enforcement officials and the community. . . .

Our records show that anywhere from 1 to 9 complaints are filed with the NAACP during the period of a month, with the largest number of complaints being recorded in July of each year. . . .

The most frequent type of police misconduct involved in these complaints is physical assault, followed by insulting epithets:

a) The common use of profanity and a reference to the complainant's race in a derogatory manner.

b) The indiscriminate searching of citizens' pockets and wallets on public streets.

c) When citizens question the violation of their rights the officers resort to physical assault, followed by arrest.

Rank order of the various types of police misconduct involved in these complaints.

Our reports show that out of 103 cases, 33 were physical assault, and 23 were cases of both physical and verbal assault. Our reports show 12 cases of insulting epithets used by arresting officers, and 12 cases of illegal search of home or car, and 4 cases of false arrest.

a) In 19 of these assault cases, victims were held without charge (usually overnight) and released. 3 were dismissed in court for lack of evidence.

b) Women were the victims of 18 of these assault cases.

c) One case involved a 16 year old boy.

d) Our files show an additional 8 cases of threats and intimidation on the part of police officers.

The central problem . . . seems to be the unprovoked attack by the police while questioning them. This, followed by false charges of "resisting arrest" has created distrust and bitter resentment of the police department on the part of the complainants.

Do the attitudes of the complainants toward the police reflect any common factors or prejudices of interest to this inquiry?

Our reports show that 90% of the complainants are working people without a previous record, who believe they are subjected

452

to unwarranted abuse because of their race. They feel that their freedom and well-being is in constant jeopardy since they are exposed to the sadist whims of race-baiting police officers. This is evident because of the similarity in the complaints where the officer is quoted as demanding that the complainant say "yes sir and no sir when answering a white man," or "I can see that you are one of those smart niggers."

Do the attitudes of policemen toward complainants reflect any common factors or prejudices of interest to this inquiry?

Our reports show a total disregard, on the part of the policemen, for the complainant's rights as a citizen in every case recorded. Example:

1) Searching of citizens in public streets for minor traffic violations.

2) Physical assault.

3) The common use of racial slurs.

4) The common practice of assault and arrest of those friends or relatives who attempt to intervene on behalf of the person being attacked by the police.

5) Abuse of complainants in police precincts.

6) The search and destruction of property, without a warrant, in citizen's homes.

7) The use of profanity in the presence of women.

8) The prevalent indication that the complainant has no rights that he (the police officer) has to respect.

9) The intimidation and abuse of interracial couples, while expressing their opposition to mixed personal associations.

10) Assumption that complainants are guilty of some crime, if not, they should be, without any evidence.

11) Hostile references to the NAACP in an effort to intimidate complainants.

12) The indiscriminate and common practice of stopping women on the street and accusing them of prostitution or of writing numbers.

Do the complaints show that any particular police precinct stations are involved more often than others?

Our records show that out of 98 complaints, 23 were made against officers from the Woodward Station; 15 against officers from the Vernor Station; 13 against officers from the Petoskey Station and 12 against officers from the Hunt Street Station. This shows a total of 63 complaints against the officers of these four precincts, which is 64% of the complaints of the entire 15 precincts.

What conclusions can be drawn from the Branch records regarding the official attitude of the police department to the complaints reported by the NAACP?

The most significant official attitude of the police department is the reluctance to take stern disciplinary measures in dealing with officers who have exceeded their authority.

1) The attempt, by the Department, to defend the behavior of police officers even when there is reasonable doubt of their innocence.

2) The failure of the Department to curtail the practice of strong-arm methods in making arrests.

3) The failure to replace those officers who bully underprivileged and unpopular elements of the community; who think their badge gives them authority to judge and punish a suspect, and who do not hesitate to enforce not only the "law" but their own prejudices as well.

4) Criticism of the NAACP and other community leadership, by the Department, for not being "cooperative" when they point out existing police brutality, and the danger of this practice if it is not corrected. An example of this is the statement made by the Police Commissioner in defense of police officers who were unduly violent in dispersing a crowd of people who had gathered on the street to hear a group of speakers from the Muhammad Temple. In a statement to the press the commissioner said: "The officers are to be highly commended for their alertness and patience in preventing what might have been a much more serious incident. A minimum of force was used and only the perpetrators were apprehended. The assembly was not only unlawful, but constituted a breach of the peace."

This statement was made after receiving a protest from Arthur L. Johnson, Executive Secretary of the Detroit Branch NAACP, who arrived on the scene along with Congressman Charles C. Diggs, Jr., a few minutes after it began. Another example of the official attitude of the police department was the failure to acknowledge a complaint where the complainant, a Mr. Marvin Petit of 3529 Nottingham, reported that an officer requested his signature on a petition for Mayor Orville Hubbard [of Dearborn] on the basis that Mayor Hubbard "is against Colored People." Despite the fact that a letter urging that this matter be looked into and the offending Officer be dealt with accordingly, no disposition of this case was reported to the Branch.

[The report then details the methods used by the branch to follow up on complaints and gain cooperation from the department by letter writing and requests for reports. As shown in the following, these efforts had little success.]

What are the weak points as indicated by the records in Branch approach to the police-community relations problem?

The weak points indicated by the records are:

1) The lack of an opportunity to examine the claims of both sides in complaints made to the police department, including:

    a) The record of police officers accused by the complainants.

    b) The number of complaints made by Negro citizens against these officers.

    c) The number of complaints made by white citizens against these officers.

    d) The common reasons for arrest of the complainants by these officers?

    e) The common reasons for arrest of white persons by these officers?

In summarizing . . . the victims of these assaults, for the most part, are working people without any previous police record. The records also show that the complainants live in various sections of the city rather than in supposedly "crime" areas! This seems to suggest that the manhandling and 3rd degree methods revealed in these cases [are] unnecessary and reflect the need for a thorough and impartial investigation of police methods in this city, if the Department is to have the confidence and respect of law-abiding citizens. . . .

The following suggestions might help to establish good police-community relations:

1) Increase the number of Negro policemen at all levels in one department by a completely "open" hiring policy.

2) Integrate the police. (mixed details)

3) Conduct human relations programs in neighborhoods surrounding each precinct. This program should place special em-

phasis on courtesy by the police and respect for the police by the citizen.

4) Organizing of a representative interracial citizens group to make a survey of the police department and recommend improvements based on their findings. This survey should be as much in the interest of favorable working conditions for the police as in the civil rights of the citizens. This group should publicize the achievements of the police department in an effort to establish pride in their work and at the same time build respect for intelligent law enforcement.

5) Investigation of police brutality complaints by an independent representative committee, so as to avoid the hazards and pitfalls of the Department investigating itself—an inherently wrong procedure.

Editor's Note

1. I was given a copy of this report at the time of its issue by Charles Wartman, then editor of the *Michigan Chronicle*. As a white "liberal," I am still grateful to him for an embarrassing encounter with reality.

4. The Cobo-Edwards Choice

Wayne County Democratic Political Action Committee

This ad and similar campaign material was sharply criticized by Edwards's opponents for injecting party politics into a "nonpartisan" election. In retrospect, it provided a rather accurate assessment of the issues of the day.

YOU Decide Who Ought to be Mayor
Then Vote Next Tuesday

EDWARDS is for lower taxes on homes—higher taxes on downtown office buildings.

REPUBLICAN COBO is for higher taxes on houses and for lowering the tax "burden" of corporations and owners of downtown property.

EDWARDS will use federal funds for a slum clearance and housing program already OK'd by the federal government.

REPUBLICAN COBO is for a private real estate deal to provide profits to private real estate companies. (Cobo is a real estate man himself—Cobo Realty Co.)

EDWARDS would reorganize the DSR to serve the people and make downtown business pay its share of the costs through taxes.

Wayne County Democratic Political Action Committee (1949), Mildred Jeffrey Collection, Box 9, folder 9, Reuther Library, Wayne State University.

457

REPUBLICAN COBO plans curtailed DSR service—higher fares "if necessary."

EDWARDS would fire police boss "Headline Harry" Toy.

REPUBLICAN COBO would "conduct a survey" of the police department.

EDWARDS has a plan under way for more playfields and public swimming pools for your kids. A playground within leg reach of every child.

REPUBLICAN COBO'S main support comes from Ohio, California and Grosse Pointe. Why should he want more playfields in Detroit? There is no profit in playfields.

EDWARDS is for development of a City-operated Detroit River Front (as in Chicago and Milwaukee) to beautify the city and use profit from the commercial property to reduce taxes.

REPUBLICAN COBO is for turning the river front over to private real estate owners for private profit.

EDWARDS comes from the ranks of labor.

REPUBLICAN COBO comes from an anti-union open shop company—Burroughs Adding Machine.

EDWARDS is against the payroll tax. Fair assessment and taxing of big real estate holdings would pay for his city improvement plan.

REPUBLICAN COBO is backed by those who would raise taxes the "easy way" by direct deductions from your pay— the payroll tax.

EDWARDS is supported by the people of Detroit—the home-owners, the small business men, THE PEOPLE WHO LIVE AND WORK IN DETROIT. Edwards has 8 years experience in the Detroit Common Council, 4 years as Council President.

THE REPUBLICAN candidate represents owners of downtown office buildings, the real estate interests, the automobile manufacturers, the Republican newspapers—the gang that fought against the interests of Detroit workers year after year. THE PEOPLE WHO LIVE OFF OF DETROIT BUT NOT IN IT.

Don't let the newspapers tell you how to vote—

MAKE UP YOUR OWN MIND—AND VOTE NOV. 8

5.   History of Schoolcraft Gardens

Schoolcraft Gardens Cooperative Association

In July 1950, the cooperative dissolved. A press release prepared at the request of some church leaders who urged clarification for their parishioners actually was a last-ditch effort to build the homes. It records the months of disaster that followed the euphoria of 1947–48, when everyone from Governor Mennen Williams on down had seemed enthusiastic.

Date: March 7, 1950

Schoolcraft Gardens Housing Cooperative is a non-profit corporation organized to provide its members with adequate-sized, well built homes at the lowest possible cost. It was started three years ago when a small group of families bought a 70-acre tract of land at the northwest corner of Schoolcraft and Lamphere and started making plans for a neighborhood of 400 to 500 homes, complete with playgrounds, shopping center and community facilities.

The site bought for the development was one of some twenty vacant tracts later studied by a Committee of the Common Council for possible development with rental-type or multiple housing

Schoolcraft Gardens Cooperative Association, "Statement on Schoolcraft Gardens Co-operative Prepared for the Presbytery and Presbyterial of Detroit," Halbeisen Collection, Reuther Archives, Wayne State University.

(row houses or apartments). The Committee, which consisted of Councilmen Oakman, Rogell and McNamara, recommended the site for re-zoning from R-1 (single free-standing houses).

Nothing further happened on the matter, until, shortly after an article appeared in the *Michigan Worker* indicating the "bi-racial" character of the group, the Tel-Craft Association [a neighborhood group of homeowners south of Schoolcraft at Telegraph Road] on December 13, 1949 petitioned the Common Council for a hearing to change the zoning of the site back to R-1, charging that there had been irregularity in the zoning procedure in 1947. The matter was referred to the City Planning Commission, which held a hearing and unanimously voted to deny the petition. The Commission's recommendation was given to the Common Council, which on December 29, 1949 voted unanimously to deny the petition, Messrs. Kronk, Garlick, Miriani, Edgecomb [former housing director, by then on the council] and Smith voting.

On December 22, 1949 and each week thereafter, a series of inflammatory articles appeared in the *Redford Record* and Floyd McGriff's other newspapers in which various appeals to racial prejudice were made under such banner headlines as "Cooperatives Seeking Conflict? Move to Bring Racial Housing into Area. Will Start with 500 Units for Unrestricted Tenancy" (December 22); "Socialists Force Multiple Housing Clash. More Details on Plan to Build Biracial Flats Here" (December 29); "Tel-Craft Group Demands Hearing on Multiple Flats" (January 5); "Bi-Racial Group Seeks Tax-Payer's Cash" (January 19).[1]

With the approval of Council President Miriani, the Tel-Craft Association secured another hearing before Common Council on January 18, 1950. . . .

At about this time the Council began to be flooded with printed post cards and letters urging the re-zoning of the land. It has been said that as many as 7,000 pieces of mail were received by each Councilman. In spite of this, members of the Cooperative were repeatedly assured by at least six members of Council that they would support the Cooperative. As a three-quarters majority (seven votes) is needed to re-zone property over the owner's protests, it did not appear as if the campaign would be successful.

Meanwhile, the Cooperative had been perfecting its building plans and completing its membership lists for the first group of fifty-four homes to be built. In order to secure a building permit, it has submitted to the Common Council a site plan calling for acceptance by the City of dedication of land for streets. . . . Although normally a routine matter, the motion to approve the site plan was on February 8, 1950 recommitted to the Council's Committee of the Whole, Councilmen Garlick, Kronk, Oakman, Rogell, and Smith voting to recommit while Councilmen Beck, Connor, Jeffries and Miriani voted no.

At the same meeting, Councilman Kronk introduced a resolution to re-zone the site back to R-1 and a public hearing was set for March 10th. . . .

The issue here is plain: Shall a group of Detroit citizens be deprived, by improper use of the zoning ordinance, of their legal rights to use their property, when the admitted real reason for the opposition to the development is the fact that the group, in accordance with the laws of the land, refuses to bar from membership an otherwise qualified family solely for reasons of race, color, creed, or national origin? Will the responsible elected officials of the City Government bow to the demands of a small group of bigoted citizens who have stooped to a campaign of lies, misrepresentation and appeals to religious and racial prejudice in their determination to keep other citizens from building their homes on land they own, and according to a plan which meets every legal requirement?[2]

Editor's Notes

1. Floyd McGriff was the flamboyant, Hearst-trained editor of a chain of widely read community newspapers that were the bane of Detroit liberals for years. McGriff had been in Paris during the latter part of World War I and had been the original bureau chief of what eventually became United Press International. Detroit's outer fringes must have seemed dull in contrast. Certainly McGriff did his best to add the spice of excitement to local politics.

    It was, in fact, the *Brightmoor Journal,* serving the community adjacent to the cooperative, that had first followed the *CIO News* with its own form of investigative reporting. One of the Fall, 1949, stories suggested that the cooperative site had been deliberately chosen because it was on the route to the new race track in Livonia. "Race mixing," sex, and gambling were injected as items to be

461

feared. The young cooperative members were slow to discover the existence of the *Brightmoor Journal*, however. McGriff's *Redford Record*, serving a middle-class neighborhood, was more widely known. Many of the cooperative members did not understand blue-collar Brightmoor; they assumed that since it was a neighborhood of unionized workers, they would follow union policies of racial equality. Those who had themselves been labor organizers knew better. Sophie Reuther and Mildred Jeffrey, for instance, expected no miracles of instant understanding.

2. The public appeal to churches and other liberal organizations for help staved off disaster for a few weeks. On March 15 a majority of those present at a council meeting supported the Cooperative's multiple zoning label; on March 17 Mayor Cobo vetoed it. Among the shifting supporters, there were no longer enough votes to override a veto.

6.   History of Lafayette Park

Robert J. Mowitz and
Deil S. Wright

> It would never have happened without Walter Reuther. Lafayette Park would still be under rocks and weeds without him. People forget that the land lay there a wasteland and a dump for six years after Cobo was elected . . . until we got CRDC [Citizens' Redevelopment Corporation] going, and Walter started pushing people to get together and get it done. . . .
>
> His leadership was also responsible for putting to rest an all-too-prevalent idea that this land was to become a "containment area" for the Negro people. At the time this concept was promoted by both the city Administration and the Private-Builder-Real Estate community.
>
> —*James W. Bell, coordinator for CRDC*
> *(Oral interview, August, 1987)*

During and following World War II, the city of Detroit was beset by a number of problems that stemmed in part from the prewar depression and in part from wartime conditions. The depression had brought the construction of private dwellings to a virtual standstill, and the wartime influx of workers plus an increase in the number of births created a serious housing shortage. The results followed the pattern familiar in American urban centers: a high concentration of low-income families in the older residential setions near the entral business district of the core city. At the same time, middle- and upper-income families had begun the exodus to the suburbs as fast as available housing would permit. The "Detroit Plan" was designed to deal with these two conditions, urban slum and suburban flight.

The Detroit Plan was made public on November 18, 1946, by Mayor Edward J. Jeffries, Jr. The substance of his proposal was that the city acquire approximately one hundred acres of land a few blocks northeast of the central business district, . . . demolish the slum residences and other buildings, and prepare the land for resale to private developers for residential use. . . . The city would recapture its $2,000,000 investment through a net annual gain in tax revenue amounting to $134,200 from the same hundred acres once redevelopment had been accomplished. Thus, the argument went, the city would recover its investment in fifteen years. . . .

In February, 1947, condemnation proceedings were begun on the first ten of the site's forty-three blocks. . . . A taxpayer's suit was filed in November, . . . and halted further action until the legality of the condemnation was clarified by the court. Land acquisition for slum clearance and eventual resale to a private developer was an innovation. . . . In October of 1948 . . . the Michigan Supreme Court handed down a decision upholding the right of the city to proceed with condemnation. . . .

[The 1949 election of Mayor Cobo intervened, creating vital shifts in housing policy.] Late in 1951, labor leaders were convinced that Mayor Cobo and his new housing director, former builder and real-estate developer Harry J. Durbin, were involved in a plan to turn over the Gratiot site to private developers eager to exploit the land as soon as it became available. It was feared that this pattern would be followed in the future to the detriment of public housing projects. The mayor's opposition to public housing was no secret and had been an issue in his successful election campaign. Soon after he took office in January, 1950, not only was a new housing director [Durbin] named, but also three new commissioners were appointed by the mayor to the five-man Housing Commission.[1] During the previous year the Housing Commission had submitted a plan to the Detroit Common Council for public housing on twelve new sites, eight of which were vacant land. Before 1950 was over, the "Cobo Commission" had recommended that the council abandon the eight vacant sites and two of the slum sites from further consideration. The council obligingly complied, leaving only two slum sites. . . .

It had taken almost five years to acquire 129 acres, but in the process clear legal precedents had been established which would facilitate further projects. . . . The long-pending federal legislation finally emerged from Congress as the Housing Act of 1949 and was signed by President Harry S. Truman on July 15, 1949. . . .

The election of Mayor Cobo in the fall of 1949 had a direct bearing upon the future of urban redevelopment in the city. . . . It meant that public housing programs were to be deemphasized and that slum clearance leading to private development of cleared land would receive the major emphasis. . . .

The deletion of the vacant sites for public housing, all of which were located in the outlying areas of the city, meant that low-income families would continue to be concentrated in the city's core area, and the elimination of the projects slated for slum sites meant that public housing would not be used as a vehicle for slum clearance. Thus, these decisions meant that projects such as Gratiot would have to bear the brunt of urban redevelopment to accommodate low-income families. . . . The two conditions that were to prove most demanding to city officials were the requirement that a local development plan be prepared that would require local approval, meet federal standards, and at the same time [be] attractive to private capital, and the requirement that adequate provision be made for the relocation of families displaced through the demolition. . . .[2]

That the Gratiot site should be redeveloped for residential use was never seriously questioned. The persistent question was, For whom?. . .

Mayor Cobo had his own ideas about how the site should be developed, and he was quick to voice them after learning of the commission's decision. The mayor immediately met with the commission and expressed his disapproval of their failure to include single-residence units in the plan. The builders reacted to this suggestion by arguing that the site was too small to permit inclusion of single residences. For that matter, they felt that the

465

present plan calling for practically all row housing on small lots was a waste of land. . . .

With the beginning of demolition and relocation in the fall of 1950, Negro housing problems had to be faced. Was the Gratiot site to be redeveloped for the former residents who could not qualify for public housing [mainly those with incomes above the poverty level]? All available evidence up to the end of 1950 indicated that providing housing for former Gratiot residents was a major goal of the project. This goal was clearly stated in the informational letter sent to families to be relocated. If facilities were to be built for this clientele, density standards had to be relatively high in order to make the building of low-rent units a profitable investment. Many of the local builders and real-estate men believed that low-cost housing, or at least Negro housing, was the only possible residential use for the site. They felt that since the site was almost completely surrounded by slum housing occupied by Negroes, only Negroes would live in the area, regardless of the type or quality of housing construction. Thus construction had to be for the Negro market, which was predominantly low-income. These businessmen felt that site planning had to recognize these circumstances in setting density and other restrictions in order to attract private investment.

The professional planners on the Plan Commission staff recognized the goal of rehousing former residents, but they wanted to accomplish this in a way which would maintain "good planning" standards. These standards seem to defy explicit articulation, but they include population-density criteria as well as engineering and aesthetic considerations. The commission itself, which included by law an architect, civil engineer, structural engineer, real-estate dealer, builder, attorney, and physician, did not share all the professional planners' values, but they tended to defend them. . . .

[Plans were drawn and redrawn in the months ahead to satisfy Washington's concern as to relocations as well as the local divisions over land use and density, phrases that became inextricably tied in with housing for blacks. At last a compromise was reached that seemed to offer something for everybody, and much more park space. This plan was approved by Washington in April, 1952. "A little over two years," state the authors, "had been consumed in the planning and approval process."]

A prospectus was prepared, and the council approved the holding of an auction at 2:00 P.M., July 30, 1952 in the council chambers of City Hall. The auction came off on schedule. Some fifty builders and brokers appeared, but all sat in silence when the call came for bids. No bids were offered, and no property was sold.

Density standards were the main reason publicly cited for failure to offer bids. . . . Privately, doubt was expressed over the likelihood that middle-income whites would not move into the project area; therefore to be realistic, construction had to be for the Negro market. . . . None of the builders who were interviewed were optimistic about the chances of selling or renting to both Negroes and whites in the same area. . . .

[A second auction was scheduled for May 6, 1953. Compromises were tried. In December, 1952, the *Detroit News* claimed the "idealists" at the plan commission had given into the "realists" of the housing commission. Durbin this time tried to line up at least one bidder in advance of the auction. Not only was the New York-based company he contacted on hand to bid, but also a local group, headed by a builder of goodwill, Bert L. Smokler. The New York firm captured the bid, but both sides soon became disenchanted, and the agreement was revoked. The whole operation was once again on hold, and seemed doomed to remain there. In 1954 a market survey, paid for by the housing commission, was made of people employed in the downtown area, who were considered the best potential prospects. It brought the discouraging news that seventy-six percent of the whites surveyed did not want mixed occupancy. At about this time there arrived a "white knight," the Citizens Redevelopment Committee (later Corporation).]

The Citizens Redevelopment Corporation traces its origin to the spring of 1953, when, in anticipation of the second auction, a brochure was prepared by Walter J. Gesell, mortgage broker and consultant, entitled, "Constructive Housing Program for Detroit's Gratiot Redevelopment Area." The key person behind the brochure, however, was James W. Bell. Bell had become interested in urban redevelopment some time earlier when he served on the staff of the Plan Commission. Bell was not a professionally

467

trained planner. In fact, his formal education ended when he graduated from Cass Technical High School in 1932, but in addition to his job on the Plan Commission staff, his experience included work with a firm of architects and employment with one of Detroit's largest builders. The brochure prepared by Bell and Gesell, who was at the time a member of the Housing Commission, proposed that a non-profit corporation be formed for the purpose of acquiring and retaining control of the entire redevelopment area in order to "promote its redevelopment under highest standards of design and construction." The specific plan, illustrated with a map and photographs, called for a number of multi-story apartment buildings which would provide "high density without crowding the land." It was pointed out that high construction costs made cooperative ownership the best possible financing method.

The authors took their plan to Mayor Cobo, but he urged them to forget about it, since negotiations had cleared the way for a firm bid from the Housing Corporation of America. When this agreement fell through a year later, the time was ripe to revive the non-profit corporation plan. This time, instead of going to the mayor, Bell contacted *The Detroit News*, with the result that the plan . . . was a feature story in the Sunday, June 27, 1954 edition of the *News*. The next day the mayor and the council received a long telegram from Walter Reuther, president of the United Auto Workers. Reuther urged that action be taken to set up a citizen's committee to deal with the Gratiot project. "It is economically and morally wrong for an industrial community with the wealth and power and the know-how of Detroit to tolerate the social cess-pools of our slums, which breed crime and disease," he wrote. . . . Reuther backed his interest with an offer of $10,000 from the UAW to help finance the work of a citizen's committee. . . .

Mayor Cobo found himself in a difficult position. Any endorsement of a citizens' committee authorized to dispose of the Gratiot site was public acknowledgment of lack of confidence in his housing director, Durbin. . . . Added to this was the Cobo distaste for being pressured into anything, compounded by the fact that the pressure was being applied by Walter Reuther, for whom Cobo had little liking. Nevertheless, the Gratiot site was now being referred to in the press as "Ragweed Acres" and privately as "Cobo's Acres," so something had to be done.

468

On July 12, Housing Director Durbin recommended that the mayor and council jointly appoint a citizen's committee to study site layout, consider the creation of a non-profit corporation, and work out a redevelopment program for the Gratiot area as a whole, which would include the area to the east that had been designated for public housing and the area directly south that had been earmarked for an extension of the original project. The following day the council passed a resolution authorizing the mayor and president of the council to appoint jointly a Citizens Redevelopment Committee of twelve members. . . . the committee [was to] include one *ex officio* member of the city government to maintain liaison with the various governmental agencies. This post went to Harry Durbin, who was also made committee chairman. The four key citizen appointees were Gesell, Reuther, Walter Gehrke, chairman of the board, First Federal Saving and Loan Association of Detroit, and Foster K. Winter, vice-president, the J. L. Hudson Company. These four made up the executive committee. . . . James Bell was appointed full-time coordinator.

By September 13, the Citizens Redevelopment Committee. . . . reported that a working agreement had been reached with two Detroit architectural firms (Victor Gruen Associates and Leinweber, Yamasaki, and Hellmuth) along with the Philadelphia architect, Oskar Stonorov to prepare a comprehensive plan for the Gratiot area. The committee requested an additional ninety days . . . and asked that during this period the council refrain from selling "or otherwise disposing of said land". . . . The council granted the request.

[After publicly blaming the committee for delays, Durbin resigned his chairmanship. On December 20, 1954, the committee formally presented its plan, and in a report to the council said:]

> Our committee is convinced that a successful program—for now and in the future—is completely dependent upon the city obtaining an integrated residential community of the most advanced design, of the highest possible standards; a community that, on a completely competitive basis, can attract back to the heart of the city people who are finding their housing in the outlying sections of the city and its suburbs. Anything short of attaining that objective would be of dubious value from both an economic and social point of view. . . .

469

On April 6, 1955, the Citizens Redevelopment Corporation of Detroit was incorporated as a Michigan non-profit corporation, and James Bell was hired as its full-time coordinator. . . . The corporation soon decided that they would prefer to work with only a single developer for the whole site, if one could be found. The proposals made by Cities Redevelopment Inc., owned by Herbert S. Greenwald and Samuel N. Katzin . . . so impressed the trustees that early in November 1955 they decided that this firm would be the exclusive co-developer of the site, with Architect Luwig Mies van der Rohe as the chief designer of the redevelopment construction. . . .

When the Citizens Redevelopment Committee first took over the Gratiot project, it was intent on preventing the area from becoming a low-income ghetto. In its various pronouncements it stressed the need for what it called an "integrated" community with a range of income levels. The award-winning plan of the committee's architects [a casualty of the CRDC's decision to go with Greenwald and the plans of the eminent Mies van der Rohe] stressed low-cost housing, including public housing, integrated with more expensive housing. . . .

The area due east, the St. Aubin extension, had been earmarked for public housing since 1949. Some 3,800 units were planned for this area. This prospect now disturbed the committee's planners, for it would guarantee that one boundary of the Gratiot site would consist of a large, Negro public housing project. (It was taken for granted that the project would be Negro, since Negroes substantially outnumbered eligible white applicants for public housing, and since the area had been occupied by Negroes.) This large Negro housing project was considered a threat to the development of the desired integrated neighborhood, and the committee prevailed upon the council to reduce the number of authorized units for St. Aubin to about twelve hundred. By 1960, plans for a public housing project had been dropped. . . .

The first unit of Lafayette Park-University City [the name given the development by CRDC], a twenty-two story apartment building, began receiving tenants in the fall of 1958. . . . By early 1959, construction had begun on an expressway [the Chrysler] which would give the western side of the site a new and secure physical boundary. Just east of the expressway, the new buildings of the

Wayne State University Medical School and Lafayette Clinic (a research unit of the Michigan Department of Mental Health) gave the site an institutional tone, the reason for the "University City" part of the site's new name. Construction had also begun on ten two-story "Townhouse" apartments, and the developer had filed an FHA application for another twenty-two-story apartment and was preparing to apply for an FHA approved mortgage for three twenty-seven-story apartments. There was still a long way to go before the eighteen hundred to two thousand families contemplated for the area could move in, but the repopulation of the Gratiot site had begun. . . .

The role of James Bell, promoter of Citizens Redevelopment Committee, is worthy of special note. It is rather extraordinary for a private citizen to move in and take over control of a project from two major city agencies, the Housing and Plan Commissions, but Bell's excellent contacts at the operating level of the community decision-making system permitted him to literally play the role of coordinator. The interest of the department store executive, the mortgage consultant, and the banker in urban redevelopment was obvious, whereas labor's interest was less obvious. . . .

They welcomed the opportunity to aid in taking the initiative from Durbin and Cobo, in whom they had little confidence. Reuther was interested in the prospects of an integrated neighborhood which would include all income groups as well as racial groups. He felt that cooperative ownership arrangements would help achieve this. With the support of Reuther, combined with that of Winter, representing Detroit's largest department store, the J. L. Hudson Company, [now Dayton-Hudson, headquartered in Minneapolis], plus support from mortgage and banking circles through Gesell and Gehrke, Bell was able to put together a formidable combination, which, in fact, took over the Gratiot project.

There were other reasons for the Citizens Committee's success. Bell was careful to avoid stacking the committee with members who played the role of official ambassadors of various interests whenever citizens' committees were organized. The mayor's Detroit Tomorrow Committee, with over a hundred members, was filled with this kind of talent. Bell's committee was composed of decision-makers. . . . The original Detroit Plan was hopefully designed to cope with the problem of housing low-income families. Although racial attitudes conditioned the various plans for the Gratiot site, in the long run economic values prevailed. It proved economically impossible to obtain private development of housing for low-income families, regardless of their race. Even the "integrated" plan of the Citizens Committee had to give way to the development of units for middle- and upper-income families. There is no evidence that Negroes will find difficulty in obtaining units on the rebuilt site, if they can afford the rents; eight of the first two hundred tenants of Lafayette Park-University City were Negro.[3] But the problem of decent housing for the former residents remains unsolved.

Editor's Notes

1. Mayor Cobo, on taking office, appointed realtor Harry Durbin to head the housing commission and quickly replaced the highly respected commissioner, the Reverend Bradby. Both actions were certainly within the mayor's powers, but the replacement of the Reverend Bradby sent unexpected shock waves through the defeated liberal and black communities. Some who had welcomed Cobo's self-proclaimed businessman's approach to government suddenly realized the new mayor was playing for keeps. Years later, in Coleman Young's administration, a drive winding through Elmwood Park on the city's near east side was given the name Bradby Drive. It serves as a memorial to the man who had fought, not only against slum housing, but for integrated housing and equality of access to the city's most attractive land.

2. The effort to relocate families was perhaps the least successful of any part of the work as, Harold Norris indicates in a following section. The Mowitz account makes clear that once the decision to abandon outlying housing sites was made, the options of inner city residents disappeared.

3. Of the eight families mentioned, several were among those who once hoped to live in Schoolcraft Gardens. Eleanor Wolf and Mel Ravitz, Wayne State University sociologists, did studies of the first dwellers in Lafayette Park and those who were there three years later. [See Eleanor P. Wolf and Mel J. Ravitz, "Lafayette Park: New Residents in the Core City," *Journal of the American Institute of Planners* (August 1964): 234–39. On the whole, they found a singularly happy neighborhood, whose residents for the most part had deliberately

chosen to live in a community that had among its other qualities racial integration. For once, time had outrun many of the barriers created by prejudice.

Wolf and Ravitz prophesied that the weak spot of the area would be its schools, specifically at the middle school level. Lafayette Park remains one of the city's good neighborhoods, though the glamour of the "urban pioneers" has faded, but its children are usually enrolled in private schools, regardless of rising costs.

7.   Dislocation without Relocation

Harold Norris

Harold Norris, attorney, professor, and longtime activist in civil right causes, delivered a speech in the fifties that summarized the failure of the city to come to grips with the problem of relocating the people who lived in the Gratiot Redevelopment Area.

The Cobo Administration is proceeding to evict some 6000 people from the Gratiot-Orleans area. The ostensible purpose for this removal program is to clear the land and permit the private development of housing. Mayor Cobo states that some of the housing to be built will be available at rents that some of the displaced people can afford. We must remember that these 6000 people are being added to some 17,000 people being displaced by the expressways. We have seen very little done to assist the relocation of the people displaced by the expressways. If past is prologue, it can be reasonably predicted that very little will be done to assist the relocation of the 6000 people in the Gratiot-Orleans

Harold Norris,"Dislocation without Relocation, Excerpts from Talk Opposing Mayor Cobo's Urban Renewal Policy; to the Greater Detroit Public Housing Tenants Council, 1952," in *Some Reflections on Law, Lawyers, and the Bill of Rights: A Collection of Writings, 1944 to 1984* (Detroit: Michigan Law Book Society, 1983), 813–15.

area. What is really happening is that poor people, mostly Negro people, are being removed from what little housing they have. This really amounts to Negro removal, not urban renewal. . . .

I have been representing many of the evicted families in proceeding before the Wayne County Circuit Court Commissioners. This is the court with jurisdiction over landlord-tenant matters; this court is the forum for non-payment of rent and eviction cases. I have been able to get some additional time for many of those being evicted. We've held up the city's ill-designed plan for some months now. But the tragic and pervasive impact of this inhuman policy of what I call "dislocation without relocation" is overwhelming. Mothers testify in court, in response to my questioning, that faced with eviction and dislocation their families are being split up. "I've had to send my son to live with my sister in Alabama, and my daughter to my mother in Chicago. . . . I don't have any place to move to now. . . ."

I believe this policy of "dislocation without relocation" is terribly wrong and ought to be opposed, opposed vigorously. . . . it is a policy that is wrong, wrong legally, wrong pragmatically, and it is dangerous. There must be a price to pay down the line sometime in some way for something that is so wrong.

Dislocation without relocation is wrong legally. I submit that the Federal Housing Act of 1948 squarely places a duty upon the city to find accommodations for renters before evicting them. The city is just going through the motions of complying with this law. After our protests the city has established a store front office and placed one brand new lawyer in that office . . . to get some qualifying displaced renters into limited public housing. But this is no remedy for the great mass of displaced people. And most of this audience knows of all the income-determination problems associated with public housing. The city is just not making a good faith effort to comply with the relocation requirements of the Housing Act of 1948. The city's policy is plainly illegal.

Second,. . . [it] is clearly immoral. It places the prodigious burden of change in our city disproportionately upon the backs of those people least able to bear it. . . . What is really being done is kicking people out. The city is creating refugees. Mayor Cobo has been quoted as saying to those protesting these evictions. . . "we don't want them here." This crude, heartless, and inequitable policy is just plain wrong, just plain immoral.

Third, this policy of dislocation without relocation is pragmatically wrong. It simply won't work. The city will either meet the problem now with a plan, or meet a crisis later without a plan. . . . There will be a price to pay. For every choice there is a price. And for every bad choice there will be a bad price. Where are the 17,000 people displaced by the expressways to go without adequate assistance? Where are the 6000 people displaced by "urban renewal" in the Gratiot-Orleans area to go without adequate assistance? They must live, they must survive. They will split-up and double-up. They will find attics and basements. They will move in with others—relatives and friends. There will be increased density of use elsewhere. And any housing, no matter how good, will deteriorate with density of use. Hence, all that will be accomplished will be the transfer of one area of relatively poor housing to the making of another area of relatively poor housing. This is not slum clearance. This is slum creation. I do not want to be misunderstood. I do not disparage the people forced out. I am merely saying this, that no matter how good the housing, if you put a lot more people in that good housing than that housing can accommodate, the good housing becomes bad housing. The costs of maintenance go up and revenues are not proportionate. Needed repairs will not be made. Bad housing will breed other problems. There is the danger of unrest. The situation has the potential for strife and combustibility. Prediction is not desire. But danger can be predicted. There will be a price for this inhumane eviction policy.

In short, Mayor Cobo's policy of dislocation without relocation, of urban renewal, of what is factually Negro removal should be opposed and changed. That policy is illegal, immoral and dangerous. . . .

Part XIV

Camelot, Riot, and
Renaissance: The
Sixties and Seventies

Camelot, Riot, and Renaissance: The Sixties and Seventies

Detroit during the sixties seemed more open to revolution than it had been at any point since the depression. It is, on the whole, not surprising that the Black Manifesto, made famous at Riverside Church in New York, was first presented at the National Black Economic Development Conference held at Wayne State University some five months earlier, or that its details were worked out in sessions at St. Joseph's Episcopal Church.

For some time there had been unease in labor unions, symbolized in the UAW by the split between the rank and file membership and its salaried executives. The city's neighborhoods, too, were restless, especially within the inner three-mile circle of Grand Boulevard. There was talk of getting a grip on the "establishment," of having more to say about planning decisions, police actions, zoning. The phrase "Urban renewal means Negro removal," frequently used by the Reverend Albert Cleage, caught on. It serves as an indicator of the wide distrust of local government, even though these were supposed to be the Camelot years.

A wave of new acronyms began to spread around the town. There was WCO, the West Central Organization; GOAL, Group on Advanced Leadership; PAR, People against Racism; WRO, the Welfare Rights Organization. In the auto plants there were DRUM, the Dodge Revolutionary Movement, and ELDRUM, its chapter formed at the Mt. Elliot Avenue Dodge plant. Then there were the Black Panthers, with rhetoric, but also with a program. In 1970 a dozen young people affiliated with the Panthers barricaded themselves in a house on the near west side; a confrontation with the police brought about a charge of first-degree murder. On that day Councilman Mel Ravitz, among others, intervened to secure their safe-conduct out of the house. Months later when all the evidence came in, the murder charge was dismissed. If some of the police seemed somewhat trigger-happy in those years, it is no less true that revolt had become to them just a middle-class act. No doubt the police felt harassed when some of the nicest people in town, including many clergy, insisted on bringing a broken toilet seat to the office of the head of the Detroit Housing Commission as a demonstration of the ills of Hobart Street, a neighborhood taken over by the city.[1]

Some successes for citizens grew out of the turmoil. The Cavanagh programs were built around community demands: defense lawyers available to the poor,[2] consumer watch programs and nutrition agencies in housing projects, field trips in the schools, exploring the city's Cultural Center (often seen only by suburban students in the past).[3]

Government response to demands for radical reform eventually included a new city charter, the rebuilding of the general city hospital in the medical center, useful redefinition of some functions of county and metropolitan government, and the reorganization of city welfare services under the new state Department of Social Services, in the hope of delivering more efficient and more humane services. If the social service reorganization accomplished nothing else, it enabled the very poor to leave neighborhoods that had long disenchanted them for the cheapest of the green fields beyond the city limits. Sadly, during the years of demand for change there *was* a great deal of outward flight—both white and black—that served to diminish the gains that might have been made by a focused effort on reform.

One change that occurred and lasted was a general opening to African-Americans of jobs at every level of employment in government, and an authentic but more limited integration of the corporate world, stopping somewhat short of top management.

Revolutionary moods do end in time. Members of the League of Revolutionary Workers viewed some of their colleagues' absorption into middle-class jobs as a "sell-out," condemning even

480

those who took jobs with the new mayor, Coleman Young, in 1974.[4]

In this study of the sixties I have included B. J. Widick's "Mayor Cavanagh and the Limits of Reform," a chapter from his *Detroit: City of Race and Class Violence*. That selection ends in 1967, when the Camelot years ended sharply.

I continue with a statement of radical prophecy that I term "Eyewitness to Disaster," by the Reverend David Gracie, whose church east of the riot scene ministered to many black and white Detroiters in the area. He was healing and comforting, trying to prevent the spread of violence, but his statement here is a plea for understanding of the root causes of rebellion. This is followed by a section of a Pulitzer Prize-winning account, published in the *Detroit Free Press*, of the meaningless deaths of July, 1967.

Risking some repetition, I include a play-by-play account of three of those deaths, which startled the nation as well as the city. It has been my experience that many Detroiters, then and later, chose to block the deaths at the Algiers Motel from their minds. I thank John Hersey, author of *The Algiers Motel Incident*, for making it harder to forget, with "The Death Game" and "The Death Game Played Out."

The years after 1967 were noted for the politics of "participatory democracy" and still more efforts at radical reform. However, the federal funds of the Cavanagh years that had made possible the major experiments of the Model Cities program ended abruptly, with disillusionment for many Detroiters who had taken part.[5]

In May, 1970, came another major turning point when May and Walter Reuther died in a plane accident in northern Michigan. Some revolutionists, convinced that Reuther had lived beyond his time, felt little reason to mourn, but the courage and common sense he brought to both labor and civic problems have been missing from many crises ever since, and the loss cannot be adequately measured. The limitations and strengths of both May and Walter Reuther deserve the best of historical study.

Both participatory democracy and rebellion hit the schools in 1969–70. More than was generally realized at the time, student unrest was closely tied to some of the radical factions of the UAW. Unlike the demands of the mid and late sixties for higher standards (as at Northern High's "Freedom School"), the violence was directed at language laboratories, study carrels, and science equipment considered to be part of the white man's elitist learning systems. The enablers of this wave of unrest were young adults, including a few teachers.

In April, 1970, the labor-liberal coalition that had worked for some seventeen years came to an end in a bitter struggle over educational integration. William Grant, at that time education writer for the *Detroit Free Press*, tells the story succinctly in "Integration's Last Hurrah," first published in the *New Republic*.

Meanwhile, "black schools for black students" became the cry of many urban students of 1969–70. Out in the larger metropolitan area, candidates for public office had to convince their constituents that they were absolutely opposed to cross-district integration.

As the struggle over school integration escalated, the NAACP brought a law suit, *Bradley v. Milliken*,[6] charging the state of Michigan of condoning and prolonging the racist practices in the public schools. After NAACP victories in both the court of federal judge Stephen Roth and the U.S. District Court of Appeals at Cincinnati, the case was lost in the United States Supreme Court. Published here is an abridgment of the dissenting opinion of Justice Thurgood Marshall, with its grim prophecy for the schools of metropolitan Detroit.

Editor's Notes

1. Detroit planned to locate a "research park" on Hobart Street near the site of the Burroughs Corporation (now Unisys). The idea created instant anger among neighbors, who resented the city's condemnation of their homes. There were long delays during which they were allowed to rent their homes on a temporary basis, but the houses received little maintenance or repairs. A number of groups from across the city kept vigil in organized protest for months.
2. Among the young, radical defense lawyers who found time to offer free and constructive legal advice to high school students in the spring and fall of 1967 were attorneys Justin Ravitz (later a Recorder's Court Judge), Dennis Archer, (later Chief Justice of the Michigan Supreme Court), and the late Kenneth Cockrel.
3. MCHRD, the Mayor's Commission on Human Rights Development; arranged field trips for students of both public and parochial schools,

perhaps the concept skirted close to the wind on the doctrine of separation of church and state, but teachers welcomed the imaginative flair of Rosemary Dolan, (later Mrs. Judd Arnett) in suggesting outings, and the free buses. A bus is the last item to be included in any school budget, but provides access to the world.

4. See Georgakas Collection, Reuther Library, Wayne State University.

5. The Model City/Model Neighborhood programs suffered not only from the loss of federal funding after the Johnson years, but from a stylized jargon of bureaucracy that was little understood among the poor who were being helped, or by anyone else.

6. After the first courtroom victory by the NAACP, the state joined the Detroit Board of Education in the appeal. At that time the case became titled *Milliken v. Bradley.*

1. Mayor Cavanagh and the Limits of Reform

B. J. Widick

Widick, an astute observer of Detroit's political scene, is a labor economist and writer who for some years watched local politics as a reporter and factory worker before looking back at Detroit from academia. In 1972 he undertook to describe the Camelot years of Mayor Jerome Cavanagh.

At the beginning of the 1960's, "public opinion" in Detroit was excited by newspaper headlines about a "crime wave." According to newspaper accounts, the number one problem was crime on the streets. . . . What Detroit needed, Mayor Louis C. Miriani insisted, was more vigorous law enforcement to curb the criminal elements roaming the streets, and he ordered a police crackdown. The police responded zealously.

Frisks and searches, mass arrests, and "holding on suspicion" became the standard practice of police operations, which were concentrated in the black community. Soon feelings of fear, humiliation, and then anger developed among the Negro people—feelings to which the white community was largely insensitive. . . .

B. J. Widick, *Detroit: City of Race and Class Violence* (Chicago: Quadrangle, 1972), 154–65.

Mayor Miriani (who was later convicted on criminal charges of income tax evasion) disregarded the protests and maintained his assertion of police "impartiality." Yet City Hall received reports of incidents involving prominent black leaders. . . . Many white policemen had learned not to call blacks "niggers," for there were now influential black municipal judges, a federal judge, and some business and union leaders. Instead they would be called "boy". . . .

. . . The persistence with which the racial issue permeated local politics, long before the issue of "white backlash" became widespread, was reflected in every mayoral campaign. In 1947 the CIO endorsed incumbent Mayor Jeffries against Eugene Van Antwerp, a conservative councilman. Van Antwerp won. In 1949 the racial issue caused the UAW to suffer its most important defeat, when George Edwards was beaten by Albert Cobo, the city treasurer, in the contest for mayor. Edwards was the most attractive candidate to appear on the Detroit scene since Mayor Frank Murphy in the 1930's. A former UAW organizer and close friend of Walter Reuther, he had returned from army service to win the presidency of the Common Council by the highest vote of any candidate. He was a law school graduate, articulate, and capable. Cobo swamped him primarily because he had stood for open housing. At dozens of property owners' meetings Edwards was denounced as pro-Negro. The AFL endorsed Cobo. To the astonishment of secondary UAW leaders, the new homeowners in Detroit among the autoworkers spoke openly in the shops against "labor's man". . . .

When the time came to face reelection in 1961, Mayor Miriani was the picture of self-confidence, if not smugness. He was the unanimous choice of the entire power structure in Detroit: the UAW, the Teamsters, the AFL-CIO council, the Chamber of Commerce, the auto companies, the newspapers. Moreover his opponent was a comparatively unknown young lawyer, a newcomer in city politics. No one in the Establishment took Jerome P. Cavanagh seriously.

Perhaps the most significant aspect of the 1961 mayoralty campaign was not the fact that the 33-year-old Cavanagh beat Miriani by over 40,000 votes, or that it was the biggest political upset in Michigan politics in 32 years, but rather its disclosure of a growing gap in attitudes between institutions, such as unions, and the people they ostensibly represent—in particular the split between white liberals and the black community.

Considerable credit for Cavanagh's victory went to TULC [Trade Union Leadership Council] which mobilized the black community against Miriani, protesting his support of discriminatory police practices.[1] The long-neglected city employees, particularly the firemen, worked hard for Cavanagh. In a postmortem, the *Detroit Free Press*, which opposed Cavanagh, stated that he "owes his victory to Detroit's Negroes, blue-collar workers and the unemployed." Five liberal councilmen also won in this tide of protest. The growing division between labor leaders and the ranks was indicated by the campaign [by UAW executives] to fire Horace Sheffield, the head of TULC. The victory of Cavanagh gave TULC too much prestige for that kind of bureaucratic stupidity.

Suddenly it appeared as if a new day had dawned for Detroit. Almost overnight the city gained a new image under the direction of the talented, articulate, and personable mayor, who soon became a favorite of the nation's press and television. It seemed that Detroit had also found the road to racial peace in the programs and policies instituted by Cavanagh, with assistance from the Democratic administrations in Washington.

As a first act in office Cavanagh persuaded Alfred Pelham, an acknowledged and successful Negro expert on municipal finance, to leave Wayne State University and the county auditor's office and direct city finances. Cavanagh made another shrewd political move in persuading George Edwards, the one-time mayoral candidate who had become a justice of the Michigan Supreme Court, to accept the tough post of police commissioner. Both the police and the black community knew this meant the end of the overt police harassment of blacks. As Edwards told a TULC audience one night, "My first job was to teach the police they didn't have a constitutional right to automatically beat up Negroes on arrest."

Soon Henry Ford, Walter Reuther, and the press were praising Cavanagh's administration, and the beginning of $360,000,000 in federal assistance started pouring into the city.

Filled with euphoria at the national economic growth and prosperity, the nation came to see the formerly distressed city as a model of social progress—the harbinger of the future for solving urban problems. This was the illusion of the early 1960's. . . .

486

This rosy outlook extended to the area of racial relations. While outrages against blacks in Selma and Birmingham shocked many people, and Rev. Martin Luther King, Jr., aroused the conscience of the nation to begin the mass civil rights movement, Detroit felt it was an exception because it had what it assumed to be an effective program for racial progress. Detroiters were fond of contrasting the calm in the auto city with the turbulence elsewhere.

Any doubts on this score were dispelled on July 23, 1963, when a massive civil rights demonstration led by Reverend King took place in Detroit. Between 150,000 and 200,000 people participated, about 90 per cent of them black. . . . Mayor Cavanagh, Governor George Romney, and Walter Reuther were among the prominent whites marching with Reverend King. The size of the march surprised everybody. About 50,000 were expected, and at least triple that number showed up. . . .

Social reform seemed to be working. . . . The Institute of Labor and Industrial Relations, of Wayne State and the U. of M. recalled that Michigan's Civil Rights Act had predated that of the federal government and praised the "broad community leadership". *Fortune* magazine included the UAW in its praise of local leadership, and pointed out that more than 40% of the Negro population were homeowners, and Michigan alone among states, had two Negroes in its congressional delegation. . . .

The role played by TULC in Detroit's comeback was a major one. In the 1960–1967 period its membership rose at one point to over 9,000, and its achievements led Bayard Rustin, the civil rights leader, to comment, "I wish there was a TULC in every industrial city in the country." The concept of a labor-liberal-Negro coalition seemed to be working. Mayor Cavanagh appointed Negroes to prominent positions. Industry consulted TULC for assistance in hiring people. Even the building trades found it expeditious to talk with TULC about Negro apprentices. When UAW opponents of Sheffield tried to have him removed from the Detroit scene or ousted from his UAW staff job, the daily press and many black and white leaders insisted that Reuther allow him to remain active in the city.

But nothing fails like success, and TULC was soon divided and fragmented by new issues. A congressional seat opened in the predominantly Negro first district, and John Conyers, Jr., the legal counsel of TULC, wanted it. His father, John Conyers, Sr., a long-time UAW activist and staff member, argued in TULC for an endorsement. Sheffield and Battle, [Robert or "Buddy" Battle, co-founder of TULC] however, had their own choice: Richard Austin, an outstanding businessman and civic leader. Conyers won the primary by 32 votes, but the election split TULC deeply.

A rival organization was set up to further fragment the power of black unionists. The Negro church leaders who had sponsored the June 1963 Freedom March in Detroit began exerting independent political pressure, vying with the NAACP, TULC, and other organizations for a dominant role in the city. Meanwhile a dynamic black nationalist spokesman, Rev. Albert Cleage, was drawing larger and larger audiences with his scornful attacks on TULC's "Uncle Tomism." Most white community leaders treated the struggles within the black community as a case of "too many black Napoleons." But this superficial analysis ignored the conflicting pressures building up behind the various black leaders. Whites underestimated the impact of national events on Detroit's black community.

TULC didn't win its fight with the building trades. George Edwards, the police commissioner and a member of TULC, resigned in 1963, and his successor, Ray Girardin, never established the firm control over the police that Edwards had, even though he was well liked in the Negro community and was a "Cavanagh man". . . .

In 1965 Mayor Cavanagh won reelection, but on the issue of "law and order." Councilman Mary Beck had attacked Cavanagh for being too friendly with the Negro community. Thomas Poindexter, whom all Negroes considered a racist, defeated a Negro for the council in a special election.

These local events were partly a reflection of the national turmoil. Newspaper reports, TV coverage, and personal accounts of friends and relatives throughout the country kept the Detroit black community in a constant state of agitation. Who could forget the ordeal of James Meredith, or the figure of Bull Connor of Birmingham, Alabama, with his police dogs, fire hoses, and cattle prods? Or the murder of four children in a Negro church by a bomb explosion, the burning of the freedom buses, and the near-murder of Detroiter Walter Bergman because he had joined the Negroes on the bus? Or the murder of Mrs. Viola Liuzzo, the idealistic Detroit housewife, and the humiliations of Rev. Martin

Luther King, Jr., who insisted that Christians practice their religion? Or the riots that kept breaking out in the Eastern cities, in Cleveland and Chicago, and then, like a grand finale, in Watts, California?

Detroit was not an island unto itself. For the black community it was a time of memorial meetings and protest rallies, of shame and anger and despair. In this atmosphere the gains of Detroit blacks—and there were some gains—seemed more like mere tokenism than true social progress.

For closer examination showed that most of the gains benefited the Negro middle class. Economic progress was reflected in the enrollment of more than 2,500 Negro students at Wayne State University—more than in the Big Ten and the Ivy League combined. Ownership of homes rose to over 60 percent among black dwellers. Yet a survey showed that 90 per cent of the graduates of a Negro high school were unemployed, as compared with only 50 per cent of the dropouts.

The deterioration of the Detroit public school system was another sore point in the Negro community. The increase in the black population from 30 to 40 per cent of the total population created de facto segregation in the schools. The number of children rose by 50,000, adding to the already overcrowded conditions. And the 50 per cent drop-out rate among black youth is hardly surprising when one considers that the white teachers and principals were totally unprepared—either by education or experience—to handle black students. "Baby sitting" rather than education, and discipline rather than influence over youth, became the frequent pattern of work for the frightened or helpless school teachers. The contrast with the suburban school system was obvious. In one case, students at the all-Negro Northern High School struck in a demand for a better education.[2]

No significant attention was paid to the new mood of dissatisfaction among the black youth. No organization had attracted them in real numbers. No program really involved them as full participants.

The disparity between the poor blacks and the whites increased in this period of prosperity. With all the publicity about housing programs and model cities, only 758 low-income units were built in Detroit in the decade beginning in 1956. Unemployment averaged about 30 per cent for Negro youth. In 1960 the

489

median income in the ghetto was $2,640 for a household, compared to the median family income in Michigan of over $6,000. This was the period when everybody but the poor seemed to make money on the poverty programs.

New programs and massive federal assistance may have changed certain trends in Detroit, but the escalation of the war in Vietnam reduced the federal aid at a time when it was most needed. No man knew this better than Mayor Cavanagh. Unless a drastic shift in national priorities took place, Detroit and other urban centers were doomed to failure. Cavanagh decided to run for Senator on a peace and social reform program, but he was ahead of his time. His opponent in the Democratic primary, [former Governor] G. Mennen Williams, proved too strong, with the backing of labor hierarchy, and he defeated Cavanagh in the primary only to lose to Robert Griffin in the fall of 1965.

The black community was upset by Cavanagh's decision to seek a higher office so soon after his reelection as mayor. They had a fondness for "Soapy" Williams, and they were concerned over a possible successor to Cavanagh. The frank dialogue and rapport between the mayor and the black community were somewhat strained at the time when each needed the other the most.

In the fall of 1966, Detroit barely avoided a race riot. A handful of black nationalists clashed with police on the east side, but the populace didn't join with the youths. Neighborhood and community leaders convinced the blacks to stay at home, and the scuffle was confined to a minor incident.

However, the storm signals appeared in the spring of 1966, and no one recognized them more clearly than Mayor Cavanagh. The killing of a young Negro war veteran by a gang of white youths infuriated the Negroes. The police arrested only one of the gang. . . . A prostitute was killed by a pimp, according to police; by the police, according to Negroes. Friction between the police and the blacks was visible everywhere.

In private sessions Cavanagh met with both Negro and white leaders to find ways of alleviating the tension, but their efforts were fruitless. In May 1967, the mayor and I discussed the situation and concluded that it would be a miracle if Detroit escaped what already appeared inevitable in other cities: a major riot.

The disintegration of cohesive social and political forces suggested events were getting out of hand.

In June the Detroit Police Officers Association, led by Carl Parsell, staged a blue-flu strike in which hundreds of Detroit policemen, for the first time since the Boston police strike in 1919, walked off their jobs for five days to support demands for higher pay.

The city was a keg of social dynamite. Yet a public warning by Cavanagh that Detroit had not eliminated any of the causes of a potential riot was not taken seriously. The people were too busy with business-as-usual, politics-as-usual, and unionism-as-usual, to listen. The illusion that Detroit was different was too strong to dispel.

Only two days before disaster struck Detroit, the highly respected Negro councilman, Rev. Nicholas Hood, reflected the views of most Detroiters when he denounced the "long hot summer mongers." Reassuring the white community, he added, "I haven't heard any Negroes talk about the possible violence this summer—only white people are talking about it."

And this is not the least of the reasons why the riot in July 1967 shattered Detroit like a terrible earthquake. The shock was to prove painful indeed.

Editor's Notes

1. The TULC grew largely out of the UAW Ford Local 600 and was organized by black leadership within the factory at the time of the Ford strike of 1940. Leaders included Horace Sheffield and the late Robert "Buddy" Battles. Both men remained active in politics.
2. Even so, a "revolution of rising expectations" might be a reason for the perceived deterioration of the Detroit Public Schools during the fifties and early sixties. Certainly the black community began to have more active participation in the schools following the election of labor-endorsed candidates.

   Black teachers and administrators made up an increasing proportion of the staff, for the most part leaning toward "basic education" rather than the wider curriculum favored by the labor-reform group. There was a new emphasis on testing, with demonstrable competence as a goal.

   For another view of the schools during this period, see the article by William Grant, "Integration's Last Hurrah ," later in this section.

2. Eyewitness to Disaster

Reverend David Gracie

David Gracie, rector of St. Joseph's Episcopal Church, was no new convert to radicalism in July of 1967. A year earlier he had offered the church for use by a "Freedom School" for student protesters from nearby Northern High. There were other radical churches in Detroit, of many faiths, with leaders trying to be in step with the new times. What is notable about the Reverend Gracie was his skill in defining the terms, the frame of reference for blacks and whites in what he saw as the revolution immediately ahead.

During the week which began on Sunday, July 23, Father Gracie lived on the tense streets near his church and in the homes of his distressed people. This sermon was preached on July 30, one week after the outbreak.

A Final Call to Repentance

We must sense the judgment in what has happened to us in Detroit. I believe the events of this week are in themselves a call to repentance, perhaps a final call to this nation.

We are called to repent from consumerism. The looting teaches us that. We have devised an economy which has as its aim consumption, an economy which will only remain stable if consumer desires are continually pumped up by advertising. This constant barrage of advertising teaches people that they are nothing without the products, that to possess the products is the goal of life. This anxiety to possess makes looters of us all. I sat

Reverend David Gracie, sermon at St. Joseph's Episcopal Church, 30 July 1967, St. Matthew's and St. Joseph's Church Archives, Detroit.

and watched from my office window the continual stream of people going through the broken windows of the drug store across Woodward helping themselves to all the products they could carry. I went home then and happened to see an afternoon TV show. There was a studio full of white housewives, screaming and quite hysterical with delight and anticipation, because some of them might win the gleaming washers and dryers and other appliances hidden behind a curtain on the stage. This was white middle-class looting and the atmosphere was not a "carnival atmosphere", it was one of hysteria.[1] And so our consumer-oriented economy tends to destroy us all. It puts tremendous strain on every class, but mostly on the lowest classes, and the marginal workers, who have to listen to the advertising day in and day out but cannot buy. . . .

We are called upon to repent from violence, which has become in so many ways an accepted part of our nation's life. I spent a night in the Church House, trying to sleep, but listening all night long to the shooting down Woodward Avenue, then closer, then finally at the A&P around the corner. I heard that shooting out of one ear and with the other heard the shooting from the TV western in the next room. We spend a good part of every day listening to gun fire and we accept the fact that our sons are going to be taught to shoot and kill anywhere in the world our government orders them to do so. When President Johnson came on TV to address us in our hour of need, we had to condemn him as a hypocrite for his words. "We oppose violence under any slogan", he said. The slogan he meant was "Black Power", but the slogans he forgot were the ones he and his staff invent every week to justify continuing violence in Vietnam. . . . Let us oppose the violence of our armies, of our police, and the "frozen violence" of our institutions which crushes the lives of the poor in our land.

How many of us had guns in our hands this past week? A State Representative had a gun in his hand and used it to kill to protect his store. A group of white snipers had an arsenal on a roof and excused themselves by saying they were just trying to help the National Guard. By way of contrast . . . I shall never forget our neighbor at the Standard gas station on Holbrook. I asked him if he had spent the nights at his station trying to protect it. He said he didn't. "I know all the kids in this neighborhood. How could I shoot one of *them* if he came at my place?

493

We must repent of our neglect of the poor. The relief center which ran so well at St. Joseph's did not just supply food and clothing to those who had been burned out. We also met the needs of ADC mothers who missed their checks by a day or two because the mails were disrupted, or who couldn't cash their checks because the banks were closed. People on ADC and other forms of relief are apt to be kept at such a subsistence level that a day's delay in the check can work a terrible hardship. Our welfare system keeps the poor alive, but barely, with their chins just above water all the time. So an emergency relief center would be welcome anytime. It is important, too, that we recognize that the slums did not just start to burn last week. They are smoldering and burning always. The rate of burning accelerated last week, that's all. When I drove down Oakland [Avenue] after the worst night there, it was as if I were seeing an apocalyptic vision. The flames seemed to be worst where I had known conditions to be worst. It was as if an artist had drawn a symbolic painting of the way Oakland always is, with its broken homes, broken dreams, its tendency toward self-destruction in crime and dope and aimless violence. . . . A nation and a city which consigns people to live under the conditions which prevail on 12th and on Oakland must repent.

Finally, we must repent of the domination of the poor by the wealthy, of blacks by whites, which prevails in our land. The explosion was kicked off by a police raid on a blind pig on 12th street. Now, the police are perceived by the poor black communities as agents of domination. They are not the police of that community, but rather the police of the white community sent there to control the lives of black people. When they pull something as blatant as that raid, . . . an explosion of resentment is likely to occur. It is my understanding that that kind of raid was not supposed to occur anymore. The Commissioner had realized that hauling great numbers of people into the paddywagon like that could be provocative action. But it did occur, and the trouble started. . . . It is only with a sense of identity that a police force of a few thousand men could hope to be effective in a city of many thousands. When this identity breaks down, as it has in the ghettos, there is little to be gained in discussing police techniques in dealing with troubled situations. Prior to that discussion must come a realization that the police force must once again belong to the people. A man will not fight his own police department.

Nor will a man smash his own store or the stores of his own people. The exceptions to the inviolability of the stores marked "soul brother" just proved the rule. If they are ours we are going to protect them. If they belong to "the man', he can try to protect them with his own police force. In rebuilding the city the number one priority should be given to efforts to turn control of the communities over to the residents of those communities. This will mean allowing the growth of strong community organizations and their sponsorship of community controlled shops and housing. Can we do this? Will a blue ribbon committee headed up by J. L. Hudson be likely to relinquish our grip of power and domination in the economic area?[2]

Our choice is between real economic and political power by the ghetto dwellers or firepower. . . . Community organization efforts in Detroit have been maligned, misunderstood and undercut, but there is real hope.

Political reorganization is called for as well. Here is a voice from Jackson Prison commenting on the meaning of what has happened: ". . .riots are a necessary evil, showing that the present form of representative government is unjust. It fails to represent properly the lower and lower-middle classes of people."

Will we heed or will this city become "a curse for all the nations of the earth", with "not one stone standing on another"?

Editor's Notes

1. The phrase "carnival atmosphere" had been used by the media early in the week to describe the looting.
2. As it turned out, few individuals in Detroit would pay a higher price for social commitment than Joseph L. Hudson, Jr. His leadership on the New Detroit Committee was backed by a very thorough program of equal opportunity in the stores, which he then served as president and chief executive officer. Hudson's reforms did not please all his colleagues, nor could he hold off the forces that led to Hudson's merger with Dayton's of Minneapolis and his own withdrawal from the business.

3.   Newsgathering during Turmoil

Detroit Free Press

During the weeks following July 23, 1967, though both major news-papers and the airwaves were filled with accounts of rioting, looting, snipers, and the arrivals of or delays in getting help from outside the city, there was still an urgent need for trustworthy news. Rumors and contradictions took on new outlines by the hour. For a time, the News followed a conspiracy theory, while the Free Press was practicing investigative journalism on riot deaths, learning that they had been preventable. On Sunday morning, September 3, 1967, this article—written by reporters Barbara Stanton, William Serrin, and Gene Goltz—appeared in the Detroit Free Press. The newspaper would later receive a Pulitzer Prize for the story.

The 43 Who Died; An Investigation into How and Why Detroit's Riot Victims Were Slain

William Dalton

William N. Dalton, a 19-year-old ex-Job Corps trainee, was killed by a police shotgun blast.

A number of witnesses claim Dalton was goaded by into making a break, then shot when he ran. Investigators from the Detroit homicide Bureau say the case is hardly that simple.

They say they have no doubt that Dalton was an arsonist, along with several of his companions that night. They also say

"The 43 Who Died," *Detroit Free Press* (3 September 1967): 1–5B.

that Dalton may well have been attempting to escape arrest, although this theory seems riddled when it is noted that no police report was ever filed on the shooting. Nevertheless, if Dalton was attempting to evade apprehension, the officer had every right to fire, the officers point out.

The investigators also note that of the number of persons who say they witnessed the incident, not one has been able to provide information that might help identify the officer they say fired the shot.

. . . The incident took place shortly after midnight on July 28, the fourth day of the riot.

According to witnesses, Dalton had been sitting on the porch of a Fernwood Street home until shortly after midnight, when he left, perhaps to go to the home of his girlfriend, Marcia Kitchen, 15, daughter of Mrs. Martha Kitchen, of 4871 Fernwood. The homes are just two doors apart.

As he walked between the homes, witnesses say, he was arrested by three policemen, probably as a curfew violator.

Philip Hyde, 23, of 4852 Fernwood, who says he observed the arrest from his porch across the street, claims that the officers put Dalton against a tree and searched him. He says they "tried to make him run, but he said he wasn't going to do it."

Hyde and another witness, Willie Arnold, 26, say the officers then walked Dalton towards Grand River, and forced him to turn down an alley which runs on the south side of Grand River between Fernwood and Edmonton. He and other witnesses say they later heard a single shot.

Other witnesses say Dalton was marched to the intersection of the Fernwood-Edmonton alley with the Grand River alley, where he was forced against the wall of a warehouse, his hands on his head.

From the warehouse, witnesses say, Dalton was marched across Edmonton to the vicinity of a parking lot, just west of Wild's Cleaners, at 8687 Grand River.

Picking up the story here is Mrs. Alberta Jones, who lives at Grand River and Arcadia, directly across from where Dalton was shot.

She claims she saw officers take Dalton into an alley on the west side of Edmonton. There, she says, she heard Dalton cry: "I didn't set no fires. You didn't see no fires."

She says Dalton was then brought into the parking lot, where a police officer pushed him against a wall, shoving him with a shotgun.

Then, they say, officers ordered Dalton to run. They say he ran along the building and vaulted over the hood of a car. As he did, a policeman raised his shotgun and fired one shot, felling Dalton on the sidewalk in front of a cleaners.

Mrs. Jones says the officer then yelled, "Let's get out of here." She says. "Everyone jumped in their cars and went off in every direction. . . . "

[In the case of George Talbert, which follows, one of the witnesses is Julian Witherspoon, the same Julian Witherspoon who was wounded by police gunfire at the St. Antoine Y.M.C.A. in the 1943 riot, and whose story appeared in the NAACP report by Walter White and Thurgood Marshall included in Part XII.]

George Talbert

George Talbert was shot and mortally wounded by a National guardsman as he walked down a West Side street in broad daylight, unarmed and innocent.

The shooting occurred about 5 p.m. on Wednesday, July 26, as Talbert, 20, of 4451 Thirtieth Street, walked east on La Salle Gardens South, a residential street near the devastated Twelfth Street area.

One of the witnesses is Julian F. Witherspoon, 47, 1978 La Salle Gardens South, an area chairman for the Mayor's Committee on Human Resources Development. Witherspoon calls himself an "eyewitness to murder."

At about 4:30 p.m., Witherspoon says, he heard shouting and shooting and went to his porch to investigate. He says he saw two Guardsmen proceeding up the street, waving back cars that were trying to go east to 12th St. When cars failed to stop, the Guardsmen squeezed off rounds over the cars from their M-1 rifles.

"You could see the drivers duck," Witherspoon says. "One minute you'd see their heads. The next minute you wouldn't."

Witherspoon says the two Guardsmen also yelled at residents on porches to get back in their houses.

The Guard's procedure that day is confirmed by a Free Press reporter assigned to that area. He says that several of the streets approaching 12th Street were closed by the Guard. He says the technique of closing them consisted of "standing in the middle of the street, shouting obscenities at whoever they were trying to move. If they didn't instantly obey, they'd fire over the car or over people's heads as they stood on their lawns."

At about 5 p.m., Witherspoon says, he saw a man—Talbert— walking east on La Salle Gardens South. His companion, Lance Smith, 28, of 3010 Gladstone, walked several paces behind. Talbert had just left his car, a 1965 Chevrolet, on Dunedin.

Witherspoon says he was frightened for Talbert but had no chance to wave him back. A moment later, one of the Guardsmen raised his rifle, aimed directly at Talbert and shot.

Talbert fell hard on the sidewalk, bleeding profusely. "Help me, I'm dying," he cried. He died 10 days later, on Aug. 5, in Henry Ford Hospital. An autopsy attributed death to pneumonia caused by the wound.

Witherspoon's version is corroborated by numerous La Salle Gardens residents. One of them is Frank Morrow, 34, of 1974 La Salle Gardens South, a combat veteran of Korea who disobeyed a Guard order to go to Talbert's aid.

By the time he got there, Morrow said, five other Guardsmen had arrived. He says he asked a Guard captain to take Talbert to the hospital, but the captain said that he was "not authorized."

Two priests from St. Agnes Catholic Church, Father John Markhan and Father Norman Thomas, came up, administered the last rites to Talbert and took him and Smith to the hospital in Smith's car. Smith had been struck by the same bullet that hit Talbert, but his wound was less serious.

Why Talbert was shot is a mystery. He had broken no law and carried no weapon. He was no curfew violator; the time was 5 p.m. He could not be mistaken for a looter; he carried nothing with him, and there are no stores in the immediate area where he was shot.

According to the Guard, Talbert was shot for refusing to heed a command to halt. The Guardsman who fired the shot told police that his guard companion had repeatedly ordered these men (Talbert and Smith) off the street. He says that one of the men, either Talbert or Smith had earlier told him, "I'm going to cut your throat, you sonofabitch." He says that "his man (Talbert) continued to come forward" so he aimed and fired at him.

Even if one accepts the National Guard's story, and none of the witnesses do, Talbert's death must be called inexcusable.

Talbert had a legal right to be where he was and to do what he was doing. Martial law had not been declared; the Guard had no arrest power whatever and its authority to give orders to anyone was sharply limited.

The Guardsman himself disobeyed a standing order—a court-martial offense—when he fired the shot that killed Talbert. Lt. Gen. John Throckmorton, commander of the Federal troops during the riot, had ordered the Guard to unload its weapons and told Guardsmen to fire only on command of an officer. This order was not followed.

Prosecutor William Cahalan has not yet ruled on Talbert's death.

Tonia Blanding

Tonia Blanding, a four-year-old Negro girl, paid for the crimes and mistakes others.

The corner of Euclid and Twelfth was like a battlefield the night of July 25.

National Guardsmen said there was sniper fire originating from the second floor of the apartment building at 1756 W. Euclid. A part-time employe of Bowman Private Police, John W. Bryant, said in a sworn statement that he had been fired on from the building a half hour before Tonia was killed and also the night before.

Guardsmen said one of their 2½-ton trucks was under fire by a sniper who was apparently shooting from the second floor apartment where Tonia was killed. The Guardsmen said they returned the fire.

During this time Cpl. Danny Kwieczinski reported to a tank commander, Sgt. Mortimer J. LeBlanc, 41, that he had seen a flash in the apartment window.

Huddled on the living room floor of a second-floor apartment were June Blanding, Valerie and William Hood, William Hood, Jr., James Matthew Blanding and several other children, including Tonia.

LeBlanc, while moving his tank to a position on Euclid directly opposite the apartment building, said the vehicle was under fire from the apartment. Once in position, LeBlanc fired short bursts from his 50-caliber machine gun into the windows he believed the sniper fire had come from.

Occupants of the apartment said later that they were not fired on until William Hood lighted a match for a cigarette.

Detective David Mason of the Detroit Police Department investigated later and decided that the Guard's firing had been directed only at the apartment from which they believed they were fired on.

Tonia died from bullets believed fired from the machine gun.

Mason said he later found one spent .38 caliber hull next to one of the windows in the apartment and a box of .38 caliber shells with some rounds missing. Police said Hood testified he owned a .38 caliber revolver.

Mason said he found in the apartment 20 men's coats, 35 pairs of men's trousers, 40 shirts, four overcoats, 23 paint brushes, two portable record players, a tape recorder, a portable television set, three portable radios and a movie camera.

There are discrepancies between the version given by the occupants of the apartment and the National Guard investigation.

The occupants said they were not fired on until after the match was lighted, yet the guardsmen from the 2½-ton truck were reported to have fired at the apartment also. Nowhere is it explained why the private guard, Bryant, did not report being fired on the day before from the apartment which he said he had pinpointed.

Finally, the wisdom of turning a .50 caliber machine gun, which fires a slug that will cut through a quarter-inch steel, on a frame dwelling is questionable. Certainly, the men in the tank did not require protection from snipers, and no sniper was found in the building.

Police procedure calls for tear gas to be used on snipers wherever possible, a technique used on sniper Sydnor. If that fails or is impossible, officers are directed to rush the building, armed with shotguns, as long as other citizens will not be endangered by their doing so.

The police were never involved in the death of Tonia Blanding. No one asked them for help.

Auburey Pollard, Carl Cooper, Fred Temple

At midnight Tuesday, July 25 three Negro youths were shooting craps on the second floor of the three-story annex of the Algiers Motel.

Two white girls who had run out on a $308.17 bill at the Ponchartrain Hotel were in the Algiers Annex, and seven or eight other persons were mingling and visiting between floors.

A little more than an hour later the three crap shooters were dead from shotgun blasts.

Carl Cooper, 17, was lying face down in a pool of blood in Room A2. Fred Temple, 18, and Auburey Pollard, 19, were lying dead in Room A3.

The girls were crying, one had a cut on her head, and both they and other guests claimed they had been beaten and threatened by officers in blue uniforms.

It had been a night of horror and bloodshed, with rioting and gunfire in all areas outside, and shotgun blasts along with reports of sniping—and worse—from inside.

The motel guests said that half a dozen uniformed men broke open the front door with gun butts, spread through the building and rounded up the occupants.

The guests said they were lined up against the wall, threatened and beaten. They heard gunshots, but none said they saw any of the youths get killed, and when the police told them to leave, they all fled into the night.

A pre-trial examination was begun Aug. 14 in Recorder's Court to determine whether Detroit Patrolmen Ronald W. August, 28, and Robert N. Paille, 31, should be held for trial in the killings of Pollard and Temple.

A youth who was in the motel, Michael Clark, testified that Paille and August had taken him into a room where Paille put a cocked pistol against his head and threatened to kill him.

Clark testified he later saw August take a youth into another room and that he heard a shot and someone fell to the floor.

August, charged with killing Pollard, submitted a statement that said he shot the youth in self-defense when the youth tried to wrest the gun away.

August was ordered to stand trial for first degree murder. No trial date has been set.

A National Guard warrant officer, Theodore J. Thomas, testified that he saw a policeman lead a man into a room and make him lie on the floor. Then the policeman fired a shot into the air, Thomas said. He could not identify the policeman.

He also said he saw August lead a man into a room and then heard a body fall. He said he had seen one body in room A-2 and one in A-3 but did not see the other body in A-3.

Days later, when confused testimony from witnesses was pieced together, one Detroit policeman was charged with first degree murder in the death of one Negro youth.

Another policeman was freed after a pre-trial examination failed to turn up enough evidence to hold him for trial.

Two policemen and a private guard were charged with conspiracy in connection with alleged beating, intimidation and abuse of persons in the motel.

The Algiers Motel had a shadowy reputation even before the events of that awful night. The police had made arrests for prostitution, and narcotics users were known to frequent the place.

An investigation was begun by the Free Press the day after the shootings when stories began to circulate among the Negroes, stories containing allegations of brutality and unwarranted killings.

A pathologist hired by the Free Press, Dr. Warren Sillery, examined the bodies of the three dead youths with the consent of relatives.

Dr. Sillery concluded that all three men were shot from inside the building from a range of 15 feet or less by 12-gauge double-0 buckshot. All the men were shot more than once. None could have been killed while engaged in a sniper battle with authorities outside the building.

Two of them, Temple and Pollard, were shot while lying or kneeling. The county medical examiner's autopsy reports agreed substantially with Sillery's finding.

A search of the motel annex failed to turn up any weapons.

Almost the only thing that persons in the motel and law officers are agreed on is that the policemen burst into the motel about 2 a.m. The police said they were investigating sniper fire from the motel.

Paille, charged with slaying Temple, was released because of insufficient evidence. His defense attorney, Norman Lippitt, argued at the examination that all that had been proved was that Paille was in the motel that night.

No charges were filed in the death of Cooper. The evidence indicated that Cooper was the first to die in Room A-2. The other two were shot later in A-3.

On August 24 the county prosecutor brought conspiracy charges against Paille, a private guard named Melvin Dismukes, and Patrolman David Senak. August was named as a co-conspirator but not a defendant.

Cahalan charged that some of the lawmen in the annex had beaten, intimidated and abused the witnesses. He said they had engaged in excesses in obvious violation of the criminal statutes.

No trial date has been set on the conspiracy charges.

Senak was under investigation by Cahalan's office in two other riot deaths but was cleared of wrongdoing last week in the death of Joseph Chandler. Cahalan is still investigating Senak's part in the death of Palmer Gray.

Dismukes is also awaiting trial on a felonious assault charge involving the Algiers Motel.

4. The Death Games at the Algiers Motel

John Hersey

During the revelations about the events at the Algiers Motel, John Hersey, the eminent author of Hiroshima, *became interested in the reports. Hersey spent many weeks in Detroit interviewing those involved: police and National Guard officers, the victims' families and their friends. His lengthy journal became* The Algiers Motel Incident, *a book that should be read and reread by all citizens of metropolitan Detroit. In two chapters, titled "The Death Game" and "The Death Game Played Out," Hersey deals with the core of the evening's events as they were relayed to him later by witnesses and from official records.*

Those who were present at the time Carl Cooper, Fred Temple, and Auburey Pollard died included Michael Clark, Lee Forsythe, James Sortor, Roderick Davis, Larry Reed, Juli Hysell, Karen Malloy, Robert Greene, an army veteran, private guard Melvin Dismukes, Warrant Officer Theodore Thomas of the National Guard, and Detroit police officers Ronald August, Robert Paille, and David Senak, plus, as Hersey had indicated, a large cast of others.

This material is present in Hersey's brief, rather staccato format, which lends itself to the illusion of a theater script.

John Hersey, "The Death Game" and "The Death Game Played Out," in *The Algiers Motel Incident* (New York: Knopf, 1968), 273–76, 277–80.

505

The Death Game

1 One at a Time

"Then," Lee [Forsythe] said to me, "they started killing us one by one."

"They were going to shoot us," Michael testified, "one at a time."

2 It Was All Right

"One of the Detroit officers," Thomas told the police, "pulled the 'big man'—Roderick Davis—out of the line and took him in A-4." In court Thomas was more explicit. "Officer Senak," he testified, "took the first man out of the line . . . into the front room, one to the left in front." "When they went in," Greene told Eggleton, [a member of the county prosecutor's staff] "he closed the door." Roderick Davis said to me, "They told me, 'Lie on the floor face down and if you make a move or say a word, we'll kill you.'" "I followed them to the doorway," Warrant Officer Thomas testified, "and Officer Senak told the man to lay on the floor and he fired a round through the wall. I seen him point the gun to the other direction. He didn't shoot him. He scared him. . . . He winked at me. He didn't say nothing." "I thought," Roderick testified, "he shot in the floor because I felt like vibration reaction by my feet." . . . "In the floor or through a chair or something," Roderick said to me:

Attorney Kohl; "Now, you were in a room with David Senak when he took a prisoner in there?"

Warrant Officer Thomas: "Yes, sir."

Kohl: "And is it not true that the told the man to lie down on the floor? He fired a shot but he didn't shoot at the man, did he?"

Thomas: "Definitely not."

Senak fired, Thomas testified, "right in the corner."

"He looked at me," Thomas testified, "and winked, indicating it was all right. . . . When we took the first man in I realized what he was doing. And it was better than letting these people be beaten; seriously. I felt somebody was going to really get hurt seriously, and I felt this was the best thing at the time."

"Then," Roderick told me, "they said, 'Don't budge an inch or you'll be dead.'" And the men left him alone in the room.

3   Want to Kill One?

"The warrant officer," Greene told Eggleton, "came out, and the policemen asked the other officer, 'Did he kill him?' And the officer said 'Yes.' " This was for the ears of the people in the line.

"This officer . . . " the Thomas synopsis said, "asked Thomas if he wanted to kill one. Thomas said 'Yes,' and took one of the men"—Michael Clark— "into A-4 and fired a rifle shot into the ceiling, forcing the man to remain in the room."

"I also took one person into that front room," Thomas testified. " . . . I used my M-1 rifle . . . I also told the man to lay on the floor, and fired a round through the ceiling . . . toward the corner so that anybody upstairs wouldn't get hit. I didn't think there was anybody upstairs around at the corner of the house.

"Let's see," Michael testified—once again he seems to err; even Senak's lawyer placed Senak in this role—"told the soldier to shoot me or something. Anyway, the soldier told me to lay down. Then he shot. I think he shot out the window or in the hall somewhere. Then he told me just to lay there and be quiet. And he said if I make any noise, he going to come back and shoot me for real."

4   Announcement

"Clark and an unknown man were taken into room A-4," the Sortor synopsis says of this first phase of the death game, "shots were heard, and the officers returned, saying, 'We killed those two.' " Telling me the story, Sortor said, "And so they said they were going to kill us, you know. They said they were going to kill us niggers, you know, so they picked Michael and this other guy out, so they said they were going to kill these two niggers, so they took them in this room in there, we heard two shots, so the police come out, so he said, 'I killed them two motherfuckers.' "

Karen told the detectives, "she believed the police killed Michael Clark." From the synopsis of Juli Hysell's statement: "They . . . made Hysell believe Clark was dead."

5 Rational, Reasonable Explanation

Thomas testified,"Immediately after the officer shot into the wall, into the floor, or corner, or wherever you want to call it, and laid the man down, they"—the people against the wall—"thought this man had been shot and they were willing to talk . . . I believe it was one of the girls—I wouldn't swear to it—said, 'Why don't you tell him about the gun? Carl is dead anyway.' And this is one of the statements I specifically heard to this effect."

"One boy spoke up," Juli testified, "and said that the boy that was dead was the one that had the pistol, and that's the only thing to my knowledge that was said about the pistol."

"One of the persons" Karen told Allen Early [an attorney who acted on behalf of Juli and Karen], "who had been in A-2 & come up to A-4 said, 'Go on and tell them anything you want because they've already killed him.' This was with reference to the blank pistol. This other person then said, 'The guy in there on the floor' (referring to Carl in A-2) 'had a blank pistol.' Policeman said, 'Why didn't you tell us that before we killed the other guy?' "

Having elicited from Juli, in the conspiracy hearing, an estimate that the ordeal in the hallway had been going of for about twenty minutes before this first mention of the starter pistol, Attorney Kohl asked, "Now, if in fact there was simply a blank pistol that had been fired, will you advise this Court, please, what rational, reasonable explanation there could be for not telling the police who would have the gun and who had done what for a period of twenty minutes?"

Juli answered: "Because everybody was scared."

6 Next?

Karen told Early, "The talking policeman then said, 'Who shall we get next?' "

The Death Game Played Out

1 I Want One?

"Then the first officer," the Thomas synopsis said, "asked the officer with the OCD type helmet (who was dark complx w/m),

508

'Do you want to kill one now?' He said, 'Yes,' and the first officer gave the gun to the second officer, who took a Negro youth from the line. . . . "

"He said it," Thomas testified, "loud enough for everybody to hear in the room, 'Do you want to shoot one?'—or to this effect."

Thomas testified that August had not been particularly active along the line-up. "Patrolman August," he said, "was very refined. He didn't say anything that I can recall." But it was August to whom Senak now turned; Thomas testified that Senak handed his shotgun to August and told him "to take a man into the back room or into a room."

"Then the guy next to me," Greene told Eggleton, "they took him to A-4. The officer told him not to take him to A-4. He said 'Take him to another room.' And he took him to A-5, I think it was A-5, that's the back room there." (It was A-3.)

"The game was going on," Thomas testified, "and I said, 'You can't kill any more in here. There are too many now.' And that is when I believe the other policemen handed Patrolman August the gun."

2 A Thing to Scare People With

Assistant Prosecutor Avery Weiswasser asked Thomas: "Did Senak hand a gun to August?"

"Yes, sir."

"What did he say when he handed him the gun?"

"To the effect this was a game. I mean, this is a thing to scare people with."

But in other testimony Thomas said, "I can't recall what was said. I know there was a conversation. I won't deny this. The idea was to give the impression that these people were being shot."

Yet again Weiswasser asked, "Did you know if anybody bothered to tell August it was only a game?"

"No, sir," Thomas replied.

3 Don't Shoot

From the Michael Clark synopsis: "Clark then heard someone take Pollard into Apt. A-2 and heard Pollard yell, 'Don't shoot. Don't shoot.' He then heard a gunshot."

From the Lee Forsythe synopsis: "Forsythe stated he heard Pollard yell, 'Don't shoot,' and a door slam, Forsythe believed in room A-3. A few seconds later, Forsythe heard a shot fired."

4 A Brush of Clothing

"Then I believe Officer August took this man to the rear of the room," Thomas, who followed August into the room, testified, "and I heard a shot. And Officer August had his back to me. I seen a brush of clothing, and I heard something fall. At this time I got scared."

"Did I see him fall? . . . " Thomas asked himself in testimony. "I won't say that. I seen movement. Officer August was standing between myself and him, and I seen a flash of clothing, what I thought was a flash."

Prosecutor Weiswasser asked at one point: "Did you hear any struggle going on prior to that time?" "No," Thomas answered, "I can't say I did."

"I want to be honest with you," Thomas testified later on. I have seen the pictures of the room after the two bodies were discovered in there. And I believe the man that Officer August took back there had a shirt on, dark gray shirt. And the pictures don't show this. And that is why I was confused on this point. You can see something or think you've seen something and think about it, and you don't know if you've seen it or not. And I thought I seen that flash of clothing. And it looked like a gray shirt."

5 Announcement

From the James Sortor synopsis: "A shot was heard and an officer returned, saying, 'That one didn't kick.' "

From the Robert Greene Synopsis: "Then a shot was heard and the Warrant Officer returned, saying, 'That nigger didn't even kick.' "

Sorter said to me, "Aubrey didn't lose his temper in that room; he was too scared. I figure if he would have lost his temper, he would have lost it when they was hitting him with the rifle. It was too quick for him to be in there tussling with the guy. It was too quick. He went in there, I heard the shot, and the guy came out, and he said, 'That one didn't even kick.' "

6 Strictly Their Business

"At this time," Thomas had said, "I got scared. . . . It scared me. I was scared. I will be honest with you. . . . As far as the conversation goes, I believe I told the policeman that this was strictly their business, and I called Henson [PFC Wayne Henson, a National Guardsman], who was outside at this time. And there was more shooting in the street. In fact, more shooting, and I told him we were going to leave. . . . "

511

5. Integration's Last Hurrah: "Where Did Everyone Go To?"

William Grant

The coalition of labor/liberal political power effectively ended in April, 1970, when the adoption by the board of education of an integration plan for high schools provoked a recall of the liberal majority the coalition had achieved. This end of an era in Detroit political life was analyzed by William Grant, at that time education writer for the Detroit Free Press.

The stage here is set for what could become integration's last hurrah. Perhaps the final blow was struck in August when the liberal bloc that has controlled the city's board of education since 1964 was voted out of office in an unusual recall election.

The board had hired an egalitarian superintendent, aggressively recruited black teachers, promoted black administrators, and purged the schools of books that did not reflect a multi-racial society and did not adequately portray black contributions to history.

School boundaries were adjusted and student transfers were approved only if they improved integration. But the board was

William Grant, "Integration's Last Hurrah: 'Where Did Everyone Go To?' " *The New Republic* (12 September 1970): 20. Reprinted by permission of *The New Republic*, © 1970, The New Republic, Inc.

unable to integrate classrooms in a system that this year is 62 per cent black. A few high schools in the corners of the city were white enclaves. Last April 7 the board moved against them. Its plan involved redrawing attendance boundaries for half of the city's high schools. Protests, student boycotts and hurriedly called neighborhood meetings followed. When the board met, angry white parents chanted "Hell no, we won't go." Speakers denounced the plan for five hours, before the board voted 4–2 to adopt it.

"All the trouble was because for the first time we devised a plan that not only moved black students into white schools, but also required white students to go to black schools," said the board president, A. L. Zwerdling, a labor lawyer and former administrative assistant to the late Walter Reuther. Zwerdling was elected to the board in 1964, with liberals Peter F. Grylls, a Michigan Bell Telephone executive, and the Rev. Darneau Stewart, a black minister. The three joined Dr. Remus Robinson, a physician, who in 1955 was the first black elected to the Detroit board and who for a decade fought almost alone for integration.[1] Dr. Robinson was hospitalized when the April 7 meeting was held and died two months later; the critical fourth vote for integration came from Andrew Perdue, a black attorney elected to the board in 1968.

The plan involved boundary changes, not busing. But the board was accused of busing and of "forcing integration to drive the white people out of town." A Citizens Committee for Better Education was formed to organize a recall of Zwerdling, Grylls, Stewart and Perdue and to press the state legislature to overturn the integration plan. The committee produced 114,000 signatures on each of four separate petitions to get the issue on the ballot.

The recall survived three law suits in federal and state courts and was ordered on the ballot by the State Court of Appeals three days before the election. The legislature voted the citizen's group virtually everything it asked. The debate in the legislature was more emotional than in Detroit. The high school integration plan was companion to board action dividing the school system into seven regions for decentralization. Conservatives in the legislature attacked both decentralization and integration. The legislature stopped the integration plan, and significantly changed the decentralization plans.

If the board was startled by the action in the legislature, it was dumbfounded by the response of its usual supporters. Republican Governor William Milliken had a few ambivalent comments about the integration plan, and said nothing at about the recall. The mayor stayed on the fence. The United Auto Workers, long the cement in Michigan's liberal politics, managed to put up the money for the single newspaper ad opposing the recall when, as one union official put it, "we couldn't raise a dime anywhere else."

"Where is everybody?" Mr. Perdue agonized a few days before the election. "Where are the people who helped us get elected—the UAW, the NAACP and the others? Don't they care anymore?"

The four did managed to attract support from black voters on election day, but the recall carried by 59 percent in a city where white voters still hold a 58–42 edge in voter registration. Only 180,000 voters managed to make their way to the end of a long primary ballot and vote on the recall, and the percentage of whites voting on the issue was much higher than the black percentage.

The four will be replaced by interim board members appointed by the governor, and permanent replacements will be elected in November, as will members of regional school boards who will take office when decentralization begins next January.[2] The Citizens Committee for Better Education intends to stay around long enough to see that as many as possible of those new board members share its views. "We have a two-year battle ahead of us to take over this school system and turn it around," said Aubrey Short, a General Motors metallurgist who is the group's chairman.

"I had a right to fight," said a somewhat defensive Edward Zaleski, a policeman who was one of the early organizers of the recall drive. "My daughter was being sent to a black school. We knew we were going to win, because we were fighting for our children. They were only fighting for an idea."

Editor's Notes

1. The meeting of April 7, 1970, was stormy indeed, with several hundred people, unable to get into the room, packing the hallways and

crowding Woodward Avenue in front of the building. One moment of quiet came when the board secretary read Robinson's letter:

> To my fellow Board members—
>
> I am sorry that I cannot be with you as you make an important de-cision that will affect the educational opportunity of thousands of De-troit youngsters. I recognize that my unavoidable absence makes it impossible for me to cast an official vote, but I hope that my thoughts—arrived at after much searching of my conscience and my commit-ment—will be given serious consideration during your deliberations regarding the regional boundaries to be drawn in compliance with act 244.
>
> I have been a member of the Detroit Board of Education since April, 1955. During these past fifteen years I have tried—to the best of my ability—to serve fairly the needs of all children from all segments of Detroit's population. I have believed—and have tried to act always from that belief—that every youngster in the city of Detroit deserves to find in our schools the unprejudiced opportunity to develop his talents in such a way as to become a self-motivated, productive citizen in a dem-ocratic, pluralistic society. . . .
>
> I am deeply troubled by the forces within society—both black and white—which would continue to foist segregated regional patterns upon future generations of Americans. I cannot, with a clear con-science, submit to these doctrines.
>
> Therefore, I support the proposed plan as providing the best oppor-tunity for quality, integrated education for our students and for effecting the most cooperation among the various racial, religious, and ethnic populations of our city. I believe this plan can work; I believe it is fair; I believe it is in the best interests of the total community. . . .
>
> This plan will enable more black and white students to attend senior high school together; it will also enable more citizens of the future to recognize—from firsthand experience—that in plura, and that in equal opportunity there is the possibility for all men to rise to the level of their best talents.
>
> My thoughts are with you.
>
> Sincerely,
> R. G. Robinson

2. The change from citywide to local school districts was the first real use of that system since 1916, when the reformers of those days elim-inated neighborhood "school inspectors."

   Among the recalled board members, The Reverend Darneau Stew-art channeled his anger into running for reelection, this time in his new local district, and won handily. Stewart served with distinction for several years until his death.

6.   The *Milliken v. Bradley* Dissent

Thurgood Marshall

Known by many as "the school busing case," by others as "Bradley-Milliken," the suit begun by the NAACP in 1970 to desegregate the Detroit Public Schools was won by the NAACP and those who joined its efforts in two lower courts before reaching the U.S. Supreme Court on appeal as the "Milliken-Bradley" case. The court rejected by a 5–4 vote in August, 1974, that section of the lower courts' opinion that had called for a metropolitan remedy involving integration plans for both city and suburban school districts.

Mr. Justice Marshall, with whom Mr. Justice Douglas, Mr. Justice Brennan, and Mr. Justice White join, dissenting:

In *Brown v. Board of Education,. . .* (1954), this court held that segregation of children in public schools on the basis of race deprives minority group children of equal educational opportunities and therefore denies them the equal protection of the laws under the Fourteenth Amendment. This court recognized then that remedying decades of segregation in public education would not be an easy task. Subsequent events, unfortunately, have seen that prediction bear bitter fruit. . . .

After 20 years of small, often difficult steps toward that great end, the court today takes a giant step backwards. Notwithstand-

Thurgood Marshall, Milliken v. Bradley, *418 U.S. Reports* (October Term 1973): 781–815.

ing a record showing widespread and pervasive racial segregation in the educational system provided by the state of Michigan for children in Detroit, this Court holds that the District Court was powerless to require the State to remedy its constitutional violation in any meaningful fashion. . . . thereby guaranteeing that Negro children in Detroit will receive the same separate and inherently unequal education in the future as they have been unconstitutionally afforded in the past.

I cannot subscribe to this emasculation of our constitutional guarantee of equal protection of the laws and must respectfully dissent. Our precedents, in my view, firmly establish that where, as here, state-imposed segregation has been demonstrated, it becomes the duty of the State to eliminate root and branch all vestiges of racial discrimination and to achieve the greatest possible degree of actual desegregation. I agree with both the District Court and the Court of Appeals that, under the facts of this case, this duty cannot be fulfilled unless the State of Michigan involves outlying metropolitan area school districts in its desegregation remedy. . . .

We deal here with the right of all of our children, whatever their race, to an equal start in life and to an equal opportunity to reach their full potential as citizens. Those children who have been denied that right in the past deserve better than to see fences thrown up to deny them that right in the future. Our Nation, I fear, will be ill served by the Court's refusal to remedy separate and unequal education, for unless our children begin to learn together, there is little hope that our people will ever learn to live together. . . .

Nowhere in the Court's opinion does the majority confront, let alone respond to, the District Court's conclusion that a remedy limited to the city of Detroit would not effectively desegregate the Detroit city schools. I, for one, find the District Court's conclusion well supported by the record and its analysis compelled by our prior cases. . . . The focus of this case was from the beginning, and has remained, the segregated system of education in the Detroit city schools and the steps necessary to cure that condition which offends the Fourteenth Amendment. . . .

The State of Michigan, through its instrumentality, the Detroit Board of Education, engaged in widespread purposeful acts of racial segregation in the Detroit School District. Without belaboring the details, it is sufficient to note that the various techniques used in Detroit were typical of methods employed to segregate students by race. . . . Exacerbating the effects of extensive residential segregation between Negroes and whites, the school Board consciously drew attendance zones along lines which maximized the segregation of the races in schools as well. Optional attendance zones were created for neighborhoods undergoing a racial transition so as to allow whites in these areas to escape integration. Negro students in areas with overcrowded schools were transported past or away from closer white schools with available space to more distant Negro schools. Grade-structure and feeder-school patterns were created and maintained in a manner which had the forseeable and actual effect of keeping Negro and white pupils in separate schools. Schools were also constructed in locations and in sizes which ensured that they would open with predominantly one-race student bodies. . . . [The evidence] showed that Negro children had been intentionally confined to an expanding core of virtually all-Negro schools immediately surrounded by a receding band of all-white schools. . . . [1]

The [district] court concluded that responsibility for segregation in Detroit city schools rested not only with the Detroit Board of Education, but belonged to the State of Michigan itself and the state defendants in this case—that is, the Governor of Michigan, the Attorney-General, the State Board of Education and the State Superintendent of Public Instruction. . . . Under Michigan law and practice, the system of education was in fact a *state* school system, characterized by relatively little local control and a large degree of centralized state regulation, with respect to both educational policy and the structure and operation of school districts. . . .

The District Court then turned to the difficult task of devising an effective remedy. . . . The District Court first considered three desegregation plans limited to the geographical boundaries of the city of Detroit. All were rejected as ineffective to desegregate the Detroit city schools. Specifically, the District Court determined that the racial composition of the Detroit student body is such that the implementation of any Detroit-only plan "would clearly make the entire Detroit public school system racially identifiable as Black" and would "leave many of its schools 75 to 90 per cent Black." The District Court also found that a Detroit-only plan

518

"would change a school system which is now Black and White to one that would be perceived as Black, thereby increasing the flight of Whites from the city and the system, thereby increasing the Black student population." Based on these findings, the District Court reasoned that "relief of segregation in the public schools of the City of Detroit cannot be accomplished within the corporate geographical limits of the city, . . . [but that the court] must look beyond the limits of the Detroit public schools. . . ."

. . . The District Court's decision to expand its desegregation decree beyond the geographical limits of the city of Detroit rested in large part on its conclusions A) the State of Michigan was ultimately responsible for curing the condition of segregation within the Detroit city schools, and B) that a Detroit-only remedy would not accomplish this task. In my view, both of these conclusions are well supported by the facts of this case and by this Court's precedents. . . .

The State had also stood in the way of past efforts to desegregate the Detroit city schools. In 1970, for example, the Detroit School Board had begun implementation of its own desegregation plan for its high schools, despite considerable public and official resistance. The State Legislature intervened by enacting Act 48 of the Public Acts of 1970,[2] specifically prohibiting implementation of the desegregation plan and thereby continuing the growing segregation of the Detroit school system. Adequate desegregation of the Detroit system was also hampered by discriminatory restrictions placed by the State on the use of transportation within Detroit. While state aid for transportation was provided by statute for suburban school districts, many of which were highly urbanized, aid for intracity transportation was excepted. One of the effects of this restriction was to encourage the construction of small walk-in neighborhood schools in Detroit, thereby lending aid to the intentional policy of creating a school system which reflected, to the greatest extent feasible, extensive residential segregation. . . . When the Michigan Legislature amended the State Transportation Aid Act to cover intracity transportation [it] expressly prohibited the allocation of funds for cross-busing of students within a school district to achieve a racial balance. . . .

Michigan, unlike some other States, operates a single statewide system of education rather than several separate and independent local school systems. . . .

The state's control over education is reflected in the fact that . . . there is little or no relationship between school districts and local political units. To take the 85 outlying school districts in the Detroit metropolitan area as examples, 17 districts lie in two counties, two in three counties. One district serves five municipalities; other suburban school districts are fragmented into as many as six school districts. Nor is there any apparent state policy with regard to the size of school districts, as they now range from 2,000 to 285,000 students.[3]

Centralized state control manifests itself in practice as well as in theory. The State controls the financing of education in several ways. The legislature contributes a substantial portion of most school districts' operating budgets with funds appropriated from the State's General Fund revenues raised through statewide taxation. The State's power over the purse can be and is in fact used to enforce the State's powers over local districts. . . . The State also establishes standards for teacher certification and teacher tenure; determines part of the required curriculum; sets the minimum school term; approves bus routes, equipment, and drivers; approves textbooks; and establishes procedures for student discipline. . . .

Most significantly for present purposes, the State has wide-ranging powers to consolidate and merge school districts, even without the consent of the districts themselves or the local citizenry . . . Indeed, recent years have witnessed an accelerated program of school district consolidations, mergers, and annexations, many of which were state imposed. . . .

In sum, several factors in this case coalesce to support the District Court's ruling that it was the State of Michigan itself, not simply the Detroit Board of Education, which bore the obligation of curing the condition of segregation within the Detroit city schools. The actions of the State itself directly contributed to Detroit's segregation. Under the Fourteenth Amendment, the State is ultimately responsible for the actions of its local agencies. . . .

Under a Detroit-only decree, Detroit's schools will clearly remain racially identifiable in comparison with neighboring schools in the metropolitan community. Schools with 65% and more Negro students will stand in sharp and obvious contrast to schools in neighboring districts with less than 2% Negro enrollment. Negro students will continue to perceive their schools as segregated. . . . School district lines, however innocently drawn, will surely be perceived as fences to separate the races when, under a Detroit-only decree, parents withdraw their children from the Detroit city schools and move to the suburbs in order to continue them in all-white schools. The message of this action will not escape the Negro children in the city of Detroit. . . .

Desegregation is not and never was expected to be an easy task. Racial attitudes ingrained in our Nation's childhood and adolescence are not quickly thrown aside in its middle years. But just as the inconvenience of some cannot be allowed to stand in the way of the rights of others, so public opposition, no matter how strident, cannot be permitted to divert this Court from the enforcement of the constitutional principles at issue in this case. Today's holding, I fear, is more a reflection of a perceived public mood that we have gone far enough in enforcing the Constitution's guarantee of equal justice than it is the product of neutral principles of law. In the short run, it may seem the easier course to allow our great metropolitan areas to be divided up each into two cities—one white, the other black—but it is a course, I predict, our people will ultimately regret. I dissent.

Editor's Notes

1. Justice Marshall, as had Judge Roth before him, lacked a careful chronology of precisely when these acts of segregation occurred. For over fifteen years, progressive board members had fought for equality. *De jure* segregation was never the policy of the boards elected by the Serve Our Schools Committee. A thorough analysis of the time factors involved in Detroit discriminatory practices is available in Eleanor P. Wolf, *Trial and Error: The Detroit School Segregation Case* (Detroit: Wayne State University Press, 1981) Wolf also notes with cool accuracy the frustrations imposed on liberal efforts at integration both by bureaucracy and by the loss of integration as a goal by an important segment of black leadership. With careful detail, she notes areas in which the court records show that the truth remained elusive.

   Wrongs had been committed, however, in whatever year, and Justice Marshall's basic arguments stand on their merits.

2. *Public Act 48*, cited here, had begun as one of several bills that were introduced in the legislature by State Senator (later Mayor) Coleman Young, who had long pursued the idea of "community control" of

the schools. In the fall of 1970 the interests of community-control advocates coincided with those of white parents in outlying Detroit areas who wished to avoid any change within their all-white neighborhood schools. The bill abruptly became law. The part of it barring the use of the Detroit Board's desegregation plan was declared unconstitutional, but by that time the question was moot.

3. The number of 285,000 represents the enrollment in the Detroit public schools just before 1970. At this writing, it is about 110,000 less.

Part XV

Playing by New Rules: Grand Plans for Downtown

Playing by New Rules:
Grand Plans for Downtown

After the advent of the New Detroit Committee in the fall of 1967, most Detroiters became more conscious of the role of business and industry in shaping directions for the city and in choosing the players in the game. It was a role that they had always filled—it was clearly perceived by the French farmers of the 1830s when their lands were crossed by new roads—but it was a role ignored by many. Detroit's movers and shakers have in recent years been examined.

One critic is the young black artist and poet Leisia Duskin, who portrays in "Business" how some leaders, hopefully lesser ones, spend their days.

The political definition of the changes from the "city of homes" that Myron Adams saw in 1911 to the developers' game plan of the late seventies is set out for us by attorney Kenneth Cockrel in "Downtown Detroit," a section of a tour guide written for a field trip sponsored by DARE (the Detroit Alliance for a Radical Economy) in September, 1979. I note that former Councilman Cockrel's remarks on the lack of democracy in decision-making seem particularly valid, and are of the sort rarely heard in civics classes. (I *do* give government teachers full marks for effort, but this is not information easily obtained by anyone.)

The last of the "downtown" items is chosen from Wolf Von Eckardt's *Back to the Drawing Board: Planning Livable Cities*, in which he gives us an out-of-town architect's view of the Renaissance Center and bolsters the opinion of many Detroiters that the Emperor-Architect of the RenCen lacked a few stitches of clothing.

1. Business

Leisia Duskin

the big shit office
workers and execs
get up early,
shower,
put on their corporate
dress.

They sign in early
in order to see
who will sign in late.
They read journals
for lunch and
listen to
MUZAK.

The rest of the
day spent staring out
windows perfecting
coffee and
cigarette butt dreams.

Leisia Duskin, *Lights Out in 10* (Detroit, 1986), 29.

2.　Downtown Detroit

Detroit Alliance for a Rational Economy

At the time Kenneth V. Cockrel prepared this material, he was serving on the Detroit City Council and frequently questioned tax abatements given to industry and to downtown developers, such as the backers of the proposed Millender Center and of the expansion of the Renaissance Center. The essay was written for the use of DARE (the Detroit Alliance for a Rational Economy). Attorney Cockrel gave his permission to reprint it here shortly before his death in 1989.

Introduction

People who don't come downtown much often are impressed with all of the new "developments." Something is always happening—new buildings are going up, and old ones are coming down. There are new public facilities, such as the Hart Plaza and the Joe Louis Arena. The amount of money being invested is considerable.

Since 1973, over $543 million was spent on downtown construction, with another $630 million earmarked for the next decade. There was never any question that there would be a Detroit "renaissance." The questions that faced the economic elite of De-

Detroit Alliance for a Rational Economy, Georgakas Collection, Box 2, file 21, Reuther Library, Wayne State University. Reprinted by permission of Kenneth Cockrel.

troit were when, how, and consistent with what priorities. But we must look beyond the glass, concrete, and glitter for the essence of the reshaping process.

The Major Goal

The present development of the downtown area pursues many of the same goals as were advanced by Mayor Cobo. The major objective is for Detroit to serve as the major administrative center for the region.

Downtown Detroit is still the most appropriate location for this center. All major roads and freeways originate downtown. . . . In addition, downtown is sufficiently compact to serve the particular needs of administrative and financial businesses. . . . These arrangements cannot be reproduced in the sprawling suburbs. . . .

How It's Done

The means for downtown Detroit's development is the much heralded private-public coalition. This unequal relationship combines the profit agenda of major investors with the political needs of the local leadership. . . .

To implement this new mechanism, a variety of hybrid organizations of business people and local political leaders has been formed. They have impressive titles: Detroit Development Authority (DDA), Economic Development Corporation (EDC), Detroit Renaissance, Inc., and Central Business District (CBD), to name a few of the most significant.

The single most important organization to downtown development is the Detroit Economic Growth Corporation (EGC). Its Board of Directors is appointed by the Mayor, and seats the chief executive officers of virtually every major area corporation. There is token representation from trade unions and the community, but the EGC is primarily directed by Detroit's corporate elite. The EGC was initially chaired by James Roche, of General Motors, and Lynn Townsend, of Chrysler Corporation. That power is now

[1979] in the hands of Arthur Seder, Jr., of American Natural Resources and Michigan Consolidated Gas.

The Economic Growth Corporation is a private corporation; its meetings are not open to the public. Nevertheless, its annual budget comes primarily from public sources: $375,000 from the State of Michigan, and $375,000 from the City of Detroit, but which is extracted from the Community Development Block Grant Funds!

This primarily publicly funded but privately controlled corporation also directs the work of two of the development agencies in Detroit: the Economic Development Corporation (EDC) and the Downtown Development Authority (DDA). To be sure, both are public entities. But the Executive Vice-President of the DDA and the EDC and all of their staffs are, in fact, employees of the EGC! They work under the direction of the EGC President; they are the people directly involved in downtown projects. . . .

These boards are justified as places where "coalitions" of powerful interests can be built, enabling them to work on projects in a coordinated fashion. Critical decisions are made by a few people who are insulated from public control. There are public officials and labor union leaders on many of these boards, but their priorities are clearly established by the business representatives. These organizations are not places where community input can be made, but are organizations whose primary function is to "facilitate" the investment of private capital in downtown Detroit.

The world of federal grants and special state legislation to aid investors is a complex one that has a language of its own. Words and phrases such as UDAG, P.A. 198, Urban Systems Grant, Community Development Block Grant, 22d Mortgage Loan, P.A. 255, P.A. 438, are casually used at these meetings, and the uninitiated will wonder what is being discussed. All of these deal with federal and state taxpayers' money. In the case of tax abatement plans . . . corporation developers are allowed to escape paying taxes, which means someone else must pick up the tab. While the language and details are often complex, the basic concept behind these grants and tax exemptions is simple: *to give public money* to private investors as inducements, thus foreclosing the use of these funds for services for the rest of us. . . .

What Is Downtown Detroit?

There are no signs or borders to mark the passage, but as we cross the Fisher Freeway, we enter a separate city. The Downtown Development Authority is a tax district separate from the rest of Detroit. Under a recently passed state law (Public Act 197 of 1975), all new revenues generated in the downtown development area after 1978 are given to the Downtown Development Authority to reinvest in that development area *only*! The result is that the increasing property tax revenues of the new private buildings are spent only within the borders of this separate city. . . .

3.   Renaissance and *Risorgimento*

Wolf Von Eckardt

Perhaps it began in the New Detroit Committee. Suddenly there was a sense of power felt by community leaders, telling each other they could begin a new city in a world of change. Perhaps, as some said, the whole thing began with the restlessness of Henry Ford II, irreverently nicknamed by Detroiters "Hank the deuce." At any rate, in the mid-seventies a decision was made to tamper with the old city and its river on a grand scale. Suddenly great round towers were climbing skyward. As the work neared completion, average citizens, whose opinion no one had asked, began to wonder. What was it all for? Why the gray bunkers in front? Why was it so hard to walk around it?

It remained for architect and critic Wolf Von Eckardt to visit the scene and put together the thoughts of many.

If Detroit ever has a renaissance—and God knows it needs one—it will happen despite its flashy, new Renaissance Center. Completed in 1977, the skyscraping bundle of glass tubes on the Detroit River is really a counter-Renaissance Center. It is at best an example of modern city planning's exclusive reliance on the "perfection of physical equipment," as Mumford called it, without regard for the intricacy of the urban fabric. It cuts the city off from its river as effectively as the nineteenth-century industrial plants and warehouses. And, in keeping with LeCorbusier's and CIAM's misguided notions it concentrates and segregates one vital urban function—high-style commerce and tourism—from the rest of the city's life to the detriment of both.

Excerpt from *Back to the Drawing Board: Planning Livable Cities* by Wolf Von Eckardt (1978) reprinted by permission of New Republic Books.

At the time the Detroit Renaissance Center was built, New York city planners began the revitalization of a frisky, but declining (mostly lower middle-class) neighborhood in an altogether different spirit with altogether different methods. The *risorgimento* of Little Italy which is roughly between Greenwich Village and Chinatown in Lower Manhattan, is hardly comparable in terms of expenditure and scale with what was done in Detroit. But it illustrates a new approach to the rejuvenation of declining cities, an approach that preserves and strengthens the integration of a variety of people and activities that make neighborhoods and cities lively.

RenCen, as Detroiters call it, consists of a 73-story, 1400-room hotel; meeting rooms and halls for large conventions; four office towers with 2.2 million square feet of rentable space; parking for 6,000 cars; and a carnival of four movie theaters, 13 restaurants, a suburban shopping-center worth of shops, cocktail lounges, splashing water, greenery, glitter, and Muzak-drenched confusion.

All this obviously draws business, people, and vitality from Detroit's already decaying downtown, six or seven blocks away. Once you have entered RenCen, there is no reason to leave it again until it is time to go home, or your money runs out. But entering the glass doors is extremely difficult if you attempt it on foot. My excuse for being so maladroit in Detroit is that before my visit I had dinner with a friend nearby and there weren't any taxis. So, with much apprehension (Detroit has one of the highest crime rates), I negotiated several deserted and partly abandoned blocks of urban no-man's land until I came to a formidable barrier—ten-lane Jefferson Avenue, a nasty highway that clearly was not designed to be crossed by anything.

A pedestrian must pass two more tests before he may be admitted to architect John Portman's never-never megastructure. First, he must prove his courage by walking the driveway through a forbidding "berm," a concrete rampart that looks suspiciously like a Berlin Wall erected to keep the natives out, but built, I am told, to house heating and air-conditioning machinery. Next, he must prove his ingenuity by finding his way through a labyrinth of driveways, without signs or sidewalks, until he finds the all but hidden entrance into drive-in Portman-land.

The reward is that, once inside, you may plunk into any one of a myriad of cushiony seats on any of six levels—by the pond, under

533

a waterfall, perching on a daringly cantilevered "cocktail pod"—looking up into dangling greenery or down into teeming humanity—and that at the flash of your credit card, an apparition will appear on a motorized refreshment wagon and sell you a drink.

The scene is at once lively and monotonous. You are inside the huge platform from which all the glass tubes sprout. It is an enormous, exciting space, filled with giant concrete columns that support the skyscrapers above, as well as elevator shafts, a multitude of escalators, spiral staircases that mesh the various levels and galleries and pods and ends. Portman is famous for these grand, somewhat adrenalized courts. He used them at the Peachtree Center in Atlanta, and the Embarcadero Center in San Francisco.

The space is monotonous once you walk around. In Detroit, the combined hotel lobby and shopping mall form a circle. You walk around and around expecting some surprise, but it is always the same. You get dizzy and confused. I never quite knew where I was. The poor graphics did not help.[1] Different shops and window displays might have helped. But at the time of my visit in the spring of 1978, few shops had opened, although the offices were renting well and conventions were booked for years.

RenCen is touted as one of the largest privately financed urban developments in the nation's history. It was launched on the initiative of Henry Ford II for the often expressed purpose of helping Detroit out of its despair, of showing confidence in the city. By the time it was finished, it showed over half a billion dollars worth of confidence. Ford was joined by fifty other corporations.

Wayne Doran, the amiable and frank spokesman for these investors, says the demonstration of confidence is as much psychological as physical. Psychologically, it may indeed have accelerated plans for other skyscrapers and shopping centers in downtown Detroit, and a federally assisted "people mover" system, linking the central business district with the cultural center—the Art Institute, the library, and Wayne State University with its various institutions—further up Woodward Avenue.[2] Psychologically, it is also true, no doubt, that the sight of the gleaming glass tubes makes many a Detroit heart beat faster, although the more impressive view of this fortress is from the Canadian side of the river.

But while Mayor Coleman Young is loudly and frequently praising RenCen, I heard much bitter talk about it on the part of Detroit housing and planning officials. Some see it as a capitalist plot against the city. The bitterness is understandable if you travel about in what one writer has called "the city of urban despair." Block after block of abandoned, looted, and burned cottages on weedy, littered plots look even more depressing than abandoned, looted, and burned-out tenements in Brooklyn. The shocking sight is one occupied house, in a sea of dead ones, with a horde of children playing in the debris of a broken-down porch.

RenCen does nothing for these children and Doran says irrefutably that it never promised to solve the city's social problems. It provides 3,000 jobs, he says, and is bringing thousands of conventioneers into the city. The trouble is, few of them venture across Jefferson Avenue.

The city, together with RenCen, will have to spend thought and money on building links to downtown, if the half billion dollar investment is to stop hurting Detroit and start helping. Well-lit greenways and walkways and minibus service to the restaurants and boutiques of Greektown and other attractions are imperative.[3] The sooner that silly "berm" is buried, the better.

I am sure the deplorable insularity of RenCen is not due to ill will, as some people charge, but to the naivete of American business in city planning and architecture. The riverfront site was easily available (although the city planners wanted it turned into a park). There was no need, as Doran pointed out, to displace anyone. It had a good view. Nor could Ford and his partners conceive of a manifestation of power and confidence that did not scrape the sky. Even Paris and London have succumbed to the Promethean temptation.

But just think what Henry Ford II and his 50 partners might have accomplished for Detroit if they had laid their half-billion dollar towers on end. It would have yielded at least 12-square blocks of new buildings—plazas, covered malls, greenery, splashing water, glitter, Muzak-drenched confusion, motorized barmaids, and all.

Editor's Notes

1. At the urging of merchants, those graphics were reassessed, and there have been some improvements. It is still possible, however, to get lost in the RenCen.

2. A beautiful, though smaller, People Mover opened in the summer of 1987. It has delightful art work by Detroit artists, but goes only on a downtown circuit—no runs to the Cultural Center.
3. Greektown is an enormous success, and everyone is happy to walk or ride the People Mover to it from the RenCen. Greektown pleases everyone, that is, except for a few old-time Greeks who remember the coffeehouses and grocery stores now displaced by rows of restaurants and the huge tourist center created in Trapper's Alley, the old Traugott Schmidt furrier's warehouse.

Part XVI

A Shrinking City

A Shrinking City

Detroit, within its city limits, is today unquestionably a shrinking city. Arguments about the accuracy of U.S. Census employees do not change the fact that there will be even fewer people in 1990. In 1950 there were 1,800,000; in 1980, 1,300,000. It is reasonable to project that Detroit may have less than one million in 1990. The loss of a half million people in thirty years was primarily due to the emptying of the central city, a six-mile square bounded by Livernois, McNichols, Conner, and the river.

It is useful to discard the widely quoted tales of suburbanites returning in great numbers to riverfront apartments. Some do return but never enough to cancel out earlier losses.

The six counties that roughly comprise the Detroit metropolitan area are something else again. Surprisingly, this area still maintains about the same level of industrial employment as it had during World War II. This is definitely not a "rust belt."[1]

Industrial employment has been relocated into many small plants with about five thousand to ten thousand workers. The new workplaces have spread out over a fifty-mile radius from the old city center. Detroit auto production has spread out into such places as Ypsilanti, Wixom, Flat Rock, and new sites north of Pontiac.

Along with scaled-down heavy industry, there are to be found in the outlying areas many corporate headquarters, principal re-

539

tail activities, and newer growth industries. It is these service sector growth industries that are drawing newcomers to all southeastern Michigan. They include government administration, financial services, higher education, and the arts.

In contrast with the old smokestack industries of the city, which around 1900 became chiefly automotive, the new suburban workplaces do not need to look as ugly as the old, though they sometimes manage to. Most of the work is done behind glass and cement walls lining the major highways.

For a view of the movements of people and their work throughout southeastern Michigan, we turn to a research document produced by the Long Range Planning Committee of the Episcopal Diocese of Michigan, titled "The Emerging Pattern: A Regional Perspective."

As we have seen a number of jobs move to the suburbs and a number of Detroit factories close or leave town, there have been efforts to keep big industry here, or to entice it with tax abatements. The Cadillac plants in southeast Detroit are gone, the Burroughs Company is now Unisys and lives in Pennsylvania. Opinion is still divided about General Motor's effort to create a new factory in Poletown, but it is clear that employment goals there have been far from realized, though old neighborhoods, churches, and shopping areas were destroyed in Detroit and Hamtramck.

One of the most imaginative efforts to meet the challenge of the jobs and factories that have gone was a series of proposals by Dan Luria and Jack Russell in *Rational Reindustrialization*. Their sensible creativity has been largely ignored by the area's power structure in the several years since their study was written.

A city is, or should be, made up of homes. Detroit has come a long way since Myron Adam's 1911 exuberance over the city of homes and trees. For a current countdown of homes and statistics of our housing supply, we turn to the Catholic Interracial Council, which in a May, 1988, newsletter brought together statistics from several sources and tied them in with the current plight of the homeless.

Another view of the results of arson, vandalism, and official neglect is that of Ron Williams, editor of *Metro Times*, in "Detroit Loves a Good Demolition." Between them, Williams and the Catholic Interracial Council make clear that "gentrification" by young preservationists is not one of Detroit's problems; arson is. The largest item in the mayor's proposed "action grant" budget for 1988–89 was ten million dollars for the demolition of already half-destroyed and unsafe buildings.

Turning from shelter to another of the basic problems of people—hunger—we introduce the 1982 report of the Michigan Task Force on Hunger, written by Councilwoman Maryann Mahaffey, chairperson of the Michigan Statewide Nutrition Commission, for Congressional hearings.[2]

As Ken Cockrel strongly suggested in a previous chapter, the city's movers and shakers, its large committees, are reluctant to share power. Over the last year or two there has developed a short list of problems that the present mayor seems unwilling to address. When the responses of the city administration began to turn to charges of "white racism" on the part of its critics, a retired UAW staffer, himself black and experienced in political action, entered the arena. "Ernie" Dillard's call for accountability on the part of blacks in government and shrewdness on the part of black voters is here excerpted under the title "The Cry of White Racism."[3]

Editor's Notes

1. See reports of the Michigan Employment Security Commission, published under the titles *Detroit Manpower Review* and *Detroit Labor Market Review* (March 1974–March 1988). The 1974–80 reports had as their executive editor S. Martin Taylor, later head of the New Detroit Committee. There were certainly variations in manufacturing employment over the years, but overall the counties neighboring Detroit have maintained their manufacturing employment totals to an amazing degree.

2. A word about Councilwoman Mahaffey: Mahaffey has spent some years on the council, serving also as a professor of social work at Wayne State University. She has been active in the national and local Welfare Rights Organization and has served as president of the National Association of Social Workers. She is a persistent advocate of those who have no other place to go for help. In the last few years, she has been actively engaged in preparing handgun control, or "gun freeze," ordinances for the city, each of which, until a minor compromise resolution in July, 1989, was shelved by her colleagues

when it became clear that there was not enough strength to override the usual vetoes of Mayor Young. Mahaffey is liberal, but also practical; her understanding of the budget process goes well beyond several of her colleagues, and those who try to dismiss her as a "little lady" usually learn better, to their sorrow. Her quality shows in this hunger report.

3. Dillard and his wife, Jessie, who served for several years on the State Board of Canvassers, the agency dedicated to keeping Michigan elections honest, are shrewd and perceptive observers of the political scene and determined Democrats. Ernest Dillard, with years of political experience behind him in his work with the UAW, had clearly reached his boiling point when he wrote "The Cry of White Racism."

1. The Emerging Pattern: A Regional Perspective

Episcopal Diocese of Michigan

In 1987, the Episcopal Diocese of Michigan (then mainly composed of the eastern half of the Lower Peninsula) undertook a study of its people and their movements. The report, written by Merle E. Henrickson, is both history and projection.

There will continue to be urbanizing development in broad bands along the principal freeways, especially along I-94, I-96 and 696, I-75 and I-275. This urbanizing development will not necessarily result in net growth, but the greatest numerical growth in the state will occur in Livingston, Oakland, Washtenaw [Ann Arbor area] and *western* Wayne Counties.

The northern part of the lower peninsula may have the greatest percentage increase, but this will be in the range of 10,000 to 20,000 per county north of the Muskegon-Bay City line. It will consist of a combination of retirees and persons supported by the recreational use of the area.

Episcopal Diocese of Michigan, "The Emerging Pattern: A Regional Perspective," Report of the Demographics Task Force, Long Range Planning Committee (Unpublished MS, 1987), Episcopal Diocese of Michigan Archives, Detroit.

The inner core of both Detroit and other pre-World War II industrial cities will continue to decline.

The church will face a major separation and social stratification of people, with particular implications for the main line denominations.

The acquaintance with the world for young newly formed families living along the individual corridors will have been formed from television and shopping malls. They will be without memory of depression, sit-down strikes, war and the social unrest of the sixties. Their computers will flash, "Document not found."

Many older retired people and much rural poverty will be located in the area north of the Muskegon-Bay City line. A residue will remain in the old inner city areas of people who can not make their way in the society in which they are living. The highest incidence of unemployment, under-employment and dependence on various welfare programs will be in these areas.

Changes since World War II in the organization of the industrial work place, as well as changes in the transportation of materials and workers to that place, have profoundly affected the patterns of industrial and residential location in the Detroit Metropolitan area.

Industrial plants built in Detroit prior to World War II were dependent on water and rail transportation to receive their essential raw materials and to ship their manufactured products. Industries in Detroit were located along the Detroit or Rouge Rivers, or along the railroad belt lines which were roughly parallel to Grand Boulevard and the circle with a six mile radius formed by Livernois, McNichols [old Six Mile Road] and Conner Avenues.

Prior to World War II there were 400,000 to 500,000 industrial work places in the Detroit area, and 85% of them were located along these railroad lines. Industrial plants were sometimes enormous concentrations of work stations, with 75,000 employed at the Ford Rouge Plant and 40,000 at the Dodge Main Plant.

The people who worked in these plants depended principally on public transportation for the trip to work, and lived as close as possible to street car or bus lines. During World War II and until 1950, there were over 1,300,000 people who lived inside the Livernois, McNichols, Conner belt in Detroit, Highland Park, and Hamtramck. Another 600,000 lived within the city of Detroit outside this belt, and the balance of the metropolitan area population consisted of 1,000,000, mostly living beyond the Detroit city limits.

Beginning with World War II, new industries broke from their reliance on railroad transportation, and came to use trucks to move materials to and between plants. Construction of freeways extended to fifty or seventy-five miles the distances which plants might be separated from their related and supplier plants. At the same time the functioning size of major industrial plants was generally reduced to a range of 3,000 to 10,000 workers.

The number of industrial jobs in the metropolitan area has remained substantially the same—in the 400,000 to 450,000 range. However, the location pattern is now reversed. At least 80% of the work places have moved outside the city and less than 100,000 remain along the old industrial corridors.

With work places moved twenty-five to fifty miles out of the city, and little public transportation, workers traveled to work in their own cars, and parked in lots provided by their employers. As new families formed, they sought homes near their work places, and gradually emptied out the old city with its housing crowded into two and four flat units. Between 1950 and 1980, the area between the Livernois, McNichols, Conner belt lost half its people—about 650,000. Over that same period, Oakland County added 600,000, *western* Wayne County added 550,000 and Macomb County added 500,000.

The outward movement was selective. People who bought new houses had regular income, either as industrial or white collar workers, frequently with two incomes in the family.

Four groups of people remained in the inner city, which experienced the greatest population loss:

Those persons who could not afford to buy a house, who had to remain where rental housing of some sort was available. Since the principal supply of rental housing in Detroit has been the two and four family flats built in the 1920's, these were the places that were available. However, the oversupply resulting from a 50% population loss meant that many were vacant, became vandalized, and have been demolished.

The elderly who chose to remain in their old homes, but also the elderly for whom new senior citizen housing was scattered around in the older part of the city.

People released from institutions for whom many of the large older houses were taken over to become adult foster care homes, or unregulated rooming houses.

A few middle class families who lived in new housing on urban renewal lands near downtown or along the Detroit River.

2.   Rational Reindustrialization

Dan Luria and Jack Russell

In 1981 Luria and Russell outlined a plan for redeveloping Detroit industry through new products, mainly "energy hardware" such as natural gas drilling and coal gasification equipment. They urged an immediate inventory of Detroit's capital goods, believing that it would show both tools and industrial capacity adaptable to these uses. They suggested that new industries might well exist in old buildings threatened by the wrecking ball, and that these industries could provide jobs for the still-available pool of highly skilled workers.

Detroit is wounded. For thirty years we have bled jobs and capital to the suburbs, to the South, and overseas. During the past five years, Detroit's condition has become critical. New wounds have been opened. We have hemorrhaged economic life as never before. In the 1980's, a city once the vital hub of America's Great Lakes industrial heartland is becoming a grim monument to the waste of an unplanned economy. While the mayor exhorts the taxpayers to save our City, a Presidential Commission has concluded that America's Detroits are disposable containers of economic activity which, now nearly empty, may be cast aside.

Detroit's economy is being killed by industrial disinvestment. Detroit's major manufacturers have not returned to the city the

Dan Luria and Jack Russell, *Rational Reindustrialization: An Economic Development Agenda for Detroit* (Detroit: Widgetripper Press, 1981), 5–12.

wealth we have created. On the contrary, the profits produced by Detroit labor have built new factories elsewhere, or been distributed to stockholders, or funded often ill-advised corporate adventures. In 1947, the city held over 280,000 manufacturing jobs in some 3,300 firms. Today, Detroit hosts less than 100,000 such jobs in fewer than 1,700 firms.

This industrial disinvestment has eroded our tax base and distorted our expenditure priorities. It is *the* fundamental cause of the municipal fiscal crisis we now confront and with which we will continue to struggle for years.

Proclamation of Detroit's Renaissance will not end the trauma of industrial disinvestment. Downtown recommercialization can replace neither the number nor the quality of the jobs lost as our industry dies. The family of the unemployed auto worker is not saved by employing one daughter as a file clerk at Renaissance Center or one son as a security guard at Riverfront West. . . .

We believe that the 1980's will determine Detroit's fate: either industrial Detroit will be rebuilt and recover an important position in the national economy, or disinvestment will destroy the life chances of our youth, our capacity for local self-government, and much of the useful wealth created by three generations of Detroiters. By the 1990's, Detroit will either be a diversified manufacturing center of a new kind, or it will be a discarded city of vacant factories and abandoned homes from which the remaining affluent shield themselves in residential enclaves and a well-fortified downtown.

If Detroit is to survive as a city in which working people can prosper, we must redefine and reorder our development priorities. We believe that a rational economic development program for Detroit must be a least-cost program to retain and create tens of thousands of high-wage, cyclically insensitive industrial jobs. This essay is a first sketch of such a program. . . .

First, we are not opposed to the relocation of investment capital within cities of a metropolis, regions of a nation, or even the nations of a world. We oppose only its unplanned, socially wasteful, and privately controlled movement. Once the relatively high wages enjoyed by Detroit auto workers had filled up the city's available space with single family homes, it was inevitable and desirable that those forms of auto production requiring extensive space would subse-

The flag left behind: scene in an abandoned factory. (Courtesy of Bob McKeown, 1988.)

quently be built in suburban and rural greenfields. But it was neither inevitable nor desirable that metropolitan Detroit be politically balkanized into hostile municipalities differentiated by class and race; that metropolitan tax base sharing would thus become impossible; that a powerful auto/oil/construction/consumer durables lobby would decree the federal highway and mortgage policies that replicated the suburban phenomenon section by section to 26 Mile Road and beyond; that Detroit would be gutted by freeway trenches rather than served by mass transit; nor that the city's commerce would be mauled by the placement of major shopping centers just beyond its borders. The spatial catastrophe of metropolitan Detroit is a sufficient argument for greater social control of investment.

Similarly, the siting of some new auto plants in the West and the South has been a logical and desirable response to regional growth and the development of new markets. But it is hardly in the interests of society as a whole that some firms leave Michigan because unionized workers can claim a greater share of the wealth they produce and because our citizens have organized politically for better protection from unsafe work and the vagaries of the capitalist business cycle.

We will not advocate the socially irrational imprisonment of private capital within Detroit or southeastern Michigan. We *will* argue for radically increased government authority in the economy. . . .

Second, we are not opposed to Detroit's Renaissance. We *do* believe it should be demystified. The much-celebrated re-birth is in essence an attempt to protect the value of existing investments and future profit opportunities in the downtown hub. The banks, retailers, utilities and other businesses downtown have been threatened by the disinvestment of Detroit, especially since 1967. The Renaissance was their self-interested redevelopment strategy, long before it became the keystone policy of the administration of Mayor Coleman Young. By logic and law, many of the downtown businesses are less mobile than industry. They must stay and protect their futures. We hope they build and succeed.

We do challenge, however, the terms they offer for development, the logic of their strategy, and the absurd conceit that somehow their success will be the salvation of a city ravished by industrial disinvestment. . . . When and if just the beachhead projects (Trolley Plaza, Riverfront West, the Millender Center, and the Cadillac Mall) are completed, hundreds of millions of federal and local public revenues will have facilitated these private developments.

Even with this huge taxpayers' subsidy, the downtown commercial renaissance is a risky business. . . .

The grand designs for the future development of downtown Detroit are based upon the questionable belief that many thousands of salaried professionals and managers can be induced to settle there with their families. Some will surely be attracted to the amenities of the river and the hub, but with Detroit's extraordinary upper-middle-class home bargains and the comfortable, secure suburbs just minutes away by freeway, we believe the downtown Renaissance may well abort. Given the high risk, the developers' current terms, the narrow strata of the population served, and the limited impact on the local economy, we do not believe that the downtown strategy should have priority claims on the City's precious economic development resources. . . .

Unfortunately, even a booming commercial Renaissance on the riverfront and downtown would not meet the needs of working class Detroit. It would not deliver the jobs. . . . It is fantasy to hope that hotels, a shopping center, some office buildings, and the service needs of wealthy condominium owners will be able to employ the workers, the children of workers, who have been discharged from our closed factories. Moreover, the jobs that the commercial Renaissance may provide will contribute far less to the families of the employed and to the economy of the city than have the high-wage, national market, industrial jobs they "replace."

During the past 30 years, Detroit has lost 27% of its population but nearly 70% of its jobs in manufacturing. In 1981, over 400,000 Detroiters—one in every three—receives some form of public assistance. . . .

Third, we acknowledge the important efforts at community development in Detroit, but argue that these efforts at best only partially balm the wounds of disinvestment; they do not constitute a cure for the disease. Detroit needs all the housing dollars and programs we can get, but we should understand that the neighborhoods created by a high-wage, high-employment industrial economy between 1910 and the 1950's will not be renewed, especially at today's costs, in an economy based on transfer payments from the federal government and on low-wage service employment. The best housing program for Detroit would be one that reopens our plants and employs our homeowners.

Similarly, most neighborhood commerce cannot survive drained by the suburban malls and dependent on the Detroit poor. If Detroit can reindustrialize and employ our people, then neighborhood merchants will have a chance. If industrial disinvestment continues unchecked, we will have boutiques for the downtowners and party stores for the people.

What *will* rebuild [Detroit's economy]? . . . Let us begin with a paradox: the very severity of Detroit's industrial disinvestment may create an opportunity. . . . Tens of thousands of workers have been permanently dismissed. Several major plants have closed; more will follow. Smaller plants that built components for obsolete technologies or products have been abandoned. Orders from smaller parts suppliers have ceased. Tool and die shops are without work. In less than 30 months, multiple shocks have broken many of the crucial links that held together Detroit's ailing but still viable automobile industry.

Are these links permanently broken or can they be reforged? In some quarters, optimism about *Michigan's* future in the automotive economy runs high. Transport economies and attempts to emulate Japanese-style inventory management may recentralize in our State some of the previously lost major elements of the industry. Southeastern Michigan still has important comparative advantages in labor skills, transport infrastructure, abundant water, and the substantial remaining share of auto production. But *Detroit* cannot hope to win back what *we* have lost; our built environment is a huge barrier to major new industrial construction. The staggering public costs borne to prepare the new Cadillac Plant site indicate the price extracted for merely retaining 6,000 of the 14,000 Cadillac jobs we had less than a decade ago. . . .

Much of our auto industry, then, is gone or going. . . . Capital leaves, but labor skills remain. Plants are closed, but not razed. Railways and freeways still tie the factories together and connect them to the nation. The links between the hundreds of small- and medium-sized vendors and the major facilities are damaged, but not broken beyond repair. The engine of production that was built over the span of half a century has not yet been scrapped, nor should it be. Detroit can still bend metal. . . .

We believe that currently there exists *no* workable program for inducing privately financed economic development. There is, moreover, no self-correcting process by which urban disinvestment creates the conditions necessary for expanded reinvestment of the kind and on the scale required. From this outlook flows the need to project our own concept of "rational economic development," one which transcends wishful thinking about an orderly transition from an industrial economy to a service economy and seeks to build upon the actual history of Detroit as a producer of durable goods for the national and international economies.

Others before us have, to be sure, seen the need to preserve and revitalize Detroit's aging industrial base through planned conversion to the production of socially useful goods needed by America and the world. Walter Reuther, for example, popularized demands for reorienting facilities supplying the 1941–1945 war effort to making building supplies for low-cost housing. Our effort seeks to supply this legacy of intent to the now very much more difficult circumstances of Detroit in the 1980's. . . .

3.   Conscience and Housing

Catholic Interracial Council

In May, 1988, the Catholic Interracial Council of Detroit, a small but highly respected group, issued a newsletter containing the results of a study of housing and the homeless. Mainly the work of Robert Selwa and Marie Oresti, it is reprinted here.

Will Housing Opportunity Grow or Diminish for Detroit?

The 1980 census showed that Detroit had a net loss of 58,696 homes! This was the largest loss of housing for any city in the United States. Detroit has had this enormous loss while other older northern and eastern cities were expanding their housing opportunity.

Detroit: net loss of 58,696 homes. *New York:* net gain of 21,000 homes.

Toledo: net gain of 13,000 homes.

Philadelphia: net gain of 11,000 homes.

Catholic Interracial Council of Detroit (May, 1988). Reprinted by permission of Robert Selwa and Marie Oresti, editors.

Boston: net gain of 8,000 homes.

Milwaukee: net gain of 7,000 homes.

Detroit's staggering rate of destruction of its homes is continuing throughout the 1980's. Here are the annual housing reports on Detroit by the Southeast Michigan Council of Governments:

Year	New Homes Built In Detroit	Homes Demolished In Detroit	Net Loss In Homes In Detroit
1980	928	4,387	-3,459
1981	1,372	6,002	-4,630
1982	1,263	3,814	-2,551
1983	165	4,037	-3,872
1984	69	3,656	-3,587
1985	217	4,301	-4,084
1986	223	5,016	-4,793
1987	262	4,796	-4,534

In the entire city of Detroit, a city of 140 square miles, during 1987 only two single family homes were built! There were 260 multiple housing units built. And there were 4,796 dwellings destroyed, for another enormous loss in housing of 4,534 homes.

This is while thousands of homeless people wander the streets of Detroit. This is while housing destruction is practiced in Detroit instead of housing rehabilitation. The net loss in housing translates into this fact: on the average, another 12 homes are destroyed every day in Detroit!

To shelter the homeless is one of the Corporal Works of Mercy. To expand housing opportunities is one of the goals of this country. What are we going to do about reaching this goal in this city? How are city, state and federal governments going to address this problem? How are business, civic groups and individuals going to address it? Are we going to let the dream of Dr. Martin Luther King die in the rubble of a bulldozer?

4.   Detroit Loves a Good Demolition

Ron Williams

Detroit maintained until recently a unique disregard for the elegant but rotting Gilded Age mansions remaining near downtown and the great architectural triumphs of the twenties. Commenting on the recent successful effort of Detroiters to save Orchestra Hall, Ron Williams, editor and publisher of Metro Times, Detroit's strong alternative weekly, wrote the following.

In 1970, when Detroit Symphony bassoonist Paul Ganson learned that Orchestra Hall was targeted to make way for a pizza parlor, he became very angry. And determined.

Mustering a group of equally angry and determined musicians and preservationists, Ganson succeeded in having the venerable hall—which just happens to be a shade this side of acoustically perfect—placed on the National Historic Register in 1971. Then the chamber concerts began, the preservation jazz series and much later the guest concerts by the DSO itself. In that sorry excuse for a decade, with the city crumbling down around them, a small group of Detroiters dug in their heels and simply said no. They said, "Save Orchestra Hall."

Ron Williams, "Detroit Loves a Good Demolition," *Metro Times* (25 February–3 March 1987): 18–20.

The Feb. 20 [1971] press conference was very crowded. . . . Some of Detroit's most powerful movers and shakers, all smiles and with good reason: they were there to announce something very right. The DSO was coming home to Orchestra Hall. Sure there had been talk of a state-of-the-art performing arts center on the riverfront with a revolving something or other. But the symphony board—which means a cross section of the most influential citizens in our community—chose to dig their own well-heeled shoes into one of the most ravaged and desolate stretches of urban landscape in a city which has virtually redefined the meaning of the words urban renewal. I hope Paul Ganson was there. He should have had the biggest smile of all. . . .

The city of Detroit is rotting. Its roof is caving in—plaster, dust and debris occasionally shower down through the sunlight and pigeon feathers admitted by the hole in the roof. Mildew and dry rot are in control now. Much of the time plywood is a formality easily dispensed with. "Detroit's buildings are getting debricked to provide patios in Dallas," says Preservation Detroit President William Colburn.

Detroiters stopped caring about their city a long time ago. When the Republicans came to town in 1980 to nominate Ronald Reagan, we boasted through bloodshot eyes and stupid grins that Detroit loves a good party. Well, the sad fact of the matter is that what Detroit really loves is a good demolition.

There is probably not another city in this country with a more shameful track record in preserving its past. Go ahead. Wander into the Burton Historical Archives of the Detroit Public Library in the cultural center and discover the truth for yourself. Or if the library isn't your style, head down to one of my favorite watering holes, Old Detroit on Beaubien in Bricktown. Order a Signature and take a hard look at the photos on the wall. It should come as no surprise that half the magnificent buildings pictured were razed long ago to make way for yet another parking lot.

History, you say? Wrong. For every Orchestra Hall, there are 20 other historically significant structures steadily degenerating, moving precariously closer to the point of no return.

The white financial structure isn't giving mortgages to restoration efforts. They are liars if they say they aren't redlining.

556

(Michael Farrell, University of Windsor; art history professor and urban pioneer)

There is no other conclusion to be drawn: Detroiters, urban and suburban alike, have permitted the physical soul of this community to be decimated. Now, as a small vanguard of preservationists and developers have begun to take stands across the city to save what is still left, the weight of decades of indifference is being felt. Detroit's financial community reflects the attitude of the people of this city and, down to almost the very last institution, turns away those proposals.

I accuse the Detroit financial community—and specifically the banks of this city—of willfully redlining preservation and restoration projects. As developers and financial analysts trip over each other to assemble projects in Oakland County, world-class theatres and historically important structures of all kinds are literally rotting in this city. What has changed in the last decade? The presence of urban pioneers, preservationists and developers of every stripe with sophisticated and viable packages who simply cannot get a penny from Detroit banks. We are allowing our own institutions, holding our money, to pursue lending policies that continue to weaken this community. Detroit banks will not lend money to Detroit.

> The Monroe block has been a long learning process. We'll preserve the facades. . . . 10 years ago, we could have preserved the whole buildings. (Dorothy Wrigley, Co-developer of the Monroe Block project)

The buildings in question are some of the oldest left standing in Detroit: Civil War-era structures adjacent to the Kern block. It took a progressive Cleveland-based developer (Forest City Dillon) joining the project to finally give it the right chemistry of public and private funding to move ahead. Also included in that historic block and incorporated into the Monroe redevelopment is the National Theatre. Built in 1911, it is the only theatre designed by internationally renowned architect Albert Kahn and is on the National Register of Historic Places.

Indifference and redlining are just terms. What they have done to this city can be viewed in stark relief . . . [at the National Theatre today]. That is what Detroit has done to its heritage.

An exception, you say? A few blocks away from the National on Bagley sits the empty United Artists Theatre. Some say water damage has made demolition inevitable; others hold out hope. Built in 1928 and designed by architect C. Howard Crane (who also designed Orchestra Hall), the United Artists could face, if not outright destruction, a far worse fate. For only a block south of the United Artists is what is perhaps the perfect metaphor for Detroit's dark struggle with its past—the remains of the Michigan Theatre, now a parking structure. Words cannot describe the feeling one gets to see the spectacular art deco ceiling and then the rows and rows of cars parked beneath. The Grand Circus Theatre . . . ? Shuttered. The Madison Theatre? Dark. All threatened.

What happens when someone comes forward, puts their own money where their mouth is and looks to Detroit's financial community for support? Chuck Forbes and his son Jim purchased the Fox, State (formerly the Palms) and Gem (formerly the Vanguard) theatres in the historic theatre district north of Grand Circus Park. After stabilizing the structures with new roofs, adequate winter heating, etc., they have searched locally and nationally in vain to secure financing to move ahead with their dream of a revitalized entertainment district. Their plan is viable. The Fox alone is inarguably one of the top two or three historic theatres in this country. But no Detroit financial institution will touch them.[1]

Debbie and Joe Grella bought the historic David Whitney Building several years ago with earnings from New York real estate transactions. With a stunning four-story marble atrium, a solid tenant base and an interior People Mover stop, the Grellas set out to refinance the building. Although, according to Debbie Grella, they had financed $300 million worth of projects in New York city, she and her husband were turned down by over 70 lending institutions when it came to this project in this city. Financing was recently acquired through an innovative Build America Bond, the first such bond sale of its kind in Detroit.

Even the prominent and powerful Southfield-based Shostak Brothers real estate firm may have met its match in the city. Despite commitments from Michigan Bell and Blue Cross / Blue Shield to lease office space, the Shostak plan to convert the old flagship Hudson's store (itself saved by preservationists in the late 70's) into luxury atrium office and retail space, perhaps downtown's single most pivotal redevelopment project, appears stalled. The reason? Lack of adequate financing. . . .

In 1981, Mike Farrell purchased a threatened Gothic home just three blocks south of Orchestra Hall. Built in 1868, the house is listed on the National Register of Historic Places.

The mansion on Alfred Street is resplendent in leather wallpaper, marble counters, hand-carved ebony bookcases and 25-foot ceilings. It is a veritable castle surrounded by a moat of modern antagonists—crack houses, prostitution dens, plasma donor centers, boarded-up buildings, rusting auto carcasses, dead hotels and weed-choked fields. "When our house was broken into, the cops said 'tough luck,' we were nuts to live here anyway," Farrell said. "Some sympathy for all the money we've spent on restoration."

Farrell needs to lower the monthly payments on the mortgage so he can replace the roof and stabilize the house. He has been to one bank three times, a second twice and tried a third bank once. He talked to officers at other banks and savings and loans. While he says the inspectors the banks send invariably fall in love with the house, when the formula for financing is run through the computers back at the office, the answer is always the same.

To most of us, that home may be viewed as an important link with the past, part of this city's heritage that should be respected and restored. . . . [Farrell sees] it as something more. "That building is the future of Detroit. And the banks don't have faith in the future of Detroit."

Editor's Note

1. Since then Michael Ilitch, owner of Little Caesar's pizza chain, has purchased the Fox from Forbes, and completed its restoration in the grand style Detroiters remember. Mr. Forbes remains an interested owner of other properties in the old theater district.

5. Hunger in Michigan

Maryann Mahaffey

I am a member of the State health coordinating council, tenured professor of the School of Social Work at Wayne State University. I did research into hunger in Detroit in 1969, and as a result, became the founder of both the Detroit and the State nutrition commissions.

Today the unemployment rate in Detroit, Mich., actually in January 1982, was 20 per cent. It is estimated that two-thirds of our black youth in Detroit are unemployed. On February 25, 1982, we were informed that two General Motors plants in Detroit will close before the end of the year, laying off 2,100 work-

Maryann Mahaffey, *Oversight Hearings on the President's 1983 Budget Recommendations for Child Nutrition: Hearings before the Subcommittee on Elementary, Secondary, and Vocational Education of the Committee on Education and Labor, House of Representatives*, 97th Cong., 2d sess., 16–18 March 1982, 111–15.

ers. McLouth Steel Co. in southeast Michigan may be saved if the creditors agree not to foreclose.

In December, 1981, we estimated—based on our 1980 population—28 per cent of Detroiters were receiving either AFDC, general assistance, or supplemental security income. These figures do not include those working at the minimum wage who are eligible for food stamps or other benefits.

Of the 9.3 million people in Michigan, currently 34.7 percent can be presumed to be economically vulnerable and barely capable of providing for their own maintenance.

. . . The most recent report documents that the highest unemployment in Michigan is not in Detroit. It is in Flint, followed by Muskegon, Saginaw, and Pontiac, with Detroit as No. 5. The Michigan Department of Commerce's slightly different approach to measuring the statewide economic distress released in November 1981, showed 15 cities in Michigan with a per capita income of less than $4,087 in 1980, and 15 with an unemployment rate above 19 per cent in 1980, including the cities of Pontiac and Flint. Using the department of commerce 1980 data, more than 15.4 percent of the population of 15 cities lived below the official poverty level. Of the estimated 18,000 terminated [from Michigan social service benefits] in Michigan last fall, 77 percent live outside Detroit.

. . . A study by the Michigan Statewide Nutrition Commission of emergency food depots and kitchens in June 1981 documented that all of them across the State of Michigan were out of food by the end of the month, most of them by the middle of the month. . . .

The end result is that some of the emergency food depots get much more restrictive as to who is admitted, and they draw their boundaries across smaller and smaller territories.

The Detroit School Board fed almost 20,000 children in the summer school lunch program. . . . We face a number of problems for the summer of 1982. The program's financing has been cut, we understand, from $122 million to $61 million. Last Year Detroit had $1.5 million to operate the program. USDA representatives told our Detroit Health Department the other day that we will receive one-half of our 1981 allotment for 1982, and yet the problem is increasing. More layoffs are occurring, and more people are running out of their unemployment benefits. . . .

561

In Detroit, the board of education has told us that 80 to 85 percent of our school-age children in Detroit qualify for free meals. The new regulation that, in effect, eliminates private, non-profit organizations as sponsors will wreak havoc in Michigan. In the summer of 1980 in Michigan, 23 churches served an average of 4,274 children per day. Eight community action agencies served 10,142 children per day, and 53 other private, nonprofit organizations such as Boys' Clubs served 23,499 meals per day. That's 84 private nonprofit sponsors serving 38,000 children every day across the State of Michigan, and they cannot be sponsors and serve the children meals in the summer lunch program in 1982 in Michigan or anywhere else in the country. . . .

The administrative costs [under new regulations] will go up, and if we don't come up with the extra money for monitoring, we could be accused of not following the regulations and face further cuts. Detroit passed an increase in its income tax last June to show that we are willing to sacrifice to save our beloved city. We have continued to lay off city workers. We had about 33,000 workers on the city payroll in the 1950's and now have 18,000.

The drop in our population is not enough to account for that much loss in workers other than representing the cutbacks in services to our citizens.

Thus, the new regulations and assignments lead us to believe that there are those who would like to find reasons to justify more cuts at the same time that we face more unemployment and more need. . . .

The program has benefits beyond the serving of meals to children. In Detroit and Michigan we have relied on volunteers as well as hiring people to work in the program. In Detroit, we have employed 40 to 50 people with 20 to 25 of those in college and high school. For many, it's their first job; it also makes it possible for them to continue in school. This is crucial for many, given the severe cutbacks in loans and grants. . . .

Why is the summer lunch program so important in meeting a child's health and nutrition needs? A nutritionist who operates the WIC program in a health center in a community southwest of Detroit has reported that the children she sees suffer primarily from anemia. A vitamin supplement is not only expensive, it is not a substitute for an adequate nutritious diet. If the children the nutritionist sees were not getting the summer lunch program, in addition to the school lunch program, they would be eating only one meal a day, and inevitably, their anemia will worsen.

A mother in another southern Michigan city reported that she sends her children to her sister's house during the summer to get the summer lunch. She does not have one in her area, for less than 50 percent of the children in her community are classified as "needy."

I worry about the children who do not have aunts or contacts in an area with 50 percent of the children classified as "needy."

When asked what she would do if the children could not get the summer lunch, the mother said they would be reduced to one meal per day. The nutritionist pointed out that summer is the time when children burn up energy and need this program. Obviously, we are also dealing with the interrelationship between programs. The food stamp allotment is inadequate. Commodities are not the answer, either, whether cheese, peanuts, or peanut butter, whatever it might be.

A study, conducted since 1978, by Shirley Nuss, Ph.D., Detroit, documents that when people face reduced incomes they first pay the rent and utilities and cut back on food. Parents generally cut back on their own food intake in order to feed their children. One father reported in the food survey this year that he takes Tylenol to cut his hunger pangs so he will eat less in order to more properly feed his children.

The need to insure a roof over one's head is exemplified in another case that we were presented with this fall, where the mother spent the rent money on food for a sick baby. Her husband, who had carefully gathered the money together to pay the rent, when he found out she had used it for food for the baby and not to pay the rent, blew up and walked out: family breakup.

When people do shift from meat to such items as noodles and rice, or using them as fillers, they often do not have access to enriched noodles and rice in their local groceries. The Michigan Statewide Nutrition Commission has advocated legislation to restore nutrients [to] processed food through the enrichment processes. But Michigan, along with a number of other States, has still not acted. It would be lovely if Congress would do so.

The lines of people selling their blood are getting longer. Grocery store personnel across the State report layoffs as food sales are down.

In the meantime, more people in Michigan are going through the McDonald's "Golden Arches" garbage for food, and the managers are complaining about people coming into their restaurants and begging for money to buy food, people who come in and eat what is left over on somebody's plate. . . .

How on Earth can anyone contemplate reducing the summer lunch program or eliminating it? Or any other nutrition program?[1]

Editor's Note

1. On December 9, 1983, Mahaffey attacked old myths that sought to place the blame on the victims of hunger. "Yesterday, Edwin Meese, White House Counselor [later attorney-general], stated that there are lines in soup kitchens simply because the 'food is free.' Mr. Meese went on to say that many of the recipients are working, and that it's easier to go to a soup kitchen than it is to shop for food. We are outraged by this cavalier approach to the problems of the unemployed and poor families. . . . I propose that a moral society will not reduce its population through starving people."

6.   The Cry of White Racism

Ernest Dillard

Since blacks have held the highest political offices in this city for 15 years, the questions voters should ask about political power in Detroit are:

Has it provided Detroit citizens (70-percent black) safety and security for their persons and property?

Has it provided clean, safe, decent and reliable public transportation?

Has it provided well-kept litter-free public parks and safe, sanitary and open rest rooms?

Has it provided safe, dope-free and properly maintained public housing for the homeless and poor as well as management that administers these complexes in compassionate but firm, business-like fashion?

Ernest Dillard, "The Cry of White Racism" (unpublished MS, 1988), 1–3.

Has it cut down the increasing rate of black infant mortality?

The answers to these questions are no. What reason tends to be given? "White racism." (Yet) the constituency is predominately black. Mayor Coleman Young has often blamed "media hype" or "white racism" when troubling issues such as crime, housing and black unemployment are raised.

But are these problems caused by "white racism" or is this cry a vote-getting, political ploy? The latter seems more plausible. Because of the long history of real racism in this country even in the best of circumstances blacks are likely to charge "white racism" before distinguishing fact from fiction.

Consider, for example, that there is a hemorrhaging exodus of the black middle class from Detroit to the suburbs. Is this caused by "white racism"? The participants in the "black flight" will not hesitate to tell you that they are leaving because the elected black political leadership has failed to provide protection for them and their families.

It is common knowledge that a significant percentage of black teachers in Detroit public schools send their own children to schools in the suburbs. . . . The parents say they fear the violence in Detroit schools.

At some point, black politicians must be held accountable. In the case of Detroit, the city charter centralizes much of the power in city governance in the office of the mayor. He appoints department directors, including the chief of police, who is black.

If this is not enough, there are more than 30 black judges in Detroit's criminal justice system. There are also 14 black state representatives, three black state senators and two black U.S. representatives. This Detroit juggernaut of black political, police, judicial, and legislative power is unmatched in the nation. Nevertheless, the hoodlum element in Detroit has been allowed to impose upon its citizens a citywide curfew that kicks in at sundown.

The problem is that the black community views the election of black public officials as tantamount to solving problems that plague the black community. Being black, candidates will be more sensitive and dedicated to the "struggle" because they "have been there." Yet, upon the slightest criticism, black elected officials tend instinctively to respond "the white folks did it," and black voters fall into this "white" trap.

What black voters are forgetting is that the reason they voted for blacks in the first place was that they didn't like what the "white folks" were doing. Yet Detroit black voters have not held black elected officials accountable for their actions. If the office of the mayor of Detroit were held by a white mayor under the circumstance of today, there would be wall-to-wall blacks marching around the City-County Building with clenched and upraised fists demanding the mayor's head.

Besides holding black politicians accountable, there must be an honest effort by black politicians to work with white mainstream groups to help improve the condition of the white and black underclass. After all, poverty and welfare are not a "black problem." True, the percentage of blacks in poverty is higher than that for whites in Michigan. But the number of whites in poverty is much greater than that for blacks.

Unfortunately, the misperception of poverty being "a black problem" allows white politicians—under the guise of fighting "big government" and "runaway welfare costs"—to vote against effective social legislation, which their white constituents sorely need. Through widespread educational programs in the white community, whites and blacks would recognize the common denominator of their need—jobs for those willing and able to work.

This would enable well-intentioned but politically sensitive white candidates or public officials to work with blacks on finding solutions to today's problems. It could significantly mute, if not silence, the cry of "white racism." And it would refocus attention on a principle that Martin Luther King introduced long ago: "Color has nothing to do with the contents of a man's character."

Epilogue: Trade-Offs and Hopes

All of us tend to ignore the lessons of history. Among the folktales related by Marie Hamlin in *Legends of le Detroit* is that of a little red creature, *le rouge nain*. Call him trickster, imp, or devil, what you will. All the peoples of the earth have one in their folktales. Cadillac was warned by the voyageurs on his arrival at Detroit to beware of offending the red devil. In spite of this, when he saw a small ugly dwarf in his path as he was leaving a large banquet in his honor, he kicked the creature out of his way, to the horror of Madame Cadillac. She reminded him that the imp had the power to put a curse both on him and the entire settlement. Cadillac refused to listen. Soon his fortunes took a sharp turn for the worse. He lost money, position, and reputation. The French blamed it on the red devil.

How effective or long-lasting the curse of *le rouge nain* on Detroit was is still uncertain. An intermittent curse at most, I think, for the city has had its share of good fortune. The legacy of unthinking arrogance epitomized by Cadillac has, however, remained over many periods of Detroit's history.

All in all, the condition of Detroit is not good as it enters the 1990s. Its major perceived troubles are crime and drugs, especially crack cocaine; poor health conditions; its schools, seen to be ineffective and prone to violence; its burned out and vandalized homes; the despair of joblessness; and a widening gulf of black-white antagonism, augmented by talk of racism.

These are the most widely perceived problems. No one can deny their existence, but there may be different shadings of reality.

My own list to examine begins with the nature of unemployment, moves to crime, including arson and "drug-related" crimes, then physical health, especially that of children. Only then do I look at the schools, which exist to serve those lucky enough to survive to age five. I propose to return last to the damage to the beautiful natural world Cadillac described, and to the river where it all began.

Each of these troubles must be considered within the context of where it occurs, the pattern of decision-making that led to it, and whether there are, even now, some ways to alleviate it. The question of where becomes all-important when we recall the tremendous growth of suburbs in the six counties surrounding Detroit proper. Executive recruiters admit to working skillfully to conceal Detroit city destinations from the outside talent they are hiring.

As indicated in "A Shrinking City," heavy automotive industry has all but vanished within the city proper, and has largely been replaced by service and high-tech industries throughout the metropolitan area. Unemployment, however, is not a significant problem in the suburbs. The shift to service industries has lined the highways with new office buildings: corporate head offices, insurance and banking firms that have migrated from Detroit's financial district, and many new hotels specializing in serving the executive traveler. For Detroiters, the problem of access to suburban jobs, especially at entry level, is acute. In August, 1989, an official in southeastern Michigan's transportation authority had an innovative idea—that buses should be rescheduled to provide more opportunities for Detroiters to reach suburban workplaces! Although determined corporations, such as K-Mart, which has its world headquarters in Troy, Michigan, have been able to negotiate outward transportation for their workers, the general pattern has been to take suburban clerical workers into Detroit workplaces, and take a few household helpers to wealthy suburbs. The late Senator Philip Hart's mass transit hearings in 1974 should have been required reading for all transportation planners since then. Senator Hart's committee saw the dangers of an isolated work force dependent on the automobile.[1]

The city government of Detroit has paid its full share, and more, in job creation by tax benefits to employers. Among significant lapses has been the city's failure to take seriously the notion of readapting its sleeping industrial capital, as described by Luria and Russell in the section from *Rational Reindustrialization*.

There are jobs in the suburbs, good jobs, but lack of access defeats many. It is the problem of which Zachariah Chandler despaired in his struggles with Congress for access to livelihood. Chandler would not hesitate to call today's situation racism.

Drugs are involved in the city's high crime rate. Yet even the city's epidemic of crack cocaine, a cheap profit maker that builds violence into its users, is not the whole story of crime. Crack has created new developments, however. Among them are more teen-age killings; children are not only victims but often killers. An element of shock and horror seems to add a depth of mystery to the new local crimes. A decade ago, citizens were aware of an increasing crime rate, yet the sad happenings were almost predictable. There were purse-snatchings, muggings, car theft, and a murder rate that drew national attention, yet was described by local police as mainly involving acquaintances. Detroiters, women in particular, gave up the evening, gave up downtown, gave up the choice of solitude away from home. Today, by contrast, crime has entered a far less predictable phase. Crime has intruded into homes, particularly those of the elderly. Child abuse, or public awareness of it, has been growing. So has the number of abandoned babies. Teen-age drug dealers are said to be commonplace; a ten-year-old dealer is found sitting on a pile of heroin in a closet. Everyone talks of his age as if it were a first-ever item. Yet there were eight- and ten-year-olds determined to murder during the Faulkner riots of 1863.

The new, improved modern crime leaves no margin for error or lack of judgment by law officers. The revitalization of the police department by Mayor Coleman Young appeared to be one of the greatest accomplishments of the 1970s. Integrated and efficient, the department went far toward wiping out memories of brutality and racism. It is only recently that there are questions. There are rumors that some officers have been involved in the drug trade. There are absolute certainties that young off-duty officers with guns can play the part of fools.

Possibly the police cannot win against the current random crime. Expressway bridge shootings, street corner shootings, gun shots from a passing car, the bullets sweeping across children on a front porch—many of these will probably remain insoluble. A partial solution would be the control of handguns. Ordinances have been proposed several times in the council (usually by Maryann Mahaffey), but until the summer of 1989 even the weakest of them, asking simply for gun registration and training for

571

owners, failed to receive a majority or has lost by a veto or threat of veto from the mayor.

As with many other city functions, the difficulty in getting crime information seems worst of all. Ordinary citizens and the council alike feel powerless.

A crime not ignored by the police and fire departments, but quickly forgotten by the public, is arson. Arson is responsible for the destruction of an unknown number of vacant homes and the loss of potential housing stock throughout the city. A decade ago, much of it was blamed on insurance fraud, as apartment after apartment disappeared along the inner city's Cass Corridor. Now it is simply the fire in the night, the end result of drugs, vandalism, or, latest of all, neighborhood anger that an empty house, open and dangerous, has stood too long.

Health can be defined by the infant mortality rate, which is one of the worst in the western world; in 1983, thirty-four per thousand. In one inner-city area, infant and neonatal deaths reached sixty-three per thousand. Death comes more certainly to babies who are black, who are poor, or whose mothers are under twenty and failed to finish high school. Many are also listed under the Health Department euphemism I.F.U. (Information on Father Unknown). This means only that the couple had not married at the time of birth, usually because they didn't believe they could afford to. All too often, the insecurity is prolonged and results in another single-parent family.

Another summer
Browns to fall, children grow up
calling grandma
"mama" and
themselves grown.

—Leisia Duskin

A spokesperson for Hutzel Hospital's neonatal clinic reported in September, 1989, that they were seeing a record percentage of mothers who had no prenatal care before coming for delivery.

As with other Detroit trouble spots, the difficulty of getting information makes reform more difficult. In a 1988 request for information, the council learned that for the second successive year, money they had appropriated for maternal and child health care had not been spent by the Department of Health.

Those 1983 statistics for infant mortality were used here be-cause in 1988 they were the latest available. Credit should go, however, to a team on the Department of Health's Substance Abuse Division for its effort to bring together data from its own department and other public agencies.[?]

As for the schools: at best, the city has lost belief in them. The media clearly see the schools as a shambles and a drawback on the city's image. It was the fiscal irresponsibility and arrogance of board members that brought the general public to the breaking point.

In the fall of 1988, four board members were replaced by a slate committed to reform. The exact nature of the change re-mains cloudy. There has been almost total acceptance by the me-dia and the public of the notion that principals should have more power. Most citizens seem to favor simplistic reforms, such as more stress on basic skills. As in Mathilde Coffin's day, there is a large coterie who wants the minimum for entry-level jobs. Low test scores draw attention, but methods of testing or the self-defeating emphasis put upon tests are rarely questioned. The high school dropout rate is deplored by all, but in-house research and some workable staff proposals to cut it have been ignored by the bureaucracy and are unknown to the citizenry.[3]

The newly elected board soon replaced the superintendent and initiated sweeping changes. Sadly, many excellent programs of the former superintendent, Arthur Jefferson, had lost by one vote. After first insisting that he would not accept the position without total board approval, John Porter, former state Superin-tendent of Instruction, became superintendent by a narrow mar-gin and has since also won or lost a few key issues by a margin of one vote.

We do not see among the proposed reforms any true aware-ness of the despair of teachers in the face of the continued nep-otism and cronyism that controls their careers. There has been an adversarial relationship between labor and management in the schools for about fifteen years.[4] (The plan to "empower princi-pals" is seen by many teachers as opening the gate of the chick-enyard to the wolf.) There is also confusion. Principals are urged to apply uniformly the rules contained in the vague and unreal-istic "Student Conduct Code." It seems not to have occurred to anyone that a valued power of any principal should be the right to form judgments on students, and even sometimes to use the quality of mercy.

There are strains in the parent-teacher relationship. Detroit has never been a take-a-teacher-to-lunch town. On the other hand, most major school ills go with society's failure to give meaningful support to the single-parent family.

Recent added stress comes from the political strength of some parents in some districts. Regionalization created power that was quickly seized upon by parents in disadvantaged districts. This was to be expected and appropriate. Less expected was the continuance of many of the same parents of self-perpetuating school committees for almost two decades. Many have long since ceased to be volunteers and are entrenched in lower-level staff positions. These parent groups have successfully upset recommendations of the superintendent, board, and staff at angry board meetings. School closings are tense; so is the placement of a program for unmarried mothers.

As to the "excellent suburban schools," as the executive recruiters term them, some are wonderful, but they vary as much as schools anywhere and suffer mainly from the racial isolation predicted by Thurgood Marshall. So, of course, do Detroit children. At this writing, the chance of Detroit schools becoming once again places of "good learning" is uncertain.

The natural environment of metropolitan Detroit has of course changed, but there has been more effort spent to maintain it than in many other parts of the country, beginning with the brave purchase of Belle Isle. Anger still flares quickly at the suggestion of any change there. An ill-advised comment by Mayor Young early in his first term that it could be a wonderful site for apartments led to the formation of the Friends of Belle Isle, fighters every one.

In the suburbs there are well-organized efforts to retain the natural heritage. Here there are the Sierra Club, SEMEAC (the Southeast Michigan Environmental Action Council), Michigan Audubon, the Nature Conservancy, and others, all struggling to preserve green space against the encroaching ugliness of glass-walled office buildings. The struggle here is to enforce state laws protecting the wetlands. The enemy is the developer.

Within Detroit, there are many enemies. It is easy to blame those who don't pick up litter. That absolves everyone else. But

Fisherman, west side Detroit. (Courtesy of Bob McKeown, 1988.)

how much blame need Detroiters accept for the frequent lack of trash bins? The most common complaints of Detroit's neighborhoods concern the irregularity of trash pickup and accusations that ordinary neighborhoods are passed over for wealthy ones.

Still more basic to the environment is land use and the river. The trend noted by Kenneth Cockrel has continued unabated. The profits of developers have fueled the growth of downtown at neighborhood expense and have determined many of the decisions made about the shoreline of the Detroit River. However, with the help of a determined Canadian government, the expansion of Cobo Hall into the Detroit River was partly cut back from its original encroachment.

In spite of the growth of Detroit shoreline parks, ordinary pedestrian access is increasingly barred in other places. The explanation given is always "security." Only the personal intervention of owner/developer Peter Stroh made possible a public walkway connecting city-owned parklands on either side of his riverfront development. Riverfront West, in contrast, permits no pedestrian access whatever to any part of its lavish apartment complex. In

575

general, along the river both public access and public decision-making have been minimal.

The river is a showcase for the general sense of powerlessness felt by Detroiters. In the areas we have discussed, there is little access to power and barely access to timely information that might strengthen the citizenry. Yet there is a sense of awakening. We note that the arts have benefited from controversy and excitement for several years. There may be a stirring in the body politic as well. The board of education was one symptom. A lively mayoralty campaign is another. Who knows what the city might become if one-twentieth of the media attention given to professional sports were diverted to government? Perhaps the catalyst will be the emerging struggle over whether the people of Detroit will be allowed to keep their beloved ballpark, Tiger Stadium, or be faced with yet another developer's bill.

Still, Mayor Young, at the urging of the Central Business District Association, arranged for festoons of light across the Ambassador Bridge to Canada. For that good deed we thank him, remembering Clara Ward's saying: "La belle Paris is not more beautiful than Detroit when the lights are shining on the river."

Editor's Notes

1. U.S. Congress, Senate Judiciary Committee, Antitrust Sub-Committee, *Hearings on S. 7767*, 93d Cong., 2d sess., 1839–51.
2. *Detroit Youth: "Harmonies of Liberty" or "Drunk with the Wine of the World?": A Summary and Interpretation of the Data Recorded by Public Institutions* (Detroit: Department of Health, Bureau of Substance Abuse, 1987).
3. Most school leavings occur at the ninth-grade level, and for that reason the catchall phrase "high school dropout rate" is often heard. It is, however, misleading, as it is subject to many statistical variations in computing it. More useful and no less grim is the fact that among students who enter the Detroit Public Schools approximately 40 percent graduate. Some of the others, of course, have successfully completed the twelfth grade in private schools, or have received an alternate diploma under the schools' GED program. Still, it is estimated that both of these groups together do not exceed 10 percent of the whole.

4. This period does not coincide at all with the earlier arrival of the Detroit Federation of Teachers, but rather with the appointment of a strongly antiunion deputy superintendent, who during his term in office managed to make a number of executive appointments and set a certain tone of contentious hostility to labor. That union negotiations have been unnecessarily difficult is only one result. The schools were probably more deeply affected by a growing reluctance to listen to suggestions from the lower ranks of staff.

Bibliography

Abrams, Charles. *The City Is the Frontier*. New York: Harper, 1965.

Anderson, Carlotta. "Jo Labadie, Detroit's Gentle Anarchist." *Michigan History* (June-July 1986): 32–39.

Angelo, Frank. *Yesterday's Detroit*. Miami: E. A. Seamann, 1974.

Ashworth, William. *The Late Great Lakes*. Detroit: Wayne State University Press, 1988.

Babson, Steve, with Ron Alpern, Dave Elsila, and John Revitte. *Working Detroit: The Making of a Union Town*. Detroit: Wayne State University Press, 1986.

Bald, F. Clever. *Michigan in Four Centuries*. New York: Harper & Row, 1954.

Barnard, Harry. *Independent Man: The Life of Senator James Couzens*. New York: Charles Scribner's Sons, 1958.

Barone, Michael, and Grant Ujifusa. *Almanac of American Politics*. Washington, D.C.: National Journal. [Issues of 1974–1990]

Bingay, Malcolm W. *Detroit Is My Own Home Town*. Indianapolis: Bobbs-Merrill, 1946.

Bluestone, Barry, and Bennett Harrison. *The Deindustrialization of America*. New York: Basic Books, 1982.

Boggs, James. *The American Revolution: Pages from a Negro Worker's Notebook*. New York: Monthly Review Press, 1963.

Bontemps, Arna, and Jack Conroy. *Anyplace but Here*. New York: Hill and Wang, 1966.

Boykin, Ulysses. *A Handbook on the Detroit Negro*. Detroit: Minority Study Associates, 1943. [Available at BHC]

Burton, Clarence M., William Stocking, and Gordon K. Miller, eds. *City of Detroit, Michigan, 1701–1922*. 4 vols. Chicago: S. J. Clarke, 1922.

Capeci, Dominic. *Race Relations in Wartime Detroit: The Sojourner Truth Housing Controversy of 1942*. Philadelphia: Temple University Press, 1984.

Casey, Geneviere. *Father Clem Kern, Conscience of Detroit*. Detroit: Marygrove College Press, 1989.

Conot, Robert. *American Odyssey*. New York: Morrow, 1974. Reprint. Detroit: Wayne State University Press, 1986.

Cornell, George, James M. McGlurken, and James A. Clifton. *People of the Three Fires: The Ottawa, Pottawatomi and Ojibway of Michigan*. Grand Rapids, Mich.: Grand Rapids Inter-Tribal Council, 1986.

Crathern, Alice Tarbell, ed. *In Detroit Courage Was the Fashion: Women in the Development of Detroit from 1701 to 1951*. Detroit: Wayne University Press, 1953.

Dain, Floyd Russell. *Every House a Frontier: Detroit's Economic Progress, 1815–1825*. Detroit: Wayne University Press, 1956.

Dancy, John. *Sand against the Wind*. Detroit: Wayne State University Press, 1966.

Detroit Department of Health, Bureau of Substance Abuse. *Detroit Youth: "Harmonies of Liberty" or "Drunk with the Wine of the World?": A Summary and Interpretation of the Data Recorded by Public Institutions*. Detroit: Department of Health, Bureau of Substance Abuse, 1987.

Detroit Free Press. *Great Pages of Michigan History from the Detroit Free Press*. Detroit: Wayne State University Press, 1987.

Edwards, George. *The Police on the Urban Frontier*. New York: American Jewish Committee, 1971.

Ewen, Lynda. *Corporate Power and Urban Crisis in Detroit*. Princeton, N.J.: Princeton University Press, 1978.

Farmer, Silas. *History of Detroit and Wayne County and Early Michigan*. Detroit: Farmer & Co., 1890. Reprint. Detroit: Gale Research Co., 1969.

Fine, Sidney. *Frank Murphy: The Detroit Years*. Ann Arbor: University of Michigan Press, 1975.

Fountain, Clayton. *Union Guy*. New York: Viking, 1949.

Gabin, Nancy. "Women Workers and the UAW in the Post-World War II Period, 1945–1954." In *The Labor History Reader*, edited by Daniel J. Leab, 407–32. Urbana: University of Illinois Press, 1985.

Georgakas, Dan. *Detroit, I Do Mind Dying*. New York: St. Martin's Press, 1974.

Georgakas, Dan, and Albert Blum. *Michigan Labor and the Civil War*. Edited by Sidney Glazer. Lansing: Michigan Civil War Centennial Observance Commission, 1964.

George, Emily. *William Woodbridge, Michigan's Connecticut Yankee*. Lansing: Michigan Department of State, Michigan Historical Division, 1979.

Grant, William. "The Detroit School Case: An Historical Overview." *Wayne Law Review* (March 1975): 851–66.

Grier, Eunice, and George Grier. *Privately Developed Interracial Housing*, 133–43. Berkeley: University of California Press, 1956.

Hamlin, Marie C. Watson. *Legends of le Detroit*. 2d ed. Detroit: Thorndike Nourse, 1884.

Hanawalt, Leslie L. *A Place of Light: The History of Wayne State University*. Detroit: Wayne State University Press, 1968.

580

Hill, Daniel G. *The Freedom-Seekers: Blacks in Early Canada*. Agincourt, Canada: The Book Society, 1981).

Holli, Melvin G. *Reform in Detroit: Hazen S. Pingree and Urban Politics*. New York: Oxford University Press, 1969.

Howe, Irving, and B. J. Widick. *The UAW and Walter Reuther.* New York: Random House, 1949.

Jackson, Kenneth T. *The Ku Klux Klan in the City, 1915–1930*. New York: Oxford University Press, 1967.

Jacobs, Jane. *The Economy of Great American Cities*. New York: Vintage, 1961.

Jameson, Anna Brownell. *Winter Studies and Summer Rambles in Upper Canada*. Toronto: Thos. Nelson and Sons, 1837.

Katzman, David. *Before the Ghetto: Black Detroit in the Nineteenth Century*. Urbana: University of Illinois Press, 1973.

Kraus, Henry. *The Many and the Few*. Los Angeles: Planta Press, 1947.

Larrie, Reginald R. *Makin' Free: African-Americans in the Northwest Territory*. Detroit: Blaine-Ethridge Books, 1981.

Lee, Alfred McClung, and Norman D. Humphrey. *Race Riot*. New York: Dryden Press, 1943.

Levine, David Allan. *Internal Combustion: The Races in Detroit, 1915–1926*. Westport Conn.: Greenwood Press, 1976.

Linck, Orville E., ed. *Kelsey the Commentator: The Affirmations and Dissents of a Distinguished Columnist*. Detroit: Wayne State University Press, 1963.

Locke, Hubert. *The Detroit Riot of 1967*. Detroit: Wayne State University Press, 1969.

Lodge, John C., with Milo M. Quaife. *I Remember Detroit*. Detroit: Wayne University Press, 1949.

Lovett, William P. *Detroit Rules Itself*. Boston: R. G. Badger, 1930.

Luria, Dan, and Jack Russell. *Rational Reindustrialization: An Economic Development Agenda for Detroit*. Detroit: Widgetripper Press, 1981.

McLauchlin, Russell. *Alfred Street*. Detroit: Conjure House, 1946.

McRae, Norman. *Negroes in Michigan during the Civil War*. Edited by Sidney Glazer. Lansing: Michigan Civil War Centennial Observance Commission, 1966.

Mary Rosalita, Sister. *Education in Detroit Prior to 1850*. Lansing: Michigan Historical Commission, 1928.

May, George S. *Michigan: An Illustrated History of the Great Lake State*. Northridge, Calif.: Windsor Publications in cooperation with the Historical Society of Michigan, 1987.

Meyer, Katherine Mattingly, ed. *Detroit Architecture: AIA Guide*. Rev. ed. Detroit: Wayne State University, 1980.

Michigan Department of Labor. *Annual Reports*. 1891–1906 and 1912–17. Lansing: Michigan Department of Labor.

Moehlman, Arthur. *Public Education in Detroit*. Bloomington, Ill: Public School Publishing Co., 1925.

Moran, J. Bell. *The Moran Family: 200 Years in Detroit*. Detroit: Alved of Detroit, 1949.

Motley, Mary Penick, ed. *Invisible Soldier: The Experience of the Black Soldier, World War II*. Detroit: Wayne State University Press, 1975.

Mowitz, Robert J., and Deil S. Wright. *Profile of a Metropolis: A Case Book*. Detroit: Wayne State University Press, 1962.

Myers, Gustavus. *History of the Great American Fortunes*, 93–121. New York: Modern Library, 1937.

National Advisory Commission on Civil Disorders, Chairman Otto Kerner. *Report*. New York: E. P. Dutton & Co., 1968.

New Detroit Committee. *Progress Report of the New Detroit Committee*. Detroit: New Detroit Committee, 1968.

Palmer, Friend. *Early Days in Detroit*. Detroit: Hunt & June, 1906.

Parkinson, Almon Ernest. *Historical Geography of Detroit*. Lansing: Michigan Historical Commission, 1918.

Player, Cyril Arthur. "Pingree." BHC, Detroit Public Library. Typescript.

Rich, Wilbur. *Coleman Young and Detroit Politics: From Social Activist to Power Broker*. Detroit: Wayne State University Press, 1989.

Rogin, Michael Paul. *Fathers and Children: Andrew Jackson and the Subjugation of the American Indian*. New York: Random House, 1976.

Ross, Robert Budd. *The Patriot War*. Detroit: Detroit Evening News, 1898.

Ross, Robert Budd, and George B. Catlin. *Landmarks of Detroit*. Detroit: Detroit Evening News Association, 1898.

Satz, Ronald N. *American Indian Policy and the Jacksonian Era*. Lincoln: University of Nebraska Press, 1975.

Schoolcraft, Henry. *The Literary Voyager, or Muzzeniegun*. Edited by Philip Parker Mason. East Lansing: Michigan State University Press, 1962.

Schucter, Arnold. *Reparations: The Black Manifesto and Its Challenge to White America*. Philadelphia: Lippincott, 1970.

Serrin, William. "God Help Our City." *Atlantic Monthly* (March 1969): 115–21.

———. *The Company and the Union: The "Civilized Relationship" of the General Motors Corporation and the United Auto Workers*. New York: Knopf, 1973.

Sexton, Patricia, and Brendan Sexton. *Bluecollars and Hard Hats: The Working Class and the Future of American Politics*. New York: Random House, 1971.

Shaw, Virginia W. V. *O, Call Back Yesterday*. Detroit: Privately printed, 1936. [Available BHC]

Sinclair, Upton. *The Flivver King: A Story of Ford-America*. Emaus, Penn.: Rodale Press, 1927.

——— . *The Goslings: A Study of the American Schools*. Pasadena: Privately printed, 1924.

Streeter, Floyd B. *Political Parties in Michigan, 1837–1860*. Lansing: Michigan Historical Commission, 1918.

Sward, Keith. *The Legend of Henry Ford*. New York: Rinehart, 1948

Sword, Wiley. *President Washington's Indian War: The Struggle for the Old Northwest, 1790–1795*. Norman: University of Oklahoma Press, 1985.

U.S. Congress. Senate Judiciary Committee, Antitrust Subcommittee. *Hearings on S. 1167*. 93d Cong., 2d sess., 1839–51. [Hearing on mass transit]

Warren, Francis H. *Michigan Manual of Freedmen's Progress*. Lansing: State of Michigan, 1915.

Washington, Forrester. *The Negro in Detroit: A Survey of the Conditions of a Negro Group in a Northern Industrial Center during the War Prosperity Period*. Detroit: Associated Charities, 1920. Detroit Public Library. Typescript.

——— . *The Negro in Detroit, 1926*. Report of the Mayor's Interracial Commission. Detroit: Bureau of Governmental Research, 1926. Detroit Public Library. Typescript.

White, Walter. *How Far the Promised Land?* New York: Viking, 1955.

Widick, B. J. *Auto Work and Its Discontents*. Baltimore: Johns Hopkins University Press, 1976.

——— . *Detroit: City of Race and Class Violence*. Rev. ed. Detroit: Wayne State University Press, 1989.

Wolf, Eleanor P. *Trial and Error: The Detroit School Segregation Case*. Detroit: Wayne State University Press, 1981.

Wolf, Eleanor P., and Mel Ravitz. "Lafayette Park: New Residents in the Core City." *Journal of the American Institute of Planners* (August 1964).

Wolf, Eleanor P., and Charles LeBeaux, with Shirley Terreberry and Harriet Sapirstein. *Change and Renewal in an Urban Community: Five Case Studies of Detroit*. New York: Praeger, 1969.

Woodford, Arthur M. *Detroit and Its Banks: The Story of Detroit Bank and Trust*. Detroit: Wayne State University Press, 1974.

Woodford, Frank B. *Lewis Cass: The Last Jeffersonian*. New Brunswick, N.J.: Rutgers University Press, 1950.

Woodford, Frank B., and Arthur M. Woodford. *All Our Yesterdays: A Brief History of Detroit*. Detroit: Wayne State University Press, 1969.

Woodson, June Baber. "A Century with the Negroes of Detroit: 1830–1930." Master's thesis, Wayne State University, 1949.

Wylie, Jeanie. *Poletown: Community Betrayed*. Urbana: University of Illinois Press, 1989.

Zunz, Olivier. *Beyond Inequality*. Chicago: University of Illinois Press, 1986.

Index

Wilma Wood Henrickson is a historian and free-lance writer. She holds the B.A. and M.A. degrees from Wayne State University. For fifteen years she was chairman of the social studies department at Murray-Wright High School, Detroit, and is currently active in a number of historical, cultural, civic, and political organizations.

The manuscript was edited by Robin DuBlanc. The book was designed by Mary Primeau.

Manufactured in the United States of America.